AN ATLAS OF BELLS

An Atlas of Bells

Ron Johnston, Graham Allsopp,
John Baldwin and Helen Turner

Blackwell Reference

First published 1990

Basil Blackwell Ltd
108 Cowley Road, Oxford OX4 1JF, UK

Basil Blackwell Inc.
3 Cambridge Center
Cambridge, MA 02142

British Library Cataloguing in Publication Data

An Atlas of bells
1. Churches. Bells. Ringing
I. Johnston, Ron
789'.5'0714

ISBN 0–631–15143–5

Library of Congress Cataloging in Publication Data

An Atlas of Bells / Ron Johnston . . . [et al.].
p.   cm.
Includes bibliographical references.
ISBN 0–631–15143–5
1. Bells—Atlases.   2. Change ringing.
I. Johnston, R. J.
(Ronald John)
CC205.A75   1990
786.8'845'0223—dc20   89–48766   CIP

Typeset in 10 on 12pt Palatino
by Opus, Oxford
Printed in Great Britain by
Butler and Tanner Ltd, Frome, Somerset

Contents

Preface

ONE of the many characteristics of British culture which is different from those of neighbouring countries is the way in which bells are used to announce the time of a service at a parish church. Bells are not peculiar to the Church of England, of course; they are used in many religions and can be found in churches and temples in most parts of the world. But the British (really the English!) have developed a method of ringing bells that is different from that used anywhere else – although the British way has been exported and is practised in a little less than a hundred churches in other parts of the world, notably in Australasia and North America.

This book is not a comprehensive study of the English art of ringing, nor a handbook to guide those who want an introduction to its esoteric intricacies. (Such a volume has recently been written by Ron Johnston: *Bell-Ringing: the English Art of Change-Ringing*, Viking Books, London, 1986.) Instead, it is a guide to where that art is practised, to the location of the 5,600 or so churches (and the small number of secular buildings) which have bells that are ringable to changes. As such, it is designed as something that will be used by members of the ringing community to locate towers where they have been invited to ring, to plan outings, and to find where they might seek to join the local band when on holiday or on a business trip. But it has also been put together in a way that will inform a wider public of the campanological art, hopefully encouraging them not only to enquire further into its many details but to learn to ring and follow the call of the bells. Change-ringing is a fascinating art, with new goals always beckoning. No two rings of bells are the same, so that the potential for new experiences is great. It is no wonder that many ringers are obsessed with their particular art-form, availing themselves of the many opportunities to advance their expertise and expand their horizons, while providing a pleasant sound that reverberates across the landscape and through the city streets, and ever-mindful of the true purpose of church bells – to bear public witness to the church and announce its activities.

The book is in three parts. The first is an introductory section of three chapters which provides background material. The nature of the English art of change-ringing is the subject of chapter 1, whereas chapter 2 discusses how bells operate and the changes are rung; chapter 3 provides an exploration of the intriguing geography of bells – why there are more in some parts of the country than others. The second part of the book is its core: an atlas comprising 60 maps which show the distribution of all towers with four or more ringable bells in each of the counties of England, in Scotland, Wales and Ireland, and in the rest of the world. Each map is accompanied by a short piece of text that highlights some of its major features and presents interesting local detail. Finally, the third part consists of a gazetteer, giving a county-by-county listing of every tower, complete with its six-figure National Grid reference. Used in conjunction with the atlas, this will enable people to locate churches exactly (though we have been unable to indicate all the one-way streets and culs-de-sac that traditionally hamper ringers as they search either for the tower that is producing such a beautiful sound or for the church where they are expected to ring a peal!).

Production of this volume has been a team effort. The launching and directing of the enterprise was undertaken by Ron Johnston, who has also provided the text and selected most of the photographs. Production of the maps was Graham Allsopp's task, and he is entirely responsible for the clarity and attractiveness of the final product, as well as for producing the listings in the format employed in the gazetteer. His work would have been immeasurably greater were it not for the massive effort that John Baldwin has put in over recent decades compiling the complete list of National Grid references and putting them into a computer file, from which it was possible to produce all the lettering for the maps as well as the gazetteer. Last, but by no means least, Helen Turner undertook the task of producing the line drawings to illustrate the text and which show the great variety of churches that contain rings of bells.

Our work has been much assisted by many others, to whom we express our thanks. Particular appreciation must be given to Ronald Dove, for long of Leeds but now resident in York. He it was who conceived the idea of publishing a full listing of all rings of bells and who did all the work compiling and checking the great mass of detail. 'Dove's Guide', as it is widely known, is an invaluable aid to ringers, and is already in its seventh edition, only 32 years after the first was produced. We are particularly indebted to Mr Dove for letting us draw on his labours of love and to William Viggers, his publisher, for without them not only would our task have been much greater but ringers as a whole would have been impoverished. We hope that they like this companion to their work. We are also indebted to the Department of Geography at the University of Sheffield, for the use of its cartographic and other facilities; to our publishers, for their encouragement and help; to Caroline Richmond for her great assistance in seeing the book into print; to the many ringers who have answered our queries; to Chris Pickford of Bedford, who shared with us his wide knowledge of the history of bells, and carefully checked all the county chapters; and to JANET (the Joint Academic Network), who facilitated the transfer of information between Cardiff and Sheffield.

Acknowledgements

THE Authors and Publishers are grateful to the following persons and institutions for permission to reproduce photographs and other illustrations on the pages specified below.

W. G. Field: *drawing of the bell cage at East Bergholt*, p. 8

Laura Dickerson: *bells at Old North Church, Boston*, p. 8

Historic Churches Preservation Trust: *Crowland Abbey*, p. 9

Whitechapel Bell Foundry Ltd: *bells at Guildford Cathedral*, p. 19; *bells for Harare Cathedral*, p. 47

News Team, Birmingham: *bellringers at Birmingham Cathedral*, p. 22

John Gilbert: *bell with silencer*, p. 24

from Thomas North's *The Church Bells of Northamptonshire*: *bellfounders' marks*, p. 32

J. F. Stocker (for John Taylor and Co.): *bell mould*, p. 33

Hopcraft Photographers: *All Saints, Worcester*, p. 46

Greater London Photograph Library: *S Sepulchre, High Holborn*, p. 46

Royal Commission on the Historical Monuments of England: *S Peter Mancroft, Norwich*, p. 46

Hulton Picture Library: *S Martin, Birmingham*, p. 48

They are also grateful to John Murray (Publishers) Ltd for permission to quote from John Betjeman: *The Best of Betjeman* (collected poems), and to Collins for permission to quote from John Betjeman: *Collins Pocket Guide to English Parish Churches*.

INTRODUCTION

1   English Church Bells

BELLS can be sounded, or rung, in a great variety of ways, as is illustrated in Percival Price's magisterial world survey, which includes only seven pages covering the English fashion.[1] The major distinction is between fixed and movable bells, between those hung in a tower or similar building and those carried from place to place, as by a town crier. We are concerned only with fixed bells.

Two basic principles are included in sounding a fixed bell. The first involves striking it with a hammer, with sufficient force so that the contact results not only in sound being issued but also in the bell vibrating for a period of some seconds and giving out a resonant sequence of notes (which reflects the shape of the bell and the differential vibration rate along that shape). Furthermore, the hammer should not stay in contact with the bell, otherwise it will reduce the vibrations and dampen the sound and lead potentially to the bell being cracked; a deep hum is much preferable to a solid clunk.

With a single bell, a person could simply strike it with a hammer or similar instrument. But climbing up to use the hammer may be neither convenient nor safe, and is probably uncomfortable too. Apparatus has therefore been developed, usually involving some form of lever, which allows a bell to be struck without close personal contact by the ringer. (With clocks, of course, it is done automatically, to ensure accuracy.) Apparatus is also available for the ringer to strike several bells in sequence, using a keyboard or some similar arrangement. From this evolved the carillon, a set of bells on which tunes can be played either from a keyboard or by a pre-programmed mechanism. Development of carillons and the art of the carilloneur is particularly associated with Belgium and the Netherlands, where the craft of tuning bells was enhanced in the seventeenth and eighteenth centuries; British bellfounders learned much from their Low Countries' counterparts in the nineteenth century. Carillons have become relatively popular in the United States, though interestingly many of them have been provided by English founders whose main work has been the production of bells for other forms of ringing. European founders have made little impression on the English market, although some bells have been imported in recent years; the ring of twelve at East Grinstead in West Sussex is one of the few complete rings not cast in England.

The other basic principle used in sounding a bell involves using a clapper which swings freely inside it; the bell, although fixed in place, must also swing, otherwise the force of the impact of the clapper would weaken it, until eventually the bell might crack. The two can be brought into contact by swinging either the clapper or the bell itself. The former method was used in Russia before the 1917 revolution which led to restrictions on religious practice. There were many very large bells, such as the Tsar Kolokol in the Kremlin: some remain, but they no longer sound their deep notes over city and steppe. A rope was attached to the clapper, which in the largest bells may itself have weighed several tons; the latter was then pulled on to the bell, striking it at the lip.[2] Swinging the clapper clearly involved much less effort than swinging the bell; even so, large numbers of people were involved, as a picture in Williams's book shows.[3]

Swinging the bell rather than the clapper is the method that developed throughout most of Southern and Western Europe, including Britain. For this, the bell is hung on a frame, on bearings, and the clapper hangs freely within it. A lever is used to swing the bell; as the bell swings, so does the clapper, and when the two momentarily come into contact, the bell sounds. If a tower contains several bells of different sizes, and hence of different notes, they are likely to sound at different intervals, since smaller bells have shorter periods (or swings) than their larger counterparts. Thus when several such bells are set swinging, the resultant set of sounds will be equivalent to a random sequence of notes with no set time between each. Such a random clangour is typical of what one hears emanating on a Sunday morning from most French and Spanish churches, in many of which the bells are set in motion (rotating on their axes) by electric motors rather than by ringers with ropes.

The English Method of Ringing Bells

Swinging bells to make them sound was typical in all British churches until at least the fifteenth century (as far as we know), and in the great majority of them until the eighteenth. But during the decades after the Reformation (from about 1540 onwards) the method evolved slowly from swinging to what we now know as ringing. Today, when a bell sounds from an English church with a ring (or peal) of four or more bells, it is almost certainly not a consequence of its having been swung by a tug on

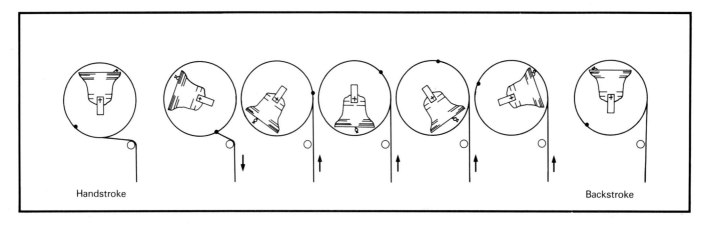

Figure 1.1 This sequence of diagrams, produced by the Whitechapel Bell Foundry, illustrates what happens when a bell is rung. It starts in the left-hand diagram with the bell mouth-upwards and the clapper resting against the bell. The rope is tied to one of the wheel's spokes, passing through the rim at the dot in the bottom left; it is guided into the ringing room below by a pulley. As the bell rotates anticlockwise the rope moves down over the pulley until the point shown in the second diagram, and then goes up as the bell's rotation continues. When the bell is mouth-upwards again, the rope is wrapped around most of the wheel, with the entry-point through the rim (the 'garter-hole') back in the bottom left. As the bell rotates, the clapper travels separately; it 'catches up' with the bell and strikes it just before the vertical position. The next time that the bell rings, it will rotate clockwise, in the reverse of the sequence shown.

a rope attached to a lever – that is known locally as chiming – but rather of its having revolved through a full circle of 360 degrees. The result is a very regular sequence of notes, which is produced by the application of human mental and physical skill with no assistance other than that of the bearings on which the bells hang and the fittings (including the rope) that allow it to be rung.

The principles of such ringing are as follows, and are illustrated in figure 1.1. The bell begins mouth-upwards – not downwards as in all other methods. It is set in motion by a pull on a rope attached to a spoke of a wheel that is fixed to the bell. Enough impetus is given in the pull so that the bell will rotate through the full circle, returning to the mouth-upwards position, at which point its motion is stopped by the ringer holding the rope. As the rotation begins, and the bell moves downwards, the clapper remains in contact with the trailing edge of the bell. Because it is much lighter than the bell, however, towards the nadir of the rotation it begins to move away from the bell. Then, as the bell climbs up towards the mouth-upwards position again, the clapper catches up with the leading edge, striking it and causing the rich sound to emanate just before the apex of the rotation is reached. The bell's rotation is then stopped before being set in motion again, this time in the opposite direction: the rotations are alternately clockwise and anticlockwise, so that the clapper always begins at the trailing edge and ends at the leading edge.

The great benefit of this system of sounding a bell over that produced by swinging it is that it allows the ringer precise control over when the clapper strikes the soundbow (hence good ringing is known in the vernacular as good striking). The ringer knows that the bell will only sound just before it completes each rotation. When a bell is swinging freely through perhaps 40 or 50 degrees from the mouth-downwards position, the ringer can make sure that the bell meets the clapper regularly but cannot alter the period between each strike very easily. When one bell is being rung this ability to control the exact time of the striking is perhaps of little importance. But when several bells of different sizes and notes are involved the sounding of the bells can be coordinated, so that instead of creating a random clangour English ringers can produce set sequences. It is possible to compose what we describe below as 'rounds' when swinging – or chiming – bells, but not to ring changes.

There are disadvantages to this means of sound production, however. Because each bell takes several seconds to rotate, and the larger the bell the longer the rotation, it is not possible for the same bell to sound again before any other does, unless the bells are rung at an extremely slow pace. Thus, unlike on carillons, conventional tunes composed for other instruments cannot be 'played' on bells rung English-style. Instead, particular types of tunes have been evolved which involve most of the bells in the ring sounding before any one does so again. The sequence of bells can alter, however, so that you can get 123, 213, 231 etc., but not 123, 322, 131.

Why this form of bell-ringing evolved in England and

not elsewhere is far from clear. Nor is it apparent why it was not exported to the European mainland, although, of course, it developed after the Reformation and was associated with the renegade Church of England and not with the Roman Catholic Church (which in England was denied the use of bells by law until emancipation in the 1830s). Certainly there is nothing in the nature of the English church that necessarily stimulated such a development, let alone demanded it. Indeed, the requirement for bells is very small; according to canon law, all churches must have one bell to call the faithful to prayer, but that is all. (Unfortunately, that requirement is now interpreted as allowing churches to install recordings of bells.) In the past, bells were used for a great variety of purposes other than announcing service times, as antiquarians have recorded, and church bells were frequently put to secular uses too, such as sounding the curfew, broadcasting the execution of a prisoner, and indicating that a market could be opened (this last still happens with the London Stock Exchange, of course, though it isn't a church bell that is employed).[4] Such uses are now rare, with the virtually universal ownership of watches and rapid transmission of detailed information via the mass media.

Like so many features that are peculiar to individual cultures, the English art of bell-ringing developed not because it was necessary but simply because some people decided that that was how it should be done, and others followed them. The decision was not a single choice, of course; it involved a slow process of trial and error, at any stage of which failure may have led to the developing procedures dying out. The methods of ringing, and of hanging the bells, evolved slowly as committed individuals carried them forward, until the practice was mastered if not perfected, and slowly it spread across the face of the country. Those individuals remain anonymous, for we know very little of the history of ringing before the mid-seventeenth century, by which time many of the crucial technical developments had taken place. Even then, change-ringing as it is practised today in 5,000 or more churches was a feature of a very small number of places only. The basic principles were developed in the century or so after the Reformation, but as a widespread art change-ringing blossomed only in the nineteenth century, when the number of rings of five or more bells increased very rapidly and a much greater number of people took up the art of campanology.

Bell-ringing has been described as the last authentic sound of medieval England, but unfortunately this is not really so, and the roots of the present practice are more recent. The sounds of today, as the bells ring out their set sequences of changes, bear little resemblance to those heard only 250 years ago in most towns and villages.

Table 1.1 The church bells of Buckinghamshire

Number of bells in tower	1553[a]	1638[b]	1714[c]	1897[d]	1950[e]	1982[f]	1988[g]
Fewer than 3	24	20	36	73			
3	57	44	59	57			
4	41	31	28	14		5	4
5	13	34	69	45	29	22	20
6	0	2	14	47	62	64	63
8	0	0	3	13	25	24	28
10	0	0	0	1	1	0	0
12	0	0	0	0	1	1	1
Total	135	131	209	250			
(5 or more)	(13)	(36)	(86)	(106)	(118)	(111)	(112)

Sources:

[a] Inventories of Goods belonging to various churches, 6/7 Edw. VI (reproduced by Cocks, p. xiv).
[b] Visitation of Churches ordered by Bishop of Lincoln (reproduced by Cocks).
[c] Brown Willis, quoted by Cocks, p. xvii.
[d] A. H. Cocks, *The Church Bells of Buckinghamshire* (Jarrold: London, 1897).
[e] R. H. Dove, *A Bellringer's Guide to the Church Bells of Britain*, first edition (Viggers: Aldershot, 1950).
[f] Dove, sixth edition (Viggers: Aldershot, 1982).
[g] Dove, seventh edition (Viggers/Seven Corners Press: Guildford, 1988).

Some idea of the relative recency of the widespread provision of rings of bells is provided for the county of Buckinghamshire in table 1.1. This draws on inventories of all bells in the county taken in each century from the sixteenth to the nineteenth inclusive, to which is added information on the number of rings of four or more bells since the Second World War. (To most change-ringers, five is the minimum number of bells on which their art can be practised with any great interest, and the *Guide* published by Dove did not list four-bell towers in 1950.) Until the eighteenth century, according to this compilation,[5] even a ring of five bells was a rarity and eight was unheard of in the county; most of the rings of three bells and fewer will not have been hung for ringing as we describe it here, but rather for chiming only. From 1714 on, however, the number of six-bell towers increased substantially, no doubt heralding much greater change-ringing activity, and the number of eight-bell towers increased many times over. A ring of ten was installed in High Wycombe in 1802; this was increased to twelve in 1963. A further ring of ten, at Slough, was later transferred to Berkshire.

Buckinghamshire is not necessarily typical of the whole country in every respect, but it illustrates the relative recency of the spread of change-ringing on five or more bells, and certainly on the higher numbers, which is generally the case. Whether change-ringing was practised in many of those towers with five and six bells at the end of the nineteenth century is doubtful, however. In Shropshire, for example, Walters remarked in 1915 that a large number of the bells were rarely, if ever, rung, and a survey of ringing in several counties in 1885 contained comments such as 'Cambridgeshire is somewhat short of bells and decidedly backward in change-ringing', and 'Cornwall is well off for bells, but . . . has very few change-ringers.[6]

Table 1.2 Recent growth in the number of rings of bells: Devon and Northamptonshire

Number of bells in ring	Devon 1872[a]	Devon 1988[c]	Northamptonshire 1878[b]	Northamptonshire 1988[c]
Fewer than 3	129		65	
3	96		39	
4	64	15	50	23
5	122	23	107	85
6	137	251	39	74
8	19	88	9	25
10	1	4	0	3
12	0	2	0	1
Total (four or more only)	342	383	205	211

Sources:
  [a] H. T. Ellacombe, *The Church Bells of Devon* (Pollard: Exeter, 1872), p. 68.
  [b] T. North, *The Church Bells of Northamptonshire* (Clarke: Leicester, 1878).
  [c] R. H. Dove, *A Bellringer's Guide to the Church Bells of Britain*, seventh edition (Viggers/Seven Corners Press: Guildford, 1988).

The growth in the number of eight-, ten- and twelve-bell towers since the late nineteenth century is shown in table 1.2, which refers to the two counties with the highest densities of bells at present.[7] (The comparisons are not exact because of changes in county boundaries, which have not been compensated for.) The greater the number of bells, the greater the challenge to ringers, and, according to many, the more musical the output. Clearly in both Devon and Northamptonshire ringers have been able to convince church authorities of the desirability of more bells, and have been able to raise the money – through their own efforts, by public subscription and by obtaining wealthy donors – to meet their desires; many will have been aided by sympathetic vicars, including some keen ringers among their number. In some cases, gifts of bells have been made by non-ringers, who love the sound that they make and want to hear it in their local church. As the table indicates, relatively few churches have been added to the list with four or more bells over the last hundred years or so, but many have been recipients of augmentations, from four to five or six, from five to six, from six to eight, and so on. In Devon, for example, the number of four- and five-bell towers has declined to no more than 20 per cent of the 1872 figure, while the number of six-bell towers nearly doubled, that of

eight-bell towers increased nearly fivefold, and six towers obtained rings of ten and twelve. Not quite as much activity is reported for Northamptonshire, which has the largest number of five-bell towers in the country at the present time.

What we can infer from these figures is that relatively few churches have had their number of bells increased to a change-ringing set since the late nineteenth century, but that among the churches with such a set augmentations have been quite common. In Northamptonshire, for example, of the 94 identified augmentations between 1878 and 1982 only one involved a tower with fewer than three bells at the former date: this was at St Edmund's church in Northampton, which was later declared redundant; the bells were transferred to Wellington, New Zealand, where they form the core of a ring of twelve in the new cathedral. Ten other augmentations involved rings of three being increased to four, five or six, and the other 83 involved augmentations where the tower already possessed at least four bells – 21 with four alone. The geography of where the changes ring was thus firmly established by the end of the last century. Undoubtedly a major reason for this was the decline of the village from then on, as rural depopulation increased apace. Parishes without rings of bells were probably among the poorest and, with falling attendances, would be unable to raise the money for more bells and their fittings; they would also find it difficult to raise bands of ringers from among their congregations. In many, too, the fabric of the church would have been unable to withstand the introduction of a ring of bells, and perhaps lacked a tower in which they could be placed; many of the churches with only one or two bells have just an open turret within which bells can be swung but not rung. In the burgeoning towns, on the other hand, most of the older parish churches had a ring of bells, but the money was rarely available for a tower and contents in the newer, twentieth-century churches of the expanding suburbs.

Since the Second World War, the publication of seven editions of Ronald Dove's *A Bellringer's Guide to the Church Bells of Britain* has provided a continuing detailed census of the availability of bells. The *Guide* initially covered only rings of five or more, but the author included a bare listing of four-bell towers from the third edition on, noting that 'Ringers who are interested in four-bell ringing represent only a small minority and those towers where a regular practice is held are so few . . .'[8] Table 1.3 shows the number of rings recorded in each edition, and indicates a remarkable stability over the 38-year period. This is a net figure, however, because some rings of bells have been lost, in most cases through redundancy of the church building. In the 1982 edition Dove recorded 124 postwar losses, although in 38 cases the entire ring was transferred to another tower and in a further 18 the metal was used for casting new

Table 1.3 The church bells of England since 1950

Number of bells in tower[a]	1950	1956	1962	1968	1976	1982	1988
4				496	443	441	420	397
5	1,048	980	938	890	826	772	732
6	2,484	2,488	2,521	2,547	2,551	2,579	2,610
8	1,482	1,524	1,537	1,551	1,562	1,589	1,589
10	158	161	165	171	182	190	188
12	54	55	59	60	68	76	89
Total				5,689	5,662	5,630	5,626	5,605
(5 or more)	(5,226)	(5,208)	(5,220)	(5,219)	(5,189)	(5,206)	(5,208)

Sources: the various editions of R. H. Dove, *A Bellringer's Guide to the Church Bells of Britain* (Viggers: Aldershot, dates as shown). The figures include the Channel Islands and the Isle of Man.

[a] There is a small number of instances of towers with seven, nine and eleven bells. Most of these are interim (i.e. a tower with six is to have eight, but currently can afford only seven); there has, however, been a ring of nine at All Saints, Basingstoke, since 1916. Rings of seven are included with eights here; nines with tens and elevens with twelves.

bells. Not surprisingly, many of these losses were from city churches (Dove lists twelve in London alone), which together with the wartime loss of 21 rings following enemy action (including seven in London, four in Bristol and three in Plymouth) has meant a considerable decline in the number of inner-city churches from which the call of the bells is now heard.[9]

Clearly the major change in the last 38 years has been with the number of augmentations to six, eight, ten and twelve. There has been a 20 per cent decline in the number of four-bell towers since 1962, and a 30 per cent fall in the number with five bells over the slightly longer period 1950–88. There are over a hundred more towers each with six and eight bells, a 20 per cent increase in the number with ten, and a 65 per cent increase in the number with twelve.

What this brief survey shows, therefore, is that over the last century there has been only a small increase in the number of churches where change-ringing can be practised but a very substantial increase in the numbers of bells involved. Why should this be? Clearly it is not a consequence of any liturgical or other developments in the Church of England, since how the bells are rung is irrelevant to the Church's needs. The more bells the more sound, but it is unlikely that more people hear them too. The answer must be with the ringers themselves, who have promoted the large number of augmentations in order to advance their own interests. Such interests do not run counter to those of the Church, of course, so long as the money can be found, and there is little doubt that change-ringing on eight or ten bells, say (and especially on nine with a tenor covering: see below) is more melodious than it is on four

or five. But the main difference is that the ringers themselves find it more interesting, and they have successfully promoted their cause in a large number of cases.

We are left with a further question: why is this development so recent? Five linked reasons are suggested as an answer. The first is the rapid advancement in the technology of hanging bells, which makes them so much easier to ring now and much less demanding of physical strength. Until the nineteenth century ringing was an activity open only to able-bodied men; the young, women, and old men were excluded because, in general, they weren't strong enough. Today, with ball bearings and stable bell frames, strength is much less important, certainly for the lighter bells in each ring; the age-range of ringers is now from seven to over 90, and in many towers there are at least as many female as male ringers (though the acceptance of women was much slower than it need have been and they faced much prejudice and discrimination until well into the present century). Thus ringing is now something that virtually any person can take up and enjoy.

Secondly, and perhaps most importantly, within the Church of England in the late nineteenth century major reforms led to the re-establishment of ringing as part of the church activities. Until then, in many places the ringers had no contact with the church authorities, rang when they wanted to and not necessarily for the church services (indeed often the bells were chimed just by the sexton on Sundays), and had reputations for drunkenness and general bad behaviour. With the Oxford Movement such practices were outlawed, and ringers were incorporated with the church organization. This meant that church authorities were more likely to aid ringers in their search for funds to augment their rings and to promote ringing (like choral singing and organ playing) as an integral part of church life. The ringers reciprocated, and organized a series of territorial societies covering the whole of England to promote *church* bell-ringing and the use of bells to announce divine service; many of those societies have 'recognition of ringers as church workers' among their aims and objectives. By 1891 they had a national body – the Central Council of Church Bell Ringers – which promoted ringers' interests within the Church, and which has done much to advance the art of campanology.

The third reason is the rapid development in the methods of ringing changes. The twentieth century has seen a great blossoming of new methods for people to learn and practice. These provide much greater stimulation to ringers; their art is one of unending opportunities. The better quality of bells makes it easier to ring these methods and to ring them for long periods. For centuries a peal of 5,000 or more changes (separate pulls on the rope) taking about three hours to complete has been accepted as a standard of ringing excellence, and

The bell-cage at the Church of St Mary-the-Virgin, East Bergholt, Suffolk: built in 1531, it stands at the side of the church to house the bells originally intended for the church tower; the bells are rung by swinging the wooden headstocks.

Bells hung mouth-downwards: those at Old North Church, Boston, USA, were cast in 1744 but now have modern fittings.

Up and ready to ring: one of the bells at Sheffield Cathedral in the mouth-upwards position.

The big and the small: both Pershore Abbey and the former church of S Andrew have a ring of eight; perhaps not surprisingly, the tenor bell at the abbey is two and a half times the size of that of its smaller neighbour.

peals are rung to celebrate many occasions. But peal-ringing on bells calling for considerable strength is hard work, and to ring one was a major feat of physical as well as mental endurance. Today the physical demands are much less, and many more peals are rung – averaging over 4,000 a year at the present time compared with less than 1,500 40 years ago. The mental demands are not reducing – indeed with the greater complexity of methods rung they are increasing – but ringers can now gather to ring a peal and master the mental problems of continued concentration for three hours or more without having to bother too much about their physical stamina. Several hundred ringers have rung more than 1,000 peals each.

The fourth and fifth reasons relate to changes in society at large. The first of these is the greater mobility that all people enjoy, as a consequence of both relatively cheap public transport and, even more so, the wide availability of cars. Until recent decades the great majority of ringers probably only ever rang at their local, probably village, church and at a few others nearby; even in the 1950s an annual one-day coach outing to towers 100 miles away was a major event. Today ringers travel far and wide to sample different bells (for no two rings are the same) and to practise their art with others. Again, the stimulations have been increased, making ringing a more attractive pastime for many – who nevertheless still realize that their major task is to ensure that the bells are rung each Sunday before the major services.

Finally, linked to greater geographical mobility has been social change, and in particular the almost complete removal of class divisions among ringers. Until the nineteenth century there were two main groups. The first, undoubtedly a minority numerically but the most influential in the development of change-ringing, were the 'gentlemen ringers' who manned the relatively small number of eight-, ten- and twelve-bell towers in the towns and cities. Most of them were drawn from the middle classes (especially the professions) and the gentry (remember that Lord Peter Wimsey was a ringer);[10] the great majority of the band at York Minster in 1705 could sign their names, for example, and when a new ring of bells was opened there in 1765 this was announced publicly by giving 'notice to all gentlemen ringers and others'.[11] The society of ringers with the largest continuous history – the Ancient Society of College Youths – was founded on 5 November 1637 and probably drew many of its early members from the Law Courts and other offices in and around the City of London.[12] These people developed change-ringing, invested substantially themselves in the provision of bells and rang the early peals. The second group, and undoubtedly the majority, were the village ringers, who manned the three-, four-, five- and (rarely) six-bell towers of rural England. They may have done some rudimentary change-ringing (as described below), but in general what they did was very different from the activities of their urban contemporaries – of whose efforts they may never have heard. Some rural residents did promote change-ringing, such as Squire Proctor of Benington in Hertfordshire, who augmented the local ring to eight in 1838 and employed his workers and their dependants as ringers. But this was rare, and it was only with the formation of the territorial societies, the

Crowland Abbey, Lincolnshire, believed to have housed the first-ever ring of bells.

greater mobility and education of rural residents, and the improvement in the 'go' of many rings that change-ringing as described in the next section was widely practised in town and countryside and the major era of augmentations to sustain it was launched.

The Nature of Change-Ringing

What, then, is change-ringing, this activity that upwards of 30,000 people of all ages and backgrounds find not only an attractive way of serving their church but also an enjoyable and time-consuming pastime, even, for more than a few, an obsession? Basically it involves the sequence of bells being altered every time that they are sounded, according to set rules that the ringers memorize.

The nature of change-ringing can be illustrated readily by tracing briefly what is believed to be its origins. We take a tower with three bells – the commonest number (other than one) before the eighteenth century. The bells are tuned to the notes me, ray, doh; the lightest is bell 1 (or the treble) and the heaviest is bell 3 (or the tenor). When they are being rung other than in changes the sequence is 123 – which ringers know as 'ringing rounds'.

There are six ways in which three bells can be ordered:

1 2 3	2 1 3	3 2 1
1 3 2	2 3 1	3 1 2

How can these six ways be put into a sequence? Clearly there are several possibilities, but the principles on which change-ringing is based severely constrain the choice. Those principles evolved over many years of trial and error, and are represented by the following three rules:

The sequence should start and end with 'rounds' (i.e. the bells in the order 123);

No row (ordering of the bells) should occur more than once in the sequence;

Between any pair of adjacent rows (i.e. a change) no bell should move more than one position in order.

The last of these rules was imposed for technical reasons. As outlined above, bells rotate through a full circle each time before they sound, so that ringing would have to be very slow if the same bell were to sound twice in succession or if one bell were to move several places in the order at one change (e.g. from 123 to 321); on more than three bells, it is extremely difficult to move a bell, especially a heavy one, through several places at successive changes (e.g. from 12345 to 53124 and then to 24135 etc.), and also to delay (or 'hold up') pulling a bell again. The other two rules are not absolutely essential, but were decided on by ringers as

pragmatic constraints to the development of their art. The decision was not a democratically taken one, of course, nor even necessarily an explicit choice. It emerged as the one of several practices that was widely accepted, and eventually universally so.

The application of these rules to three bells severely limits the number of changes. The sequence must start with 'rounds' (123), and it can be followed only by either 213 or 231. If 213 is chosen, then the next possibles are either 123, which is 'rounds' again and hence the end of the sequence (rule 2), or 231. And so the sequence of rows can be built up as a set of six changes:

either	1 2 3	or	1 2 3
	2 1 3		1 3 2
	2 3 1		3 1 2
	3 2 1		3 2 1
	3 1 2		2 3 1
	1 3 2		2 1 3
	1 2 3		1 2 3

The two possibilities are the reverse of each other, so the choice was a simple one!

How, then, were these sequences rung? Taking the first option, the initial step was undoubtedly what we now know as 'call changes', in which one of the ringers (or another person who was not ringing at the time) called out the changes – not necessarily changing the order at every row, so that each order might have sounded several times before another change was called. Thus to move the bells from 123 to 213, the 'conductor' might call out 'one after two, three after one' or just 'one after two', and at the next pull the ringers would put them in that order. For the next change, the call might be 'three after two, one after three', and so on. Undoubtedly other methods were used: for example, the conductor might call out the row (e.g. 'two, one, three', 'two, three, one', etc.), or the sequence of rows might have been remembered by the ringers, so that the conductor could just call 'next' and they would implement the next change. Another possibility is that the ringers had the sequence laid out on a card or board in front of them, so that when 'next' was called they would see what the next change was. This last method assumes literacy, of course. It is still used in some places where call-change ringing is practised, but is totally frowned upon by change-ringers, who insist that ringers use no aids to memory.

The next step from call-change ringing is to ring the sequence unaided, with the changes coming consecutively and the ringers implementing them having memorized what they involved. This perhaps initially meant memorizing the whole set of numbers as in the list above, but it was realized that this was unnecessary (in part, undoubtedly, because of the demands made on the memory when ringing four or more bells: see below). If we look at the sequence of six changes again,

There is a ring of ten in the south-west tower of Westminster Abbey, and another at S Margaret's Church alongside.

and concentrate on bell number one, we readily identify a clear pattern:

```
1 2 3
2 1 3
2 3 1
3 2 1
3 1 2
1 3 2
1 2 3
```

The bell proceeds from the front of the row to the back, and then returns to the front: its position in the sequence is first place, second place, third place, third place, second place, first place, first place. This could be committed to memory quite easily, and once the conductor said 'go into changes' the ringer of the first (or treble) bell would go through that pattern. And he would find a guide to help in that, because as the treble moves from the front of the row to the back it follows bell number 2 and then bell number 3; as it returns to the front, it follows them in that same sequence again.

If we follow each of the bells through the set of rows, we find that all do the same work, except that they start in a different position:

```
1 2 3      1 2 3      1 2 3
2 1 3      2 1 3      2 1 3
2 3 1      2 3 1      2 3 1
3 2 1      3 2 1      3 2 1
3 1 2      3 1 2      3 1 2
1 3 2      1 3 2      1 3 2
1 2 3      1 2 3      1 2 3
```

Each is moving from front to back and from back to front again, in a smooth pattern. And so it was realized that the ringers did not need to learn the particular route for each bell, but just the general principles, which they should be able to practise on any one of the bells.

On three bells, the set of changes is small and the method of ringing them not too hard to learn (though

it is not as easy as it perhaps seems, and certainly putting it into practice is not straightforward to the novice). As the number of bells increases, so does the number of possible rows. For three bells, there are six rows and thus six possible changes. For four bells there are 24 (i.e. the number of different ways of ordering four items, which is calculated as the factorial of four or 4 × 3 × 2 × 1 = 24); for five there are 120; for six, 720; and so on up to twelve and 479,001,600. (It is estimated that it would take 37 years and 355 days to ring all of the changes on twelve bells!)

On the higher numbers, the problem for ringers was to compose all of the possible changes, since the simple procedure outlined for three bells was insufficient. If we apply them to four bells, we get:

```
1 2 3 4
2 1 4 3
2 4 1 3
4 2 3 1
4 3 2 1
3 4 1 2
3 1 4 2
1 3 2 4
1 2 3 4
```

which is only eight changes. To get the full 24, a new rule has to be introduced: when the treble bell is in first place at the end of a set of eight changes, the bell in second place stays there, and then the sequence starts again. This produces

```
1 2 3 4
2 1 4 3
2 4 1 3
4 2 3 1
4 3 2 1
3 4 1 2
3 1 4 2
1 3 2 4
1 3 4 2
3 1 2 4
3 2 1 4
```

and so on.

The line dividing two rows is known as the 'lead end'; it divides off segments of rows at the point where the treble bell (1) returns to where it started. The full sequence of 24 changes of Plain Bob Minimus is shown in box 1. In it, the treble bell follows the straightforward sequence from front to back and from back to front again, three times: this is known as 'plain hunting'. But the other three do not, because at each lead-end that smooth path is interrupted. This is illustrated for bell 3. At the end of the first lead it rings twice in second place and then returns to first place again, without going up to third and fourth places. At the end of the second lead, its path to the front is blocked by bell 4 making the two blows in second place, so it returns to fourth place before proceeding to the front. This produces a kink in its path which is known as a dodge: because it is a kink on its way down to the front it is known as a 'dodge down'. At the end of the third lead it makes a similar dodge on the way from the front, which is known as a 'dodge up'. Bells 2, 3 and 4 all do the same set of work at lead-ends, in the same sequence, but starting at different places in the sequence.

```
1 2 3 4
2 1 4 3        3 1 2 4        4 1 3 2
2 4 1 3        3 2 1 4        4 3 1 2
4 2 3 1        2 3 4 1        3 4 2 1
4 3 2 1        2 4 3 1        3 2 4 1
3 4 1 2        4 2 1 3        2 3 1 4
3 1 4 2        4 1 2 3        2 1 3 4
1 3 2 4        1 4 3 2        1 2 4 3
1 3 4 2        1 4 2 3        1 2 3 4
```

Box 1 Plain Bob Minimus

Learning the work for the full set of changes on four bells is clearly a harder task than that for only three. (It is known technically as Plain Bob Minimus: Plain Bob describes the rules that govern the sequence of changes; Minimus indicates that they are being implemented on four bells.) Learning and effecting it does not come automatically to beginners today; in the early days of ringing, much effort must have been expended on mastering its apparent complexity. Indeed, it was probably not Plain Bob Minimus – or the Plain Bob method on any number of bells – that was first rung. The method shown in box 2, known as Grandsire Doubles, is one of the oldest. In it, as shown by the path of bell 5, a place is made in third place at the lead-end and there is a dodge in fourth and fifth places.

```
1 2 3 4 5 6
2 1 3 5 4 6      2 1 5 4 3 6      2 1 4 3 5 6
2 3 1 4 5 6      2 5 1 3 4 6      2 4 1 5 3 6
3 2 4 1 5 6      5 2 3 1 4 6      4 2 5 1 3 6
3 4 2 5 1 6      5 3 2 4 1 6      4 5 2 3 1 6
4 3 5 2 1 6      3 5 4 2 1 6      5 4 3 2 1 6
4 5 3 1 2 6      3 4 5 1 2 6      5 3 4 1 2 6
5 4 1 3 2 6      4 3 1 5 2 6      3 5 1 4 2 6
5 1 4 2 3 6      4 1 3 2 5 6      3 1 5 2 4 6
1 5 2 4 3 6      1 4 2 3 5 6      1 3 2 5 4 6
1 2 5 3 4 6      1 2 4 5 3 6      1 2 3 4 5 6
```

Box 2 Grandsire Doubles

Methods such as Grandsire Doubles were almost certainly initially rung as call-changes, with the conductor changing a single pair of bells each time. Thus the first few changes might have been achieved as follows:

```
1 2 3 4 5
2 1 3 4 5
2 1 3 5 4
2 1 3 4 5
2 3 1 4 5
2 3 4 1 5
3 2 4 1 5
  etc.
```

Box 3 illustrates what Fabian Stedman called his 'Plain Changes' on five bells, in which only one pair of bells is moved between adjacent rows. The treble bell is a member of that pair in every change except where it pauses in either first or fifth place. No row is repeated, so that all 120 are rung, but the music produced is very 'static' because one bell can stay in the same place for up to eight changes.

```
1 2 3 4 5
2 1 3 4 5      4 1 2 3 5      5 1 4 3 2      5 1 3 2 4
2 3 1 4 5      4 2 1 3 5      5 4 1 3 2      5 3 1 2 4
2 3 4 1 5      4 2 3 1 5      5 4 3 1 2      5 3 2 1 4
2 3 4 5 1      4 2 3 5 1      5 4 3 2 1      5 3 2 4 1
3 2 4 5 1      2 4 3 5 1      5 4 2 3 1      5 3 4 2 1
3 2 4 1 5      2 4 3 1 5      5 4 2 1 3      5 3 4 1 2
3 2 1 4 5      2 4 1 3 5      5 4 1 2 3      5 3 1 4 2
3 1 2 4 5      2 1 4 3 5      5 1 4 2 3      5 1 3 4 2
1 3 2 4 5      1 2 4 3 5      1 5 4 2 3      1 5 3 4 2
1 3 4 2 5      1 2 4 5 3      1 5 2 4 3      1 3 5 4 2
3 1 4 2 5      2 1 4 5 3      5 1 2 4 3      3 1 5 4 2
3 4 1 2 5      2 4 1 5 3      5 2 1 4 3      3 5 1 4 2
3 4 2 1 5      2 4 5 1 3      5 2 4 1 3      3 5 4 1 2
3 4 2 5 1      2 4 5 3 1      5 2 4 3 1      3 5 4 2 1
3 4 5 2 1      4 2 5 3 1      2 5 4 3 1      3 5 2 4 1
3 4 5 1 2      4 2 5 1 3      2 5 4 1 3      3 5 2 1 4
3 4 1 5 2      4 2 1 5 3      2 5 1 4 3      3 5 1 2 4
3 1 4 5 2      4 1 2 5 3      2 1 5 4 3      3 1 5 2 4
1 3 4 5 2      1 4 2 5 3      1 2 5 4 3      1 3 5 2 4
1 4 3 5 2      1 4 5 2 3      1 2 5 3 4      1 3 2 5 4
4 1 3 5 2      4 1 5 2 3      2 1 5 3 4      3 1 2 5 4
4 3 1 5 2      4 5 1 2 3      2 5 1 3 4      3 2 1 5 4
4 3 5 1 2      4 5 2 1 3      2 5 3 1 4      3 2 5 1 4
4 3 5 2 1      4 5 2 3 1      2 5 3 4 1      3 2 5 4 1
4 3 2 5 1      4 5 3 2 1      5 2 3 4 1      2 3 5 4 1
4 3 2 1 5      4 5 3 1 2      5 2 3 1 4      2 3 5 1 4
4 1 3 2 5      4 1 5 3 2      5 1 2 3 4      2 1 3 5 4
1 4 3 2 5      1 4 5 3 2      1 5 2 3 4      1 2 3 5 4
1 4 2 3 5      1 5 4 2 3      1 5 3 2 4      1 2 3 4 5
```

Box 3 Stedman's Plain Changes

Fabian Stedman was one of the prime movers in the development of change-ringing. He lived in the late seventeenth century, in both Cambridge and London, and published one of the earliest books on ringing (Richard Duckworth's *Tintinnalogia*); he was trained as a printer but later joined the Excise Department and wrote a book of his own (*Campanologia*, 1677). The bells that he rang were at S Benedict's Church (or S Bene't's) in central Cambridge. He is remembered mainly by the popular principle named after him.

Eventually, ringers responded to the challenge of learning the method and ringing it as an unbroken sequence of changes from memory, with nobody calling out the individual changes. And so was born the modern method of change-ringing, applying the basic rules outlined above. This probably occurred in London, early in the seventeenth century.

Having mastered the plain course of Grandsire Doubles, ringers had merely taken the first step on a then-uncharted voyage of discovery into the vast complexity and fascination of change-ringing that awaited them. They first had to find a way of ringing all the changes. The plain course of Grandsire Doubles contains only 30 changes, and yet they knew by writing them out that 120 different rows were possible. To get the others they had to invent new rules. The first was what is known as a 'Bob', which changes the work at a lead-end. For the first lead-end, we get the following with and without a Bob:

5 1 4 2 3	with a Bob	5 1 4 2 3
1 5 2 4 3		1 5 4 3 2
1 2 5 3 4		1 4 5 2 3
2 1 5 4 3		4 1 5 3 2
2 5 1 3 4		4 5 1 2 3
5 2 3 1 4		5 4 2 1 3

The Bob makes another bell stop in third place and return to the lead (bell 4 in the example); the bells above third place perform a 'double dodge'. Ringers discovered that if they had a Bob at every other lead-end they could get 60 changes but no more. To get the full 120 they had to introduce a further rule, known as a 'Single'. This produced the following at the first lead-end:

5 1 4 2 3	with a Single	5 1 4 2 3
1 5 2 4 3		1 5 4 3 2
1 2 5 3 4		1 5 4 2 3
2 1 5 4 3		5 1 4 3 2
2 5 1 3 4		5 4 1 2 3
5 2 3 1 4		4 5 2 1 3

in which one bell (5 in the example) stayed in second place at the lead-end and another (bell 4) stayed in third place for four successive rows. And then, if they substituted a Single for one of the Bobs in the set of 60 changes, and repeated the set, they achieved the full 120.

Having composed the full set of changes, two problems faced the ringers who tried to implement it. The first was to learn what to do at the Bob and at the Single, which involved more complex rules. The second was to know when to implement Bobs and Singles. The former involved developing the memory and a whole gamut of terms – 'double-dodging', 'long thirds', 'dodge 5–4 down out of the hunt' etc. – with which to commit the rules to mind: like most other activities, change-ringing has its own, somewhat arcane, vocabulary which visitors to towers find perplexing, to say the least. The latter involved a conductor, who learned when the Bobs and Singles were to be made, and called out 'Bob' or 'Single' at the relevant moment.

In change-ringing, as in so many different activities, there were soon people who were not satisfied with the current practices but sought new challenges, developing new methods of organizing changes and, as already suggested, introducing larger numbers of bells. Over time, to cater for the exponents, further rules were introduced, the most important of which was that each change should involve as many pairs of bells as possible. On eight bells, this meant that

$$2\ 1\ 4\ 3\ 6\ 5\ 8\ 7$$
$$2\ 4\ 1\ 6\ 3\ 8\ 5\ 7$$

was much preferred to

$$2\ 1\ 4\ 3\ 6\ 5\ 8\ 7$$
$$2\ 1\ 4\ 6\ 3\ 8\ 5\ 7$$

although it was realized that occasionally a number of bells would have to stay in the same place for two rows in order to achieve the required number of changes. Similarly, to avoid a proliferation of calls, the convention was introduced that only two – a Bob and a Single – would be allowed in any method. Of course these rules are not laws, and nobody enforces them on ringers. They simply became the standard practice, either because they seemed eminently sensible or because it seemed a good thing to do at the time. They are now accepted by the Central Council of Church Bell Ringers as the norms, and ringing that lies outside those standards is not accepted by the Council (e.g. in its officially accepted 'records'). This does not prevent bands of ringers adopting other norms if that is how they want to ring. When many bands were isolated and rarely if ever rang with others, undoubtedly many did have their own. Today, however, ringers are mobile; visitors and migrants can be readily accommodated only if they accept the same principles.

There have been two basic elements in the development of change-ringing over the last 250 years or so. The first is the proliferation of methods. Change-ringing is now practised in towers with from four to twelve bells, although very few have seven, nine or eleven and four is not popular for change-ringing because the range of

A ringer's membership certificate

methods available is so small. (Some towers have more than twelve bells – York Minster has 14, for example. This, however, is to enable different rings of six, eight and ten to be selected which are in the diatonic scale associated with the tenor being rung; thus at Sheffield Cathedral there is a 'flat 6th' to enable eight bells to be rung with bell 9 as the tenor.) Changes on each number of bells have their own name, as follows:

3 – Singles	4 – Minimus
5 – Doubles	6 – Minor
7 – Triples	8 – Major
9 – Caters	10 – Royal
11 – Cinques	12 – Maximus

The sequence for even numbers of bells indicates an increase in 'superiority' or 'status' from the 'minimum' to the 'maximum' (though there are plans for a ring of at least 16 at S Martin's Parish Church in Birmingham). That for odd numbers has names reflecting the maximum number of pairs of bells that can change position between any two rows: on three bells only one pair can change; on five bells, two; and so on.

Change-ringing on odd numbers of bells probably preceded developments on even numbers. Today, even-bell ringing dominates, largely because of the much greater range of methods available. With odd-bell ringing on seven or more bells, it is conventional to ring with what is known as 'tenor covering', i.e. the heaviest bell is not involved in the changes but always sounds at the end of each row. This helps to give a regular beat to the ringing and many ringers believe that it produces the most attractive music, especially when changes are being rung on nine bells (i.e. Caters). There is, of course, no necessity for this practice, which has just become the convention. As a consequence, although there are towers with five bells, there is only one with seven, one with nine (at All Saints, Basingstoke; installed in 1916), and none with eleven. (There have been brief periods of towers having eleven – for example, at S James, Accrington, Lancashire, in the early 1970s – as an intermediate stage between having ten and twelve.) And so strong has been the convention that until 1986 the Central Council would not recognize for its records either peals rung on odd numbers greater than five without a tenor covering or peals on even numbers plus a tenor covering. The change of heart in 1986 did not herald a revolution in ringing practices, and very few peals within the new rules have since been rung.

As indicated above, Plain Bob (see box 4 for the Major version) is the simplest of all methods of change-ringing: it can be rung on any number of bells (odd or even), and is usually the first that a learner tackles. It is known as a 'plain hunt method' because the treble bell (number 1) follows the simple path from the front to the rear of the row and back again throughout (i.e. it makes no dodges) and is unaffected by the calls of Bob and Single. Relatively few other 'plain hunt' methods are rung, however. Much more common are those based on the 'treble bob hunt' principle, in which the treble dodges in each pair of places (i.e. 1–2, 3–4, etc.) both on the way to the rear of the row and then again on the way back to the front. Box 5 shows one of the most straightforward treble bob methods, Kent Treble Bob Major, with the path of the treble highlighted. The path of the treble is shown as a line – known to ringers for some reason as the 'blue line' – and it is that which ringers must learn. As in plain hunt methods the work of the treble bell is fixed and is unaffected by the Bobs and Singles: it provides the fulcrum around which the other bells are rung.

Within the 'treble bob hunt' group, by far the most popular methods are those of the Surprise family. A Surprise method is one in which an internal place is made (i.e. a bell remains for two blows in a place in the row other than the first and the last) whenever the treble is moving from one dodging position to another. Thus, for example, in a Surprise Minor method,

```
1 2 3 4 5 6 7 8      5 1 3 7 2 8 4 6      8 1 7 6 5 4 3 2      4 1 6 2 8 3 7 5
2 1 4 3 6 5 8 7      5 3 1 2 7 4 8 6      8 7 1 5 6 3 4 2      4 6 1 8 2 7 3 5
2 4 1 6 3 8 5 7      3 5 2 1 4 7 6 8      7 8 5 1 3 6 2 4      6 4 8 1 7 2 5 3
4 2 6 1 8 3 7 5      3 2 5 4 1 6 7 8      7 5 8 3 1 2 6 4      6 8 4 7 1 5 2 3
4 6 2 8 1 7 3 5      2 3 4 5 6 1 8 7      5 7 3 8 2 1 4 6      8 6 7 4 5 1 3 2
6 4 8 2 7 1 5 3      2 4 3 6 5 8 1 7      5 3 7 2 8 4 1 6      8 7 6 5 4 3 1 2
6 8 4 7 2 5 1 3      4 2 6 3 8 5 7 1      3 5 2 7 4 8 6 1      7 8 5 6 3 4 2 1
8 6 7 4 5 2 3 1      4 6 2 8 3 7 5 1      3 2 5 4 7 6 8 1      7 5 8 3 6 2 4 1
8 7 6 5 4 3 2 1      6 4 8 2 7 3 1 5      2 3 4 5 6 7 1 8      5 7 3 8 2 6 1 4
7 8 5 6 3 4 1 2      6 8 4 7 2 1 3 5      2 4 3 6 5 1 7 8      5 3 7 2 8 1 6 4
7 5 8 3 6 1 4 2      8 6 7 4 1 2 5 3      4 2 6 3 1 5 8 7      3 5 2 7 1 8 4 6
5 7 3 8 1 6 2 4      8 7 6 1 4 5 2 3      4 6 2 1 3 8 5 7      3 2 5 1 7 4 8 6
5 3 7 1 8 2 6 4      7 8 1 6 5 4 3 2      6 4 1 2 8 3 7 5      2 3 1 5 4 7 6 8
3 5 1 7 2 8 4 6      7 1 8 5 6 3 4 2      6 1 4 8 2 7 3 5      2 1 3 4 5 6 7 8
3 1 5 2 7 4 8 6      1 7 5 8 3 6 2 4      1 6 8 4 7 2 5 3      1 2 4 3 6 5 8 7
1 3 2 5 4 7 6 8      1 7 8 5 6 3 4 2      1 6 4 8 2 7 3 5      1 2 3 4 5 6 7 8
1 3 5 2 7 4 8 6      7 1 5 8 3 6 2 4      6 1 8 4 7 2 5 3
3 1 2 5 4 7 6 8      7 5 1 3 8 2 6 4      6 8 1 7 4 5 2 3
3 2 1 4 5 6 7 8      5 7 3 1 2 8 4 6      8 6 7 1 5 4 3 2
2 3 4 1 6 5 8 7      5 3 7 2 1 4 8 6      8 7 6 5 1 3 4 2
2 4 3 6 1 8 5 7      3 5 2 7 4 1 6 8      7 8 5 6 3 1 2 4
4 2 6 3 8 1 7 5      3 2 5 4 7 6 1 8      7 5 8 3 6 2 1 4
4 6 2 8 3 7 1 5      2 3 4 5 6 7 8 1      5 7 3 8 2 6 4 1
6 4 8 2 7 3 5 1      2 4 3 6 5 8 7 1      5 3 7 2 8 4 6 1
6 8 4 7 2 5 3 1      4 2 6 3 8 5 1 7      3 5 2 7 4 8 1 6
8 6 7 4 5 2 1 3      4 6 2 8 3 1 5 7      3 2 5 4 7 1 8 6
8 7 6 5 4 1 2 3      6 4 8 2 1 3 7 5      2 3 4 5 1 7 6 8
7 8 5 6 1 4 3 2      6 8 4 1 2 7 3 5      2 4 3 1 5 6 7 8
7 5 8 1 6 3 4 2      8 6 1 4 7 2 5 3      4 2 1 3 6 5 8 7
5 7 1 8 3 6 2 4      8 1 6 7 4 5 2 3      4 1 2 6 3 8 5 7
5 1 7 3 8 2 6 4      1 8 7 6 5 4 3 2      1 4 6 2 8 3 7 5
1 5 3 7 2 8 4 6      1 8 6 7 4 5 2 3      1 4 2 6 3 8 5 7
1 5 7 3 8 2 6 4
```

Box 4   Plain Bob Major

whenever the treble moves between places two and three or between four and five (in either direction) another bell must make a place in either the second, third, fourth or fifth position in the row. Clearly, if the treble is moving between second and third place, another bell cannot remain in either, so the place must be made in either fourth or fifth. It will probably be in fourth place, since, as the examples below show, if it were fifth place then other bells would have to make fourth and sixth places too.

Fifth's place made:	Fourth's place made:
2 1 3 4 5 6	2 1 3 4 5 6
2 3 1 4 5 6	2 3 1 4 6 5
3 2 4 1 6 5	3 2 4 1 5 6

Again, there is no need for the second alternative to be preferred: that it has become the convention reflects ringers' general desire that as many pairs of bells change

between each pair of rows as possible, giving more musical variety.

The range of Surprise methods that can be rung is very great, especially on eight or more bells, because of the availability of several internal places each time the treble moves dodging places. (Surprise methods, like all 'treble bob hunt' methods, can be rung only on even numbers of bells, because each dodging position requires two places.) The earliest rung, and still that tackled first by most ringers, is Cambridge Surprise – the name indicating where it almost certainly originated. As comparing boxes 4 and 6 shows, a course of Cambridge Surprise Major is much more complicated to learn than Plain Bob Major (and is twice as long, since the treble bell occupies each place four times in a lead, not twice). In Plain Bob, it is only at the lead-end that a dodge or second's place are made; for the rest of the lead, each bell is plain hunting like the treble. In

15

```
12345678   41268375   61487253   81675432   71853624   51732846   31524768
21346587   14623857   16842735   18764523   17586342   15378264   13257486
12435678   41628375   61847253   81765432   71583624   51372846   31254768
21436587   46182735   68174523   87156342   75138264   53127486   32145678
24163857   64817253   86715432   78513624   57312846   35214768   23416587
42618375   64182735   86174523   78156342   57138264   35127486   23145678
42163857   46817253   68715432   87513624   75312846   53214768   32416587
24618375   48671523   67851342   85731264   73521486   52341678   34261857
26481735   84765132   76583124   58372146   37254168   25436187   43628175
62847153   84671523   76851342   58731264   37521486   25341678   43261857
62481735   48765132   67583124   85372146   73254168   52436187   34628175
26847153   47856312   65738214   83527416   72345618   54263817   36482715
28674513   74583621   56372841   38254761   27436581   45628371   63847251
82765431   74856312   56738214   38527416   27345618   45263817   63482715
82674513   47583621   65372841   83254761   72436581   54628371   36847251
28765431   45738261   63527481   82345671   74263851   56482731   38674521
27856341   54372816   36254718   28436517   47628315   65847213   83765412
72583614   54738261   36527481   28345671   47263851   65482731   83674521
72856341   45372816   63254718   82436517   74628315   56847213   38765412
27583614   43527186   62345178   84263157   76482135   58674123   37856142
25738164   34251768   26431587   48621375   67841253   85761432   73581624
52371846   34527186   26345178   48263157   67482135   85674123   73856142
52738164   43251768   62431587   84621375   76841253   58761432   37581624
25371846   42315678   64213857   86412735   78614523   57816342   35718264
23517486   24136587   46128375   68147253   87165432   75183624   53172846
32154768   24315678   46213857   68412735   87614523   75816342   53718264
32517486   42136587   64128375   86147253   78165432   57183624   35172846
23154768   41263857   61482735   81674523   71856342   51738264   31527486
21345678   14268375   16487253   18675432   17853624   15732846   13524768
12346587   41623857   61842735   81764523   71586342   51378264   31257486
21435678   14628375   16847253   18765432   17583624   15372846   13254768
12436587   16482735   18674523   17856342   15738264   13527486   12345678
14263857
```

Box 5 Kent Treble Bob Major

Cambridge, on the other hand, there are places and dodges being made throughout the lead. To ring it, that sequence of work must be committed to memory. It looks daunting, and usually is to the relative novice. The exact sequence must be remembered – and there is a substantial vocabulary to describe the various parts of the line – and then it must be rung with the ringer placing his or her bell in the right place in each row. Trial and error, and help from others, is the only way of succeeding.

The possibilities for composing Surprise methods seem endless. At the beginning of the present century relatively few had been devised, and few ringers ever attempted to ring those that had. Over the years, however, more and more have been tackled successfully, and Surprise ringing is now considered by many the acme of ringing. Some stick to the other (not necessarily simpler) methods, especially those rung on odd numbers with tenor covering, because they prefer the music. And many, probably a majority, never try Surprise, because the people that they ring with in their local tower have not been able to tackle such methods. (It is relatively easy for one person to learn to ring Surprise if all of the others are already proficient; for a whole band to learn it together is much more difficult.) Among those who do learn it, the challenges of new methods present ever-opening vistas. And there are other possibilities too: 'Spliced Surprise' ringing, with the method being changed in mid-course, at the lead-end, by an instruction from the conductor, is becoming more popular.

Apart from the plain hunt and treble bob methods, only two others are frequently rung; both are odd-bell methods and are thus rung with tenor covering. The first is Grandsire, which was introduced earlier as one of the initial methods composed: it is peculiar in that it has two hunt bells – i.e. doing the work that only the treble does in Plain Bob – which in the plain course are bells 1 and 2; when a Bob or Single is called, only the treble bell is never affected. Box 7 illustrates this with a short touch of Grandsire Triples. The final method is Stedman Triples (see box 8), named after one of the earliest-known ringers. This is a 'principle', in which all of the bells do the same work, and is very popular because of its musical qualities.

Change-ringing itself is a major challenge. To master

16

```
12345678   51372846   81765432   41628375   31254768   71583624   61847253
21436587   15327486   18756342   14682735   13245678   17538264   16874523
12463857   51234768   81573624   41867253   31426587   71352846   61785432
21648375   52137486   85176342   48162735   34125678   73158264   67184523
26143857   25314768   58713624   84617253   43216587   37512846   76815432
62418375   25134678   58173264   84167523   43126857   37152486   76185342
62148735   52316487   85712346   48615732   34218675   73514268   67813524
26417853   25361478   58721364   84651723   43281657   37541286   76831542
62471835   52634187   85273146   48567132   34826175   73452168   67385124
26748153   56231478   82571364   45861723   38421657   74351286   63781542
27641835   65324187   28751346   54687132   83246175   47532168   36875124
72468153   56234817   82573416   45867312   38426715   74352618   63785214
27648513   65328471   28754361   54683721   83247651   47536281   36872541
72465831   63582417   27845316   56438712   82374615   45763218   38627514
74256813   36854271   72483561   65347821   28736451   54672381   83265741
47528631   63582471   27845361   56438721   82374651   45763281   38627541
74256831   36854217   72483516   65347812   28736415   54672318   83265714
47528613   38645271   74238561   63574821   27863451   56427381   82356741
45782631   83462517   47325816   36758412   72684315   65243718   28537614
54876213   38642157   74235186   63578142   27864135   56423178   82357164
45786123   83461275   47321568   36751824   72681453   65241387   28531746
54871632   84362157   43725186   37658142   76284135   62543178   25837164
58476123   48631275   34271568   73561824   67821453   26451387   52381746
85741632   84613257   43217586   37516842   76812435   62415378   25318764
58714623   48162375   34125768   73158624   67184253   26143587   52137846
85176432   48612735   34215678   73518264   67814523   26413857   52317486
85716342   84167253   43126587   37152846   76185432   62148375   25134768
58173624   81462735   41325678   31758264   71684523   61243857   21537486
51876342   18647253   14236587   13572846   17865432   16428375   12354768
15783624   81674523   41263857   31527486   71856342   61482735   21345678
51738264   18765432   14628375   13254768   17583624   16847253   12436587
15372846   18674523   14263857   13527486   17856342   16482735   12345678
15738264
```

Box 6 Cambridge Surprise Major

a method and to ring it well is the goal that many ringers set for themselves and for the bands with which they practise. Ringing it well is crucial, since all ringing can be heard not only by the ringers themselves but by the general public in the vicinity. Discordant clanging, when two or more bells sound together, is unpleasant – or so English ringers believe – as is uneven ringing when the rhythm is broken. But for nearly 300 years just ringing a method has not been enough for some: the goal has been to ring a peal in the method.

To ringers a peal is an unbroken sequence of at least 5,000 changes (5,040 on seven or fewer bells), which takes a little less than three hours to ring, on average. In general, the length of time reflects the number and the size of the bells: more bells take longer to ring, as do heavier bells. Why 5,000? There is some logic to this. On seven bells, 5,040 is the maximum number of changes possible, and it is feasible physically to ring for about three hours. On eight bells, the maximum number is 40,320, which should take about 24 hours; for most people, the mental and physical commitment would be too great, and clearly it could not be done regularly – to the relief of the listening public! On six bells, the maximum is 720 changes, which takes only half an hour. Thus the maximum for seven seemed a reasonable compromise: it was long enough to pose a substantial challenge but not so long that most ringers would never even attempt it.

The early peals rung were of Triples. The first was rung at Norwich in 1715; the first in London was achieved in 1718.[13] At that time most change-ringing was on either five or seven bells, and clearly 5,040 was a greater challenge than 120. The initial test was to compose a peal that was true – i.e. that contained all of the rows, with no repetition. The next challenge was to ring it, which in those days was physically much more difficult than it is now. To succeed was a great event, and, because the initial successes were in Triples, the target of 5,000 or so changes (exact 5,040s cannot be obtained for most methods on eight or more bells) became the norm. This meant that for peals of Minor, seven 'extents' of 720 changes had to be rung, whereas for Doubles, 42 'extents' of 120 changes are necessary. Peals of Doubles and Minor were relatively rare until the twentieth century.

In the early years, ringing a peal was something that

```
1 2 3 4 5 6 7 8
2 1 3 5 4 7 6 8        5 1 6 4 7 3 2 8        4 1 2 7 3 6 5 8             3 1 5 2 7 4 6 8
2 3 1 4 5 6 7 8        5 6 1 7 4 2 3 8        4 2 1 3 7 5 6 8             3 5 1 7 2 6 4 8
3 2 4 1 6 5 7 8        6 5 7 1 2 4 3 8        2 4 3 1 5 7 6 8             5 3 7 1 6 2 4 8
3 4 2 6 1 7 5 8        6 7 5 2 1 3 4 8        2 3 4 5 1 6 7 8             5 7 3 6 1 4 2 8
4 3 6 2 7 1 5 8        7 6 2 5 3 1 4 8        3 2 5 4 6 1 7 8             7 5 6 3 1 4 2 8
4 6 3 7 2 5 1 8        7 2 6 3 5 4 1 8        3 5 2 6 4 7 1 8             7 6 5 4 3 2 1 8
6 4 7 3 5 2 1 8        2 7 3 6 4 5 1 8        5 3 6 2 7 4 1 8             6 7 4 5 2 3 1 8
6 7 4 5 3 1 2 8        2 3 7 4 6 1 5 8        5 6 3 7 2 1 4 8             6 4 7 2 5 1 3 8
7 6 5 4 1 3 2 8        3 2 4 7 1 6 5 8        6 5 7 3 1 2 4 8             4 6 2 7 1 5 3 8
7 5 6 1 4 2 3 8        3 4 2 1 7 5 6 8        6 7 5 1 3 4 2 8             4 2 6 1 7 3 5 8
5 7 1 6 2 4 3 8 SINGLE CALLED   4 3 1 2 5 7 6 8 SINGLE CALLED   7 6 1 5 4 3 2 8 SINGLE CALLED   2 4 1 6 3 7 5 8
5 1 7 2 6 3 4 8        4 1 3 5 2 6 7 8        7 1 6 4 5 2 3 8             2 1 4 3 6 5 7 8
1 5 7 6 2 4 3 8        1 4 3 2 5 7 6 8        1 7 6 5 4 3 2 8             1 2 3 4 5 6 7 8
1 5 7 2 6 3 4 8 SINGLE MADE   1 4 3 5 2 6 7 8 SINGLE MADE   1 7 6 4 5 2 3 8 SINGLE MADE
5 1 7 6 2 4 3 8        4 1 3 2 5 7 6 8        7 1 6 5 4 3 2 8
5 7 1 2 6 3 4 8        4 3 1 5 2 6 7 8        7 6 1 4 5 2 3 8
7 5 2 1 3 6 4 8        3 4 5 1 6 2 7 8        6 7 4 1 2 5 3 8
7 2 5 3 1 4 6 8        3 5 4 6 1 7 2 8        6 4 7 2 1 3 5 8
2 7 3 5 4 1 6 8        5 3 6 4 7 1 2 8        4 6 2 7 3 1 5 8
2 3 7 4 5 6 1 8        5 6 3 7 4 2 1 8        4 2 6 3 7 5 1 8
3 2 4 7 6 5 1 8        6 5 7 3 2 4 1 8        2 4 3 6 5 7 1 8
3 4 2 6 7 1 5 8        6 7 5 2 3 1 4 8        2 3 4 5 6 1 7 8
4 3 6 2 1 7 5 8        7 2 6 1 5 4 3 8        3 2 5 4 1 6 7 8
4 6 3 1 2 5 7 8        2 7 1 6 4 5 3 8        3 5 2 1 4 7 6 8
6 4 1 3 5 2 7 8        2 1 7 4 6 3 5 8        5 3 1 2 7 4 6 8 BOB CALLED
6 1 4 5 3 7 2 8        1 2 4 7 3 6 5 8        5 1 3 7 2 6 4 8
1 6 5 4 7 3 2 8        1 4 2 3 7 5 6 8        1 5 3 2 7 4 6 8
1 5 6 7 4 2 3 8        1 4 2 3 7 5 6 8        1 3 5 7 2 6 4 8 BOB MADE
```

Box 7 A touch of Grandsire Triples

was not attempted very frequently and success was far from guaranteed. Failure could come about for a variety of reasons: problems with the bells or their fittings, notably the ropes; physical or mental exhaustion on behalf of the ringers; errors in the ringing which the conductor could not correct, so that the changes were not rung and ringing had to cease; or an error by the conductor in failing to call a Bob or Single at the right place. Today problems with the physical conditions of the bells are less frequent than they were in previous centuries, although ropes still break. Most peals that fail do so because of human error, either by individual ringers who make mistakes which lead to the conductor ending the attempt, or by the conductor failing in calling the peal. Very few peals are completely error-free: most ringers make occasional mistakes (called 'trips') which are immediately corrected, either by the ringers themselves or by the conductor. Most conductors will end an attempt if there are lots of errors, both in the method and in the quality of the ringing (the 'striking'); they have their own standards for what is acceptable.

It is the conductor who bears the heaviest burden, because all peals involve Bobs and Singles and most contain a substantial number. (The average peal of Triples, for example, will contain well over a hundred calls.) The conductor must learn where these come, and call them all at the right moment: one omission is sufficient for the peal to be lost. (There are many examples of unnoticed errors – a Bob missed, or one put where it was not needed – and the peal continued, only to find that it didn't finish in rounds, and so was invalid.) All this must be done by memory, while the conductor is ringing the method too and correcting errors that others make (and trying not to make any personally). The art of conducting peals, because of the demands that it makes, is one that the majority of ringers never tackle. It involves even more memory-work and concentration than just ringing in the peal: but for those who do take up the challenge, it adds to the fascination and stimulus of the activity.

For ringers, peals are personal challenges. For some, they are challenges spurned, since they cannot face the

```
1 2 3 4 5 6 7 8
2 1 3 5 4 7 6 8
2 3 1 4 5 6 7 8
3 2 4 1 6 5 7 8    1 7 2 4 6 5 3 8    5 6 2 4 7 1 3 8
2 3 4 6 1 7 5 8    1 2 7 6 4 3 5 8    6 5 2 7 4 3 1 8
2 4 3 1 6 5 7 8    2 1 7 4 6 5 3 8    6 2 5 4 7 1 3 8
4 2 3 6 1 7 5 8    2 7 1 6 4 3 5 8    2 6 5 7 4 3 1 8
4 3 2 1 6 5 7 8    7 2 1 4 6 5 3 8    2 5 6 4 7 1 3 8
3 4 2 6 1 7 5 8    7 1 2 6 4 3 5 8    5 2 6 7 4 3 1 8
4 3 6 2 7 1 5 8    1 7 6 2 3 4 5 8    2 5 7 6 3 4 1 8
4 6 3 7 2 5 1 8    7 1 6 3 2 5 4 8    2 7 5 3 6 1 4 8
6 4 3 2 7 1 5 8    7 6 1 2 3 4 5 8    7 2 5 6 3 4 1 8
6 3 4 7 2 5 1 8    6 7 1 3 2 5 4 8    7 5 2 3 6 1 4 8
3 6 4 2 7 1 5 8    6 1 7 2 3 4 5 8    5 7 2 6 3 4 1 8
3 4 6 7 2 5 1 8    1 6 7 3 2 5 4 8    5 2 7 3 6 1 4 8
4 3 7 6 5 2 1 8    6 1 3 7 5 2 4 8    2 5 3 7 1 6 4 8
3 4 7 5 6 1 2 8    6 3 1 5 7 4 2 8    5 2 3 1 7 4 6 8
3 7 4 6 5 2 1 8    3 6 1 7 5 2 4 8    5 3 2 7 1 6 4 8
7 3 4 5 6 1 2 8    3 1 6 5 7 4 2 8    3 5 2 1 7 4 6 8
7 4 3 6 5 2 1 8    1 3 6 7 5 2 4 8    3 2 5 7 1 6 4 8
4 7 3 5 6 1 2 8    1 6 3 5 7 4 2 8    2 3 5 1 7 4 6 8
7 4 5 3 1 6 2 8    6 1 5 3 4 7 2 8    3 2 1 5 4 7 6 8
7 5 4 1 3 2 6 8    1 6 5 4 3 2 7 8    3 1 2 4 5 6 7 8
5 7 4 3 1 6 2 8    1 5 6 3 4 7 2 8    1 3 2 5 4 7 6 8
5 4 7 1 3 2 6 8    5 1 6 4 3 2 7 8    1 2 3 4 5 6 7 8
4 5 7 3 1 6 2 8    5 6 1 3 4 7 2 8
4 7 5 1 3 2 6 8    6 5 1 4 3 2 7 8
7 4 1 5 2 3 6 8    5 6 4 1 2 3 7 8
4 7 1 2 5 6 3 8    5 4 6 2 1 7 3 8
4 1 7 5 2 3 6 8    4 5 6 1 2 3 7 8
1 4 7 2 5 6 3 8    4 6 5 2 1 7 3 8
1 7 4 5 2 3 6 8    6 4 5 1 2 3 7 8
7 1 4 2 5 6 3 8    6 5 4 2 1 7 3 8
```

Box 8 Stedman Triples

hours of physical and mental effort. For others, they are challenges to be taken up rarely, because the personal satisfaction that they bring is not great. For a few, they become an obsession, and people collect peals like others collect train-numbers. A small number ring at least 100 a year; a handful have rung over 2,000 each; some want to ring a peal on every ring of twelve; and so on. For this last group, peal-ringing almost becomes an end in itself. But most church authorities limit the number of peal attempts allowed – if only to protect themselves from the wrath of parishioners and others who, however much they may enjoy the sound of the bells, do not want to hear them every Saturday afternoon and perhaps on two evenings in the week as well.

Although some peal-ringing is done simply as ringers' indulgence, many peals are organized to mark

The bells in motion at Guildford Cathedral; ten bells are shown, as the photograph was taken before the addition of two further trebles.

special occasions, either of local or of wider significance. It is the way in which ringers celebrate a birth, a marriage or a church ceremony (such as the installation of a new vicar), and they may ring with the bells muffled (placing leather on the clappers of the bells to deaden the sound) to mark a death. All peals rung are reported in the ringers' weekly paper, *The Ringing World*: in most weeks, these occupy six or seven of the 20 or so pages, and the annual total is now over 4,000.

Peal-ringing offers many new challenges: the first peal in a method; the first attempt at a new composition; and so on. Occasionally, special peals are attempted, such as longer lengths than the norm. The longest length possible on eight bells has been achieved only once: it took eight men (seven of them bachelors) 17 hours and 58 minutes of continuous ringing at Loughborough Bell Foundry in July 1963. (It was rung at Leeds, Kent, in April 1761, but by 14 different ringers working in relays, who exchanged ropes while the ringing continued. The rules of the Central Council do not accept such 'performances' as peals.) Other long lengths have been rung, on all numbers of bells, as groups of ringers decide to press their physical and mental capacities to the limits, while always maintaining high standards of striking.

The majority of people who take up ringing never attempt a peal, let alone succeed: many give up ringing before they become proficient enough; some never have the opportunity because peal-ringing is not common in their area. Some prefer not to try; for them, just to ring is sufficient pleasure in itself, and involves them in the work of their church. But other goals are available. One is the ringing of quarter-peals, of 1,250 or so changes taking about three-quarters of an hour. This is much less demanding physically and mentally, can more readily be fitted into a busy schedule, and can be done in the period immediately before a particular service. Not all quarter-peals rung are reported in *The Ringing World*, but certainly there are more each year than there are peals.

Summary

It is usually very difficult to describe in words the fascination that an activity can have for people who develop an interest in it. To outsiders, their absorption into an esoteric practice seems inexplicable. As with so many hobbies, people get 'hooked' on bell-ringing. It is a utilitarian hobby, of course, since ringing has an important role to play in the life of the Church and the great majority of ringers respect that role by ensuring that bells are always rung for Sunday service, even if, as Sir John Betjeman describes it,

It is a classless folk art which has survived in the church despite all arguments about doctrine and the diminution of congregations. In many a church when the parson opens with the words 'Dearly beloved brethren the Scripture moveth us in sundry places . . .' one may hear the tramp of the ringers descending the newel stair into the refreshing silence of the graveyard. Though in some churches they may come in later by the main door and sit in the pew marked 'Ringers Only', on others they will not be seen again, the sweet melancholy notes of 'the exercise' floating out over the Sunday chimney-pots having been their contribution to the glory of God.[14]

All we have been able to do here is provide a brief introductory insight to the subject of the ringers' fascination, showing how the practice of change-ringing evolved and what it involves.

Notes

1 Percival Price, *Bells and Man* (Oxford University Press: New York, 1983).
2 The clappers of Russian bells weighed, on average, some 2.25 per cent of the weight of the bells, some of which were tens of thousands of kilograms. See E. V. Williams, *The Bells of Russia* (Princeton University Press: Princeton, 1986).
3 Williams, op. cit., p. 146.
4 See J. R. Nichols, *Bells, thro' the Ages* (Chapman and Hall: London, 1928), and J. Camp, *In Praise of Bells: the Folklore and Traditions of Britain's Bells* (Robert Hill: London, 1988).
5 A. H. Cocks, *The Church Bells of Buckinghamshire* (Jarrold: London, 1897).
6 H. B. Walters, *The Church Bells of Shropshire* (Woodall, Minshell, Thomas and Co.: Oswestry, 1915). The 1885 surveys were conducted by F. W. J. Rees and published in *The Bell News*: the quotes are from the edition of 20 June 1885.
7 The data for Devon in 1872 are taken from H. T. Ellacombe, *The Church Bells of Devon* (William Pollard: Exeter, 1872), and those for Northamptonshire in 1878 from T. North, *The Church Bells of Northamptonshire* (Samuel Clarke: Leicester, 1878). The 1982 figures are from the sixth edition of R. H. Dove, *A Bellringer's Guide to the Church Bells of Britain* (Viggers: Aldershot, 1982). Dove's *Guide* does not give any details for churches with three or fewer bells.
8 Dove, op cit., fourth edition (1968), p. 194. (In the 1982 listing, Dove notes that in 147 of the towers – almost exactly one-third of the total – the rings of four 'are reputed to be in an unringable condition': p. 191.)
9 Dove, op. cit., sixth edition (1982), pp. 197–200.
10 In Dorothy L. Sayers's excellent mystery novel *The Nine Tailors*.
11 David E. Potter, *The Bells and Bell Ringers of York Minster* (privately pubd: York, 1987).
12 W. T. Cook, 'The Society of College Youths 1637–1987', *The Ringing World*, no. 3957 (27 February 1987), p. 197. See also his *The Society of College Youths 1637–1987: a New History of the Society* (privately pubd: London, 1987).
13 F. W. J. Rees claimed that the first peal was rung at Norwich in 1718, although the peal board at S Peter Mancroft Church reports the date as 2 May 1715. He also claimed – in *The Bell News* (16 May 1885, p. 56) – that this fact 'was not generally known to the Exercise until more than 160 years had elapsed', because of the 'decentralized' organization of ringing. He also published a 'Chronology of Change Ringing' in the 1884 volume of *The Bell News*.
14 Sir John Betjeman in his 'Introduction' to *Collins Pocket Guide to English Parish Churches* (Collins: London, 1968), pp. 20f.

2 How the Bells are Rung

In the previous chapter we looked at change-ringing very much as a theoretical activity based on mathematical principles, with no reference to how the theory is put into practice. Thus we turn now to the application of those principles – we shift from 'pure mathematics' to 'applied mathematics'. This involves discussion of two questions: first, how are bells rung in changes?; and, second, how do the bells work?

Ringing the Changes

One cannot walk into a ringing-room off the street and expect to be able to ring a bell, let alone ring one in changes. Ringing a bell in the English fashion is a skill that has to be carefully taught and practised. The first stages of the learning process involve acquiring expertise in bell-handling; this is usually taught with the bell 'silenced' (i.e. the clapper is prevented from striking the bell), and the novice learns alone, without the other bells being rung too. Only when the learner is a proficient 'bell-handler' will he or she then be started on the next stage, ringing a bell with others. This is known as 'ringing rounds' (with the bells sounding in the descending diatonic sequence each time), and involves not just pulling the rope in the right way but also at the right moment. Only when one is an accomplished 'rounds-ringer' can one move into change-ringing, probably after learning to ring call-changes: it will most certainly be several months after the first lesson before the novice gets to this stage.

How, then, does one start? Visitors to a ringing-room (the term belfry is usually reserved for the room containing the bells themselves) will see that it contains a set of ropes that fall from the ceiling in a circle. In some the circle is perfect, with each rope at the end of an imaginary spoke of a wheel whose axle would be in the centre of the ringing-room; most are imperfect in some way (some pairs of ropes closer to each other, some 'spokes' slightly longer than others, and so on); a few are very odd. The ropes usually comprise three strands, but those attached to the heavier bells are slightly thicker than those on the lighter bells. At about head level there is some woollen padding, about one metre long, woven into the rope: this is known as the sally, and is probably striped red, white and blue. Below the sally is about six feet of rope so that it falls to the floor with some to spare; above it, the rope passes through a hole in the ceiling.

The bells are almost certainly organized in the circle so that they fall clockwise in the order of the descending notes (in about one per cent of towers they fall anticlockwise). Thus, if there are eight bells in the key of C, they start with the treble C^1 and go in sequence B, A, G, F, E, D, B, C around the circle. But before you can ring in that sequence, you must learn bell-handling.

Handling a bell

As pointed out in the previous chapter, every time a bell sounds it is after it has rotated almost a full 360 degrees on its axis, starting and finishing in the mouth-upwards position. The task of the ringer, therefore, is to pull the bell over the balance, make it rotate fully, and then stop it (under control) before pulling it back. The bell alternately rotates clockwise and anticlockwise: if it were to rotate clockwise every time it sounded there would be problems with the rope, as described below.

The ringer starts with the bell mouth-upwards (for the moment, we don't ask how it got to that position and how it stops there until you want to ring it). The bell is set in motion by gripping the sally and pulling it downwards. After it reaches about knee level the sally ceases to move downwards any further, and begins to proceed up towards the ceiling. This is because, after the bell has rotated so far, the place at which the rope is attached to the wheel passes closest to the pulley which directs it into the right place in the ringing-room; as it moves upwards, it takes the rope with it, as illustrated in figure 1.1. The ringer must let it go up; indeed, there is no way it can be stopped. Since at the end of the rotation the sally is higher than it was at the start – in ringing rooms with low ceilings it will have disappeared from sight – the ringer must not only let it go up, but must release it; the alternative is to be lifted off the floor (perhaps to make contact with the ceiling), since the impetus of all but the very smallest of bells is too great for any ringer's weight to counter. Thus the ringer pulls the sally downwards, and then lets go at the moment when it reaches its lowest point.

This is far from all, however: if the ringer lets go of the rope, how can the rotation of the bell be halted and then set off again in the opposite direction? The answer is that, although the sally is released, the ringer always keeps hold of the end of the rope. Its length below the sally is adjusted so that, with the arms at full stretch above the head, the rope-end is just reachable by the ringer when the bell is back at the mouth-upwards position. Keeping a tight hold of the rope, the ringer is able to halt the progress of the bell on its revolution, hold it still for a moment if necessary, and then pull it back in the opposite direction. As the bell rotates again, so the sally comes back down nearly to the floor, before starting to rise as the bell approaches the mouth-upwards position. The ringer catches the sally as it rises, while keeping hold of the rope-end in one hand (usually the left). When the sally is at head level, the ringer grips it tight – again at full stretch of the arms above the head, so the sally must be caught in the correct position – and halts the bell's rotation. (The rope-end is held between thumb and first finger; when the sally is gripped, it is pressed against the palm and cannot slip out of the hand.) The bell is then ready to start the sequence all over again.

It all sounds fearfully complicated and as such it is likely to result in many possible errors. What happens if you don't catch the sally, or let go of the rope, or pull it too hard, or don't catch the sally in the right place, or don't pull hard enough? The answer is that you lose control of the bell. But if you are well taught this won't happen. In your early lessons you will master, first, pulling the rope-end only; second, catching, pulling and releasing the sally only; and third, when you are proficient at both, combining the two. (When you are pulling only the rope-end, the person teaching you will pull the sally, and vice versa.) You learn how hard to pull the bell, so that it completes its rotation but can then be stopped. If you don't pull it hard enough, it will have insufficient impetus to go round the full circle; if you pull it too hard, then you will be straining to stop it continuing for another rotation. You learn not only how to catch the sally, but to catch it

(*Top*) David Ingram, at Birmingham Cathedral, ready to pull a bell at the backstroke

(*Top right*) Bells being rung at the handstroke: the rope-end is firmly trapped between the ringer's left hand and the sally, which is firmly gripped by both hands.

(*Right*) Three bells being rung in sequence at backstroke: that on the left has already been pulled, the one in the centre is just being pulled, and that on the right will follow.

22

consistently at the right moment and in the right place. And then, after a few hours' practice (perhaps spread over several weeks), your instructor will invite you to try and combine both: what ringers call the 'handstroke' (pulling the sally) and the 'backstroke' (pulling the rope-end). Very few do it successfully first time, but the vast majority soon master it, and learn how to keep hold of the rope-end while catching the sally.

As with many activities, handling a bell looks difficult – and sounds even more so when it is described in words! But it is not that hard, otherwise many would-be learners would fail – and very few indeed do. It needs careful instruction and it cannot be taken lightly; the potential for injury is always there if people are careless or 'play' at ringing. Mastering the skills, separately and then together, gives the recruit a sense of achievement, because he or she has now become proficient at a relatively arcane and esoteric art.

Earlier, we decided to leave until later a discussion of how a bell is placed in the mouth-upwards position and how it remains there until you want to ring it. The answer isn't that it is balanced there; indeed that is virtually impossible, since although the bell itself is symmetrical the clapper is always on one side of it. What happens is that, just beyond the balance, a piece of wood (called a stay) attached to the headstock – which in turn is fixed to the crown of the bell and therefore pointing down when the bell is mouth-up – is used to rest the bell against another piece (called a slider) which is attached to the bell-frame. This prevents the bell from toppling over the balance, as figure 2.1 (see p. 30) shows. When the bell rotates, the stay rotates with it. As it approaches the mouth-upwards position, the stay comes into contact with the slider before the bell is quite vertical. This should stop the rotation, but the slider can move horizontally through about 30 degrees, pushed by the stay, so that the rotation ends when the bell is just beyond the balance. It then goes back in the opposite direction, and the slider is pushed back to its original position.

This, then, answers one of the questions; the ringer is provided with a rest. If the bell is pulled too hard, the stay will shift the slider across fast and, if it isn't slowed by the ringer, will then find a buffer in its way. It may bounce back, and rotate again out of the ringer's control, or the stay and/or the slider may break. This is the preferred result, since it is likely to produce less damage to the bell than the jarring at the sudden end of the rotation; stays and sliders are accordingly made of relatively soft wood. Some learners break a stay or two during their early lessons, but they soon learn not to over-pull and that they should never let the bell rotate quite as far as the position when the slider has stopped moving. The stay and slider assembly provide a way of resting the bell when it is not being rung, not a cushion on which the impetus of the bell's motion can be absorbed.

With the stay/slider assembly (a relatively recent tech-nological innovation) bells could always be left mouth-upwards. A few are, but most aren't, because of the inherent danger either of the rope being pulled by a visitor to the ringing-room when there are no trained ringers there or of the bell being set in motion when somebody is working in the belfry. In addition, in many towers bells are also part of a clock apparatus, and there are hammers which strike the hours and quarters on them: these only work when the bell is mouth-downwards, which is clearly less dangerous.

Other than at intervals during a ringing session and between two such sessions (notably between ringing for morning and evening service on a Sunday), the bells are usually left mouth-downwards. Putting them into that position involves what ringers term 'ringing the bells down'. The rope is pulled in the usual way, except that after every pull it is shortened slightly by the ringer. This restricts the rotation, and eventually the bell becomes like a pendulum that is slowly running down as the angle of swing decreases. Returning them to the mouth-upwards position ('ringing the bells up') involves exactly the opposite procedure, with the rope being made longer (i.e. the ringer, who begins with it coiled in one hand, slowly lets it out) and the swing wider. This is relatively hard work, because extra energy has to be imparted to the bell each time to increase its angle of swing.

Ringing a bell up and down comes later in the learner's progress than the more straightforward task of ringing it once it is up. It is, as we said, relatively hard work to pull a bell up, and indeed for heavier bells – those weighing about a ton or more – it is usual for two people to be involved. It takes only a couple of minutes, however. In 'normal' ringing, the amount of energy required is not great and involves little more effort than one exerts in polishing shoes. Physical tiredness is not a common problem for ringers – unless they ring very heavy bells (especially in peals) or bells that, for a variety of technical reasons, don't 'go well'.

Ringing 'rounds'

Once the learner has mastered the skills of bell-handling, the next big step is learning to ring in 'rounds', which involves not just pulling the rope to make the bell sound but pulling it at the precise moment so that the bell sounds at the correct point in sequence. The basic feature of English ringing is that the bells ring to an exact rhythm. When rung well, bells sound as if they are activated by clockwork – but of course they are being rung by skilled individuals. Ringing to the rhythm – what ringers call 'striking well' – is again something that is learned, and it can be learned only through experience (an experience which is very public, of course). It involves coordination of hand (for pulling the rope), eye (for watching when others pull theirs) and ear (for checking that you get it right).

In rounds, bells are rung in the sequence of the

descending scale. As the ropes are organized clockwise in that sequence, each rope is pulled after that to the right of it. The skill that the ringer has to learn is exactly when: slightly too soon, and the rhythm will be broken by the two bells either 'clashing' (i.e. ringing together) or sounding too close, in staccato-like form; slightly too late, and the rhythm will be broken because the gap between them is too wide. Getting it exactly right involves judgement and learning. Usually, each rope is pulled no more than a split-second after that preceding it, so that as the two move down the sallies are no more than a few inches apart.

The basic rhythm of the bells is that of a perfectly consistent beat; the pace never alters and the gap between each pair of bells is the same. It isn't easily achieved, but to produce that perfect set of sounds is a substantial challenge that all ringers want to meet. In most places, the listener will perceive that the steady rhythm includes a regular gap – what to ringers is known as 'open handstroke leading'. Take a ring of five bells. If they were being rung at a steady beat without such a gap then they would sound

1 2 3 4 5 1 2 3 4 5 1 2 3 . . .

or, if you like,

soh fah me ray do soh fah me ray doh so fah me . . .

With the gap, however, represented by g, you get

1 2 3 4 5 1 2 3 4 5 g 1 2 3 4 5 1 2 3 4 5 g 1 2 3 . . .

Note that this comes before every second blow of the first, or treble, bell – which is before it is pulled at handstroke – hence the term for this kind of ringing. For the ringer of the treble this calls for special skills, since the gap between 5 and 1 at backstroke for 1 is different from that between 5 and 1 before the handstroke. Note, too, that the treble handstroke comes after the last bell's backstroke – i.e. the ringer of 1 pulls the sally after the ringer of 5 pulls the rope-end – which is an added slight complication.

Although 'open handstroke leading' is the norm in most places, in some districts – notably in Devon and around Barnsley at the present time – the perceptive listener will notice that the rhythm lacks the gap. This is 'closed handstroke leading', or 'cartwheeling' as it is known in the Barnsley area. The pace is consistent, and the rhythm regular, but the punctuation mark is missing.

Into changes

Ringing in rounds, and certainly ringing in rounds well, needs practice, because you have to time your pull to perfection. The bell must be sent up to the balance – but not against the stay/slider – and then there will be a slight pause, near the balance, before it is pulled again. (A good ringer can 'hold' as bell on the balance, without leaning it on the stay/slider, for as long as necessary; before stays

A silencer placed in a bell to prevent the clapper striking it

and sliders were invented, this was the only way bells could be silenced between spells of ringing without the effort of ringing them down and then up again.) It is easy to pull slightly too hard and produce a gap in the rhythm; and it is just as easy to pull slightly too little, and so not to be able to delay the next pull long enough. As with all aspects of ringing, however, the skill is slowly acquired. When the ringer can constantly place a bell in rounds it is time to progress to change-ringing.

In change-ringing, as described in the previous chapter, the position of the bell in the sequence alters at nearly every pull. For example, you may have

1 2 3 4 5

2 1 4 3 5

where the position of bell 1 is altered so that it has to delay and that of bell 2 means that it has to hurry slightly. If the changes are laid end to end you get

1 2 3 4 5 2 1 4 3 5

so that five bells (2, 3, 4, 5 and 2 again) sound before 1 sounds once more, but only three (3, 4, 5) sound between the two pulls on 2. Thus in change-ringing the ringers must learn to alter the position of their bells in the sequence without breaking the rhythm. They can do it in one of two ways: either by 'ringing by ear' so that their sense of rhythm and the speed of the ringing indicates exactly when the pull should be made; or by knowing which bell to follow, and pulling the rope at the correct moment relative to it. Most people favour the second.

Knowing which bell to follow means either remembering or working out the sequence. In plain hunting on four bells, for example, bell 1 follows bell 2 after the first change, bell 4 after the second, and bell 3 after the third; it then follows bell 2 again, then bell 4, then bell 3, as the sequence shows:

```
1 2 3 4
2 1 4 3
2 4 1 3
4 2 3 1
4 3 2 1
3 4 1 2
3 1 4 2
1 3 2 4
1 2 3 4
```

The ringer might remember this as a simple sequence: 243. Most learners do. In putting it into practice, they will appreciate that exactly when they pull 1 to follow 2 will involve a smaller gap than when 1 follows 3, which in turn will be smaller than when 1 follows 4. The reason for this is that, the heavier the bell, the bigger its wheel and the longer it takes to rotate. So ringing changes means not just following a different bell each time, but following it at the right moment in order to sustain the rhythm and ensure good striking. Achieving both takes practice. Moving the bell from one place to another means having full control of it, so that you can either delay or hasten the next pull accordingly, and this takes time before mastery is achieved; it is very easy to pull too hard and delay the next pull too long, or not pull hard enough and be premature with the next. And, of course, you have to remember whether you have to delay or hurry, and which bell you have to follow next – all in a split second!

If you are ringing simple methods like plain hunt, it is possible to remember the sequence of bells to follow, but it would be a major feat to remember the sequence for, say, Kent Treble Bob Major (p. 16), not to mention Stedman Triples (p. 19). And in any case, if bobs and singles are to be called, the demands would be impossible, and so ringers don't try. Instead, for at least some of the time, they rely on general knowledge of the order that the bells move from the back of the row to the front, and then to the back again. This is known as the coursing order, which in most methods on eight bells involves the sequence 2 4 6 8 7 5 3 – i.e. all the evens followed by all the odds. In addition, the art that is known as 'ropesight' helps in spotting the bell that you are going to follow next. If you are moving from the front of the row to the back this is relatively straightforward, since the bell that follows yours at one stroke is the one that you follow at the next and the ringer of the bell you are going to follow is following you, and so looking at you. Thus in

```
1 2 3 4
2 1 4 3
```

1 is followed by 2, and 1 then follows 2. If you are moving from back to front, you have to spot the bell coming towards you in the opposite direction, which for bell 4 is bell 1 in the above example.

It all sounds inordinately complicated. You must learn the line for the method, as described in the previous chapter, and then trace it through the rows by spotting the bells that you have to follow after each change. And you have to follow each at exactly the right moment, to ensure good striking. It involves coordination of memory, eye and hands. Clearly it is not something that comes naturally; it must be practised, and in the early stages of learning change-ringing you must be prepared for many failures and people shouting at you to tell you what to do. (They shout not because they are cross but because they want your attention immediately – you have to pull again in a second or so – and want to make sure you hear above the sound of the bells.) But once you grasp the basic principles, then the challenges that you can tackle are never-ending. To those for whom change-ringing becomes an obsession, it is the challenge of learning new methods and ringing them well, perhaps in peals, that brings the interest, that leads them to travel far and wide to satisfy their curiosity as to the nature of different rings as well as methods and compositions. All the while they are concentrating on producing good striking, for any change-ringing is a public performance heard not only by the performers but also by many members of the general public. (Some of the most popular churches for peal-ringers are not suprisingly those with few residents within earshot.) The result is the glorious sound of changes pealing out over the fields of rural England and the rooftops of the city streets.

And Up Above?

How do the bells themselves work, to produce that sound? We know that bells have their own particular shape – indeed 'bell-shaped' is a term that has entered the English language. But not all bells are the same shape, though they are constructed to the same general principle of being a hollow vessel which is wider at its open end.[1]

The bells

The particular shape of bells rung to changes in the English fashion evolved over many centuries of trial and error; indeed, it is still evolving today as the bellfounders introduce slight modifications in their attempts to improve the quality of the sound. The benefit of the general shape that has developed is that when the bell sounds, although one note is dominant, several others are also heard as the impact of the clapper on the soundbow is transferred through the whole body of the bell. The goal of the bellfounder and tuner is to produce a bell whose shape is such that a particular combination of notes is heard.

The notes produced by a bell are a product of its size, in exactly the same way that the note produced by the string of a violin is a product of its length. The longer the string, and the larger the bell, the deeper the principal note; thus,

25

to produce a sequence of different notes violin players change the length of the string, whereas bellfounders produce bells of different sizes. The violin string is straight, however, whereas the bell is curved, so that the bell has more than one vibration length and thus several notes sound; one dominates, because it is produced by the impact of the clapper. The details of the shape determine the different lengths of the various subsidiary notes, and the precise identification of those notes is introduced by the tuner, who shaves off thin layers of metal from inside the bell in order to get the correct thickness.

Over time, one particular set of notes has been selected as providing what founders and ringers believe to be the best combination. This is known as the Simpson sequence, which was introduced in the late nineteenth century; the first full set of bells to be tuned to the Simpson principle is at S James's Church, Norton, a suburb of Sheffield. If a bell is to be tuned to the note C, then the full five are

Nominal	C^1
Quint	G
Tierce	E flat
Strike	C
Hum	C^{-1}

The strike note – that produced by the clapper hitting the bell – is the dominant one. There are three above it and one an octave below; the latter is termed the hum because it is the longest-lasting, a product of the continued vibration of the full length of the bell. Not all rings of bells are tuned to this principle by any means, however, for precision machinery to produce exactly the correct bell-shape and to remove exactly the right amount of metal was introduced only in the nineteenth century. Before that time the craft of bellfounding was both skilled yet haphazard. The only way bells could be tuned before the nineteenth century was to chip small bits out, so that if too much was removed there was no way to compensate for the loss; and if the bellfounder chipped away too hard he could crack the bell. Removing metal from the outside of the lip raised the strike note; removing it from inside the soundbow lowered the note. Today, tuning is so well developed that founders can cast bells for augmentations so that the new ones fit perfectly with the old, without involving any retuning of the latter: contrast the two trebles added to the former ten at Rotherham in 1986 (those two weigh more than the old treble bell which is now number 3) with the two added to the former six at nearby Hope, in Derbyshire, several decades earlier, where the older bells were not Simpson-tuned.[2]

Bells are produced by the use of moulds. The inner mould defines the hollow part of the bell, the outer mould defines its external shape, and the gap between the two is the bell itself. Production of the mould is thus a highly skilled task. It is done by using materials that are very pliable while damp, but extremely heat-resistant and unyielding when dried. The internal mould – or core – is built up by applying loam to a stone or brick heart, and shaping it by the use of a metal or wooden gauge, or crock. The external mould – the cope – comprises a basic metal case on the inside of which loam is applied and also shaped by a strickle; any inscriptions and decorations for the bell are impressed in this mould. The crock and strickle are thus crucial, and founders have developed their own sets for rings of bells of different weights and sizes.

Once the core and cope have been shaped they are bolted together. Molten metal is poured into the gap between them from the top, which is then sealed, and the bell is left to cool for several days before the cope is removed and the bell lifted off the core. The metal is an alloy developed at least 3,000 years ago to produce the particular qualities needed for a bell: it must be very strong, to withstand being struck by a clapper whose speed can be up to 600 m.p.h. at the moment of impact, and also elastic, so that it vibrates and produces the resonant sound that we associate with bells, especially the hum that lasts seconds after the strike note is heard. A combination of 77 per cent copper, to provide the elasticity, and 23 per cent tin, to provide the strength, is the traditional alloy used for British bells, and no better alternative has been produced. (Steel bells have been cast – mainly at Sheffield – and 14 rings still exist, though most are unringable; their sound does not compare, and they rust.) The clapper has traditionally been made of wrought iron, which is a relatively soft material that also vibrates; in recent years wrought iron has not been made (though a foundry was opened at the Ironbridge museum in 1987) and most modern clappers are now made of either cast iron or special steel.

Bells are bulky objects and difficult to move; they are fragile too. The materials with which they are made are more readily transported, and so it is not surprising that for several centuries most bells were cast where they were to be hung, or nearby. In some cases, it was possible to move them by water, but it was certainly the eighteenth century before this became widespread. Thus many early bells were cast by craftsmen whose trade incorporated several aspects of metalwork; it is almost certain that for the great majority bell-founding was a sideline only. (This was not peculiar to England. In pre-Revolutionary Russia the main bellfoundry in Moscow was also the arsenal; when demand for cannon was high, production of bells fell.[3]) Not surprisingly, many of their products were of inferior quality: poor in tone because of imperfections of shape; poorly tuned; difficult to ring; and liable to fracture. Extant sets of churchwardens' accounts illustrate the problems, and the number of recastings that were necessary. But since each foundry had only a small market area, few founders had sufficient experience to develop the craft; whether or not they produced a good bell (they were rarely asked to produce a full ring) was a matter of chance, and on many occasions they broke up the product before it ever reached the belfry and tried again. (Consider

The source of it all: copes at Loughborough Bell Foundry

the case of Thomas Bartlet, who went from London to Durham in 1631 to cast new bells for the cathedral. The bells that he produced were recast in 1639, 1664, 1675 and 1682, before being replaced in 1693.[4])

Some founders worked as itinerants, proceeding from parish to parish in search of work and setting up a foundry in a convenient yard or even in a field. Christopher Hudson was one such. He was trained in London, and in 1680 cast the seven-ton Great Tom, the clock bell at Christ Church, Oxford. In 1693 he went to Durham and cast eight new bells for the cathedral; he followed this with other local contracts, of which we know of six.[5] But until the seventeenth and eighteenth centuries the characteristic pattern was of a large number of small foundries serving local areas only. For the great majority we have no record, since they left no papers; the markings and inscriptions on their bells have been used to identify founders. Much work was done in the late nineteenth century by antiquaries – many of them members of the clergy – recording inscriptions and marks on bells and cataloguing their founders. For those of which we know, David Struckett's comprehensive listing provides the material for map 2.1, which shows how widespread an activity bell-founding was until the present century.[6]

It was the development of water transport, with the improvements in river navigation and the construction of canals, that allowed the growth of full-time foundries serving wide hinterlands. This is illustrated by the work of Henry Penn, who started as a founder at Ecton, North-amptonshire, in 1703 and moved to Peterborough in 1708. More than 240 of the bells that he cast between 1703 and 1729 have been recorded by Michael Lee: most of them (as map 2.2 indicates) are in churches close to the foundry whence they came, but there are examples of his work at Kingston-upon-Hull, Leicester and Ely.[7] Penn's Peterbor-ough foundry was in Bridge Street, no more than 200 yards from the River Nene, to which it was joined by a canalized stream called the Bell Dyke which passed the back of his property. By this means, he was able to ship his bells far and wide, though the movement was slow and there were undoubtedly difficulties taking them from a convenient wharf at the destination to the church.

Penn's sphere of influence fades into relative insignifi-cance when contrasted with that of the Gloucester foundry run from 1622 till 1835 by members of the Rudhall family. Walters claims that more than 4,500 church bells were cast there.[8] By the eighteenth century the quality of their work was becoming widely known, especially that achieved by Abraham Rudhall, and Walters notes that

his reputation during the early years of the 18th century spread rapidly up the valleys of the Wye and the Severn, into Hereford and Worcester, and so into Shropshire, Cheshire, and even Lancashire. This was doubtless due to the facilities for carriage up these water ways; and it is interesting to note that Rudhall bells are rare in Warwickshire, the Avon being presumably less navigable.[9]

At that time (1915) some 300 of the bells recorded in Shropshire, nearly one-third of all the bells there, were cast by the Rudhalls at Gloucester. But the Rudhalls had a much wider market area: in 1744 they cast the first ring of bells for North America, the destination being Old North Church in Boston, from where Paul Revere set off on his famous ride during the War of Independence.[10]

By the nineteenth century, using the waterways (includ-ing coastal vessels) and then the railways, founders were able to meet orders for bells from most parts of England. A location close to a navigable waterway was thus very desirable, and was one of the reasons that a foundry run by the Taylor family was moved from Oxford to Lough-borough in 1839. The choice of Loughborough followed an order to provide a new ring of bells for the parish church there, the contract stipulating that the bells must be cast in the town. Taylors established a foundry in an inn yard, but then stayed (eventually closing the Oxford foundry in 1854), benefiting from local business and the accessibility of the town via the canal and railway systems. The foundry is now one of only two left in the country, the other being at Whitechapel in East London (close to the docks), where the activity has been carried out con-tinuously since 1574.

Today, because they are cast at only two foundries, bells are standardized, certainly much more so than in the past, and we no longer have the profusion of founders' marks that adorned the products of earlier centuries. But every ring of bells, even a modern ring, is unique, because it must be custom-built, designed to fit into a specific setting – a particular tower. Thus, for example, the rings of twelve at Sheffield and Canterbury cathedrals were both pro-duced by the Whitechapel Foundry (the former in 1970 and the latter in 1981). Sheffield's tenor weighs 34.0.8 (cwt., quarters, pounds) and Canterbury's 34.3.4; ringers can tell the difference, even if others cannot.

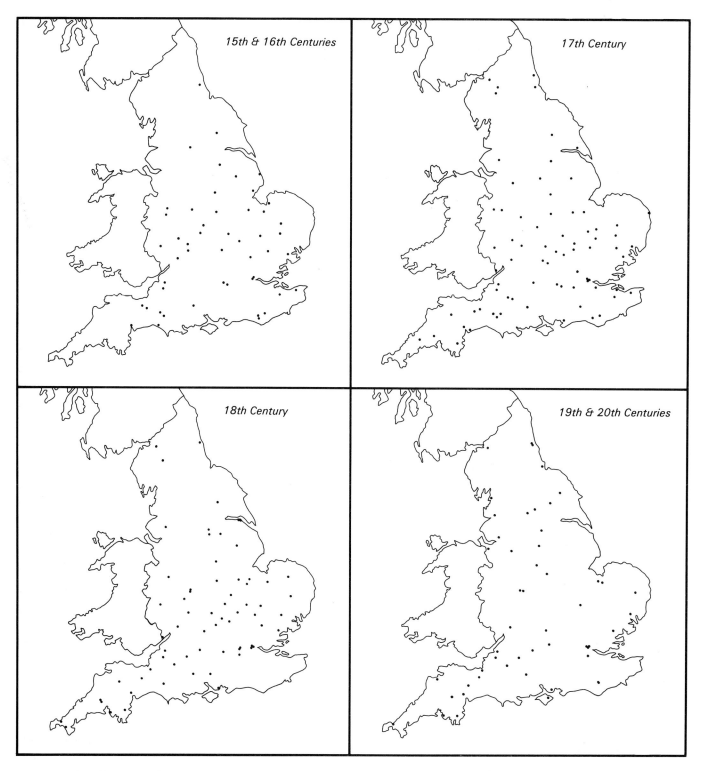

Map 2.1 The geography of known bellfoundries in (a) the sixteenth century and earlier; (b) the seventeenth century; (c) the eighteenth century; and (d) the nineteenth and twentieth centuries (David W. Struckett, *A Dictionary of Campanology*, privately published, 1985).

Fittings

As indicated, in order to sound the bell must rotate through a full circle, and this is achieved by using a rope attached to a wheel that is part of the bell's fittings. The bell is hung on a wooden or metal frame by a pair of gudgeons which fit into bearings that are attached to the frame. These gudgeons form the axis of rotation, and they

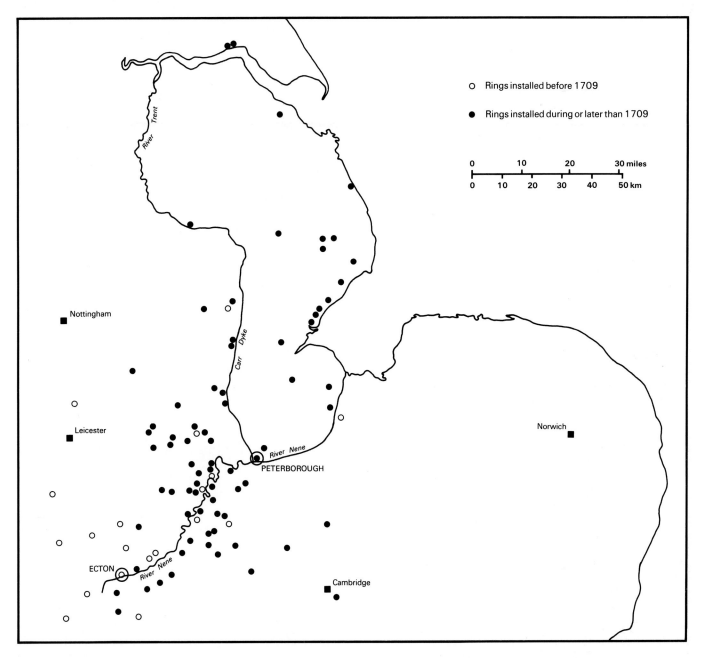

Map 2.2 The geography of the bells cast by Henry Penn of Ecton and Peterborough, 1703–29 (Michael Lee, *Henry Penn: Bell Founder*, privately published, 1986).

are attached to the bell by a headstock (formerly made of wood, now of metal) fixed to the crown of the bell – as shown in figure 2.1. The wheel is attached to the headstock, and the rope is tied to one of the spokes of that wheel.

The nature of all these fittings has evolved with time. The wheel is a particular case. Initially bells were swung by pulling on a rope attached to a lever, but this did not allow them to swing through a very wide arc; as the angle of swing increases, so problems are created as more rope goes up into the belfry. To allow a wider swing, first

quarter, and then half and three-quarter wheels were attached to the levers to control the rope. The particular feature of these wheels was their wide and deep rims, designed so that, as the lever moved upwards, the rope – which passed into the wheel's rim through a hole – fell into the rim and didn't interfere with the bell mechanism. Eventually, full wheels were introduced, which allowed the bell to rotate full circle and the rope to occupy just about the full circumference of the rim when the bell was balanced at backstroke – as shown in figure 2.1. In this way, the rope could be controlled, and was virtually

29

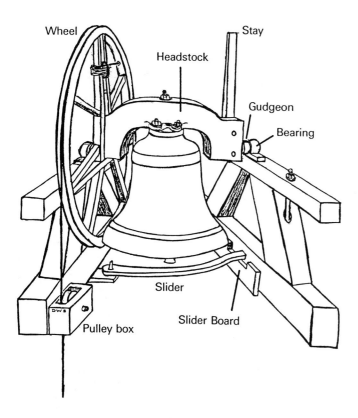

Figure 2.1 A sketch diagram of a modern bell hung in a wooden A-frame. As the bell rotates, the stay can move the slider within the slider board, so that it can pass the vertical position in both directions; the pulley in the pulley-box ensures that, wherever the bell is in its rotation, the rope always falls vertically into the ringing-chamber. (Sketch by David W. Struckett)

Clappers for S Peter, Raunds, Northamptonshire, await collection from the Loughborough foundry.

guaranteed to be in the correct position for the next pull.

The frames on which the bells hang have traditionally been made of wood, especially oak. Strength has been a crucial factor in the choice of this material, not simply because the frame has to carry the weight of the bell, but much more importantly because it has to withstand the stresses created by the movement of the bell. Even the smallest bells create a large impulsive force as they rotate at substantial speeds (of several hundred m.p.h. at the peak of acceleration), much more than that implied by their mass alone. As a bell rotates, it sets up both a horizontal and a vertical force. The latter is the more substantial, being something over four times the weight of the bell; the horizontal force is about twice the bell's weight. The frame has to withstand these forces, both downwards and sideways, which come in quick succession with any one bell and in a great variety of sequences with several bells being rung to changes. If the frame is not strong, the combination of horizontal and vertical forces will very soon destroy its rigidity and lead to its collapse.

Many frames have failed over the centuries because they have not been either strong or rigid enough to withstand the forces of rotating bells. The failures are usually slow; as the frame distorts more, so the bells become difficult to

ring, until eventually ringers will deem them unringable. The fittings by which the bells are attached to the frame can also fail: the headstock, fixed to the crown and to the gudgeons which rest in the bearings and form the axis of rotation, may break free, or even break; the gudgeons may fracture; the bearings may give out. Any of these failures may happen while a bell is being rung, with the consequence that it falls into the frame, probably damaging the bell and perhaps others too. Long before such a collapse, however, the wear of the fitting could make the bell difficult to ring; a bell with a worn and mis-shapen gudgeon is hard work for a ringer, for example.

Development of frames and fittings has been a long evolutionary process, paralleling the development of bells themselves, and is still continuing. Most wooden frames comprise very thick beams and cross-beams, for example, and may have additional members added at later dates to provide extra strength and support.

In many cases, the basis of the frame was an A-shape (as in figure 2.1), with the diagonal members spreading the impact of the forces away from the point on the main beams immediately under the bearings. These frames were constructed of many sections, and the bolts had to be tightened regularly to ensure no warping of the shape. Modern frames are made of steel, which must be painted routinely to prevent rusting.

It isn't just the bell-fittings and the frame that must withstand the forces set up by the rotating bells, of course. Those stresses are not absorbed simply by the frame but are transmitted through it to the structure of the tower. The two different forces have to be assimilated by the tower in different ways. The vertical forces are more readily accommodated. They set up a downwards pressure which creates compaction forces; as long as the tower and its foundations are solid enough, these can be withstood. The horizontal forces, though less in magnitude, are more problematical because they impact directly

(*Top*) Wheels great and small

(*Right*) Preparing the moulds: the cope has been placed on the core of the nearest mould, but the others still await their covering.

(*Top right*) Steel bells aren't worth very much at Loughborough. Alongside are a modern bell and a traditional one; the latter has the canons to which the headstock was attached, whereas on the former the headstock is bolted to the crown.

on the walls of the tower itself. If the frame were not firmly embedded in the tower wall, then it would act as a battering ram and would soon destroy the tower. There are many examples of failures that reflect this phenomenon. Raven reports that the steeple of All Saints' Church, Fulbourn, Cambridgeshire, fell on Trinity Sunday, 1766, for example, and that the tower of Isleham Church, in the same county, fell in the 1870s – though 'It is worthy of note that . . . not one of the bells was broken' and they were rehung in the new tower.[11] Such collapses are rare today, though there are towers where ringing cannot take place because of architectural defects. The slender tower of the church at Baldersby S James in North

Yorkshire contains a heavy ring of eight bells (tenor nearly 26 cwt.), for example. They were installed when the church was built by Lord Downe in 1856; because the tower is so slender (only ten feet square) the bells are in three tiers, high in the tower. They were very difficult to ring, and an article in *The Bell News* for 1885 claims that they were rung in May of that year to 720 changes for the first time.[12] They have not been rung in the twentieth century.

The tower itself must be well constructed so that it withstands the forces as a whole and transmits them as low down its structure as possible, thus reducing its motion. If it did not, then the walls could readily break

Plate XIV.

Some characteristic bellfounders' marks (from Thomas North's *The Church Bells of Northamptonshire*): no. 79 is by John Keene of Woodstock and is on a bell dating from *c.* 1640 at Towcester; no. 80, by Johannes de Yorke of York, dates from *c.* 1320 and is on a bell at Waslip, Leicestershire; no. 81 is also John Keene's and is found on several bells; no. 82, by an unknown founder and of unknown date, is on a bell at Wonsford; Richard Sanders of Bromsgrove produced no. 83, which is on a bell dating from 1714 at Kettering; the origin of no. 84, at Harringworth, is unknown; the church at Hinks on the Hedges has both nos. 85 and 87 on different bells, but their provenance is unknown; no. 86 was placed on a bell at Clipston in *c.* 1590 by E. Newcombe of Leicester.

away from one another. (In many towers, remedial action has had to be taken to ensure that this does not happen. At the Church of S Sepulchre, High Holborn, for example, a concrete ring beam was built into the tower in 1985 to allow the silent bells to be rung again.) With several bells rotating, perhaps at different angles depending on the organization of the frame, then horizontal forces are set up in different directions every second or so.

Design of the frame is crucial, therefore. It must be so arranged that the ropes fall into the ringing-room in a circle (or approximately so), otherwise ringing will be difficult. And it should be organized so that the bells do not all rotate in the same direction. The maximum force in any one direction at any moment should be minimized – by, for example, having the two heaviest bells rotating in different directions (in most frames either N–S or E–W) so that they do not all impact on the same wall at the same time.

A further problem concerns the position of the bell-frame in the tower. The higher up it is, the further the sound will be thrown. Thus it is an advantage to have the bells as high as possible, especially if the sound can be released through louvres in the roof as well as in the window-openings. Unfortunately, there is a disadvantage too, because the higher the bells are hung, the greater the lateral deflection and thus the stress on the structure as a whole. Towers are designed with this in mind, and most move slightly – to the discomfort of visitors who lean on the ringing-room wall during ringing – but the heavier and higher the bells, the more solid the construction must be.

Over the centuries, the problems posed by placing heavy bells in church towers and then ringing them in the English style were tackled through a long process of trial and error. Many frames proved too weak; many fittings failed and bells were broken; many towers had to be strengthened to withstand the stresses. In true pragmatic style, adjustments were made and ingenuity brought to bear on some apparently intractable problems. Thus, for example, in order to get rings into relatively small towers, frames were designed that placed the bells at two levels – even three in some instances – with the ropes from the upper tier being guided through the lower tier in order to ensure a proper circle below. By careful design, it is possible to install and ring bells where the possibility looks bleak. At Papanui, New Zealand, for example, a massive kauri frame was constructed which carried all the forces – horizontal and vertical – down to ground level and had no impact at all on the wooden outer cladding. (Papanui was beset by problems in its early days. The first ring of bells was lost in transit in a shipwreck, and the tower that housed the second ring proved insubstantial; the present structure was built in 1912 and the kauri frame was replaced by steel in the 1980s.) After the Second World War circular frames were introduced. A number of these are based on the transportable belfry designed in hollow structured steel sections by the Whitechapel Foundry for Expo 67 in Montreal: it weighed two and a half tons, could be erected in two days by two men, and supported a ring of eight with a tenor of four and a quarter cwt. Such frames transmit all the forces to the base of the tower and allow light rings of bells to be installed in slender, weak structures. In addition, circular frames in reinforced concrete have been cast to carry very heavy rings. A prime example is at Liverpool Cathedral, where the massive neo-Gothic central tower (reached by two lifts) contains the heaviest ring of bells in the world: the tenor weighs 82 cwt. (dwarfing the next largest – the tenor at Exeter Cathedral – which weighs in at a mere 72 cwt.). These circular frames provide a perfect rope circle, of course, as well as transmitting the horizontal forces at all angles and not just at two, which is characteristic of all other types.

Summary

All we have been able to do in this chapter is provide a brief outline of the mechanics of change-ringing, in both the belfry and the ringing-room. In the belfry we have substantial yet delicate bells, produced now by only two English foundries, each of which closely guards its trade secrets (about how it tunes bells, for example). They are the sole survivors of a long line of founders, some itinerants, some amateurs, many of whom were failures, all of whom have contributed in some way to the development of this accomplished craft, even if their products are no longer part of our soundscape. The development of bells, their fittings and their environments has been a long, skilled process involving technical and structural ingenuity to produce a musical instrument that contributes a glorious sound to the towns and villages of England. Change-ringing is not just a marvellous musical rhythm, it is also a testimony to the expertise of English craftsmen.

Below the bells is the ringing-room, which in about one-third of churches is at ground level, at the foot of the tower; with a few central towers, this means that the ringing takes place in full view of the congregation, as at Ashbourne and Melbourne in Derbyshire. Here the ringers pull on the ropes to produce that marvellous sequence of notes. They are combining the physical skills of coordination and, to some extent, strength to make the bells sound with the mental skills of learning methods and applying ropesight to ensure that those methods are rung accurately. The result is a rhythmic music beloved not only of the ringers themselves but of many listeners too, some of whom have recorded their appreciation in prose and verse. Sir John Betjeman wrote:

I make no apology for writing so much about church bells. They ring through our literature, as they do over our meadows and roofs and few remaining elms.[13]

Sir John lived in Wantage. Nearby is Uffington, where the thirteenth-century church houses a ring of five in its octagonal central tower, and his poem about the village bells reads:

> Tonight we feel the muffled peal
>   Hang on the village like a pall;
> It overwhelms the towering elms –
>   That death-reminding dying fall;
> The very sky no longer high
>   Comes down within the reach of all.
> Imprisoned in a cage of sound
>   Even the trivial seems profound.[14]

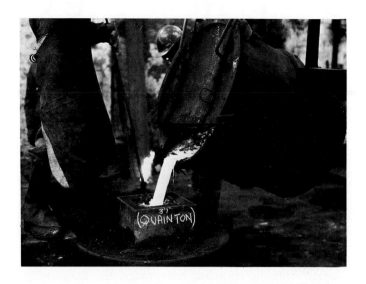

Pouring the molten metal into a mould at Loughborough foundry for one of the bells at Quainton, Buckinghamshire

Notes

1 Percival Price, *Bells and Man* (Oxford University Press: New York, 1983).

2 For a full treatment of tuning, and also of other aspects of bell-founding, see George Elphick, *The Craft of the Bellfounder* (Phillimore: Chichester, 1988).

3 Edward V. Williams, *The Bells of Russia* (Princeton University Press: Princeton, 1983).

4 Peter L. Rivet, *Bells of the Durham and Newcastle Dioceses* (Durham and Newcastle Association of Church Bell Ringers, 1979), p. 4.

5 ibid., pp. 4–5.

6 David W. Struckett, *A Dictionary of Campanology* (privately pubd, 1985).

7 Michael Lee, *Henry Penn – Bell Founder* (privately pubd, 1986).

8 H. B. Walters, *The Church Bells of Shropshire* (Woodall, Minshall, Thomas and Co.: Oswestry, 1915), p. 442.

9 ibid.

10 Interestingly, another ring of bells was shipped to North America at about the same time and hung in S Michael's Church, Charleston, South Carolina. It was taken down during the War of Independence and shipped back to England. After hostilities ceased the bells were returned and hung for ringing again. They were taken down during the Civil War (the church was an artillery target) and destroyed in a warehouse fire in 1865. *The Bell News* (11 August 1906), p. 218.

11 J. J. Raven, *The Church Bells of Cambridgeshire* (George Bell and Sons: London, 1881).

12 *The Bell News* (13 June 1895), p. 87.

13 In his 'Introduction' to *Collins Pocket Guide to English Parish Churches* (Collins: London, 1968), p. 30.

14 In J. Guest, *The Best of Betjeman* (Penguin Books: Harmondsworth, 1985), p. 110.

3 Where the Changes Ring

ALTHOUGH churches with rings of bells are common in England, they are by no means ubiquitous elements of the landscape. Thus this final introductory chapter presents an initial exploration of the geography of rings of bells, describing where they are most commonly found and suggesting reasons for their locations as a prelude to the atlas and gazetteer that follow.

In total, as table 1.3 (p. 7) shows, there are about 5,600 rings of four or more bells in England at the present time. The great majority of them are in the cathedrals and parish churches of the Church of England. Some 25 Roman Catholic churches have rings, the majority of them in the north of England: this includes three cathedrals, all with rings of eight – S Chad's, Birmingham; S Anne's, Leeds; and S Marie's, Sheffield. In addition there is a ring of six in the United Reformed Church at Hebburn, Tyne and Wear; rings of eight in the Unitarian churches at Brookfield, Greater Manchester, and Todmorden, West Yorkshire; a ring of eight in the Undenominational Church at Port Sunlight, Merseyside; and a ring of six in the Greek Orthodox Church at Tor Mohun, Torquay. (The last-named church was until recently Anglican and was transferred when it was made redundant; the Roman Catholic Church at Malton, North Yorkshire, with a ring of eight, was also an Anglican church until recently.) In addition there are about 20 secular rings. Some of them are in former churches that are now used for other purposes – such as the Library at Lincoln College, Oxford, the Arts Centre at York and the Parish Centre at Pershore. Others are in public buildings, such as Manchester Town Hall (a ring of twelve), Liverpool Municipal buildings (only four) and the Commonwealth Institute in Kensington (ten). And there are several private rings, ranging from the twelve in the Waterloo Tower at Quex Park, Birchington, Kent, built by Squire Powell so that he could practise twelve-bell ringing without going to London, through the ten in the Loughborough Bell Foundry of John Taylor and Co. (on which more peals have been rung than on any other ring), to the ring hung in a cottage by Arthur Jopp at Stoulton in Worcestershire and those rings in Frank Mack's loft and garage in Exmouth.

The 5,600 rings in Church of England churches mean that a majority of the Anglican places of worship in the country are without a ring of four or more bells. Just about 40 per cent of all parishes have a ring on which change-ringing can be practised,[1] so that although we are talking about a widespread activity we are not dealing with one that is typical of all Anglican parishes.

Where, then, are the rings of bells? Are they evenly spread over the country? The answer to the latter question is a resounding no, and the maps presented in this chapter illustrate why. Because of difficulties in compiling the data, these maps are based on slightly different sources and use different spatial units; nevertheless they give a clear picture of the geography of rings of bells.

The Geography Described

Map 3.1 shows the location of each ring of four or more bells separately, and gives a very clear impression of variations in the density of rings across Great Britain. The dominant feature is the almost total lack of bells in Scotland and much of Wales. For Scotland, this reflects the end of a northward trend within Britain as a whole, for the north of England is relatively empty also. For Wales, the trend is largely within the country; the density of rings in the Welsh Marches is similar to that in the English West Midlands, but as one moves west into Wales so it declines rapidly.

England, too, has areas where there are many more rings of bells than there are in others. The gaps representing Dartmoor, the New Forest, the Fenland, the High Peak, and much of the northern Pennines are to be expected from the terrain and settlement there. Less explicable are the clusters of dots in the East Midlands, Oxfordshire, the London and Bristol areas, and the Somerset–Devon border. Why are there more rings of bells there than, for example, in Kent and Sussex?

Map 3.1 gives a good initial feel for the geography of bells in England; it tells us that the changes ring out more frequently in some areas than others. But to appreciate why that is so, we need to refine the presentation of the data. Map 3.2 does this in a simple way, by indicating the number of rings in each of the present administrative counties of England, including Greater London and the six metropolitan counties.[2] The numbers there are derived from the atlas and gazetteer; the counties that stand out as having most rings are Devon, Somerset, Suffolk, Norfolk, Hereford and Worcester, and Northamptonshire.

Raw numbers are somewhat misleading, of course, because counties differ in their size, their populations, the number, age and size of their settlements, and so on. Thus we have produced a number of other maps of the density of bells, relating the number of rings to some

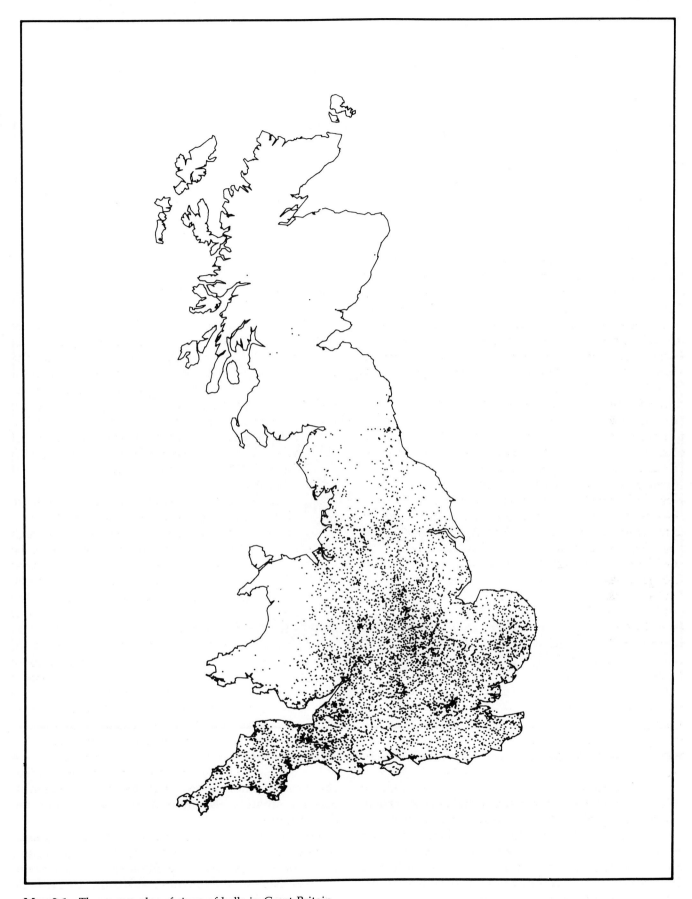

Map 3.1 The geography of rings of bells in Great Britain

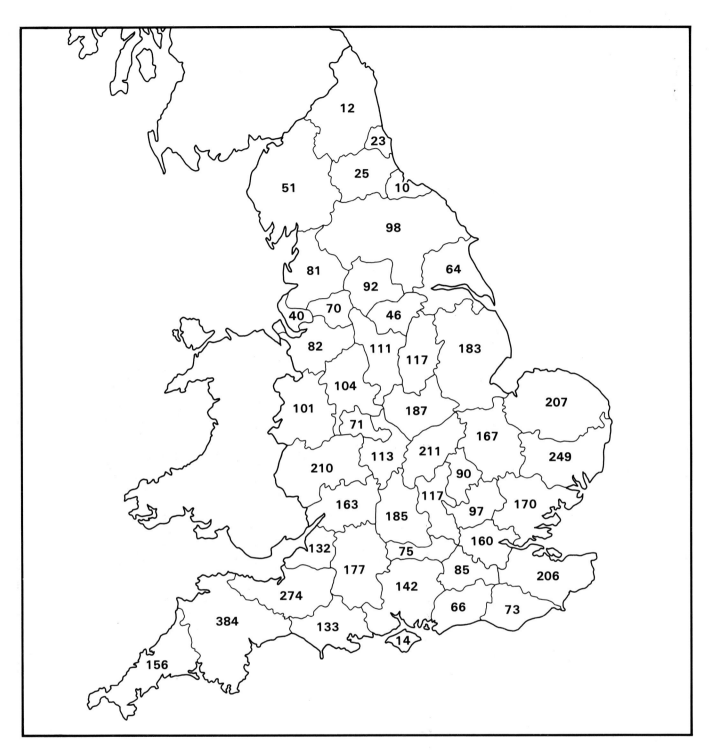

Map 3.2 The number of rings of four or more bells in each English county, 1989

aspect of each county's size. Map 3.3 shows the number of people per each ring of bells, according to the present counties. Three major features can be discerned. First, as with so many aspects of the social and economic geography of England, there is a north/south divide. A line joining the Mersey to the Humber delineates the two halves: north of it, no county has a ring of bells for every 8,000 or fewer residents; to the south of it, most of the counties fall into the two highest-density categories. Secondly, there is also an urban/rural divide, with the cities having many more people per ring of bells than the rest of the country. Each of the seven metropolitan counties is in the lowest-density category of only one ring per 20,000 or more people, for example, and the county of Avon is also less well-provided with bells, relative to its population, than its more rural neighbours. Finally,

36

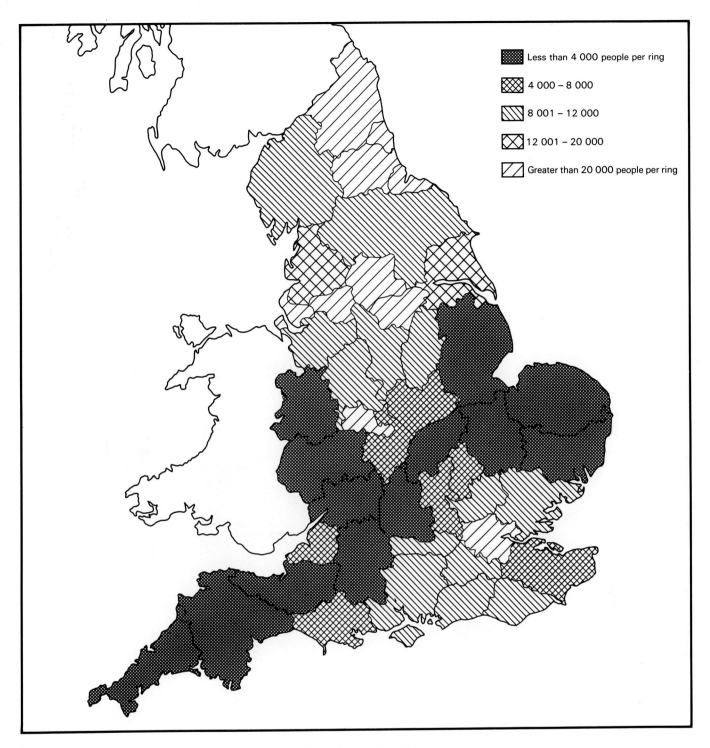

Map 3.3 Population per ring of bells in each of the English counties, 1989

within the south of England there is a band of counties running diagonally from Cornwall to Norfolk and Lincolnshire, and with a salient stretching through the counties of the Welsh Marches, which has the highest densities of all. The counties to the south-east of this belt have densities similar to those of the North Midlands.

Instead of expressing the density of rings of bells relative to population we can represent it using area as the denominator, portraying the number of rings by, say, each one hundred square kilometres. To do this we have used the National Grid, which is the basis for the Ordnance Survey maps and the six-figure grid references that we publish in the Gazetteer.[3] Maps have been produced at two different scales: for 50 km squares (2,500 square kilometres) and for 25 km squares (625 square kilometres).[4] With the former scale, if there are 50 rings of

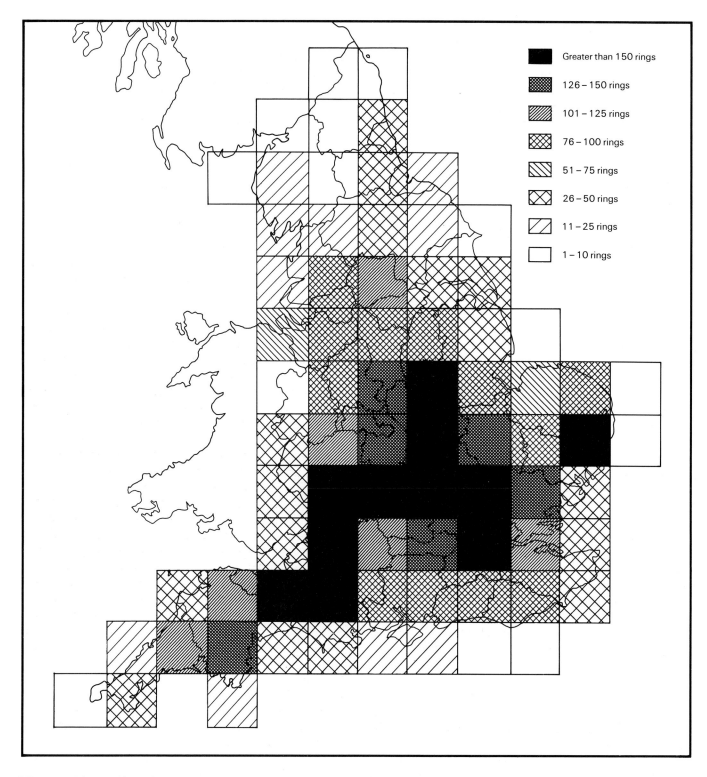

Map 3.4 The number of rings of four or more bells per 50 km square, 1989

bells per square, then on average there is about eight kilometres between each tower and its nearest neighbour: if there are 100 rings, the towers are only five and a half kilometres apart on average; and if there are 200, the average distance between neighbouring towers is only four kilometres. At that last density, everybody should

have at least one ring of bells within earshot. With maps drawn using the smaller squares, if there are 25 towers in a square the average distance between neighbouring towers is 5½ kilometres and if there are 50 then it is only four kilometres.

Map 3.4 shows the distribution of all rings of four or

more bells according to the 50 km square grid. The majority of the 77 squares that cover part of the land area of England contain fewer than 75 rings. Some of these are coastal squares, parts of which are not occupied by land. In the south of England, all the squares with fewer than 75 rings are either coastal or include part of the Welsh border; in the remainder of the squares there, the average number of bells per square is 140, or one tower every 4¾ kilometres. North of the Mersey–Humber line all squares fall into the category of 75 towers or fewer, irrespective of whether they are coastal or not, with two exceptions – the squares covering the metropolitan counties of Greater Manchester and South and West Yorkshire.

The highest density of all on this map (221 towers, or one every 3¾ kilometres) is in the square covering the area between Leicester and Northampton. The second peak (214) covers central and west London, and the third the area of central Somerset around Taunton. With the exception of central London, the urban/rural divide in southern Britain stands out again, as does that SW/NE trending stripe: rings of bells, it seems, are most characteristic of the towns and villages of that belt of country.

If we shift to the smaller grid (map 3.5), not surprisingly we get the same general picture. There are some features which the broader sweep of map 3.4 hides, however. The most important is that the urban/rural divide is apparently inverted, because the two squares with the highest densities cover the centres of London (80 towers) and Bristol (66) respectively. Four other squares have more than 50 rings of bells each (i.e. one every four kilometres): the area south and east of Taunton; the areas to the north-west and the south-east of Northampton; and the city of Leicester and its environs. In general, the concentration of bells in the SW/NE trending diagonal across the country is confirmed, but, as well as this largely rural pattern, certain major towns also have substantial concentrations of rings of bells. The north/south divide continues to stand out, but it is noticeable that the densities along the south coast of England to the east of Bournemouth are similar to those of Cheshire, Derbyshire, Lancashire and Yorkshire.

Returning to the larger squares, the four sections of map 3.6 show the density of rings of different numbers. That for rings of ten and twelve shows the dominance of the big cities. London, with 40 towers, stands out as the major centre of ten- and twelve-bell ringing; the only other substantial concentrations are in the West Midlands and in Bristol. Nearly half the squares have no more than one such ring, so that the residents of many parts of the country must travel if they are to hear the glorious sounds of Caters, Royal, Cinques and Maximus. The London area also stands out in the map of all towers with eight or more bells; it has 159, more than twice as many as the 75 of the next major concentration, covering northern Greater Manchester. The rural heart of England is not as well provided with rings of the higher numbers, but instead,

as the map of five- and six-bell towers shows, is where the smaller rings are commonest. The adjacent counties of Leicestershire and Northamptonshire have the highest densities, followed by Somerset, Gloucestershire and Oxfordshire. Finally, the map of four-bell rings shows that there are many parts of the country where these are rare: the major concentration is in the East Midlands.

Our last set of maps is based on neither population nor area but on the territorial units for church organization – the ecclesiastical parishes. Each of them has its parish church, and so the larger the number of parishes in an area the greater the potential number of rings of bells. Map 3.7 indicates the percentage of ecclesiastical parishes in each county with a ring of four or more bells. It uses the pre-1974 counties rather than the modern administrative units employed in maps 3.2 and 3.3, because they were the only ones for which the number of parishes was readily obtainable.[5]

Map 3.7 shows very substantial variability across the counties of England in the percentage of ecclesiastical parishes with a ring of four or more bells. The range is from less than 20 per cent in the four northernmost counties plus Greater London to over 70 per cent in Devon. The latter stands out as the only county where as many as three in every four of the parishes contain a ring. Four others approach that figure, with rings in more than 60 per cent of the parishes – Cornwall, Somerset, Oxfordshire and Northamptonshire – and a further nine counties have rings in at least half of their parishes.

The major features of the geography of bells in England identified in the earlier maps are present in map 3.7 too. The north/south divide is very clear; each of the six ancient counties north of the Mersey–Humber line has a ring in under 30 per cent of its ecclesiastical parishes, a figure matched only by London further south. (The pre-1974 London County contained only the inner twelve boroughs of the later Greater London County, thus including the city and adjacent areas but excluding most of the twentieth-century suburbs.) The SW/NE diagonal stripe of counties with the highest densities is also present, though comparison with the map based on population (map 3.3) indicates several major differences. First, the counties at the north-eastern end of the diagonal (Cambridgeshire, Huntingdonshire, Lincolnshire and Norfolk) have lower densities than their neighbours (below 50 per cent of parishes with bells in the first two). They have more rings of bells relative to population than relative to parishes than do Northamptonshire and Oxfordshire, suggesting a greater number of small (in population) parishes without rings in the former group. Similarly, the counties of the Welsh Marches north of Gloucestershire have relatively low densities, again suggestive of many small, ring-less parishes. Thirdly, the stripe is shown to have two cores, one in the south-west and the other in Northamptonshire and Oxfordshire; between the two, the density falls slightly in the counties

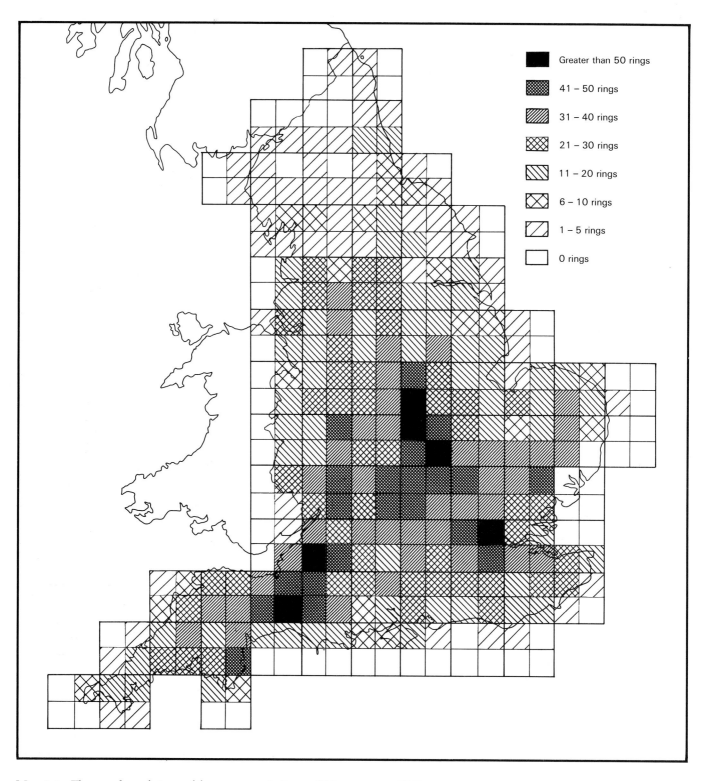

Map 3.5 The number of rings of four or more bells per 25 km square, 1989

of Gloucestershire, Wiltshire and Berkshire, where more of the land area comprises relatively high and unpopulated chalk and limestone country.

Comparing the counties on either side of the stripe, map 3.7 shows a clear difference between those in south-east England and those in the Midlands. Of the former group only Kent has a ring of bells in as many as 40 per cent of its ecclesiastical parishes, whereas Hampshire, Surrey, Sussex, Middlesex and Essex have between 30 and 40 per cent. All the counties lying north of Gloucestershire, Oxfordshire and Northamptonshire and south of the Mersey–Humber line, on the other hand, have not

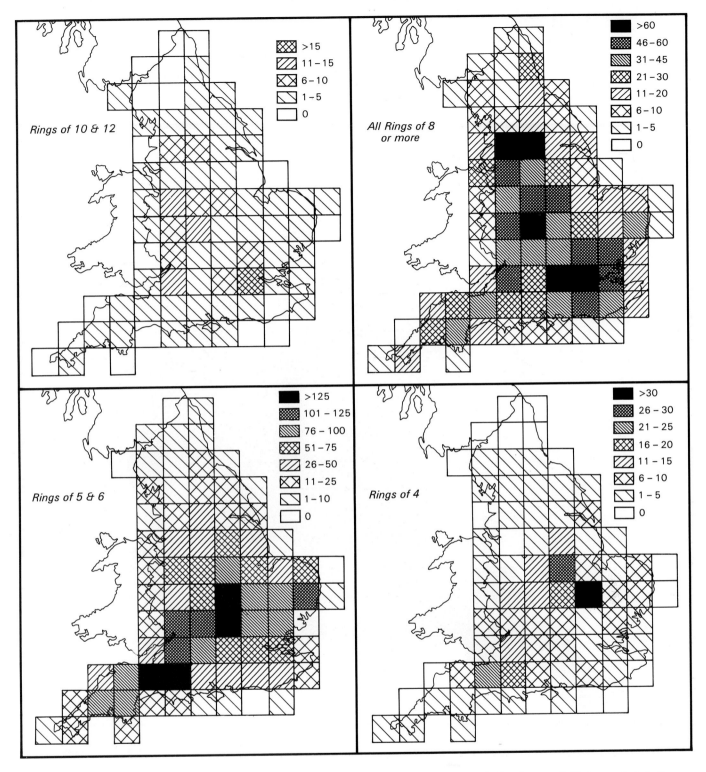

Map 3.6 The number of rings of (top left) ten and twelve bells, (top right) eight or more bells, (bottom left) five and six bells and (bottom right) four bells, per 50 km square, 1989

only at least 30 per cent of their parishes with rings; in all but four cases they have at least 40 per cent, and in two (Leicestershire and Rutland) over half. In relative terms, the south-east of England – considered by many to be the country's core – has fewer rings of

bells than the counties further from London; the sound of bells being rung in changes is less typical of England's capital and neighbouring counties that it is in the rural areas of the 'heart of England' and the far south-west.

41

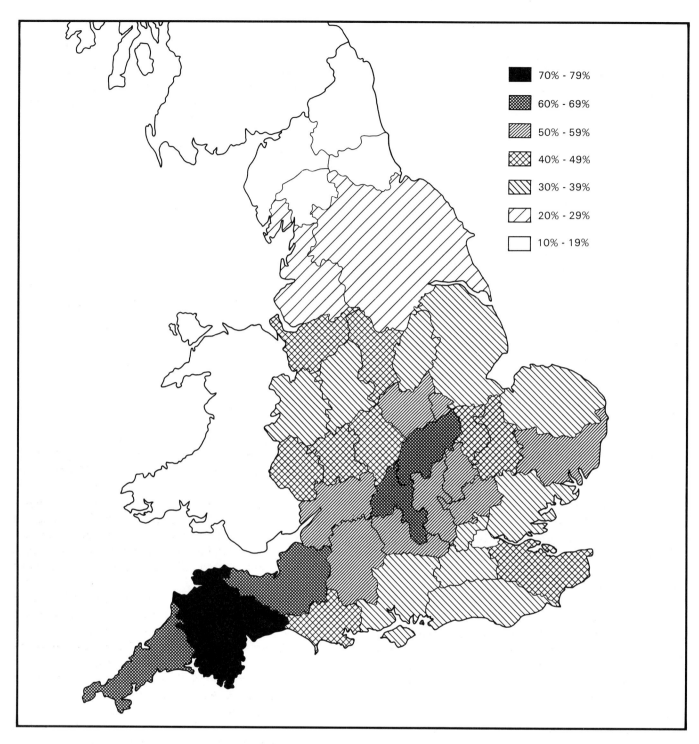

Map 3.7 The percentage of ecclesiastical parishes with a ring of four or more bells, 1989, using the pre-1974 administrative counties

Accounting for the Geography

The preceding maps have identified a clear geography. How do we account for it? Why is it that the south has many more rings of bells than the north; the south-east has fewer rings than the Midlands; the rural areas have greater densities of bells than do urban areas; but that the large cities contain most of the rings of ten and twelve?

The urban/rural division is the easiest to account for. First, urban parishes, especially those of the large cities, have much larger populations than their rural counterparts: many of the latter have only a few hundred inhabitants while the former average many thousands. In the towns, the main parish church – in or close to the town centre – is usually old and well endowed, and has a ring of eight or more bells. But, and here is the second element, in the more recently developed suburbs the parishes are modern and their churches no more than a century old. Many of these newer parishes have been relatively poor since their institution, and have never housed affluent residents who, individually or together, could afford to finance the building of a well-endowed church complete with a substantial tower and ring of bells. Thus most urban parishes are large, in terms of potential congregation, and relatively recent and poor. They contrast sharply with the rural parishes (including the country towns), where the churches are several centuries old and the wealth derived from agriculture and trade has been drawn on over a long period to provide both substantial buildings and rings of bells.

The urban/rural distinction is illustrated if we separate out those ecclesiastical parishes created in the nineteenth century from those with longer histories.[6] With the former group, only in four counties (Devon, Dorset, Leicestershire and Wiltshire) do as many as 30 per cent of the 'new' parishes have rings of bells. In the great majority of counties under 20 per cent of nineteenth-century parishes have rings. Of course, most of those parishes were created in the great towns and cities that burgeoned with the Industrial Revolution. Not all of their new churches lack bells, though the great majority do, because donors were relatively few and the parishioners were not inclined to raise money to adorn their new churches with rings of bells. Thus most of the nineteenth- and twentieth-century suburbs are 'bell-less regions'.

This nineteenth-century situation contrasts strongly with that in the older-established parishes of the English countryside, especially in the diagonal stripe. On average, about half of the pre-nineteenth-century parishes in each county have rings of four or more. Map 3.8 shows the percentages of those parishes without bells on which change-ringing can be practised. They range from fewer than 30 in the three south-west counties of Cornwall, Devon and Somerset, and also in Cheshire, to almost 90 in the three northern counties of Cumberland, Northumberland and Westmorland. But why such a difference? And why is Cheshire as well provided as Cornwall and Devon, which is not what maps 3.2 and 3.3 suggest? The reason seems to be that Cheshire's parishes are much larger on average than is the case for the country as a whole. Only 14 per cent of pre-nineteenth-century parishes had populations of 2,000 or more in 1901 in England as a whole, whereas 25 per cent contained fewer than 250 residents; in Cheshire, the respective percentages were 38 and 6. By contrast, the percentages for Gloucestershire were 10 and 30, and for Rutland they were 7 and 41.

We might conclude, therefore, that the larger the population of a pre-nineteenth-century parish, the greater the likelihood that it has a ring of bells today. Table 3.1 shows this to be the case: very few of the smallest parishes have rings, whereas over three-quarters of the largest do. The reason for this is presumably that the larger the parish, the greater its ability to raise the money for a tower and a ring of bells,[7] either from a rich donor (a local landowner, probably) or by subscriptions raised from the population at large. Thus the counties with the smaller parishes should be those with fewest rings of bells.

Table 3.1 Percentage of pre-nineteenth-century parishes with rings of bells

Population	Percentage	Population	Percentage
1–99	4.5	750–999	66.3
100–249	21.9	1,000–1,499	71.2
250–499	44.2	1,500–1,999	76.3
500–749	59.6	2,000 +	75.1

This generalization is insufficient to account for all the differences shown on our maps, however. Map 3.9 indicates why. In England as a whole, just over 20 per cent of the parishes with populations of 100–249 have rings of bells today. In 14 of the counties, however, under 10 per cent do, whereas in the four with the highest densities (Cornwall, Devon, Northamptonshire and Somerset) the percentage is over 50. So why is it that in some rural areas there are many more small parishes with rings of bells than is the case elsewhere?

Our answer is tentative and far from complete. One part of it is to suggest that it is the wealthier rural areas that have the greatest densities of bells. Since most rings were installed (or were augmented to four or more) in the eighteenth and nineteenth centuries, we would expect the areas of agricultural wealth then to be the best provided with bells. To some extent this is true, but no clear correlation can be identified. Certainly the poorest farming areas in the moorlands of the north have very few substantial churches, but there are relatively few in the richer areas nearby either; the Vale of York is little better provided with rings than the North Yorkshire Moors, for example.

Any ring of bells requires a tower and, until recent developments in bell-hanging technology, a substantial one was needed. Little work has been done on the distribution of such towers in England, but one analysis has suggested that the pattern of churches with substantial towers (especially those of perpendicular design) corresponds quite closely with the SW/NE

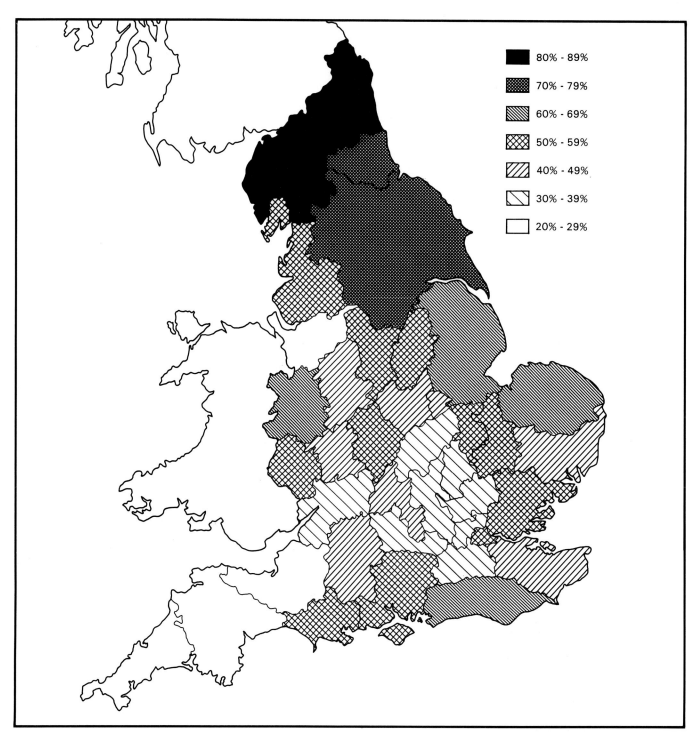

Map 3.8 The percentage of pre-nineteenth-century ecclesiastical parishes without rings of four or more bells, 1989, using the pre-1974 administrative counties

diagonal band that we have identified in our maps. In contrast, Frank Allen points out that

the parts of England deficient in important towers and spires are the whole of north-west England, most of Wales, the counties of Hampshire, Surrey and Sussex, and a part of Kent.[8]

This corresponds very closely to the areas that we identified as having relatively low densities of bells.

Substantial towers were not necessarily built to house bells, and certainly not the majestic rings of eight, ten and twelve that many now contain. After all, the origin of the term belfry has nothing to do with bells; it refers

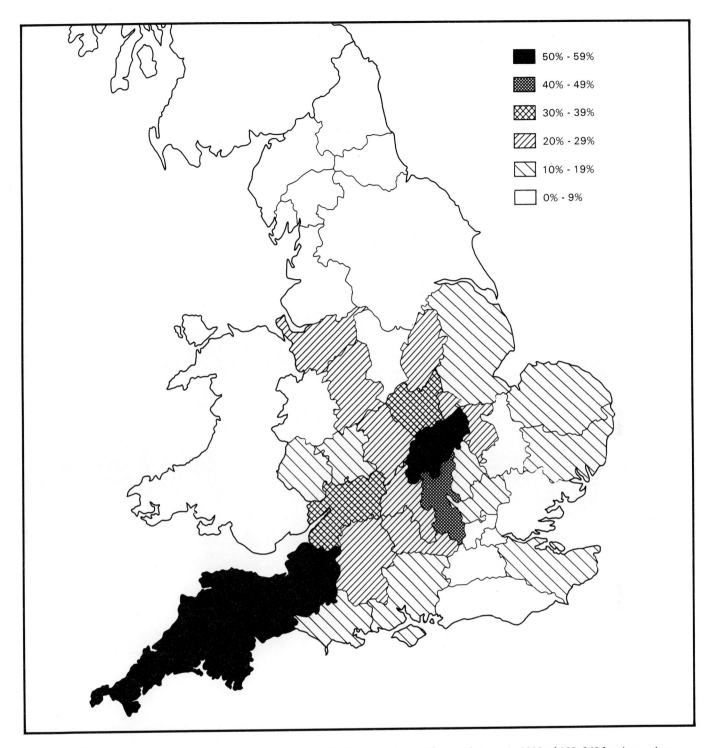

Map 3.9 The percentage of pre-nineteenth-century ecclesiastical parishes with populations in 1900 of 100–249 having a ring of four or more bells, 1989

to a watch tower, and many of the oldest belfries were constructed to provide both a prospect and a refuge for the locals, from which they could see potential aggressors approaching and in which they would barricade themselves. But why build such towers across the Midlands and not in the North? Clearly, most were not constructed to fulfil such functions, for they long postdate the pacification of England (although some were used as places of refuge in the Wars of the Roses and the Civil War). Basically most were built by those who saw a large tower as a status symbol for the parish, a clear statement of religious adherence, or both. And once one or a few parishes in an area had built such a tower, others would have sought to match or outdo them, encouraged no doubt by the masons who were looking for further work and the local clergy who wanted to demonstrate their status. The availability of suitable raw materials nearby would have been an additional spur: thus one finds an outlier of the diagonal stripe extending into East Yorkshire, using the limestone available in various parts of the county, and containing such superb examples of perpendicular towers as Hedon and Howden in the old East Riding and Tickhill and Wadworth in what is now South Yorkshire.

Where the church-builders had provided substantial towers, therefore, there was a greater probability that over time the locals would replace the two or three bells hung in them for chiming by a change-ringing set. In other parts of the country, different architectural styles were less conducive to the installation of such rings. Norfolk and Suffolk, for example, have large numbers of round towers, many built of flint.[9] Relatively few of them have rings of bells; Morris identified only 17 of the 129 existing round towers in Norfolk as having five or more bells; of the Suffolk examples, 15 had one bell, five

(*Above*) The church of S Sepulchre, High Holborn, home of the 'bells of Old Bailey'

(*Above right*) The church of All Saints, Worcester, whose twelve bells have been rung to several long peals in recent years; Worcester Cathedral, also with twelve bells, is in the background.

(*Right*) S Peter Mancroft Church, Norwich, where the first-ever recorded peal was rung, in 1715

46

had two, eleven had three, two had four, four had five and another four had six, according to his list.[10]

The existence of a tower doesn't mean that the parishioners will necessarily have endowed it with a ring of bells, of course, and it could well have been that a local 'copycat' pattern developed with the installation of bells too. We should recall that the development of change-ringing in the countryside was in many areas entirely separate from that in the towns. For example, York Minster has long had a ring of bells, and one authority claims that it was the first church to install a complete ring of twelve – although that is countered by those whose claim primacy for London.[11] But the area around York has very few rings of bells even today. There are rings at the suburban villages of Acomb, Bishopthorpe, Clifton, Huntington, Strensall and Stockton in the Forest (the last two are very recent) but the villages to north and south have not invested in rings of more than three, with one exception – the relatively modern ring at Escrick. And yet change-ringing was being practised in York and developments there led to its introduction in neighbouring towns. The London founders of Lester and Pack installed new bells at York Minster in 1765, and at the same time secured orders for rings of eight in the nearby towns of Helmsley, Howden and Malton. Here we have further evidence of the difference at the time between the 'gentlemen' change-ringers of the towns and the call-change ringers of the countryside. This was common throughout the country; during the eighteenth and nineteenth centuries, however, some rural areas (along the SW/NE diagonal stripe) took up call-change ringing and installed rings of five or more bells, whereas in others (such as the Vale of York) augmentations of the existing rings of three (most of which were probably chimed only) were rare.

The example of the city of York points to the dominance of urban centres in the development of change-ringing. Indeed, although rural parishes are in general more likely to have rings of bells than are their urban counterparts, we should not forget that some of the highest densities of all are recorded in England's cities. Prominent among these are those that dominated the country, in population but especially in wealth, in the century before the onset of the Industrial Revolution. London was pre-eminent then, in ringing as in so many other aspects of life, and by the seventeenth century the City alone had more than 80 rings of bells.[12] Today it has only 13, including the rings of twelve at S Paul's Cathedral, S Giles, Cripplegate (now in the heart of the Barbican development), S Mary-le-Bow, Cheapside (Bow Bells), S Michael, Cornhill, and S Sepulchre, Holborn Viaduct (the 'Bells of Old Bailey'). This concentration of bells in the City reflects the large number of churches there, many of them closely linked to the nearby mercantile wealth: donors for rings of bells could readily be found, and they were encouraged by the many ringing societies then in existence, such as the Ancient Society of College Youths.

Bristol, Ipswich and Norwich, too, have long histories of change-ringing and large numbers of inner-city churches with rings, and contrast strongly with the upstart cities of the Industrial Revolution, such as Manchester and Sheffield. Most of the latter have a large parish church that has been upgraded to cathedral status and houses a ring of ten or twelve, and many have been centres of change-ringing activity since the eighteenth century. But their inner cities are otherwise almost empty of rings of bells, and although each has a few in its suburbs the urban areas as a whole are not well endowed with rings.

The existence of a ring of bells in a church reflects a great variety of influences, therefore, many of which are particular to the place. Thus, for example, the city of Oxford has 13 rings within the old town, including five in churches associated with university colleges (Christ Church – where the college chapel is also the cathedral – and Lincoln, Magdalen, Merton and New Colleges; Merton College bells are rung from a balcony with only a low balustrade). Cambridge, on the other hand, has only five, none of them in a church or chapel associated with a college. And, of course, what happens in one place is very much influenced by occurrences nearby. Undoubtedly the augmentation of the bells in one rural parish in many cases spurred their neighbours to do likewise; local and itinerant bellfounders will also have encouraged augmentations, to advance their own interests. Similarly, the development of change-ringing in London appears to have stimulated the installation of rings of eight in neighbouring Kent relatively early: there were at least 27 established in the eighteenth century, and a further 27 before 1887.[13] Kent was a centre of early peal-ringing, notably at the village of Leeds, east of Maidstone, where the 40,320 changes of Plain Bob Major were rung in relays in 1761.

Outside England

Beyond the boundaries of England, bells hung for change-ringing are few and, generally, very recent. Scotland currently has only 15 rings, including a new eight in S Machar's Cathedral, Aberdeen; that city heard the first peal rung in Scotland in 1859, on the bells of S Nicholas, which were destroyed in a fire in 1874. During the eighteenth century Episcopalianism was outlawed, which probably prevented installation of bells in the country; the first Scottish ring was provided only in 1789, at S Andrew's, Edinburgh. But there is very little ringing immediately across the border in England either, and it is not surprising that the art did not spread into Scotland. Wales has more than 160 rings, mainly in the east and south of the country, where the influence

The church of S Michael, Coslany, Norwich, whose band of ringers competed with their neighbours at S Peter Mancroft in the 1730s to ring the first peal of Stedman Triples

The bells for Harare Cathedral assembled in their frame at Whitechapel foundry before their long journey

The parish church of S Martin, Birmingham, known to most ringers as the 'Bull Ring' church: its 36¾ cwt. ring of twelve is soon to be replaced by the first-ever diatonic ring of 16.

'Bow bells' ring out from S Mary-le-Bow, Cheapside.

of England and its established religion is greatest; further west, where parishes are generally poorer, rings are rare, and the ancient county of Cardiganshire has only two – a ring of six at S Mary's Church, Cardigan, and one of eight at S Padarn's, Llanbadarn Fawr.

Beyond the shores of Great Britain, Ireland, with 35, has most rings of bells, 20 of them in the Republic, including five in Dublin, two in Cork and two in Limerick; only five of these are in Roman Catholic churches. Australia will soon overtake Ireland, however. Its first bells were taken to Sydney in 1795, though they were not hung until 1805; the tower fell down two years later. The bicentennial celebrations in 1988 were used as the focus of a campaign to obtain several more rings, in places as far apart as Brisbane and Perth. Across the Tasman, in New Zealand, there have been rings of bells in the South Island city of Christ-church for over a century: there were five 'ringable' rings in the country when Dove's first edition was published in 1950; today there are nine. Change-ringing is also becoming increasingly popular in the United States. The bells in Old North Church in Boston, recently restored, were cast in 1744. In 1950 there were eight rings, but the first peal of Major was achieved only in 1965; in 1972 there were 19, with several others proposed: one of the recent installations was a ring of ten placed in the tower of Washington's Old Post Office building by the Ditchley Foundation to mark the American Bicentennial.

Only six other countries have bells hung for change-ringing in the English style. South Africa has six rings, Zimbabwe two and Kenya one; India and Pakistan have one each (at Poona and Lahore respectively), though neither can be rung, and there are eight rings in Canada. Finally, although they cannot be rung 'English-style', there are bells in parts of Italy that are somewhat similar, and we cover these in the last section of the Atlas.

Conclusion

Change-ringing is an aspect of the social history and social geography of England which has received relatively little attention. At the end of the nineteenth century a number of scholars with antiquarian interests – many of them Church of England clergy – compiled detailed records of the founders and inscriptions of bells in various counties and published books containing the results of their labours: unfortunately they covered only parts of the country and there are major areas, such as Yorkshire, for which there is no complete record – either for then or for now. Others have researched various aspects of the history of ringing, most of them focusing on particular churches,[14] and the fruits of this work (and much more that remains unpublished) are now being brought together in the first major history of campanology.[15]

This chapter has thrown a little light on one aspect of the history of change-ringing, which has been almost entirely ignored up till now – its changing geography. It has shown that rings of bells are much more characteristic of certain parts of England than others, and has suggested reasons why. Only a great deal more pain-staking investigation will fill out the general picture that it has provided: meanwhile, we are left with the question of why most rural parishes in Devon have rings of bells but few of their Yorkshire counterparts do.

Notes

1 This figure assumes that each parish has only one church. Some have more, of course, so the percentage is a slight overestimate.

2 Although the Greater London Council and the six metropolitan county councils were abolished in 1986, the counties themselves remain.

3 The grid references (except for the four-bell towers) were compiled by John Baldwin and are published in his *Where's that Tower? A Church Bellringer's Index to the Towers of Britain* (privately pubd: Cardiff, 1986).

4 We use the basic 100 km squares of the Ordnance Survey as our grid; a key to their location is in the *Ornance Survey Atlas of Great Britain* (Book Club Associates: London, 1982).

5 It would have been a mammoth task to reconstruct the list of ecclesiastical parishes for the present counties. Indeed, the only lists available refer to the end of the nineteenth century. (After 1901 the Census volumes list ecclesiastical parishes by diocese but not by county.) Thus the maps are based on the number of ecclesiastical parishes per county in 1901; the number of rings of bells per county is taken from the latest (1968) edition of Dove's *Guide* to use that set of counties.

6 The 1901 Census lists identify the nineteenth-century parishes, enabling this separation. Unfortunately, twentieth-century parishes are not considered.

7 Some of the small parishes with rings will have been larger, but suffered substantial depopulation during the nineteenth century. Many more of the larger ones will have grown rapidly during that century, notably in the towns, but may not have acquired bells.

8 F. J. Allen, *The Great Church Towers of England* (Cambridge University Press: Cambridge, 1937), p. 3.

9 Ernest Morris, *Towers and Bells of Britain* (Robert Hale: London, 1955), p. 138, reports 135 in Norfolk and 45 in Suffolk.

10 Ibid., p. 142.

11 D. Potter, *The Bells and Bellringers of York Minster* (privately pubd: York, 1987). See also the correspondence between David Potter and Andrew Wilby in *The Ringing World* in the first half of 1986.

12 W. T. Cook, 'The Society of College Youths 1637–1987: Part I', *The Ringing World* (27 February 1987), p. 197.

13 The estimates are derived from J. C. L. Stahlschmidt, *The Church Bells of Kent* (Elliott Stack: London, 1887).

14 For example, C. J. Pickford, *The Steeple, Bells and Ringers of Coventry Cathedral* (privately pubd: Bedford, 1987).

15 Earlier attempts at such a history – notably Ernest Morris, *The History and Art of Change-Ringing* (Chapman and Hall: London, 1931) – contain much useful material but lack any detailed analysis.

THE ATLAS

This Atlas comprises 60 maps designed to show the distribution of the rings of four or more bells in every English county, in the other countries of the British Isles, and in the rest of the world. Each map is accompanied by a page of text which describes the geography shown and gives a brief history of bells and ringing in the area.

The bulk of the Atlas is the set of 47 maps of the counties of England, which contain some 96 per cent of the world's rings of bells. There is a separate map for each county, with three exceptions: Cleveland and Durham, Hampshire and the Isle of Wight, and Northumbria and Tyne and Wear are combined into single, two-county maps. The maps of the largest counties in terms of rings of bells – Devon and Somerset – are divided into two, with a consequent increase in the amount of textual material. Insets to a number of the maps show the central areas of towns and cities with several rings of bells. In two cases – the centre of London within Greater London and the City of Oxford within Oxfordshire – insets could not show the large number of towers, so separate maps have been prepared; again, this is complemented by an increase in the amount of text.

The counties used in the maps (and the regions in Scotland) are those introduced by the local government reorganizations of Greater London (1964) and the remainder of Great Britain (1974). Thus counties such as Huntingdonshire, Middlesex and Rutland do not appear; Herefordshire and Worcestershire are combined; the new metropolitan counties of Greater Manchester, Merseyside, South Yorkshire, Tyne and Wear, West Midlands and West Yorkshire are included, along with Avon (the metropolitan counties still exist even though their county councils were abolished, along with that for Greater London, in 1986); and the eastern part of Yorkshire is shown as the northern part of Humberside. Some ringers, along with many other people, prefer to use the old counties, in part because many of the ringing associations are based in them (e.g. the Lancashire and Yorkshire Associations): Dove's *Guide* partly meets their objections, by treating Herefordshire and Worcestershire separately, retaining Middlesex, and reducing Greater London to the London postal area. We have decided to stick entirely to the new counties, however, since they form the reality of the administrative geography of Great Britain at the present time.

The county maps have been reproduced at different scales in order to maximize the use of space, but they have a common key. On each, the main built-up areas are shown by shading, and the major roads are indicated.

The location of every ring is shown by a bell symbol, with the size and shading of the bell representing the number in the ring. The smallest symbols represent rings of four (open) and five (shaded); the next largest indicate rings of six (open) and eight (shaded); and the largest are reserved for rings of ten (open) and twelve (shaded). (The one ring each of seven and of nine are indicated by a number alongside the place-name, as are the two 'true' rings of more than twelve – at Birmingham and Perth.) The lettering of the place-names also reflects the number of bells in the ring. For rings of four, five and six we use a small type-size in upper and lower case; for rings of eight we use the same type-size, but upper-case letters only; for rings of ten a larger-type size in upper and lower case is used; and for rings of twelve again the same size is used but with upper-case letters only. Where a settlement (village, town or city) has more than one ring within its built-up area, the lettering of its name reflects the size of its largest ring: the dedication or district of each church is then shown using the smallest type size. (In two cases there are two rings of bells in one home, at Exmouth, Devon, and at Stoulton, Hereford and Worcester: these are shown overlapping. The church of S Andrew, Rugby, Warwickshire, has a ring of bells in each of its two towers.)

For settlements with several rings of bells in a small area (invariably the centre), an inset map is provided, using the same symbols and lettering conventions; the area covered by the inset is shown on the main map. These insets are not detailed street maps, but sufficient detail (the main roads and waterways) is provided on them to give a clear indication of where each ring is located.

The maps of England, Scotland and Wales have been designed to give a general picture of the pattern of bells in those countries and also to act as a guide in locating each ring. For the latter, the Atlas must be used in conjunction with the Gazetteer and the relevant Second Series 1:50000 sheets of the British Ordnance Survey (the Landranger Series). Detailed instructions on how that can be done are given in the introduction to the Gazetteer.

The Atlas is organized in six sections. The first four refer to England and cover the South-west, South-east, Midlands and North of the country successively. The fifth covers the rest of the British Isles – Wales (with three maps), Scotland, Ireland, the Channel Islands and the Isle of Man. Finally, the sixth contains maps for the rest of the world, with particular treatment of Australia, New Zealand, Africa, North America and the Verona district of Italy.

The text associated with each map has been produced drawing on a very wide range of sources, including the ringers' weekly newspaper, *The Ringing World*. Particular use has been made of the listings of bells produced for most of the (pre-1974) English counties (the majority of them in the late nineteenth century). For those wishing to do further research, a list of those sources is appended.

Bibliography

This bibliography lists all the sources drawn upon in producing the textual commentaries. They are given alphabetically by author, and the relevant modern county (counties) to which they refer is (are) indicated in brackets at the end of the title.

Baldwin, John, *Where's that Tower? A Church Bellringer's Index to the Towers of Britain* (privately pubd: Cardiff, 1986).

Bliss, M. and Sharpe, F., *The Church Bells of Gloucestershire* (privately pubd for the authors, 1985) [Avon, Gloucestershire].

Boulter, W. C., 'Inscriptions on the church bells of the East Riding', *Yorkshire Archaeological and Topographical Journal*, 2 (1871–2), pp. 82–6, 216–25; 3 (1873–4), pp. 26–32, 403–7 [Humberside, North Yorkshire].

Cheetham, F. H., 'The church bells of Lancashire', *Transactions of the Lancashire and Cheshire Antiquarian Society*, 33–44 (1915–25) [Cumbria, Greater Manchester, Lancashire, Merseyside].

Clarke, J. W., 'Cheshire bells', *Transactions of the Lancashire and Cheshire Antiquarian Society*, 60 (1948); 61 (1949); 62 (1950–1); 63 (1952–3); 65 (1955) [Cheshire, Greater Manchester, Merseyside].

Clouston, R. W. M., 'The church bells of Flintshire', *Archaeologensis Cambriensis* (1951), pp. 129–62 [Clwyd].

Cocks, A. W., *The Church Bells of Buckinghamshire* (Jarrold: London, 1897) [Buckinghamshire].

Colchester, W. E., *Hampshire Church Bells* (Warner: Winchester, 1920) [Hampshire, Isle of Wight].

Cook, W. T., *The Society of College Youths 1637–1987: a New History of the Society* (privately pubd: London, 1987).

Daniel-Tyssen, A., *The Church Bells of Sussex* (Sussex Archaeological Society: Lewes, 1864) [East Sussex, West Sussex].

Deedes, C. and Walters, H. B., *The Church Bells of Essex* (privately pubd for the authors, 1909) [Essex, Greater London].

Dunkin, E. H. W., *The Church Bells of Cornwall* (Bemrose: London, 1878) [Cornwall].

Ellacombe, H. T., *The Church Bells of Devon* (Pollard: Exeter, 1872) [Devon].

——, *The Church Bells of Somerset* (Pollard: Exeter, 1875) [Avon, Somerset].

——, *The Church Bells of Gloucestershire* (Pollard: Exeter, 1881) [Avon, Gloucestershire].

Elphick, G., *Sussex Bells and Belfries* (Phillimore: Chichester, 1970) [East Sussex, West Sussex].

Holmes, D. A., *Church Bells of the Basingstoke District* (privately pubd by the author: Overton, 1987) [Hampshire].

Jennings, T. S., *A History of Staffordshire Bells* (privately pubd by the author: Kingston upon Thames, 1970) [Staffordshire, West Midlands].

——, *Master of my Art: the Taylor Bellfoundries 1784–1987* (John Taylor and Co.: Loughborough, 1987).

——, *A Short History of Surrey Bells and Ringing Customs* (privately pubd by the author: Kingston upon Thames, 1974) [Greater London, Surrey].

Jowitt, L., 'The church bells of Derbyshire, described and illustrated', *The Reliquary*, 13–19 (1872–9) [Derbyshire].

Ketteringham, J. R., *Lincoln Cathedral: a History of the Bells, Bellringers and Bellringing* (privately pubd by the author: Lincoln, 1987) [Lincolnshire].

L'Estrange, J., *The Church Bells of Norfolk* (Miller and Levins: Norwich, 1874) [Norfolk].

Lynam, C., *The Church Bells of the County of Stafford* (pubd by the author, 1889) [Staffordshire, West Midlands].

Morris, Ernest, *The History and Art of Change Ringing* (Chapman and Hall: London, 1931).

North, T., *The Church Bells of Leicestershire* (S. Clarke: Leicester, 1876) [Leicestershire].

——, *The Church Bells of Northamptonshire* (S. Clarke: Leicester, 1878) [Northamptonshire].

——, *The Church Bells of Rutland* (S. Clarke: Leicester, 1880) [Leicestershire].

——, *The Church Bells of Lincolnshire* (S. Clarke: Leicester, 1882) [Humberside, Lincolnshire].

——, *The Church Bells of Bedfordshire* (Elliot Stock: London, 1883) [Bedfordshire].

North, T. with Stahlschmidt, J. C. L., *The Church Bells of Hertfordshire* (Elliot Stock: London, 1886) [Greater London, Hertfordshire].

Owen, T. M. N., *The Church Bells of Huntingdonshire* (Jarrold and Sons: London, 1899) [Cambridgeshire].

Park, G. R., *The Church Bells of Holderness* (Andrews: London, 1898) [Humberside].

Phillimore, W. W. P., 'Church bells of Nottinghamshire', *The Reliquary*, 19–20 (1878–80) [Nottinghamshire].

Pickford, C. J., *The Steeple, Bells and Ringers of Coventry Cathedral* (privately pubd by the author: Bedford, 1987) [West Midlands].

Poppleton, J. E., 'Notes on the bells of the ancient churches of the West Riding of Yorkshire', *The Yorkshire Archaeological Journal*, 16 (1900–1), pp. 46–83; 17 (1902–3), pp. 1–32, 192–236 and 434–462; 18 (1904–5), pp. 88–104 [North Yorkshire, South Yorkshire, West Yorkshire].

Potter, D. E., *The Bells and Bellringers of York Minster* (Friends of York Minster: York, 1987) [North Yorkshire].

Raven, J. J., *The Church Bells of Cambridgeshire* (Cambridge Antiquarian Society: Cambridge, 1881) [Cambridgeshire].

——, *The Church Bells of Suffolk* (Jarrold and Sons: London, 1890) [Suffolk].

——, 'The church bells of Dorset', *Proceedings of the Dorset Natural History and Archaeological Society*, 23 (1904), pp. 33–128; 24 (1906), pp. 103–48; 26 (1908), pp. 204–21; 27 (1909), pp. 93–137 [Dorset].

Rivet, P. L., *Bells of the Durham and Newcastle Dioceses* (Durham and Newcastle Diocesan Association of Church Bell Ringers: Newcastle, 1979) [Cleveland, Durham, Northumbria, Tyne and Wear].

Robinson, F. E., *Among the Bells: the Ringing Career of F. E. Robinson, Written by Himself* (privately pubd: Guildford, 1909).

Sharpe, F., *The Church Bells of Radnorshire* (pubd by the author: Brackley, 1947) [Powys].

——, *The Church Bells of Oxfordshire* (pubd by the author:

Brackley, 1953) [Oxfordshire].

——, *The Church Bells of Cardiganshire* (pubd by the author: Brackley, 1965) [Dyfed].

——, *The Church Bells of Berkshire* (Kingsmead Reprints: Bath, 1970) [Berkshire, Oxfordshire].

——, *The Church Bells of Herefordshire* (pubd by the author: Brackley, 1976) [Hereford and Worcester].

Stahlschmidt, J. C. L., *The Church Bells of Kent* (Elliot Stock: London, 1887) [Greater London, Kent].

——, *Surrey Bells and London Bellfounders* (Elliot Stock: London, 1884) [Greater London, Surrey].

Struckett, David W., *A Dictionary of Campanology* (privately pubd, 1985).

Thompson, B. L., 'Westmorland church bells', *Transactions of the Cumberland and Westmorland Antiquarian and Archaeological Society*, 76 (1970), pp. 51–68 [Westmorland].

Thow, W. A., *The Rings of Twelve* (privately pubd by the author, n.d., *c.* 1982) [general].

Tilley, H. T. and Walters, H. B., *The Church Bells of Warwickshire* (Cornish Brothers: Birmingham, 1910) [Warwickshire, West Midlands].

Walters, H. B., *The Church Bells of Shropshire* (Woodall, Minshall and Thomas: Shrewsbury, 1915) [Shropshire].

——, *The Church Bells of Wiltshire* (Kingsmead Reprints: Bath, 1969; first pubd 1929) [Wiltshire].

——, *The Church Bells of Worcestershire*, reprinted from the *Transactions of the Worcestershire Archaeological Society* (1932) [Hereford and Worcester, West Midlands].

Wright, A., *The Church Bells of Monmouthshire* (William Lewis: Cardiff, 1942) [Gwent].

S. MARY, BROWNSEA ISLAND, DORSET

SS PETER & PAUL, BISHOPS HULL, SOMERSET

Gloucestershire

Avon

Wiltshire

Somerset

Devon

Dorset

Cornwall

PART 1

—

SOUTH-WEST ENGLAND

WEST CAMEL, SOMERSET

S JAMES, TROWBRIDGE, WILTSHIRE

Avon

THE county of Avon was created in 1974 from what were formerly parts of Gloucestershire and Somerset. Its core is the cities of Bath and Bristol, but it also includes much magnificent countryside where the Cotswolds meet the Mendips. As a well-urbanized county, its ratio of rings of bells to population is smaller than that of its neighbours, but is much greater than that of, say, the West Midlands. In part this is because of the wealth of provision of bells in the ancient, prosperous trading city of Bristol; in part, too, it reflects the richness of the countryside around, the architectural traditions of the area, with the many superb church towers, and the place of this part of England in the development of ringing in country churches. This is seen on the map particularly in the south of the county, where virtually every village in the rich area of the Yeo valley, on the northern flanks of the Mendip Hills, has a ring of at least six bells. Indeed, that district is superbly described by John Betjeman, who wrote in *Collins Pocket Guide to English Parish Churches* that 'Over orchards and elms and willows, wherever you are in Somerset [now Avon], you can hear church bells, for few towers contain less than six of them and this is the chief county of ringers.'

As in Somerset and Gloucestershire, the basis of this wealth of bells was laid down two centuries or more ago, although outside Bath and Bristol there were few rings of eight or more before the present century. Ellacombe's Somerset listing (*The Church Bells of Somerset*, 1875) indicates only two of eight outside Bath – at Keynsham and Midsomer Norton – before 1800, with that at Yatton being installed in 1824; Almondsbury and Thornbury, formerly in Gloucestershire, also had eights by 1800. Midsomer Norton's included three treble bells given by King Charles II in 1750; they were augmented to twelve in 1976, by the purchase of the six bells from the redundant church of S Mark, Lyncombe, Bath, and using the metal to provide the extra four trebles.

Bath and its surrounding settlements have long had rings of bells. In the city itself, the abbey had a ring of eight by 1700, which was augmented to ten in 1774 (these are hung anticlockwise); S James's (destroyed in 1942) ring of eight was installed in 1729; All Saints, Weston, acquired six in 1739, and the eight at S Michael's was obtained in 1757. There are several nineteenth-century installations: Christ Church, Walcot, had its single bell replaced by six in 1867 and augmented to eight six years later; at S Saviour, Larkhall, a complete ring, the gift of W. Harper, was presented in 1830; and at S Mary the Virgin, Bathwick, a five was augmented to eight in 1819 (it was increased to ten in 1987). The other rings of eight in the area are recent augmentations: Twerton had had a ring of six since 1724, however, and Batheaston attained its six exactly a century later. (A further ring of eight was installed at S Andrew's in 1879 and destroyed in the Second World War.)

Compared with most English cities, Bath is very well supplied with rings of bells, but its near-neighbour outshines it. Ellacombe's book *The Church Bells of Gloucestershire* (1881) lists twelve rings of eight or more bells in Bristol at that time (including three of ten and one of twelve, undoubtedly the greatest number of such 'higher' rings outside London then), plus four rings of six (three of them, plus the ring of eight at nearby Clifton, were lost during the Second World War). Three foundries dominated in providing these bells: that of the Bilbie family of Chew Stoke just south of Bristol, which was casting bells between 1698 and 1814; that of the Rudhall family, in Gloucester; and that of the Evans family, which operated in Chepstow from 1686 to 1770. (Bristol's own founders, such as the Purdue family – 1601–88 – have few remaining bells in the city, largely on account of later recasting.)

All the rings listed by Ellacombe were in place, though not necessarily as large as they were in 1881, by the end of the eighteenth century, indicating the extent to which Bristol's rich merchants were prepared to endow churches in their home city with towers and bells – at a time, of course, when Bristol was England's second largest city. Christ Church acquired its ring of ten in 1727, eleven years after Rudhalls recast an earlier ring of eight in 1716 (the trebles were recast by Bilbies in 1789). The augmentation took place in the same year as Rudhalls provided an eight for nearby All Saints. S Mary Redcliffe had a ring of eight installed by Rudhall in 1698; this was augmented to ten in 1823 and became Bristol's first twelve in 1872 (the other, at S Stephen's, was completed only in 1971, having been increased from eight to ten by the local foundry, Llewellin and James, in 1891). The other rings of ten still present are those at S Ambrose, Whitehall, an eastern suburb, where the light eight received two new trebles in 1980, and S James, Horsefair, where the Rudhall eight of 1754 was augmented in 1866 (using a new bell from Taylors of Loughborough plus a clock bell already in the tower): that lost from S Nicholas as a result of Second World

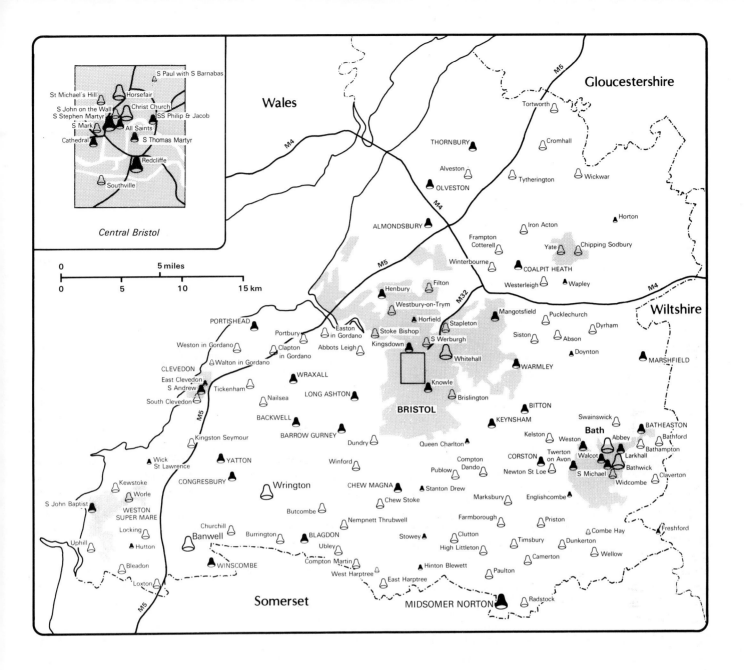

War bombing is believed to have been created in 1810, building on the heavy eight provided by Rudhalls in 1764.

So many rings of six or more bells within such a small area would surely seem enough for Bristol, but that is not all. Until 1958 the city's cathedral contained a ring of only four; the bells remain in the central tower, but in addition the north-west tower now contains the 21 cwt. ring of eight which formerly hung in the Temple Church, where the leaning tower was unsafe. (Two other Bristol rings were moved in the 1960s: the eight now at Warmley was initially at S George's, Bristol East, and the six at S Paul's, Bedminster, was formerly at S Luke's, Bedminster; the latter ring has now been removed.) At S Nicholas, in 1957 four of the original ten

(3, 4, 6, 10) were recast and rehung in the old frame for the clock, hour and curfew bell in the church, which was restored as the City Museum. Finally, there is another ring of four at S Paul's, Portland Square. The plan was for the church to have a ring of ten, and bells 1, 6 and 10 were installed, with a sanctus bell, in 1795, in a frame for ten; only the heavy two (9½ and 26 cwt.) are hung for ringing.

Many would doubt whether Bristol 'needs' more bells. Those in place are regularly rung by active bands, and Bristol is a major centre of peal-ringing. The most popular tower in the area for peals is that at Barrow Gurney, to the south-west of the city, where the relatively isolated ring of eight is the locale for between 19 and 25 successful attempts each year.

Cornwall

CORNWALL is the one part of Great Britain's Celtic periphery in which rings of bells are common: indeed, the county has one of the highest densities of rings, with about two-thirds of its parishes having four or more bells in the church tower. In part, this is because – in comparison with many other parts of rural England – there are few small parishes (in 1900, for example, only four of the 267 had populations of fewer than 100 and 23 more had between 100 and 249 residents). But, even among the smaller parishes, the installation of a ring of bells was common: in eleven of the 23 with 100–249 residents and 28 of the 44 with 250–499.

Many of the rings have been in place for 150 years or more. Of the 39 rings of five listed by Dunkin in 1878 (in *The Church Bells of Cornwall*), 21 were installed before 1800, as were 34 of the 54 rings of six (and four of the other 24 were based on eighteenth-century rings of five). Compared with Devon, Cornwall has relatively few medieval bells (Ellacombe in *The Church Bells of Devon* lists the number in each county), suggesting relatively late development, but by the middle of the eighteenth century the installation of five or more was clearly catching on fast.

Like most other relatively remote rural areas, Cornwall had very few rings of eight before the present century. The oldest was at Kenwyn, cast in 1747 by Thomas Lester; these were followed by the eight at S Petroc's Church, Bodmin, installed in 1767; this tower had one of the earliest rings of five (1691) and six (1699) in the county, too. The only other ring of eight before 1800 was provided in 1771 for the large village of Stoke Climsland in the Tamar valley inland from Plymouth, where the Pennington family had a foundry at the time, and just four more were installed between then and 1878 – for St Austell (1810), St Columb Major (1825), Penzance (1865) and Fowey (1870). The church at Penzance was built in 1833, and the separate parish was created only in 1871. The bells were a mixture of gifts, including one from the town council, and the result of public subscription; when they were replaced in 1930 the borough council donated the cost of another of the bells. (Canon Roberts has claimed – *Ringing World*, 22 January 1982 – that a ring of eight was installed at St Buryan as long ago as 1638, but by 1878 there was only a ring of three there, which was increased to four in 1801.)

Over the last 100 years there have been many augmentations, for Cornwall now has only six rings of five but 45 rings of eight, as well as its nearly 100 rings of six. Of the 62 rings of three in Dunkin's list, 30 had been augmented a century later, a much greater proportion than in most other counties, where the augmentations are usually to the larger foundations; of those 30, eleven are new rings of eight and 17 rings of six. Similarly, nine of the 13 rings of four had been augmented, seven to rings of six and two to rings of five. But the main change was with the rings of five, for of the 39 listed by Dunkin only four were in the same state a century later; 29 were rings of six and six were rings of eight. Finally, one-third of the rings of six were augmented to eight over the same period. At Redruth, for example, the 1744 ring of six (cast at Whitechapel) was increased to eight in 1935, and the four at Luxulyan was recast and augmented to six in 1902, as the gift of a local architect.

Change-ringing was introduced late to the county. A quarter peal of Grandsire Triples rung at Penzance by a local band (the Penzance Band of Scientific Changeringers) in October 1872 is believed to have been the first in the county; their peal in the following June was certainly the first in Cornwall. Call-change ringing was the norm, rung with closed handstroke leads: indeed the Penzance band was affiliated to the Guild of Devonshire Ringers.

This situation has changed somewhat, but there are still many churches today where only call-changes are rung. In welcoming the Central Council of Church Bell Ringers to Penzance in 1979, the President of the Truro Diocesan Guild noted that 'Cornwall has not many strongholds of method ringing'; on the other hand, by then a peal had been rung on every ringable set of bells, and two members of the guild had rung one in every tower.

One of the strongholds of method and peal-ringing in Cornwall is the church of S Anta and All Saints, Carbis Bay, just outside St Ives. Canon A. S. Roberts was appointed priest-in-charge there in 1940, when the church was incomplete and lacked, among other things, the top stage of the projected tower. A light ring of eight (tenor 9½ cwt.) was dedicated in October 1946: each bell was a gift (the seventh being paid for by the ringers of Cornwall), and the Church Council (the parish was created only in 1948) paid for the frame. In 1959 another gift enabled the tower to be completed, and two trebles were given by the Emma Barron Bell Trust.

The only other tower in Cornwall with ten bells is Truro Cathedral. This was built only in the late nineteenth century, incorporating the old parish church of S Mary as the south aisle. (S Mary's had but two bells.) It was in 1910 that the ten bells (all donated) cast by Taylor were installed, and the first peal on them (tenor 33¾ cwt.) was rung by a Plymouth band in the following year.

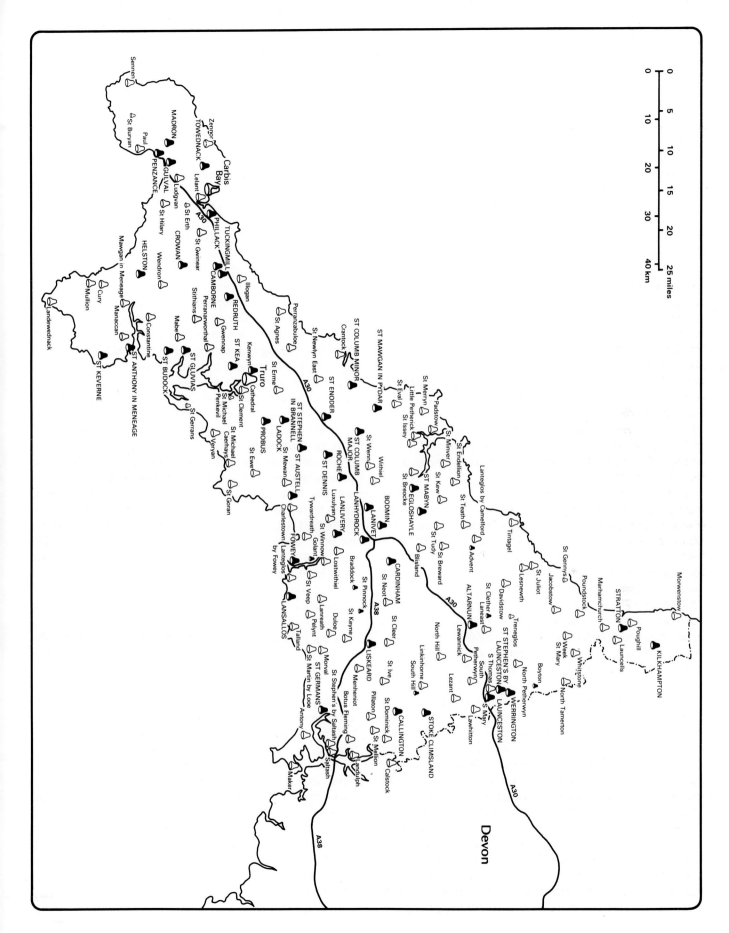

Sennen

St Buryan

MADRON
Zennor
TOWEDNACK
Carbis
Bay

Paul
GULVAL
PENZANCE
Ludgvan
Lelant

St Hilary
St Erth
A30
PHILLACK
TUCKINGMILL

Mawgan in Meneage
HELSTON
Wendron
CROWAN
St Gwinear
CAMBORNE

Cury
Mullion
Manaccan
Constantine
Stithians
Perranarworthal
REDRUTH
ST KEA
Illogan

Landewednack
ST ANTHONY IN MENEAGE
ST BUDOCK
Mabe
Gwennap
Kenwyn
St Agnes
Perranzabuloe

ST KEVERNE
ST GLUVIAS
St Gerrans
St Clement
St Erme
Truro
Cathedral
St Michael Penkevil
ST ENODER
St Newlyn East
Cranock
ST COLUMB MINOR

Veryan
St Ewe
PROBUS
St Mewan
ST AUSTELL
ST COLUMB MAJOR
ST MAWGAN IN PYDAR

St Goran
LADOCK
ST STEPHEN IN BRANNELL
ROCHE
St Wenn
St Eval

St Michael Caerhays
Charlestown
ST DENNIS
LANHYDROCK
LANLIVERY
Withiel
St Issey
St Endellion
Padstow
St Merryn
Little Petherick

Lanteglos by Fowey
by Fowey
Tywardreath
Luxulyan
LANIVET
BOODMIN
ST MABYN
St Breocke
St Minver

Lantic
Golant
St Winnow
Braddock
EGLOSHAYLE
St Kew
St Teath
St Tudy

FOWEY
St Veep
Lostwithiel
St Pinnock
CARDINHAM
Blisland
St Breward
Advent
Tintagel

LANSALLOS
Lanreath
Duloe
St Keyne
St Neot
North Hill
Lesnewth

Talland
Pelynt
St Cleer
Lewannick
St Juliot
Jacobstow

St Martin by Loo
Morval
LISKEARD
Menheniot
St Ive
St Clether
Laneast
Davidstow
St Gennys

Antony
ST GERMANS
Botus Fleming
Pillaton
St Dominick
CALLINGTON
Linkinhorne
South Hill
Lezant
North Petherwyn
Trenegios
Week
St Mary

Maker
St Stephen's by Saltash
Saltash
Landulph
Calstock
STOKE CLIMSLAND
Lawhitton
S Thomas
St Mary
LAUNCESTON
ST STEPHEN'S BY LAUNCESTON
WERRINGTON
Boyton
Whitstone
North Tamerton

South
Petherwyn
Marhamchurch
Launcells
STRATTON
Poughill
KILKHAMPTON
Morwenstow

A30
A38

Devon

0 5 10 20 30 40 km
0 5 10 15 20 25 miles

61

Devon

In terms of rings of bells, Devon is England's most populous county, having over 100 more than its nearest rival, Somerset. In terms of density Devon wins, too, with over 70 per cent of its parishes having a ring of four or more bells in the church tower. Not surprisingly, then, the map is a very full one, with Dartmoor the only obviously empty area (the only settlement of any size on the moor – Princetown – lacks a ring). In some districts, such as that inland of Torbay, the density of towers is very high indeed.

The eighteenth century saw many churches acquire a ring of at least five bells: before 1700 the evidence of Ellacombe's lists (*The Church Bells of Devon*, 1872) suggests that there were only six rings. Thus, of the rings of five that Ellacombe lists which can be dated, 85 were in place by 1800, and another 35 were installed during the first 70 years of the nineteenth century; for the rings of six, too, the majority were of pre-1800 provenance – 84 of the 135 that could be dated. Clearly, ringing as we understand it was widespread at least 150 years ago (although almost certainly it was not change-ringing). There were also 18 rings of eight present when Ellacombe drew up his list, plus one ring of ten (at Exeter Cathedral). Several of these were old, too, with those at Alphington, Crediton, Cullompton, Exeter S Sidwell, Plymouth Charles Church (now lost), Plymouth S Andrew, Tavistock, Tiverton and Totnes having been installed in the eighteenth century.

Even older was the ring of ten at Exeter Cathedral. At the time of the inventory of church furnishings in 1552 there were eight bells in one tower and five in the other, and it is probable that the former were provided with full wheels and hung for ringing by 1678. The ten was installed in 1729, including a 62 cwt. tenor called Grandison after a bishop of that name (an earlier bell, cast in 1396, had been the first to carry his name); it was recast by Taylors in 1902, with 10 cwt. of metal being added to it, and 20 years later became the tenor of a ring of twelve. For just over 200 years this was the heaviest ring of bells in the world, being surpassed in 1939 by those of Liverpool Cathedral (which were not hung and rung until the 1950s). No peal was rung, or even attempted, at Exeter until 1902, not just because of the weight of the bells but also because of their arrangement in the tower; the bells all swung in the same direction in the timber frame, and the ropes fell into four rows in the ringing-room, which made change-ringing extremely difficult. The new frame installed in 1902 removed this

problem, and a peal of Grandsire Caters was rung in October of that year. The first peal on the twelve was Stedman Cinques in 1924, and the first with the tenor rung to changes was Cambridge Surprise Maximus; two men rang the tenor, for four hours and 25 minutes.

Eleven further rings of eight were installed in the first 70 years of the nineteenth century. Since then, the number of eights has increased fivefold, as the result of augmentations. A great deal of this activity has been associated with the expansion of change-ringing in the county. For long, Devon was dominated by call-change ringing, with closed handstroke leads, emphasizing not only the striking of the changes but also ringing the bells up and down in peal. Indeed, Ernest Morris claims (in *The History and Art of Change Ringing*) that it was not until 1865 that a band of Devon ringers first rang 120 changes of Grandsire Doubles, at Kelly, near the Cornish border, at the instigation of the local vicar. Change-ringing in Devon today is associated with the Guild of Devonshire Ringers, and, of its 59 affiliated towers in 1985, 32 were rings of eight or more. This is in contrast to the call-change ringers, who are affiliated to the Devon Association of Ringers: of the 68 towers in their 1981 list, 18 were rings of eight. (Three towers are on both lists.) The map showing the location of towers affiliated to the two bodies indicates that they operate largely in separate areas. The Devon Association has a virtual monopoly of the central part of the county, particularly the area to the north of Dartmoor, and also in the south, around the Sal estuary. Thus call-change ringing dominates the more remote parts of the county. The Guild of Devonshire Ringers, on the other hand, is strongest in the Exeter area, in the east of the county, and in the coastal strip between Dawlish and Torbay. Outside those areas, only the city of Plymouth provides a further focus of change-ringing activity.

The popularity of call-change ringing, and the rural nature of the county, no doubt accounts for the small number of rings of more than eight. Outside Exeter and Plymouth, only Cullompton (1920) and Brixham (1970s) have rings of ten in churches. But Devon does have the only ring of twelve in a Roman Catholic church in England, at the Abbey Church of S Mary at Buckfast. A ring of twelve was cast by Warners in 1910 for the monks, but was not hung until 1921; it was replaced by Taylors in 1935.

A county with so many rings of bells installed in the eighteenth century, and, apart from the coastal settle-

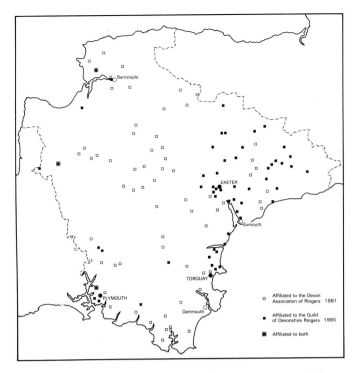

Towers affiliated to the two Devonshire ringing associations

ments, not very accessible at that time to the rest of England, would have needed local founders. (Nevertheless, medieval bells from London, usually provided singly, reached remote inland villages – as at Brentor on Dartmoor, which had a fourteenth-century bell until it was recast in 1909.) The lists produced by Ellacombe indicate the extent to which the development of bell-ringing in Devon was dependent on local bell foundries. Of the 2,010 bells listed, nearly half (923) were cast either by a Devon foundry or by a firm with Devon links (such as Taylors; see below). A further 593 were cast in an adjacent county (489 in Cornwall and the rest in Somerset), 405 elsewhere, and 89 at unknown locations. Of the Devon founders, the Bilbie family of Cullompton (and Chew Stoke, in adjacent Somerset) was responsible for 352 bells, including the ring of eight for Tavistock in 1769, 18 rings of six and 19 of five: Thomas Bilbie was based at Cullompton from 1787 to 1813, during which time 132 of the Bilbie bells hung in Devon were cast; the remainder were presumably cast in Chew Stoke and transported to the south-west. The Bilbies were succeeded at Cullompton by William Parnell and his son, and Ellacombe lists 54 examples of their work, of which only the six at Arlington was a complete ring. (The son, Charles, also cast bells in Exeter.)

The family which produced most bells for Devon churches before 1870 was the Penningtons. Three having the Christian name John and two called Thomas had a foundry in Exeter between 1618 and 1741, and together cast 174 bells, nearly all of them single, which was the norm in those days. (Indeed, of the 174,

surviving evidence suggests that in only eleven cases did they manufacture two for the same church at one date; they produced three on one occasion – for Widecombe in the Moor, in 1632; and one ring of four, for the Church of S Mary Steps, Exeter, in 1656.) The family's main founding activities took place at two villages in east Cornwall south of Launceston – Lezant and Stoke Climsland (the latter village was the second in Cornwall to have a ring of eight). In total, 489 bells were cast in those villages for Devon churches, many of them in complete rings of five or six, between 1702 and 1818. Finally, the only other firm of Devon founders to produce more than 100 bells for local churches was Taylors. Between 1825 and 1839 John Taylor I operated a foundry at Buckland Brewer, just south of Bideford. One of his first contracts was to produce a ring of six for the church of SS Mary and Benedict there, having made rings of six for the nearby churches at Roborough and S Giles in the Wood two years earlier. During the years in which the Buckland foundry was in operation, 78 of the 115 Taylor bells listed by Ellacombe were cast. Much of the early work was for churches in the remote part of North Devon close to the foundry (including rings of five for Ashreigney and Downland and of six for Hartland and Woolfordisworthy), but in the late 1820s several contracts were won in the area between Oke-hampton and the Cornish border, including the six at Bridestowe, the five at Bradstone, and the eight at nearby Lifton. (More detail about the Buckland Brewer foundry is provided in T. S. Jennings, *Master of my Art*, 1987.)

The greatest concentration of rings of bells in Devon, not surprisingly, is in the county town and ancient city of Exeter, which at present has four rings of eight and one of six in churches within the town itself – plus the twelve at the cathedral and rings in suburban villages. Several others have been lost: the two rings of eight in Ellacombe's list (at S Sidwell's – augmented to ten in 1891 – and S Edmund's) have both gone, the latter since the Second World War, as has a six from S John's (a ring of five established in 1740 and augmented to six in 1843), which was recast as part of the modern ring of eight at S Mark's. Another which might have been lost is the light ring of six (tenor 6 cwt.) in the Church of S Petrock. Those were retuned and rehung in 1987 so that they could be used to train ringers for other churches in the area, as well as to be the centre of a church bell-ringing information centre. The bells from S Sidwell's were one of five rings lost by enemy action in the Second World War – the others being the rings of ten at Plymouth Charles Church and the rings of eight at Plymouth Stonehouse, Devonport Dockyard Chapel (where the author William Banister was a ringer) and Aveton Gifford (a village north of Kingsbridge). Outside London and Bristol, the county of Devon lost most rings during those hostilities.

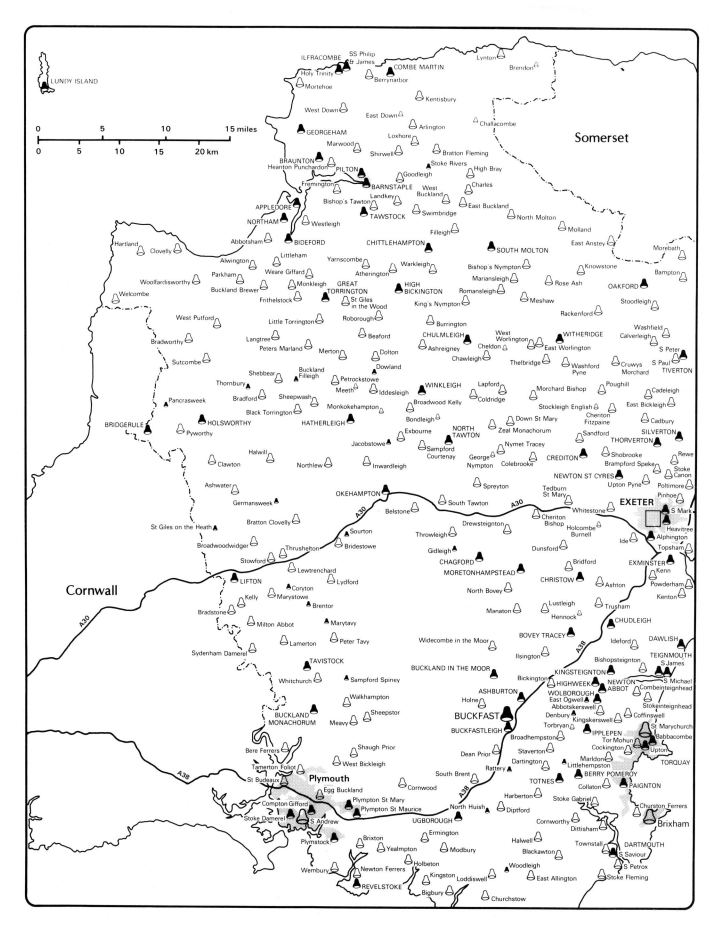

LUNDY ISLAND

0   5   10   15 miles

0 5 10 15 20 km

Somerset

Cornwall

ILFRACOMBE SS Philip & James   COMBE MARTIN   Lynton   Brendon
Holy Trinity   Berrynarbor
Mortehoe   Kentisbury
West Down   East Down   Arlington   Challacombe
GEORGEHAM   Marwood   Loxhore   Bratton Fleming
BRAUNTON   Shirwell   High Bray
Heanton Punchardon PILTON   Goodleigh   Stoke Rivers   Charles
Fremington   Landkey   West   East Buckland   Molland
BARNSTAPLE   Buckland
APPLEDORE   Bishop's Tawton   Swimbridge   North Molton   East Anstey
NORTHAM   TAWSTOCK   Filleigh
Westleigh   CHITTLEHAMPTON   SOUTH MOLTON   Morebath
Hartland   Clovelly   Abbotsham   BIDEFORD
Alwington   Littleham   Yarnscombe   Warkleigh   Bishop's Nympton   Knowstone   Bampton
Parkham   Weare Giffard   Atherington   Marlansleigh   Rose Ash   OAKFORD
Woolfardisworthy   Monkleigh   HIGH   Romansleigh   Stoodleigh
Welcombe   Buckland Brewer   GREAT   BICKINGTON   Meshaw
Frithelstock   TORRINGTON   King's Nympton   Rackenford   Washfield
West Putford   St Giles   Burrington   WITHERIDGE   Calverleigh
in the Wood   CHULMLEIGH   West   East Worlington   S Peter
Bradworthy   Little Torrington   Roborough   Cheldon   Worlington   Washford   Cruwys   S Paul
Langtree   Beaford   Ashreigney   Pyne   Morchard   TIVERTON
Sutcombe   Peters Marland   Merton   Dolton   Chawleigh   Thelbridge   Poughill
Shebbear   Dowland   Morchard Bishop   Cadeleigh
Thornbury   Buckland   Petrockstowe   WINKLEIGH   Lapford   Stockleigh English   East Bickleigh
Pancrasweek   Filleigh   Meeth   Iddesleigh   Coldridge   Cheriton   Cadbury
Bradford   Sheepwash   Broadwood Kelly   Fitzpaine
BRIDGERULE   Black Torrington   Monkokehampton   Bondleigh   Down St Mary   SILVERTON
HOLSWORTHY   HATHERLEIGH   Exbourne   Zeal Monachorum   Sandford   THORVERTON
Pyworthy   NORTH   Nymet Tracey   Shobrooke   Rewe
Halwill   Jacobstowe   TAWTON   George   CREDITON   Brampford Speke   Stoke
Clawton   Northlew   Sampford   Nympton   Colebrooke   Upton Pyne   Canon
Ashwater   Inwardleigh   Courtenay   NEWTON ST CYRES   Poltimore
Germansweek   Spreyton   Tedburn   Pinhoe
OKEHAMPTON   South Tawton   St Mary   EXETER   S Mark
St Giles on the Heath   Belstone   Cheriton   Whitestone   Heavitree
Bratton Clovelly   Drewsteignton   Bishop   Holcombe   Ide   Alphington
Broadwoodwidger   Sourton   Throwleigh   Burnell   Topsham
Stowford   Bridestowe   Gidleigh   Dunsford   EXMINSTER
Thrushelton   CHAGFORD   Bridford   Ashton   Kenn
Lewtrenchard   MORETONHAMPSTEAD   CHRISTOW   Powderham
LIFTON   Lydford   North Bovey   Lustleigh   Trusham   Kenton
Coryton   Manaton   Hennock   CHUDLEIGH
Kelly   Marystowe   Ideford   DAWLISH
Bradstone   Brentor   Widecombe in the Moor   BOVEY TRACEY   TEIGNMOUTH
Milton Abbot   Marytavy   Ilsington   Bishopsteignton   S James
Lamerton   Peter Tavy   BUCKLAND IN THE MOOR   KINGSTEIGNTON   S Michael
Sydenham Damerel   ASHBURTON   Bickington   HIGHWEEK   NEWTON   Combeinteignhead
TAVISTOCK   Sampford Spiney   Holne   WOLBOROUGH   ABBOT   Stokeinteignhead
Whitchurch   Walkhampton   East Ogwell   Coffinswell
BUCKFAST   Denbury   Abbotskerswell   St Marychurch
Meavy   Sheepstor   BUCKFASTLEIGH   Torbryan   Kingskerswell   Babbacombe
BUCKLAND   Broadhempston   IPPLEPEN   Upton
MONACHORUM   Dean Prior   Tor Mohun   TORQUAY
Shaugh Prior   Staverton   Cockington   Marldon
Bere Ferrers   West Bickleigh   Dartington   Littlehempston   BERRY POMEROY
Tamerton Foliot   South Brent   Rattery   TOTNES   Collaton   PAIGNTON
St Budeaux   Egg Buckland   Cornwood   Harberton   Stoke Gabriel   Churston Ferrers
Compton Gifford   Plympton St Mary   North Huish   Diptford   Cornworthy   Dittisham   Brixham
Stoke Damerel   Plympton St Maurice   UGBOROUGH   Halwell   Townstall
S Andrew   Ermington   Blackawton   DARTMOUTH
Plymouth   Brixton   Modbury   Woodleigh   S Saviour
Plymstock   Yealmpton   Cornworthy   East Allington   S Petrox
Wembury   Holbeton   Kingston   Stoke Fleming
Newton Ferrers   Bigbury   Loddiswell
REVELSTOKE   Churchstow

64

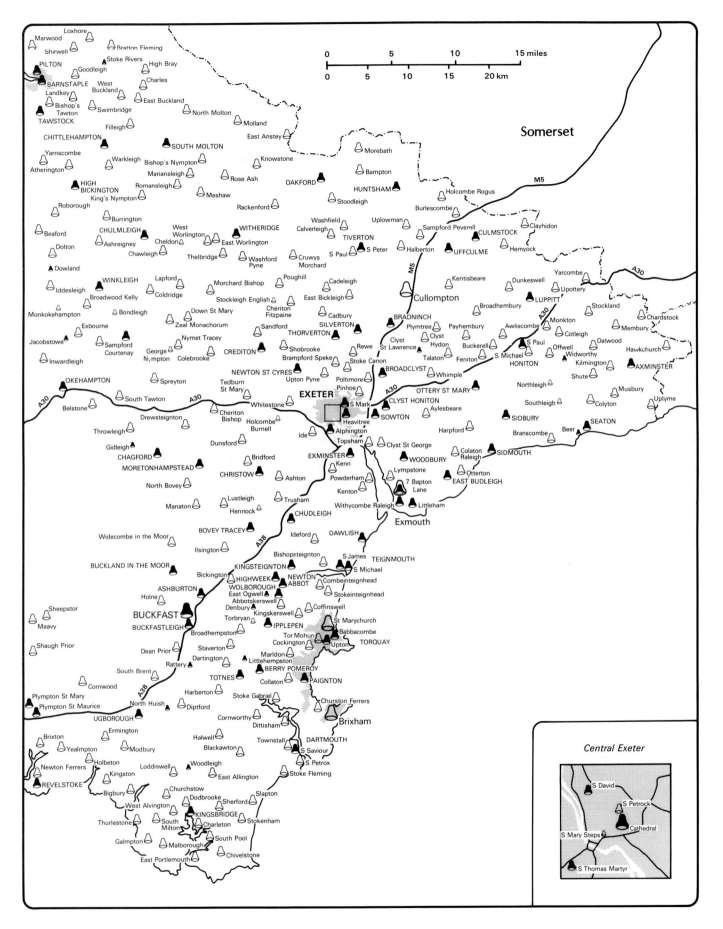

Loxhore
Marwood
Shirwell
PILTON
BARNSTAPLE
Landkey
Bishop's
Tawton
TAWSTOCK
CHITTLEHAMPTON
Yarnscombe
Atherington
HIGH
BICKINGTON
Roborough
Beaford
CHULMLEIGH
Dolton
Ashreigney
Chawleigh
Dowland
Iddesleigh
WINKLEIGH
Broadwood Kelly
Monkokehampton
Jacobstowe
Inwardleigh
OKEHAMPTON
Belstone
Throwleigh
Gidleigh
CHAGFORD
MORETONHAMPSTEAD
North Bovey
Manaton
Widecombe in the Moor
BUCKLAND IN THE MOOR
ASHBURTON
Holne
BUCKFAST
BUCKFASTLEIGH
Sheepstor
Meavy
Shaugh Prior
Plympton St Mary
Plympton St Maurice
Cornwood
UGBOROUGH
Ermington
Brixton
Yealmpton
Modbury
Newton Ferrers
Holbeton
Kingston
REVELSTOKE
Bigbury
West Alvington
Thurlestone
Galmpton
East Portlemouth

Bratton Fleming
Goodleigh
Stoke Rivers
High Bray
Charles
West
Buckland
East Buckland
Swimbridge
Filleigh
North Molton
Molland
East Anstey
Morebath
Bampton
SOUTH MOLTON
Knowstone
Warkleigh
Bishop's Nympton
Mariansleigh
Rose Ash
King's Nympton
Meshaw
Rackenford
Burrington
West
Worlington
East Worlington
Cheldon
Thelbridge
Washford
Pyne
Lapford
Coldridge
Bondleigh
Down St Mary
Zeal Monachorum
Sandford
Nymet Tracey
George
Nympton
Colebrooke
CREDITON
Spreyton
South Tawton
Drewsteignton
Cheriton
Bishop
Holcombe
Burnell
Dunsford
Bridford
CHRISTOW
Ashton
Lustleigh
Hennock
Trusham
BOVEY TRACEY
Ilsington
KINGSTEIGNTON
Bickington
HIGHWEEK
WOLBOROUGH
East Ogwell
Abbotskerswell
Denbury
Torbryan
Kingskerswell
IPPLEPEN
Broadhempston
Dean Prior
Staverton
Rattery
Dartington
South Brent
North Huish
Harberton
Diptford
Stoke Gabriel
Cornworthy
Halwell
Dittisham
Townstall
Blackawton
DARTMOUTH
S Saviour
S Petrox
Stoke Fleming
Churchstow
Dodbrooke
Sherford
Slapton
KINGSBRIDGE
South
Milton
Charleton
Stokenham
Malborough
South Pool
Chivelstone

OAKFORD
HUNTSHAM
Stoodleigh
Holcombe Rogus
Burlescombe
Washfield
Calverleigh
Uplowman
Sampford Peverell
CULMSTOCK
Clayhidon
TIVERTON
S Paul
S Peter
Halberton
UFFCULME
Hemyock
Cruwys
Morchard
Kentisbeare
Dunkeswell
Yarcombe
Upottery
Poughill
Cadeleigh
Stockleigh English
East Bickleigh
Cheriton
Fitzpaine
Cadbury
SILVERTON
Shobrooke
THORVERTON
Brampford Speke
NEWTON ST CYRES
Upton Pyne
Rewe
Clyst
St Lawrence
Stoke Canon
Tedburn
St Mary
Whitestone
EXETER
Heavitree
Alphington
Ide
Topsham
EXMINSTER
Kenn
Powderham
Kenton
Withycombe Raleigh
CHUDLEIGH
Ideford
DAWLISH
Bishopsteignton
S James
TEIGNMOUTH
S Michael
Combeinteignhead
NEWTON
ABBOT
Stokeinteignhead
Coffinswell
St Marychurch
Babbacombe
Tor Mohun
Cockington
Upton
TORQUAY
Marldon
Littlehempston
BERRY POMEROY
TOTNES
Collaton
PAIGNTON
Churston Ferrers
Brixham

Cullompton
BRADNINCH
Plymtree
Clyst
Hydon
Payhembury
Broadhembury
BROADCLYST
Whimple
Clyst
St Lawrence
SOWTON
CLYST HONITON
Aylesbeare
Harpford
Clyst St George
WOODBURY
Lympstone
7 Bapton
Lane
Littleham
Exmouth
Colaton
Raleigh
Otterton
EAST BUDLEIGH

Somerset
M5
A30
M5
A30
A30
A38
A38
A30

LUPPITT
S Michael
S Paul
HONITON
Awliscombe
Monkton
Cotleigh
Offwell
Widworthy
Kilmington
Shute
AXMINSTER
Buckerell
Feniton
Talaton
Northleigh
Southleigh
SIDBURY
Branscombe
Beer
SEATON
Coif on
Musbury
Colyton
Uplyme
SIDMOUTH
Stockland
Chardstock
Membury
Dalwood
Hawkchurch

Central Exeter
S David
S Petrock
S Mary Steps
Cathedral
S Thomas Martyr

Dorset

DORSET typifies the general image of rural southern England. Apart from Poole and Bournemouth (the latter formerly in Hampshire) there are no major urban areas: the county is characterized by chalk downlands and green valleys, with lines of villages following the clear streams, and the occasional market town. It is a county where rings of five and six predominate, and one that played no part in the early development of change-ringing; the first peal of Surprise in the county was not rung until 1909, at Milton Abbey.

Parts of the map are virtually empty; most of those areas are relatively empty of people, too, notably the coastal strip south of the A35, where one community lost its bells as a consequence of the area around it being used as an artillery range: West Lulworth had a ring of six, but the tower was weakened by the continual reverberations of gunfire, and the replacement contains a chime of two bells. Further north, the fertile valleys support lines of villages, some of whose names were celebrated in Sir John Betjeman's poem *Dorset*. Ryme Intrinsica has a ring of three, and so is not on the map, but the rings of four at Melbury Bubb and Toller Porcorum are there, as are those at Stourton Caundle and Stour Provost.

As a rural county Dorset has a predominance of rings of five and six; its only twelve, at Christchurch Priory, was in Hampshire until 1974. Just under one-half of its parish churches have rings of four bells or more. Dorset was not one of the richer counties in the south; most of its parishes have small populations, and there has been no bellfounding tradition.

In his survey of Dorset parish churches published early in this century (in the *Proceedings of the Dorset Natural History and Archaeological Society*) Canon Raven identified 14 rings of eight (excluding Bournemouth and Christchurch), 31 of six, 53 of five and 39 of four; in addition, there were 42 rings of three. Many of the smaller rings had been in place for a century or more: of the rings of five, more than half were pre-1800 installations (with the occasional bell recast since), although only eight of the rings of six dated from the eighteenth century or earlier. Thus until the present century relatively few villages invested in bells on which change-ringing was likely to be practised: most of the rings of five in Raven's survey have since been augmented. At Lytchett Minster, on the outskirts of Poole, for example, the seventeenth-century ring of four was augmented to five in 1903, with a further bell added seven years later. And at nearby Sturminster Marshall the medieval ring of four was augmented to six only in 1911. Netherbury, north of Bridport, on the other hand, has what is probably the county's third-oldest ring of six (those at Wimborne S Giles, cast by Rudhall in 1737, and S Peters, Shaftesbury, are certainly older). The tenor bell was recast in 1810 and the age of its predecessor is unknown; the remainder were installed in 1610, 1636, 1740, 1748 and 1750, the oldest two at least having been cast in the churchyard, where a mould was found during excavations.

Just as there were few rings of six in this relatively remote rural area before the nineteenth century, so there were even fewer rings of eight. Indeed, of the 14 recorded by Raven, only three, those at Beaminster, Dorchester and Wareham, were installed before 1800 (though Raven omits a 1750 ring of eight by Robert Catlin at Blandford Forum, and a nine was installed at Christchurch Priory in 1755); there were only four rings of eight in Dorset in 1850, plus that in Poole (1821 – then in Hampshire). The first eight was installed at S Peter's in Dorchester, with Thomas Bilbie of Chew Stoke, Somerset, getting an order to replace the old ring of five in 1734. The treble had to be recast 16 years later, and the second in 1800. Beaminster's ring of eight was installed in 1765, and Wareham's 20 years later; both now have rings of ten, as does Poole (augmented in 1937).

Of the later rings of eight, the most prominent is that at Sherborne Abbey, which is the heaviest ring of eight in the world, the tenor weighing 46 cwt. The abbey has long had very heavy bells, the original tenor having been cast at Tournai in France and donated by Cardinal Wolsey. Before the eight was installed by Warners of London in 1858 there was a ring of six with a tenor reputed to weigh 52 cwt.: Ellacombe claimed that early in the century it took 21 people to ring the bells, with six on the tenor and two on the treble. The original tenor (by Purdue) remained, but soon cracked, and was recast by Warners in 1865 (to 46 cwt.); Mears and Stainbank recast again in 1934.

Other heavy rings of eight in the county include that at Kingston, which was installed in 1878 in the as-yet unfinished church: the tenor weighs 26¾ cwt. At Wimborne Minster, the augmentation from six to eight in 1856 provided a tenor of 29½ cwt.; the bells were recast and two trebles were added in 1911, after a fire. Charminster has had three twentieth-century augmentations; the original ring of five by the Purdue family of Somerset was increased to six in 1933, to eight in 1961 and to ten in 1981. And at Cattistock, a ring of eight replaced a carillon of 35 bells (cast at Louvain in Belgium), of which eight were hung for ringing, too, after a fire in 1940.

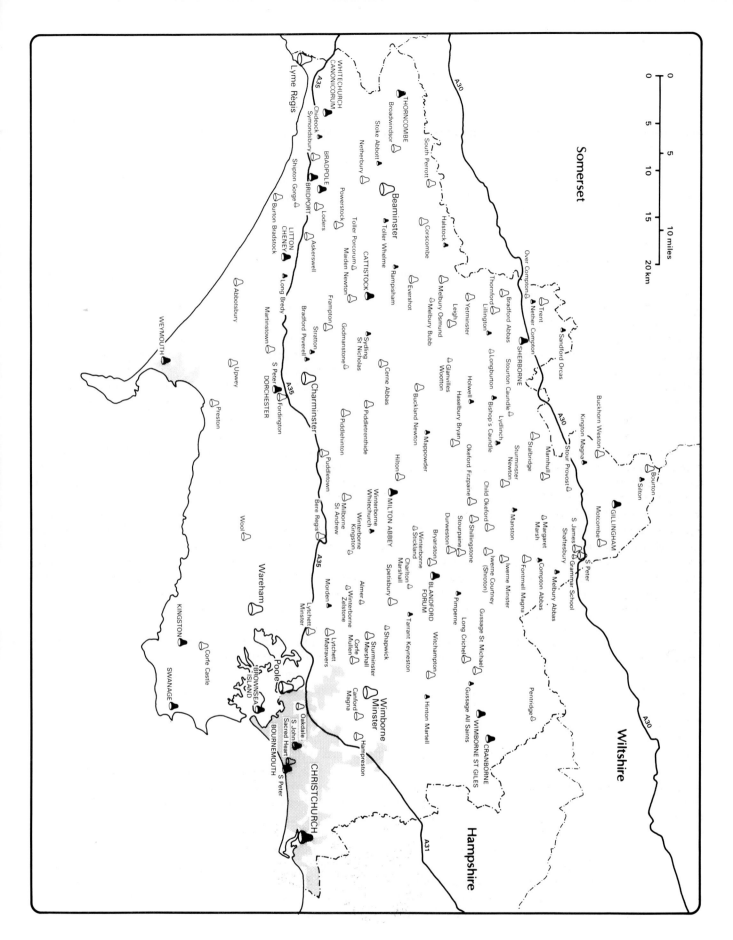

Somerset

Wiltshire

Hampshire

Lyne Regis
WHITECHURCH
CANONICORUM
Broadwindsor
THORNCOMBE
Stoke Abbott
Netherbury
South Perrott
Chideock
Symondsbury
Shipton Gorge
BRADPOLE
BRIDPORT
Loders
Askerswell
Burton Bradstock
LITTON
CHENEY
Long Bredy
Abbotsbury
Martinstown
Bradford Peverell
Stratton
Fordington
S Peter
DORCHESTER
WEYMOUTH
Upwey
Preston

Beaminster
Toller Whelme
Corscombe
Halstock
Leigh
Melbury Osmund
Melbury Bubb
Rampisham
Toller Porcorum
Maiden Newton
CATTISTOCK
Frampton
Godmanstone
Evershot
Yetminster
Sydling
St Nicholas
Cerne Abbas
Puddletrenthide
Piddlehinton
Charminster
A35
Bere Regis
Puddletown
A35

Over Compton
Trent
Nether Compton
Sandford Orcas
SHERBORNE
Thornford
Lillington
Bradford Abbas
Stourton Caundle
Longburton
Bishop's Caundle
Holwell
Haselbury Bryan
Glanvilles
Wootton
Buckland Newton
Mappowder
Hilton
Okeford Fitzpaine
Child Okeford
MILTON ABBEY
Winterborne
Whitechurch
Winterborne
Kingston
Milborne
St Andrew
Morden

A30
Kington Magna
Buckhorn Weston
Stour Provost
Marnhull
Stalbridge
Sturminster
Newton
Manston
Shillingstone
Stourpaine
Durweston
Bryanston
Winterborne
Stickland
Charlton
Marshall
BLANDFORD
FORUM
Spetisbury
Almer
Winterborne
Zelstone
Tarrant Keyneston
Sturminster
Marshall
Shapwick

Gillingham
Silton
Bourton
Motcombe
S Peter
S James
Grammar School
Shaftesbury
Margaret
Marsh
Compton Abbas
Melbury Abbas
Fontmell Magna
Iwerne Courtney
(Shroton)
Iwerne Minster
Pimperne
Long Crichel
Witchampton
Gussage St Michael
Gussage All Saints
Hinton Martell
Pentridge

Wareham
KINGSTON
Corfe Castle
SWANAGE
Wool
Lytchett
Minster
Lytchett
Matravers
Poole
BROWNSEA
ISLAND
Oakdale
S John
Sacred Heart
S Peter
BOURNEMOUTH
CHRISTCHURCH
Hampreston
Corfe
Mullen
Canford
Magna
Wimborne
Minster
WIMBORNE ST GILES
CRANBORNE

A30
A31

Gloucestershire

THE county of Gloucestershire has been well served by amateur historians interested in recording the details of all its church bells: the Rev. H. T. Ellacombe's detailed survey (published in Exeter in 1881 as *The Church Bells of Gloucestershire*) was followed a century later by an even more comprehensive compilation, the joint work of Mary Bliss and Frederick Sharpe (and published in 1985 under the same title). The Gloucestershire that Ellacombe was concerned with contained most of the city of Bristol, now part of Avon. Nevertheless, there is much of campanological interest in what remains as largely a county of prosperous towns and farming areas.

Parish churches with rings of four or more bells are to be found in most parts of the county, but there are some empty areas, most of which are devoid of substantial settlements. In the west, the largest of these areas is the Forest of Dean to the north of Lydney, where villages are few and the modern mining town of Cinderford, where the parish was established only in 1843, has just one bell in the parish church of S John the Evangelist. Around Cirencester, the higher dip slopes of the Cotswolds are dry and the valleys do not carry permanent streams; further down-valley, alongside the tributaries of the Isis, are lines of villages – as along the Coln, with rings at Withington, Chedworth, Coln St Denys, Bibury, Coln St Aldwyns and Hatherop, as well as at the major market town of Fairford.

Some of the towers in this Cotswold county played major parts in the early development of change-ringing, especially peal-ringing. The parish church of S Laurence, Stroud, was the site of the first recorded peal rung outside Norwich and London, in 1722; by 1815 it had a ring of ten. Nearby Painswick acquired a ring of twelve only six years later, having had a ten for 90 years. Within a year of their installation those ten bells were being rung to record-length peals (8,064 Grandsire Caters in 1734; 10,080 in 1735), and long lengths on twelve bells were rung there in each of the next two centuries. And the Painswick habit clearly spread a few miles to the north-east, to S Mary's, Cheltenham, which had eight from 1697 (recast in 1823) and ten in 1833. Here record lengths of Stedman (13,054 changes) and Grandsire (15,227) Caters were rung in 1888 and 1889 respectively. The bells at Cheltenham were augmented to twelve in 1911. A similar event occurred at Cirencester in 1722 (where there were ten in 1713).

These early centres of peal-ringing must have been isolated islands of activity, for rings of eight or more were relatively rare in the rest of the county before the nineteenth century; only at Chipping Campden (1737), Gloucester Cathedral (early sixteenth century) and S Mary de Crypt, Gloucester (1749), Mitcheldean (1760), Tetbury (1722), Tewkesbury (1696) and Wotton under Edge (1756) were there also rings of eight in 1800. The first half of the nineteenth century saw only three more rings of eight added: at St Briavels (1831), Dursley (1824) and Longney (1824). The present rings of ten at Berkeley and Lydney were not even hinted at during the whole of the century, for each church had six only at the time of Ellacombe's survey.

Other than the rings of eight, ten and twelve, Ellacombe records 41 rings of five in 1881, of which 31 were in place by the end of the eighteenth century; he also records 104 churches (excluding the city of Bristol) with rings of six bells, of which 79 had rings of at least five by 1800.

A very substantial proportion of the rings of bells in Gloucestershire churches are pre-nineteenth century, therefore. There have been many augmentations since (comparison of Ellacombe's survey with the present situation indicates at least 60 since 1881, excluding Bristol), but bells have been available for change-ringing in well over 100 Gloucestershire churches since 1800.

Why should this be? What is peculiar about Gloucestershire that it should have been a leader? Certainly, it had the available materials for building church towers that could hold rings of bells in massive oak framess, and its agriculture –- based on woool – was extremely prosperous. But the same was true elsewhere, so why was Gloucestershire in the vanguard? An important, almost certainly the most important, factor was the presence in Gloucester – the cathedral and county town – between 1684 and 1835 of the extremely successful foundry run by the Rudhall family. It produced bells for the whole world, and the county's churches placed many orders with the foundry. Ellacombe's recording of the founder of every bell in the county iin 1881 indicates that, excluding Bristol, Ruddhall bellss could be foound in 115 of the 166 churches withh five or more bells; inn 52, the Ruudhall bells comprised the complete ring.

The presence of such a successful foundry in the county would have been a major stimulus to the installation of bells there, both through the salesmanship of the Rudhalls themselves and the desire of parishioners, rich and poor, to obtain sets of bells at least the equal of their neighbours. This family of six bellfounders probably contributed more than any other to the presence of rings of bells in much of western England; they are responsible for much of the pleasure that people get there as they regularly heed to the call of the bells.

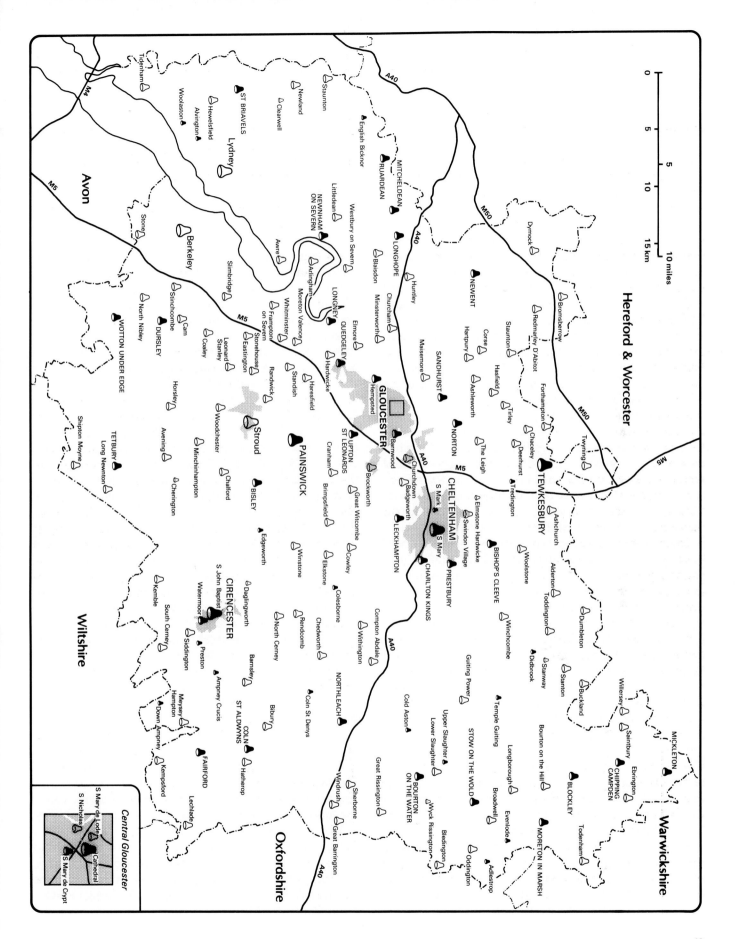

Hereford & Worcester

Warwickshire

Oxfordshire

Wiltshire

Avon

0
5
5
10
15 km

5

10 miles

Tidenham
Woolaston
Newland
Staunton
Alvington
Hewelsfield
Clearwell
ST BRIAVELS
Lydney
English Bicknor
Westbury on Severn
MITCHELDEAN
RUARDEAN
LONGHOPE
Littledean
NEWNHAM ON SEVERN
Blaisdon
Minsterworth
Churcham
Huntley
Dymock
Bromsberrow
Redmarley D'Abitot
Staunton
Corse
Hartpury
NEWENT
Forthampton
Ashleworth
Hasfield
Tirley
Chaceley
Deerhurst
The Leigh
Twyning
TEWKESBURY
Ashchurch
Tredington
Aldertton
Toddington
Dumbleton
Willersey
Saintbury
Ebrington
CHIPPING CAMPDEN
MICKLETON
Todenham
MORETON IN MARSH
Adlestrop
Oddington
Bledington
Evenlode
Broadwell
STOW ON THE WOLD
Lower Slaughter
Upper Slaughter
Longborough
Bourton on the Hill
Buckland
Stanton
Didbrook
Starway
Winchcombe
Woolstone
BISHOP'S CLEEVE
Swindon Village
Elmstone Hardwicke
S Mary
PRESTBURY
CHELTENHAM
S Mark
CHARLTON KINGS
Temple Guiting
Guiting Power
Wyck Rissington
BOURTON ON THE WATER
Cold Aston
Great Rissington
Sherborne
Windrush
Great Barrington
NORTHLEACH
Compton Abdale
Withington
Chedworth
Colesborne
North Cerney
Rendcomb
Coln St Denys
Bibley
Coln St Dennis
COLN ST ALDWYNS
Hatherop
Quenington
Hampton
Meysey Hampton
FAIRFORD
Lechlade
Kempsford
Down Ampney
Ampney Crucis
Siddington
Preston
South Cerney
Kemble
CIRENCESTER
S John Baptist
Watermoor
Daglingworth
North Cerney
Barnsley
Winstone
Edgeworth
Elkstone
Cowley
Great Witcombe
Brimpsfield
Cranham
UPTON ST LEONARDS
Brockworth
Churchdown
Badgeworth
LECKHAMPTON
S Mary
Leckhampton
NORTON
Maisemore
SANDHURST
The Leigh
Ashleworth
Barnwood
GLOUCESTER
Hempsted
Hardwicke
QUEDGELEY
LONGNEY
Elmore
Hareffield
Standish
Randwick
Stonehouse
Eastington
Leonard Stanley
Coaley
Horsley
BISLEY
PAINSWICK
Stroud
Woodchester
Minchinhampton
Chalford
Avening
Cherington
TETBURY
Long Newnton
Shipton Moyne
Whitminster
Frampton on Severn
Moreton Valence
Arlingham
Awre
Standish
Cam
Stinchcombe
DURSLEY
North Nibley
WOTTON UNDER EDGE
Slimbridge
Stone
Berkeley

Central Gloucester
S Mary de Lode
S Nicholas
Cathedral
S Mary de Crypt

M4
M5
M5
M50
M50
A40
A40
A40
A40
A40

69

Somerset

CHURCHES in two-thirds of Somerset parishes have a ring of at least four bells, placing the county in fourth place for density of rings behind Devon, Northamptonshire and Oxfordshire: only Devon has more rings of bells, however. Given that high overall density, it is not surprising that most of the map shows a church with a ring of bells every few kilometres. The only empty areas are the largely unpopulated districts, such as the Somerset Levels north of Bridgwater and Glastonbury and the nearby recently drained areas of the Cary and Parrett valleys, plus the Brendon Hills and Exmoor in the far west of the county. The highest densities are in the Vale of Taunton and the south-eastern corner of the county, on the Dorset border.

As is typical of the more rural parts of England, the great majority of the rings in Somerset are of four, five or six bells only. A century ago this was even more the case, and the Rev. H. T. Ellacombe's survey (*The Church Bells of Somerset*, 1875) shows that, of the 326 churches with four or more bells, fully 150 had a ring of five and another 72 had a ring of four; in comparison there were only 85 rings of six, plus 18 of eight and one of ten (at Bath Abbey, now in the new county of Avon). The great majority of those rings of four and five have since been augmented, for the present county of Somerset has only 30 of the former and 52 of the latter (with another four and 15 respectively in Avon). Twenty of the 68 rings of three have been augmented, too: six are now parts of rings of five, eleven of rings of six, and six of rings of eight.

Creation of the county of Avon removed the northern part of Somerset and nine of the rings of eight present in 1875, plus Bath Abbey. (Parts of Bristol were initially in Somerset, including Redcliffe.) Of the 13 rings of eight that were in what we now know as Somerset in 1875, all but two (those at East Coker and at Mells) were in the county's market towns, though not all the towns by any means had a ring of eight by then (Chard, Evercreech and Glastonbury had rings of six, for example, and Street a ring of five). Only eight were in place before the end of the eighteenth century (at Bridgwater, East Coker, Dunster, Frome, Bishop's Lydeard, Shepton Mallet, Yeovil and Wells Cathedral), with the county town of Taunton not getting a full octave until 1840: these were augmented to ten by Taylors in 1885 and to twelve by Mears and Stainbank in 1922. Those early rings of eight included that installed at Wells Cathedral in 1757, with a tenor of 44 cwt.

What we have, then, is a rural county with a large number of rings of bells early on, but most of them small in number. Many of them were fairly old: of the 150 rings of five that can be dated in Ellacombe's survey, for example, 88 were apparently in place before 1800, as were 38 of the 85 rings of six. Clearly, developments in one village influenced what happened in neighbouring ones. South Cadbury acquired a ring of five in 1769, for example, which was the same year in which neighbouring North Cadbury secured a ring of six and nine years before nearby Queen Camel gained its six bells; West Coker obtained a ring of six in the same year (1770) East Coker gained eight – and two years after a ring of eight was installed in the nearby town of Yeovil. (The area just south-west of Yeovil was clearly an early focus of ringing: nearby Hardington Mandeville had a ring of five in 1742, seven years after Haslebury Plucknett.) Another early concentration of rings was in the area south-west of Bridgwater, where S Mary's obtained a ring of eight in 1745. Rings of five were installed at Spaxton, Broomfield, Cannington and Nether Stowey in 1734, 1739, 1756 and 1769 respectively, and Goathurst had a ring of six by 1783.

Over the last century, augmentations have seen not only a very substantial reduction in the rings of four and five in favour of sixes, but also the number of rings of eight has more than tripled and there are five rings of ten, as well as the twelve at Taunton. The rings of ten include Minehead, where S Michael and All Angels Church had only four bells in 1875, and Wells Cathedral, which has the heaviest tenor of any ten-bell ring in the world (at 56¼ cwt.: the ten was installed in 1891).

Somerset and adjacent areas contain by far the largest concentration of heavy rings of bells in the country. Of the rings of ten, in addition to that at Wells, Yeovil has the seventh heaviest tenor bell (40½ cwt.), while those at Wrington (36½ cwt.) and Bath Abbey (33¼ cwt.) – now both in Avon but for long in Somerset – rank ninth and fourteenth respectively. (On the other hand, the county also has the lightest ring of ten but one, the private ring hung at the Potters Yard in Taunton, where the tenor weighs 1¼ cwt.; the lightest is the private ring at Exmouth, with a tenor of 5 lb. 8 oz. only.)

Three of the four heaviest rings of eight in the world lie just outside Somerset (at Sherborne Abbey in Dorset, Westbury in Wiltshire, and Congresbury in Avon; the last was in Somerset until 1974, as was Long Ashton, which ranks twelfth). The heaviest in modern Somerset

The city of Wells from the air, looking west: the cathedral, whose south-west tower contains the heaviest ring of ten in the world, is in the foreground; the tower of the Church of S Culbert is close to the city's western edge.

is at Frome, where the tenor of 31 cwt. puts it in eleventh position, six places above Wedmore (30 cwt.).

It is with heavy rings of six and five that Somerset's pre-eminence is unchallenged, however. The village of Queen Camel, just north of Yeovil, has the heaviest in the world (the tenor of 36¾ cwt. is more than 7 cwt. larger than the next heaviest, at Brailes in Warwickshire). In his autobiography, *Among the Bells*, F. E. Robinson reports visiting Queen Camel in 1894 and achieving the first-ever change-ringing on the bells. The fifth and sixth both had two ropes attached, and were normally rung by two men each; in Robinson's band, however, each was rung by one person, who had to grip a double thickness of rope at the tail-end. Out of a total of 58, 14 other Somerset rings of six have a tenor weighing more than one ton (the heaviest are at Bruton, Doulting, Kingsdon, Montacute and Stogursey). In addition, the county of Avon has seven rings of six with

tenors weighing one ton or more, of which four (Easton-in-Gordano, Portbury, Publow, and Wellow) were formerly in Somerset. Thus the ancient county contains one-third of all of the heavy rings of six in the world!

Somerset doesn't do quite as well with the heavy rings of five, but of its 46, twelve have a tenor weighing 15 cwt. or more, which place them in the top 72 (and there is another at Wick St Lawrence, now in Avon but long in Somerset); Suffolk has 77 rings of five, but only five in the top 72, and Northamptonshire has nine of its 85 in the list. Relatively, therefore, Somerset clearly wins out. Furthermore, at East Pennard, near Evercreech, it has the heaviest ringable set of five bells, as most campanologists would understand the term. Its tenor bell is 24¾ cwt., whereas that at East Bergholt in Suffolk is 26 cwt. But, as visitors to the 'cage' in the churchyard of the latter will know, East Bergholt's bells

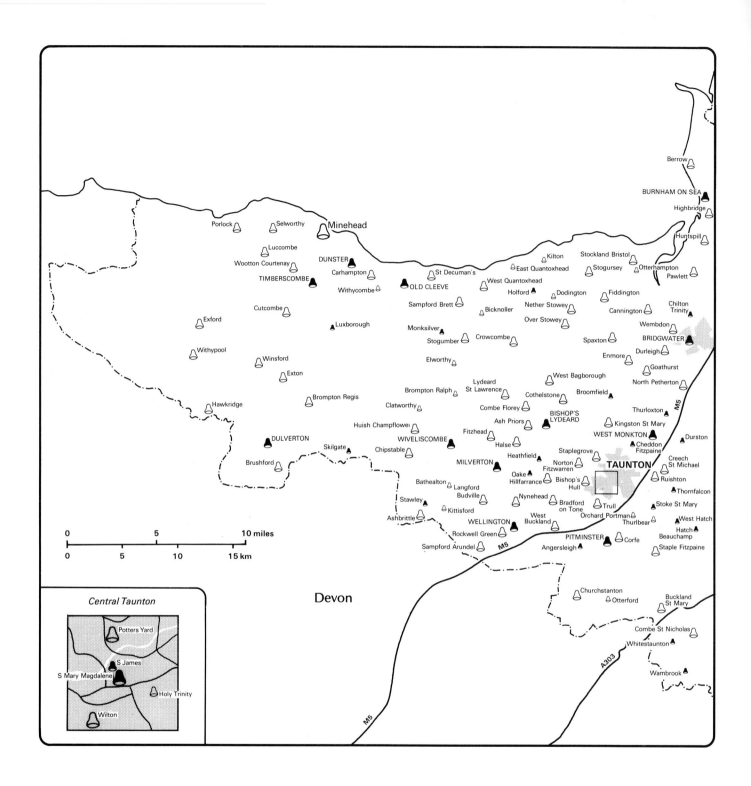

are not rung by ropes but by standing on a beam and working the wheel by hand.

Why this part of England should have such a concentration of heavy bells is unclear. Certainly, its churches are well able to carry them, for the county's ecclesiastical architecture is renowned for the many Perpendicular towers constructed from the local stone. Presumably a local culture that favoured heavy bells

developed in the eighteenth and nineteenth centuries, fostered perhaps by the founders who benefited from the trade. There may even have been competition between villages to outdo each other in the size of their bells (and the local cider industry may have benefited too from the effort used to ring them!). Whatever the reason, there can be no better part of rural England for a visit if you want to hear the deep, resonant tones of

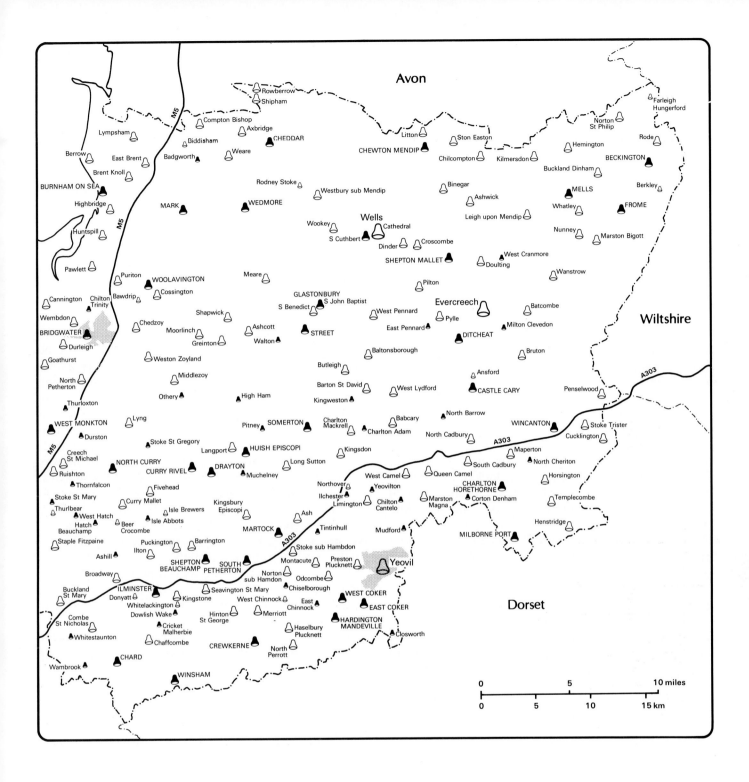

well-tuned heavy bells pealing across a beautiful countryside.

Today, many of those rings are pealed regularly, both by locals and by visiting bands who come to enjoy their marvellous sounds. But Somerset did not play a large role in the early development of either change-ringing or peal-ringing: when the new ten was opened at Wells in 1891, the Oxford Diocesan Guild was invited to provide the band for the first peal. (The conductor was James Washbrook, who rang the tenor for the first 3¼ hours and then handed it over to an assistant, while continuing to call the peal. Four years later he rang it single-handed to a peal of Kent Treble Bob Royal, and on the next day rang the tenor at S Cuthbert's to a peal of Major – before moving on to ring two more peals on the third day!).

Wiltshire

It could well be claimed that Wiltshire is the least noteworthy of the counties of southern England with substantial densities of rings of bells, because its ringers have made little impression on the history books until very recently. Nevertheless, over half of the county's parishes have rings, and although a large number of them are relatively modern there is a well-documented history of bell-founding in the county from the sixteenth century on.

Pre-eminent in this bell-founding activity was the cathedral city of Salisbury, and there are records of bells being cast there in every century from the fifteenth to the present. The earliest founder for whom full details have been published (by H. B. Walters in *The Church Bells of Wiltshire*, 1929) was John Wallis (1581–1624). Walters lists 263 bells known to have been cast by him; almost all are in Wiltshire or one of the adjacent counties, including bells for the ring at Windsor Castle, of which three survive. As was usual at the time, nearly all Wallis's work involved the provision of a single bell, but he did produce the (now unringable) four at Southwick in Hampshire, the front four of the present ring of five at Burbage, four bells (the present 2, 3, 4, 5) of the six at Collingbourne Kingston, and four (the present 2, 3, 5, 6) at Bishop's Cannings; this last village had a ring of eight in 1602, which was probably the first produced after the Reformation. Wallis's successors cast other bells, though not as many as he himself.

The other major Wiltshire foundry was at Aldbourne, a large village in the north of the county, close to the edge of the chalk downs. Here the Cor and Wells families were active from 1694 to 1830, producing a large number of bells for churches not only in Wiltshire and adjacent counties but also in Middlesex, Warwickshire and Worcestershire. Their home village church contains several of their bells; Robert and James Wells made them up to eight in 1787, with Robert donating the treble himself. They are heavy bells (tenor 19 cwt.) which until the 1960s were rung from the ground floor of the tall Perpendicular tower.

One church for which neither foundry provided a ring of bells was the county's finest, Salisbury Cathedral, for, like Norwich, this major structure has only a clock chime of five bells. There was a detached campanile in the cathedral grounds (a wooden structure, 200 feet high, with spire) containing eight bells; because of negligence these were unringable after 1740, and all but one (retained as a clock bell) were sold in 1777. The campanile was taken down in 1789. (Some say that it was not replaced because of the drunkenness and bad behaviour of the ringers!) Elsewhere in the city there are four rings of eight, only one of which – that at S Thomas of Canterbury church – is of any age, having been installed in 1771. Two others (at S Edmund of Abingdon – now the Arts Centre – and S Martin) were augmentations of sixes in 1884 and 1886 respectively, and the fourth, S Paul in the suburb of Fisherton Anger, is a twentieth-century augmentation. Other early rings of eight in the county include Urchfont (by 1664), Calne (1689), Highworth (1716) and Chippenham (1734).

The only ring of twelve is in the county town, Trowbridge. The original ring of eight was provided by James Wells of Aldbourne in 1800, and two trebles were added by Llewellin and James of Bristol in 1923. All ten were recast in 1934 by Taylors, when two more trebles were added. Christ Church, Swindon, was for a long time the only other tower in the county to have a ring of more than eight. Its nineteenth-century church by Sir Giles Gilbert Scott, on the edge of the hill where the Old Town sits, was provided with a ring of eight in 1881, augmented to ten in 1924. Down the hill, in the railway town, is the Church of S Mark, built by the Great Western Railway Company in 1846. A ring of six was installed in 1904, with two trebles added in 1927. Finally, there is the village of Edington, under the Westbury White Horse. Its church is believed to be one of the very few pre-Reformation monastic buildings still largely in its original form; its central tower for a long time contained a heavy ring of six in a deteriorating wooden frame; these were rehung and augmented to ten in 1968.

As mentioned above, Wiltshire ringers have not made a major impact on the development of change-ringing until recently, and there is not a single mention of ringing at a Wiltshire church in Ernest Morris's comprehensive *The History and Art of Change Ringing* (1931). The recent contributions came in the early 1980s, when a band based on the light eight at the Swindon suburban village of Stratton St Margaret set a number of records for the most Major methods rung in a peal; they finished the sequence with 400. Wiltshire retains a long tradition of ringing in the villages and market towns, and, as the map shows, most parts of the county are within the call of the bells. Those that aren't are the empty areas of Salisbury Plain, where there are few villages outside the valleys: Everleigh is a major exception, though one other, Imber, was closed by the armed forces to use as a firing range and the five bells were removed from the church; the metal was used in the augmentation at Edington Priory.

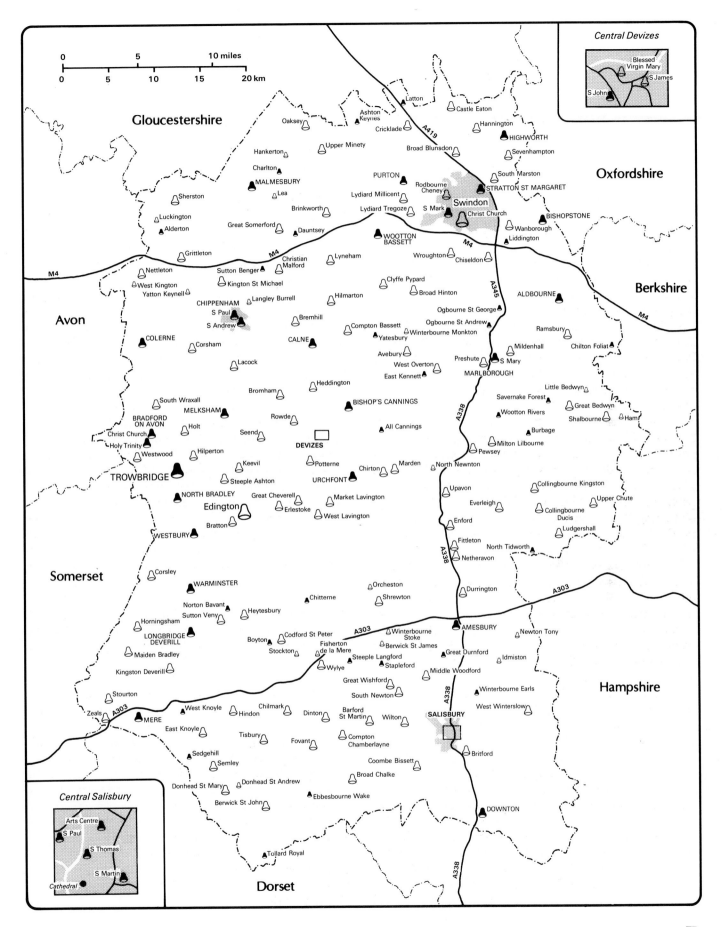

Central Devizes

Blessed Virgin Mary
S James
S John

Gloucestershire

Oxfordshire

0 5 10 miles
0 5 10 15 20 km

Latton
Castle Eaton
Oaksey
Ashton Keynes
Cricklade
Hannington
Upper Minety
HIGHWORTH
Broad Blunsdon
Sevenhampton
Hankerton
Charlton
South Marston
MALMESBURY
PURTON
Lea
Rodbourne Cheney
STRATTON ST MARGARET
Brinkworth
Lydiard Millicent
Sherston
Great Somerford
Lydiard Tregoze
S Mark
Swindon
BISHOPSTONE
Luckington
Dauntsey
Christ Church
Alderton
WOOTTON BASSETT
Wanborough
Grittleton
M4
Liddington
Nettleton
Christian Malford
Lyneham
Wroughton
Chiseldon
Sutton Benger
West Kington
Yatton Keynell
Kington St Michael
Clyffe Pypard
Berkshire
Hilmarton
Broad Hinton
ALDBOURNE
M4
CHIPPENHAM
Langley Burrell
S Paul
Bremhill
Compton Bassett
Ogbourne St George
S Andrew
Ramsbury
Avon
Winterbourne Monkton
Ogbourne St Andrew
Chilton Foliat
COLERNE
Yatesbury
Mildenhall
Corsham
CALNE
Avebury
Preshute
S Mary
Lacock
West Overton
MARLBOROUGH
Heddington
East Kennett
South Wraxall
Bromham
Little Bedwyn
MELKSHAM
BISHOP'S CANNINGS
Savernake Forest
Great Bedwyn
BRADFORD ON AVON
Holt
Rowde
Wootton Rivers
Shalbourne
Ham
Christ Church
Seend
All Cannings
Burbage
Holy Trinity
DEVIZES
Milton Lilbourne
Hilperton
Westwood
Pewsey
TROWBRIDGE
Keevil
Potterne
Chirton
Marden
North Newnton
Steeple Ashton
URCHFONT
NORTH BRADLEY
Collingbourne Kingston
Great Cheverell
Market Lavington
Upavon
Edington
Erlestoke
Upper Chute
Bratton
West Lavington
Everleigh
Collingbourne Ducis
WESTBURY
Enford
Ludgershall
Fittleton
North Tidworth
Netheravon
Somerset
Corsley
WARMINSTER
Orcheston
Durrington
A303
Norton Bavant
Chitterne
Shrewton
Newton Tony
Sutton Veny
Heytesbury
Horningsham
Winterbourne Stoke
Idmiston
LONGBRIDGE DEVERILL
Codford St Peter
AMESBURY
Boyton
Berwick St James
Maiden Bradley
Stockton
Fisherton de la Mere
Great Durnford
Steeple Langford
Middle Woodford
Kingston Deverill
Wylye
Stapleford
Great Wishford
Winterbourne Earls
Stourton
South Newton
West Winterslow
Zeals
West Knoyle
Chilmark
Dinton
Barford St Martin
Hampshire
MERE
Hindon
Wilton
SALISBURY
East Knoyle
Tisbury
Fovant
Compton Chamberlayne
Sedgehill
Britford
Semley
Coombe Bissett
Donhead St Mary
Donhead St Andrew
Broad Chalke
Berwick St John
Ebbesbourne Wake
DOWNTON

Central Salisbury

Arts Centre
S Paul
S Thomas
S Martin
Cathedral

Tollard Royal

Dorset

75

S MARY, STREATLEY, BERKSHIRE

ALL SAINTS, DEANE, HAMPSHIRE

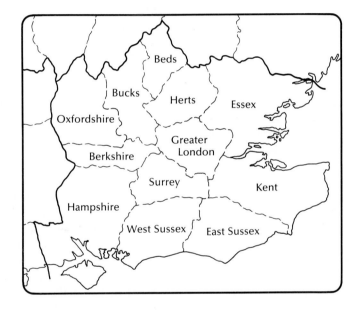

PART 2

—

SOUTH-EAST ENGLAND

S MARY-LE-BOW, CHEAPSIDE, CITY OF LONDON

S PETER, BRIGHTON, EAST SUSSEX

Bedfordshire

BEDFORDSHIRE contains only slight topographical variations, which are nevertheless clearly seen in the map of rings of bells. To the south and north of Bedford itself are the clay vales of the upper Great Ouse and its tributaries; these are relatively empty of settlements and parish churches with rings of bells. There are also low ridges between the marshy valleys, however, on which the pattern of settlement is both older and of higher density. Overall, just under 60 per cent of the ancient county's parishes have rings of bells.

As is typical of this part of rural England, the basic pattern of the campanological map was laid down in the eighteenth century, with the provision of rings of five and six in many country churches, but with only a few rings of eight in the main towns. A survey of *c.* 1710 showed 66 rings of five, five or six rings of six, and no rings of eight or more; at the time of North's survey (*The Church Bells of Bedfordshire*, 1883) there were still only eight rings of eight. Four of these were in the county's main towns: at Bedford, where eight replaced a ring of five at S Paul's Church in 1744; at Dunstable, where another five was replaced in 1776; at Luton, where a similar event occurred in 1775; and at Leighton Buzzard, where a number of gifts enabled the installation of eight to replace a heavy six in 1787. The large village of Cardington, just outside Bedford, also installed a ring of eight (in 1785), having previously had a six, and another early installation of an eight was at the large village of Toddington north-west of Luton (in 1792). At Clifton, augmented to six in 1867, five chiming bells were added in 1869, and two of them were hung for ringing in 1880; when the bells were restored in 1931 only six were hung for ringing, and the full eight was restored in 1953.

At Woburn, the parish church built from the sixteenth century onwards included a 'semi-detached' tower, which contained a ring of five by 1663. In 1787 there was an accident when one bell fell into the ringing-room. One other was found to be broken in 1829, when all of them were recast into a ring of six (of the cost of £384, the Duke of Bedford subscribed £100). In 1864 the old church was taken down, to be replaced by a new one paid for by the Duke. The old tower was retained, and the bells were augmented to eight in 1877, largely owing to the efforts of a local ringer, Charles Herbert. The new church had a tower, and a 55 cwt. bell hung for ringing, which three men rang up half an hour before each service: after a ten-minute pause they rang it for ten minutes, and then lowered it, for which they were paid 3/- (15p) per Sunday by the Duke. But in 1892 a crack in the masonry from top to bottom was discovered. The spire was dismantled, barely 25 years after it was erected. The bell was retained, and in 1910 the metal from it, plus that of seven of those in the old tower, was used to cast a new ring of eight (tenor 24 cwt.), which was presented to the new church by the eleventh Duke.

The number of rings of eight in Bedfordshire has more than doubled since North's survey (the only other in place then was at Clifton), but at most of the churches where augmentations have taken place there was no equivalent of the Duke of Bedford to meet much of the cost. At Linslade, for example, S Barnabas's church was opened in 1849 to replace S Mary's, Old Linslade, whence in 1869 it received the ring of five bells which had been in place since 1781, and at the same time added a new treble. Two further bells were installed in 1904. Most of the twentieth-century augmentations have been in villages, notably on the greensand belt to the east of Woburn. An exception to this was in the county town, where S Peter's church gained a ring of eight in 1948, the two trebles being added to a six installed in 1894, itself a successor to a five created in 1825 by the addition of a treble to an earlier ring of four. These bells were not as old as the six at S Mary's, created out of an old five (1612) in 1748; the church was made redundant in 1976 and the bells now ring as the back six of a light eight at the new church of S Andrew.

In the centre of Bedford is S Paul's Church, probably the first in the county to get a ring of eight. These bells were rehung in 1868, following the total reconstruction of the tower and spire, but in the 1890s it was decided to replace them. Plans were made for a new ten, with a 47 cwt. tenor, but in the end cash constraints meant that several of the bells were recast, and two trebles were added in 1896 and 1897. Plans to augment to twelve were thwarted by the Second World War (which the bells spent out of the tower in the churchyard); they were fulfilled in 1977, to commemorate the Queen's Silver Jubilee and the centenary of the formation of the Diocese of St Albans.

The county has two other rings of twelve. At Luton, two trebles were added in 1983 to the ring of ten cast by Taylors in 1948. At Leighton Buzzard the ring of eight (1787) was augmented to ten in 1906. In the early 1980s it was decided to rehang the bells; the restoration was completed in 1984. A year later the bells, fittings and frame were destroyed by fire. In 1987, a new ring of twelve was installed; insurance paid for replacing the old ten and an anonymous donation of £10,000, plus other gifts, allowed three further bells to be cast, making a ring of twelve plus semitone.

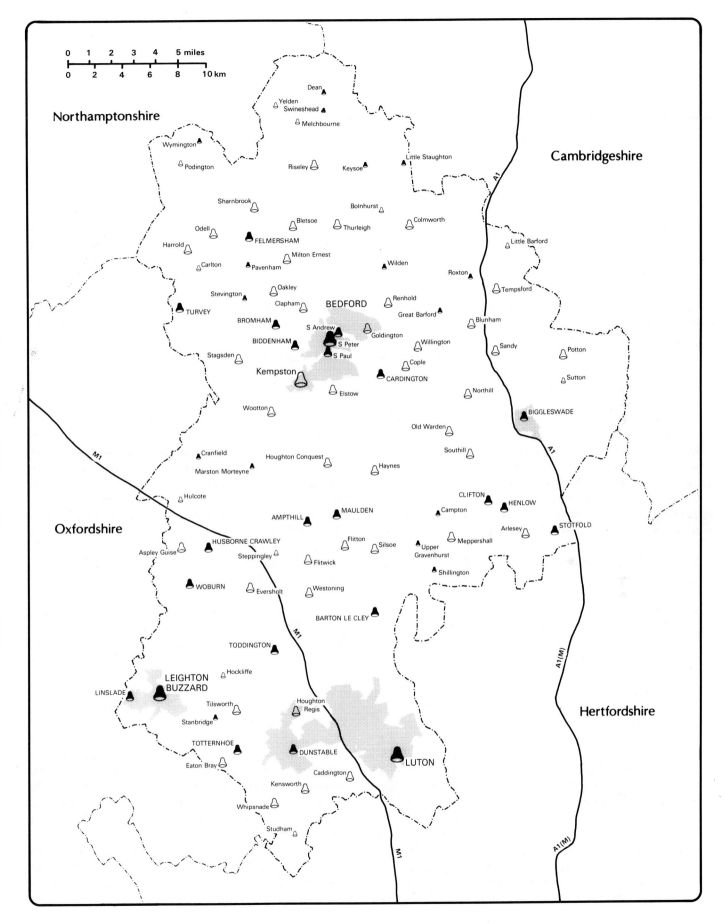

Northamptonshire

Cambridgeshire

Dean
Yelden
Swineshead
Melchbourne

Wymington
Podington
Riseley
Keysoe
Little Staughton

A1

Sharnbrook
Bolnhurst
Colmworth
Odell
Bletsoe
Thurleigh
Little Barford

Harrold
FELMERSHAM
Milton Ernest
Wilden
Roxton
Tempsford
Carlton
Pavenham

Stevington
Oakley
Renhold
Blunham
TURVEY
Clapham
BEDFORD
Great Barford
Sandy
Potton
BROMHAM
S Andrew
Goldington
BIDDENHAM
S Peter
Willington
Sutton
Stagsden
S Paul
Cople
Kempston
CARDINGTON
Northill
Elstow
BIGGLESWADE
Wootton
Old Warden
Southill
Cranfield
Houghton Conquest
CLIFTON
Marston Morteyne
Haynes
HENLOW
Campton
Hulcote
Arlesey
STOTFOLD
Oxfordshire
AMPTHILL
MAULDEN
Meppershall
Aspley Guise
HUSBORNE CRAWLEY
Flitton
Silsoe
Upper
Steppingley
Gravenhurst
Flitwick
Shillington
WOBURN
Eversholt
Westoning
Hertfordshire
BARTON LE CLEY
TODDINGTON
Hockliffe
LEIGHTON
BUZZARD
LINSLADE
Houghton
Tilsworth
Regis
Stanbridge
TOTTERNHOE
DUNSTABLE
Eaton Bray
LUTON
Caddington
Kensworth
Whipsnade
Studham

M1

A1(M)

A1(M)

M1

79

Berkshire

THE ancient county of Berkshire was 'beheaded' in the 1974 reorganization of local government, losing the Vale of the White Horse to Oxfordshire and gaining only the town of Slough from Buckinghamshire in small recompense. The present county now comprises a narrow east–west tract with the M4 motorway as its major axis. There is a reasonable density of rings of bells throughout most of Berkshire; while much of the Lambourn Downland is empty of settlement, there are villages in the valleys, many of which have rings of bells.

Although Berkshire has relatively few ancient churches, and only a small number of big medieval churches – such as those at Lambourn (eight bells by 1742) and Newbury – bell-ringing is long established there. Of the four rings of five in the county, for example, three were in place by the middle of the eighteenth century; similarly, of the 35 rings of six, twelve were in place before 1800 and in another nine cases there was a ring of five in the tower by that date. Many of the larger rings are recent; eleven of the rings of eight are twentieth-century augmentations, and the rings of ten at Thatcham and Warfield (augmented from eight in 1970 and 1968 respectively) are in towers which have long contained bells (six at Thatcham from 1624 and five at Warfield from 1718), but obtained rings of eight only early in the twentieth century. Several other churches achieved a ring of eight only during the second half of the nineteenth century. At All Saints, Boyne Hill, in Maidenhead, the tower's foundation stone was laid in 1864 and the spire was completed 18 months later. A ring was installed, but a fire shortly after destroyed the bells. The metal was used to recast another ring in 1868.

Berkshire was a relatively remote rural area until the last century, when the expansion of London and its hinterland stimulated rapid urbanization along the main transport corridors. But in the old market towns eight-bell ringing is a long-established practice. At Newbury, a ring of six, in place before 1680 (possibly by 1602), was recast into a ring of eight by a Reading bellfounder (Henry Knight) in 1680, at a cost of £67; the Aldbourne founder James Wells recast the bells in 1803, at a cost of £400; they were augmented to ten in 1933 at a cost of £190. At Slough, a ring of six installed in 1855 was augmented to eight in 1886; these were replaced by a heavier eight before augmentation to ten.

Further east at Reading, where there was an almost continuous tradition of bell-founding during the sixteenth and seventeenth centuries, notably by members of the Knight family, there are currently three rings of eight plus one of twelve. That at Caversham is the result of an augmentation in 1891 to a ring of six which had been in place since the seventeenth century; that at S Giles is also the result of a late nineteenth-century augmentation (1890) to an earlier ring of six, cast by Thomas Mears at Whitechapel in 1793. But there have been rings of eight at the other two churches, for at least 200 years in one case and 300 in the other. At the Minster church of S Mary the Virgin, with its checkerboard appearance, there were five bells by 1553, though for some years between then and 1603 there were only three. The new ring of five formed at the start of the century was augmented to six in 1617, and thus was one of the earliest of such rings in the county. In 1740 two new trebles were added, and the first peal of Triples was rung on them in December of that year. Nearby, at the church of S Laurence, there was a ring of five by 1574; in that year the third bell was recast twice, suggesting that the first attempt was a failure, although the founder was paid twice. These bells were very heavy – the tenor weighed 34 cwt. – and they may not have been ringable in changes. In 1662 they were replaced by a ring of eight, which in 1748 was recast and augmented to ten; in 1929 Mears and Stainbank provided two new trebles and recast the existing treble to make the present ring of twelve.

The other town in Berkshire with several rings of bells is the royal city of Windsor, where there is a ring of ten, two rings of eight, plus a ring of six at 'suburban' Clewer. In Old Windsor, a ring of five installed in 1775 was augmented to six in 1870 and eight in 1892, while at New Windsor the church of S John the Baptist was provided with eight as early as 1711. The founder, Richard Phelps, recast two of the bells 18 years later, and four (including one recast in 1729) were recast in 1822; augmentation to ten began in 1987, involving two treble bells which had formerly hung in three London towers (S Dionis, Blackchurch; All Hallows, Lombard Street; All Hallows, Twickenham). Most interesting, however, is the ring of bells in the detached tower of S George's Chapel, Windsor Castle. The five largest bells there have been in place since 1612, when they replaced a set of medieval bells (believed to be heavy) cast in the fourteenth century. In 1614 these were augmented to six, and a further two bells were added in 1650, making a heavy ring of eight (tenor 26 cwt.) which is hung anticlockwise. (Two of the bells have since been recast, one of them on two occasions.) The first peal on the eight was rung in 1748; today the bells are normally rung only on special occasions linked to the Royal Family.

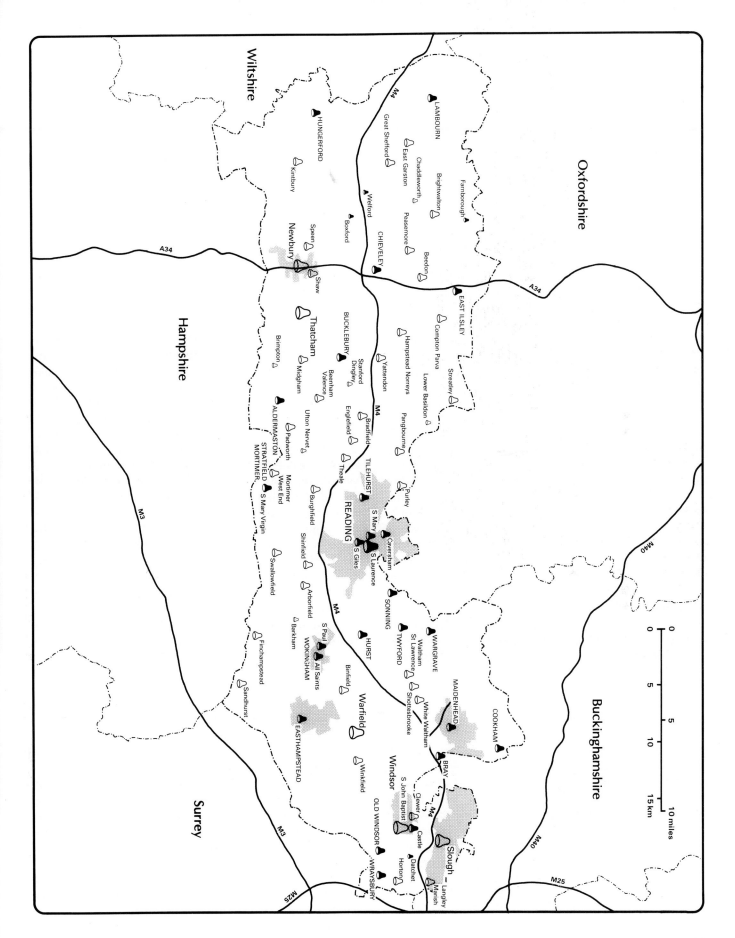

Wiltshire

Oxfordshire

Hampshire

Buckinghamshire

Surrey

HUNGERFORD

Kintbury

Great Shefford

LAMBOURN

Chaddleworth

Brightwalton

East Garston

Farnborough

Peasemore

Welford

Boxford

CHIEVELEY

Beedon

Speen

Newbury

Shaw

Thatcham

Brimpton

Midgham

BUCKLEBURY

Stanford Dingley

Beenham Valence

Englefield

Yattendon

Hampstead Norreys

Lower Basildon

Compton Parva

Streatley

EAST ILSLEY

Pangbourne

Bradfield

Ufton Nervet

Padworth

ALDERMASTON

STRATFIELD MORTIMER

STRATFIELD MORTIMER

Mortimer West End

S Mary Virgin

Theale

TILEHURST

Purley

Burghfield

Shinfield

Swallowfield

Finchampstead

Sandhurst

READING

S Mary

S Giles

S Laurence

Caversham

SONNING

Arborfield

Barkham

S Paul

All Saints

WOKINGHAM

Binfield

HURST

TWYFORD

WARGRAVE

Waltham St Lawrence

White Waltham

Shottesbrooke

MAIDENHEAD

COOKHAM

Warfield

EASTHAMPSTEAD

Winkfield

Windsor

BRAY

S John Baptist

Clewer

Castle

OLD WINDSOR

Datchet

Horton

Slough

WRAYSBURY

Langley

Marsh

A34

A34

M4

M4

M4

M4

M3

M3

M25

M25

M40

M40

0

0

5

5

5

10

10

15 km

10 miles

Buckinghamshire

THE county of Buckinghamshire sits athwart the limestone belt which has been the source of building stone for many of the country's fine churches. The main scarp of the Chiltern Hills crosses the county to the north-west of High Wycombe.

The south-east of the county comprises a series of deep valleys draining the Chiltern scarp, along which settlement is concentrated. Some of these communities – such as High Wycombe – were industrial centres in the nineteenth century; today many of them are commuter settlements, with fast rail links to London. To the north-west of the scarp is the Vale of Aylesbury, a densely populated rural area with many small villages, a considerable number of which, as the map shows, have rings of bells. A rural character is typical of much of Buckinghamshire, but in the far north – based on the formerly independent small towns of Bletchley, Wolverton and Stony Stratford – is the major new town of Milton Keynes. Here, in the low undulating country, typical also of the neighbouring counties of Northamptonshire and Oxfordshire, is the highest density of rings of bells, putting that part of Buckinghamshire clearly in the campanological heart of rural England.

As part of that heart of England's bell-ringing regions, Buckinghamshire has long had many small rings in its villages. This is shown by table 1.1 (reproduced on p. 5, taken from A. H. Cocks's *The Church Bells of Buckinghamshire* (1897): in 1714, of 209 churches listed, 114 had a ring of four or more bells, with a majority having five. By 1897, the numbers of rings of five and six were approximately equal, as a result of augmentations: today there are three times as many rings of six as five, and almost none of four. One late installation, however, was the ring of five steel bells (cast in Sheffield) installed at Thornborough in 1861, to replace four bronze bells. After being unringable for more than 30 years, these were restored in 1986. There is another ring of steel bells in the county, the six at Waddesdon.

Being close to London, Buckinghamshire was well placed to benefit from the early developments of change-ringing there, particularly with the growth of commuters in the nineteenth century as the railways opened up the county. Thus by the end of the nineteenth century it had more rings of eight than was typical of more distant counties, such as Northamptonshire. Many of those rings are quite old. As far as can be discovered from dates given by Cocks, the oldest of all is in the church closest to London, S Mary's, Denham, where an eight was installed in 1683. High Wycombe gained eight in 1711, two years before Bletchley and 38

before Newport Pagnell. Another early eight was installed in 1768 at the village of Long Crendon, near the Oxfordshire border, which was an early centre of change-ringing as early as 1752 on the heavy five; Aylesbury acquired a ring of eight in 1773, as did Buckingham in 1782, Hadenham in 1809 and Marlow in 1834, all early centres of peal-ringing.

With the outward expansion of London, and the growth of the dormitory towns, more augmentations to eight took place. In the 1880s, for example, the rings of six at Beaconsfield and Hughenden were increased (with the two trebles at the latter being in memory of Lord Beaconsfield, the former Benjamin Disraeli). In the twentieth century several new eights have been inaugurated in the part of the county south-east of Aylesbury – at Aston Clinton, Burnham, Farnham Royal, Iver, Stoke Poges and West Wycombe. At Wooburn, the ring of eight was created in 1914 by the addition of two trebles. These were cast by T. Mears, who in 1902 had recast the sixth – originally cast in 1868 by J. Murphy of Dublin. In some places the churches have been remodelled or new ones have been built to meet the needs of the expanding population. The latter was the case at Lane End, where the first church (built in 1832) was replaced in 1878 by a new one, in which the opportunity was taken to replace the original single bell with a ring of six. And the same process is happening today: *The Ringing World* carried an article in its issue of 13 March 1987 concerning the dedication of the first new church in Milton Keynes designed to have a ring of bells. Meanwhile, at High Wycombe, the ring of eight had been increased to ten in 1788 (thanks to a gift from the Earl of Wycombe), but the tenor was found to be too heavy for the tower: it was removed in 1802 and the ring restructured, with a new treble being added. The ring was again restructured in 1909, providing a new, heavier tenor; two more trebles were added, so that the only tower in the county with more than eight bells (following the departure of Slough to Berkshire) is a ring of twelve.

Further out, in the Vale of Aylesbury and beyond, the usual augmentation was from five to six, with only Hanslope and Olney in the far north and Stewkley and Newton Longville just south of Bletchley getting rings of eight; several new rings of five or six were installed here in the late nineteenth and early twentieth centuries. Thus the county is very much divided by the Chiltern scarp, into a typical five- or six-bell area of rural England to the north-west and a metropolitan eight-bell area to the south-east – but it is doubtful whether geology had much to do with the division!

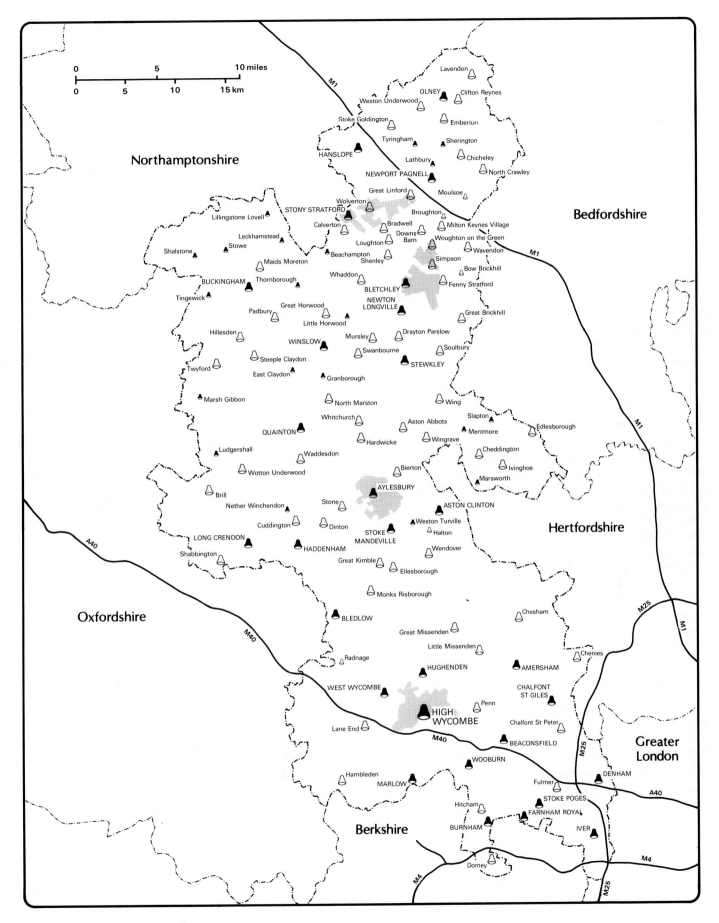

Northamptonshire

Bedfordshire

Lavendon
Weston Underwood
OLNEY
Clifton Reynes
Stoke Goldington
Emberton
Tyringham
Sherington
HANSLOPE
Lathbury
Chicheley
NEWPORT PAGNELL
North Crawley
Great Linford
Moulsoe
Wolverton
Broughton
STONY STRATFORD
Milton Keynes Village
Lillingstone Lovell
Calverton
Bradwell
Woughton on the Green
Leckhamstead
Downs
Barn
Wavendon
Stowe
Loughton
Shalstone
Beachampton
Simpson
Maids Moreton
Shenley
Bow Brickhill
BUCKINGHAM
Thornborough
Whaddon
BLETCHLEY
Fenny Stratford
Tingewick
NEWTON
LONGVILLE
Padbury
Great Horwood
Great Brickhill
Hillesden
Little Horwood
Mursley
Drayton Parslow
WINSLOW
Swanbourne
Soulbury
Steeple Claydon
STEWKLEY
Twyford
East Claydon
Granborough
Marsh Gibbon
North Marston
Wing
Whitchurch
Aston Abbots
Slapton
Edlesborough
QUAINTON
Hardwicke
Wingrave
Mentmore
Ludgershall
Waddesdon
Cheddington
Brill
Wotton Underwood
Ivinghoe
Bierton
Marsworth
Nether Winchendon
Stone
AYLESBURY
Cuddington
Dinton
ASTON CLINTON
LONG CRENDON
Weston Turville
Hertfordshire
HADDENHAM
STOKE
MANDEVILLE
Halton
Shabbington
Wendover
Great Kimble
Ellesborough
Monks Risborough
Chesham
BLEDLOW
Great Missenden
Oxfordshire
Little Missenden
Chenies
Radnage
HUGHENDEN
AMERSHAM
WEST WYCOMBE
CHALFONT
ST GILES
HIGH
WYCOMBE
Penn
Lane End
Chalfont St Peter
Greater
London
BEACONSFIELD
DENHAM
WOOBURN
Hambleden
Fulmer
MARLOW
Hitcham
STOKE POGES
IVER
FARNHAM ROYAL
Berkshire
BURNHAM
Dorney

83

Essex

ESSEX has two main regions, which are reflected in the settlement pattern and architectural styles, and in the density of rings of bells. In the north and west are low hills; to the south and east are the claylands. This regional division stands out very clearly in the map of churches with rings of bells. The claylands are part of that 'stoneless district' of the London basin where village churches with substantial towers capable of carrying four or more bells are relatively rare, especially in the area between the Blackwater and Thames estuaries.

To the west of the A12 and the main railway line to Colchester and Norwich there is a very regular pattern of settlements whose parish churches have rings of bells. Many of these are in villages typical of the prosperous areas of rural England. Others are in the former market towns, where substantial handsome churches, many with Perpendicular towers, were built to reflect the local wealth and were endowed with rings of bells. Dedham, for example, had a ring of eight by 1754, Finchingfield by 1781, Hatfield Broad Oak a year later, Great Tey in 1794, Thaxted in 1778 and Great Waltham in 1796. Saffron Walden, too, had a ring of eight by the end of the eighteenth century. These were augmented to twelve in 1914, when Bowells of Ipswich provided four new trebles to add to those cast by John Briant of Hertford; Bowells' bells were clearly unsatisfactory, for in 1928 they were replaced by four products of the Whitechapel Foundry.

During the nineteenth century the south-western corner of Essex was invaded by the rapidly advancing suburban tide of London. With suburbanization came new churches and bells. In some places a new church was provided with a complete ring of bells – as at Brentwood in 1877 and at S Mary Magdalene at Harlow Common in 1905 (the church was opened in 1834). In others, population growth provided the basis both for expansion of the church and the installation of further bells. The village of Prittlewell on the north bank of the Thames had a ring of six in its church by 1773. By the late nineteenth century it had become part of Southend-on-Sea; in 1895 its church received two new treble bells, and a further two were added in 1902, to give a ring of ten with a tenor weighing just under 18 cwt. The rings of ten at Bocking and Braintree are even more recent; Bocking had six in 1682 but the augmentation to eight came in 1904, five years after Braintree's, where six were installed in 1858. Waltham Abbey achieved a ring of eight a century earlier, in 1796, and in 1914 John Taylor of Loughborough augmented them to twelve, leaving only two of the original bells (the present 6th and 7th).

London's expansion was halted by planning policies after the Second World War, but these did not stop population growth in Essex, creating dormitory suburbs for London, as with Chelmsford. There, several former villages with rings of bells now form part of the built-up area; the cathedral, which had contained a ring of eight since 1777 and of ten since 1810, received a new set of twelve bells in 1913, cast by Warners of Cripplegate.

Although many of the rings of bells in Essex are relatively recent installations, reflecting the recent population growth, Colchester had a flourishing bell foundry in the seventeenth century. The area around the town has relatively few rings even today, but the Graye family contributed substantially to the soundscape of East Anglia in general if not to their immediate home neighbourhood in particular. Genealogical research by Deedes and Walters (reported in *The Church Bells of Essex*, 1909) has identified five Colchester residents with the name Miles Graye over the period 1567–1694. The middle three were bellfounders; their work ranges in date from 1600 to 1686 according to recorded dates on the bells. Deedes and Walters identified 451 cast by the brothers, of which 36 had been recast. Almost all of those cast before 1649 carry the inscription MILES GRAYE MADE ME; of those 268, most were cast for local churches, with 134 in Essex and 91 in Suffolk, but they also provided the bell which formed the tenor for the original ring at Newcastle upon Tyne Cathedral (no doubt carried there by coastal vessel). After 1649, Miles Graye III (grandson of the original founder) produced at least 157 more bells, most for churches in either Essex (71 bells) or Suffolk (39). Early in his career, however, he must have spent considerable time away from Colchester, for between 1649 and 1657 he produced 36 bells for churches in Bedfordshire, Cambridgeshire, Hertfordshire and Huntingdonshire.

As was normal in the seventeenth century, most of the contracts for bellfounders were for individual bells to augment those already in place, and it was rare for a full ring of even four to be purchased. Thus there are very few Graye rings extant. One early such ring was the five cast for Feering in 1624, which was augmented to eight some 175 years later; the only Essex church that has a complete set cast by Miles Graye I and II is at Great Leighs, where the five are hung anticlockwise in a round tower. Miles Graye III produced no full set for a church in his home county, though there are rings of five by him in two Suffolk churches and one in Cambridgeshire.

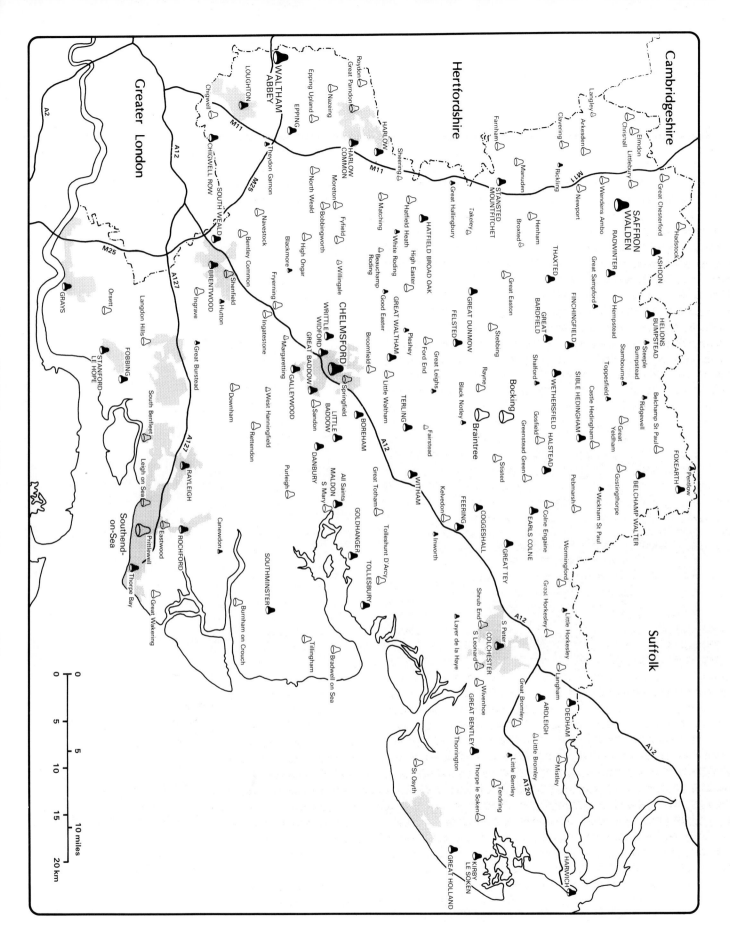

Cambridgeshire

Hertfordshire

Suffolk

Greater London

Saffron Walden

Waltham Abbey

Loughton

Epping

Chelmsford

Brentwood

Southend-on-Sea

Grays

Fobbing
Stanford le Hope

Rayleigh
Rochford

Colchester

Harwich

Kirby le Soken

Great Holland

Southminster

Maldon
Tollesbury

Witham
Coggeshall
Great Tey
Feering

Braintree
Bocking

Halstead

Great Dunmow
Felsted

Great Waltham
Great Baddow
Little Baddow
Gallewywood
Widford
Writtle

Thaxted
Finchingfield
Great Bardfield

Radwinter

Ashdon

Foxearth
Belchamp Walter

Dedham
Ardleigh
Great Bentley

0   5   10   15 10 miles
0   5   10   15 20 km

85

Greater London

THE county of Greater London was created in 1964, incorporating the former, and much smaller, London County plus all of Middlesex and parts of Essex, Hertfordshire, Kent and Surrey. Relative to its population, the county has few rings of bells.

In the early development of change-ringing, when it was very much a secular sport and rings of bells were provided by affluent donors so that they and their friends could indulge in this new pastime, London predominated. The City, in particular, was a major centre and its many churches were among the first to be endowed with rings of bells. The number of rings in City churches before the Great Fire of 1666 is not known, and the great majority of them were destroyed then. A substantial number was replaced in the ensuing decades, and in 1733, according to Cook (in his *The Society of College Youths 1637–1987: a New History of the Society*), when a band called 'The Rambling Ringers' was established to ring at all the churches with between three and six bells, they rang at 35 different towers in the next 16 months – excluding the several rings of eight or more. Indeed, a ring of five in the City, at the Church of S Bartholomew, Smithfield (next to the hospital), has the oldest complete ring, cast by Thomas Bullidon in about 1510.

Most of the City's rings postdate the fire, and many of the earliest are enshrined in the nursery rhyme 'Oranges and Lemons'. The bells of S Clements, on which the tune is played, are at the Church of S Clement Danes in the Strand (just outside the City proper and so in the City of Westminster). The church was rebuilt by Wren in 1680–2 and a spire added in 1719; a ring of eight was installed in 1693 and augmented to ten in 1843. Like those of so many other London churches, the bells were lost as a result of enemy action in the Second World War, but the church was restored (it is now the church of the Royal Air Force) and a new ring of ten was provided in 1958. The next church mentioned in the rhyme is S Martin's (which announced the debt of five farthings). The 1721 church (by the same architect as S Clement Danes) was provided with a ring of ten in 1725 – cast by the Rudhalls of Gloucester – and augmented to twelve two years later; these bells have recently been removed and sold to the University of Western Australia, and were replaced by a new ring in late 1988. 'When will you pay me?' was asked by the bells of Old Bailey, undoubtedly those of the Church of the Holy Sepulchre without Newgate, which stands opposite the Central Criminal Court. This church originally obtained a ring of six from the Priory of S Bartholomew, Smithfield, at the time of the Reformation; these were lost in the Great Fire, and were replaced in 1667/8 by a new six, which was augmented to eight in 1671. Four years later they were augmented again, to ten, and this was believed to be the first ring of ten on which change-ringing was practised. The bells were never easy to ring – they were recast in 1739 – and were silent for about 40 years after the Second World War. They were restored in the early 1980s, however, and augmented to twelve in 1985. Finally, the 'great bell of Bow' refers to the tenor bell at the Church of S Mary-le-Bow, Cheapside, just east of S Paul's Cathedral. According to some, Bow had the first true (i.e. diatonically tuned) ring of twelve in the country, in 1653, but others attribute that to York Minster, and argue that Bow acquired a heavy eight after the Great Fire, which was augmented to ten in 1762 and to twelve in 1881, and recast in 1933. It was one of the three rings of twelve in the City lost during the Second World War, and the replacement twelve (cast in 1956; hung in 1961) has a tenor some 12 cwt. lighter than its predecessor.

The second ring of twelve lost by enemy action was at S Giles, Cripplegate; this church, now in the centre of the Barbican complex, received a new ring in 1953; its initial twelve was a 1792 augmentation of a 1726 ring of ten, itself replacing an eight of 1668. The third ring has not been replaced, even though the church, S Bride's, Fleet Street, has been rebuilt, complete with tower. This church played an important role in the early development of change-ringing. The ring of ten was installed there – by the Rudhalls of Gloucester – in 1710, and in 1717 what was possibly the first peal in London (Grandsire Caters) was rung there. In 1719 it was augmented to twelve, with each of the two local societies (the London Scholars and the College Youths) giving one of the new bells: interestingly, the bells were chained up to prevent others ringing them, an indication of the competitiveness of London ringing at the time and the rarity of a ring of twelve.

Although the rings of twelve in the City form one of the major concentrations of such rings in the country, there have been many other rings – lesser in number but not necessarily in either quality or importance. Several of them were lost in the Second World War – a further tragedy to hit London's bells, nearly three centuries after the Great Fire – and not all have been restored. The fine ring of six at S Vedast, Foster Lane – in the shadow of S Paul's, and possibly closer to the altar of that cathedral than its own bells – has been restored, as has the majestic ring of eight at S Lawrence Jewry, in the

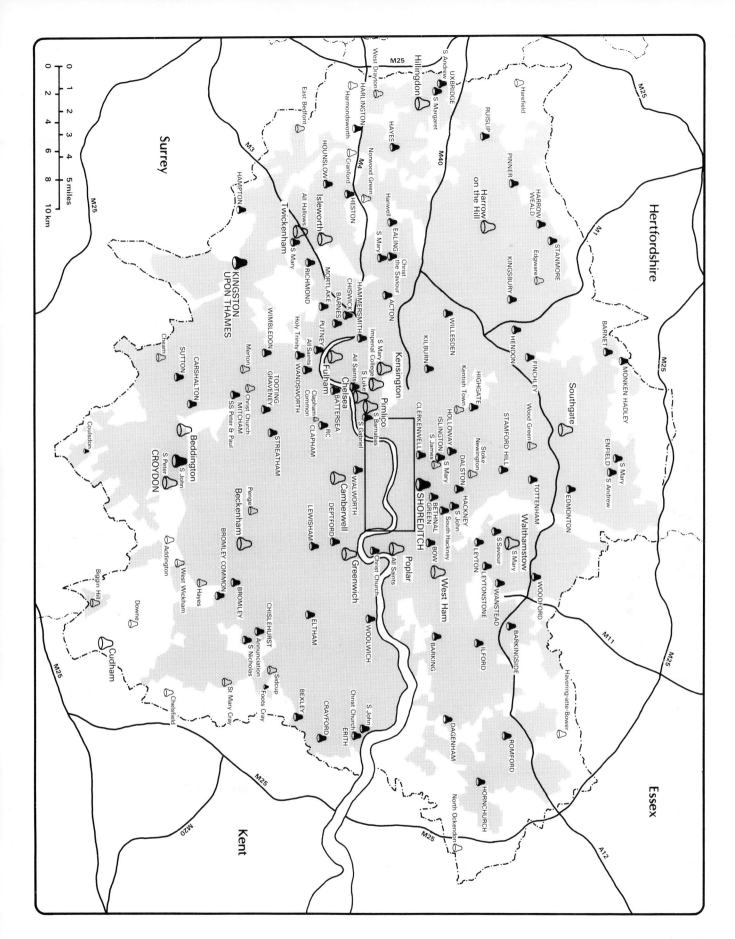

Surrey

Hertfordshire

Essex

Kent

M25
West Drayton
M25
M40
M1
M3
M4
M11
M25
M20
A12

Hillingdon
S Andrew
UXBRIDGE
S Margaret
HARLINGTON
Harmondsworth
East Bedfont
HAYES
Cranford
Norwood Green
HOUNSLOW
HESTON
HAMPTON
Isleworth
All Hallows
S Mary
Twickenham
RICHMOND
MORTLAKE
BARNES
CHISWICK
HAMMERSMITH
Hanwell
EALING
S Mary
Christ the Saviour
ACTON
Harefield
RUISLIP
PINNER
HARROW
WEALD
Edgware
STANMORE
Harrow
on the Hill
KINGSBURY
HENDON
FINCHLEY
WILLESDEN
KILBURN
Kentish Town
HIGHGATE
Wood Green
STAMFORD HILL
Southgate
MONKEN HADLEY
BARNET
ENFIELD
S Mary
S Andrew
TOTTENHAM
EDMONTON
S Mary
Imperial College
S Mary
Kensington
Holy Trinity
WANDSWORTH
All Saints
PUTNEY
Fulham
All Saints
S Luke
Chelsea
S Barnabas
S Gabriel
Pimlico
BATTERSEA
RC
Clapham
CLAPHAM
Common
CLERKENWELL
S James
ISLINGTON
HOLLOWAY
Stoke
Newington
DALSTON
S Mary
Hackney
S John
South Hackney
BETHNAL
GREEN
SHOREDITCH
BOW
Poplar
West Ham
LEYTON
S Saviour
S Mary
LEYTONSTONE
WANSTEAD
WOODFORD
Walthamstow
BARKINGSIDE
ILFORD
BARKING
DAGENHAM
ROMFORD
HORNCHURCH
North Ockendon
Havering-atte-Bower

KINGSTON
UPON THAMES
WIMBLEDON
Merton
Christ Church
MITCHAM
SS Peter & Paul
TOOTING
GRAVENEY
STREATHAM
Penge
Beckenham
BROMLEY COMMON
Cheam
SUTTON
CARSHALTON
Beddington
S Peter
CROYDON
S John
Coulsdon
Addington
West Wickham
Hayes
BROMLEY
CHISLEHURST
Annunciation
S Nicholas
Sidcup
Foots Cray
St Mary Cray
Chelsfield
Biggin Hill
Cudham
Downe
BEXLEY
CRAYFORD
ERITH
Christ Church
S John
WOOLWICH
ELTHAM
Greenwich
DEPTFORD
Christ Church
All Saints
LEWISHAM
Camberwell
WALWORTH

87

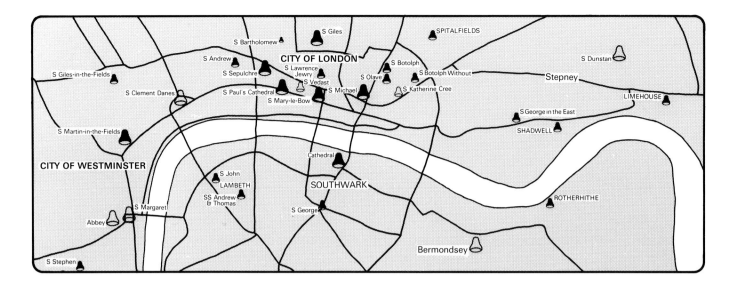

courtyard of the Guildhall. At S Dunstan-in-the-East, where many early peals were rung on the 1700 Rudhall eight (four were recast within 50 years), the bells were replaced in 1951 but rarely rung. It was then decided not to rebuild the church, and the bells were sold back to the founders (Taylors) in 1970; they now hang as a chime in three towers at Stirling Winery, California. The 1714 ring of ten at S Magnus the Martyr, in Lower Thames Street, are still stored, awaiting hanging, having been removed from the tower just after the war started.

One ring of twelve which miraculously survived the blitz was that at S Paul's Cathedral. This is a relatively modern ring, having celebrated its centenary in 1978. The predecessor of Wren's magnificent cathedral did not have a ring of bells at the time of the Great Fire (the earlier ring having been lost in 1561 when the spire was struck by lightning) and there was no pressure to instal bells in the new cathedral: the London ringing societies were fully engaged at other towers, it seems. It was not until the 1870s that the question of a ring was raised – after the absence of bells was noted at a service to give thanks for the Prince of Wales's recovery to health in 1872. By 1876 all of the money had been raised – with eleven of the bells donated by City livery companies and the tenor by the City Corporation – and Taylors of Loughborough secured the contract to provide the ring: the tenor, at 62 cwt., was the second largest in the world (though the later installation at Liverpool means that it now occupies third place; S Paul's tenor is lighter than Exeter's, but the entire ring is heavier than Exeter's. When the bells were to be installed, the cathedral authorities negotiated with the College Youths to provide a band to ring them for Sunday services. The College Youths is the oldest extant London ringing society – having been founded in 1637. It had not been very active early in the nineteenth century, and the society had never before been involved with the provision of a regular Sunday service band. At the time, the society had been criticized by other ringers for this lack of such a commitment – one that was becoming central to the role of bells in the reformed Church of England – but this link to the capital city's major cathedral gave the society a *raison d'être* and new life, with the S Paul's Cathedral Guild of Ringers being a subset of the College Youths. (The latter is, to all intents and purposes, a male-only society, though it is no longer the socially exclusive group that it was in earlier centuries.) Another wartime survivor was the nearby church of S Michael, Cornhill, whose original twelve (of which three remain) was cast in 1728.

Compared with the City, the West End of London – traditionally the home of the court and the government – has many fewer rings of bells, suggesting that it was successful businessmen who were most likely to donate bells. Indeed, there are only three rings of bells in Westminster proper – the twelve at S Martin-in-the-Fields already referred to, and the two rings of ten in Parliament Square. Westminster Abbey initially had a separate campanile, but this was removed in 1750 and the six bells were transferred to Hawksmoor's new north-western tower. These were augmented to eight in 1919, to commemorate the peace of 1918, and then recast and augmented to ten in 1971. In the shadow of the abbey is the small church of S Margaret, which for long had a ring superior to that of the abbey. In 1751 John Holt called the first performance of his famous peal of Grandsire Triples (Holt's Original) there, and the ring of eight was augmented to ten in 1971.

Across the river from Westminster and the City, the south bank from Lambeth to Southwark is well provided with rings. They include the twelve at S Saviour's, Southwark – Southwark Cathedral since 1905. Here there was a heavy ring of eight (tenor 47 cwt.) by 1673, and peals were being rung there by 1730. Five years later a ring of twelve was provided – being cast by Samuel Knight in a yard next to the church. Eight of those bells are still in the tower, but the other four (7, 10, 11, 12; the last weighed 48 cwt.) have been recast. Many early peals were rung here – a number by the College Youths – including several records; one, a peal of 12,675 Stedman Cinques, which took 9 hours 47 minutes in 1923, was found false 13 years later. A little to the east is the modern, brick-built church of S Andrew, Lambeth, which replaced an earlier church (lacking bells) destroyed in the Second World War. In 1971 the nearby church of Holy Trinity, Southwark, was declared redundant and the vicar of S Andrew sought to move the bells to his church. The eight, with a tenor of 19½ cwt., was much too heavy for the tower, however, but some of the metal was used to make a new eight, with a tenor of only 3¾ cwt., which was installed in 1971. Also lost from the south bank was the church of S John, Horsleydown, whose 1783 ring of ten resounded to the first ever peal of Stedman Caters in 1787.

Outside central London, the density of rings of bells is generally low, and there are substantial areas of the map with very few rings at all; indeed, only about 10 per cent of the parish churches in Greater London have a ring of bells. Much of inner south London is almost bereft of rings, for example, as is also the case with the outer eastern suburbs. As elsewhere in the country's major urban regions, the rings present can be roughly categorized into three types: those in the churches of old settlements later incorporated within the Greater London conurbation; those in new churches built to serve expanding suburbs that were swamping old villages; and new churches built for areas formerly lacking a place of worship.

The church of S John the Baptist, Hillingdon, in west London, is an example of the first type. Its tower was built in 1629 to house a pre-existing ring of five. In 1731 the then ring of six was augmented to eight; the bells were recast several times. In 1911, at the time of a further recast, they were augmented to ten; a churchwarden paid for all this work, and 50 years later his daughter covered the cost of an overhaul: as in so many towns and villages of England, the generosity of parishioners who loved the sound of bells, even though not ringers themselves, has been instrumental in providing the rings we now enjoy. The tower is unusual, in that it is topped by a hexagonal wooden cupola containing a sanctus bell. Some towers acquired substantial rings early, however. At Fulham, for example, Rudhalls provided an eight in 1729 which was augmented to ten in 1746. Kensington obtained eight in 1772, and similarly Chelsea, Hackney, Rotherhithe, Shoreditch and West Ham attained eights early.

Just north of Hillingdon, at Uxbridge, are two nearby churches. One, S Margaret's, is the old parish church, which has had a ring of six since 1716 – though the tower was rebuilt in 1820; this was augmented to eight in 1902. S Andrew's is a new church, built in 1865 to serve a newly created parish: it was provided with a ring of six at the outset, which became eight just twelve years later. A few miles closer to the centre of London is an example of a nineteenth-century church built to serve a rapidly expanding parish where formerly there was a small village. S Mary's, Hanwell, was designed by Sir Gilbert Scott and built in 1841, replacing a smaller Georgian building erected in 1785 to supersede an even smaller church. Only two bells were provided, however, and it was not until 1975 that a ring (of eight) was provided.

Several of the churches built for new settlements are to be found in eastern London. The parish of Poplar in London's Docklands was created in 1817, for example, and the Georgian church of All Saints (one of the 'Waterloo' churches) was built in 1822. It was provided with a ring of ten at the outset. (Other 'Waterloo' churches with bells include S John's, Waterloo Road, Bermondsey, Shadwell and Walworth.) A few miles to the north, at South Hackney, the Church of S John of Jerusalem was built in 1842, replacing the original church (designed to hold 750 people) erected in 1810. A ring of eight was provided in 1848 – one of the donors being the Bishop of Armagh. Kentish Town is to the west of Hackney, near the southern end of Hampstead Heath, and the church of S Martin, Gospel Oak, was built in 1865, being provided with a ring of six cast by Warners of Cripplegate. Later in the century new suburbs such as Dalston, Deptford and Southgate obtained rings. More recently, some of the new churches have received bells from closed churches in the inner areas. Caterham Valley in Surrey took eight from S Mary's, Lambeth, for example; Kingsbury's eight came from S Andrew's, Wells Street; and, as early as 1890, the ring of six from All Hallows, Staining, was recast for Hackney.

The ring of six at Kentish Town is a relatively rare occurrence in Greater London, where the great majority of the rings comprise eight or more bells. In the inner part of the county (what was London County until 1964), only 9 per cent of the rings of bells are fives or sixes, compared with, for example, over 80 per cent in Cambridgeshire. Greater London has more than 10 per cent of England's rings of ten and twelve, compared with only 6 per cent of the rings of eight, and less than 1 per cent of the rings of five and six. The campanological wealth of London was demonstrated in September 1986 on the 'Grand Day' arranged to celebrate the 75th anniversary of the first appearance of *The Ringing World*. Ringing took place at more than 80 towers, with at least 1,000 ringers participating in the special service at Southwark Cathedral. At S Mary-le-Bow alone, 300 different people rang during the afternoon, and 650 visited the Whitechapel Foundry. The vitality of campanology at the present time was clearly demonstrated.

Hampshire and the Isle of Wight

THE density of rings of bells is not high in these two counties – with rings in only just over one-third of the parishes. The main area of emptiness on the map reflects the settlement pattern, however, for most of the south-western part of Hampshire comprises the New Forest, in which Minstead, Brockenhurst and Lyndhurst are virtually the only communities. (One village on the edge of the forest – Dibden, on the west bank of Southampton Water – lost its ring of eight, installed in 1887, as a consequence of enemy action in the Second World War.) Elsewhere in the county, much of the landscape comprises chalk downlands, in which settlement is relatively sparse; major strings of villages with rings occur, either along the spring line at the foot of a chalk scarp (as in the line stretching south-east from Winchester through Bishop's Waltham to Havant) or along a valley (as with that of the Test north of Romsey).

In many ways, the Isle of Wight is also an 'empty area' in terms of rings of bells, having only 14. The western part of the island particularly lacks bells, but overall nearly half of the parishes have a ring of five or more (there are no rings of four). The five rings of eight or more are, not surprisingly, all relatively recent: Carisbrooke's is the oldest, having been installed in 1770; Newport's (augmented to twelve in 1989) was provided in 1808 – there was a strong six-bell band there at the time; and the three in the seaside resorts were installed in close succession (Ryde, 1886; Brading, 1887; Shanklin, 1888). Some of the rings of six were also installed in the 1880s. The ring at Brighstone – relatively isolated on the south-west coast – is fairly old, however, with a recast ring of five hung in 1740; the treble was added in 1960 by a local resident in memory of his wife. In 1985 local ringers were able to announce – with a great deal of understandable pride – that, with the restoration of Shanklin bells, all 14 sets of bells on the island were now ringable. In Hampshire the main early rings were eights in Portsmouth (1703) and Southampton, Holy Rood (1742); these latter were lost in the war and the metal salvaged to increase the eight at S Michael's (1878; recast 1923) to ten. The other ten in Southampton, at S Mary's, was a 1933 augmentation of a 1914 ring of eight; they were destroyed in 1940 and then replaced. Ringwood acquired eight in 1763, Alton in 1785, and Alresford in 1811.

When W. E. Colchester undertook his survey of the bells of the two counties in the early part of this century (published in *Hampshire Church Bells*, 1920), he identified 1,416, of which 266 were cast before 1700. Very few had been cast in the county, and the majority of them dated

from the seventeenth century; most have been recast since. Colchester suggests that this was because 'many of the bells were weak from years of chiming, and tended to crack when hit by the clapper in ringing; many of the frames were built for chiming bells only, and could not withstand full ringing, and many of the early bells had locally made half-wheels and bearings that were not true.' Thus most of the bells heard sounding through Hampshire today are imports.

Almost all the major settlements in Hampshire contain at least one church with a ring of eight or more bells. One of the oldest rings of eight is at S Michael's, Basingstoke, where there has been a ring of that number since 1751. Several of the bells have been recast. The majority were recast in 1938, 22 years after the town became unique in the annals of ringing. It was then that Mears and Stainbank cast a ring of nine for the new church of All Saints. Why nine were installed is not clear; what is known is that for many years these bells caused problems for the Central Council of Church Bell Ringers, whose rules until 1986 did not recognize peals of Caters on nine bells without a tenor covering, and bands would persist in ringing them there. Indeed, the county was quite a headache for the council for a period. At Liss, north of Petersfield, there are two churches, one with a ring of eight and the other with six, but these were insufficient for some local ringers. In 1982 a 'ring' of four galvanized buckets was hung in somebody's garage there, and when they were augmented to twelve, peals were rung. The buckets were later replaced by porcelain bells (tenor 7¼ lb.), but the council still refused to recognize peals on them as having been rung on bells as it defined them!

Nothing could be more different from the Liss garage than the massive central tower at Romsey Abbey, which houses a 24 cwt. ring of eight. The bulk of the tower is not matched by its height, however, for it only just protrudes above the roof of the nave. The bells are hung in an octagonal wooden turret on the tower roof, having been placed there in 1791 by Thomas Mears, and the ringing-room is reached via a narrow, dark stairway. This is much less frightening than the open wooden spiral staircase in the centre of the tower at S Mary's, Andover, which is in full view of the rest of the church and sways considerably; the church was rebuilt in the 1840s but the ring of eight dates from 1758.

Hampshire has no particularly heavy rings, though the tenor of the twelve at Winchester Cathedral (eight in 1734; ten in 1892; and twelve in 1921) weighs 35 cwt. But it does have one of the lightest rings of ten in a church.

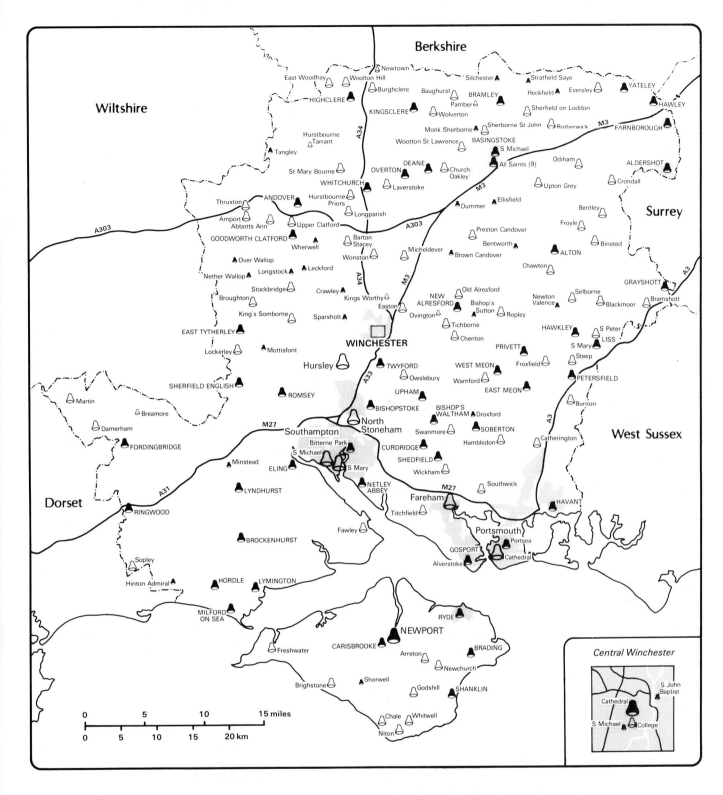

Until 1893 S Nicholas at North Stoneham (near Southampton) contained only three bells; three more were added then, to make six, with a 7¼ cwt. tenor. Sixteen years later these were joined by a new treble and a new tenor (9¼ cwt.), and George Williams worked to develop ringing of a high quality. In 1931 he and his wife gave two further bells to mark their Golden Wedding Anniversary, making the lightest ring of ten in a church at the time; the treble of the eight was recast then too. The back seven were recast in 1956, and the tenor now weighs 10¼ cwt.; there are seven ecclesiastical and four non-ecclesiastical lighter rings of ten now, but only two of the former (at Taunton and Grundisburgh) are lighter than North Stoneham's original ten.

Hertfordshire

THE small county of Hertfordshire is in the treeless district that surrounds and incorporates London, and has little good local building stone. Sir John Betjeman (in *Collins Guide to English Parish Churches*) wrote that, as a consequence, 'like the landscape in which they are set' most of the county's churches 'are distinguished rather for their seemliness and moderation than for more dramatic qualities.' But in more than half of the county's parishes those churches have a ring of four or more bells – including one of twelve and six of ten. Two main reasons for that can be identified. The first was the presence in Hertfordshire between 1782 and 1825 of a major bellfounder, John Briant, himself a competent change-ringer; the second was the growing suburbanization of much of the county as London expanded northwards, introducing considerable wealth (initially landed; later commercial), some of which was invested in bells and other fittings for the local churches.

Many Hertfordshire villages and small towns were prosperous enough to instal towers and rings of bells in their churches before these two factors came into play, however. Thomas North's survey of the county (completed by J. C. L. Stahlschmidt and published in London in 1886 as *The Church Bells of Hertfordshire*) identified three rings of ten, 16 of eight, 35 of six, 28 of five and five of four, making 87 churches in all, out of a county total of 186. Of the rings of five, 22 were in place at the start of the nineteenth century. (One of them, Westmill, had a ring of eight installed in 1759 but the three trebles were sold in the 1830s to pay for repairs to the church.) Similarly, 20 of the rings of six were in place in 1800, and another seven churches had rings of five augmented to six during the nineteenth century.

John Briant came to this area of established bell-ringing from his home in Suffolk in 1782, and his first major contract was for the new ring of eight for S Andrew's church in the county town. He cast only six other complete rings for churches in the county: eight for Hatfield, six for Barkway and North Mimms, and five for Codicote, Rushden and Wallington; all but the ring at Rushden have since been augmented. He produced 16 other complete rings, including four each for churches in Oxfordshire and Essex, plus a ring of six for Barnstaple in Devon and eight for S Alkmund's in Shrewsbury. Briant manufactured many other bells, however, most of them for local churches where he was contracted for augmentations. His reputation for this work (plus that of his caster, Henry Skerman, and his

tuner, Henry Symondson) was such that Thomas North wrote of 'his chief merit . . . as a "splicer". He was almost unrivalled in adding trebles to rings of bells.' He was responsible for the two trebles both at All Saints, Hertford, and at S Peter's, St Albans (where he also recast the 7th bell) as well as the three treble bells for the twelve at S Giles, Cripplegate, in London, and he recast the treble of the old eight at St Albans Abbey.

The number of rings of eight has more than doubled since North's survey. Ten of the rings of six identified in the 1880s had been augmented to eight a century later, as had four of the rings of five and two of the rings of three; in addition, four churches with only a single bell in 1886 (at Bushey Heath, Hoddesdon, Oxhey, and Welwyn) later obtained rings of eight. (S Mary's Welwyn, had five in the eighteenth century when the tower fell. The bells were later sold after complaints about the noise, and a turret for a single saunce – or sanctus bell – was built. The new ring of eight was installed after the Second World War.) But of the rings of eight or more present in 1885, 13 were in the towers before 1800, including rings of ten at S Peter's, St Albans, and All Saints, Hertford, installed in 1787 and 1791 respectively. (The bells at the former were augmented to twelve in 1868, following a donation. Thirteen years later it was discovered that the 10th and 11th bells were cracked, and it was decided to give the trebles to the founders in part-exchange to cover the cost of recasting.) A peal was rung at All Saints, Hertford, as early as 1724, and local bands rang peals at Baldock, Braughing, Aspenden and Essendon in 1737, 1746, 1764 and 1777 respectively: the Braughing Youths rang 12,240 Plain Bob Major in 1779, taking seven hours and 34 minutes. Hertford was the county's main centre of ringing during the eighteenth century, and in 1767 the All Saints ringers founded The Hertford College Youths; by 1822, however, ringing had lapsed there and a Waltham Cross ringer had been engaged to train a new band.

Nineteenth-century augmentations included the donation of two treble bells at Benington in 1838 by the local landowner Squire Proctor, who employed ringers on his estate and encouraged the development of change-ringing at the church: this village in the rural heart of the county resounded to some of the earliest peals of Surprise Major in the middle of the century. (The squire didn't like the two trebles very much, and had them recast in 1853.) Their achievements included

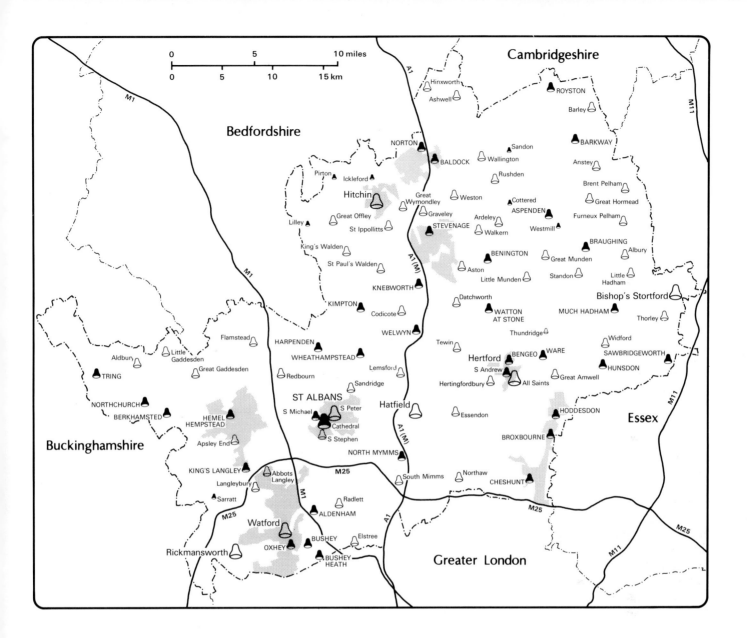

the first ever true peal of Cambridge Surprise Major (the now famous Charles Middleton composition), in 1873, and the longest peal (6048 changes) then rung of London Surprise Major. Ernest Morris also records (in *The History and Art of Change Ringing*, 1931, p. 388) that they pioneered the ringing of long touches in 'various methods continuously', a precursor of the now common practice of splicing methods (especially Surprise).

The twentieth-century augmentations have almost all been in the suburbanized parts of the county, particularly its southern borders plus the A1 corridor that bisects Hertfordshire from south to north, passing the new towns of Stevenage and Welwyn. Thus nearly every augmentation to eight has been in a major dormitory settlement – at Bushey and Bushey Heath,

Aldenham and Oxhey in the south-west around Watford; at Broxbourne, Cheshunt and Hoddesdon alongside the A6 in the Lea Valley, and at Bengeo in Hertford; at North Mymms, Welwyn, Stevenage, Knebworth, and Norton in the A1 corridor; and at S Michael's in St Albans and S Nicholas in nearby Harpenden. Only in the relatively isolated town of Royston on the Cambridgeshire border and the neighbouring village of Barkway have rings of eight been introduced to the more rural parts of the county, where rings of five and six are the norm. Similarly, the augmentations to ten at Hatfield, Rickmansworth and Watford are in suburban towns; Bishop's Stortford's ten was installed in 1820, a century after the 1671 ring of six was augmented to eight.

Kent

KENT has rings of bells in just under half of its parish churches. Most of those without such rings are small parishes in the more wooded parts of the county, where presumably local resources were insufficient to provide the necessary investment in towers and churches. Timber was occasionally used to build substantial towers, as with the pagoda-like detached campanile at Brookland, but such extravaganzas are rarities.

Kent contained several early centres of change-ringing on higher numbers, and by the time of Stahlschmidt's survey (*The Church Bells of Kent*, 1887) there were five rings of ten and 52 of eight in the county, in addition to 80 of six, 61 of five, and 26 of four. Four of the rings of ten were in major towns – at Canterbury Cathedral, where the eight was augmented in 1802; at Hythe, which gained eight in 1802 and two more in 1861 (but the ten was reduced to eight in 1891); at Maidstone, dating from 1784; and at Greenwich (now part of Greater London), where the ten were first rung in 1734.

The exception was the village of Leeds, to the east of Maidstone, which had a population in its joint parish with Broomfield of fewer than 1,000 as late as 1900, but by then had enjoyed a ring of ten bells for 150 years. The nearby tower of Lenham obtained a ring of eight bells in the same year as Leeds acquired its ten (1751) and together the ringers at the two towers (the Leeds Youths and the Lenham Society) rang a large number of peals in the middle and late eighteenth century (including, for example, the first peal on the new ring of eight bells at Bromley in 1773). Many of these were remarkable for either the novelty of the method or the length; most were peals of Major, rather than the Triples that were popular elsewhere. Two of the performances at Leeds are particularly remarkable. In 1793 a peal of Plain Bob Major was rung in three hours twelve minutes by a band in which the average age of the ringers was 73; the youngest was 65 and the oldest (who rang the tenor) was 86. Some 32 years earlier, 14 men rang the full 40,320 changes of Plain Bob Major, in relays, in 27 hours; this was achieved just two weeks after an earlier attempt, which failed after about eleven hours ringing when a bell (presumably lacking a stay) overturned.

Leeds and Lenham were not alone in being relatively small settlements with rings of at least eight bells by the end of the eighteenth century. In Harrietsham the eight was inaugurated in 1744; nine of the peals recorded in James Barham's pealbook (and listed in Ernest Morris's *The History and Art of Change Ringing*) were rung there, including his first three, which were rung with the Lenham Society before their tower had its ring augmented to eight. Another group of neighbouring villages in east Kent had rings of eight before 1800 – Ash (1790), Sandwich (1779) and Wingham (1720); the Leeds Youths visited Wingham for a peal in 1747 but Barham records no visit to the other two. The first peal on Sandwich bells was rung in 1823 by a band from Wye; the Wye ringers' first peal on their own bells – Grandsire Triples – was recorded in 1742 and the band was described as 'ye first set that ever rang it in the county without the assistance of Londoners or others'.

There were several other Kentish villages with rings of eight by 1800 – Biddenden (1784), nearby Cranbrook (1782) and Goudhurst (1775), Elham (1763), Hadlow (1775), Headcorn (1766) and Wrotham (1754) as well as Wye (1742). The towns of Bromley (1773) and Deptford (1701) – both now in Greater London – also had eight bells in their parish churches, as did Ashford (1762), Faversham (1748), Gravesend (1771), Sevenoaks and Tenterden (1769) and Tonbridge (1774).

This early start was capitalized on in the nineteenth century when many more towns and villages had their bells increased to eight in number, and many more augmentations have taken place in the twentieth century. Since Stahlschmidt's survey at least 26 of the rings of six have been increased to eight, many of them in villages, whereas the sixes at Rochester Cathedral and at S Laurence (Ramsgate) have been increased to ten. Ash next Sandwich now has ten, and Canterbury Cathedral has twelve (the augmented twelve of 1923 was replaced by a new ring from the Whitechapel Foundry in 1981). There is also a ring of twelve at Quex Park in a country estate outside Birchington, which is a suburb of Westgate on Sea. These bells were installed in 1819 by the landowner, John Powell Powell, in a specially built tower, for which Mears provided bells at a cost of £824. Powell wanted to be able to practice change-ringing on twelve bells without travelling to London, so he provided the bells and trained a local band. He invited both the Ancient Society of College Youths and the Royal Society of Cumberland Youths (the two main London societies) to the opening in 1819, with the Cumberlands ringing the first peal on the bells. Powell didn't ring, but later took part in several peals himself. Powell's heirs paid for the front four to be recast in 1951.

The developments in Kent owe much to the county's proximity to London and the growth of commuter settlements. But it was also a major centre of development in its own right, for there were few prodominantly rural areas with eight-bell ringing practised as widely as it was in Kent before 1900, even though the county has never had thriving bellfoundries.

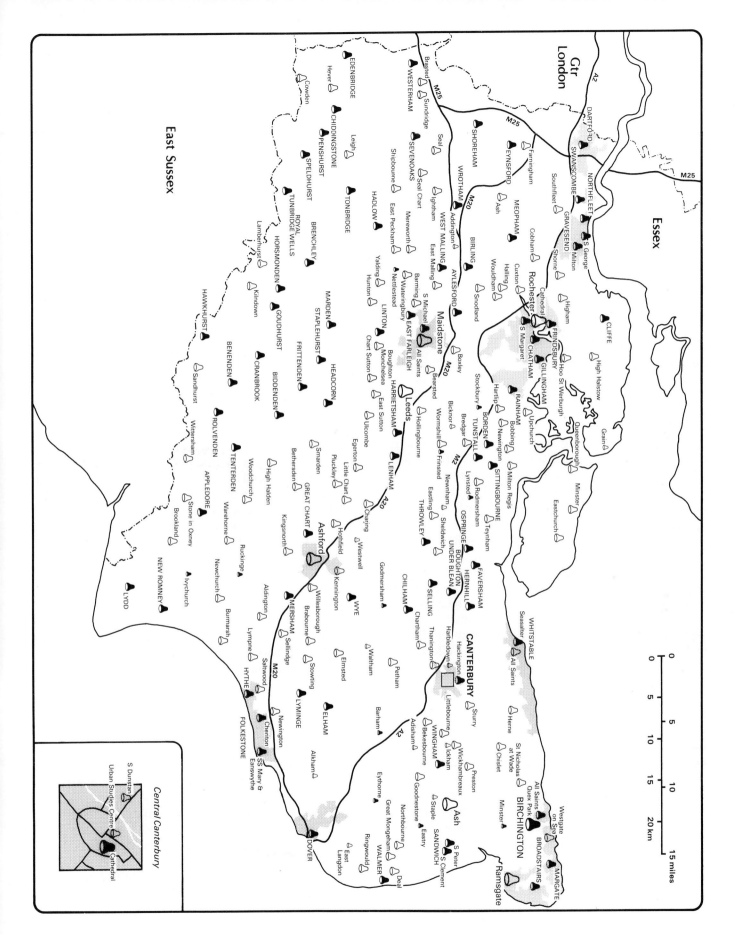

Gtr
London

Essex

East Sussex

A2

DARTFORD

M25

M25

Cowden

Hever

EDENBRIDGE

Sundridge

Brasted

WESTERHAM

Leigh

CHIDDINGSTONE

PENSHURST

SPELDHURST

ROYAL
TUNBRIDGE WELLS

Lamberhurst

HORSMONDEN

BRENCHLEY

Kilndown

HAWKHURST

Sandhurst

GOUDHURST

CRANBROOK

BENENDEN

BIDDENDEN

Wittersham

ROLVENDEN

TENTERDEN

APPLEDORE

Stone in Oxney

Brookland

Warehorne

NEW ROMNEY

Nychurch

Newchurch

Burmarsh

LYDD

Seal

SEVENOAKS

Seal Chart

Shipbourne

Ightham

Mereworth

East Peckham

HADLOW

TONBRIDGE

SHOREHAM

EYNSFORD

WROTHAM

M20

Addington

WEST MALLING

East Malling

BIRLING

Yalding

Hunton

Nettlestead

Wateringbury

Barming

S Michael

All Saints

EAST FARLEIGH

Maidstone

Boughton
Monchelsea

LINTON

Chart Sutton

Sutton

East Sutton

MARDEN

STAPLEHURST

FRITTENDEN

HEADCORN

Ulcombe

Egerton

Little Chart

Pluckley

Smarden

High Halden

Bethersden

Woodchurch

GREAT CHART

Kingsnorth

Aldington

Ruckinge

Farningham

Southfleet

Cobham

MEOPHAM

Ash

Wouldham

Halling

Cuxton

Snodland

Boxley

Bearsted

HARRIETSHAM

Leeds

Stockbury

Bicknor

Wormshill

Frinsted

LENHAM

A20

Charing

Westwell

Hothfield

Ashford

Kennington

Willesborough

Brabourne

MERSHAM

Sellindge

Saltwood

Chenton

HYTHE

FOLKESTONE

SS Mary &
Eanswythe

SWANSCOMBE

NORTHFLEET

GRAVESEND

Milton

S George

Shorne

Higham

Rochester

Cathedral

S Margaret

CHATHAM

FRINDSBURY

GILLINGHAM

BORDEN

RAINHAM

Upchurch

Bobbing

Newington

Hartlip

Bredgar

TUNSTALL

SITTINGBOURNE

Milton Regis

Rodmersham

Teynham

Lynsted

Newnham

OSPRINGE

Throwley

Eastling

Sheldwich

SELLING

BOUGHTON
UNDER BLEAN

HERNHILL

FAVERSHAM

Hoo St Werburgh

High Halstow

CLIFFE

Grain

Queenborough

Minster

Eastchurch

Minster

Eastchurch

WHITSTABLE

Seasalter

All Saints

Swalecliffe

Herne

St Nicholas
at Wade

Chislet

Preston

WINGHAM

Ickham

Wickhambreaux

Littlebourne

Sturry

Hackington

CANTERBURY

Harbledown

Adisham

Bekesbourne

Bishopsbourne

CHILHAM

Chartham

Thanington

Petham

Waltham

Barham

Elmsted

Stowting

LYMINGE

ELHAM

Alkham

Newington

DOVER

East
Langdon

Ringwould

WALMER

Deal

Eastry

SANDWICH

Goodnestone

Northbourne

Great Mongeham

Eythorne

Nonington

Ash

Staple

S Peter

S Clement

Minster

All Saints

Westgate
on Sea

Quex Park

BIRCHINGTON

BROADSTAIRS

MARGATE

Ramsgate

0   5   10   15   20 km

0   5   10   15 miles

S Dunstan

Urban Studies Centre

Cathedral

Central Canterbury

95

Oxfordshire

SITTING astride the limestone belt that crosses England from south-west to north-east, Oxfordshire (including, in its south-western part, the Vale of the White Horse which was formerly in Berkshire) has one of the highest densities of bells in the country. Most of its churches are built of Cotswold limestone, either quarried locally or moved along the Thames and its tributaries. The city of Oxford itself contains many such churches, and the old town to the west of the Cherwell/Isis junction probably has one of the highest densities of rings in the country. The city itself had a foundry for just a short period between 1821 and 1854, when the Taylor family practised their craft there; other Oxfordshire foundries included that operated by the Bond family at Burford from 1862 to 1947, two centuries after Edward Neale cast bells there. Most of the county's bells are 'imports', however, including several complete rings by the Bagley family, who worked from Chacombe, just north of Banbury, from 1631 to 1782, as well as from Chipping Norton and Witney.

In Oxford itself, some of the stimulus for installing rings of bells in the city's many churches will have been provided by the colleges of the university, some of which have their own rings. New College had a ring of eight installed in 1655; it was probably the first complete such ring cast by any founder – Michael Darbie, an itinerant – and he followed this by providing eight for Merton College in 1657. The latter was not a success, however, and was replaced by a ring cast by another itinerant, Christopher Hodson (who later cast bells for Durham Cathedral) in 1680: those bells, which are rung from a gallery some 60 feet above the church floor and with a 20 feet square gap, are the oldest complete ring of eight. In 1712 the six bells at Magdalen College were augmented to eight, which apparently spurred the New College authorities into action: they asked Abraham Rudhall, who had cast Magdalen's new bells, to provide them with two trebles to make ten, a development that was matched by Magdalen only in 1740 when William Freeman, a ringer and member of the college, gave the extra bells. (A Hertfordshire squire, Freeman also gave bells to Aspenden and Braughing in that county.)

The year 1680 was important at another college, too, for it was then that Christopher Hodson cast some new bells for the Cathedral Church of Christ, which is also the chapel of Christ Church College. The history of the bells here is a very long and complex one, as Frederick Sharpe makes clear in his *The Church Bells of Oxfordshire* (1953). The original ecclesiastical foundation in Oxford was Oseney Abbey, sited to the south of the present railway station. This was dissolved at the Reformation and its bells – including the original Great Tom – were placed in the central tower of Christ Church Cathedral. In all eight bells were moved, but they did not make a ring. Great Tom was removed in 1678, for recasting and placing in Tom Tower, and Hodson's contract was to cast four new bells to make a ring of ten. He made them too light relative to the existing heavier bells, and they were virtually inaudible when rung in changes, so they were either recast or replaced by the Rudhalls at the beginning of the eighteenth century. The first peal in the county was rung on these, in 1733. In 1872 the bells were moved to a new tower then being built over the staircase to the dining hall. The stonework for the tower was not complete when the transfer occurred, and the bells were hung in a massive wooden structure (called the 'meat safe' by Lewis Carroll), around which the masonry was built. In 1897, to mark Queen Victoria's Diamond Jubilee, the two trebles were added.

Besides these four college rings, there are nine other rings in the centre of Oxford. S Ebbe's Church has a light ring of eight (tenor 4¾ cwt.), the two trebles having been added to the original six (cast in 1790) to honour the memory of the famous local ringer James W. Washbrook. (The original six were cast by John Briant at Hertford when he was also producing bells for Hanwell and for Littlebury, Essex: the inscriptions suggest that some of the bells were placed in the wrong church!) There are also rings of eight at S Giles's (augmented from six in 1927), S Martin's and All Saints (now the Library of Lincoln College – also augmented in 1927) and at S Mary Magdalene (another light eight, augmented in 1973); a further eight at S Peter in the East, which had not been rung for many years, was transferred to Stanford in the Vale when the church was made redundant. There are rings of six at S Aldate's, S Cross's, Carfax Tower (formerly S Martin's Church), S Mary the Virgin and S Thomas's. (S Michael's also had a ring of six, a 1668 ring of five augmented 40 years later, which are now hung dead.) At S Aldate's, S Cross's, S Mary Magdalene's and All Saints the ring of five was augmented to six in 1874, in each case by Mears and Stainbank.

The city of Oxford has long resounded to the ringing of bells in changes, therefore. So, too, have many of the nearby villages, most of them now incorporated into the expanding urban area. Cowley, Headington, Iffley, Old Marston and Wolvercote all had rings of five by the end of the eighteenth century; only North Hinksey's bells are modern.

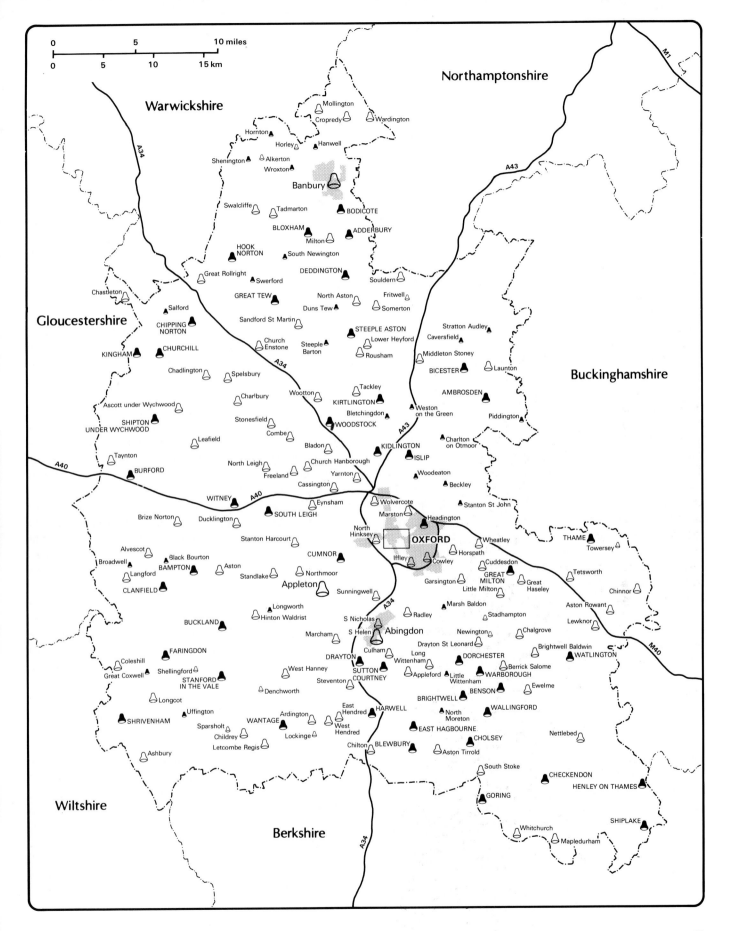

Warwickshire

Northamptonshire

Gloucestershire

Buckinghamshire

Wiltshire

Berkshire

Mollington
Cropredy
Wardington
Hornton
Horley
Hanwell
Shenington
Alkerton
Wroxton
Banbury
Swalcliffe
Tadmarton
BODICOTE
BLOXHAM
ADDERBURY
Milton
HOOK NORTON
South Newington
Great Rollright
DEDDINGTON
Swerford
Souldern
Chastleton
GREAT TEW
North Aston
Fritwell
Duns Tew
Somerton
Salford
CHIPPING NORTON
Sandford St Martin
STEEPLE ASTON
Stratton Audley
Caversfield
KINGHAM
CHURCHILL
Church Enstone
Lower Heyford
Middleton Stoney
Launton
Chadlington
Spelsbury
Steeple Barton
Rousham
BICESTER
Ascott under Wychwood
Charlbury
Wootton
Tackley
AMBROSDEN
Piddington
SHIPTON UNDER WYCHWOOD
Stonesfield
KIRTLINGTON
Bletchingdon
Weston on the Green
Leafield
Combe
WOODSTOCK
Taynton
Bladon
Charlton on Otmoor
BURFORD
North Leigh
Church Hanborough
KIDLINGTON
ISLIP
Freeland
Yarnton
Woodeaton
WITNEY
Cassington
Beckley
Brize Norton
Eynsham
SOUTH LEIGH
Wolvercote
Stanton St John
Ducklington
Marston
Headington
Stanton Harcourt
North Hinksey
OXFORD
Wheatley
THAME
Alvescot
Horspath
Towersey
Broadwell
CUMNOR
Iffley
Cowley
Cuddesdon
Tetsworth
Langford
BAMPTON
Aston
Northmoor
Garsington
GREAT MILTON
Great Haseley
Chinnor
Black Bourton
Standlake
Little Milton
CLANFIELD
Appleton
Sunningwell
Marsh Baldon
Aston Rowant
Longworth
Radley
Stadhampton
Lewknor
Hinton Waldrist
S Nicholas
Chalgrove
BUCKLAND
Marcham
S Helen
Abingdon
Newington
Coleshill
FARINGDON
West Hanney
Culham
Long Wittenham
Drayton St Leonard
Brightwell Baldwin
Great Coxwell
Shellingford
DRAYTON
Appleford
DORCHESTER
WATLINGTON
STANFORD IN THE VALE
Steventon
SUTTON COURTNEY
Berrick Salome
Longcot
Denchworth
Little Wittenham
WARBOROUGH
Uffington
BRIGHTWELL
BENSON
Ewelme
SHRIVENHAM
Ardington
HARWELL
Sparsholt
WANTAGE
East Hendred
North Moreton
WALLINGFORD
Childrey
Lockinge
West Hendred
EAST HAGBOURNE
Letcombe Regis
Chilton
BLEWBURY
CHOLSEY
Nettlebed
Ashbury
Aston Tirrold
South Stoke
CHECKENDON
GORING
HENLEY ON THAMES
Whitchurch
Mapledurham
SHIPLAKE

97

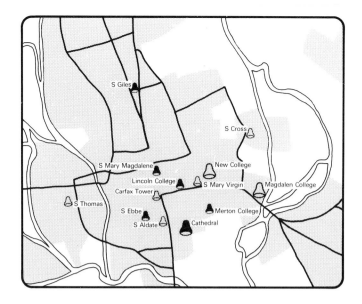

Outside the city there are many parish churches which have had rings of bells for 200 years of more. Of the present rings of five, for example, more than half were in place (or predecessors were) by 1800, and, although many of the rings of six were completed in the nineteenth century, most of them were in churches with at least five at the outset of the century. New churches are a rarity in this long-settled part of rural England, and new rings of bells were almost as rare, it seems. If Britain is the 'ringing isle', then rural Oxfordshire in the nineteenth century will have characterized it very well, for very few parts of the county were even a small number of miles from a church where changes could be rung. The heathlands around Nettlebed at the Southern edge of the Chilterns between Wallingford and Henley on Thames and an area to the north of Bicester are the only real gaps where residents and travellers would have been beyond the call of the bells.

There are several rings of eight outside Oxford that were installed more than 200 years ago. Most are in the prosperous market town churches, such as S John the Baptist Church in Burford (1932), S Mary, Wallingford (1738), S Helen, Abingdon (1764; augmented to ten in 1888), S Edburg, Bicester (1782), and S Mary Magdalene, Woodstock (1785). But several relatively small settlements also had rings of eight very early, including Great Tew (1709 – a ring cast by Rudhall of Gloucester, like the new ring of eight at Chipping Norton in 1825) and Kirtlington (1718; cast by Bagley of Chacombe). East Hagbourne has had a ring of eight since the 1770s, as has Great Milton (where a ringing contest was held on the earlier six in 1764); Benson acquired a ring of eight in 1781, cast by the Chelsea foundry of Thomas Janaway, and Adderbury's was installed in 1789 by Briant of Hertford, replacing a ring of six with a 30 cwt. tenor. Most of the other rings of eight are twentieth-century augmentations, however; only at Banbury (where a new

church was built in 1820, complete with a ring by Briant; the bells were recast as ten in 1930), Dorchester (1867), Henley (1813), Hook Norton (1899), Kidlington (1897), Shipton (1893), Thame (1876) and Witney (1815) was a full octave provided during the nineteenth century.

But Oxfordshire, like its Midlands neighbours, is basically a county of rich rural areas, characterized by sturdy village churches built of Cotswold stone. More than half of them have a ring of five or more bells, and in well over 100 of the towers there is a ring of five or six only. In his 1953 book (*The Church Bells of Oxfordshire*) Frederick Sharpe listed 28 rings of five. Of these, ten were in place by the end of the sixteenth century, with the oldest at Aston Rowant (1625), Old Marston (1665), Wroxton (1676), Shenington (1678), Wood Eaton (1680) and Salford (1687). The last four of these obtained their bells from the foundry of the Bagley family at Chacombe, Northamptonshire, which is just east of Banbury. Shenington and Wroxton are only a few miles from Chacombe, as also are Horley (which has a 1706 ring of four from the Bagley foundry), Hornton (a 1741 Bagley ring of five), and Swalcliffe (which obtained a ring of six from the same source in 1685).

Of the 67 rings of six in Sharpe's list (recall that he was working in the pre-1974 county excluding the Vale of the White Horse), nine were installed by 1700, and a further 16 by 1800; 26 became rings of six in the nineteenth century, and 16 in the twentieth (the figures for the last two centuries for rings of five are eight and nil respectively). Of the 42 completed after 1800, 30 were rings of five by that date. In addition, of the 34 rings of eight listed by Sharpe, 31 were rings of at least five by 1800, so at the turn of the nineteenth century there were at least 60 rings of five in the county, plus some 45 rings of six. Many of the augmentations to six occurred late in the nineteenth century; there were also some new rings, such as that at Leafield (north-east of Burford), where the tenor bell was the gift of Queen Victoria.

In a county with so many rings of bells, it is not surprising to find a number of the country's most renowned ringers of the past, and some of its towers as the scenes of their exploits. One of these has already been mentioned. James W. Washbrook spent most of his life in Oxford, and rang many peals in the county, including record lengths of 10,080 Double Norwich Court Bob Major at Appleton in 1888 and three peals of Caters, each over 12,000 changes long. In 1899 he was recruited to teach a band to ring the new bells at Arklow in Ireland, where he was the first person to ring two bells to a peal, in 1901. (He rang bells 3 and 4, and also called the peal – Grandsire Triples.) Another local worthy was Canon G. F. Coleridge, who was President of the Central Council of Church Bell Ringers from 1921 to 1930 and who died in 1949; the two trebles at Christ Church Cathedral were recast in 1952, and are inscribed in his memory.

Both Washbrook and Coleridge rang in the late nineteenth century with another Oxfordshire clergyman, who in 1905 became the first person to complete 1,000 peals. This was rung on 9 August at S Peter's Church, Drayton, where F. E. Robinson was vicar from 1878 to 1908. It was planned to ring a peal of Stedman Triples, silent and non-conducted, two days earlier with Washbrook ringing two bells. That attempt failed, however, so Robinson called another attempt, but a rope broke near to the end. Both Washbrook and Coleridge rang in the successful peal, in which Robinson called Thurstan's peal of Stedman Triples, something which he did many times: of Robinson's 1,241 peals, 861 were of Stedman Triples, and he called 719 of them.

Robinson's peal-ringing record is well known, since he provided full details in an autobiography, *Among the Bells* (1929). In it he recalls that when he was presented to the benefice of Drayton (then in Berkshire) in 1878 he found a new ring of six installed by Mears and Stainbank. Two years later a new treble and a new tenor were added, both – as the inscriptions indicate – the gift of Robinson. The bells were dedicated on 27 May, and in the afternoon he called a peal of Grandsire Triples on them, being the first incumbent to conduct a peal on his own church bells. He rang many peals on the bells, including the longest length of London Surprise Major then rung (11,320 changes; six hours six minutes) in 1896 and, on August Bank Holiday 1888, three peals in a day (Cambridge and Superlative Surprise and Double Norwich Court Bob Major: they also lost one!).

Not far from Drayton is the village of Appleton (also formerly in Berkshire). A new ring of six was put in the tower in 1818 to replace a former ring of three. In 1854 these were augmented to eight, which involved hanging two bells on a second layer because of the small size of the nine-foot square tower. Leading the fundraising for this work was Alfred White, a member of a family of wheelwrights and smiths, who founded a bell-hanging firm in 1842. He rang in the first 720 on the six in 1821 and, along with three other members of his family, in the first peal on the eight in 1855. In 1859 it was decided to recast the front three bells, and the cost of this was met by F. E. Robinson; two years later Robinson gave two new tenors (at a cost of £254), producing a light ten with a tenor of 13 cwt., and he rang in the first peal on them in October of that year.

In 1888 this light ring of ten was one of those involved in what Frederick Sharpe has called a 'fever pitch' of record-breaking attempts. In January a band including Robinson and Washbrook rang 10,000 Double Norwich Court Bob Major; in March they were in the band that rang 12,041 Stedman Caters; in April they rang in 13,265 Grandsire Caters; and on the last day of the year, together with Coleridge, they rang what Robinson called 'a brilliant peal' of 15,041 Stedman Caters, thereby regaining the record which they had lost in the previous May to a Cheltenham band. (The last peal started 1½ hours late, as the tenor ringer did not arrive. He was found in the next village, threshing corn. According to Robinson, only two mistakes were made.)

Appleton is found again in the record books after the First World War, with a peal of 21,363 Stedman Caters in 1922, which regained the record from a band which rang 18,027 at Loughborough in 1909. Richard and Fred White rang 9 and 10 respectively in this peal, as they did ten years later when the record length of Grandsire Caters (16,271 changes) was also rung on the bells. Then, in 1978, a peal of 22,899 Stedman Caters was rung in twelve hours and twelve minutes.

Oxford from the air looking east, showing many of the towers in the city centre with bells. In the centre background, at the end of the High Street, is Magdalen College. On the north side of the street are the spires of the University Church of S Mary the Virgin and Lincoln College Library (formerly the Church of S Martin and All Saints), and Carfax Tower (formerly the Church of S Martin of Tours). The tower of Christ Church is on the far right of the picture, with the spire of S Aldate's Church opposite the college; Merton College tower can be seen between Christ Church and Magdalen. New College tower is in the left background of the picture.

Surrey

THE small, though densely populated, county of Surrey has relatively few rings, and the great majority of its parishes lack four or more bells in their church. As with the other more urbanized counties, a substantial proportion of the rings are of eight bells or more. The proportion was even greater before the reorganization of Greater London's local government in 1964 led to one ring of twelve (at S John Baptist, Croydon), three of ten (Beddington; S Peter's, Croydon; and Kingston upon Thames, the last a ring of twelve since 1972), five of eight, and two each of six and five being transferred out of the county.

Much of the Surrey landscape comprises relatively barren country of heathland and infertile soils, although an impressive narrow ridge of chalkland runs from west to east through the county. It was not, then, an area rich in church architecture before the suburban invasion of the nineteenth century, and Jennings (in *A Short History of Surrey Bells and Ringing Customs*) notes that one-sixth of Surrey churches have a wooden belfry. Nevertheless, the map of rings of bells was well established prior to that period, and the major activity since has been augmentation. Stahlschmidt's survey (*Surrey Bells and London Bellfounders*, 1884) identified 13 rings of five in the area which is now Surrey, of which nine were in place before 1800 (only one, at Chipstead, has not since been augmented). Four new rings of five were provided during the nineteenth century – at Buckland (1860, now six), Hascombe (1854), Tandridge (1870) and Witley (1842, now eight); all four are in the south of the county. Similarly, of the 33 rings of six listed by Stahlschmidt, 17 were in place by 1800, and in a further six it is known that there was a ring of five in the tower by that date. Of the ten 'new' rings of six installed (as far as can be told) during the nineteenth century, the great majority were in villages beyond the suburban towns, the only exceptions being Egham, Esher and Kingswood.

Some of the earliest Surrey bells were cast by the Eldridge family, who operated a foundry in Gilford Street, Chertsey, from 1619 to 1714; for three years (1656–8) they also ran a branch foundry at Coventry. Richard Eldridge started founding at Wokingham in 1593, when he produced a bell for Capel in the south of the county (Wokingham is now in Berkshire). The most common inscription used by him on a bell was 'Our Hope is in the Lord', whereas his successor, Brian, preferred 'Gloria Deo in Excelsis' [sic]. Chertsey parish church contains a much older bell, cast in 1310, according to Ernest Morris (in *The History and Art of Change Ringing*), for the local abbey; it was tolled when Henry VI was buried there.

The present county of Surrey had only eleven rings of eight in 1884, plus the ten at Leatherhead. Most of these were relatively recent installations, with only the eights at Farnham (1723) and S Nicholas, Guildford (1736), in place before 1750, and four more (Epsom, 1761; Godalming, 1792; Holy Trinity, Guildford, 1764; and Reigate, 1784) before 1800. (At Reigate, as at Chertsey 54 years earlier, the town's Member of Parliament presented a bell. The three bells at Ashtead were recast into six in 1725 with finance provided by Lord Dudley, whose name was recorded on both treble and tenor.) There have been many augmentations since, for the county now has six rings of ten and 42 of eight, plus the twelve at Guildford's cathedral, which started with a ring of ten in the mid-1960s and obtained the additional trebles a decade later. The city of Guildford is indeed the main ringing centre in the county. Apart from its new, brick-built cathedral on a hill outside the town, next to the new university, there are three towers close together in the city centre, plus rings at the former villages of Merrow, Shalford and Stoke now all but absorbed into the expanding urban area.

The augmentations to eight have been in villages and towns alike – though many of the villages are basically dormitory suburbs and are as urbanized as the commuter towns. The new rings of ten, joining Leatherhead, are all in major towns, however: Egham, Epsom, Guidford (S Nicholas), Haslemere and Reigate.

Although nearer to London, which was the main

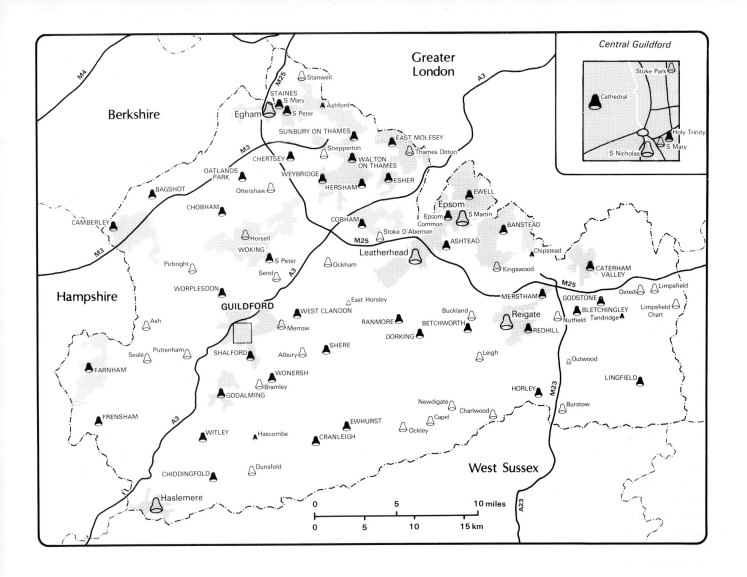

centre of change-ringing, especially peal-ringing, in the eighteenth century, than most of the churches in Kent, in general Surrey towers contributed much less to the early developments. Morris mentions Epsom, Leatherhead and Guildford in his *The History and Art of Change Ringing*. Leatherhead ringers 'have assiduously followed the art' since six bells were installed in 1792; and after the ten were in place, 'a large number of peals in all methods have been rung'. Epsom had its first peal in 1766, and 'a large number' of others, especially after installation of the ten; and Guildford 'has long had notable ringers to perform on the various church bells of the town'. But no notable performances are reported for any one of the three and no other Surrey tower is mentioned in the book. In the early twentieth century, however, a Guildford band of handbell ringers led by Alfred Pulling set a number of records. (Pulling was also an excellent tower-bell ringer, taking part in several early peals of Spliced Surprise: he also rang a peal in 1925 in which all of the ringers were 6 feet or more tall.) Their main successes were peals of Stedman, especially Caters; they rang the record length of 19,738 changes in 1912, having set out to ring 22,222 but ending the peal early because of time problems.

East Sussex

THE ancient county of Sussex was not well provided with rings of bells, and had five or more in only one-third of its parishes. The division of the county into two in 1974 put about an equal number of towers in each part. Neither has many fine examples of church architecture: as Betjeman describes it, 'The churches of Sussex are many and various. They are not among the most magnificent since, unlike East Anglia and Gloucestershire, there was no flourishing local industry here when Gothic architecture reached its zenith in the 15th century' (*Collins Pocket Guide to English Parish Churches*).

The area now occupied by the county of East Sussex had eight towers with eight bells when Daniel-Tyssen published his survey (*The Church Bells of Sussex*) in 1864, plus 20 rings of six and 18 of five. The eight-bell rings were nearly all in place by the end of the eighteenth century: the oldest dated from 1739 (at Battle), followed by four more in the 1770s (at S Nicholas, Brighton, Rye, Salehurst and Waldron); Seaford, Brightling and Southover (Lewes) joined the group in the early nineteenth century. Those at S Mary's Church, Rye, a Norman foundation which is the largest church in the county, replaced a ring of six supposedly installed in 1360, stolen by French invaders in 1367, recaptured and rehung immediately after and recast in 1774; the trebles were added in the following year.

A second survey of Sussex bells, published by Elphick in 1970, provides more information about late nineteenth- and early twentieth-century augmentations than is available for most counties. There are no rings of twelve in East Sussex, but four rings of ten. Two are in Brighton. S Nicholas's Church, in the centre of the town, had a ring of five in 1724, augmented to eight in 1777. Two more bells were added in about 1815; they were taken to S Peter's Church in 1826, returned to S Nicholas in 1882 and recast in 1891; Gillett and Johnston provided a new ring of ten in 1922. At S Peter's, a new eight was put in the tower in 1882; J. T. Rickman offered a ring of twelve in 1914, but only ten were installed. Many peals have been rung on them – 370 between 1914 and 1967 alone – and both towers have been the sites of major performances. At S Nicholas, for example, a peal

of 11,088 Plain Bob Major was rung in May 1779 (taking six hours 50 minutes), which was the longest length in the method rung to that date. But in the twentieth century, S Peter's has been the siite of most record performances. The first peal of Bristol Surprise Major was rung there in 1901, four years after Rev. E. Bankes James devised the method; several other first peals of new Surprise Major methods were heard there in the previous decade (most of them conducted by George Attree) – a period when, according to Ernest Morris, the Brighton Company members were 'the foremost ringers in the country, assiduously practising all these higher methods' (*The History and Art of Change Ringing*). Even more noteworthy was the peal in 1926 of London Surprise Royal, Brighton Version. London Surprise Major cannot truly be extended to Royal, and several variants were produced: the Stepney version was first rung 19 years earlier.

The third ring of ten in the county is in the county town, Lewes, but not in its town centre church, which has a round tower (one of three such churches in the Ouse Valley) and only two bells. The church of S John the Baptist, Southover, in the Ouse Valley, had a ring of eight installed in 1839, which Mears and Stainbank augmented to ten in 1905.

The county's fourth ring of ten was created in 1988, at the church of SS Saviour and Peter, Eastbourne, when two new trebles (donated in memory of Frs Mckenzie and Whiting) were added to the restored octave. They were cast in the Netherlands (as are most of the new bells installed by the Derbyshire bellhanging firm of Eayre and Smith), but to the same profile as the original ring (provided by Warners of London).

In the century after Daniel-Tyssen's listing was published there were 33 augmentations according to Elphick's survey: most were to provide rings of eight (17; seven from five and nine from six) and six (13; eight of them from rings of five). There were also nine new rings, for new churches. The resort of Eastbourne was recipient of four of these, all in the 1880s: All Souls was provided with a ring of five in 1882 (these were scrapped in 1960); All Saints and Christ Church

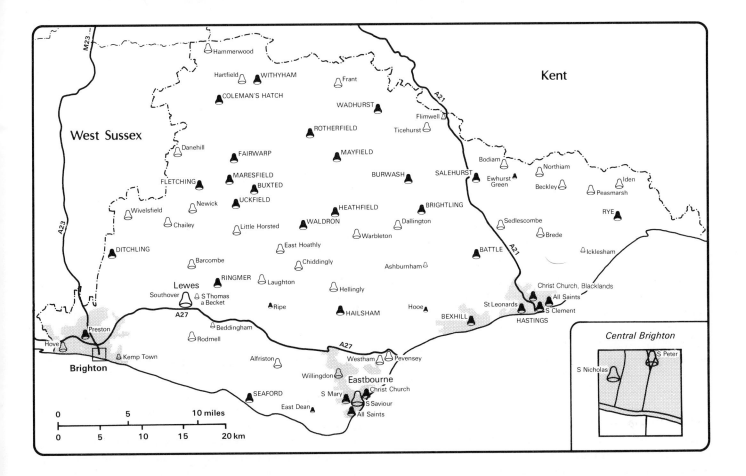

obtained rings of eight in 1883, and SS Saviour and Peter had to wait three more years for its eight, heaviest of the group (tenor 24¼ cwt.). Further along the coast, St Leonards on Sea acquired a ring of eight for its new Christ Church in 1894. Nearby Hastings had two augmentations. That at All Saints was a straightforward provision of three trebles in 1963, but at S Clement's there were two major changes. The original ring of six, installed in 1697, was replaced by a ring of eight steel bells (cast by Naylor Vickers of Sheffield) in 1860. These were replaced by a Taylor eight in 1963, the donors of the new bells including the Hastings and St Leonards' Operatic and Dramatic Society, the Residents of Hastings, New Zealand, and Hastings Grammar School. At Christ Church, Blacklands – an inner suburb – only one donor was needed: the ring of eight installed in 1897 was the gift of one lady to mark Queen Victoria's Diamond Jubilee.

In all, the greatest volume of augmentation and provision of new rings took place between 1880 and 1914. These were decades of relative prosperity when, according to Jennings's history of Taylor's foundry (*Master of My Art*, 1987), substantial tonnages of bells were produced. The decades between the two world wars were also very active ones for Taylor, but the interest then in providing new bells does not seem to have included East Sussex. There, the widespread, though relatively thin, provision of bells had already taken place.

Major accidents causing the loss of rings of bells are rare today, but the hurricane which struck south-eastern England on 16–17 October 1987 threatened several East Sussex rings. At Rotherfield, for example, the spire collapsed and much debris fell among the bells, which had been left 'up'. The top of the spire was removed at nearby Buxted, and Withyam tower was cracked. The church of S Paul, Brighton, only ever acquired one bell, although a heavy eight had been intended in 1853; the wooden octagonal structure in which it was hung is now damaged beyond repair.

West Sussex

ALTHOUGH the division of the county of Sussex into two independent units in 1974 led to about half of the churches with rings of bells going to each part, the general impression given by the map of West Sussex is of a region poorly provided with bells and with large, almost empty areas. In fact, those empty areas appear because they are very largely devoid of settlements. Most notable is the broad band of the South Downs to the north of Chichester, extending from the county boundary to the coast east of Worthing. That block of high country is pierced by river valleys in only two places – by the Arun north of Arundel and the Adur between Worthing and Shoreham-by-Sea; there are no villages in the Adur gap and those in the Arun gap lack rings of bells. The A24 does cross the downs north of Worthing, and the ring of six at Findon – augmented from four by Mears in 1870 – is the only place on the chalk where it is possible to hear the call of the bells.

Settlements with rings of bells are confined to the coastal belt, the valleys of the Arun, Adur and Rother, and a few villages in the forests of Ashdown and St Leonard's in the north-east of the county. The empty band of chalkland north of the Rother in the north-west is also a barren area campanologically.

The major feature of the pattern of towers along the coastal strip is of the relative absence of rings of bells in the modern coastal resorts – notably Bognor Regis and Littlehampton. Only at Worthing was a ring provided for a new church, S Botolph's, in the former village of Heene, which had a Warner ring installed in 1879. Elsewhere the churches with bells are in the villages that preceded the rash of villas that came with the nineteenth-century railways. Several of these – and most notably that at Bosham, picturesquely sited on the banks of Chichester Harbour, have timbered, pyramidal spires as the roofing for their towers. Most of their rings of bells are relatively old; the eight at Arundel was a gift of the Duke and Duchess of Norfolk in 1855, and the eight at Shoreham-by-Sea was augmented from five, the three trebles being cast by Mears and Stainbank in 1896.

At the western end of this coastal strip is the cathedral city of Chichester, where the eight bells are hung in a detached campanile, the only one associated with an English cathedral for many years until Chester's new one was opened in 1973. At Chichester, as at Chester and other cathedrals that have had campaniles in the past, such as Salisbury, the main tower is central and the great weight is a substantial burden for the arches that have to carry it. The downward force of ringing bells may be too great for those foundations to bear, which is why bells were not installed – even though it is claimed that it would be entirely safe with modern technology to put bells in, for example, Salisbury Cathedral's central spire. Some central towers with bells do create substantial problems (the duration of ringing is severely constrained at Worcester Cathedral, for example, where the tenor weighs 49½ cwt.).

The original six bells at Chichester were augmented to eight in 1729 with the gift of two trebles cast at Whitechapel by Richard Phelps. Two of the earlier bells were manufactured at Salisbury by William Purdue in 1665, who with his brother Roger also did some casting at a foundry in Chichester. In general, however, the south coast counties to the east of the Isle of Wight were the scenes of very little bell-founding over the last 500 years, and most of their bells are imports.

One unique set of imports in West Sussex is at East Grinstead, where the eighteenth-century tower of S Swithin's church houses the only ring of twelve in either of the Sussex counties. A ring of eight was installed there in 1813, and was recast and augmented to ten in 1972. Achieving a ring of twelve was the project undertaken by the Sussex County Association to mark its centenary in 1985, which involved raising the money for three new trebles (including a sharp 2nd to give a light eight). The treble is inscribed 'The gift of Kate and Peter Hurcombe – Master 1985. Sussex County Association . . .'; the 2nd tells that it was 'The gift of Peter and Judy Howard, Duncan and Heather Weaver'; and the sharp 2nd is inscribed 'Given in memory of our parents by Jacqueline and Peter Hunter'. The bells were cast not by an English foundry but by the firm of Eijsbouts of Assen in the Netherlands; this firm also provided the ten in 1972, and so East Grinstead parish church now has a ring of twelve which is also the only complete ring in England cast outside the country.

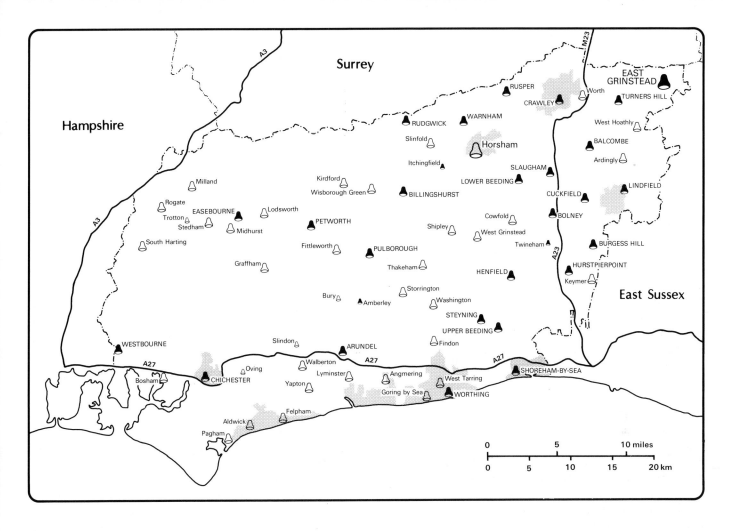

Elsewhere in the inland belt of the county, the pattern is that typical of rural England. West Sussex as a whole had twelve rings of five in place in 1864, of which only one, at Thakeham (1809) was not installed before 1800, together with 18 rings of six, the great majority of which were also eighteenth-century rings. Of the nine rings of eight, however, only those at Bolney, Chichester Cathedral, Horsham and Hurstpierpoint were in place before 1800. Four were added before 1864 (at Arundel, Cuckfield, East Grinstead and Petworth). Nine more augmentations occurred in the late nineteenth century (including Diamond Jubilee projects at Pulborough and Upper Beeding in 1897), and three in the twentieth.

In his book on the bells of the two counties of East and West Sussex (*The Church Bells of Sussex*), Daniel-Tyssen provided a year-by-year chronology of the provision of bells, which is much more detailed than that available for most other English counties. Until the end of the seventeenth century, the great majority of installations were of single bells, with only one example each of a ring of four (in 1631) and a ring of six (in 1699). After that date, complete rings became more common, with the first full ring of eight being installed in 1739 (at Battle).

Daniel-Tyssen also notes that periods of domestic disturbance were years when few bells were cast – none for Sussex churches during the Civil War (1642–5), for example, and none between 1789 and 1794. He also identifies three years – 1665, 1712 and 1724 – when there was above-average activity in Sussex because of the presence in the county of itinerant founders. Ten bells were cast for Sussex churches in the first of those years, compared with only eight in the previous four, and four in the following four; 15 were cast in 1712, after a blank period of two years; and the 16 provided in 1724 were followed by only three in the next five years. The largest number of bells installed in a year (before 1860, the last surveyed) was 19, in 1815.

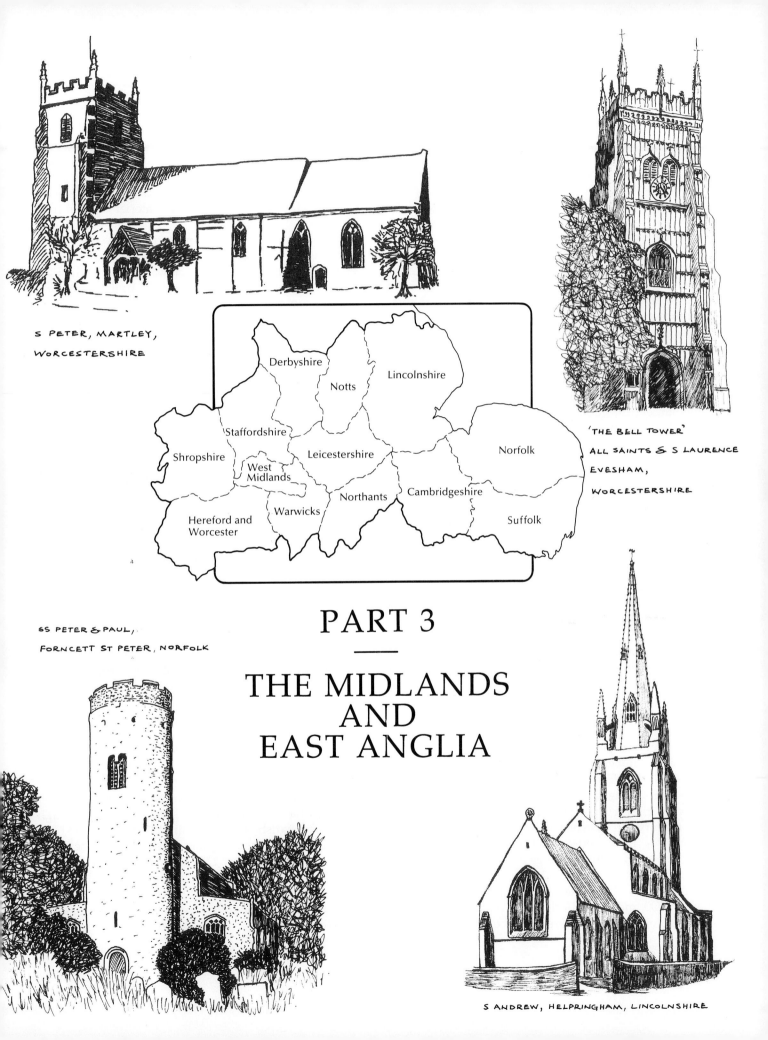

S PETER, MARTLEY,
WORCESTERSHIRE

'THE BELL TOWER'
ALL SAINTS & S LAURENCE
EVESHAM,
WORCESTERSHIRE

SS PETER & PAUL,
FORNCETT ST PETER, NORFOLK

PART 3
—
THE MIDLANDS
AND
EAST ANGLIA

S ANDREW, HELPRINGHAM, LINCOLNSHIRE

Cambridgeshire

In terms of the map showing the location of rings of bells, the modern county of Cambridgeshire (which incorporates the formerly separate county of Huntingdonshire, plus the Soke of Peterborough, once in Northamptonshire) is one of the most interesting. There are areas where the density of rings is fairly high, and others where for many miles there are no churches from which the sound of change-ringing peals out.

Much of the county comprises land which is very close to sea level, and which has only recently been drained to allow agriculture to be practised and communities to be established with some degree of security. In the south, around the city of Cambridge itself, are low hills on which there are long-established villages, and these stand out on the map alongside empty areas of only recent settlement. Thus to the south of Cambridge there is a high density of churches with rings to either side of the M11, but further west, towards the Bedfordshire border and the A1, there is a substantial empty region, which is the valley of the Upper Cam. Further north, the relatively elevated area around the triangle formed by the A1, A45 and A604 roads (and to the west beyond) is well populated, but this is succeeded by an even emptier area, with no apparent settlement at all north of Chatteris and Ramsey apart from the well-sited towns of Whittlesey, March, and Wisbech (for which the nearby Downham Market foundry provided a ring of ten). This is the Bedford Level (Middle Level), the flat land drained by the River Nene, which was drained only in the seventeenth century and lacks villages and hamlets. Further east is the Bedford Level (South Level), drained by the Great Ouse, where the history is the same and only a few settlements, such as Ely and the aptly named Sutton in the Isle, are to be found. The landscape so wonderfully evoked in *The Nine Tailors*, Dorothy L. Sayers's detective novel focused on ringing, is to be found here.

The southern part of Cambridgeshire is a westward extension, topographically, of the rich bell-ringing districts of Bedfordshire and Northamptonshire, and many of its villages have had rings of bells for at least two centuries, a large number cast by local founders. Owen's survey (published as *The Church Bells of Huntingdonshire* in 1899) shows that particular part of the present county with four rings of eight and nine of six only, plus 21 of five and 23 of four. Of the 372 bells which he was able to date, nearly half (181) were cast before 1700, indicative of the early installation of small rings: 16 of the rings of five and 17 of the rings of four

were in place by 1800, but only three of the rings of six. The situation was very similar further east, in what was the county of Cambridgeshire before 1974: 31 of the 44 datable rings of five were installed by 1800, as were twelve of the 24 rings of six (the material is taken from J. J. Raven, *The Church Bells of Cambridgeshire*, 1881). One of the oldest rings in the county (a heavy five with a tenor of 46 cwt.) was given to King's College by Henry VI in the fifteenth century but was sold to a London bellfounder by the authorities in 1756; unlike at Oxford, there is no tradition of rings of bells at Cambridge colleges. The Roman Catholic church of Our Lady and the English Martyrs has a heavy ring of eight.

The great majority of the rural towers had five bells or fewer until the mid-nineteenth century, and it is doubtful whether change-ringing was widely practised before then. It was probably pursued in the towns, however, in many of which rings of eight or more were installed relatively early. The oldest was the ring of twelve installed in Great S Mary's Church, Cambridge, in 1772 (there had been a ring of ten there since 1722); in 1788 a peal of 6,600 Plain Bob Maximus was rung, still the record for that method on twelve bells. These bells were hung anticlockwise until a restoration in 1952. At Soham, the 1790 ring of eight was augmented to ten in 1808. The band there had established a reputation for peals of Major in the previous decade, and one of their most noteworthy achievements was a peal of Oxford Treble Bob Major rung by eight members of the Tebbit family (three brothers and five of their sons) in 1809. In Huntingdonshire, there were only four rings of eight by the end of the nineteenth century, but three of them were more than 100 years old: the eight at St Ives was installed in 1723 by Henry Penn of Peterborough; that at St Neots (where the local band taught themselves to ring a peal of Grandsire Triples in 1753) 30 years later by the local founder Joseph Eayre; and Godmanchester's eight was installed in 1794 by the Downham Market founder Thomas Osborn. St Neots gained two extra trebles in 1984.

Cambridgeshire has two cathedrals, but for a long time neither resounded to the sound of bells in changes. Ely's still has only a small clock chime of five, though the nearby parish church acquired its eight in 1781. At Peterborough, after 250 years of silence, the bells are again operational. In 1709 four heavy bells were removed from the tower and used by the local founder Henry Penn to cast a ring of ten (tenor 35 cwt.); he had enough bell-metal left over to cover his payment for the job. Ringing was soon halted, because of fears that it

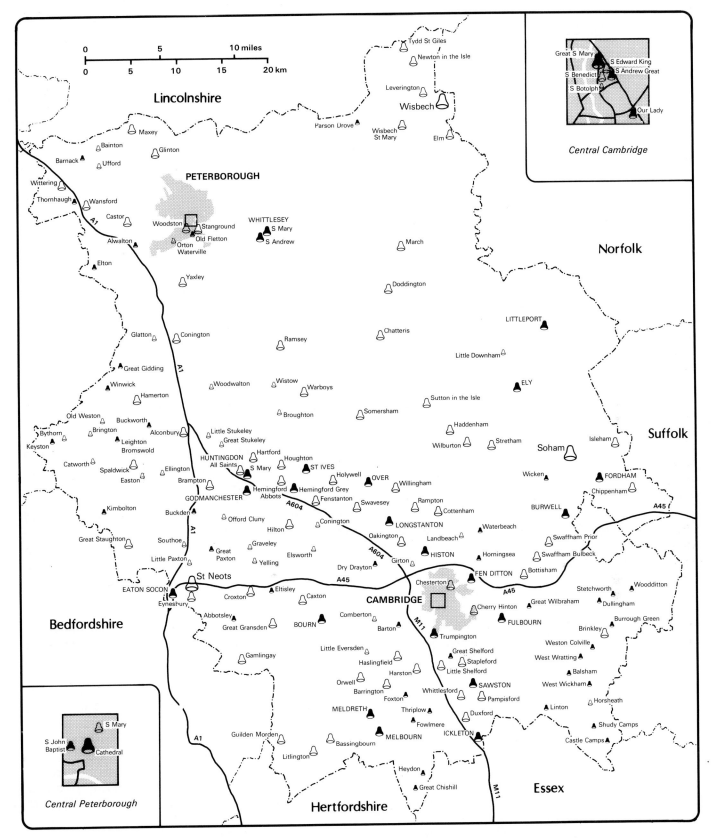

would cause the west front to collapse. In 1831 the five trebles were sold as metal to Downham Market foundry, and the heavy bells were kept for the clock. In the early 1980s it was proved that the west front wouldn't fall. The ring of ten from the closed church of S John the Divine, Leicester, was purchased, two trebles were added, and in November 1986 the bells were rededicated and rang out across the city.

109

Derbyshire

DERBYSHIRE has no major industrial conurbations. Its eastern portion contains small industrial towns, some, such as Belper, associated with textiles, others based on mining; the county town itself is a large engineering centre. The west of the county is largely rural, and the valleys are fertile and densely settled; in the far north, beyond Hope and Castleton, are the high, desolate gritstone moors of the Dark Peak, which are empty of all but a few farms and contain no villages with rings of bells in their parish churches.

A listing of the bells in most Derbyshire churches was published by Jowitt in the 1870s in *The Reliquary*. Outside the county town, there was one ring of ten (at Chesterfield), six of eight, 26 of six and 18 of five. Of those, about half of the rings of five and six were installed before 1800. Of the rings of eight and ten, however, only those at Bakewell and Chesterfield are that old, Bakewell's 1719 ring of six having been augmented to eight in 1796. At Chesterfield, the tower beneath the famed crooked spire had a ring of eight in the early 1700s, built on a 1612 ring of three. This was replaced by a new ring of ten in 1820: the bells were opened on 22 May, with three peals rung by visiting bands from Oldham, Sheffield, and Leeds/Wakefield; the following day bands from Ashton under Lyne and Mottram, and the Sherwood Youths, rang three more peals.

The other rings of eight in the county by the 1870s were Ashbourne, cast by Dobson of Downham Market, Norfolk, in 1815; Castleton, where a six installed in 1803 was augmented nine years later to eight by Harrison of Barton on Humber; Youlgreave, where the 1762 ring of five was replaced by an eight with a 26½ cwt. tenor in 1870 (when the church was extended); Staveley, where two trebles, augmenting the 1782 ring of six, were given in 1811 to mark the 21st birthday of the Marquis of Hartington; and Glossop, where another six by Harrison, dating from 1806, was augmented in 1853. Most of these are in the northern part of the county, where the valleys were attractive sites for the stately homes of aristocratic families, some of whom gave to the local churches. The most famous of those homes is Chatsworth, and the Duke of Devonshire presented a ring of six for the new church in the estate village of Edensor (which replaced an older church with a 1769 ring of four). Indeed, the northern part of the county was much better provided with rings of bells before 1800: there were only five rings of five or more of that vintage to the south of the A38 outside Derby (at Breadsall, Hartshorne, Ilkeston, Lullington and Repton).

In Derby itself, All Saints (now the cathedral) had a ring of six augmented to ten in 1677 (giving it the first ring of ten in provincial England), thanks to the work of Francis Thacker of nearby Repton, whose name is on the treble. The ring of eight at S Luke's was installed in 1875 in a church on land donated by Mrs Moss. She gave the bells, and was determined that they should be heavier than those at All Saints; the tenor is 30 cwt. and remains the county's heaviest bell. The eight at S Peter's was completed in 1901. In addition, Derby has 'lost' three rings: an eight at S Werburgh's, completed in 1848; the eight at S Alkmund's, completed in 1908 and now at Whitehaven; and the ten at S Andrew's – an eight installed in 1881 and augmented in 1927.

Just north of Derby is the village of Duffield, the home from 1872 of Sir Arthur Percival Heywood, a polymath with great enthusiasms for both railways and bells. He installed a light railway in the grounds of his home, and built one for the Duke of Westminster's estate in Cheshire too. For the local church, he had the 1799 ring of six recast into an eight in 1884; the bells were hung on bearings that he designed and made, and three years later he augmented them to ten to mark Queen Victoria's Golden Jubilee. He invented a method, which he called Duffield, and published a book about it, and encouraged the development of Surprise ringing by the local band: 100 peals were rung there between 1884 and 1892, of which Heywood called 70. He was also the driving force in the creation of the Central Council of Church Bell Ringers, was its founder president and served in that office for 28 years.

Wormhill has the lightest ring of six in use in a church. It was cast by Taylors in 1863 (as the back six of an eight) to be hung in the foundry to illustrate their work, but the bells were bought for the tiny tower in this small village (the tenor was defective, and was recast in 1864). In the north-east of the county, an association to promote the ringing of five and six bells was established at Clay Cross in 1887. The original towers in the East Derbyshire and West Nottinghamshire Association were all in Derbyshire. Initially, membership was restricted to five- and six-bell towers, but in 1899 Alfreton (whose ring of five was increased to six in 1897) obtained a ring of eight, and by 1902 four other towers (Ashover, Darley Dale, North Wingfield and Ripley) were also recipients of new trebles. For much of its existence, the association has run schemes designed to promote regular Sunday service ringing – certificates were issued and a shield competed for: not all ringing contests have been concerned with the quality of striking.

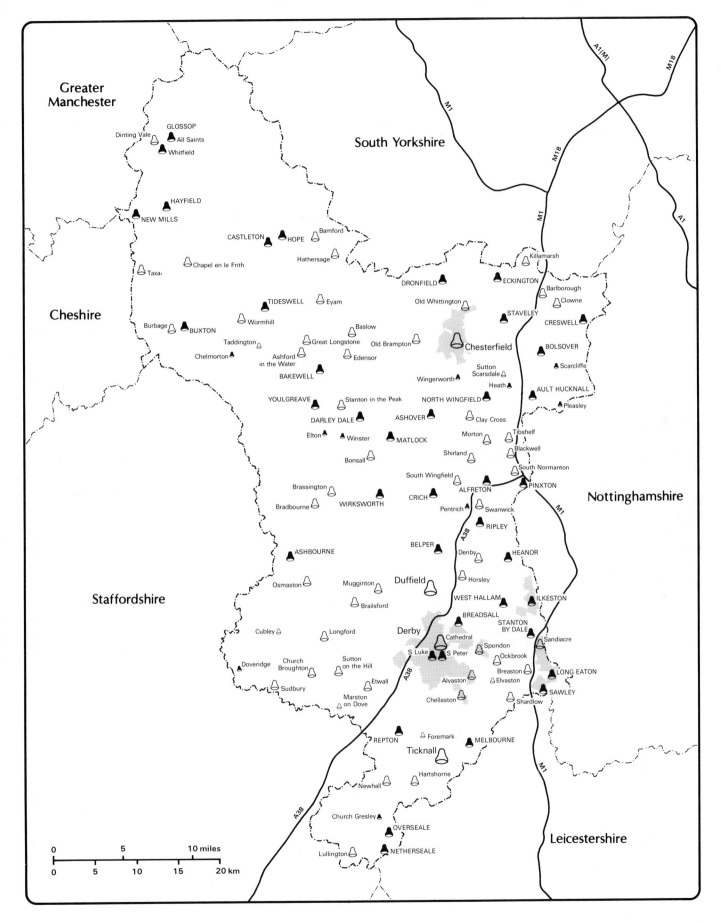

Greater
Manchester

South Yorkshire

Cheshire

Staffordshire

Nottinghamshire

Leicestershire

Dinting Vale
GLOSSOP
All Saints
Whitfield

HAYFIELD
NEW MILLS

Taxai

Chapel en le Frith

CASTLETON HOPE Bamford
Hathersage

DRONFIELD ECKINGTON Killamarsh
Barlborough
Clowne

TIDESWELL Eyam
Wormhill
Old Whittington
STAVELEY CRESWELL

Burbage BUXTON
Taddington
Chelmorton
Ashford
in the Water
Great Longstone
Edensor
Old Brampton
Chesterfield
BOLSOVER
Scarcliffe

Baslow

BAKEWELL
Wingerworth
Sutton
Scarsdale
Heath
AULT HUCKNALL
Pleasley

YOULGREAVE Stanton in the Peak
DARLEY DALE
Elton Winster MATLOCK
NORTH WINGFIELD
ASHOVER Clay Cross
Morton Tibshelf
Shirland Blackwell
Bonsall South Normanton

Brassington
Bradbourne WIRKSWORTH
South Wingfield
CRICH
Pentrich Swanwick
ALFRETON PINXTON

ASHBOURNE
Osmaston
Mugginton
Brailsford
Duffield
Denby
Horsley
BELPER
RIPLEY
HEANOR

Cubley Longford
Doveridge Church
Broughton
Sudbury
Sutton
on the Hill
Etwall
Marston
on Dove
WEST HALLAM ILKESTON
BREADSALL
STANTON
BY DALE
Sandiacre

Derby
Cathedral
S Luke S Peter
Spondon
Ockbrook
Breaston LONG EATON
Alvaston Elvaston
Chellaston Shardlow
SAWLEY

REPTON Foremark MELBOURNE
Ticknall
Hartshorne
Newhall

Church Gresley
OVERSEALE
Lullington NETHERSEALE

0   5   10 miles
0 5 10 15 20 km

111

Hereford and Worcester

THE counties of Herefordshire and Worcestershire were united in the 1974. Just under half the ecclesiastical parishes have churches with rings of four or more bells. The great majority have six bells or fewer, but the more urbanized section (the former Worcestershire) has four rings of twelve, two of them in the county town. The cathedral received a ring of twelve, cast by Taylors, to replace a 200-year old ring of eight in 1869, and these were replaced by the same foundry in 1928; All Saints nearby had an eighteenth-century ring of ten from the Rudhall foundry in Gloucester (six installed in 1692, two added in 1750 and another two in 1752) which was augmented to twelve in 1977. Evesham's twelve, in a detached bell tower (in a churchyard containing two churches, part of a third, plus the remains of a great abbey), were cast in 1951 by Taylors; the bells replaced a ten created in 1910 when two trebles were added to Rudhall's 1741 ring of seven, which had been cast to accompany the existing tenor bell.

Hereford Cathedral had a ring of ten bells by 1698. The inventory of all churches carried out for King Edward VI in 1552 records eight bells there, of which probably six were a ring as we understand the term. Three of them still hung in the central tower a century later. There were nine bells by 1697, when Abraham Rudhall was given the contract to provide a ring of ten. Six new bells were cast, but four old ones (dating from 1420, 1350, 1480 and 1500) were retained as the 5th, 6th, 9th and tenor. Two of Rudhall's bells were later recast (the 8th and the treble), as was the 1420 bell in 1865. The tenor bell, weighing nearly 34 cwt., is the largest surviving medieval tenor, having been cast (probably by Thomas Gefferies) in Bristol between 1480 and 1500. The ninth was also cast in Bristol, by William Warwick – whom some believe was also the donor.

River transport was a favoured way of moving bells before the nineteenth century. Hereford is on the River Wye, which meets the Severn at Chepstow, some miles downstream of Gloucester, so it is not surprising that Abraham Rudhall of Gloucester secured the contract for the cathedral's new ring of ten. Indeed, the Rudhall foundry placed a large number of bells in Herefordshire between 1689 (when a ring of five was provided for Eastnor, of which only the tenor survives) and 1829 (the third bell for Holme Lacy, an eight by 1709). Many of these bells were in complete sets, and a catalogue produced by John Rudhall in 1804 lists three rings of eight, 23 of six, 16 of five and three of four, as well as 34 other bells. This list is reproduced in Frederick Sharpe's *The Church Bells of Herefordshire*, and he suggests that the Rudhalls cast at least 389 bells for churches there. Although a remote part of rural England, there is evidence of change-ringers in 1699 at Leominster, and a peal was recorded in 1738 at Ross on Wye (an eight in 1695, five years after Ledbury).

Whereas rings of bells can be found in most parts of Herefordshire, with the lightest densities to the north of Leominster (an eight in 1755) and west of the A49, Worcestershire's distribution is much more uneven, with the greatest concentration in the south of the former county. There are many Rudhall bells: the 1804 listing identifies five complete rings of eight, 15 of six and ten of five as well as many other contributions of 'mixed' rings. Not included, however, is the village of Martley, north-west of Worcester, whose church of S Peter contains the oldest complete ring of six bells cast by Richard Keene of Woodstock in 1673, in a field near to the church according to local belief, but chip-tuned in 1914 and retuned in 1983.

Among the many rings provided by the Rudhall foundry for a Worcestershire church was the full ring of eight (tenor 25½ cwt.) at Pershore Abbey. The abbey is renowned among ringers not so much for the fine tone of its bells as for the nature of the ringing-room. To avoid blocking off the fine windows in the tower when the abbey was restored in the 1860s, the architect decided not to allow a normal ringing-room to be built. Instead, he provided a 'cage' – a wrought-iron 'walled' platform that is fixed to a pair of oak cross beams and 'sits' in the middle of the tower. Access to this, from inside the roof of the nave, is via an open iron spiral staircase and a 'bridge' across one of the 16-inch wide beams. All is enclosed with wire mesh, but many ringers feel uneasy there. They prefer the Parish Centre next to the abbey: formerly the Church of S Andrew, with a Rudhall six cast in 1715, this was made redundant in the 1970s; the bells were augmented to eight in 1981.

Local Worcestershire foundries supplied several early rings. John Martin of Worcester provided rings of five for Clifton upon Terne in 1668 (augmented to six in 1914) and Crowle in 1667 (augmented to eight in 1897); Grafton Flyford acquired a six in 1676, and though one was 'lost' around 1814 all the others survive. Clarke and Bushell of Evesham provided several rings between 1703 and 1711, including the present back six at Badsey, and Richard Sanders of Bromsgrove produced, among others, rings of six for Upton Snodsbury (1703) and Eckington (1721), as well as the eight for Worcester S Helen (1706; no longer there).

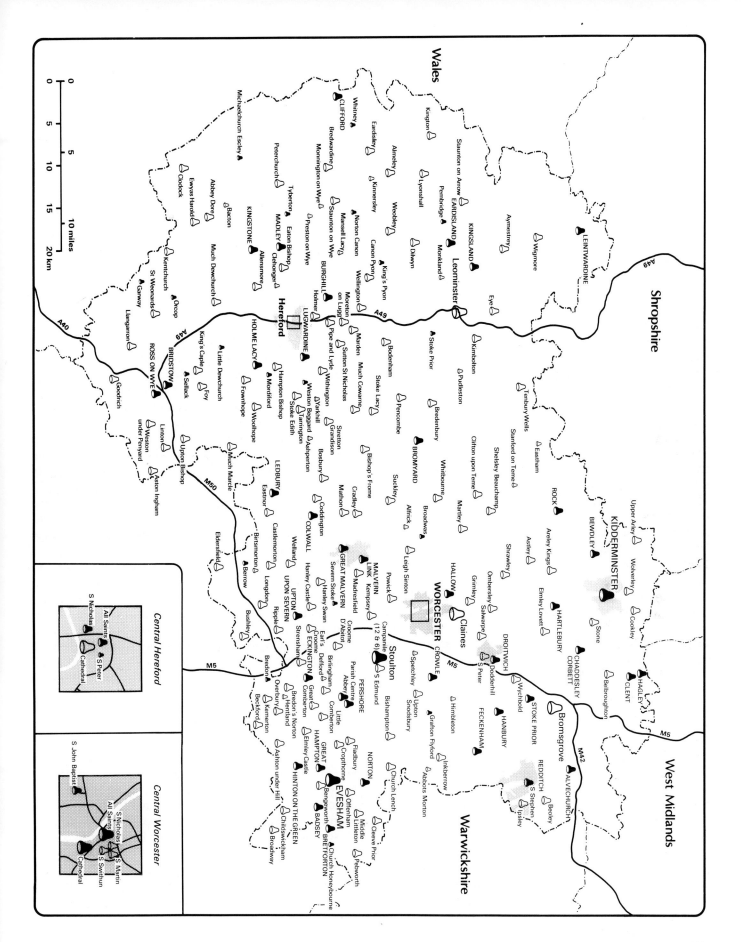

Wales

Shropshire

West Midlands

Warwickshire

Central Hereford

S Nicholas
All Saints
S Peter
Cathedral

Central Worcester

S John Baptist
S Nicholas
All Saints
S Martin
S Swithun
Cathedral

Michaelchurch Escley
Clifford
Whitney
Kington
Eardisley
Almeley
Kinnersley
Staunton on Arrow
Pembridge
EARDISLAND
Monkland
KINGSLAND
Lyonshall
Weobley
Bredwardine
Monnington on Wye
Peterchurch
Tyberton
Staunton on Wye
Mansell Lacy
Norton Canon
Canon Pyon
King's Pyon
Dilwyn
Aymestrey
Wigmore
LEINTWARDINE
Leominster
A49
Eye
Kimbolton
Diddock
Ewyas Harold
Bacton
Abbey Dore
Much Dewchurch
Kentchurch
St Weonards
Garway
Llangarron
Kingstone
Allensmore
Clehonger
Eaton Bishop
MADLEY
Preston on Wye
BURGHILL
Holmer
Wellington
Moreton on Lugg
Hereford
A49
LUGWARDINE
Pipe and Lyde
Sutton St Nicholas
Marden
Much Cowarne
Bodenham
Stoke Prior
Stoke Lacy
Pencombe
Pudleston
Tenbury Wells
Eastham
Stanford on Teme
Clifton upon Teme
Shelsley Beauchamp
Martley
ROCK
BEWDLEY
KIDDERMINSTER
Upper Arley
Wolverley
Cookley
Areley Kings
Astley
Shrawley
Ombersley
Grimley
Elmley Lovett
HARTLEBURY
Stone
CHADDESLEY CORBETT
Belbroughton
CLENT
HAGLEY
A49
Goodrich
A40
A49
ROSS ON WYE
BRIDSTOW
Sellack
Foy
King's Caple
Little Dewchurch
Fownhope
Woolhope
HOLME LACY
Mordiford
Hampton Bishop
Yarkhill
Weston Beggard
Stoke Edith
Tarrington
Ashperton
Stretton Grandison
Bosbury
Bishop's Frome
Cradley
Mathon
Suckley
Alfrick
Broadwas
Whitbourne
BROMYARD
Bredenbury
Linton
Weston under Penyard
Aston Ingham
Upton Bishop
M50
Much Marcle
Eastnor
Coddington
COLWALL
LEDBURY
Eldersfield
Birtsmorton
Castlemorton
Longdon
Berrow
Welland
Hanley Castle
UPTON UPON SEVERN
Ripple
Bushley
Hanley Swan
Severn Stoke
GREAT MALVERN
MALVERN LINK
Madresfield
Kempsey
Powick
Leigh Sinton
HALLOW
WORCESTER
Claines
CROWLE
M5
DROITWICH
S Peter
Dodderhill
Wychbold
HANBURY
FECKENHAM
STOKE PRIOR
Bromsgrove
M42
HINTON ON THE GREEN
Broadway
Campanile (12 & 6)
Stoulton
Bishampton
Spetchley
Upton Snodsbury
Himbleton
Grafton Flyford
Abbots Morton
Church Lench
Inkberrow
REDDITCH
S Stephen
Ipsley
Beoley
ALVECHURCH
Croome D'Abitot
Earl's Croome
Defford
ECKINGTON
Birlingham
Great Comberton
Little Comberton
PERSHORE
Parish Centre
Abbey
S Edmund
S Nicholas
Strensham
Bredon
Overbury
Bredon's Norton
Kemerton
Beckford
Ashton under Hill
Childswickham
Church Honeybourne
Pebworth
Cleeve Prior
Middle Littleton
Offenham
NORTON
Cropthorne
Fladbury
GREAT HAMPTON
Elmley Castle
EVESHAM
Bengeworth
BRETFORTON
BADSEY

Scale: 0 5 10 15 20 km / 0 5 10 miles

Leicestershire

THE full history of the developing sciences of bell-founding and bell-hanging, and of the art of change-ringing, will surely include many references to Leicestershire. Some of the earliest records of bellfounders refer to its county town – where Stephen Belyetere, John de Stafford, John Hose and Thomas de Melton all cast bells in the fourteenth century – and there were foundries open for part at least of each of the next four centuries. The centre of activity moved to Loughborough in 1839, when John Taylor established the foundry that still bears his name.

Modern Leicestershire incorporates the formerly independent county of Rutland. Its densely occupied map, where well over half of the ecclesiastical parishes have churches with rings of bells, is very much a product of the last century. Thomas North's survey of the county of Leicestershire (published as *The Church Bells of Leicestershire* in 1876) showed that, of 283 churches, only 125 had rings of four or more bells; of those most comprised either four or five only (48 each) and there were 18 rings of six, nine of eight and two of ten (both in Leicester itself). There have been many augmentations since, because the figures for the new county in 1988 were: three of twelve; five of ten; 52 of eight; 72 of six; 31 of five; and 23 of four. (Rutland in 1880 – according to North's *The Church Bells of Rutland* – had two rings of eight, four of six, ten of five and ten of four; 88 years later the figures were two, 13, ten and eight.) Of those 48 rings of four in what was formerly Leicestershire, only 15 remain; eight have been upgraded to rings of five, 13 to rings of six and seven to rings of eight, while three rings of three have been augmented to four. Many fewer of the rings of three have been augmented, however, and 56 of the 82 listed by North have no more bells today than they did a hundred years ago.

Rings of eight bells or more were rarities 160 years ago in Leicestershire; most of them were in sizable settlements and had been in place for some time. Some of the oldest were in small villages, however: at Staunton Harold in the north-west, where North records that the eight was given by the local landowner, Sir Robert Shirley, in 1656, though this is doubted; at Church Langton, where a five was augmented in 1763; and at King's Norton nearby, where a ring of ten given to the new church by Squire Fortrey was completed in 1781, though two bells were considered unsatisfactory and later removed. These early rural provisions were the results of individual donations; towns such as Ashby-de-la-Zouch and Melton Mowbray did not get their rings of six augmented to eight until the early nineteenth century, both as a result of public subscriptions.

Two of Leicester's city-centre churches had rings of ten before the end of the eighteenth century. At S Martin's (now the cathedral) a ring of five was augmented to six in 1657, to eight in 1781, and to ten six years later: the front four were recast in 1854, and a new ring of twelve was installed in 1937. S Margaret's had a ring of eight in 1711 and of ten in 1738; it also achieved twelve – a new ring also cast by Taylor – before S Martin's, in 1921. Peals of Grandsire Triples was recorded at S Margarets (in a Norwich newspaper) as early as 1730 and 1731, and after the two trebles were donated (by the same Squire Fortrey who provided King's Norton's bells) peals of Caters were rung; on 25 February 1777 a peal of 10,080 Grandsire Caters was rung in seven hours and twelve minutes in the afternoon following an unsuccessful attempt, over 5,000 changes long, in the morning.

Other churches in Leicester were also provided with bells in the nineteenth century. The five at St Mary-de-Castro were augmented to eight in 1830 and rings of eight were donated to the new church of S Mark in 1872 by its founder, W. Perry-Henrick, and to S Saviour's in 1877. At the church of All Saints, the old ring of five was upgraded to six in 1948 and to eight in 1952; the new church of S John the Divine received a ring of eight in 1902, augmented to ten in 1928. Neither of these latter rings is now heard in its original setting, however: S John's bells form the core of the new (1987) ring of twelve at Peterborough Cathedral, and All Saints' bells ring in the village church of Sproxton; S Saviour's bells have been scrapped and S Mark's have been sent to Goulburn in New South Wales.

The two rings of twelve in Leicester were cast by the Loughborough foundry of John Taylor and Sons, as were the ten bells of Loughborough parish church. The coming of the foundry to Loughborough from Oxford and the full history of the family is told in the company's history published in 1987: Trevor S. Jennings, *Master of my Art: the Taylor Bellfoundries 1784–1987*. In 1899 a tower containing a light ring of eight bells, later augmented to ten, was constructed as part of the foundry. These have been made available to visitors for all sorts of ringing, and more peals have been recorded there (the 2,500th was achieved in 1987; most of those have been on the back eight) than at any other tower; they include the only successful attempt to ring the full extent of 40,320 changes of Plain Bob Major, which took place in July 1963, taking 17 hours and 58 minutes.

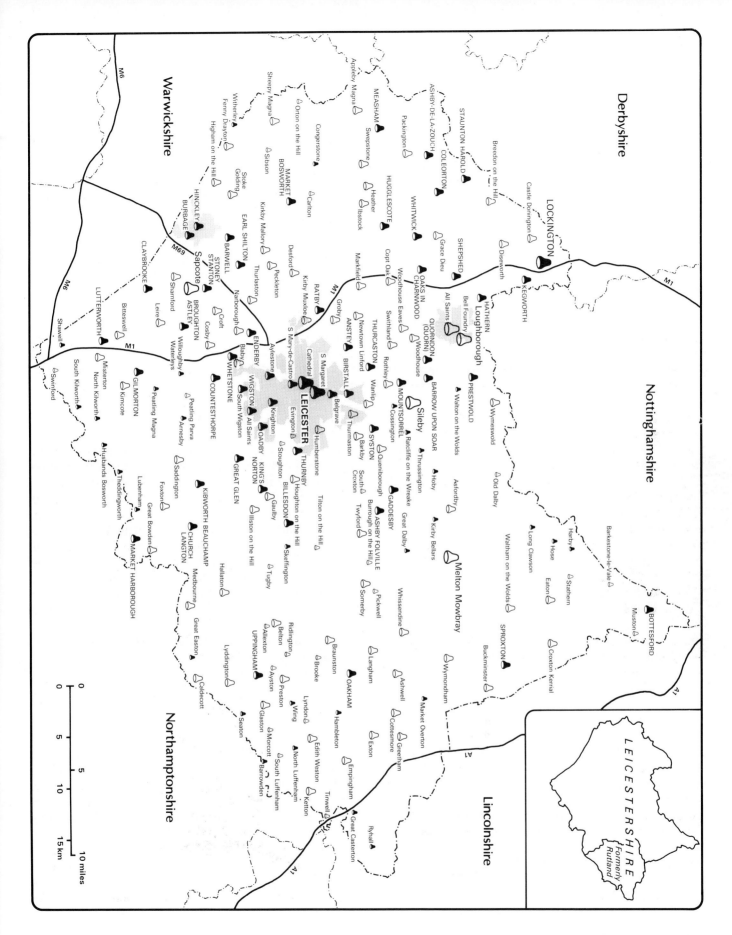

Derbyshire

Warwickshire

Nottinghamshire

Northamptonshire

Lincolnshire

M6

ASHBY-DE-LA-ZOUCH

STAUNTON HAROLD

LOCKINGTON

M1

MEASHAM

Appleby Magna
Sheepy Magna
Witherley
Fenny Drayton
Higham on the Hill
Orton on the Hill
Sibson
Congerstone
Stoke Golding
Kirkby Mallory

Packington
Swepstone
Carlton
Heather
Ibstock
HUGGLESCOTE
MARKET BOSWORTH
WHITWICK
Grace Dieu
SHEPSHED
Breedon on the Hill
Castle Donington
Diseworth
HATHERN
Loughborough
KEGWORTH
Bell Foundry
All Saints
QUORNDON (QUORN)

COLEORTON

HINCKLEY
BURBAGE
Sapcote
M69
EARL SHILTON
STONEY STANTON
BARWELL
BROUGHTON ASTLEY
CLAYBROOKE
M6
LUTTERWORTH
Shawell
Swinford
South Kilworth
North Kilworth
Misterton
GILMORTON
Kimcote
Peatling Magna
Arnesby
Peatling Parva
Saddington
Foxton
Lubenham
Great Bowden
MARKET HARBOROUGH
Theddingworth
Husbands Bosworth

Shamford
Leire
Bittesvell
Croft
Cosby
Willoughby Waterleys
COUNTESTHORPE
WHETSTONE
WIGSTON
South Wigston
All Saints
Knighton
Blaby
ENDERBY
Aylestone
Kirkby Muxloe
RATBY
Groby
Desford
Thurlaston
Peckleton
Narborough
Newtown Linford
ANSTEY
THURCASTON
Woodhouse Eaves
Woodhouse
OAKS IN CHARNWOOD
Copt Oak
Markfield
Swithland
Rothley
Cathedral
S Margaret
S Mary-de-Castro
LEICESTER
Belgrave
BIRSTALL
Wanlip
Evington
Humberstone
Thurmaston
THURNBY
Stoughton
Houghton on the Hill
KING'S NORTON
BILLESDON
OADBY
Gaulby
Skeffington
Tugby
KIBWORTH BEAUCHAMP
CHURCH LANGTON
Medbourne
Great Easton
Hallaton
GREAT GLEN
Illston on the Hill
Tilton on the Hill
Lyddington
Caldecott
Seaton
Great Casterton
Ryhall
Tinwell
UPPINGHAM
Ayston
Preston
Wing
Lyndon
Edith Weston
North Luffenham
South Luffenham
Ketton
Morcott
Glaston
Barrowden
Hambleton
Empingham
Ridlington
Belton
Alleston
Brooke
Braunston
Lyndon
OAKHAM
Langham
Ashwell
Cottesmore
Greetham
Market Overton
Exton
Whissendine
Pickwell
Somerby
Burrough on the Hill
ASHBY FOLVILLE
GADDESBY
Great Dalby
Kirby Bellars
Melton Mowbray
Waltham on the Wolds
Buckminster
SPROXTON
Croxton Kerrial
Long Clawson
Hose
Harby
Eaton
Stathern
Barkestone-le-Vale
Muston
BOTTESFORD
Wymondham
Old Dalby
Asfordby
Hoby
Ratcliffe on the Wreake
Thrussington
SYSTON
Barkby
South Croxton
Twyford
Queniborough
Cossington
MOUNTSORREL
Sileby
BARROW UPON SOAR
Walton on the Wolds
Wymeswold
PRESTWOLD

A1

A1

LEICESTERSHIRE
Formerly Rutland

0   0
5   5
10
15km
15
5
10
10 miles

115

Lincolnshire

THE county of Lincolnshire (now lacking the northern part, which became part of the new county of Humberside in 1974) is believed to have housed the first complete ring of bells (at Crowland Abbey), and for some years the cathedral in its county town boasted two rings. But it is not well provided with rings; many parts of the map are conspicuously empty of churches with four or more bells.

Parts of the county lie astride the oolitic limestone belt that has provided the raw material for many substantial town churches; villages at the foot of the west-facing scarp, along the springline, have churches with rings of bells – mainly of five and six. To the east are the low, chalky Lincolnshire Wolds, which carry only a light density of small settlements; rings of bells are few, and in the triangle joining the market towns of Horncastle, Louth and Market Rasen (about 29 km. between each pair) not a single village boasts even four bells in its church. Louth has a magnificent church, with a fine heavy ring of eight (tenor 31½ cwt.) installed in 1726, but the provision of those bells appears not to have influenced the nearby villagers to want bells too.

To the east and south of the wolds are the flat claylands of the coastal belt and the northern part of the East Anglian fens. These stoneless districts also include substantial 'bell-free' areas. Some are relatively recently settled; where there is a long history of small villages – as in the area around Boston – churches with rings are to be found.

Lincolnshire has long been a productive agricultural county, initially from the sheep raised on the wolds. The wealth obtained was concentrated in the county's major towns and ports, where it was invested, among other things, in the churches. None shows this more clearly than the south Lincolnshire town of Boston, where the famous 272-foot high tower (known as the Boston Stump) is a beacon visible for many miles – on land and sea. Today it contains a ring of ten, installed in 1932 to succeed the ring of eight hung there in 1785, itself successor to an earlier ring of eight; a peal of Triples was rung on them in 1738. Local donors were important here, as elsewhere: Caythorpe's ring of eight was presented in 1759, for example, the original ring of two having been augmented to six only 15 years earlier; Grantham augmented its six to eight in 1752, and achieved ten with the aid of money from the Duke of Rutland in 1775; and the local lord of the manor gave eight to Harmston in 1799.

Although many of those villages with rings of five and six today received their bells as long as 200 years

ago, it is unlikely that their relatively early purchases were linked to a much earlier development in the far south of the county. Crowland (or Croyland) Abbey is an ancient building at the heart of an isolated village close to the banks of the River Welland – near to an early meeting place with the Nene – a few miles north of Peterborough, in fen country that was undoubtedly very difficult to move through until the major drainage work of recent centuries. The first abbey was built there in 716, but it was burnt down in 930. A replacement was constructed, and seven bells were placed in its central tower. That abbey was burnt in 1091, when the tower fell and the bells were melted down. It was replaced by a third abbey – itself destroyed by fire in 1146 after being damaged in an earthquake 29 years previously – which had a 'humble belfry' containing only two bells, all that the monks could afford at the time. The fourth abbey was constructed in 1190, and part of it provides the village with its present parish church (dedicated to SS Guthlac and Bartholomew); it had two sets of bells, including a ring of four in a campanile that was destroyed at the time of the Dissolution. A ring of five was installed in the other tower in 1465; they were cast in London and carried to Crowland for a total cost of £160, met entirely by the abbot himself. Two of these were probably still in the western tower in 1783, but they were later recast; a third, cast later than 1465 but undated, remains as the tenor of the light six, in company with two seventeenth-century bells, two from the late eighteenth century and one dating from the twentieth century. Thus nothing remains of the fifteenth-century ring, let alone that of 900 years ago, and we can only wonder at the reasons for these early campanological innovations in such an inaccessible spot in medieval England.

Also in South Lincolnshire is the village of Surfleet, which has the second lightest ring of twelve in the world (tenor 12 cwt. 9 lbs.; the lightest is at Accrington). In 1898 Surfleet received a new vicar, Henry Law-James, who had learned to ring in Gloucester. He found an unringable five in the tower. One of the bells was recast, and a band formed; it rang its first peal on the last day of 1901. A treble was added in 1902. Eleven years later Law-James had two bells recast, and installed four new trebles in a new iron frame, at his own expense, in memory of his mother. The new ten saw many first peals in the method for the Lincoln Diocesan Guild (which Law-James was instrumental in founding in 1899). Two further trebles were added in his memory in 1932, the year of his death.

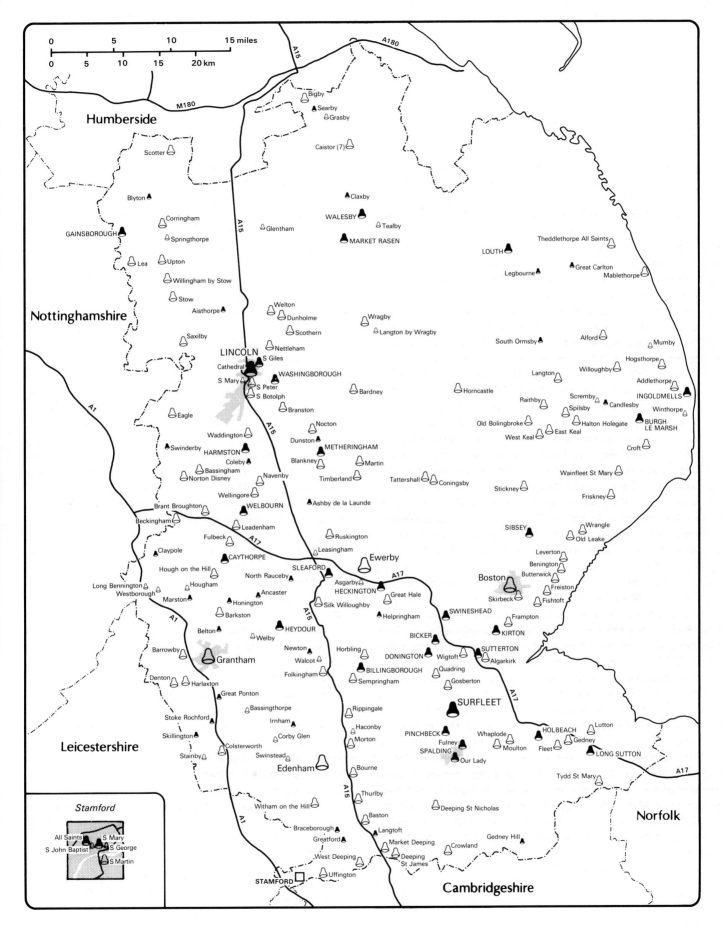

Humberside

Nottinghamshire

Leicestershire

Stamford

All Saints — S Mary
S John Baptist — S George
S Martin

STAMFORD

Cambridgeshire

Norfolk

Bigby
Searby
Grasby
Caistor (7)

Scotter

Claxby
WALESBY
Tealby
MARKET RASEN

Blyton

Corringham
Springthorpe
GAINSBOROUGH
Lea
Upton
Willingham by Stow
Stow
Aisthorpe

Glentham

Welton
Dunholme
Scothern

Wragby
Langton by Wragby

LOUTH
Theddlethorpe All Saints
Legbourne
Great Carlton
Mablethorpe

Saxilby

Nettleham
LINCOLN
S Giles
Cathedral
S Mary
S Peter
WASHINGBOROUGH
S Botolph
Branston

Bardney

Horncastle

South Ormsby
Alford
Mumby
Hogsthorpe
Langton
Willoughby
Addlethorpe
Raithby
Scremby
Spilsby
Candlesby
Winthorpe
INGOLDMELLS
Old Bolingbroke
Halton Holegate
BURGH LE MARSH
West Keal
East Keal
Croft

Eagle
Waddington
Swinderby
HARMSTON
Coleby
Bassingham
Norton Disney
Navenby
Wellingore
WELBOURN
Leadenham
Brant Broughton
Beckingham
Fulbeck
Claypole
CAYTHORPE
Hough on the Hill
North Rauceby
Long Bennington
Westborough
Hougham
Marston
Ancaster
Honington
Barkston
Belton
Welby
HEYDOUR
Barrowby
Grantham
Newton
Walcot
Denton
Harlaxton
Folkingham
Great Ponton
Bassingthorpe
Irnham
Stoke Rochford
Corby Glen
Skillington
Colsterworth
Stainby
Swinstead
Edenham

Nocton
Dunston
METHERINGHAM
Blankney
Martin
Timberland
Tattershall
Coningsby
Stickney
Ashby de la Launde
Ruskington
Leasingham
Ewerby
SLEAFORD
Asgarby
HECKINGTON
Great Hale
Silk Willoughby
Helpringham
SWINESHEAD
BICKER
DONINGTON
Wigtoft
SUTTERTON
Algarkirk
Frampton
KIRTON
Horbling
Sempringham
BILLINGBOROUGH
Quadring
Gosberton
Rippingale
Haconby
Morton
SURFLEET
PINCHBECK
Whaplode
HOLBEACH
Lutton
Fulney
Moulton
Gedney
SPALDING
Fleet
LONG SUTTON
Our Lady
Tydd St Mary
A17
Bourne
Thurlby
Witham on the Hill
Deeping St Nicholas
Gedney Hill
Baston
Langtoft
Crowland
Braceborough
Greatford
Market Deeping
West Deeping
Deeping St James
Uffington

Wainfleet St Mary
Friskney
SIBSEY
Wrangle
Old Leake
Leverton
Benington
Butterwick
Boston
Freiston
Skirbeck
Fishtoft

117

Norfolk

NORFOLK comes fourth among the counties of England in terms of the number of churches with rings of bells. But the map of the county does not suggest a high density, for only about one-third of all parish churches contain a ring. Many of those lacking four or more bells are in the small parishes that are typical of this rural county. Only in the larger parishes was a ring of bells the norm, and even so the proportion with five or more compares unfavourably with the adjacent counties of Suffolk and Cambridgeshire.

Small parishes usually lack sufficient resources for the building of large and well-furnished churches, even in relatively rich agricultural areas such as parts of Norfolk. But the towns in these areas may be very wealthy from the profits of trade, and this is frequently reflected in the churches. This is certainly the case in Norfolk, where there are many substantial town churches, many having had rings of eight or more bells for as many as 200 years. When he reported his survey of *The Church Bells of Norfolk* (Norwich, 1874), John L'Estrange listed 20 rings of eight, three of ten and one of twelve. Of those 24, all but three had been installed in the eighteenth century or earlier; the eight at Aylsham (a substantial market town of 2,500 inhabitants in 1900), for example, was installed in 1700 and augmented to ten in 1735. Since L'Estrange's survey there have been relatively few augmentations to create new rings of eight or more; only 15 have been identified, including the two in the adjacent settlements of Pulham St Mary and Pulham Market. Norfolk is one of the few counties where the number of rings of eight or more bells has not more than doubled during the twentieth century. One of the few recent augmentations was the upgrading of the ten at S Nicholas's, Great Yarmouth, the largest parish church in England, to twelve. These were lost through enemy action in the Second World War and replaced in 1958.

However, there are few rings of four, and the county is dominated by rings of five and six. Most of them are very old. L'Estrange recorded 98 rings of five in 1874, of which 28 were in place before 1700 and a further 53 before 1800; only 17 were either installed or augmented to five in the nineteenth century. Many were cast by local founders, including itinerants; there is a long list of known bellfounders practising in Norwich from the fourteenth to the eighteenth centuries, and another for King's Lynn for the fourteenth, fifteenth and sixteenth centuries. The small town of Downham Market had a very active foundry between the 1790s and the 1830s.

Why, then, do so few Norfolk churches have rings of bells, given that the practice of providing five or more was established so early and that local bellfounders were available to provide the needed instruments? One major reason is evidently the small size of so many Norfolk parishes. Another is the nature of many of the churches there. Much of the county's geology provides no solid building materials, and flint is commonly used. The typical Norfolk village church has a round flint tower, in many cases with only a small diameter. It is difficult to fit more than two or three bells into most of these, many of which in any case could not withstand the physical forces pressing outwards on the walls from several rotating bells. Thus many parts of northern Norfolk, where such architecture is common, are almost empty of rings of bells; southern villages are much more likely to have bells than their northern counterparts.

The gem of Norfolk ecclesiastical architecture is, of course, the massive cathedral in the county town, cocooned from the noise of the busy commercial centre in its large close. But Norwich Cathedral has never had a ring of bells, and in the tower beneath the glorious spire all one finds is a set of five on which the clock chimes are mechanically operated. Elsewhere in the city, however, the richness of the medieval trade was expressed in a large number of churches, many of which were provided with rings of bells: unfortunately several of them are currently unringable.

The city of Norwich has a central place in the history of bell-ringing because many early peals were rung there, notably the first recorded. This was rung on 2 May 1715 at the market-place church of S Peter Mancroft, which has had eight bells since 1672. The eight men took three hours and 18 minutes to ring the first-ever recorded true peal – 5,040 changes of Plain Bob Triples; two earlier peals had been rung, but in both cases the composition was later proved false. Their society, the Norwich Scholars, later rang the first-ever peals of Grandsire (1718) and Stedman (1731) Triples, the latter after much competition with the band at the nearby church of S Michael, Coslany – this latter group broke away from the Mancroft ringers in 1730. Many other early peals were rung at Mancroft (including Grandsire Cinques in 1775 and Norwich Court Bob Maximus in 1817, both peals taking just over four hours), Coslany and the other city-centre churches of S Giles (eight bells from 1730) and S Andrew (eight from 1704; ten from 1825). Peals at S Andrew were particularly meritorious because the ropes fell in the following order around the circle: 1, 3, 2, 7, 10, 5, 4, 6, 9, 8; yet the first-ever peal of London Surprise Major was rung on the bells in November 1835.

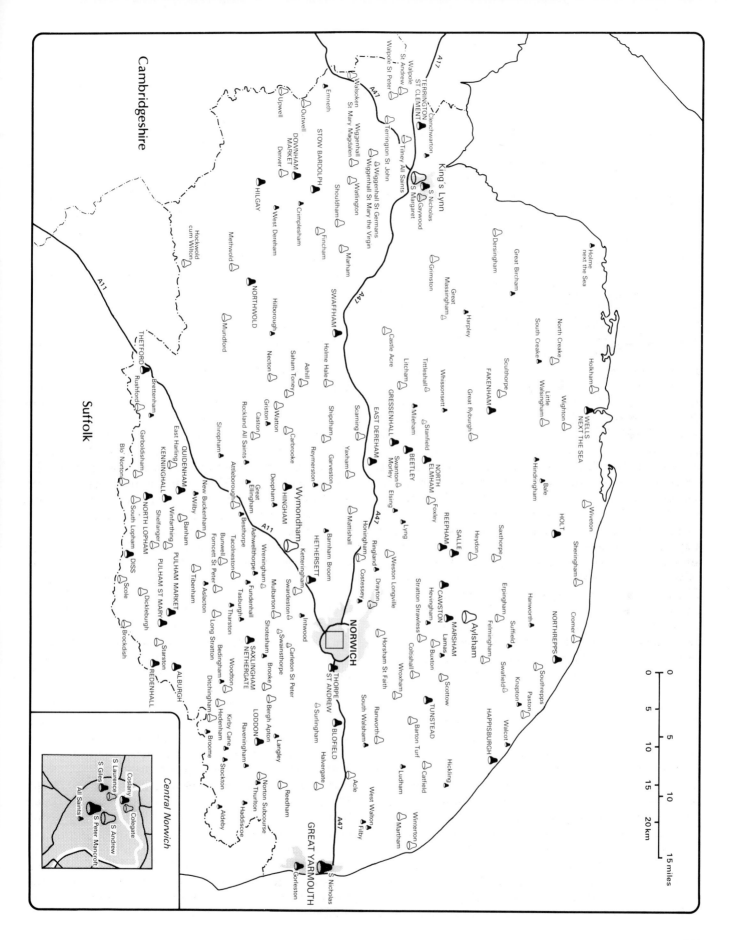

Cambridgeshire

Suffolk

Central Norwich

King's Lynn

NORWICH

GREAT YARMOUTH

Walpole St Andrew
Walpole St Peter
St Clenchwarton
Walsoken
Emneth
Upwell
Outwell
Wiggenhall St Mary Magdalen
Terrington St John
Tilney All Saints
Wiggenhall St Germans
Wiggenhall St Mary the Virgin
TERRINGTON ST CLEMENT
S Nicholas
Gaywood
Denver
DOWNHAM MARKET
STOW BARDOLPH
Shouldham
Watlington
Marham
Fincham
HILGAY
West Dereham
Crimplesham
Methwold
Hockwold cum Wilton
Hilborough
NORTHWOLD
Mundford
SWAFFHAM
Grimston
Great Massingham
Harpley
Castle Acre
Litcham
Tittleshall
Whissonsett
Great Ryburgh
Dersingham
Great Bircham
North Creake
South Creake
Little Walsingham
Wighton
Scultthorpe
FAKENHAM
Holme next the Sea
Holkham
WELLS NEXT THE SEA
Hindringham
Bale
Wiveton
Sheringham
Cromer
NORTHREPPS
Southrepps
Paston
Walcott
Happisburgh
Winterton
Martham
West Walton
Filby
Acle
Ludham
Catfield
Hickling
Barton Turf
TUNSTEAD
Scottow
Buxton
Lamas
Coltishall
Wroxham
Horsham St Faith
South Walsham
Ranworth
Swafield
Knapton
Felmingham
Suffield
Erpingham
Hanworth
HOLT
Heydon
Saxthorpe
SALLE
REEPHAM
Foxley
Lyng
Weston Longville
Drayton
Costessey
Hevingham
CAWSTON
MARSHAM
Aylsham
Thetford
Brettenham
Rushford
Garboldisham
Blo Norton
South Lopham
NORTH LOPHAM
KENNINGHALL
Shelfanger
Winfarthing
Banham
Wilby
New Buckenham
East Harling
QUIDENHAM
DISS
Scole
Dickleburgh
PULHAM MARKET
PULHAM ST MARY
Starston
REDENHALL
ALBURGH
Tibenham
Aslacton
Great Ellingham
Attleborough
Besthorpe
Rockland All Saints
Caston
Griston
Watton
Carbrooke
Deopham
HINGHAM
Wymondham
HETHERSETT
Kelveringham
Barnham Broom
Mattishall
Ringland
Honingham
Stratton Strawless
Ashill
Saham Toney
Necton
Reymerston
Garveston
Yaxham
Shipdham
Holme Hale
Scarning
EAST DEREHAM
Swanton Morley
Elsing
Mileham
Stanfield
BEETLEY
NORTH ELMHAM
GRESSENHALL
Shotesham
Swainsthorpe
Brooke
Bergh Apton
Langley
SAXLINGHAM NETHERGATE
LODDON
Kirby Cane
Raveningham
Stockton
Norton Subcourse
Thurlton
Haddiscoe
Aldeby
Broome
Ditchingham
Hedenham
Woodton
Bedingham
Tasburgh
Tharston
Long Stratton
Forncett St Peter
Bunwell
Tacolneston
Ashwellthorpe
Wreningham
Fundenhall
Mulbarton
Swardeston
Intwood
Carleton St Peter
Surlingham
Halvergate
Reedham
THORPE ST ANDREW
BLOFIELD
Costessey
Horsham St Faith
Gorleston
S Nicholas

Central Norwich
S Laurence
S Giles
All Saints
Costany
Colegate
S Andrew
S Peter Mancroft

0   5   10   15   20 km
0   5   10   15 miles

119

Northamptonshire

ONE cannot travel more than two or three miles in most of Northamptonshire without coming to a village where the parish church has at least four bells. The county can truly be described as the 'heart of this ringing isle', and it was an early heart of change-ringing in the eighteenth century, with peals on eight at Kettering as early as 1730 and the first-ever five-bell peal at East Haddon in 1756.

The county is very largely a rural one, despite some industrial impact in the Ise and Nene Valleys in the nineteenth century and at Corby and Northampton in the twentieth. But it sits directly astride the limestone belt: in parts the building stone is the typical silver colour, elsewhere it is deep brown, because of the iron content. There is thus plentiful building material, which has been used extensively in the erection of churches, many of which have spires.

A number of those churches have long contained rings of bells. North's late nineteenth-century survey lists 309 churches in all (including the small number in the Soke of Peterborough), of which only 65 had but one bell or two. There were 39 rings of three, 50 of four, 107 of five, 39 of six and nine of eight (see *The Church Bells of Northamptonshire*, 1878), indicating a very high proportion of rural churches with bells on which change-ringing could be practised. For a variety of reasons, the installation of a set of four or more bells became much more commonplace in Northamptonshire early in the development of ringing than elsewhere. Of the 51 rings of four in North's list, for example, there were four bells in at least 28 of the towers by 1700 and in another 19 by 1800. With the rings of five, there were more recent installations: nevertheless, of the 99 that have been dated from the list, 33 (or a predecessor ring of five) were in place by 1700 and a further 37 by 1800, so again the great majority were a century old. The same was true of the rings of six: of the 39, ten were in place by 1700 and a further 23 by 1800; only four were nineteenth-century installations/augmentations.

In part, the demand for rings of bells by Northamptonshire parishes in the 1600s and 1700s was probably stimulated by the activities of local bellfounders and the desire of parishioners to acquire similar (if not better) rings to those of their neighbours. The county has had several major main foundries. The Bagleys were active from 1631 to 1782, originally at Chacombe (1687–1703) but later at Ecton. Henry Penn, who learnt the trade from Henry Bagley at Ecton, was active from 1703 to 1792, being based at Peterborough from 1708. Finally, the Eayre family operated a foundry at Kettering from 1710; a branch was established at St

Neots in 1735, and all work transferred to there from Kettering in 1762.

This early provision of rings of five and six in the rural churches was not matched by a large number of rings of eight or more. At the time of North's survey the county had only eight rings of eight – plus the eight at S John the Baptist, Peterborough. Of those eight rings, all but one (Aynho, augmented from six in 1870) were in place by 1800. Three were in the county town itself: the six bells at All Saints were replaced by an eight, cast in London by Chapman and Mears, in 1782; in the next year a public subscription enabled the six at S Giles to be replaced by a new eight, cast at St Neots by Edward Arnold, a predecessor of Robert Taylor of that town. S Peter's church received its eight 50 years earlier, when Abraham Rudhall replaced the earlier ring of four. Elsewhere, Oundle's six were increased to eight in 1780, as were Kings Sutton's in 1793. At the latter, the trebles were donated by Henry Smyth of nearby Charlton who, according to North, 'was passionately fond of, and practised, as well as patronised, bell-ringing'. By then, two of the county's main towns already had rings of eight: Kettering's five were replaced by Richard Sanders of Bromsgrove in 1714 (they were augmented to ten in 1921 and twelve in 1979) and Daventry's five were superseded in 1738.

Several of the towns of Northamptonshire had rings of eight early on, therefore, but it was only in the late nineteenth and early twentieth centuries that there were augmentations to add to that early number. Two were in Northampton, where the six at Holy Sepulchre was augmented to eight in 1878, and an eight was placed in the new church of S Edmund in 1884; less than a century later the church was made redundant, and the bells formed part of the new ring for Wellington Cathedral in New Zealand. Many of the augmentations to eight were in the new, small industrial towns to the north and east of Northampton, whose prosperity and growth in the late nineteenth century was based on the boot and shoe industry; they form a line from Desborough (1923) and Rothwell (1906), through Burton Latimer (1920), Finedon (1897), Titchmarsh (1885), Thrapston (1897) and Irthlingborough (1893), to Wellingborough (1884) and Irchester (1930), Rushden (1953), Higham Ferrers (1892) and Raunds (1898).

Augmentations to eight (and also to ten, at Daventry, 1965, Northampton S Giles, 1894, and Moulton, 1973) were but a part of a great deal of late nineteenth- and twentieth-century activity in the county. Comparison of figures for 1878 and 1982 show that in just over 100

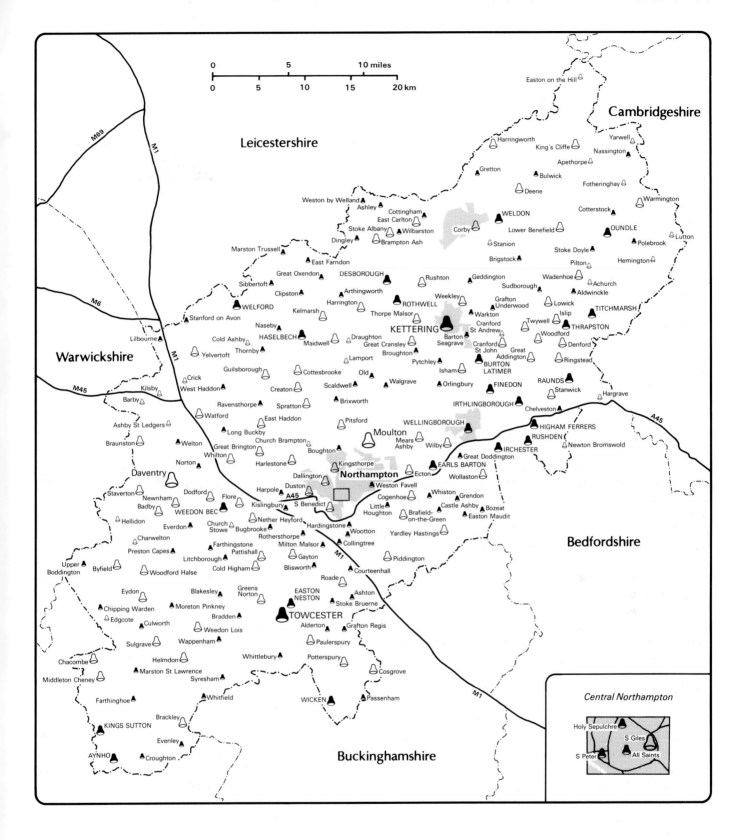

years three rings of three were augmented to four, five to six and four to eight; 17 rings of four were increased to five, nine to six and one to eight; 25 rings of five were augmented to six and seven to eight; and nine rings of six were augmented to eight. The solid base created in the seventeenth and eighteenth centuries has been built upon to create what is undoubtedly the highest density of rings of bells in rural England, and it remains the 'county of 5s', the only one to have more rings of five than of six.

Nottinghamshire

THE county of Nottinghamshire is one of marked contrast between the urban-industrial landscapes typical of so much of northern England and the rich agricultural vistas of the East Midlands. The map of rings of bells in the county illustrates this, with a clear contrast between the agricultural south (incorporating parts of the Vale of Belvoir) and east and the industrial north and west. But there is more to it than that, for the largest 'hole' in the county map (to the east of Mansfield) includes not only the relatively empty areas of Sherwood Forest but also the rich estates of the Dukeries, where only three of the settlements – Blidworth, Harworth and Edwinstowe (all to become mining villages in the 1920s) – have churches with rings of bells.

The county town of Nottingham is well provided with bells, with a ring of eight and two rings of twelve in the city centre and several of eight in the suburbs; the city was an early centre of bellfounding, with the Oldfields, William Noone and the Hedderley family all active in the medieval period. Of the two rings of twelve, the oldest is at S Peter's, where the bells were augmented to eight in 1672 by the Society of Northern Youths (their successors, the Society of Sherwood Youths, paid for the recasting of two trebles in 1771); two trebles were added in 1965 to the ring of ten created in 1919. Sixteen years later, the older ring of ten at nearby S Mary's was also augmented to twelve, with trebles cast in the Netherlands; nine of the other ten bells (originally cast in 1761) were recast in 1935, but the present eleventh – cast in 1595 by the local founder Henry Oldfield – was retained. There is one other ring of twelve in the county, in the minster at Southwell, a small country town just west of Newark. For many years this was a somewhat 'notorious' tower, for the eight bells (installed by Rudhall in 1721) were rung from a gallery around the central tower, with the ringers protected from falling the 70 feet into the minster by a wooden balcony topped by wire netting. Further, the bells were hung anticlockwise, and the 'circle' was very large, with two ropes on each side of the 40-foot square tower. In 1962 the gallery was removed when the county acquired its first ring of twelve, thanks to the generosity of a local donor: the new twelve is also hung anticlockwise, however, so Southwell Minster remains unique.

The growth of Nottingham, as with that of many other cities, has encompassed formerly separate, smaller settlements, whose parish churches now serve parts of the growing suburbs. West Bridgford, across the Trent Bridge, is an example of this: until 1956 its parish church of S Giles had only three bells, but these were then replaced by a new eight. Radcliffe on Trent is a little further out, and can perhaps be better described as a suburban village. Its church was enlarged and rebuilt in 1879, and a ring of six was installed seven years later (the old church had three); these were augmented to eight in 1947. But it is not only the big cities that expand and take over once independent villages. Balderton has now been engulfed by Newark, for example. Its village church obtained a ring of five in 1842. A six was added in 1900, being hung on a separate frame above the original bells: it was taken down and stored in the ringing-room in 1930. All six were rehung in 1951, and two further trebles were added eleven years later.

The more rural areas of the county, and especially that to the north-east of the A1, are characterized by rings of four, five and six in the village churches. Some are old buildings, such as that at Edwinstowe in the heart of Sherwood Forest: here, as in so much of rural England, a full ring of bells is relatively recent, however – six replacing three in 1889. At Selston, on the Derbyshire border, too, the ancient church had only three bells until 1905, when a ring of six was provided as part of a restoration programme. The old church at Ossington was destroyed when a wealthy Yorkshire textile merchant bought the local estate in 1768: the new Georgian church received a ring of six (incorporating one older bell) in 1784.

There is no published list of the bells of all Nottinghamshire churches, but the partial details provided by Phillimore (in *The Reliquary*) suggest that few villages had four or more bells before 1875. This was not the case with the towns, however – of which there are relatively few: both Newark and Retford have rings of ten for example. Newark obtained a Rudhall eight in 1713, which was replaced by the Taylor ten in 1842. That at S Swithin's, East Retford, was installed in 1890, augmenting a ring of eight provided by the Town Council in 1835 (which, in turn, replaced a 1771 ring of six). The mining towns in the west of the county are more recent in their growth and acquisition of bells, however. At Kirkby in Ashfield a treble and tenor were added to a ring of three in 1927 to produce a five, which was augmented to six in 1973, and at Hucknall the ring of three was replaced by a new eight (presented by a single donor) only in 1958. At nearby Eastwood, a ring of eight was installed in 1904 to replace an 1858 steel ring of six; the bells hang in the traditional tower of a church otherwise destroyed by fire in 1963, which was replaced by a modern, low, brick building.

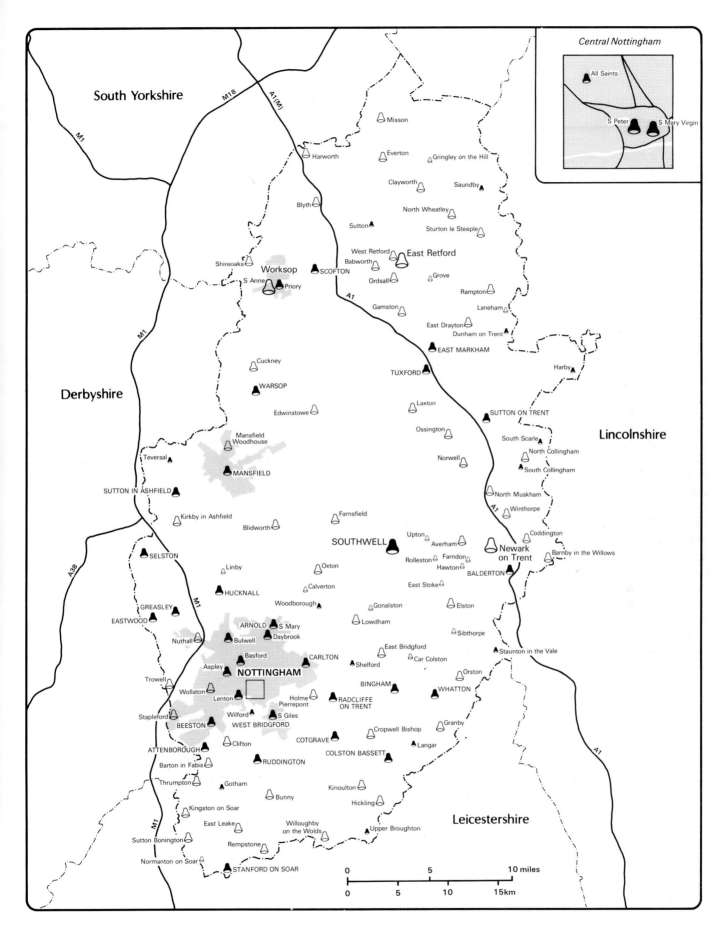

Central Nottingham

All Saints

S Peter · S Mary Virgin

South Yorkshire

Derbyshire

Lincolnshire

Leicestershire

Misson
Everton
Gringley on the Hill
Harworth
Clayworth
Saundby
North Wheatley
Blyth
Sutton
Sturton le Steeple
West Retford
East Retford
Shireoaks
Babworth
Worksop
SCOFTON
Grove
S Anne
Priory
Ordsall
Rampton
Laneham
Gamston
Cuckney
East Drayton
Dunham on Trent
WARSOP
EAST MARKHAM
Harby
TUXFORD
Edwinstowe
Laxton
SUTTON ON TRENT
Mansfield
Woodhouse
Ossington
South Scarle
Teversal
North Collingham
MANSFIELD
Norwell
South Collingham
SUTTON IN ASHFIELD
North Muskham
Kirkby in Ashfield
Farnsfield
Winthorpe
Blidworth
Upton
Coddington
SOUTHWELL
Averham
Newark
on Trent
SELSTON
Linby
Oxton
Rolleston
Farndon
Barnby in the Willows
Hawton
HUCKNALL
Calverton
BALDERTON
GREASLEY
Woodborough
East Stoke
EASTWOOD
Gonalston
Elston
Nuthall
ARNOLD
S Mary
Lowdham
Sibthorpe
Aspley
Bulwell
Daybrook
East Bridgford
Staunton in the Vale
Basford
CARLTON
Shelford
Car Colston
Orston
Trowell
NOTTINGHAM
BINGHAM
WHATTON
Wollaton
Lenton
Holme
Pierrepont
RADCLIFFE
ON TRENT
Stapleford
Wilford
S Giles
Granby
BEESTON
WEST BRIDGFORD
COTGRAVE
Cropwell Bishop
ATTENBOROUGH
Clifton
COLSTON BASSETT
Langar
Barton in Fabis
RUDDINGTON
Thrumpton
Gotham
Kinoulton
Bunny
Kingston on Soar
Hickling
East Leake
Willoughby
on the Wolds
Upper Broughton
Sutton Bonington
Rempstone
Normanton on Soar
STANFORD ON SOAR

0   5   10 miles
0   5   10   15km

123

Shropshire

SHROPSHIRE has many more rings in the east of the county than in the west, although there are 'empty' districts in the former – notably that due east of Ludlow. West of the A49 a majority of the parish churches in the valleys of the Severn and its tributaries above Shrewsbury lack a ring of four or more bells.

The Severn was for long the county's main thoroughfare, directing its links with the outside world towards the south. Not surprisingly, therefore, the Rudhalls' foundry at Gloucester was able to obtain a large number of contracts in Shropshire early on, the first in 1693 (Stanton Lacy) and the last in 1827 (Chetton). This is easily seen in a brief analysis of the rings listed in H. B. Walters's *The Church Bells of Shropshire* (1915). Of the 20 rings of eight or more bells then in existence, twelve had at least some bells cast in Gloucester, and there were complete sets cast for Whitchurch (1714), Oswestry (1717), Ellesmere (1727) and Ludlow (1732, replacing a 1688 ring; a peal was rung here in 1733, three years after one at Ellesmere); the ten at S Chad's, Shrewsbury, was also by Rudhall. Similarly, 27 of the 54 rings of six included some Rudhall bells, as did nine of the 15 rings of five; both rings of four listed by Walters were complete Rudhall installations.

The Rudhalls penetrated the whole of the county, though they were particularly successful in the southeast, and there is little evidence of other founders doing much trade in Shropshire before 1800. David Struckett's listing (in *A Dictionary of Campanology*) includes only three local foundries: Sir William Corvehill, of Much Wenlock, in the mid-sixteenth century; the Clibury family, which was active in Wellington throughout the seventeenth century and cast several local rings; and Thomas Roberts and Ellis Hughes, who worked in Shrewsbury between 1678 and 1700.

The pattern of rings of bells at the end of the nineteenth century was typical of rural England at that time, although there were slightly more rings of eight than was the case in some counties. It was the towns – most of them small market towns – that had the rings of eight, with very few exceptions: these were the villages of Condover just south of Shrewsbury (where the eight was installed in 1812 by John Briant of Hereford), High Ercall, north-east of Shrewsbury (also 1812; Rudhalls installed six in 1707), and Norton in Hales, in the far north-east of the county, which acquired an eight from Warners of London in 1867. Another village, Wistanstow, north-west of Ludlow, had its Rudhall six augmented to eight in 1903. Other small towns, such as Broseley, Clun, Madeley and Much Wenlock, had to wait until well into the twentieth century for their rings of six to be augmented to eight, however.

Few of the towns had rings of eight before the nineteenth century – only Ludlow, Oswestry, Ellesmere, Whitchurch and Shifnal (the last a Lester and Pack ring installed in 1770), plus Shrewsbury; Newport's was cast by Mears in 1812. But most achieved nineteenth-century augmentations – many of them to Rudhall rings of six. One of the exceptions was Coalbrookdale, the town adjacent to the early industrial centre of Ironbridge, where the church received its eight bells in 1852. Until those augmentations (many of them in the latter part of the century), the towns of Shropshire, like the villages, echoed to ringing on six bells only.

The main exception was the county town of Shrewsbury, which in a period of 20 years around the beginning of the nineteenth century had rings of eight and twelve installed, as well as another eight augmented to ten. The oldest bells in the town are the eight dating from 1673 at Holy Cross Abbey (some are by Rudhall), but they can be chimed only. The oldest ringable eight is at S Mary's, installed by Pack of London in 1775 and augmented to ten in 1811. The ring of twelve is at S Chad's, whose bells, cast by Mears of London, were installed in 1798 and were soon being put to use in peals by the local Union Society, formed in 1714; it rang at S Chad's predecessor (which had a ring of ten) and was responsible for the augmentation work at S Mary's. There was also a very active peal-ringing band at nearby Shifnal during this period – the Albion Society – which rang many of Triples and Major between 1770 (when the bells were installed) and the middle of the nineteenth century. The band frequently included Samuel Lawrence, reputedly one of the heaviest men in the country (it is claimed that he weighed 32 stone), who could not gain entry to some towers because of his girth; he rang peals in London (including the first ever of Stedman Cinques at S Martin-in-the-Fields), Ashton, Manchester and Birmingham, as well as in Shropshire.

Besides these two old city-centre churches, plus Holy Cross Abbey, Shrewsbury has had three other rings: two have now been removed – unfortunately so often the case with bells put in new churches in the nineteenth century, which today no longer have a congregation. A ring of eight was installed at S Alkmund's in 1812, and was soon being rung to peals by the Union Society. In the 1970s the Shropshire Association of Church Bellringers purchased these bells from

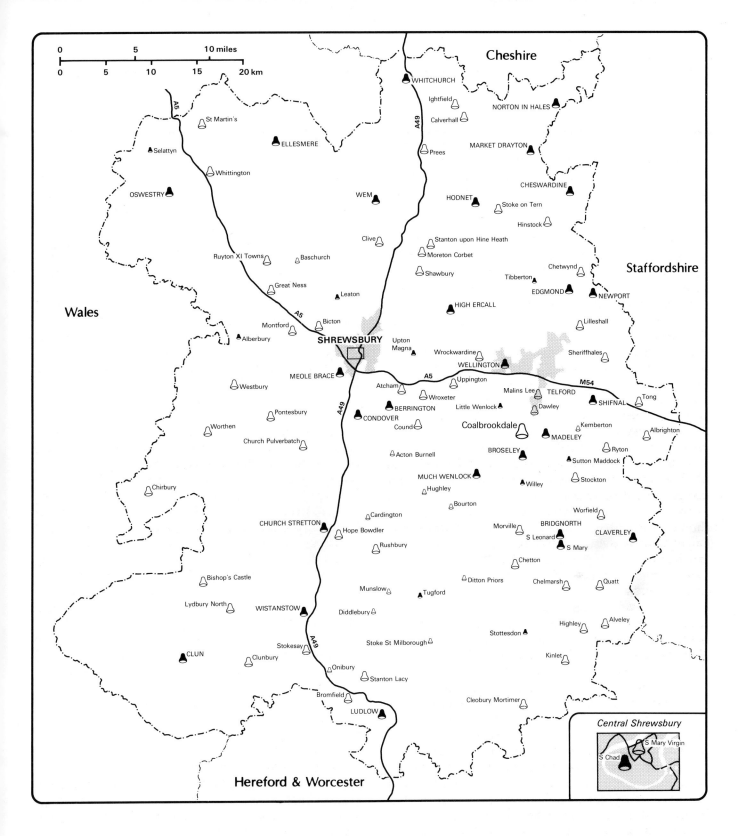

the church authorities, in the hope that a new home could be found for them; this is possibly in Australia. Also discarded is a ring of six placed in the new church of S Michael by Mears in 1830: the tower was declared unsafe in the 1960s, the bells were removed, and the metal was used for casting other bells. Finally, there is a ring of six at S Julian's: this was installed in 1868 (to replace a Rudhall six dating from 1706) in a church which is now an Arts and Crafts Centre; the bells can be chimed only.

Staffordshire

THREE types of area are clearly defined on the campanological map of Staffordshire. To the west of Stafford is a characteristic rural area; most of the towers have rings of four, five or six, and only the small towns of Eccleshall and Penkridge, plus the village of Broughton, have rings of eight. The empty moorland is to the east of Leek, where only the villages of Ilam and Sheen, deep in the Manifold Valley, have rings. Finally, the Potteries conurbation, focused on Stoke on Trent, presents the industrial face of Staffordshire, with a considerable number of churches with bells – though not many relative to the number of parishes and population.

The history of the acquisition of rings of bells in the rural areas is similar to that of many midlands counties. In the south of the county there were rings of five or six at Abbots Bromley, Ingestre, Tamworth and Tutbury by 1700, whereas further north Draycott in the Moors had five in 1678 and Stoke had six in 1682. The early eighteenth century saw a Rudhall 'invasion' – as described in Trevor Jennings's *A History of Staffordshire Bells* – which started in 1700 with the ring provided for Trysull, followed by a six for Stoke (transferred to Broadwood Kelly in Devon in 1832–3) and bells for Rugeley (1706), Biddulph (1707), Stone and Eccleshall (both 1710). A ring of six was provided in 1714 for the church at Trentham, just south of Newcastle under Lyme. In 1767 these bells were sold to S Margaret's, Wolstanton, for 9d. (3.75p) per lb. weight, in return for a single bell at the same rate: the six were augmented to eight in 1884.

According to the listings produced by C. Lynam (in *The Church Bells of the County of Stafford*, 1889), by 1800 the county had 19 rings of five, 20 rings of six, six rings of eight (including two cast in 1726 by Rudhall, for Lichfield S Mary and Burton S Modwen), and one of ten. Eight further rings of five were installed during the period 1800–78, of which only one – that at Ilam – is still a five; five of the others have since been augmented to rings of six, along with five of the eighteenth-century rings, while three of the new rings of five and three of the pre-1800 rings have been augmented to, or replaced by, rings of eight in the twentieth century. (The old five at Abbot's Bromley, for example, which was cast in 1612, was replaced in 1976 by the ring of eight from Bradley in the West Midlands: the move involved not only the bells but also their fittings and frame. At Shenstone, the ring of five cast at Edgbaston in 1704 was replaced by a Mears six in 1813. These were augmented to eight in the late nineteenth century. The bells were then scrapped; five replaced them, and they were later augmented to

six and then to eight again.) Nine of the rings of six in place in 1800 have since been augmented to eight: Tamworth's (which had been a five by 1699 and become a six in 1672) was augmented to eight in 1884 and ten in 1960, one of seven rings of ten in the present county.

The first of these was installed at Lichfield Cathedral in 1688, replacing a ring of six installed by Richard Keene of Woodstock (about which Christopher Pickford has written in detail: *The Ringing World*, 1 June and 8 June 1984). The ring of ten was provided by Henry Bagley of Ecton, Northamptonshire: the ninth was cracked in a fire in 1758, and was recast by Rudhalls; the treble and tenor were recast by Rudhalls in 1764; and the tenor recast again, by Mears, in 1813. The bells were rehung – by Barwells of Birmingham – in 1902, and were recast – by Taylors – into a new ring in 1947, paid for by the freemasons of the county to commemorate the cathedral's 750th anniversary. The other rings of ten are much more recent: at S Paul's, Burton, the eight placed in the new church in 1872 was recast and augmented in 1912; at Stafford, the eight in place since 1751 were increased to ten in 1887; Hanley had an eight provided for the new church in 1790, which became ten in 1923; the ten at Stoke S Peter was recast and augmented from an eight dating from 1832 in 1970; and at Leek, the 1721 Rudhall six was increased to eight in 1863 and to ten in 1926. The church of S Giles in Newcastle under Lyme was provided with an eight by Rudhalls in 1732; these were augmented to ten in 1928, and two further trebles in 1980 made it the only ring of twelve in the county. These, plus the rings of ten at Stoke and Hanley, are in the Potteries, the major industrial conurbation in the county: there, as E. H. Edge records (in *The Ringing World*, 26 November and 3 December 1982), eight new rings were installed between 1820 and 1890, along with nine in rural areas nearby.

Staffordshire bands have contributed substantially to the history of change-ringing, especially peal-ringing: Ernest Morris (in his *The History and Art of Change Ringing*) refers to the band at S Paul's, Burton on Trent, in the 1880s as making their town 'the Mecca of the Exercise', even though the bells were noisy and difficult to ring. Their exploits included three peals of Superlative on successive days in late 1885; they also rang the fourth-ever peal of London Surprise Major in 1887, and in the following year took a trip to Fulham to ring the first of the method in London. More recently, the Rudhall six (1722) at S Michael's, Lichfield, was rung to more than 100 quarter peals each year in the early 1980s, and the 1,000th since 1964 was rung on 25 October 1986.

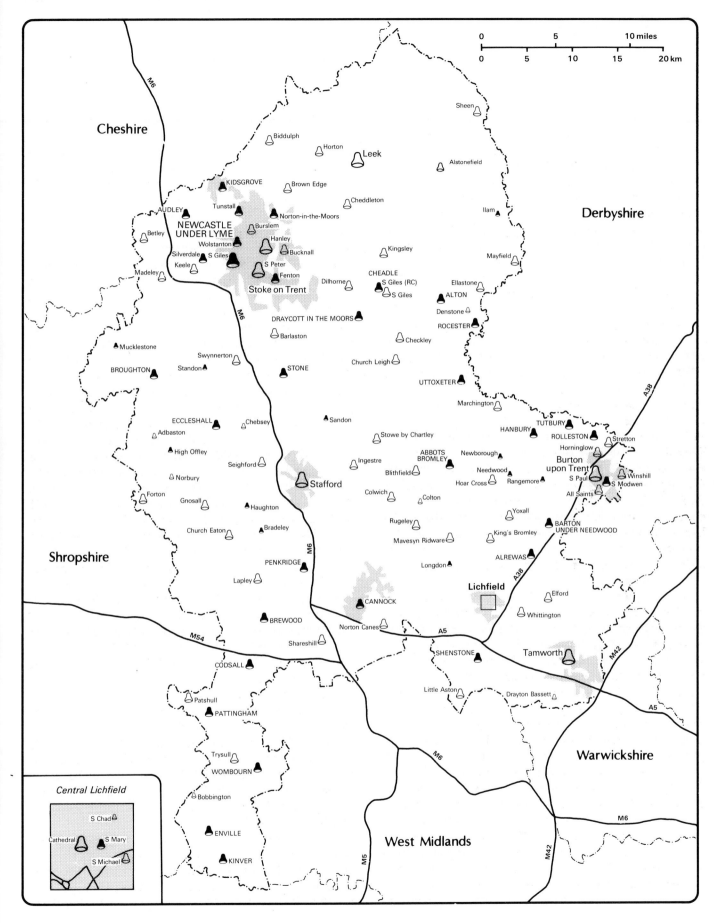

0   5   10 miles

0   5   10   15   20 km

Cheshire

Derbyshire

Sheen

Biddulph

Horton

Leek

Alstonefield

KIDSGROVE

Brown Edge

Cheddleton

Ilam

AUDLEY

Tunstall

Norton-in-the-Moors

NEWCASTLE
UNDER LYME

Burslem

Mayfield

Betley

Wolstanton

Hanley

Kingsley

Silverdale

S Giles

Bucknall

S Peter

CHEADLE

Ellastone

Keele

Madeley

Fenton

S Giles (RC)

ALTON

Dilhorne

S Giles

Denstone

Stoke on Trent

DRAYCOTT IN THE MOORS

ROCESTER

Barlaston

Checkley

Mucklestone

Church Leigh

Swynnerton

UTTOXETER

BROUGHTON

Standon

STONE

Marchington

A38

Sandon

Stowe by Chartley

HANBURY

TUTBURY

ECCLESHALL

Chebsey

ROLLESTON

Stretton

Adbaston

Newborough

Horninglow

Burton
upon Trent

High Offley

Ingestre

ABBOTS
BROMLEY

Needwood

S Modwen

Seighford

Blithfield

Rangemore

S Paul

Winshill

Norbury

Stafford

Hoar Cross

All Saints

Forton

Colwich

Colton

Yoxall

Gnosall

Haughton

Rugeley

BARTON
UNDER NEEDWOOD

Church Eaton

Bradley

Mavesyn Ridware

King's Bromley

ALREWAS

M6

Longdon

Shropshire

PENKRIDGE

Lichfield

Elford

Lapley

CANNOCK

Whittington

A38

BREWOOD

Norton Canes

A5

M54

Shareshill

SHENSTONE

Tamworth

M42

CODSALL

Little Aston

Drayton Bassett

A5

Patshull

PATTINGHAM

Warwickshire

Trysull

WOMBOURN

Bobbington

M6

Central Lichfield

ENVILLE

West Midlands

M42

S Chad

KINVER

Cathedral

S Mary

M5

S Michael

M6

127

Suffolk

LIKE its East Anglian neighbour Norfolk, Suffolk has a large number of churches with rings of bells (more than 200). Relatively, however, Suffolk has many more rings of bells, with only the heathlands north of Bury St Edmunds and the forested areas inland of Orford Ness lacking a high density of points on the map. In part, this difference reflects the lesser number of small parishes in Suffolk (only 14 with fewer than 100 inhabitants in 1900, compared with 44 in Norfolk), but in addition many more small Suffolk parishes endowed their churches with rings of bells (90 of the 166 with populations of 250 to 499, for example, compared with 66 of 213 in Norfolk).

As is the case with its northern neighbour, Suffolk is dominated by churches with five or six bells (again, there are few rings of four, most of them unringable). Many of those rings are as much as two centuries old. Raven's late nineteenth-century survey (*The Church Bells of Suffolk*, 1890) recorded 128 rings of five, of which 95 had been installed before 1800. There were 76 rings of six in place, too, of which 33 had been installed in the previous century; of the other 43, 16 were augmentations of rings of five that were in the towers before the year 1800. Since then, about 25 of the rings of five have been augmented to six, but only about ten of the towers with six bells 100 years ago now have eight. The framework for Suffolk ringing today is very largely that of the mid-nineteenth century.

The county has a substantial number of eight-bell towers, the majority of which were in place by 1890. The first, at Horham, a small village in the north and distant from any major town, and with a population of fewer than 300 in 1900, was installed in 1673, 15 years before a ring of eight was provided for S Mary-le-Tower church in Ipswich. (The 'circle' at Horham has the ropes falling in the order 1, 5, 6, 2, 3, 4, 7, 8.) Hadleigh, too, had a ring of eight before the end of the seventeenth century, and ten more had been installed by 1800. The neighbouring parishes of Framsden and Helmingham joined them in 1814 and 1815 respectively, as a result of donations from a local landowner who clearly enjoyed the sound of bells pealing over his estates: the Earl of Dysart gave two trebles to Framsden and an entire ring of eight to Helmingham.

Suffolk's major town is the port of Ipswich, which was for long a prosperous trading centre (today the larger ships dock at the modern – and bell-less – port of Felixstowe at the mouth of the River Orwell). As in so many prosperous pre-industrial trading centres, the merchants of Ipswich displayed their wealth by investing in the town's churches, which in many cases involved the provision of bells. Today, as the map shows, there are eight churches with four or more bells (one unringable: there is another church with a chime of six bells), all of them clustered together in the town centre. In total, the old town had only twelve parishes before the nineteenth century, so the provision of a ring of bells in three-quarters of them (and another has a ring of three) indicates a very substantial local interest in the ancient art. Unfortunately, four of the eight churches with bells are now redundant as places of worship.

The Church of S Mary-le-Tower is a modern (1860s) building on an ancient site close to the town's ramparts. The old church had eight bells, the new one has twelve, incorporating two seventeenth-century bells, one cast by Miles Graye of Colchester in 1610 and the other by his son-in-law John Darbie, an Ipswich founder, in 1671. In 1908 the Ipswich ringers achieved the first-ever peal of Cambridge Surprise Maximus; led by George Symonds, they extended their repertoire, and rang peals of Maximus in ten different methods during the 1920s.

Elsewhere in the town, ringers can find a complete ring of six by John Darbie at the seafarers' church of S Clement; the front five were cast in 1660 and the tenor in 1680. At the city-centre church of S Lawrence, rebuilt by the Victorians, there is the second oldest complete ring of five in the country – three of the bells having been cast in about 1450 by Richard Brayser of Norwich. S Margaret's has a ring of eight, augmented by the local founder Alfred Bowell in 1925. (Bowell cast more than 400 bells in Ipswich during the first four decades of the twentieth century; he was succeeded by his son Frederick, who ceased casting in 1950 and so was one of the last of England's provincial bellfounders.)

Another Suffolk tower to have a permanent place in the history of peal-ringing is that of the small town of Leiston, close to the nuclear power plant at Sizewell. Early in the twentieth century a family of eleven brothers called Bailey learnt to ring at S Margaret's church, and together eight of them rang a peal of Plain Bob Major in October 1911, taking only two hours 58 minutes on a tenor weighing over a ton. (The eldest of the ringers rang the tenor; the youngest rang the treble.) They rang several other tower bell peals together, including the first peals of Suffolk, Dublin and Edinburgh Surprise Major, and were also very proficient with handbells, ringing peals of Stedman Triples, Caters and Cinques as well as Kent Treble Bob Maximus. They were the first and probably the last set of brothers to achieve such ringing feats.

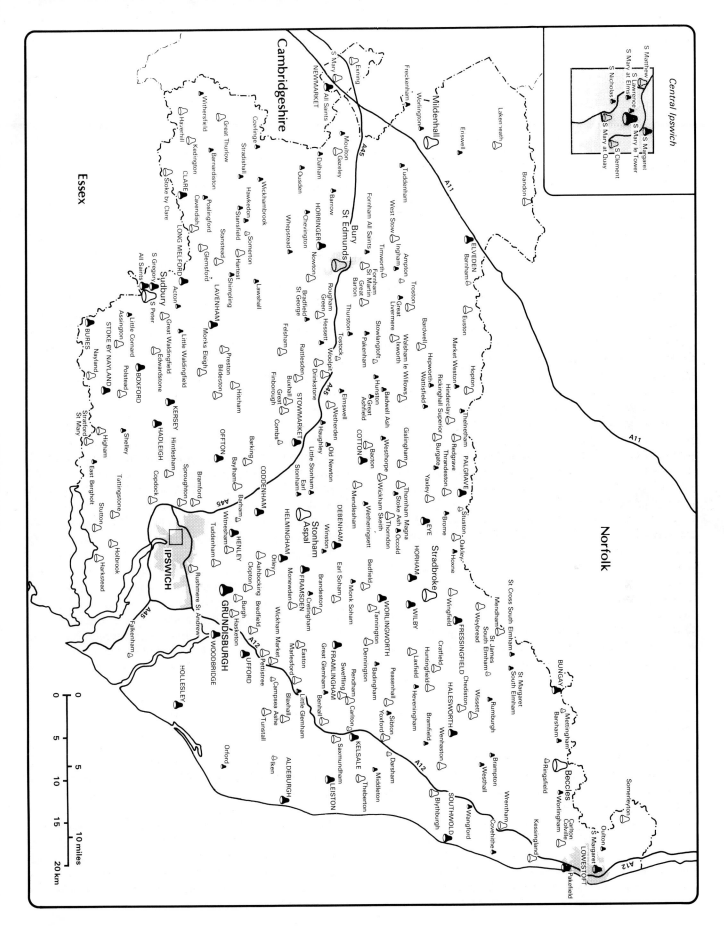

Central Ipswich

S Matthew
S Lawrence
S Mary at Elms
S Margaret
S Mary le Tower
S Nicholas
S Clement
S Mary at Quay

Cambridgeshire

Essex

Norfolk

NEWMARKET

Exning
Freckenham
Worlington
Mildenhall
Eriswell
Lakenheath
Brandon

All Saints
S Mary

Moulton
Gazeley
Dalham
Ousden
Barrow
Tuddenham
ELVEDEN
Barnham

Covington
Withersfield
Haverhill
Great Thurlow
Kedington
Barnardiston
Stoke by Clare
CLARE
Cavendish
Poslingford
Stradishall
Hawkedon
Stansfield
Glemsford
Hartest
Somerton
Wickhambrook
Chevington
Whepstead
Newton
HORRINGER
Bury
St Edmunds
Fornham All Saints
West Stow
Ingham
Ampton
Timworth
Fornham
St Martin
Great
Barton
Troston
Great
Livermere
Market Weston
Euston
Barnham
Hopton
Thelnetham
Hinderclay
Redgrave
PALGRAVE
Hepworth
Wattisfield
Rickinghall Superior
Burgate
Threadeston
Stuston, Oakley
Hoxne
Thornham Magna
Wickham Skeith
Occold
Stoke Ash
Thorndon
Brome
EYE
HORHAM
Stradbroke
Wingfield
Laxfield
WORLINGWORTH
Tannington
Badingham
Dennington
Peasenhall
Heveningham
Cratfield
Huntingfield
WILBY
Bardwell
Walsham le Willows
Ixworth
Hunston
Badwell Ash
Great
Ashfield
Gislingham
Westhorpe
Bacton
COTTON
Mendlesham
Wetheringsett
Bedfield
Monk Soham
Earl Soham
Brandeston
Cretingham
Monewden
FRAMSDEN
Marlesford
Easton
Great Glemham
Benhall
Little Glemham
Blaxhall
Campsea Ashe
Tunstall
ALDEBURGH
Iken
Orford

St Cross South Elmham
Mendham
St James
South Elmham
St Margaret
South Elmham
Weybread
Fressingfield
Chediston
Wissett
Rumburgh
Wenhaston
HALESWORTH
Bramfield
Sibton
Yoxford
Rendham
Carlton
Swefling
Sternfield
Saxmundham
KELSALE
Darsham
Middleton
Theberton
LEISTON
Blythburgh
SOUTHWOLD
BUNGAY
Mettingham
Barsham
Beccles
Ringsfield
Wangford
Covehithe
Wrentham
Brampton
Westhall
Reydon
Kessingland
Somerleyton
Oulton
Carlton
Colville
S Margaret
Worlingham
LOWESTOFT
Pakefield

IPSWICH
GRUNDISBURGH
WOODBRIDGE
UFFORD
Burgh
Hasketon
Pettistree
Wickham Market
Otley
Clopton
Ashbocking
Bredfield
Swilland
Witnesham
HENLEY
Tuddenham
Rushmere St Andrew
Falkenham
HOLLESLEY

HELMINGHAM
Stonham
Aspal
Winston
DEBENHAM
Earl Stonham
Coddenham
Barham
Little Stonham
Old Newton
Haughley
STOWMARKET
Combs
Buxhall
Great
Finborough
Stonham
Needham
Baylham
Barking
OFFTON
Sproughton
Bramford
Copdock
Bayham

Rattlesden
Drinkstone
Woolpit
Tostock
Elmswell
Wetherden
Thurston
Rougham
Green
Hessett
Bradfield
St George
Felsham
Cockfield
Lawshall
Preston
Bildeston
Hitcham
Kersey
HADLEIGH
Hintlesham
Shelley
Higham
Stratford
St Mary
East Bergholt
Tattingstone
Stutton
Holbrook
Harkstead

Sudbury
S Gregory
S Peter
Acton
Long Melford
S Gregory
All Saints
Glemsford
Shimpling
Monks Eleigh
Lavenham
Little Waldingfield
Great Waldingfield
Edwardstone
BOXFORD
Polstead
Assington
Little Cornard
Nayland
Stoke by Nayland
Bures

A45
A11
A45
A12
A12
A45

0 5 5 10 15 10 miles
0 5 10 15 20 km

129

Warwickshire

CREATION of the new metropolitan county of West Midlands in 1974 left the ancient county of Warwickshire with a very odd shape and without its major cities of Birmingham and Coventry. In terms of rings of bells, 30 towers were taken from Warwickshire, including the three twelves in Birmingham and a large number of rings of eight. This resulted in a pattern typical of rural southern England, with no ring of twelve, four of ten, 20 of eight and more than 70 of five or six. These, as the map shows, are widely distributed throughout the county, and the main towns are well provided with rings.

Most of the rings of eight and ten in the towns are relatively new: indeed, according to the survey by Tilley and Walters in the early years of the present century (*The Church Bells of Warwickshire*, 1910), there was only one ring of eight or more in 1800 in what is now Warwickshire – the ten at S Mary, Warwick, which was installed in the great Perpendicular tower in 1703. The ring of six at Hatton was increased to eight in 1817, but reduced to six again when the bells were recast in 1885. It was not until the second half of the nineteenth century that most of the rings of eight identified by Tilley and Walters were installed – in 1873 at Nuneaton S Nicholas, in 1874 at Ullenhall, in 1887 at both Warwick S Nicholas and Stratford upon Avon, and in 1891 at Bedworth (an augmentation from three). At All Saints, Chilvers Coton, Nuneaton, a light ring of eight to replace the existing three was installed only in 1907; it was augmented to ten in 1946, producing one of the lightest such rings (tenor 13¼ cwt.).

One interesting late nineteenth-century installation, creating a unique situation, took place at the parish church of S Andrew, Rugby, in 1895. Since 1711 the church had had a ring of five in its fourteenth-century tower (which incorporates a fireplace; the chimney is within the walls, invisible from the outside, and has an outlet in a battlement). In the 1890s it was decided to extend the church to meet the needs of the growing town, and the design included a new tower, in which was placed a 24 cwt. ring of eight. The original tower and its ring of five bells were retained, however, and both rings are regularly used. Further south, in the centre of the spa town of Leamington, there are two rings of eight, both augmented from six early in the twentieth century. One is in the Roman Catholic church of S Peter – one of the very small number of rings in Roman Catholic churches outside the north of England – where an 1877 ring of six was augmented to eight in 1905.

Warwickshire's map of rings of bells was less full than that of several of its neighbours at the beginning of the nineteenth century, and was then filled out very substantially by the Victorians. The early installations included heavy rings of six present by 1552 at both Brailes and Monks Kirby; rings of six were also provided for Burton Dassett, Chadshunt, Long Compton and Wellesbourne, for example, during the seventeenth century. But these early installations did not stimulate more, and of the 34 rings of five listed by Tilley and Walters 12 were established after 1800. Seven of them have not been augmented since: six are in relatively remote villages – Avon Dassett, Cherington, Ladbroke, Leamington Hastings, Oxhill and Radway – with only one close to a major town – Clifton upon Dunsmore, just east of Rugby. (There was initially a ring of four at Leamington Hastings with a tenor of 22 cwt.; that tenor was recast into two trebles to make a ring of five.)

The relatively isolated parts of the county have experienced fewest alterations to their complement of bells during the twentieth century. The most rural part of contemporary Warwickshire, and the least accessible to major towns, is the Stour Valley south of Stratford upon Avon. There are 25 rings within the diamond-shaped area south of the A41 and A46 roads, only four of which have been augmented in this century: the fives at Butlers Marston and Ilmington are now sixes; the six at Wellesbourne has been upgraded to an eight; and the three at Great Alveston, on the edge of Stratford, has also been augmented to six. This is in contrast to the situation in the more urbanized parts of the county: there are 13 towers within a few miles of the centres of Warwick and Leamington Spa, five of which have had augmentations during the present century; there are eight in the Rugby area, five of which have had augmentations, as also have five of the eight close to Nuneaton (all of them rings of three or four only before the addition of extra bells). This illustrates one of the major features of the changing map of campanology in England since 1900; most of the new bells have been placed in the towns and in the villages close to them, and ringing is, relatively at least, declining in the more rural areas.

One of the new rings is at Nether Whitacre in the north of the county. Hampton in Arden (now in the adjacent county of West Midlands) obtained a ring of eight by purchasing the bells from the redundant church of S John, Miles Platting, inner Manchester. Its bells were then transferred to Nether Whitacre's formerly bell-less church.

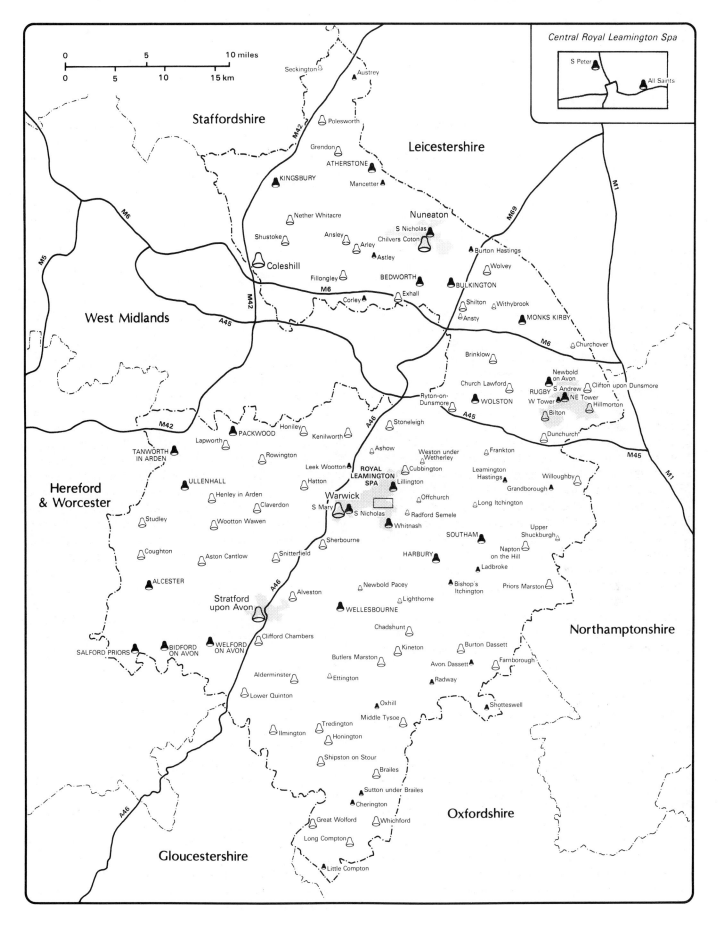

Central Royal Leamington Spa

S Peter

All Saints

0   5   10 miles
0   5   10   15 km

Staffordshire

Leicestershire

West Midlands

Hereford
& Worcester

Northamptonshire

Oxfordshire

Gloucestershire

Seckington
Austrey
Polesworth
Grendon
ATHERSTONE
KINGSBURY
Mancetter
Nether Whitacre
Nuneaton
Shustoke
Ansley
Arley
Astley
S Nicholas
Chilvers Coton
Burton Hastings
Coleshill
Fillongley
BEDWORTH
Exhall
BULKINGTON
Wolvey
Corley
Shilton
Withybrook
Ansty
MONKS KIRBY
Churchover
Brinklow
Newbold
on Avon
Church Lawford
Clifton upon Dunsmore
Ryton-on-
Dunsmore
WOLSTON
RUGBY
S Andrew
W Tower
NE Tower
Hillmorton
Bilton
Honiley
PACKWOOD
Stoneleigh
Dunchurch
Lapworth
Kenilworth
Ashow
Weston under
Wetherley
Frankton
TANWORTH
IN ARDEN
Rowington
Leek Wootton
ROYAL
LEAMINGTON
SPA
Cubbington
Leamington
Hastings
Willoughby
ULLENHALL
Hatton
Lillington
Grandborough
Henley in Arden
Warwick
Offchurch
Claverdon
S Mary
S Nicholas
Radford Semele
Long Itchington
Studley
Wootton Wawen
Whitnash
SOUTHAM
Upper
Shuckburgh
Coughton
Aston Cantlow
Snitterfield
Sherbourne
HARBURY
Napton
on the Hill
ALCESTER
Ladbroke
Alveston
Newbold Pacey
Bishop's
Itchington
Priors Marston
Stratford
upon Avon
WELLESBOURNE
Lighthorne
SALFORD PRIORS
BIDFORD
ON AVON
WELFORD
ON AVON
Clifford Chambers
Chadshunt
Kineton
Burton Dassett
Butlers Marston
Avon Dassett
Farnborough
Alderminster
Ettington
Radway
Lower Quinton
Oxhill
Shotteswell
Middle Tysoe
Ilmington
Tredington
Honington
Shipston on Stour
Bra5iles
Sutton under Brailes
Cherington
Great Wolford
Whichford
Long Compton
Little Compton

131

West Midlands

THE metropolitan county of West Midlands was created in 1974 out of the cities of Birmingham and Coventry (formerly in Warwickshire), the Black Country of Staffordshire, and the Dudley/Stourbridge area of Worcestershire. It developed as an industrial conurbation in the eighteenth and nineteenth centuries, so that, relative to its population, it has a small number of rings. However, it has one of the highest concentrations of ten- and twelve-bell towers in England, and Birmingham in particular has long been a major centre for change-ringing on twelve.

Most of the rings are relatively recent, including virtually all of the eights in the Birmingham suburbs (Erdington acquired eight in 1904, for example). Some did not stay in place for very long, following the decline of inner-city churches. The 1869 ring of eight placed in Bishop Ryder's church in Birmingham was moved to Harborne in 1962; the eight placed in the church of S John Deritend in 1779 was moved to Bishop Latimer's church in 1957 and then, in 1972, to suburban Perry Barr. In the centre of Birmingham today there are just three rings: the twelves at S Philip's Cathedral and at the parish church of S Martin (known widely as the Bull Ring church) and the eight at the Roman Catholic Cathedral of S Chad. The bells were installed in S Chad's as a ring of five in 1849 and augmented to eight in 1877 (until the emancipation acts of the 1830s Roman Catholic churches were not allowed bells, and could not 'advertise' their services accordingly). The bells at the other two have long been in place. S Philip's Cathedral was built in 1711, had a ring of eight by 1727 and of ten in 1751; there was a recasting in 1937, by Gillett and Johnston, and two trebles were added by the same foundry in 1949 when the cathedral was restored after extensive war damage. S Martin's has had twelve since 1772; the present ring was installed in 1928 by Mears and Stainbank, but the two tenors were recast only a year later (and made heavier). This ring of twelve (plus flat 6th) is in the process of being replaced by the first true diatonic ring of 16, at a cost of over £200,000. Individual bells are being provided by sponsors, including Birmingham City Council and British Gas.

A little way from the centre of Birmingham is the parish church of SS Peter and Paul, Aston (very visible to drivers on the A38(M)), which had eight bells by 1775 and ten in 1814; a new twelve was installed by Taylor's in 1935. Further out, in the formerly separate town of Solihull, a ring of twelve was created when Taylor's provided two trebles in 1969 for the ring of ten they installed in 1932; there has been a ten there since 1894, however, and an eight since 1685. The Black Country, west of Birmingham, has two further rings of twelve: at Walsall, where a Rudhall eight of 1775 was augmented to ten in 1863 and replaced by a Taylor twelve in 1929; and at Wolverhampton, where Gillett and Johnston provided a new ring in 1911. Christ Church, West Bromwich, was also once the home of twelve, installed in 1850, two years after the original ring of two was augmented to ten. In 1953 the church authorities were told that the tower was unsafe for twelve-bell ringing, and the four trebles were removed. The church was made redundant in 1975 and the bells were destroyed in a fire a few years later; some of the metal was used to cast the two trebles used to augment the ten at Newcastle under Lyme, Staffordshire, to twelve in 1980.

1987 saw the opening of a new twelve in the West Midlands, at Coventry Cathedral. The body of that fine sandstone building, though not the tower and spire, was destroyed by enemy action in 1941, but long before then the cathedral had lost its ring of bells. A ring of ten was installed in the tower in 1774 by Pack and Chapman of London. In 1885, however, plans to refurbish the church led to their being silenced. The architect (John Richard Scott, son of Sir George Gilbert Scott) wanted to open up the lantern of the tower to view from below, which meant that the bells had to be removed. Plans were drawn up for a detached campanile in the churchyard, but the scheme lapsed soon after the death of the major potential donor. Eventually the bells were rehung in the octagon at the base of the spire, where they could be chimed but not rung: they were recast by Gillett and Johnston in 1927 into a ring of twelve with two semitones. Throughout this period there was much controversy (related in detail in C. J. Pickford's *The Steeple, Bells and Ringers of Coventry Cathedral*, 1987), but it was not until 1982 that the possibility of the bells being hung for ringing became a probability, confirmed in 1985 by the donation of £88,000 by the widow of the

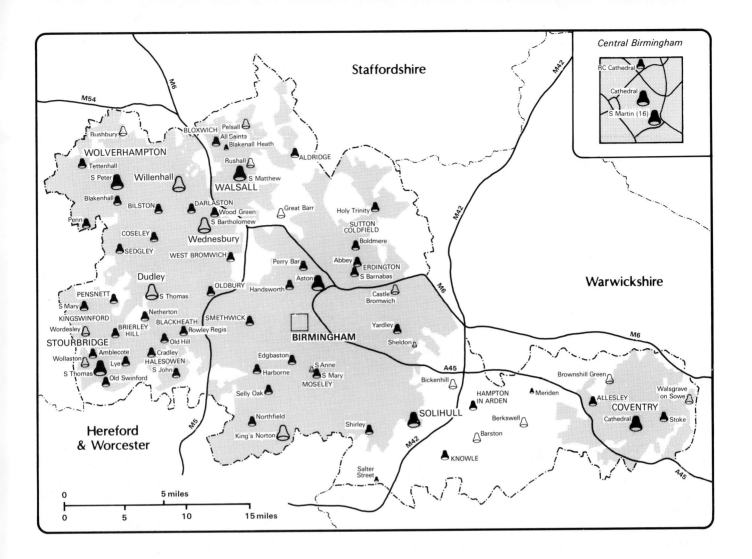

Central Birmingham

former chairman of Jaguar Cars. (The full cost was about half as much again.) The bells were rehung lower in the tower, and above them is a viewing chamber for looking down on the bells and up to the lantern. Interestingly, the 1885 decision was presaged by the recommendation to the parish of George Gilbert Scott to open up a similar lantern in the adjacent church of Holy Trinity, where a ring of eight had been installed in 1776. The bells were removed in 1856, seven were recast, and they were rehung in a temporary wooden campanile in the churchyard, but could never be rung. The campanile was demolished in 1967, and much of the bell metal was used ten years later to cast the new ring of twelve for Christchurch Cathedral, New Zealand.

The Birmingham area's ringers are organized into the S Martin's Guild for the Diocese of Birmingham, created in 1889 when the S Martin's Youths merged with the Holt Society of Aston (the diocese was not created until

1905). It has always been one of the main peal-ringing associations (921 were rung between 1889 and 1927, for example; Ernest Morris's records suggest that just under 50,000 were rung in total during that period). A major nineteenth-century ringer was Henry Johnson, who rang 140 peals – a great many for the time – and who is remembered annually at the guild's Henry Johnson Commemoration Dinner. He was followed in the twentieth century by George E. Fearn, Ringing Master at Birmingham Cathedral from 1947 to 1974. The first person to ring 2,000 peals (his total was 2,667, of which only 59 were in hand), he organized regular Thursday night peals at S Philip's Cathedral (known locally as the 'long practices'). These were so successful that Birmingham Cathedral became the first church to have 1,000 peals rung on its bells, in 1978, more than 700 of them having been rung since ringing was restarted in 1957.

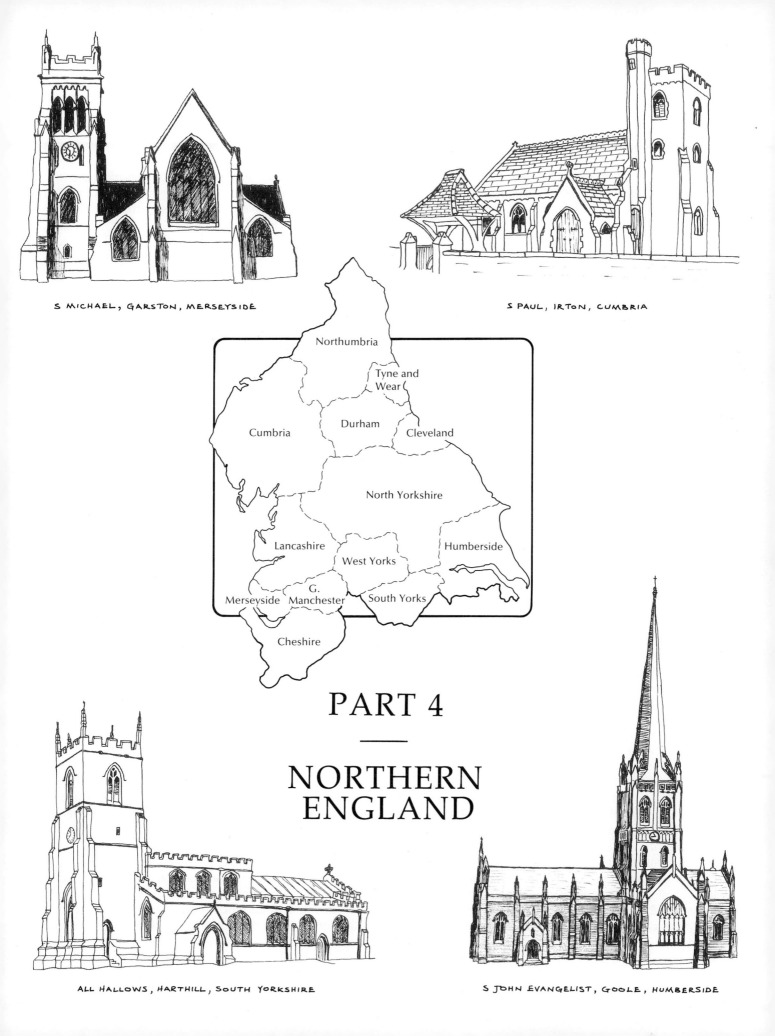

S MICHAEL, GARSTON, MERSEYSIDE

S PAUL, IRTON, CUMBRIA

Northumbria

Tyne and Wear

Cumbria

Durham

Cleveland

North Yorkshire

Lancashire

Humberside

West Yorks

G. Manchester

Merseyside

South Yorks

Cheshire

PART 4

NORTHERN ENGLAND

ALL HALLOWS, HARTHILL, SOUTH YORKSHIRE

S JOHN EVANGELIST, GOOLE, HUMBERSIDE

Cheshire

THE map of Cheshire suggests a county relatively thinly populated with rings of bells, and large empty areas covering, for example, Delamere Forest between Chester and Frodsham and the hills to the west of Crewe and Nantwich. In part, however, this appearance of emptiness is a product of the ecclesiastical organization, for there are relatively few small parishes in the county. Nevertheless, only a minority of parishes of all sizes have a ring of four or more bells, and Cheshire is clearly of the north rather than of the Midlands in this aspect of its geography and culture.

Unfortunately, no complete survey of the county's bells has been published and Clarke's detailed information (in *Transactions of the Lancashire and Cheshire Antiquarian Society*) covers only the western portion (including the parts of the Wirral now in the county of Merseyside). Although most churches had a small ring before 1800, it was only in the nineteenth century that most of the rings of eight were installed. Thus of the twelve towers covered in Clarke's survey that now have rings of eight, none was in place before 1830. (There was an earlier eight in Chester, but this no longer survives. The early augmentations to eight include Sandbach in 1858 and Congleton in 1867. Later in the century came Northwich, 1887, Lymm, 1890, Bunbury, 1895, Tarporley, 1896, Middlewich, 1897, and Grappenhall, 1899.) The reason for this was undoubtedly that until the nineteenth century Cheshire was a relatively isolated and poor rural county. Industrialization to the north in Lancashire saw the beginnings of suburban development in some areas, and the building of new churches for expanding small towns. In many cases this building activity was linked to the establishment of large country homes in the county by people made rich during the period of industrialization. The Duke of Westminster, for example, was responsible for the erection of a church in the new parish of S Mary without the Walls, Handbridge, in south Chester, where a ring of eight by Mears and Stainbank was placed in 1887 – the year of Queen Victoria's Golden Jubilee. He also gave the new trebles at Pulford when the ring of six was augmented to eight, but his major contribution to campanology was the fine ring of eight (tenor 26¾ cwt.) for the new church built in the estate village of Eccleston in 1907, close to his home at Eaton Hall. These actions of one individual contrast with the more usual way in which rings of bells slowly expand as members of a parish decide, for some reason or another, to augment their present provision. Not all were necessarily like the parishioners of Neston, however, who decided in 1724 to obtain a ring of six immediately after Rudhalls of Gloucester had installed a ring of five at the neighbouring village of Burton: squabbles within the village meant that their rivals were not outdone until 1731, but there is no evidence of similar dissent when it was decided to augment the ring to eight in 1884, in the old tower which was by then attached to a new church.

There were several early rings of five and six, however, with many being supplied by the Rudhall foundry in Gloucester, who transported the bells by river to either Bridgnorth or Shrewsbury, and then over land. Their 1804 catalogue lists 22 rings of six and ten of five in what was then Cheshire, including Marberry, Nantwich, and Tarvin. Elsewhere augmentations of smaller rings took place in the nineteenth century; at Dodleston, for example, the four was augmented to five in 1870 (and then to six in 1929), and at Backford the ring of four was increased to five and then six in 1887 and 1889 respectively.

Most cathedral cities have had several rings of bells installed long before similar developments have taken place in their rural hinterlands. This was so with the Roman town of Chester, although the city has never been rich in ringing, for a variety of reasons. The cathedral had five bells in the early sixteenth century, which were recast and placed in the massive central tower in 1605. They were heavy and lumbering, with 'no attraction for change-ringers', according to Clarke, and were not rung between 1754 and 1814. They were recast into a 29 cwt. ring of eight in 1867, and augmented to ten in 1937 through the work of the Chester Diocesan Guild. In 1963 the bells were deemed unringable. An architect's report said that, in order to prevent obscuring the internal upper arches and gallery of the central tower, a new ring of bells and ringing-room would have to be high in the tower, which would be both expensive and structurally dangerous. In 1968 it was decided to build a detached tower in the cathedral grounds, to modern design, and a new ring of twelve, including the metal from nine of the original ten, was opened in 1975.

Other than the cathedral, there are now only two other rings in Chester, plus those at the new suburban parishes at Handbridge and Hoole. There is a ring of eight in the now redundant church of S Mary, which was augmented from a six in 1895 when two bells from a

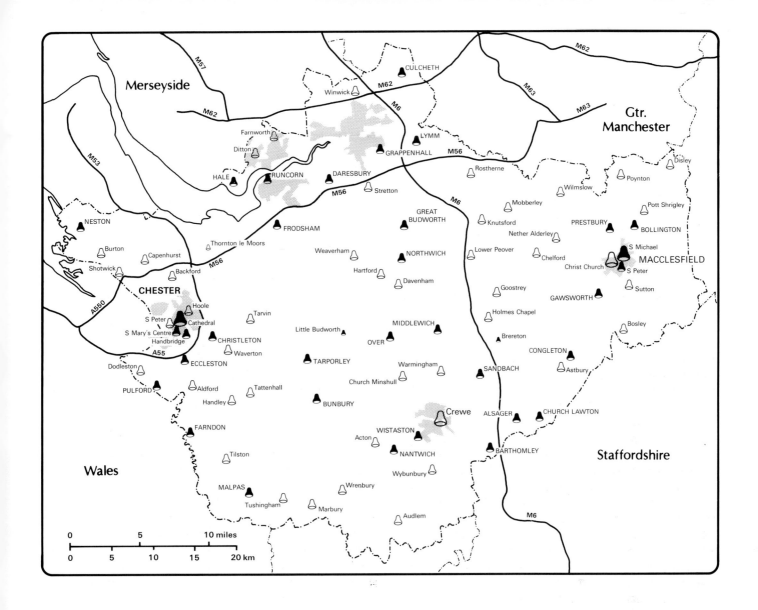

nearby church about to be demolished were made available, and there is a ring of six in S Peter's Church, which was last heard in 1897. These latter bells were augmented to six in 1708 by Abraham Rudhall, who obtained several other contracts in the city at about that time. He augmented the five at S John the Baptist Church to six in 1710, for example, and added two further bells in 1733 for the Society of Chester Scholars. Much of the north side of the tower collapsed after a storm in 1881, and was never rebuilt, so the bells were rehung as a chime. Rudhall's foundry was also responsible for a ring of six at S Michael's in 1726; the bells were placed in a new tower in 1849, but this cracked very badly in 1897 and it was decided to cease ringing.

Elsewhere in the county the history of bell installations is very similar, with many being relatively recent. The result is substantial provision in a few places, notably at Macclesfield, which has a ring of each of

eight, ten and twelve. Christ Church and S Michael both obtained their rings – ten and eight respectively – from Rudhalls in 1777; S Michael's was augmented to ten by Taylors in 1891 and to twelve in 1923. Rudhall was active further east as well, providing a new ring of six for Wilmslow in 1733, for example, but many parish councils obviously decided not to instal rings, or perhaps never even considered it. Where new churches were built in the nineteenth century, a ring of bells may have been part of the plan, especially if local donors were available. Poynton, for example, built a new church in 1858. In 1883 it was decided to add a tower with spire in memory of Lord Kernon; a bell fund was started and eventually a ring of six was purchased in 1887. In other places the ring of bells is even more recent: in 1986, for example, the three at Pott Shrigley was increased to six with the purchase of a redundant bell from Leicestershire and two new trebles from a Dutch foundry.

Cleveland and Durham

THE counties of Cleveland and Durham in north-east England, which were for long some of the most isolated parts of the country but which were transformed by the industrial revolutions of the last 200 years, are not renowned for magnificent churches and, not surprisingly as a consequence, have very few rings of bells.

The architectural gem of the area is the cathedral at Durham, built on a high spur overlooking the River Wear and including three massive towers. The bells are high in the central tower, and more than 300 steps must be climbed to reach the ringing chamber. There was a ring of six here in 1693, when Christopher Hodson, an itinerant London bellfounder, obtained the contract to recast them into a ring of eight, which had a tenor weighing 30 cwt. These were rehung in a wooden frame in 1766, and in the succeeding 200 years three were recast (the treble in 1780, the third in 1781, and the fourth in 1896). These bells were difficult to ring, and in 1979 were taken down for retuning and rehanging in a new frame, with two additional trebles. The frame sits in the centre of the tower, and it is possible to walk around it while the bells are ringing. Below is a large ringing chamber, in the centre of which is the perfect rope circle; on the walls hang several of the old wheels.

While in Durham (as recorded in Rivet's *Bells of the Durham and Newcastle Dioceses*) Christopher Hodson also cast a ring of six for S Oswald's Church, in the south of the city; these were replaced in 1977 by a ring of eight cast by Taylors of Loughborough. Hodson's work was done in 1694, seven years after James Bartlett cast a ring of five for S Nicholas's Church, which is the oldest set in the county; they were rehung in 1889, when a treble was added.

Outside Durham City very few parish churches had more than three bells before the nineteenth century. Only the churches at Staindrop, Stockton-on-Tees, Sedgefield, Darlington (S Cuthbert's) and Bishop Auckland, all in the south of the area, had rings of five or six bells. The oldest of these is probably the ring of five at Sedgefield, where the tower was built in 1490. A medieval bell dating from about 1425 was installed then, and four trebles cast by Samuel Smith of York were added in 1707. A frame was built for six bells, and Smith cast five, but the parish could not afford them all, and so one was returned to York. This left a ring of five tuned to a minor key, with the medieval bell as the tenor. The latter was found to be cracked in 1930 but renovation was carried out only in 1972. To avoid destroying a medieval bell it was not recast but rather welded, the whole bell being heated to a temperature of 1,000° for this to be achieved (it took a week). Sedgefield's bells are the only ringable five in the two counties. The five at Willington is a set of steel bells cast by Naylor and Vickers of Sheffield in 1866; currently, the tenor cannot be rung, although the fittings remain in the belfry.

Most of the other rings of bells in Durham and Cleveland are nineteenth-century castings, placed either in new churches or in towers which formerly contained only two or three bells. Many of them were cast at the Whitechapel foundry in London, and sent north in small ships returning from taking coal to the capital; Rivet refers to the 100 years after 1740 in the north-east as 'A century of Whitechapel bells'. But of the 237 pre-nineteenth-century parishes in the old County of Durham (before the creation of Cleveland and Tyne and Wear in 1974) only 27 have rings of bells, as do twelve of the 164 parishes created since then. The coast north of Hartlepool is entirely bell-less, although Hartlepool itself has three rings (including a ring of ten), all of which were installed in the first eleven years of the twentieth century. Neither Middlesbrough nor its coastal neighbour, Redcar, has a ring – indeed the entire built-up area of Teesside has only three rings, at Ormesby, Stockton – the ancient market town – and Thornaby. (There was an eight at S Hilda's Church, Middlesbrough, on which many peals were rung, but they are now hung 'dead'.) Stockton had a 9 cwt. ring of six by Llewellin and James of Bristol, which was recast and increased to ten by the addition of four tenors in 1953; two further trebles were added in 1983.

Inland, there are two minor concentrations of bells. The first is in the market-cum-railway town of Darlington, where the old ring of six at S Cuthbert's in the town centre was joined by that at S John the Evangelist's in the new development area near to the railway station in 1848 and another at Holy Trinity in the western suburbs in 1891. By the latter date, S Cuthbert's bells had been augmented to eight (in 1866, by Warners of London), and S John's were similarly augmented (by Mears, who cast the original six) in 1893. The other concentration is in and around the former steel town of Consett. In 1885 both Christ Church, Consett, and S Cuthbert's, Benfieldside, were provided with rings of six bells, with Consett obtaining two further trebles in 1887. Sixty years later Taylors provided another ring of eight for the urban area, for the Roman Catholic church of Our Lady Immaculate, Blackhill. These were installed 25 years after a ring of eight had been provided for Blackhill; in 1922 Mrs Annie Lee gave the bells to S Aidan's church in memory of her parents, husband and son.

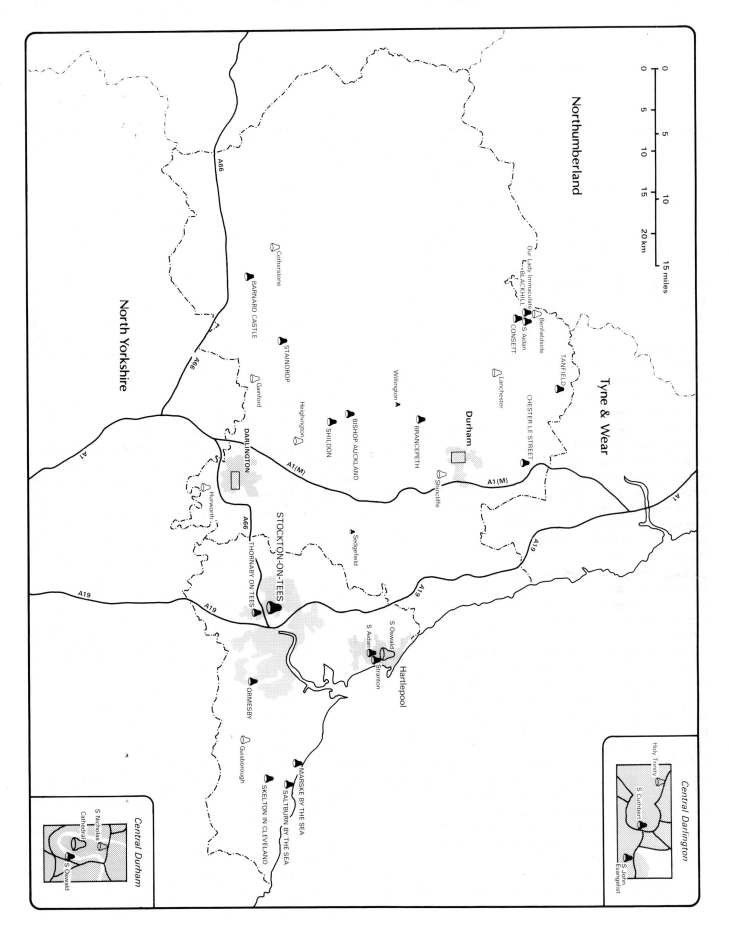

Northumberland

Tyne & Wear

North Yorkshire

Cotherstone

BARNARD CASTLE

STAINDROP

Gainford

Heighington

DARLINGTON

Willington ▲

Lanchester

Our Lady Immaculate
BLACKHILL
CONSETT
S Aidan
Benfieldside

TANFIELD

CHESTER LE STREET

Durham

SHILDON

BISHOP AUCKLAND

BRANCEPETH

Shincliffe

A1(M)

A1(M)

A1

A66

A66

A19

A19

A19

Hurworth

STOCKTON-ON-TEES

THORNABY ON TEES

Sedgefield

S Oswald
S Aidan
Stranton
Hartlepool

ORMESBY

Guisborough

MARSKE BY THE SEA
SALTBURN BY THE SEA
SKELTON IN CLEVELAND

Central Durham

S Nicholas
Cathedral
S Oswald

Central Darlington

Holy Trinity
S Cuthbert
S John
Evangelist

139

Cumbria

THE map of rings of bells in Cumbria is almost empty, but much of the county's area (the former counties of Cumberland and Westmorland, plus the district around Furness, which was in Lancashire until 1974, and the north-western part of what was the West Riding of Yorkshire) is high mountain or fell. Nevertheless, even the more populated areas have relatively few rings: in the former county of Cumberland only 11 per cent of parishes, and in Westmorland 17 per cent.

The former county of Westmorland contained 88 churches in 1970 according to B. L. Thompson (in *Transactions of the Cumberland and Westmorland Antiquarian and Archaeological Society*), with a total of 260 bells, an average of fewer than three each. Most of the rings of four or more bells were installed in the nineteenth century. Two centuries earlier, only Kendal had a ring of six, and Brough, Kirkby Stephen and Orton each had four; by the late eighteenth century the only changes were that Kendal had a ring of eight and Kirkby Lonsdale had a ring of six. The latter was augmented from three in 1724, and the bells were recast in 1826. Kendal's six was installed in 1695 by Christopher Hodson just after his work at Durham Cathedral – though the tenor, reputedly weighing 35 cwt., was recast by Rudhall of Gloucester in 1711 and by Samuel Smith of York in 1717 – and these were augmented to eight in 1775; the first peal in the county was achieved in 1796. (The new eight was placed in the church tower; before that, according to Ernest Morris, the bells had hung in a detached 'bellhouse'.) The augmentation to ten came in 1816, and the first peal of Caters was rung three years later.

Elsewhere in what was formerly Westmorland, little happened until well into the nineteenth century. (Hawkshead, then in Lancashire, acquired a ring of six in 1775; the two trebles were added in 1958.) Appleby's five was augmented to six in 1833 and Shap's three became five in 1864, with a sixth added in 1882. In the Lake District proper, both Brathay and Langdale obtained rings of six late in the century. Crosthwaite, whose original three were claimed by some to be old bells from Kendal transferred in 1773, received three more in 1885, 15 years after Heversham's three were also augmented to six and five years before nearby Beetham also acquired three more bells to make a ring of six. Milnthorpe's six dates only from 1912, eleven years after Taylors installed a ring of eight (tenor 32 cwt.) at Ambleside. The eight at Orton dates from 1917, though the tenor of the earlier ring of four had been recast by Rudhall in 1711 when he was operating from Kendal.

In the former county of Cumberland, the beginning of ringing as we know it came in the nineteenth century. Changes could have been rung before then – at Carlisle Cathedral (a six installed in 1658), Cockermouth, Penrith, and Workington – but there is no evidence that they were; Douglas Sim reports (in *The Ringing World*, 1 July 1983) that the first recorded change-ringing in the county occurred when a Liverpool band rang a peal of Grandsire Triples at St Bees in 1858, and that it was only the second peal – by a College Youths band at S Stephen's, Carlisle, in 1865 – that stimulated the development of the art locally. By then a number of churches had rings of eight. The first eight was provided when Cockermouth's six was recast in 1856. Two years later St Bees Priory also obtained a ring of eight, to replace a ring of three installed in 1815.

One of the few rings obtained in the nineteenth century was for S Paul's, Irton, in 1887, to mark Queen Victoria's Golden Jubilee; the eight bells, replacing two, were a gift of Sir Thomas Brocklebank, of a major shipping line, in memory of his wife. West Cumberland's industries boomed in the first decades of the twentieth century (based on the local iron and coal), and rings of eight were provided for Egremont in 1902, Arlecdon in 1904, Cleator Moor in 1909 (to replace an 1873 ring of six), and Hensingham in 1913. A sixth ring for the area came with the installation of ten at S James's, Whitehaven: seven of the bells came from the redundant church of S Alkmund, Derby.

The Furness area, too, is an area of recent bell installations. Cheetham identifies only two rings of eight in the 1920s, at Broughton and Dalton. Broughton's eight was provided by Taylors in 1900 and was augmented to ten in 1980. A ring of six was installed in the abbey church at Dalton in 1865 (replacing three). The bells were recast and augmented to eight in 1913, but they were soon unringable, and in 1927 Taylors recast them into ten. The two rings of six in the area were older – Ulverston's dating from 1836; the five at Kirkby in Furness (augmented to six in 1908) were installed by a Norfolk foundry in 1831. The ancient priory church at Cartmel, where the bells hang in a small square tower set diagonally on top of the squat central tower, has had six bells only since 1932: the two oldest were installed by the Wigan foundry of John Scott in 1661, and two more were added in 1729 and 1731 respectively. Today the tower contains ten bells which make two rings of six. Four new bells were provided in 1987 to blend with the two treble bells installed in 1932, so those two are common to both rings.

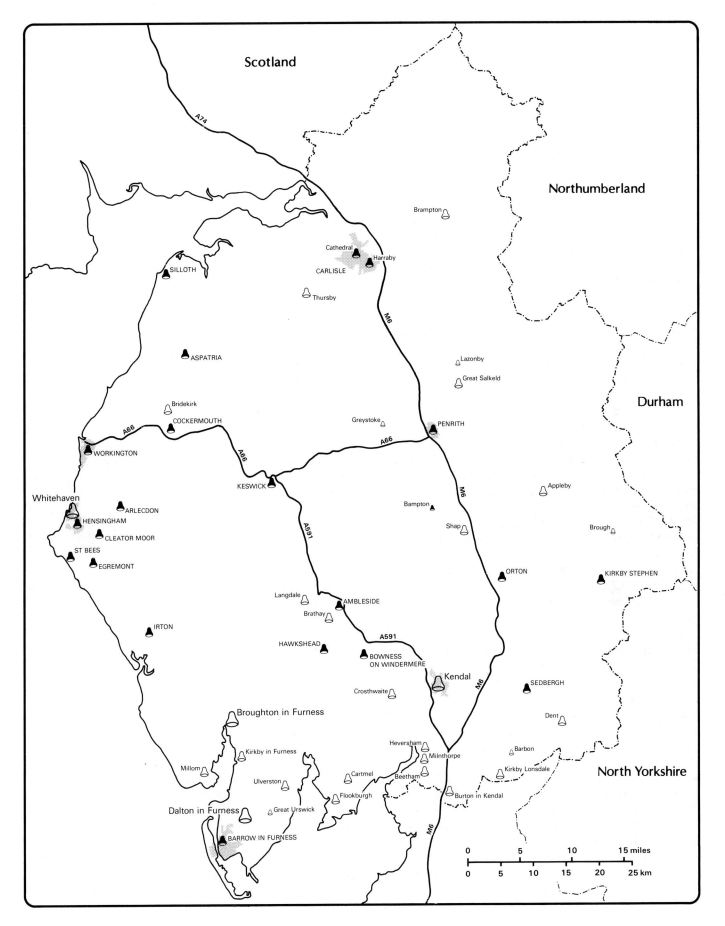

Scotland

Northumberland

Durham

North Yorkshire

A74

SILLOTH

Cathedral
CARLISLE
Harraby

Thursby

M6

Brampton

ASPATRIA

Lazonby

Great Salkeld

Bridekirk

A66

COCKERMOUTH

Greystoke

PENRITH

A66

WORKINGTON

Whitehaven

ARLECDON

HENSINGHAM

CLEATOR MOOR

ST BEES

EGREMONT

KESWICK

A591

A66

Appleby

Brough

Bampton

Shap

M6

ORTON

KIRKBY STEPHEN

IRTON

Langdale

AMBLESIDE

Brathay

HAWKSHEAD

BOWNESS
ON WINDERMERE

Crosthwaite

A591

Kendal

M6

SEDBERGH

Dent

Broughton in Furness

Kirkby in Furness

Millom

Ulverston

Cartmel

Flookburgh

Great Urswick

Dalton in Furness

BARROW IN FURNESS

Heversham

Milnthorpe

Beetham

Barbon

Kirkby Lonsdale

Burton in Kendal

M6

0   5   10   15 miles

0   5   10   15   20   25 km

141

Greater Manchester

THE new county of Greater Manchester covers the city of that name plus much of the conurbation of industrial towns that developed with it in the nineteenth century. Northwards and eastwards it extends into the cotton towns of Bolton, Bury, Rochdale, Oldham, Ashton under Lyne and Stalybridge, while to the south it includes both Stockport and a sweep of suburbia. To the west it absorbs the coalfield town of Wigan. Some of the towns incorporate old market settlements, such as Wigan, but most are nineteenth-century creations, with churches built to serve the burgeoning industrial populations. The majority of the parishioners were poor, but there were also rich industrialists who wished to record their presence and wealth in stone and in church contents.

Unfortunately, we have no complete nineteenth-century compilations of the bells in Lancashire churches to compare with those produced for most of the counties of southern England, and the listings produced in volumes of the *Transactions of the Lancashire and Cheshire Antiquarian Society* by F. H. Cheetham cover only about half the towers in the present county (some 14 of which were formerly in Cheshire). From these we get some idea of the way in which bells were provided in this heartland of 'dark Satanic mills'.

In parts of the county, several of the parish churches had a ring of five or six bells by the end of the eighteenth century, most of them 'imported' from other parts of England, because Cheshire and Lancashire were, as far as we know, almost bereft of bellfoundries. (The main exception was the foundry at Wigan run by the Scott family from 1656 to 1701 and the Ashtons from 1703 to 1750.) Wigan parish church, for example, had a ring of six provided by Rudhalls of Gloucester in 1732, eight years after the same foundry furnished a ring of five for nearby Standish and eight years before a similar delivery to the church of S Mary the Virgin at Leigh. (Rudhall bells were brought to Lancashire from Gloucester on the Severn as far as Shrewsbury, and then over land.) Rudhalls augmented the Leigh ring to eight in 1761. A similar augmentation at Rochdale S Chad occurred in 1787, where Rudhalls had installed six bells in 1752, twelve years after a similar six was provided for nearby Radcliffe. Rudhalls provided several other rings in the eighteenth century, including those at S George, Bolton (later removed to Wangaratta, Australia), at Bury and at Eccles. A new ring of eight was also provided for Flixton parish church in 1806. When the bells arrived the tenor was placed upside down in a field beside the church and ten guineas' worth of double strong ale was poured in it for 'the populace to regale themselves with'; the ale lasted one hour.

The older settlements of the eastern part of the county also had rings of bells in their parish churches. The present Manchester Cathedral – then the parish church – was in possession of a Rudhall ring of eight cast in 1706, having previously had five bells which were increased to six in 1679. The eight were augmented to ten by Rudhalls in 1825, and the tower was rebuilt in 1867. Rudhalls also provided bells for the parish church of S Mary the Virgin in Oldham, with a ring of four being augmented to six in 1722; a new church was built in 1830 and provided with a ring of twelve by Mears, which was replaced by a Taylor twelve in 1922. The Gloucester foundry was also involved in providing bells for the parish church of S Michael and All Angels at Ashton under Lyne, where a ring of eight by Rudhall was installed in 1779, augmented to ten in 1790 and remodelled in 1818, when a heavier tenor was added. Six of the original bells remain in the church, but not in the same tower: a new tower was built in 1818, and another in 1889, when the ring was augmented to twelve by Mears and Stainbank, who recast two of the original bells. (The tenor had been cast by them in the 1818 remodelling, which involved scrapping the treble and recasting two other bells.)

Rudhalls provided bells for new churches built in the early years of the nineteenth century, as with the 1806 ring of eight for S George's church at Bolton. Later in the century the Whitechapel and Loughborough foundries became the main providers (the Whitechapel foundry having taken over the Gloucester business in the 1830s, when Thomas Mears moved briefly to the West Country following John Rudhall's death in 1835). Thus Mears provided new rings of eight for Mossley S George and for S James, Birch-in-Rusholme (the latter bells were moved less than a mile to Holy Innocents, Fallowfield, in 1981), and Taylors provided an eight for West-houghton in 1870. These entire rings were mostly gifts, as with the eight donated by Higginbotham in 1871 to the church of S Peter in Ashton under Lyne, which had been built 50 years earlier. Warners of Cripple-gate also obtained business in the area later in the century, providing a ring of eight at Milnrow in 1869 (at a cost of £782) and another for Swinton three years later.

The centre of Manchester has a fine ring of twelve in

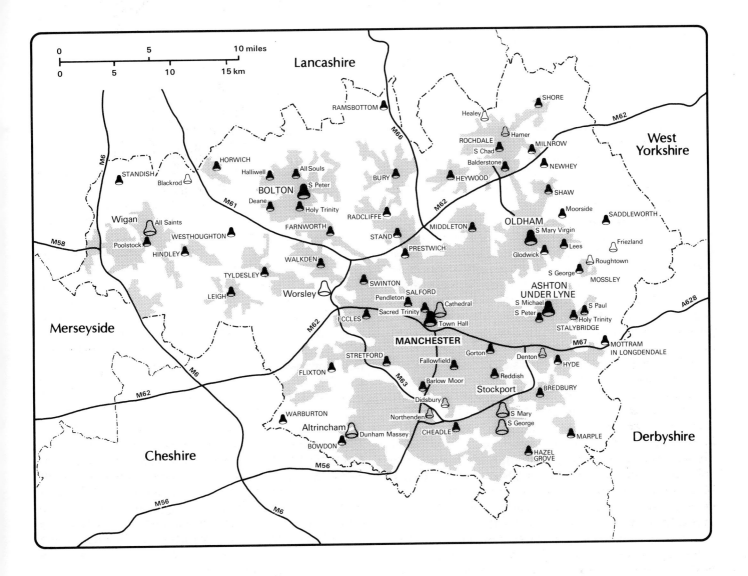

the main tower of its town hall. Before 1937 there were 21 bells there in total, installed in the 1880s, of which ten were hung for ringing (with a tenor of 52 cwt.); the gross weight of all 21 was 34 tons 6 cwt., which meant that the tower had more bell metal in it than any other in the country. Taylors recast and rehung them in 1937, creating a ring of twelve with a 42½ cwt. tenor; for many years these were rung by a band of local policemen, with helpers.

Although not renowned for a large number of rings of bells, Greater Manchester has contributed substantially to the development of change-ringing, in two major episodes. In the late eighteenth century the eastern part of the area was the focus of intense rivalry in peal-ringing striking contests, initially involving bands from S Michael's, Ashton under Lyne, and S Paul's, Oldham (from which the bells have long since gone). Some of their main contests were at the opening of new rings of bells, as at S John's, Manchester (a ring of eight provided for a new church in 1768 by Lester and Pack of

the Whitechapel foundry; the bells were later transferred to Eccles), at Saddleworth in 1781 and at Flixton in 1806. 150 years later a band focused on the church of S Thomas, Norbury, Hazel Grove, frequently hit the headlines of *The Ringing World* with a large number of pioneering peals, notably of Spliced Surprise Major; these included the longest peal ever rung at the time – 21,600 changes of Bristol Surprise Major at Over, Cheshire, in November 1950. Norbury's church was built in 1833. It obtained six bells in 1837 from the nearby parish of Disley, which was acquiring a new ring and offered its old bells to the new church for the cost of transport and installation (£60). In 1925 four of those bells were recast by Taylors, and four new trebles added (the other two original bells – both dated 1617 – were preserved in the tower as examples of seventeenth-century founding, but not hung for ringing). Up to that time Norbury was a centre of six-bell change ringing. It then became a centre for new developments; 226 peals were rung there between 1955 and 1978.

Humberside

CREATION of the county of Humberside was one of the most unpopular acts of the 1974 reorganization of local government, for it detached much of the old East Riding from the county of Yorkshire and joined it (if joined is the right term, because the Humber Bridge was not then open) to part of north Lincolnshire, around the towns of Grimsby and Scunthorpe.

Much of the county has a very low density of rings of bells. This is especially so to the north of the Humber estuary, which comprises three relatively empty tracts of country: the low-lying valley of the Derwent, draining south to the Ouse; the rolling, dry Wolds; and the low, wet lands of Holderness, where the coast is being rapidly eaten away. There are few large settlements, and the majority of churches lack a ring of bells.

No complete survey of the bells of Yorkshire has ever been published, and the only detailed compilation available for Humberside is that produced in 1898 by G. R. Park in *The Church Bells of Holderness*. He lists 53 churches, of which 19 had only one bell, 13 had two bells, and 15 had three; the only 'rings' as we understand the term were two each of four, five and six. One of the rings of six, at Sutton, had been installed only in 1890 (replacing a ring of three); one of the rings of five was established four years later (at Withernsea; the inscription on the treble indicates that the funds for those bells were 'raised by ladies' of the town), and the other was augmented from four in 1846. The two rings of four (at Leven, a new church opened in 1845, and at Swine) were nineteenth-century installations; only at Hedon, which had a ring of six from 1776, was there a long tradition of ringing. Little has changed since: both Hedon and Patrington now have eight; Burstwick and Withernsea each have six; and the rings of three at Roos and Rise have been augmented to five.

Park's survey is supplemented by a listing of the inscriptions on all church bells in the old East Riding (excluding Kingston upon Hull) published by W. C. Boulter in the early 1870s (in the *Yorkshire Archaeological and Topographical Journal*). He lists 155 churches, of which 24 had one bell, 51 had two and 62 had three. There were six rings of four; six rings of five (at North Cave, installed in 1772; North Ferriby, an 1864 augmentation; Pocklington, 1754; Escrick, 1857; Hemingborough, 1730; and Patrington; Escrick and Hemingborough are now in North Yorkshire); four of six (at S Mary's, Beverley, from 1760; Market Weighton, from 1783; Hedon; and Christ Church, Bridlington, where the steel ring is no longer present); and two of eight (the 1775 ring installed by Pack and Chapman at Howden

and that at Beverley Minster, completed in 1747). These were rare islands where change-ringing could be practised (there is little evidence that it was), and compared with counties further south very little work was done to augment the available two- and three-bell rings.

The church of S Augustine, Hedon, has a tall, central perpendicular tower which is characteristic of the rich churches of the East Riding; it contains a ring of eight augmented in 1929. Entry to the ringing-room is much easier than at Patrington – the cathedral of Holderness – where one either crawls along a plank across the north transept or ascends a wooden stair in the side of the open central tower. Here, the ring of five was augmented to six in 1909 and then to eight.

The wealthy agricultural areas of North Humberside were for many centuries the Wolds, and some of the profits earned from the wool were used to build impressive large churches in the local stone. These were provided with rings of bells, too, as at Bridlington Priory (a 26½ cwt. ring of eight), S Mary's, Beverley (ten; 34¾ cwt.), Beverley Minster (ten; 41¼ cwt.) S Mary the Virgin, Cottingham (eight; 21 cwt.) and Howden Minster (eight; 22¼ cwt.) Cottingham had only four bells until 1897, when Warners provided four trebles to mark the Diamond Jubilee of Queen Victoria. At Howden the ring of eight was installed by Taylors in 1932, and is widely recognized as one of the finest in the old county of Yorkshire; it replaces an earlier ring of eight which was destroyed by fire in 1929.

South Humberside has a much greater density of rings, especially in the coastal area to the east of the Humber Bridge. Further west is the low lying, very wet area of the Trent Valley in the Isle of Axholme. Between the two areas is the narrow limestone ridge of the Lincoln Edge, from which ironstone was obtained in the Frodingham–Appleby district to provide the base for the establishment of the industrial town of Scunthorpe. The parish church, dedicated to S John the Evangelist, was opened in 1891 with a single bell, but seven others were installed two years later (by Taylors) in memory of Lord St Oswald, who founded the church.

Close to the southern end of the Humber Bridge are the two small towns of Barton-upon-Humber and Barrow upon Humber, where the Harrison family practised as bellfounders between 1763 and 1833. They cast many of the bells in the churches on both sides of the estuary, but there were few rings of more than five on their side of the river. Barrow and Barton each had rings of six by 1750 – before the Harrisons started work – but these were not augmented until the twentieth

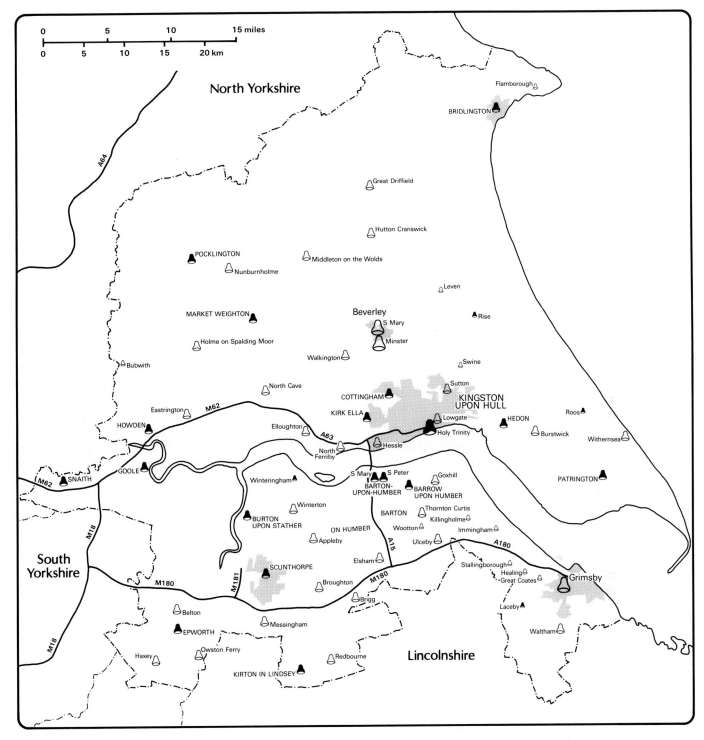

century. (Barton has two churches in adjacent church-yards, both with rings of eight; one is now closed and the bells are not rung.) Messingham, Ulceby, Winteringham and Winterton all had rings of five before 1800, and there was a ring of six at Redbourne in 1774, but most of the rings of six and eight have been installed only in the last 100 years. Grimsby had its ring of four in S James' Church increased to six in 1830 and to eight a year later, and Brigg acquired its ring of eight in 1878, but these were very rare events. More typical of the area

is the development at Laceby, a village on the edge of Grimsby. It had three bells in S Margaret's from the sixteenth century augmented to four only in 1895, when the vicar presented a new treble in memory of his brother; the fifth bell was obtained in 1928.

This part of rural England obtained most of its rings of bells relatively late, therefore. Its ancient towns with their fine churches have long had the sound of changes ringing across their roofs, but for the countryside around the sound is a modern development.

Lancashire

THE ancient county of Lancashire was very substantially truncated in the 1974 local government reorganization, losing both the Liverpool area to Merseyside and much of the south-eastern district to Greater Manchester, as well as having the Furness region transferred to Cumbria. The area left as Lancashire was not a rural remnant of those removals, however, for it includes major industrial towns, such as Preston, Blackburn, Accrington and Burnley, and the resorts of Lytham, Blackpool and Morecambe, all of which are well provided with rings of bells. But around them are many empty areas on the campanological map, the largest of which is the very thinly populated Forest of Bowland, to the east of the M6 north of the Ribble Valley; others include the relatively recently drained coastal lowlands to the north of Ormskirk, south of the Ribble, and, on the other side of that river's estuary, the similar area of the Fylde.

As is typical of the more urbanized counties, particularly those whose towns and cities grew rapidly in the nineteenth century, the majority of Lancashire's rings are of eight or more bells; there are only three rings of five, including one at Thurnham (1848), south of Morecambe, which is the only Roman Catholic church in the country with that number of bells. Indeed, the county has by far the largest number of Roman Catholic churches with rings of bells in England, indicative of the relative strength of Roman Catholicism there and its 'openness' after the Emancipation of the 1830s. The Fylde area has most of these churches, with the five at Thurnham, a six and an eight at Lytham, a six at Kirkham (1844; the oldest Roman Catholic ring) and an eight at Blackpool; the others are the six at Bamber Bridge, south of Preston, an eight at Chorley nearby, and the ring of ten at Lancaster Cathedral.

Lancashire was provided with many bells during the eighteenth century by the Rudhall family, whose foundry was at Gloucester. (The Rudhalls also provided several rings for Cheshire churches.) Cheetham's listings (in the *Transactions of the Lancashire and Cheshire Antiquarian Society*, 1915–25) identify 183 Rudhall bells in the county (including those parts now in Merseyside and Greater Manchester) in 67 different towers; the first ring provided in the present county of Lancashire was a 1711 octave for Preston, replaced in 1814. Among the Rudhall bells are the rings of six at Halsall (1786), Goosnargh (five in 1713; augmented in 1742), Cockerham (1748) and Melling (1754), as well as the original six in several towers that now contain eight – as at Poulton le Fylde. Rudhalls also provided all eight bells at several churches, including Croston (1787–1806),

Ormskirk (six in 1714; augmented in 1774), and Lancaster Priory; six bells were installed in 1744 and two more in 1747, which were replaced by the heavy Taylor ring (tenor 30½ cwt.) in 1886.

Apart from the rings of bells provided for the ancient parish churches, many of those in place today – especially the rings of eight – were obtained for new churches built for the expanding settlements of the nineteenth century. Thus Warners of Cripplegate, London, provided a ring of eight for the new church at Aughton (Christ Church) in 1878; Taylors carried out similar work for Holy Trinity, Blackburn, in 1888 (transferred to S Silas in 1982), Samlesbury in 1900 and Tarleton in 1914; Mears installed eight at Haslingden (1830), Helmshore (1851) and Kirkham in 1846 (replacing a 1714 Rudhall six). The coastal resort towns were almost all late in acquiring bells for the new or enlarged churches constructed to serve the expanding populations. At Morecambe, for example, Holy Trinity Church was opened in 1841, but the tower did not receive a ring of bells (six, cast by Charles Carr at Smethwick) until 1897; they reached the church after a procession along the promenade from the station. In 1939 Taylors recast them into a ring of eight. The same was true in some of the industrial towns, such as Oswaldtwistle. The land for Immanuel Church was given by the Lord of the Manor, Sir Robert Peel (later to be Prime Minister), in 1835, and the church was consecrated two years later. An appeal for money to purchase a ring of bells was launched in 1874, by a vicar who was himself able to ring (how many parishes owe the installation of bells to the keenness of a vicar who had learned ringing elsewhere?). A ring of six was established in 1878, at a total cost of £492 (£41 was raised in the collection at the dedication service; more was expected, but there were labour troubles in the town at the time). The church records show that the ringers twice went on strike. The reason in 1893 was a common one – for more pay – but four years earlier the ringers had declined to ring because the vicar hadn't actively supported the local Conservative candidate in the recent general election! New ringers were obtained in 1893 and kept the sound of the bells calling across the town, and in 1913 their ring was augmented to eight. But there was to be another strike, in 1964 when the ringers declined to accept the vicar's insistence that all who rang to announce a service should then attend it.

Only five Lancashire towers have more than eight bells, the oldest being Blackburn Cathedral, where the 1737 Rudhall six was augmented to ten in 1851. The other

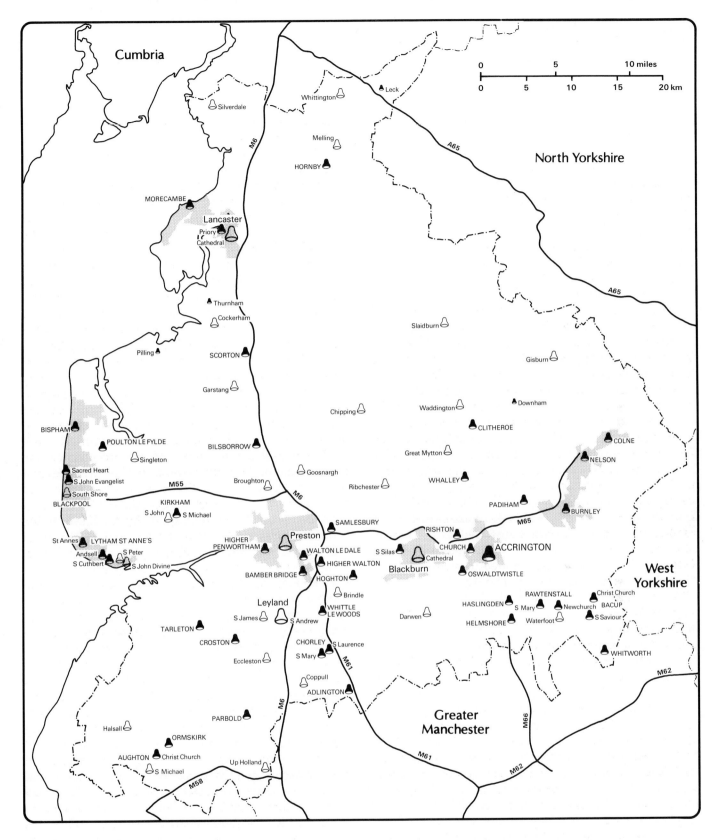

Cumbria

North Yorkshire

West Yorkshire

Greater Manchester

Silverdale

Whittington

Leck

Melling

HORNBY

MORECAMBE

Lancaster
Priory
Cathedral

Thurnham

Cockerham

Slaidburn

SCORTON

Pilling

Garstang

Gisburn

Chipping

Waddington

Downham

CLITHEROE

BISPHAM

POULTON LE FYLDE

BILSBORROW

Singleton

COLNE

NELSON

Sacred Heart

Goosnargh

Great Mytton

WHALLEY

S John Evangelist

Broughton

Ribchester

PADIHAM

BURNLEY

South Shore

BLACKPOOL

M55

KIRKHAM

SAMLESBURY

RISHTON

M65

St Annes

LYTHAM ST ANNE'S

S John   S Michael

Preston

M6

Andsell

S Peter

HIGHER
PENWORTHAM

WALTON LE DALE

S Silas

CHURCH

ACCRINGTON

S Cuthbert

S John Divine

HIGHER WALTON

S Laurence

Cathedral

Blackburn

OSWALDTWISTLE

BAMBER BRIDGE

HOGHTON

Brindle

RAWTENSTALL

Christ Church

Leyland

WHITTLE
LE WOODS

Darwen

HASLINGDEN

S Mary

Newchurch

BACUP

TARLETON

S James

S Andrew

HELMSHORE

Waterfoot

S Saviour

CROSTON

CHORLEY

S Laurence

Eccleston

S Mary

WHITWORTH

Coppull

ADLINGTON

M61

M66

M62

PARBOLD

Halsall

ORMSKIRK

Greater
Manchester

AUGHTON

Christ Church

Up Holland

M6

M62

S Michael

M58

M61

rings of ten were provided in 1929 at Leyland, in 1934 at Preston, and in 1948 at Lancaster. There is only one ring of twelve, at S James' Church, Accrington, where the tenor weighs just 11¼ cwt., making it the lightest ring of twelve in a church in the world. The new church had a ring of six installed by Mears in 1805. In 1953 there was a ring of eight, which was augmented to ten in 1967; the eleventh was installed in 1973 and the twelfth in 1974.

Merseyside

THE new county of Merseyside comprises the city of Liverpool plus nearby towns, such as St Helens and Southport, and the northern part of the Wirral peninsula. As a predominantly urban area, most of its rings are of eight bells or more, and their number is small relative to the population. Nevertheless, Merseyside is renowned throughout ringing circles because it possesses the heaviest ring in the world.

As in other parts of England that were rapidly urbanized during the nineteenth century, some of the older settlements had parish churches with rings of bells in place before the industrial revolution. In Merseyside, the focus of ringing was at S Nicholas's Church (at what is now called Pier Head), which had a ring of six by 1649. The bells were recast by Rudhall of Gloucester in 1724 and placed in a larger tower in 1750. This fell in 1810 when the bells were being rung before a service: the spire collapsed into the nave and killed 25 people. A new tower was built in 1814, with a ring of twelve cast in 1812–13 by the Downham Market foundry of W. Dobson; this was replaced by Taylors in 1952. Another early Liverpool ring – an eight at S Peter's, augmented from four by Rudhall in 1707 – was later replaced by Mears, augmented to ten and then transferred to the parish church of S Helens in 1920. The Gloucester foundry of Rudhall was very active in the area in the eighteenth century, providing rings for S Thomas, Eccleston, in 1727 and Walton in 1736, as well as rings of five for Hoylake on the Wirral in 1719, at Childwall in 1722 and at Eastham in 1757.

It was in the nineteenth century, with the building of many new churches, that most rings of bells came to Merseyside, however, as shown in the listings published in the *Transactions of the Lancashire and Cheshire Antiquarian Society* by F. H. Cheetham (1915–25) and J. W. Clarke (1948–55). Cheetham gives details for six rings of eight and seven of six in what is now Merseyside, with five of these in new churches (including Tuebrook, 1869; Garston, 1877; Halewood, 1883; and Woolton, 1887): the eight for S Luke, St Luke's Place (destroyed in the Second World War) was cast in Norfolk in 1818 for All Saints, Newton Heath, Manchester, but it was uncertain if the tower could support them, so they were sold to Liverpool Corporation and placed in S Luke's in 1829. (Liverpool Corporation – or its successor, the City Council – has its own ring of four bells in the Municipal Offices, hung in the 1860s, which

are rung to mark certain events, including election day.) Similarly, in the Wirral six of the nine rings of eight listed by Clarke were installed in new churches between 1867 and 1911.

Many of these churches have celebrated the centenary of the installation of their ring of bells in recent years, while some still have to reach that anniversary. Among the latter is Emmanuel Church, Southport, on the northern side of the centre of the resort and dormitory town. The land had been donated by the Lady of the Manor in 1876, but construction started only in 1895; the church was consecrated in 1898 but the redbrick and sandstone central tower was not completed until 1901. This contained a ring of eight bells, cast by Taylors, which was donated with the tower by a local couple in memory of the wife's father. Further down the coast, at Crosby, the church was built in 1853, but, lacking a rich donor, a ring of bells (six) could only be afforded ten years later. At about the time of their centenary, the bells fell silent, but they were restored a decade later: a fire in 1972 destroyed all of the church except the tower, and when it was opened after rebuilding in 1975, the bells announced the rededication service. Closer to the centre of Liverpool, a ring of bells (cast in Dublin, a rarity for an English church) was placed in the Roman Catholic church of S Francis Xavier at Everton in 1870; the replacement Taylor bells, dating from 1920 (like those at the Roman Catholic church in Sheffield), are kept ringing by local university students.

On the Wirral, too, nineteenth-century urbanization led to the building of new churches to cater for the expanding congregations. At Moreton, for example, a suburb of Wallasey, a new church was consecrated in 1863 and provided with a ring of four bells by Warners. These have been regularly rung in recent years, and a peal was achieved in 1973. In Wallasey itself the church of S Hilary, with a fine central tower, was built in 1859 to replace one that was burned down, save for the tower, which had a ring of five provided by the Wigan foundry in 1723 and augmented to six in 1853. The bells fell during the fire, 'clashing and clanging to the pavement', according to a contemporary press report, but the fragments of metal were rescued and used in 1859 by Taylors to produce a new ring for the new church.

In many ways all of these late nineteenth- and twentieth-century augmentations and installations pale into insignificance when compared with what hap-

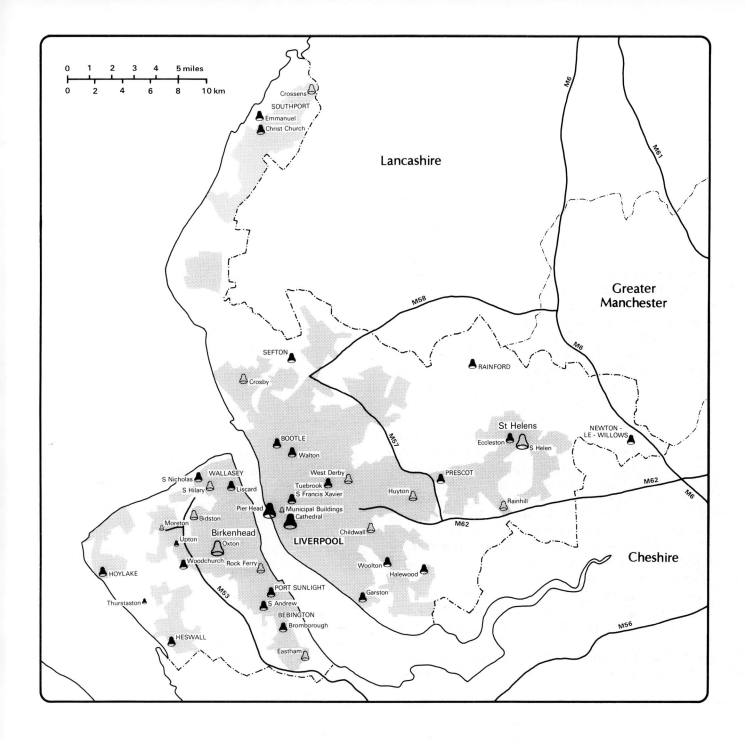

pened at Liverpool Cathedral in 1951. The cathedral was started early in the twentieth century. The massive tower was due for completion at the end of the 1930s, but delays and then the war meant that it was not ready for the bells until 1951. These had been cast in 1938–9 at the Whitechapel Foundry, however, and so the heaviest ring of bells in the world had to wait twelve years before they could be heard. The tenor bell weighs 11 lbs. over 82 cwt., and is thus just under half a ton heavier than the tenor at Exeter Cathedral. The eleventh weighs 55 cwt. and 1 lb., and is the sixth heaviest bell in a ring; only the tenors at Exeter, S Paul's Cathedral, London, York Minster and Wells Cathedral are bigger. The bells are hung on reinforced concrete piers, 6 ft. 6 ins. high, set into a circular frame which is 2 ft. thick and 42 ft. in diameter; in total, the tower contains more than 2,000 tons of reinforced concrete and steelwork to support the bells.

Northumbria and Tyne and Wear

THE two northernmost counties of England have a very low density of rings of bells. This in part reflects the low density of population, which in turn was largely a consequence of the relative inhospitability of the landscape to farming. Before the nineteenth century there were 172 parishes in Northumberland (the present county of Northumbria plus those parts of Tyne and Wear north of the River Tyne). Many of these were undoubtedly poor, and their churches small, unadorned buildings. Certainly few had bells, and only 22 have rings of five or more at present (plus another five in post-1800 parishes).

Rings of bells were extreme rarities in the area before 1800. In 1759 the Archdeacon of Northumberland wrote to a friend that there were only five rings of more than two bells in that county, including eights in Berwick, Hexham and Morpeth and three 'very bad bells' at Alnwick. The two oldest were almost certainly in Newcastle upon Tyne, at the Cathedral Church of S Nicholas and the medieval church of All Saints. The latter no longer has bells. It had five in the 1630s, which were recast into six in 1696 by Christopher Hodson; the bells were cast on land nearby made available for the task. The church was rebuilt at the end of the eighteenth century, and a new ring of eight installed by Thomas Mears in 1797; it was destroyed by fire in 1946.

Newcastle Cathedral tower was completed in 1448, when it contained a heavy ring of five bells; three of the medieval bells survive. The Town Council paid for them to be augmented to eight in 1717, and the first ever peal in Northumberland was rung on them in 1755. The church became a cathedral only in 1882, and ten years later it received a new ring of ten cast by Taylors of Loughborough, with the City Corporation a major donor; William Lister Newcombe donated two additional trebles in 1914.

There were two other rings of bells in Newcastle before the Industrial Revolution, at the city centre church of S John the Baptist, where six were installed by Smith of York in 1706 (they were augmented to eight by Warners in 1884 and all recast by Gillett and Johnston in 1926), and at S Andrew's church, where a ring of six installed in 1726 (by Phelps of Whitechapel) is now hung as a chime only; the story goes that the tenor hasn't been rung since it was cracked when being tolled for the death of Disraeli in 1881.

Outside Newcastle, the oldest record of a ring (according to the very full information in Rivet's *Bells of the Durham and Newcastle Dioceses*, 1979) is at Morpeth. A ring of six was given to the town by its successful parliamentary candidate (Edmond Maine) in 1706. There was no tower to hold the bells, so the clock tower was built by the council; the ring was augmented to eight in 1833. Tower and bells remain the property of the local district council, but the latter are rung to announce services at the parish church a mile away. Further north, Berwick upon Tweed also has a secular ring, hung in the town hall in 1754; these bells are currently unringable. Hexham's eight were installed in 1742; at North Shields (Tynemouth) a ring of six was provided in 1787 (the first set of bells was lost at sea *en route* from Whitechapel, and had to be replaced); it was augmented to eight in 1874 and to ten four years later; South Shields acquired its six in 1763, which was replaced by eight in 1885; and the eight in Gateshead was installed in 1788, replacing a 1730 ring of six.

Elsewhere, the rings of bells are nineteenth-century installations (so that most were cast in either London or Loughborough), many of them in new churches built for the rapidly growing urban populations, and there has been little activity since. Only at Bamburgh (the northernmost ringable bells in England), Gosforth (a six in 1901, augmented to eight in 1920), SS James and Basil, Fenton, in Newcastle, where a new church provided by a shipping magnate in 1928 as a memorial to his two sons killed in the First World War was provided with a ring of eight in 1930, and at Roker (where the ten was installed in the new church in 1947) have rings been installed during the present century, and there have been only six augmentations of existing rings (including Newcastle Cathedral). Indeed, ringers in the area have been struggling to keep rings of bells intact and used. Apart from the two Newcastle churches discussed above, that at Low Elswick has been closed, but the tower remains and the bells announce services at a nearby church. South of the Tyne, ringing in Gateshead was halted in 1979 by a fire that gutted S Mary's church, but in 1987 the six bells of S Peter, Jarrow – a redundant church – were installed at S Mary's, Heworth, a Gateshead suburb. And at Hebburn, nearby, where S Andrew's United Reformed Church has had a ring of six since 1872, a light ring of six has been installed in a redundant Presbyterian church now owned by South Tyneside Council. Finally, S Paul's Church, Alnwick – where the Duke of Northumberland gave the original bell and the ring of eight was completed by public subscription in 1874 in memory of his wife – has been transferred (like that at S Leonard's, Malton, North Yorkshire) to the Roman Catholic church: the bells are currently unringable, however.

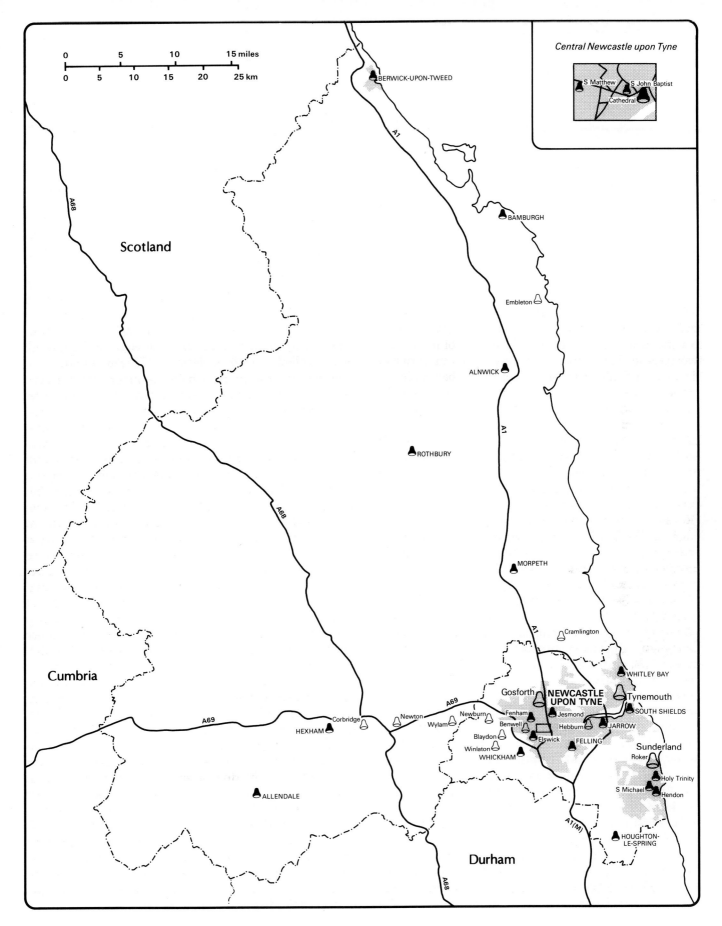

Central Newcastle upon Tyne

S Matthew   S John Baptist
Cathedral

BERWICK-UPON-TWEED

Scotland

BAMBURGH

Embleton

ALNWICK

ROTHBURY

Cumbria

MORPETH

Cramlington

WHITLEY BAY

Gosforth   NEWCASTLE   Tynemouth
UPON TYNE   SOUTH SHIELDS

A69   Newton   Fenham   Jesmond   Hebburn
Newburn   JARROW
Wylam   Benwell
Corbridge   Elswick   FELLING
HEXHAM   Blaydon
Winlaton   WHICKHAM   Sunderland
Roker
ALLENDALE   Holy Trinity
S Michael   Hendon

HOUGHTON-
LE-SPRING

Durham

North Yorkshire

THE most rural part of the old county of Yorkshire has relatively few rings of bells in its large number of parishes. Some of the empty areas on the map are largely empty of settlements, too. Occasionally one comes across a church in a remote area with a ring of bells, none more remote than those cast in 1868 in Birmingham for S Chad's, Middlesmoor.

Other empty areas cannot be accounted for by the topography. Most noteworthy among these is the Vale of York around the city of York itself, where few churches were provided with bells for change-ringing. In the triangle bounded by York, Easingwold and Malton there was until recently only one ring (the six at Whitwell on the Hill – and this is unringable). At least 13 other churches in the district have three bells, but clearly there was no local movement to have them augmented and adopt the art of ringing for so long practised in the nearby city. The Vale of Pickering, on the other side of the Howardian Hills, similarly is almost bell-less.

Rings of bells were in place in the few major town churches of the area by the end of the eighteenth century, although there is little evidence of much change-ringing outside York. Ripon Cathedral, for example, had a ring of five in the south-west tower by 1733, which was recast into a ring of eight by Lester and Pack of Whitechapel in 1761, and augmented to ten in 1891. Selby Abbey also had a ring of five by the early eighteenth century, augmented to six in 1821 and then to eight in 1863. A fire in 1906 destroyed the bells, which were replaced by the present ring of ten. Nearby, there was a ring of five installed at Sherburn in Elmet. Whitby's ten began as a six, and was augmented to eight in 1898 and to ten in 1911. Scarborough's original eight was cast by Taylors in 1851–2 (the tenor and treble won prizes in the Great Exhibition), and was augmented in 1979.

York was undoubtedly one of the earliest centres for the introduction and development of change-ringing outside London, and it could well be that York Minster was the first church to acquire a *ring* of twelve bells (though it almost certainly was not the first to obtain twelve bells). David Potter's research (*The Ringing World*, 14 February and 11 April 1986) provides evidence that they were a diatonically tuned twelve after the recasting of 1681; others claim S Mary-le-Bow's twelve predated York's.

That first ring of twelve was replaced by a ring of ten in 1765, with a tenor weighing 53¼ cwt. (Full details are given in David Potter's *The Bells and Bellringers of York Minster*.) These bells were destroyed by fire in 1840, and replaced by another, and heavier, ring of twelve, which was recast and restored in 1925. The present tenor weighs 59¼ cwt., and is the fourth heaviest ringing bell in the world.

Like other medieval cities, York was well supplied with churches, several of which had rings of bells. Centuries of neglect have had unfortunate consequences for the bells. By the 1970s only those at the minster were ringable. In some cases the situation was unredeemable; in others, it was possible to restore the bells. At S Martin le Grand the bells, silent since the previous century, fell from the tower after the church was bombed in 1942, and by 1960 all but the tenor had been stolen. The church was rebuilt with grants from the War Damage Commissioners, and in 1977 the beginnings of a new ring were obtained with the purchase of a chime of eight from Illingworth, West Yorkshire. The back four were retained, and a new set of four trebles obtained by recasting the ring of three from the redundant church of S Margaret, Walmgate.

There were several rings of six in the city besides the two that were lost earlier in the century. The former Church of S John, Ousebridge, became an arts centre, and its ring of six has been restored. At Clifton, to the north, the derelict 10 cwt. ring of six was removed, and replaced in 1978 by a much lighter six (tenor 3¼ cwt.) cast from the four remaining bells of the Illingworth chime. S Mary, Bishophill Senior, was closed in 1954; the 1770 Pack and Chapman ring of six was placed at Acomb. At S Michael, Spurriergate – which exchanged its three bells in 1765 for the front five of the twelve being scrapped at the minster and acquired another treble at the same time – ringing had ceased around 1905. The tower began to lean, and in 1969 its top 25 feet was removed. Only the tenor was rehung, but in 1986 the other five bells joined it, giving the city yet another ring on which to teach and practice, despite the church being made redundant.

Nor is this all. At S Andrew's, Bishopthorpe, a ring of four created by Taylors was augmented to five in 1988 and six in 1989; 1988 also saw the bells at S Olave's restored, and in 1989 a new ring was installed at All Saints, based on four bells obtained from a redundant chime in Sheffield. Outside the city, the ring of six at Huntington (installed as five in 1881 and increased to six in 1884) was augmented to eight in 1977, the 1895 Taylor ring of four at Stockton on the Forest was increased to six in 1984, and at Strensall a ring of five installed in 1985 was augmented to six in late 1987 when removal of the clock mechanism made room for a sixth ringer in the tiny ringing-room.

Elsewhere in the county, there are new rings of six at Sowerby, Rudby and Ainderby Steeple.

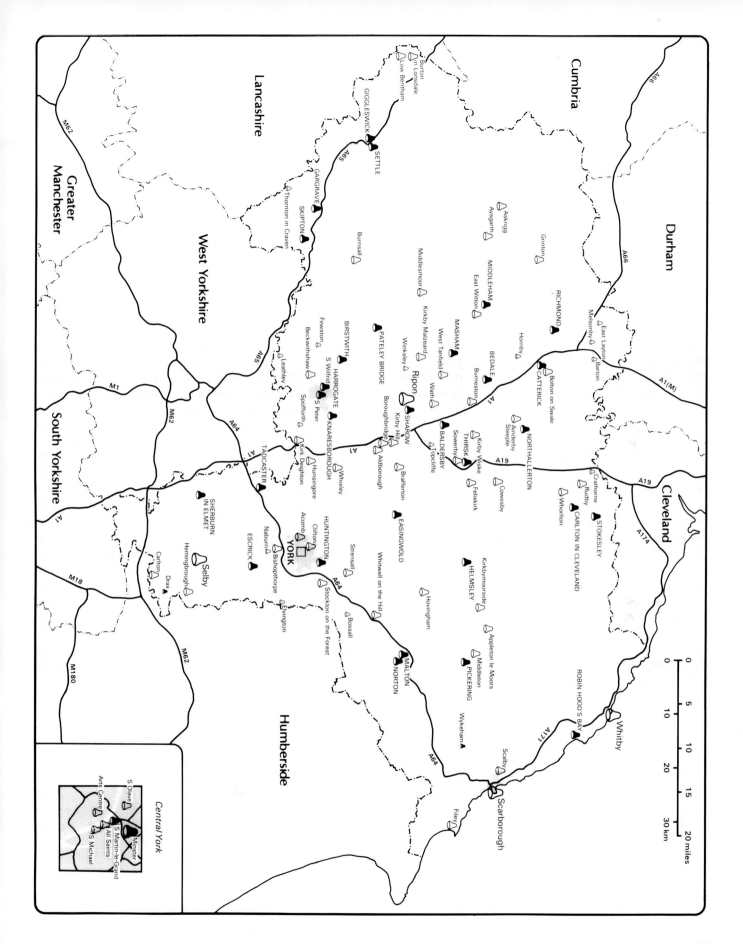

Cumbria

Durham

Lancashire

Greater Manchester

West Yorkshire

South Yorkshire

Cleveland

Humberside

Burton in Lonsdale
Low Bentham
GIGGLESWICK
SETTLE
GARGRAVE
SKIPTON
Thornton in Craven
Askrigg
Aysgarth
Grinton
Burnsall
Middlesmoor
MIDDLEHAM
East Witton
Kirkby Malzeard
West Tanfield
MASHAM
Wath
RICHMOND
Melsonby
East Layton
Barton
Hornby
BEDALE
Burneston
CATTERICK
Bolton on Swale
Fewston
BIRSTWITH
Beckwithshaw
S Wilfrid
HARROGATE
S Peter
Leathley
Spofforth
PATELEY BRIDGE
Winksley
Ripon
SHAROW
Kirby Hill
Boroughbridge
Aldborough
BALDERSBY
Topcliffe
Sowerby
THIRSK
Kirby Wiske
Felixkirk
Anderby Steeple
NORTHALLERTON
Cowesby
Whorlton
Rudby
Crathorne
STOKESLEY
CARLTON IN CLEVELAND
KNARESBOROUGH
Kirk Deighton
Hunsingore
Whixley
Brafferton
Acomb
Clifton
YORK
HUNTINGTON
EASINGWOLD
Kirkbymoorside
HELMSLEY
Middleton
Appleton le Moors
PICKERING
TADCASTER
SHERBURN IN ELMET
ESCRICK
Naburn
Bishopthorpe
Strensall
Whitwell on the Hill
Hovingham
SELBY
Hemingbrough
Carlton
Drax
Selby
Elvington
Stockton on the Forest
Bossall
MALTON
NORTON
Wykeham
Filey
Scarborough
Scalby
ROBIN HOOD'S BAY
Whitby

Central York

S Olave
Arts Centre
S Martin-le-Grand
Minster
All Saints
S Michael

M62
M1
M62
M18
M180
M62
A64
A1
A65
A65
A66
A1(M)
A19
A19
A174
A171
A64

0
5
10
15
20
30 km

0
5
10
20
30 miles

153

South Yorkshire

CREATION of the new county of South Yorkshire in 1974 brought into one unit the four cities of Barnsley, Doncaster, Rotherham and Sheffield, whose rapid growth in the nineteenth century was based on the twin foundations of coal and steel.

The rural base to nineteenth-century industrialization and urbanization was not rich in most of the county, which includes both the barren Pennine moors in the west and the marshy wastes in the lower Don valley in the east. But running through the county from north to south is a narrow band of limestone country, which divides Rotherham from Doncaster. Here, as elsewhere in England, the wealth derived from sheep-farming was invested in fine village churches made from the local stone. S Mary's, Tickhill, is probably the finest example within the county, its Perpendicular tower having been erected in the late fourteenth/early fifteenth centuries. Not surprisingly, the tower was provided with bells, and there was at least a ring of four there by the end of the seventeenth century. In 1726 the metal from those bells, plus that from the three in a nearby church, was recast in the Castle Yard to make a ring of six; this was augmented to eight in 1896. A few miles away, where the River Don cuts a deep gash through the limestone ridge, the village of Sprotbrough contains a ring of six installed in 1771 by Pack and Chapman of Whitechapel, recast and augmented to eight by Taylors of Loughborough in 1963.

The installation of these two rings at Sprotbrough and Tickhill in the eighteenth century was typical of developments in similarly placed rural districts then, but most of the churches in the area were provided with three bells only. The empty area of the map between Darfield and the A1(M) contains several such small rings – at Barnburgh, Bolton upon Dearne, Brodsworth, Hickleton, High Melton, Hooton Pagnell, Hooton Roberts, Marr and Mexborough: a number of them are rung regularly by a band based at Darfield. According to Poppleton (in his lists of West Riding bells published in *The Yorkshire Archaeological Journal* at the end of the nineteenth century), the present county of South Yorkshire then had one ring of twelve, one of ten, nine of eight, 20 of six and two of five. Of those, 20 were in place with at least a ring of five by 1800. Today there are 46 rings in the county.

In the western part of the county, the first rings of bells were in the ancient parish churches – notably All Saints, Rotherham; S Peter's Cathedral, Sheffield; and the Priory Church of S Mary the Virgin at Ecclesfield.

The last of these had a ring of four by 1617, to which two trebles were added in 1750; two further bells were appended in 1845 to make an anticlockwise ring of eight (they were rehung in 1952 and made clockwise), with the 7th and tenor two of the 1617 bells. Rotherham has had a ring of at least six since 1752. Thomas Hilton of nearby Wath augmented it to eight in 1782, and it was further augmented to ten in 1821 and to twelve in 1986.

At S Peter's, Sheffield, the ring of eight was installed in 1745 and increased to ten in 1798; the bells were recast only a few years later, and in 1868 were augmented to twelve thanks to a gift from a parishioner. In 1970 a new, lighter ring of twelve was installed; a fire in 1979 destroyed the ringing-room but fortunately was put out before it reached the belfry. In the early nineteenth century there was a great deal of change-ringing activity here, by two societies – S Peter's Youths and S Peter's Independent Youths – who shared the use of the bells. Their early peals included one of 6,048 Cambridge Surprise Major (it took four hours 18 minutes with the 33 cwt. tenor), which was claimed as the first in the method; unfortunately, the composition was false. (Cambridge is the most popular Surprise Major method, but is very difficult to compose peals for: the first true peal was not rung until 1873.) Later in the century the band was led by Charles Henry Hattersley, a local industrialist, who rang in over 200 peals and composed many more.

Growth of the towns in the nineteenth century saw the creation of several new sets of bells, some in old churches with rapidly expanding congregations and some in the new ones erected to serve the industrial populations. The former group included Treeton, which obtained a ring of six in 1892; nearby Beighton had one much earlier, and a peal was rung there in 1784. At S Mary's, Rawmarsh, a ring of four installed in 1709 was recast into six in 1856 and placed in a new tower, which proved unsafe and had to be dismantled. Another new tower was built in 1869, and a local landowner gave two trebles to create a ring of eight, recast in 1917.

New churches in the nineteenth century included those at Dore, Ranmoor, Eastwood and Pitsmoor. The church at Dore was built in 1829, but had only a single bell until 1908, when public subscriptions raised £600 for the ring of eight. S Stephen's, Eastwood, was somewhat more fortunate. The church was built in 1874, but shortage of money meant that the tower was not included; 36 years later Col. Sir Charles John Stottard provided for the tower and spire and the light ring of eight installed

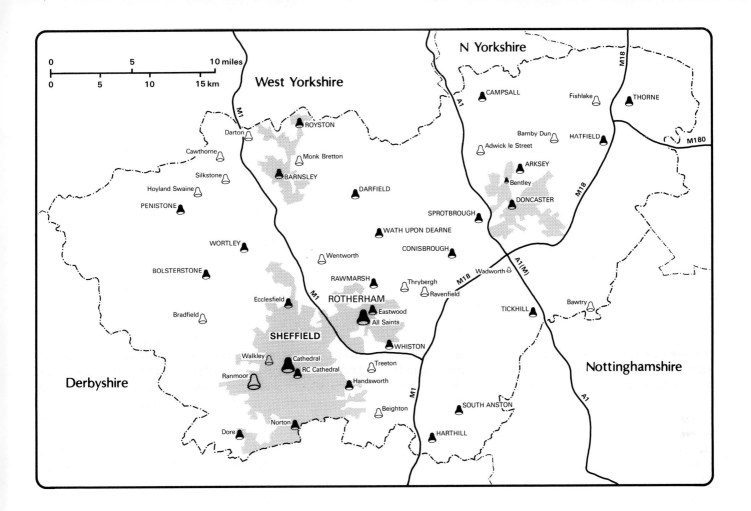

by John Warner. All Saints, Pitsmoor, was also built in the nineteenth century – by the steel industrialist John Brown – and included a ring of eight, with a ringing-room difficult of access; the church was demolished in the early 1970s, and the bells now form the back eight of the ten at S Anne's, Worksop. Also in Sheffield, and very close to S Peter's Cathedral, is a further nineteenth-century church with bells – the Roman Catholic church of S Marie, which became Hallam Cathedral in 1980. Opened in 1850, the church was provided with a ring of eight in 1861 by the Sheffield foundry of Naylor Vickers. The contract said that the congregation was to pay only for the hanging of the bells and the founders could have free use of them; if the congregation didn't wish to purchase them, they would be removed. In 1873 it was decided not to buy them, and they were removed and sent to Moseley, West Midlands, where they remain (unringable). The Duke of Norfolk, a major Sheffield landowner, gave money for four new bells, and a public subscription ensured a ring of eight, installed in 1874 by Mears and Stainbank.

Villages as well as industrial suburbs acquired bells during this period. The church of S Nicholas, Bradfield, stands high on the moors above Sheffield; its three bells were rehung in 1836 and augmented to six in 1847. Nearby, S Mary's Church was built in another isolated village, Bolsterstone, in 1879; in 1892 the death of a former vicar was marked by the raising of £585 in six weeks, sufficient to purchase a ring of eight in his memory.

In the north of the county, the boundary with West Yorkshire divides what for more than a century has been a distinctive area not so much for its bells as how they were rung. There are four features of the ringing in this area around Barnsley (where a ring of six was installed in 1769, to be augmented to eight only four years later). The first is the Yorkshire tail end, a piece of sally at the end of the rope rather than the loose part tucked back. The second is the 'closed handstroke' or 'cartwheel' method of ringing, with no gap between the tenor backstroke and treble handstroke: the bells are rung slower than in 'conventional' ringing. The third is the range of Treble Bob Minor methods rung, and the fourth is the popularity of ringing contests. In recent decades all have died out to some extent, but towers with Yorkshire tail ends where cartwheel ringing is practised still exist, and the Barnsley and District Society runs more than one striking contest annually.

West Yorkshire

THE new county of West Yorkshire combines the old woollen textile industrial areas centred on Bradford, Dewsbury, Halifax, Huddersfield and Leeds with parts of the rich Yorkshire coalfield. There are few tracts of fertile rural land in the area, and although the magnesian limestone ridge passes through the county's eastern edge – around Aberford and Bramham – there are none of the large stone towers found elsewhere on that geological outcrop.

As with most of the industrial areas of northern England, the present county of West Yorkshire was thinly populated before the nineteenth century, and had few rings of bells. Poppleton's list (in *The Yorkshire Archaeological Journal*) for the end of the nineteenth century shows one ring of five, 22 of six, 21 of eight, four of ten and three of twelve in place then. Of the rings of six, however, only half were pre-1800 installations. Indeed, there were probably only about a dozen rings of five or more bells in the county at the start of the nineteenth century, mainly in the parish churches of the old market centres. In some of these, however, change-ringing was being practised long before 1800. In 1787 a peal of Treble Bob Major by a visiting band of the Ancient Society of College Youths was claimed as the first peal in Yorkshire; the first were in 1742, however, at Leeds (on the new eight) and Wakefield. Leeds Parish Church had a ring of ten installed in 1798 – with the first peal, Grandsire Caters, rung on Christmas Day, and Wakefield Parish Church (now Cathedral) obtained ten in 1817. In the early decades of the nineteenth century the ringers at these and several other West Yorkshire towers (such as at Keighley and Sowerby, both with rings of eight installed early in the century) contributed substantially to the development of change-ringing: a peal of Cambridge Surprise Major – undoubtedly false – was rung at Keighley in 1811, for example, and the first peal of Superlative Surprise Major was rung at Huddersfield in 1821 by a local band. Perhaps the greatest of these achievements were those of the Wakefield Society, who rang the first-ever peal of Cambridge Surprise Royal in 1822 and followed it with the first of Superlative Surprise Royal four years later. (They rang a peal in the latter method in January 1825, but soon after announced that the composition had been proved false. A year passed before they succeeded in ringing a true peal, and another century passed before anybody else did.) Halifax, Leeds and Wakefield went on to instal rings of twelve (in 1857, 1841 and 1892 respectively), but Huddersfield stopped at ten; a further ring of twelve for the county was achieved in 1975, when two trebles were

added to Taylor's 1921 ring of ten for Bradford Cathedral, and 1988 saw another twelve, at Ossett.

It was the industrialization of much of the county in the late eighteenth and early nineteenth centuries that saw the introduction of rings of bells to most of the area, as old churches were either extended or replaced to cater for expanding congregations and new ones were built where previously there was nothing. In Holmfirth, for example, a parish was created in 1651. Population growth led to the need for a new church (the third on the site) in 1783, to which a tower and six bells were added in 1786/8; the bells were cast by Mears and Stainbank. For many years Holmfirth was a centre of Treble Bob Minor ringing, with its band successful in a variety of contests. Indeed, at that time West Yorkshire was renowned for its six-bell ringing, on bells from both Whitechapel (Horbury and Kildwick, for example) and Taylors (Armitage Bridge, Ilkley). At Rothwell, north of Wakefield – successively rural village, pit village and dormitory for Leeds – the first tower for the parish church was started in 1460. There were only two bells plus a clock bell by the end of the eighteenth century, however, and a ring (of six) was not installed until 1837; it was augmented to eight in the following year. At Guiseley, where there has been a church on the site of the present S Oswald's for at least 700 years, there were only three bells until 1847, when a ring of eight was installed.

New nineteenth-century churches also abound. A number of them – including those at Idle, Brighouse and Pudsey – were paid for out of the £1 million given by the government in 1818 for the building of new churches (the 'million or Waterloo churches') in the areas with rapidly expanding populations. That at Pudsey, between Bradford and Leeds, was opened in 1824; it was designed to hold 2,000 people and cost £13,360, including £1,000 for the tower. A ring of eight, partly paid for by public subscription, was installed, cast by Mears of Whitechapel, who provided many of the county's new bells at that time. Brighouse's church was opened seven years later, but had to wait until 1874 for its ring of eight bells – again from the Whitechapel foundry. Dobson of Downham Market also provided several rings of eight early in the century, including those at Birstall, Elland and Liversedge. Elsewhere, new churches depended on combinations of wealthy donors plus public subscriptions. At S Mathias, Burley, most of the money for the church was provided by a local banker and the local MP in 1854, and two other members of the MP's family provided three bells; these

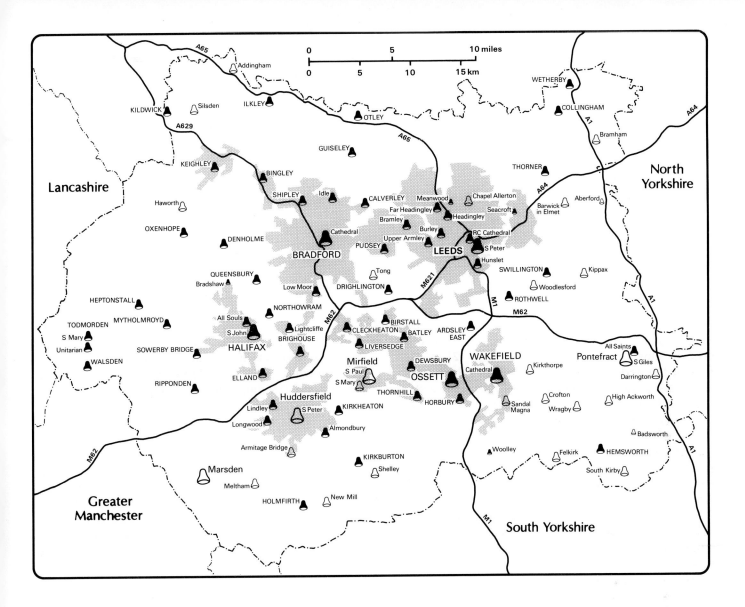

were augmented to six in 1855 and to eight in 1936.

As has all too frequently been the case, some of these nineteenth-century churches have fallen into disrepair and disuse little more than 100 years later, and the bells are no longer needed. Fortunately most have found new homes. In Leeds, for example, the eight at S Matthew's, Holbeck (an inner working-class suburb) was moved to the mining village of Swillington in 1979, 108 years after its initial installation, and the eight from the nearby Roman Catholic church of S Francis to S Anne's (Roman Catholic) Cathedral in the city centre in 1980. At Thornhill the church of S Michael and All Angels obtained a ring of six in 1873 from Mirfield parish church, where a new ring of ten was provided to replace the century-old bells. In 1979 it was decided to replace these with the ring of eight then hanging in S Paul's, Cross Stone, Todmorden, which had been cast by Charles Carr of Smethwick in 1910. The mill town of Todmorden had four rings of eight at one time (includ-ing one at the Unitarian church; there were also bells at Congregational churches at Lightcliffe and Saltaire, both now lost); others lost include a ring of nine at S John, Bradford (which included a flat fourth), the eight from Bolton in the same city, and the 1853 ring of eight at Earlsheaton; a 1794 ring of eight at S John's, Wakefield, has been hung dead since the tower was rebuilt in 1844. Meanwhile, new rings have been installed, too, includ-ing a ring of five at Woolley in 1985 and an augmenta-tion in 1986 to five of the three set up in 1865 at Seacroft.

Yorkshire ringers have contributed to the develop-ment of their art in a variety of ways. The most famous was probably Jasper Whitfield Snowdon (1844–85) of Ilkley, who in his short life wrote a number of books on ringing methods and history. He was a co-founder and first president, in 1875, of the Yorkshire Association of Change Ringers, and a tribute to his life and work is the stained glass window erected in Ilkley Church to his memory in 1887.

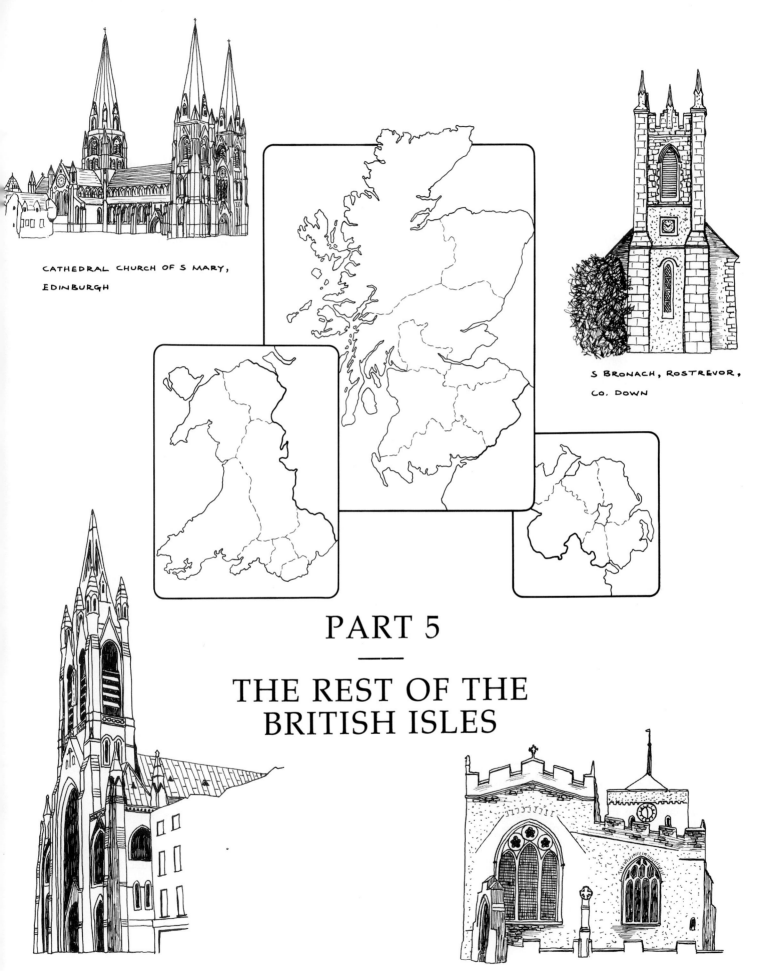

CATHEDRAL CHURCH OF S MARY,
EDINBURGH

S BRONACH, ROSTREVOR,
CO. DOWN

PART 5

—

THE REST OF THE
BRITISH ISLES

SS AUGUSTINE & JOHN, DUBLIN

S MARY VIRGIN, HAVERFORDWEST, DYFED

North Wales: Clwyd and Gwynedd

IN North Wales, as in the southern portions of the principality, it is a general rule that the further you get from England the fewer the rings of bells. Thus nowhere on the Lleyn Peninsula resounds to changes on four or more bells, and the residents must travel to Porthmadog for that pleasure. Further south, in what was formerly Merionethshire, the locals are little better served, with only the rings of eight at Barmouth (set up in 1894) and Dolgellau (where a peal was rung in 1809, the year of their installation) to entertain their ears, and anybody on the isle of Anglesey wishing to hear bells must travel to Beaumaris (installed as a six in 1819 by Dobson of Downham Market and augmented to eight in 1904).

Although rings of bells are few in these counties, there are more rings of eight than of six – because most of them are in the towns (an indication not only of the relative poverty of many of the villages but also of the dispersed settlement pattern characteristic of the area, with relatively few nucleations of any size). Even so, the visitor to many of the towns may well be disappointed on Sundays, for there are no rings in Caernarfon, Holyhead, Llanfairfechan, Penmaenmawr, Conwy, Colwyn Bay or Prestatyn; the only exceptions are the Taylor rings of eight at Llandudno (1893) and Rhyl (1876). The two cathedrals in the area are Bangor (a ring of three, including a 29¼ cwt. tenor) and St Asaph (a two, with a 25 cwt. tenor). Bangor does have an 1888 ring of eight at Glenadda, however, an 1816 ring of six at Llandegai and a chime of six at Upper Bangor.

Only one church in North Wales has more than eight bells, and has had for more than 200 years. S Giles's massive western tower in Wrexham is at least the third to stand there, one of its predecessors having fallen in a gale and another burnt in a fire: the present Perpendicular tower was built after the 1457 fire (there is an exact copy of it at Yale University, whose founder is buried in S Giles's churchyard). The ring of ten was installed by the ubiquitous Abraham Rudhall in 1726, the bells being transported by barge from Gloucester to Shrewsbury and thence over land by horse-drawn wagon. Three years later, the first peal in Wales was scored on the back eight – Grandsire Triples, only eleven years after the first-ever peal in the method.

Elsewhere in the western part of Clwyd are nearly all the rings of six in North Wales; the exceptions are Abergele (originally a 1730 ring of five, augmented to six in 1887) Rhuddlan and Llandegai (an 1816 ring from Downham Market). In what was Flintshire and Denbighshire the pattern is similar to that across the English border in Cheshire, with village churches having introduced rings in the eighteenth century, influenced by developments in nearby settlements and by the promotional activities of founders. The Rudhalls of Gloucester were by far the most successful promoters of their wares (as shown by Clouston's list published in *Archaeologensis Cambriensis*, 1951); they exploited the Severn Valley routeway, providing the rings of six for Holt in 1714 and Chirk a century later, for example. Hawarden, not far from Chester, where Rudhalls did much trade in the early eighteenth century, is one of the churches with a set of their bells, though their six was not the first to sound from the thirteenth-century tower of S Deiniol. Scott of Wigan provided an early six in 1662, which Rudhall replaced 80 years later: the bells carry the typical Gloucester inscriptions: 'Peace and good neighbourhood', 'Prosperity to all our benefactors' and 'Prosperity to this parish' are on bells 1, 2 and 3 respectively (as they are on 4, 5 and 8 at Wrexham), while the tenor (like Wrexham's tenor) carries the message 'I to the church the living call and to the grave do summon all'. Nearby Buckley was separated from Hawarden parish only in 1874 (although its church was consecrated in 1822), and a tower capable of carrying a ring of eight was not completed until 1901. Those eight were duly installed by Taylors a year later, and a Chester ringer was engaged to teach a local band in spring 1903; a year later they rang their first peal.

Clouston's listing for Flintshire (the only part of North Wales for which such a list has been published) shows rings in only 15 of the 59 churches. Of those 15, only at five (Bangor-is-y-coed, Gresford, Hanmer, Hawarden and Mold) was there a ring of five or more before 1900; the rest are modern installations, including three (Buckley, Hope and Rhuddlan) provided in the present century. There is an eight dating from 1872 by Mears and Stainbank at the 'marble church' of Bodelwyddan; in what was Denbighshire, there are also eights at Denbigh (1873) and Ruthin (1889, an augmentation of an 1843 ring of six) in the Clwyd valley, as well as in the magnificent tower at Gresford (1875) just outside Wrexham.

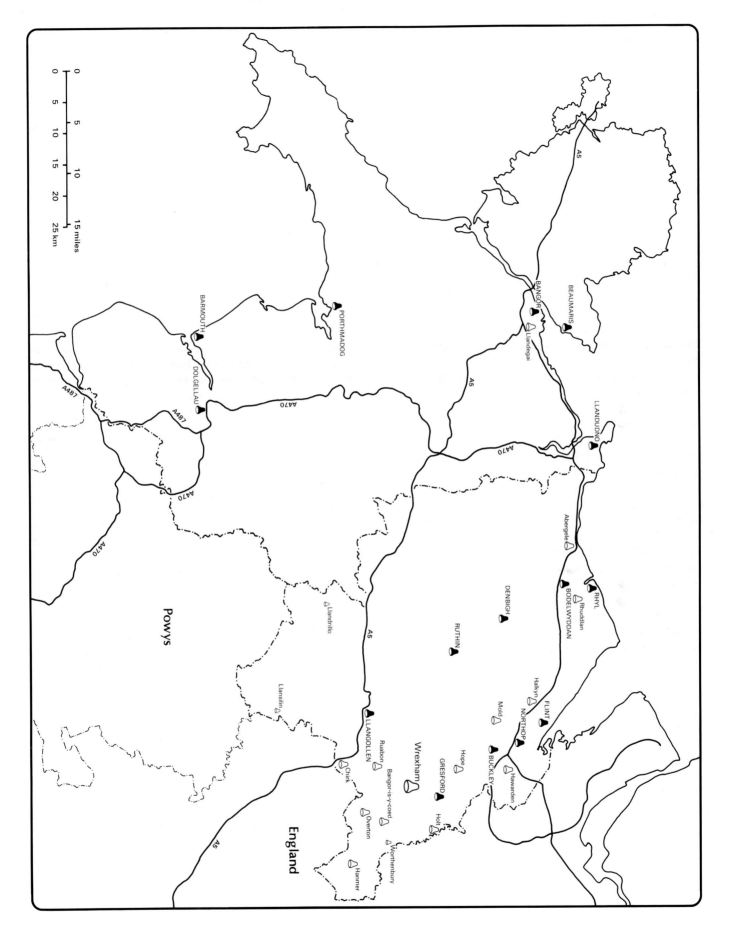

Powys

England

Wrexham

BARMOUTH

PORTHMADOG

DOLGELLAU

BANGOR

BEAUMARIS

Llandegai

LLANDUDNO

Abergele

DENBIGH

RHYL
Rhuddlan
BODELWYDDAN

Llandrillo

RUTHIN

Halkyn
FLINT
NORTHOP

Mold

Llansilin

LLANGOLLEN

Ruabon

Hope

BUCKLEY

GRESFORD

Hawarden

Chirk

Bangor-is-y-coed

Overton

Holt

Worthenbury

Hammer

A5

A470

A487

Mid and West Wales: Dyfed and Powys

THIS almost entirely rural area has a very low density of rings of bells. In part this is because large tracts are devoid of settlement. It also reflects the relative poverty of much of the settled area, so that the parish churches were small and poorly endowed.

The relative poverty of much of the counties is reflected in the ecclesiastical architecture, and clearly demonstrated in Sharpe's listings of the bells of the former counties of Cardiganshire and Radnorshire (*The Church Bells of Cardiganshire*, 1965, and *The Church Bells of Radnorshire*, 1947). For Radnorshire, on the English border, he provided details of the bells at 64 churches, of which 31 had only a turret or an open frame, 22 had but a single bell and seven others had two bells. Of the 33 churches with a tower, 21 had a ring of three or more bells, though there were only three rings of five, four of six and two of eight. The rings of eight are in two neighbouring small towns on the Shropshire border: Presteigne obtained a ring of six in 1717, four years before Knighton, and its augmentation to eight in 1906 was eight years before Knighton's. A further eight, at Glasbury, began as a Rudhall six in 1795; it was replaced in 1838 and augmented in 1905. The other settlements closest to English influence – Gladestry, Old Radnor and Clyro – all had rings early in the eighteenth century (in 1719, 1724, and 1708 respectively), but further into Wales the bells were later arriving: New Radnor acquired five in 1851, augmented to six in 1938; at Llanfihangel Rhydeithon the ring of three was increased to five in 1838, and an extra bell, donated by the then vicar, who was a keen ringer, was added in 1936; at Crossgates the ring of five was installed in 1912; at Nantmel the ring of six came in 1903.

Further south, in what was formerly the county of Brecknock, there are slightly more rings of bells, especially in the valley of the Usk and its tributary the Llynfi (although Merthyr Cynog must be one of the most isolated rings; unfortunately only one of the bells is now hung for ringing). Brecon itself has three rings of bells: an eight at S Mary's (installed in 1750 by Rudhalls), a six at S David's, Llanfaes, and a five at the cathedral. The last are unringable; they are the remnants of a Rudhall six, three of them dating from 1745, but the second is missing – presumed stolen. As in Radnorshire, many of the rings are relatively recent augmentations to an eighteenth-century foundation: at Bronllys, for example, a 1721 ring of five by Evans of Chepstow (who also provided rings of six for Llanfihangel, Cwm Du and Llangattock in 1719 and Llangorse in 1721) was augmented to six in 1939; at Llandefaelog Fach a ring of five installed by 1718 was augmented to six in 1889; at Llanelli a 1715 ring of five was augmented in 1909; at Defynnog a ring of four was augmented to six in 1887; and at Llanfeugan (Pencelli) a seventeenth-century ring of four was recast and increased to eight in 1921.

In the north of Powys, occupying what was formerly the county of Montgomeryshire, there is a small number of rings – most of them comprising six bells – close to the English border; the ring of eight at Machynlleth is extremely isolated from the rest. Rudhalls provided several of the rings, including those at Llanfyllin (six, 1714), Church Stoke (five, 1721), Montgomery (six, 1724), Newtown (six, 1727) and Welshpool (six, 1791; recast and augmented to eight, 1724). Further west, rings of bells are very few. In what was Cardiganshire, Sharpe lists 97 churches, of which only 34 had a tower: of the churches with one bell only, 19 had a tower and 63 a turret. Of the 17 churches with two or more bells, there were ten with two, two with three, and one each with four, six and eight. The ring of four (installed in 1777) at the isolated village of Llandysul was restored and augmented by Taylors in 1969. The ring of six is in S Mary's Church, Cardigan. In 1705 the tower of this church, containing five bells, collapsed; Lester and Pack used the salvaged metal in providing a new six in 1754, but five of these were replaced by Rudhalls in 1810. The fourth was cracked in 1880, and the bells were not rung again until restoration in 1961. Llanbadarn Fawr, a suburb of the university and resort town of Aberystwyth, has the ring of eight, this being an 1885 augmentation of a 1749 installation of six.

The southern part of Dyfed is positively overcrowded with rings of bells compared with Cardiganshire, including Rudhall rings at Laugharne, Llandeilo and Llandovery: even so, there are only 14 rings, half of which contain eight bells. They include S Peter's Church, Carmarthen, for which Abraham Rudhall provided a ring of six in 1722; this was augmented in 1904, with two of the original bells being recast. Further west, the former county of Pembrokeshire is often cited as more English than some of its eastern neighbours. But the provision of rings of church bells was not a characteristic widely introduced, and there are only six, including eighteenth-century rings at Haverfordwest, Nevern and Tenby. In addition there is the ring of eight in St David's Cathedral. Its central tower had at least five bells by the end of the sixteenth century, but these were removed 200 years later. The present (1930) ring of eight hangs in an octagonal gateway tower.

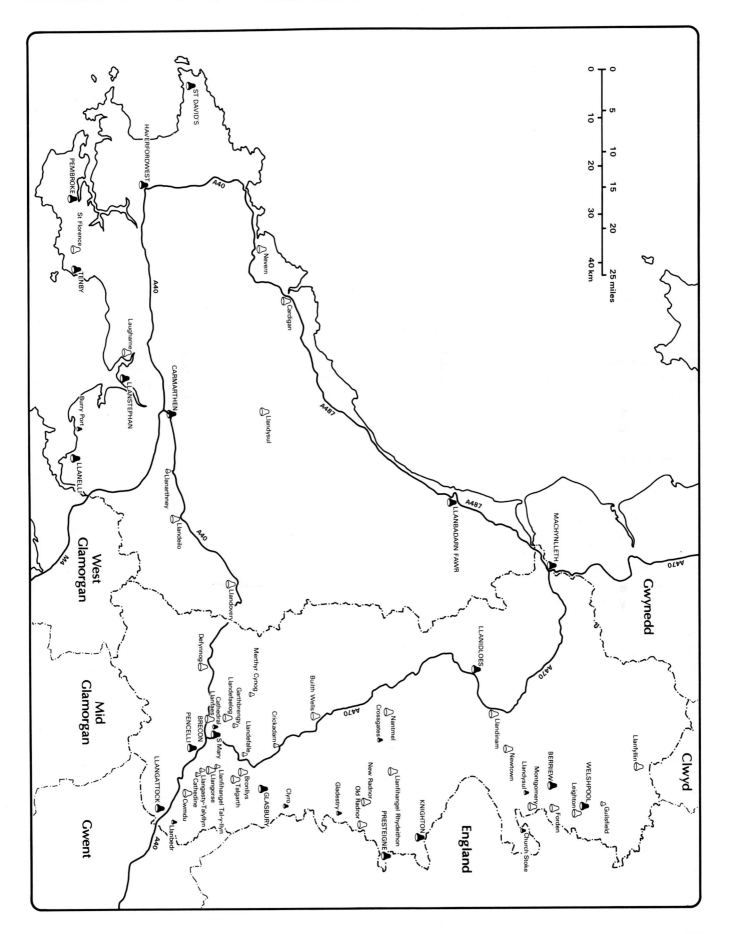

ST DAVID'S

HAVERFORDWEST

PEMBROKE

St Florence

TENBY

Laugharne

LLANSTEPHAN

Burry Port

LLANELLI

Llanarthney

Llandeilo

West Glamorgan

Mid Glamorgan

Nevern

Cardigan

A40

A487

Llandysul

A487

LLANBADARN FAWR

MACHYNLLETH

Gwynedd

A470

CARMARTHEN

Llandovery

Defynog

Merthyr Cynog

Garthbrengy
Llandefaelog

Cathedral
Llanfaes
PENCELLI
BRECON
S'Mary

Llandefalle

Crickadarn

Builth Wells

A470

LLANIDLOES

Llandinam

LLANIDLOES

Nantmel
Crossgates

Newtown
Llandysul
Montgomery
BERRIEW
Forden

Llanfylin

WELSHPOOL
Leighton

Guilsfield

Clwyd

Church Stoke

England

LLANGATTOCK

Llanfihangel Tal-y-llyn

Garthbrengy
Llangorse
Talgarth
Cathedine
Cwmdu
Llanbedr

Bronllys

Clyro

Gladestry

New Radnor
Old Radnor

Llanfihangel Rhydeithon

PRESTEIGNE

KNIGHTON

A40

Gwent

163

South Wales: Glamorgan and Gwent

ABOUT half of all of the rings of bells in Wales are to be found in the four south-eastern counties – Gwent, plus Mid, South and West Glamorgan. This is in many ways the most anglicized part of Wales, not so much because of its proximity to England as because of the industrialization of the nineteenth century, which saw the development of the major towns of Cardiff, Newport and Swansea (though early in the process Merthyr Tydfil was the largest town in Wales). Proximity to England, and the influence of the English established church (disestablished in Wales early in the twentieth century), means that Gwent (formerly Monmouthshire) has most rings of bells, however. In Glamorgan the main concentration is on the rich coastal plain to the west of Cardiff. There are relatively few rings of bells in the valley settlements of Mid Glamorgan, and only nine in the county most distant from England.

Unfortunately, no listings of the bells of these counties have been published apart from Wright's *The Church Bells of Monmouthshire* (1942). The writer on the occasion of the 80th anniversary of the foundation of the Llandaff and Monmouth Diocesan Association of Change Ringers (which covers much of South Wales) notes that in 1893 the area contained '11 rings of eight and a fair number of fives and sixes' (*The Ringing World*, 12 October 1973). The main rings included Llandaff Cathedral, now in suburban Cardiff, S John's, Cardiff, S Mary's, Monmouth, and S Woolos's, Newport – all four of which are depicted on the association's original membership certificate. S Woolos's has the only ring of twelve in the principality, dating from 1939, when Gillett and Johnston recast the front three of the ring of ten installed in 1913 and added two more trebles; these five differ in weight by only 89 pounds between the lightest and the heaviest. Llandaff obtained a ring of ten six years after Newport. Until 1879 it had but a single bell in the north-west tower, but an octave was then installed (incorporating that 1782 bell); two trebles were added in 1920. The tower at S John's, Cardiff, was built in 1473, and by 1708 it contained a Rudhall six; this became an eight in 1814, and the first ring of ten in South Wales in 1893. Monmouth's ring of eight is even older; it was recast by Abraham Rudhall in 1706.

There are two other rings of ten in Gwent. Abergavenny's was installed in 1948, replacing an eight completed in 1887 (when the existing six was found to be unringable). Chepstow acquired its ten in 1959. Its ring of six was installed in 1735 by the local founder William Evans, who augmented it to eight 14 years later. The foundry was open from 1686 to 1767, producing a

total of 508 bells, many of which are still to be heard in the local area as well as in the Wye Valley and across the Bristol Channel. William Evans also cast five bells for Exeter Cathedral, including the tenor, Grandison, for long the largest ringable bell in England, which was recast by Taylors in 1902.

On the Glamorgan plain, many of the village churches are old, and some had rings of bells before the nineteenth century. At Coity, just outside Bridgend, for example, there were four bells by 1710, when Evans of Chepstow rehung them; a fifth was added in 1723, and in 1726 a new ring of six was provided, the old bells being sent by sea to Chepstow. Those bells are still rung today, having been rehung in 1952. The small church of Porthkerry, near Barry, also had four bells about 250 years ago, but these were augmented to six only in 1950. Cowbridge received a complete ring of eight from the same foundry in 1722. Similarly at Llanishen, now a suburb of Cardiff, a ring of three was initiated by the Chepstow founders in the mid-eighteenth century; a new six was installed by the Bristol foundry of Llewellin and James in 1890, these being replaced by a new light six in 1978. Llewellin and James also cast a ring of six (now eight) for the Cardiff suburb of Whitchurch. Further west, at Swansea, a six at Morriston has been removed, but the eight at S Mary's lost by action in the war has been replaced.

Outside the main towns, there is a major difference between the small settlements of the coastal plain and the larger, newer ones of the valleys to the north. This is very clear in the contrast between South Glamorgan, where three-quarters of the rings are of six bells or fewer, and Mid Glamorgan, where the majority have eight bells. In Gwent, too, most of the valley churches with bells have a ring of eight, whereas most of those on the coastal plain have either five or six (the 1866 ring of six at Bassaleg is of steel). Ebbw Vale is typical of the valley churches. Christ Church was built in 1861, but its tower was not completed until 1880. In 1896 a Derbyshire lady gave the church a lectern – but she had given a ring of bells to Bedwellty. It was only in 1936 that Christ Church received bells, to mark the reopening of the local steelworks after seven years' idleness. The chairman of the local steel company donated £200, and the new ring was heard when the first furnace was 'blown in' in October 1937. Taylors of Loughborough provided several of these late nineteenth-century rings, including those at Merthyr Tydfil (1893) and Pentre (1890; the heaviest tenor bell in Wales at 26.3.19); there was already a Rudhall six (1807) at Blaenavon, which Taylors replaced with an eight.

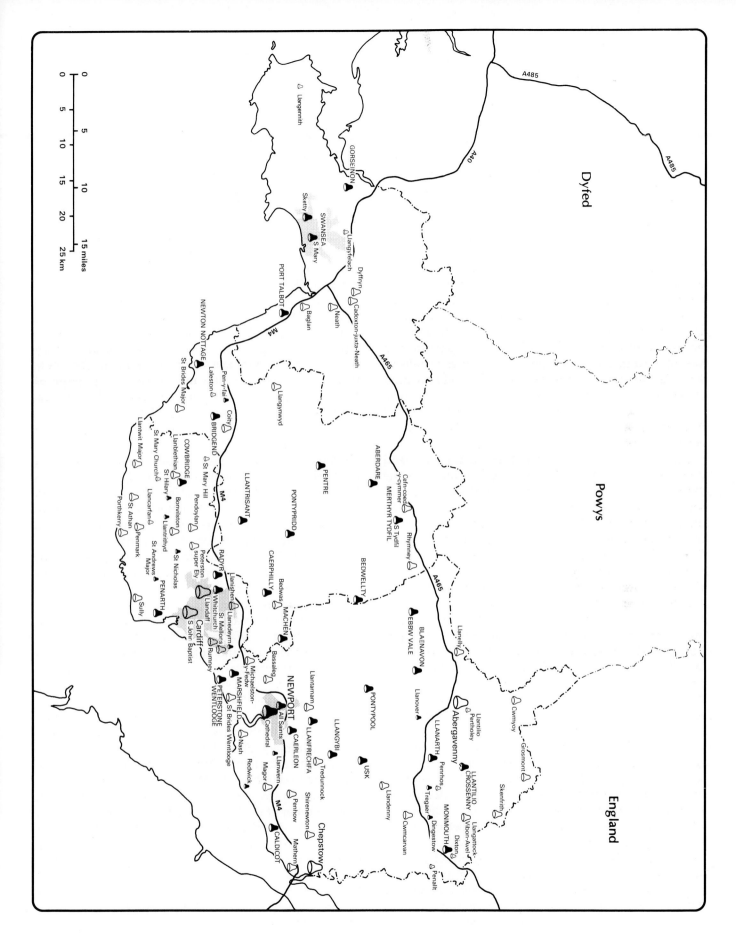

Scale bar:
0
5
10
15
20
25 km

0
5
10
15 miles

Dyfed

Powys

England

GORSEINON

Llangennith

Sketty

SWANSEA
S Mary

Llangyfelach

PORT TALBOT

Dyffryn
Cadoxton-juxta-Neath
Neath
Baglan

A40

A485

A485

A465

NEWTON NOTTAGE

St Brides Major

Laleston
Pen-y-fai

Corty

BRIDGEND

St Mary Hill

Llangynwyd

Llangynwyd

ABERDARE

PENTRE

Cefn-coed-
y-cymmer
S Tydfil

MERTHYR TYDFIL

Rhymney

Llantwit Major
St Mary Church
COWBRIDGE
Llanblethian
St Hilary
Bonviston
Pendoylan
Llantrithyd
St Nicholas

Porthkerry
St Athan
Penmark
Llancarfan
St Andrews
Major

LLANTRISANT

PONTYPRIDD

BEDWELLTY

RADYR
Peterston
super Ely

Llanishen

Whitchurch
Llandaff
Cardiff
St Mellons
S John Baptist
Rumney

CAERPHILLY

Bedwas
MACHEN
Bassaleg

Sully

PENARTH

Michaelston-
y-Fedw

MARSHFIELD

St Brides Wentlooge

PETERSTONE
WENTLOOGE

Nash

Redwick

Magor

Llanwern

Penhow

Shirenewton

Matherne

CALDICOT

Chepstow

NEWPORT
All Saints
Cathedral

Llantarnam

LLANFRECHFA
CAERLEON

Tredunnock

LLANGYBI

USK

PONTYPOOL

Llandenny

Cwmcarvan

Llanover

EBBW VALE

BLAENAVON

Abergavenny

LLANARTH

Penhos
Tregaer
Dingestow

MONMOUTH

Dixton

Penallt

Llanelly

Llantilio
Pertholey

Cwmyoy
Grosmont

Skenfrith

LLANTILIO
CROSSENNY
Llangattock-
Vibon-Avel

165

Scotland

SCOTLAND has only 15 rings, the great majority of them containing either eight or ten bells. In part, the absence of bells reflects that country's separate Christian denomination – Presbyterianism – which in general frowns upon expensive items such as bells, and certainly so if they play no significant role in the church's life. Most of the rings are in Episcopal churches (the Episcopal Church of Scotland is in communion with the Church of England, but the Presbyterian Church is the established Church of Scotland). But in part, too, the lack of bells reflects their general absence in adjacent northern England; rural ways of life were generally harsh in the northern areas, population densities low, and churches small and lacking expensive contents. Full details of the rings were published in a pamphlet 'Scottish Rings of Bells' (1949) by Ronald Clouston, updated by him in *The Ringing World* (24 and 31 December 1982). Scotland does have several carillons, however, six of the total of 19 in Great Britain (at Aberdeen, St Andrews, Perth, Dumbarton, Dunfermline and Kilmarnock).

The first ring of bells was not installed in Scotland until 1789, when an eight cast at Whitechapel in the previous year was provided for S Andrew's Church, Edinburgh. Tower problems mean these have been unringable since 1903. (S John's church in Perth has a carillon and 28 other bells, including eight bells cast before the Reformation.) Dunkeld Cathedral acquired a ring of six – also from Whitechapel – in 1814; these, too, were unringable for many years, but have recently been restored. S James, Leith (the port of Edinburgh) obtained a ring of eight in 1866, but these were removed in the 1970s when the church was declared redundant, and some were rehung at Larbert as a chime. S Nicholas's, Aberdeen, also had a nineteenth-century eight (the first peal in Scotland was rung on these bells, in 1859), having been made a four in 1795 and a five in 1803 before augmentation in 1859; it was lost in a fire in 1874.

The early introduction of rings of bells to Scotland was not particularly successful, therefore, and it was not until the middle of the nineteenth century that some of the present rings were installed. In 1879 a ring of ten was placed in S Mary's Episcopal Cathedral, Edinburgh, when that building was opened. The bells, cast by Taylors of Loughborough, have a tenor that is the fifth heaviest in the world for a ring of ten (only 21 pounds lighter than Inveraray's, which is the third heaviest; they were a gift of the Dean, and such was their novelty that a band from Leeds was brought in to ring a peal to mark the opening. S Mary's Episcopal Cathedral,

Glasgow, received its ring of ten in 1901, again as the result of a single donation – by the parents of Louise Pearson.

Scotland has three other rings of ten. The oldest is at Inveraray, in a massive tower which dominates the church in this small town. The church was built by the wife of the eighth Duke of Argyll, who lived in nearby Inveraray Castle, in 1866, but the tower was added only in the 1920s by the tenth Duke, as a war memorial; the Duke was patron of the Scottish Association of Change Ringers. The bells were cast (by Taylors) in 1920, but the tower was incomplete until 1932. The bells were almost derelict in the first two decades after the Second World War, and visiting bands who made the long journey to ring (usually a peal attempt) on what is widely recognized as one of the finest sets of ten in the world had to take their own ropes. Much has been done to improve the conditions in the 1980s, and there is now an annual ringing week each summer, but in such an isolated, small community it is difficult to sustain a local band of change-ringers.

Scotland's other rings of ten are the results of relatively recent augmentations from eight, in 1970 at S Cuthbert's, Edinburgh, and in 1973 at S Andrew's Cathedral, Inverness. The latter is Britain's northernmost tower: its nearest neighbours are the 1880 Warners' ring of four at Fort William and the new eight – installed in 1987 – at S Machar's Cathedral, Aberdeen, whose bells were obtained from the redundant church of S Stephen's, West Ealing.

Apart from the five rings of ten, Scotland has six of eight, two of which are in Dundee. Both were installed in 1872, by the Whitechapel foundry, at S Paul's Episcopal Cathedral and at S Mary's Tower, which was built and is owned by the city council; they are rung by the one society – the Dundee Society of Bellringers. One year earlier a ring of six had been installed at Alloa (which was augmented to eight in 1925), and in 1882 Sir Peter Coats gave the original ring of eight at Paisley. The bells at Dunblane Cathedral, north of Stirling, were cast as a chime by Taylors in 1908 and were hung for ringing (with the two trebles recast) in 1951.

Of the two rings of six, one is at Dunkeld Cathedral and the other at the Church of the Holy Rude, Stirling. The latter's fifteenth-century tower contained only four bells until 1970; the frame installed then allows for a ring of eight, but to date only a six has been provided. Finally, there is just one ring of five – at Fettes College, Edinburgh, where the lightest ring of five in the world (tenor 2¼ cwt.), cast by Taylors in 1956, hangs in a turret on the college roof.

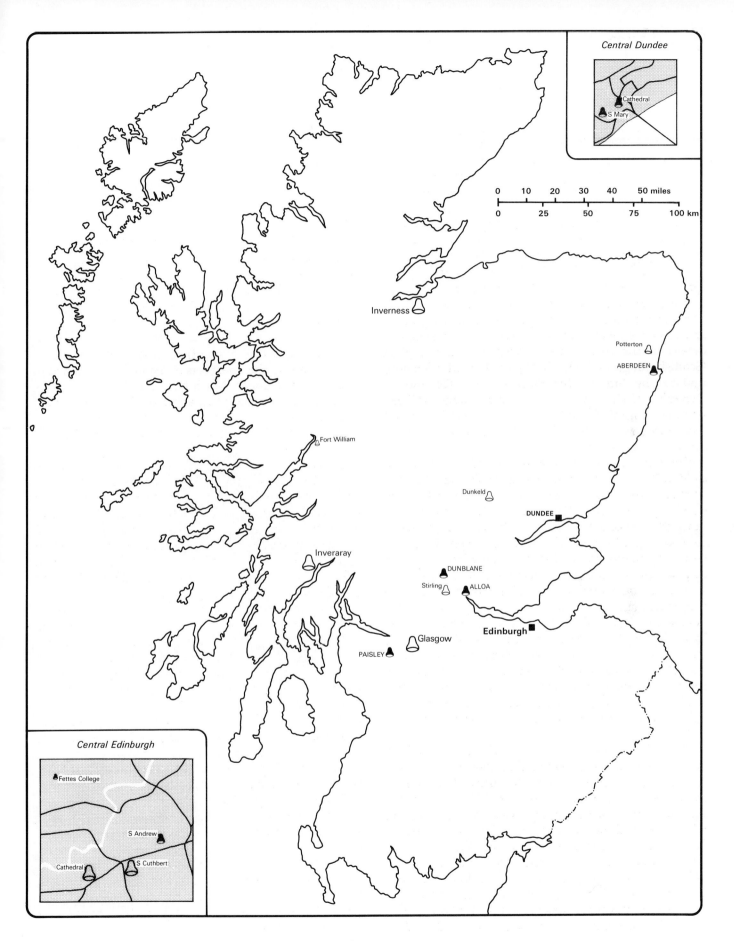

Central Dundee

Cathedral
S Mary

0   10   20   30   40   50 miles
0   25   50   75   100 km

Inverness

Potterton
ABERDEEN

Fort William

Dunkeld

DUNDEE

Inveraray

DUNBLANE

Stirling   ALLOA

Glasgow

Edinburgh

PAISLEY

Central Edinburgh

Fettes College

S Andrew

Cathedral   S Cuthbert

167

Ireland

THE map of Ireland shows very few rings more than a few miles inland. But then, Ireland's four main cities of Belfast, Cork, Dublin and Londonderry are ports.

There are two main reasons why it is basically only the coastal towns that have rings of bells. Change-ringing was developed in England, and was taken to Ireland by a colonial power whose main settlements there were the ports – especially Dublin. The further inland you go, the further you get from the influence of anglicization. In the northern province of Ulster much of the settlement was from Scotland – a virtual campanological desert until the end of the nineteenth century – so again it was only in the main centre of English influence, notably the Belfast area, that one might expect to find substantial numbers of bells. The colonists and settlers – English and Scots – brought their own religious denominations, which differed from that dominant among the native Irish population, and there was little conversion to either Presbyterianism or the Church of England (for which the Church of Ireland forms the local branch).

Only five Roman Catholic churches, all in the Republic, have rings of bells. Three are rings of ten, at the Immaculate Conception, Wexford, Mount S Alphonsus Monastery, Limerick, and the church of SS Augustine and John in Dublin, built between 1862 and 1895. In 1872 a local resident gave a ring of eight bells, which were cast just along the street by John Murphy, who traded between 1818 and 1880; Carrs of Smethwick augmented them to ten in 1898.

Whereas all three rings of ten in Roman Catholic churches are rung, this is not the case with either of the rings of eight. The heavy eight (tenor 34 cwt.) at S Mary Magdalene Cathedral, Cork, is unringable, as is the similar ring (tenor 29 cwt.) at the Cathedral of the Assumption, Thurles, where only bells 1 to 7 are hung for ringing. (Another eight, at S Paul's, Dublin, is now hung 'dead'.)

Dublin is the main centre of ringing in the Republic. The city has two Church of Ireland cathedrals, the National Cathedral of S Patrick and the Diocesan Cathedral of Christ Church; each has a tenor weighing just over 45 cwt. S Patrick's has the eighth heaviest twelve in the world, whereas Christ Church has the third heaviest ring of ten. S Patrick's bells were originally an eight, cast by Purdue, in Dublin, in 1670; they were augmented to ten in 1897 by Lord Iveagh. Instrumental in obtaining this gift was the Lord Chief Justice of Ireland, Sir Richard Cherry, who had learned to ring in Waterford (where a Whitechapel eight was

installed in 1870) and was an active ringer in Dublin for 30 years after the installation; he paid for the augmentation in 1909. He also persuaded a notable English ringer, Gabriel Lindoff, to move to Dublin in order to establish change-ringing there. Christ Church had a ring of eight cast by Abel Rudhall in 1738, which Murphy augmented to ten, plus the semitones, in 1877.

The only ring of six in Dublin (one of only three in the Republic) is in the city's only medieval church, S Audoen's. This was initially provided with three bells, but by 1790 had a ring of six which was intermittently ringable during the following century. In 1982 the church received a bequest from its late church warden, which was to be used first for rehanging the bells; they were reopened in the following year.

Outside Dublin, Arklow, Bray and Drogheda (Rudhall, 1790) all have rings of eight with tenors weighing more than a ton, and there is a six (hung anticlockwise in 1682) at the village of Blessington. The only ring of five, at S Fachtna's Cathedral, Rosscarbery, is unringable. Arklow is another tower to which an English ringer was invited to develop change-ringing. The well-known Oxfordshire ringer James W. Washbrook moved there in 1899, where he not only trained a competent peal band but rang the first double-handed peals. (Lord Carysfort, who had given the bells in 1898, employed Washbrook as both steeplekeeper and verger.)

There are two rings at Limerick. At the cathedral, a ring of six was cast by the Purdue brothers in 1673, when William Purdue died and was buried there; it was augmented in 1703. Cork has heavy rings of eight in its Church of Ireland (tenor 27 cwt.; a 1751 Rudhall ring) and Roman Catholic (34 cwt.) cathedrals, though the latter bells are unringable.

The Belfast area has the largest concentration of rings of bells in Ireland. The city itself has a ten, an eight and a six, though none is in the oldest part of the city; the oldest ring is the eight at S Thomas, installed in 1871. Nearby Bangor (1899), Carrickfergus (1920), Holywood and Lurgan have rings of eight and Hillsborough a ring of ten; only the Hillsborough ring is old, a 1772 Rudhall eight augmented in 1972. In 1987 the first ring of twelve in Northern Ireland was opened, at Ballymena. (There are twelve bells in S Columb's Cathedral, Londonderry, as well as at Christ Church, Dublin, but no true twelve for ringing: each is a ring of ten with two extra bells to make a light eight. S Patrick's Church, Ballymena, obtained a ring of eight in 1895 and replaced it by a light twelve in 1987.

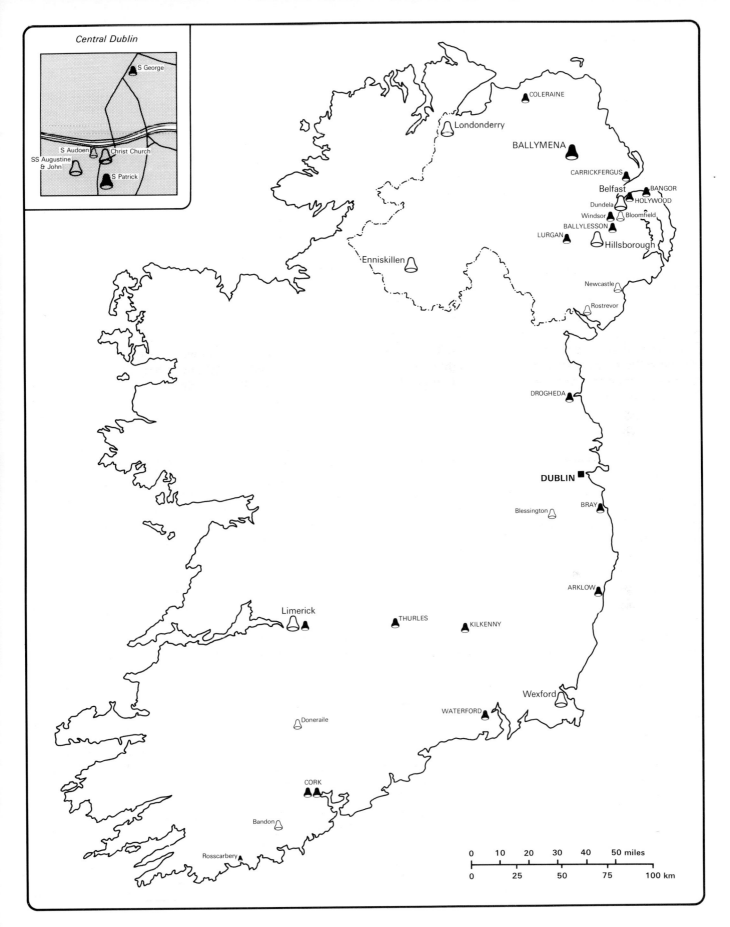

Central Dublin

S George

S Audoen   Christ Church
SS Augustine
& John
S Patrick

COLERAINE

Londonderry

BALLYMENA

CARRICKFERGUS

Belfast   BANGOR
Dundela   HOLYWOOD
Windsor   Bloomfield
BALLYLESSON
LURGAN
Hillsborough

Enniskillen

Newcastle
Rostrevor

DROGHEDA

DUBLIN

BRAY
Blessington

ARKLOW

Limerick
THURLES   KILKENNY

Wexford
WATERFORD
Doneraile

CORK

Bandon

Rosscarbery

| 0 | 10 | 20 | 30 | 40 | 50 miles |

| 0 | 25 | 50 | 75 | 100 km |

169

The Islands

THE Channel Islands are small outposts of the English way of life close to the coast of France, and their local culture includes change-ringing; indeed, in recent years that culture has been flourishing and new rings have been installed.

Jersey has twelve parishes, each with a church, but only two have rings of bells. S John in the Oaks has a ground-floor ring of eight and S Mark the Evangelist, in the main town of St Helier, has a ring of six. The latter was built in 1844, and provided with bells from Whitechapel. These could not be rung between 1880 and 1970, however, because of the installation of a clock; restoration work allowed them to be reopened in 1973.

Guernsey now has more rings than Jersey, thanks to two major projects in the early 1980s. The oldest ring on the island is at Greve (also known as St Michael du Valle, Vale), where a medieval three was recast and augmented to six by Warners in 1891. They were retuned and rehung in 1971 – providing easier bells to ring for the local call-change band. In 1985 a second ring of six was provided, with an augmentation of the unrung four at Le Bourg (St Marguerite de la Forêt). The back three were cast in 1685, and a treble was added by Warners in 1896 (a few years after the Vale job was completed). Those four were retuned in 1984, and two new trebles cast by Whitechapel foundry; the central tower is a small one, and even though the tenor weighs only 5½ cwt. the bells are hung in three tiers. A few miles away, at St Pierre du Bois (Les Buttes), a ring of ten was installed in the same year (1985), having been purchased from the redundant church of S Catherine, Feltham. One band of ringers serves both churches. There are also bells in St Peter Port, at the pro-cathedral. The originals were provided in 1736, and they were recast (at Villedieu in France) in 1913; the frame and fittings are from the eighteenth century, however. Although they have been rung at least once since the Second World War they are now chimed only.

The other Channel Island with a ring of bells is Alderney, which obtained its six for St Anne's in 1850, when the church was opened. The bells were used to warn islanders of the impending invasion in 1940, and were then removed from the tower so that it could be converted into an observation and machine-gun post. Four of the bells were sent to France to be melted for munitions, but never were, and were rescued from a dump in Cherbourg and returned to Alderney in 1947. They were not replaced in the tower but set up on trestles in the churchyard, and it was only in 1953 that sufficient money was raised to have them recast and rehung in the tower.

Ringing now flourishes in the Channel Islands, and in the local striking contest held in October 1987 the six towers entered a total of ten teams.

Lundy Island and the Isle of Man have rings of bells, but no ringing. Lundy, which is officially part of Devon (see map on p. 63), has a ring of eight at S Helen's Church, cast by Carr of Smethwick and given by the island's clerical owner in 1897. These have been rung to one peal – Stedman Triples, conducted by F. E. Robinson – in 1905. Robinson, the first person to ring 1,000 peals, complained that the steamers did not stay long enough for a peal attempt, so that the cost of a day trip for a quick 'tower-grab' was very high. The first attempt for the peal failed after half an hour because of the state of the bells, and, as Robinson puts it in *Among the Bells*, pp. 451–2, the ringers 'beaten and dispirited, prepared for their return voyage.' But a gale sprung up, they couldn't leave, so they tried again, and succeeded. Severe erosion of the fittings by salt spray led to rapid deterioration and the bells soon became unringable, and they have been dismantled.

The Isle of Man also has a ring of eight, at the Cathedral Church of S German, Kirk German, Peel. These bells were installed in 1883 by Warners and in 1888 were rung to two peals in one day, the visiting band having failed with two attempts on the previous day. (The tenor weighs only 8¼ cwt.) The bells are now unringable. Another eight, at Douglas (cast by Murphy of Dublin in 1852), was lost in a fire in 1911 and replaced by a chime in the following year; a peal was rung there by a Liverpool band in the year of installation.

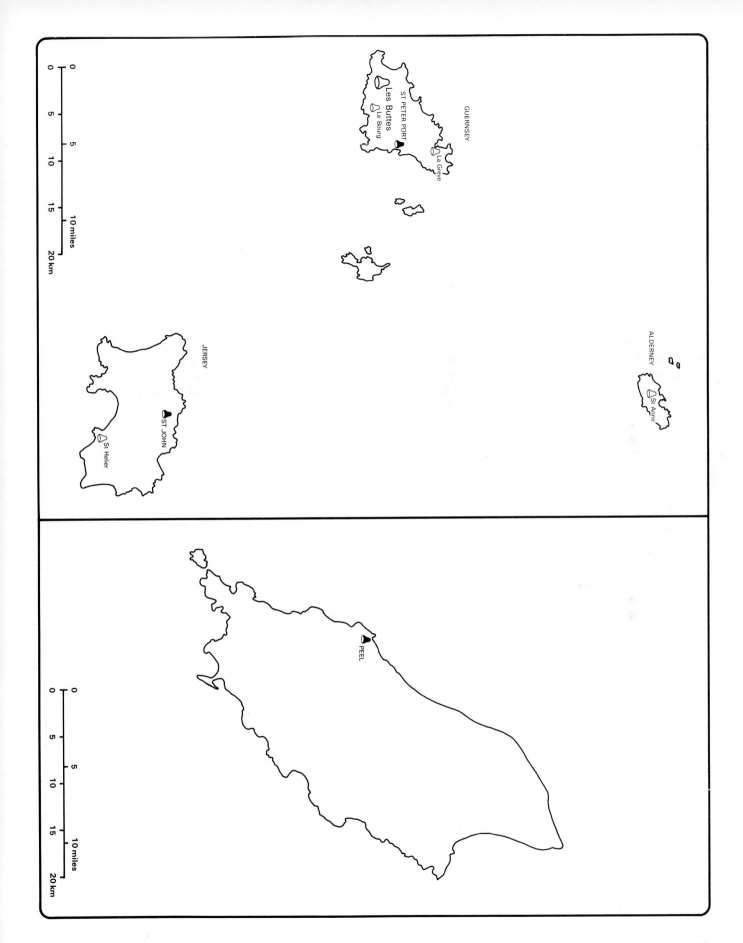

Les Buttes

ST PETER PORT

La Greve

Le Bourg

GUERNSEY

ALDERNEY

St Anne

JERSEY

ST JOHN

St Helier

PEEL

0
5
5
10
15
10 miles
20 km

0
5
5
10
15
10 miles
20 km

CATHEDRAL CHURCH OF CHRIST,
VICTORIA, BRITISH COLUMBIA,
CANADA

PART 6

—

BEYOND THE BRITISH ISLES

OLD S PAUL'S CATHEDRAL,
WELLINGTON, NEW ZEALAND

S ANDREW, WALKERVILLE, ADELAIDE,
AUSTRALIA

Australia

Australia has for long been the country outside the British Isles with most rings of bells. The majority of them are in the large cities that are the state capitals – but it is possible to find the occasional ring in a small town many miles (often hundreds) from any other.

According to tradition, ten bells were taken to Australia as long ago as 1795, to Sydney by Governor Hunter, but the tower at S Phillip's, Church Hill, was not strong enough to withstand change-ringing, and was demolished in 1856. The oldest extant ring, cast at Whitechapel in 1846, is at Holy Trinity, Hobart, Tasmania. Change-ringing was apparently introduced in 1863, following a visit by ringers from Lancashire. In 1890 two peals of Grandsire Triples were rung by a visiting band from Victoria, who had achieved the first peal in Australia (in Sydney) eight months earlier. By the mid-1970s the bells were unringable, and in 1985 a major appeal was launched to have them recast and rehung for the Australian bicentenary celebrations in 1988.

Melbourne was the first major centre of change-ringing; it has three rings in its central area – an eight at S James's Old Cathedral (initially six, installed in 1853), an anticlockwise eight at S Patrick's Roman Catholic Cathedral (these were cast by Murphy of Dublin in 1851 for S Francis's, Lonsdale Street, but the tower was never built and in 1868 they went to S Patrick's), and the first ring of twelve in Australia, hung in S Paul's Cathedral (by the Whitechapel foundry) in 1889.

Sydney has most rings of bells. S Andrew's Cathedral has a 1965 Taylor ring of ten; further bells were cast in 1982, 1985 and 1988 to make twelve (with an extra bell). S Mary's Roman Catholic Cathedral had its eight augmented to twelve in 1987. Three other city-centre churches have bells, including Christ Church, St Laurence, a small tower somewhat dwarfed by nearby buildings, which obtained a ring of six in 1853, augmented to ten in 1987. Five Sydney suburbs have rings, and there are plans for bells at more distant Windsor.

Apart from the city rings, there are a few in isolated communities. At S Clement's, Yass, the new church was provided with a locally cast bell in 1865. In 1869 five more were provided (by Blews of Birmingham) to make a ring of six, but the original had disappeared. Locals were trained to ring by others with English experience, but ringing stopped in 1880, and the bells were only restored in 1948 thanks to an enthusiastic local vicar. A new treble was provided, and in 1950 a peal of Doubles was rung to celebrate the church's centenary.

Even more isolated are the towers in Western Australia and Queensland. In the latter, until the installation of two rings at Brisbane in 1988, the only ring was the 1887 Whitechapel eight (plus a semitone) in a detached tower at Maryborough, some 100 miles north of the state capital; its nearest ring was at Maitland, some 500 miles south as the crow flies. But this was nothing to the isolation of the ringers at S George's Cathedral, Perth, whose nearest tower was at Adelaide. A tower with bells was proposed by Perth's bishop to commemorate Queen Victoria's death in 1901, and the bells were obtained from Warners in the following year. A heavy ring of eight was installed too high in the tower; it was replaced by a lighter ring in 1975. With the provision in recent decades of a six at Claremont, the bells at S Martins-in-the-Fields at the university, and an eight at York about 50 miles away, Perth's ringers are no longer quite so isolated.

A major boost to Australian ringing came in 1934 with a party of British ringers which visited all the towers and rang several peals. It led to the installation of at least one other ring: at S David's Cathedral in Hobart the original plan was for a chime, but after the visit it was decided to instal a Taylor eight, and the order was placed in 1935.

The country's bicentenary celebrations in 1988 led to a great deal of work to have bells installed as permanent, audible memorials, and every one of the mainland states will get at least one new ring. In Brisbane, for example, a ring of ten has been installed in a new tower at S John's Cathedral, eight of the bells having been cast for the original pro-cathedral in 1876; a chime of six bought from Dundee has been hung for ringing at S Andrew's, South Brisbane. Some of the bells have been purchased from redundant churches in Great Britain; those from S George, Bolton, have gone to Wangaratta Cathedral, and those from S Mark, Leicester, to Goulburn Cathedral. The major project has undoubtedly been that at the University of Western Australia, which has bought the old ring of twelve from S Martin-in-the-Fields, Trafalgar Square, London. These have been augmented to 17 (i.e., two octaves plus two other bells) and hung in a new tower overlooking the Swan River, where they form part of the instrumental collection of the university's music department. Secular rings are not new to Australia; the town halls at both Adelaide and Ballarat have rings of eight.

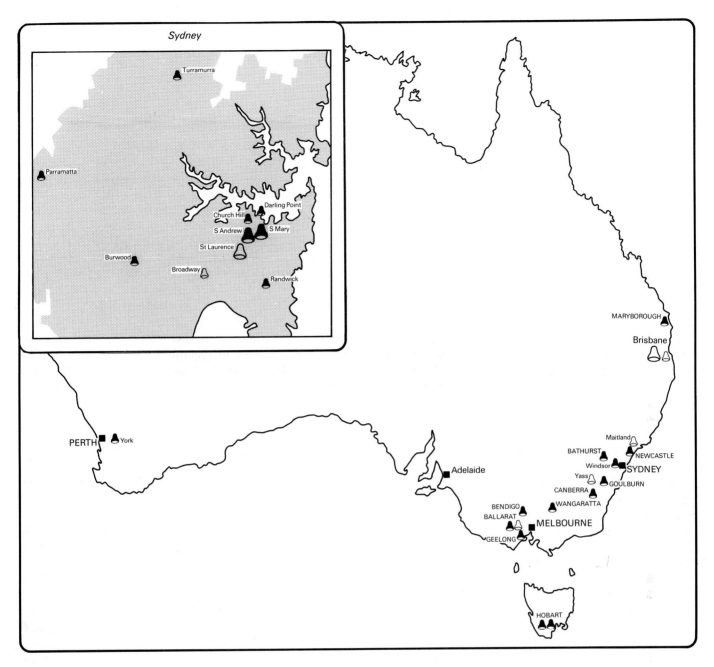

Sydney

- Turramurra
- Parramatta
- Church Hill
- Darling Point
- S Andrew
- S Mary
- St Laurence
- Burwood
- Broadway
- Randwick

MARYBOROUGH

Brisbane

PERTH ■ York

Adelaide

Maitland
BATHURST
Windsor
NEWCASTLE
SYDNEY
Yass
GOULBURN
CANBERRA
WANGARATTA
BENDIGO
BALLARAT
GEELONG
MELBOURNE

HOBART

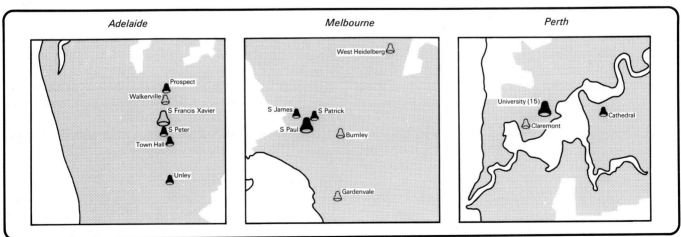

Adelaide

- Prospect
- Walkerville
- S Francis Xavier
- S Peter
- Town Hall
- Unley

Melbourne

- West Heidelberg
- S James
- S Patrick
- S Paul
- Burnley
- Gardenvale

Perth

- University (15)
- Claremont
- Cathedral

New Zealand

THERE have been rings of bells in New Zealand for more than a century, but in only one city – Christchurch in the South Island, known to many as the 'most English' of New Zealand's urban settlements – has there been a virtually unbroken history of ringing. Today, ringing thrives in each of the country's five largest cities: Auckland, Christchurch, Dunedin, Hamilton and the capital, Wellington.

The oldest ring in the South Island is at the Christchurch suburb of Papanui, where S Paul's church was provided with a ring of five in 1880 by a single donor; it would have been earlier, but the first ring was lost in a shipwreck off the South African coast, and new bells had to be cast in London as part of the insurance claim. The original tower was unsatisfactory, however, and ringing finally ceased in 1909 when the nine-foot cross fell from the steeple. A new tower was built in 1912, but ringing again ceased in 1914; in 1926 a new, heavily braced frame of kauri was built, independent of the thin cladding of the tower walls. The bells were augmented to six in 1970, and then to eight in 1985, when a steel frame replaced that of kauri.

At Christchurch Cathedral, designed by Sir Giles Gilbert Scott to a basic design familiar to those who know the nineteenth-century churches of S John, Ranmoor, Sheffield, and Christ Church, Swindon, a ring of ten was installed in 1888, having been cast seven years earlier. This was replaced by a ring of twelve, the first in New Zealand, in 1978.

The only other tower in the South Island with bells is at the First Church of Otago in Dunedin; this is a Presbyterian church, and the headquarters of that denomination in New Zealand's 'replica' of a Scottish city (the city's name, Dunedin, is an antipodean version of Edinburgh). The original church, built in 1848 (the year the city was founded), was presented with a bell, cast by Mears and Stainbank, by friends in the Free Church of Scotland (responsible for the Otago Settlement) in 1851. To mark its centenary in 1973, a donor offered a full ring of bells. The Whitechapel foundry advised that as there were no local ringers a chime would be preferable; this was announced in the local press and two ringers who had learned in England came forward and offered to train a band. The bells were cast in 1973 and hung in 1975.

In the North Island, Wellington's first ring of bells, a ring of eight reputed to weigh 15½ cwt. at S Peter's in

the city centre, was cast by Warners of London in 1879. The tower is very small, the oak frame is integrated into its fabric, and the vibration problems are such that the bells have not been rung since soon after their installation. Thus it was another hundred years before the centre of the country's capital resounded to the sound of change-ringing – from two virtually adjacent churches. At what is now known as Old S Paul's, formerly the cathedral, there is a light ring of five bells which are rung from the ground floor of the porch, and which can be seen rotating through the transparent polycarbonate panels in the ceiling. Originally there was a ring of three, also cast by Warners, which was first rung in March 1867, but ringing ceased many decades ago. The church was closed in 1964, but purchased by the government for the nation two years later. Plans to refurbish the bells were developed, and eventually the ring of five was dedicated in September 1979.

Nearby is the new S Paul's Cathedral, whose foundation stone was laid by the Queen in 1954. It was only in 1978 that plans were prepared to complete the tower and install a ring of bells. The ring of eight from the redundant church of S Edmund, Northampton, in England was obtained, a new tenor and three new trebles were cast, along with a flat sixth and an extra treble, and one of the original bells was recast. The new ring was dedicated on Easter Day 1984, exactly one hundred years after the original dedication in Northampton.

New Zealand's oldest full ring in chronological age, though not in the period during which the bells have been ringable, is at S Matthew's, Auckland. The bells were cast in 1862 by Warners and arrived in Auckland the following year; they were intended for the city's cathedral, with the cost having been raised by subscription canvassed by Bishop Selwyn's wife. But the cathedral had no tower, and the bells were thus 'lent' to S Matthew's. The bells were rung for some years but were silent for over 60 before restoration work started in the late 1960s. They were re-dedicated in 1972, after one had been recast in London in 1971.

Finally, there has been a ring of eight at the cathedral in Hamilton since 1950, when six bells were added to the tenor installed in 1932 and the treble of 1948. At Cambridge, a few miles away, there is a ring of six steel bells which are hung for ringing but cannot be rung because of the construction of the timber tower.

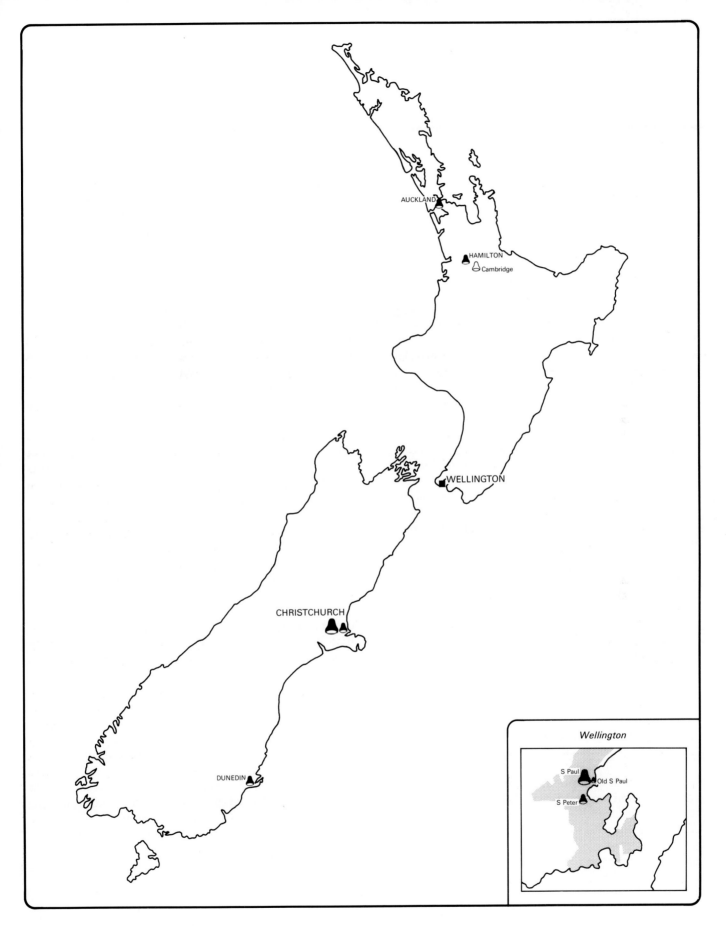

AUCKLAND

HAMILTON
Cambridge

WELLINGTON

CHRISTCHURCH

DUNEDIN

Wellington

S Paul
Old S Paul
S Peter

177

North America

As far as can be told, the North American colonies were the first places outside the British Isles to acquire rings of bells. Few rings were installed thereafter, but there has been a recent upsurge of interest in the United States, which had only eight rings in 1950 but nearly 30 by the end of the 1980s.

The oldest ring of bells on the continent was cast at Gloucester by Abel Rudhall in 1744, for Old North Church in Boston. The bells were derelict for many years, but have recently been rehung. Their installation did not start a major trend, although it could be that some rings were purchased about which we have no records. In 1973, for example, a visiting bell-hanger 'discovered' six previously unknown rings, including a twelve and two eights in Philadelphia; none is ringable. All the rest of the early trade went to Whitechapel: the 1754 eight for Christ Church, Philadelphia (the first peal in North America was rung here in 1850); a 1767 eight for Charleston; a 1797 eight for New York; an 1803 six for Baltimore; and all the early twentieth-century rings (the Church of the Advent, 1900; Groton, 1901; the Perkins Institute for the Blind and Hingham, 1912).

The Boston area is the focus of ringing in the United States. As well as the bells at Old North Church, there is an eight at the Church of the Advent, an eight in suburban Watertown (at the Perkins Institute), and tens at suburban Hingham (the Memorial Hall Campanile) and the school chapel at nearby Groton (augmented, 1962). Northampton has a ring of eight (installed in 1968) at Smith College. Indeed, schools, colleges and universities occur frequently in the list of American towers with bells – including the ten at the Mitchell Tower of the University of Chicago (Whitechapel, 1970) and a new eight at Kalamazoo College, Michigan (Whitechapel, 1983).

New York has only the unringable eight bells at Holy Trinity, Wall Street; the nearest ringable bells are the light eight at the chapel of Melrose School, Brewster. But Washington, DC, boasts two rings of ten. The central tower of the National Episcopal Cathedral has bells hung in a radial frame like that at Liverpool Cathedral. Ten British ringers were flown over for the dedication in 1964, and they rang a peal of Stedman Caters, the first ten-bell peal in the United States (on the next day the band rang the first peal of Royal – Cambridge Surprise – on the continent, at Groton). The other ring of ten, in the tower of the Old Post Office building, was given to mark the country's bicentennial by the British Ditchley Foundation; the bells – similar in weight and tone to those at Westminster Abbey – were cast, like the cathedral ring, at Whitechapel, in 1976 and hung in 1983.

As the map shows, there are several rings in the southern states – many of them new: so far, none has been installed in the west. In most cases, generous donors attracted by the English call of the bells have made possible an installation in their home town. At New Castle, Delaware, for example, a light six was installed at Immanuel Church in 1973 by Ronald and Beverly Finch (the bells were destroyed by fire in 1980 and replaced in 1982). The eight at S Thomas's Episcopal Church, Houston, resulted from Robert Ingram's hearing the bells at S Martin-in-the-Fields when visiting London; Ingram became minister at the church in 1953, and in 1971 achieved his goal of a ring of bells there. Relatively nearby is Abilene, where a ring of six Dutch bells was installed in 1983 by a local engineer – with novel clapper and other arrangements.

Most North American churches lack solid towers, so that when a church wants bells it usually has to build a tower too. This was the case at Miami's Episcopal Cathedral, whose Dean was keen to have a ring and was offered the money by a couple who were members of the congregation. A local property developer was convinced that he should donate a tower, and in December 1983 the new light ring of eight rang out for the first time.

Whereas bell-ringing has increased substantially in popularity in the United States in recent years (there were three rings of ten and five of eight in 1956, compared with six of ten and 18 of eight in 1988), there has been little activity in Canada, where in the late nineteenth century the Whitechapel foundry had an agent responsible for many orders for chiming bells. Of that country's eight rings, four are in the French-speaking province of Quebec – two unringable Whitechapel tens (of 1843 and 1910 vintage) in Roman Catholic churches in Montreal (one of which is the second heaviest ten in the world), and two rings of eight in Quebec City (that at Holy Trinity was cast by T. Mears in 1930; Warners provided the bells for S Matthew's in 1885). Further west, there is a light eight in a Calgary suburb, the only installation (1955) in the country since the Second World War; it was the last contract of the Croydon founders Gillett and Johnston. The ten at Mission City and the eights in Vancouver (1906) and Victoria are hardly near neighbours. The bells at Christ Church Cathedral, Victoria, were given in 1936 by the wife of the Dean of S Paul's in London, in memory of her brother: like the Ditchley bells in Washington, they were modelled on the old bells at Westminster Abbey – at that time a 28 cwt. ring of eight.

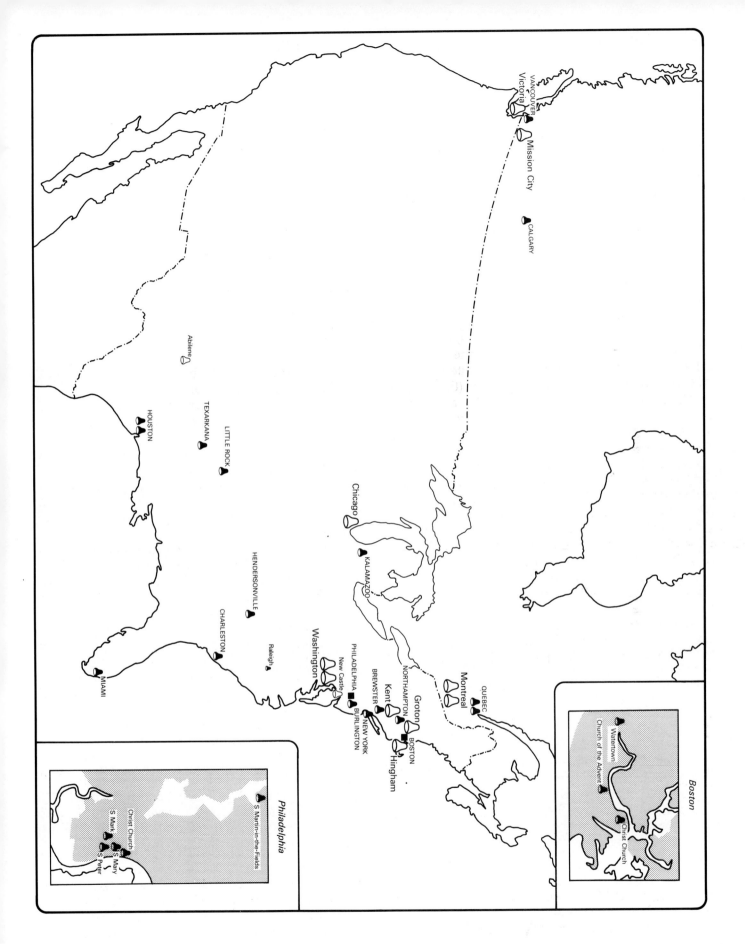

VANCOUVER
Victoria

Mission City

CALGARY

Abilene

HOUSTON

TEXARKANA

LITTLE ROCK

Chicago

KALAMAZOO

HENDERSONVILLE

CHARLESTON

Raleigh

Washington

New Castle

PHILADELPHIA

BREWSTER

Kent

NORTHAMPTON

Groton

Montreal

QUEBEC

BOSTON

NEW YORK

BURLINGTON

Hingham

MIAMI

Philadelphia

S Martin-in-the-Fields

Christ Church

S Mark

S Mary

S Peter

Boston

Watertown:
Church of the Advent

Christ Church

179

The Rest of the World

OUTSIDE the British Isles, Australia, New Zealand and North America, there are very few bells hung for change-ringing, and all those are in former British colonies. India and Pakistan each have one ring – at Poona and Lahore respectively – but they are not rung. That at Poona is a fairly heavy ring of eight (tenor 25 cwt.) hung by Taylors in a slender red-brick campanile added to an Anglican mission in 1893. (It is claimed that the campanile was designed as a clock tower, but the clock never arrived.) The bells were rung early in the twentieth century by visiting British military personnel, but there is no evidence of their having been other than chimed during the last four decades. Taylors provided the eight for Lahore in 1903.

It is possible to hear change-ringing today in Africa, as long as you go to one of just seven places. Of the nine rings on the continent, six are in the Republic of South Africa. Cape Town and Durban each have a ring of eight and a ring of ten. Cape Town's ten, at the Anglican Cathedral, was hung in 1979. The original tower, which contained a Mears eight of 1834, had to be demolished, and Whitechapel cast the new bells in 1962; these then had to await completion of the new tower. The most recently cast ring is the 1981 light eight (tenor 4½ cwt.) for the church of S George at Parktown in suburban Johannesburg. All the country's bells are regularly rung, including the 1878 Warner eight at Grahamstown Cathedral.

Zimbabwe has two rings of bells. At Harare, the foundations of S George's Cathedral were laid in 1913, but the body of the building was not completed until 1938, and even then there was no tower. In 1954 an anonymous donor gave a ring of ten bells, which meant that a tower was needed. This was completed in 1961, with more than half of the cost being met by the English Dulverton Trust. The bells were cast at Whitechapel in 1958 and hung in a temporary gantry until October 1961, when the first ringing in the country took place in preparation for the dedication on 5 November. The other ring is at Kwe Kwe, about half-way between Harare and Bulawayo. S Luke's Church was built in 1913, but the tower was donated only in 1960. Money for bells was raised at that time, and sufficient was obtained to buy bells 1, 2, 4 and 6 of a light six, on which ringers were trained. In 1972 a local doctor died and left a legacy to the church. The money had to be spent in England, and it was decided to buy the other two bells to complete the six. They were ordered in 1974, but it was two years before the British government let them be shipped to Lourenço Marques in Mozambique, where they arrived just too late to avoid the closure of that country's border with Rhodesia (as Zimbabwe then was). The bells were sent on to South Africa and eventually reached Kwe Kwe by rail in June 1976; they were first rung four months later.

The only other known ringable ring in Africa is at Kilifi, in Kenya, just up the coast from the main port of Mombasa: the light ring of six (tenor 2¾ cwt.) is hung in a wooden frame which is open to the elements high up in the church tower; ringing is now very rare at this very isolated set of bells.

There is also a ring of six in the tower of S Paul's Cathedral, Valetta, Malta, which was installed by Mears in 1845 for ringing, but it is now only a chime.

One other part of the world where people may find the sound of bells somewhat similar to that in England is Italy, where several regions have developed their own particular form of ringing; they include Romagna, Lombardia and the Verona district of Veneto. In the last of these areas, the local and English principles are very similar, with the bells turning full circle in alternate directions: they have no stay, however, and the ropes have no sallies. They are rung not to changes but to tunes, with the maestro calling out the numbers of the bells to ring at each chord: clearly, every bell must be taken to the balance each time it is pulled. The number of ringers is very large (several thousand in the Veronese area), and there are organizations with complex rules: striking contests have been held in the Verona area since 1903 (according to *Arte Campanaria*, 1985, by Mario Carregari and Gianni Mauli). Given the similarity between English change-ringing and Veronese ringing, the Central Council of Church Bell Ringers unanimously voted in favour of the Veronese association's affiliation to the council in 1988. The map on p. 182 shows where bells are rung à la Veronese.

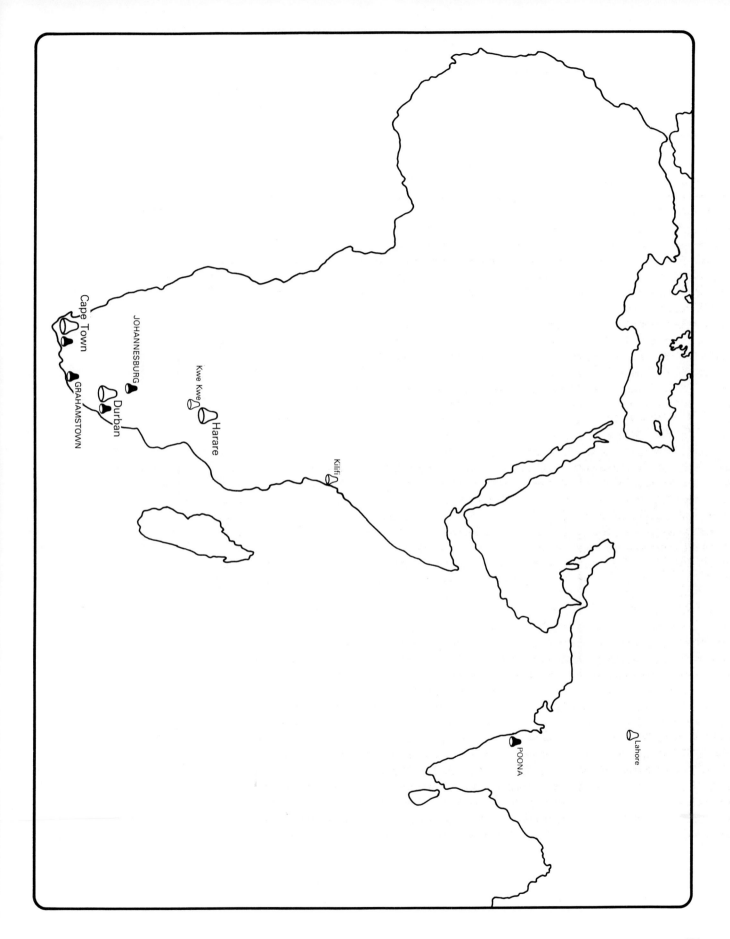

Cape Town

JOHANNESBURG

Kwe Kwe

GRAHAMSTOWN

Durban

Harare

Kilifi

POONA

Lahore

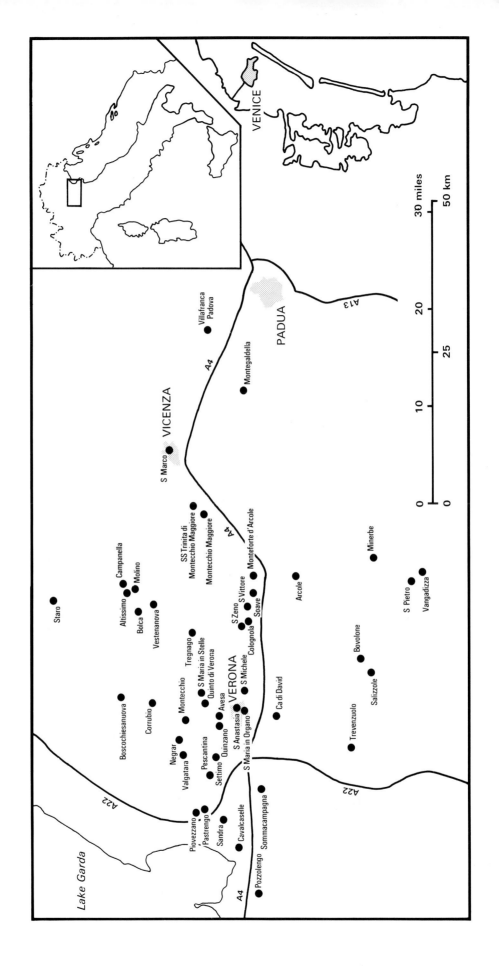

THE GAZETTEER

THE purpose of this Gazetteer, which derives from and extends John Baldwin's *Where's that Tower?*, is to provide sufficient information so that readers can, with the aid of the relevant Ordnance Survey 1:50000 maps, locate every tower in Great Britain precisely. The following information is given for every ring of bells:

name of the settlement;
dedication of the church (or nature of the building if it is not a church);
number of bells in the ring (plus number of semitone bells);
six-figure national grid reference.

The settlements are arranged alphabetically within the counties of England and Wales and the regions of Scotland.

The grid reference is a unique number referring to a location within Great Britain, which indicates where the church (or other building) is. The great majority of rings of bells are in churches, which are identified on the Ordnance Survey (OS) maps by one of two symbols – a black square with a cross on top, for a church with a tower, or a black circle with a cross on top, for a church with a tower and spire. (Other churches are shown just by a cross. A very small number of these have rings of bells, usually in a turret or similar arrangement not classified as a tower by the OS.) Thus the grid reference tells you which of the churches on the map you are looking for, and with the use of the 1:50000 map you should be able to find it on the ground without any difficulty. Full details on using the grid reference system are given below.

In any compilation such as this, there are problems of both accuracy and terminology. With regard to accuracy, we have attempted to give a correct national grid reference for every ring, but we cannot guarantee that no mistakes have been made. With regard to the number of bells in a ring, we have sought to be as up-to-date as possible; the detail given here reflects the situation as of 30 December 1989, with the exception that known changes (new rings; augmentations) for 1990 have been included. Thus the Atlas and Gazetteer refer to the situation at the start of 1990. Many augmentations occur each year, however, along with a small number of new installations, so it is certain that in a few places the information given here will soon be obsolescent.

A not-inconsiderable difficulty for a small, but significant, number of rings was determining which place they should be identified with. Our decision was that, where a ring is clearly within a built-up area, it should be associated with it. For example, within the county of Avon, many of the towers within the built-up area of Bristol are listed as in that city. The main exceptions to this are with the new towns of Milton Keynes in Buckinghamshire and Telford in Shropshire; several of the rings there are in old-established settlements (such as Stony Stratford in Milton Keynes and Coalbrookdale in Telford) and these have been separately identified.

A further problem with place-names is that the places with which ringers commonly associate certain towers are not actually the places where they are located; they are either somewhere else (usually nearby) or have a different official name. Since our purpose in producing the Gazetteer was to aid people in finding towers on the OS 1:50000 maps, we decided to use those maps as the official statements of place-names. Thus, for example, the ring at Wootton Glanville in Dorset is shown as Glanvilles Wootton and that at Wadesmill, Hertford-shire, is shown as Thundridge. More interestingly, in the county of Powys, Wales, there is a ring of eight at a church which ringers know as S Meugan, Llanfeugan. The parish that the church serves is indeed Llanfeugan, but the OS map shows no such community; instead, the church is shown as an isolated building some distance from the nearest settlement of Pencelli. Here, we use the latter name of Pencelli, rather than the ecclesiastical parish name of Llanfeugan, to indicate where that ring of eight is. (There can be no doubt where it is on the ground, as reference to grid reference SO 087246 will show.)

For the great majority of ringers, the names given to places with rings are those listed in R. H. Dove's *A Bellringer's Guide to the Church Bells of Britain*. Where our listing differs from that in the seventh (1988) edition of Dove's *Guide*, either in the name of the place or the built-up area under which it is listed, we have provided a checklist at the end of the Gazetteer. This is in two parts: in the first the left-hand column gives the place-name according to Dove, arranged alphabetically, and the right-hand column gives that which we use, based on the Ordnance Survey; in the second, the columns are reversed and the place-names that we use are arranged alphabetically.

For towers outside Great Britain, less detailed locational material is given. For Ireland, the towers are listed by county, with the relevant six-figure national grid reference relating to the Irish grid, where available; four-figure references are given for the others. For other countries, the grid reference is replaced by the latitude and longitude of the settlement and, where relevant (as in Sydney, Australia), the tower within it.

Locating a Tower from its Grid Reference

The system of grid references developed by the Ordnance Survey is based on a set of 100-kilometre squares, each of which, as indicated on the accompanying map, is identified by a two-letter code.

Within each of those squares, the six-figure grid reference is based on its subdivision into 100 smaller squares, each side of each of which is ten kilometres long. Those squares have a unique reference number. As shown on the diagram accompanying the map, the grid of lines spaced ten kilometres apart are numbered from 0 to 9, from west to east and from south to north. Thus the square in the far south-west is square 00 and that in the far north-east is 99. Together with the letters denoting the 100-kilometre square, this enables one to give the location of any point, to an accuracy of ten kilometres. Swindon, for example, is in 100-kilometre square SU; within this, it is in the second kilometre square to the east and the ninth to the north, or square 18, so that its grid reference at the ten-kilometre scale of accuracy is SU18.

More detailed referencing is obtained by dividing each ten-kilometre square into one-kilometre squares, in exactly the same way as the 100-kilometre square is divided into ten-kilometre squares. This allows a four-figure reference, which is accurate to the nearest kilometre. For Christ Church, Swindon, that reference is SU 1583; in other words, the church is 15 kilometres east of the south-west corner of square SU, and 83 kilometres to the north of that point.

Finally, each one-kilometre square is divided into 100 smaller units, with a grid that comprises lines drawn 100 metres apart. At this scale, the location of any point can be determined to an accuracy of 100 metres. For Christ Church, Swindon, the resulting six-figure reference is SU 157839; the church is 15.7 kilometres east of the south-west corner of square SU, and 83.9 kilometres north of that point.

On the 1:50000 OS maps, the ten- and one-kilometre squares are identified by light blue lines, with the edges of the former thicker than those of the latter. Thus on sheet 173 of the Landranger series, Christ Church, Swindon, is readily identified by finding the one-kilometre square whose eastern margin is denoted by line 15 and whose southern edge is line 83 (the easting – the north:south line indicating the distance eastwards from the south-west corner of the 100-kilometre square – is given first in a grid reference, and the northing – the distance north of the east:west trending line – is given second).

Christ Church is the only church in that square with a tower or spire, and so its location alongside the B4289 is readily identified once the square has been found. The more detailed six-figure reference is not needed.

This may not be the case in some towns, however, as for example with Devizes, on the same OS Landranger sheet. There are three rings in the town, including an eight at S John's church and a six at the church of the Blessed Virgin Mary. Both these are in the square denoted by the one-kilometre references 00 and 61. The full six-figure references are SU 004612 for S John's and SU 006616 for the church of the Blessed Virgin Mary. Thus S John's is 400 metres east and 200 metres north of the bottom left-hand corner of the square; the church of the Blessed Virgin Mary is 200 metres further east and 400 metres further north – i.e., towards the north-east corner of the square.

The 100-metre grid is not shown on the maps, so one has to estimate the location within the one-kilometre squares, both to produce the six-figure grid references and to use them to identify the relevant location. This is readily done, and enables the exact location of each church/building with a ring of bells to be identified.

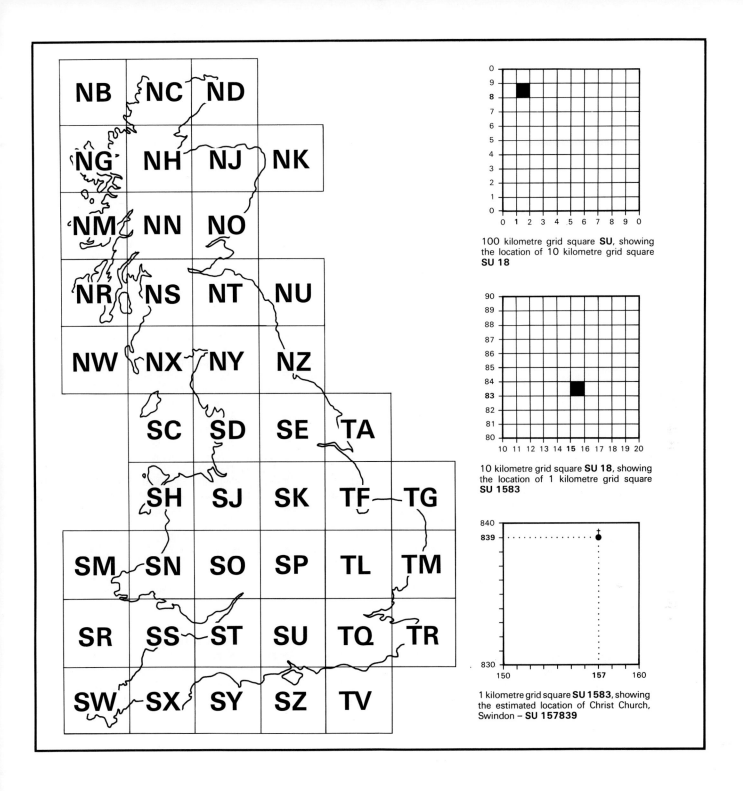

100 kilometre grid square **SU**, showing the location of 10 kilometre grid square **SU 18**

10 kilometre grid square **SU 18**, showing the location of 1 kilometre grid square **SU 1583**

1 kilometre grid square **SU 1583**, showing the estimated location of Christ Church, Swindon – **SU 157839**

England

Avon

ST 544740	6	Abbots Leigh, Holy Trinity
ST 705748	6	Abson, S James Great
ST 603841	8	Almondsbury, S Mary Virgin
ST 633874	6	Alveston, S Helen
ST 493683	8	Backwell, S Andrew
ST 399591	10	Banwell, S Andrew
ST 515684	8	Barrow Gurney, S Mary Virgin & S Edward K&M
ST 751648	10	Bath, Abbey Church of SS Peter & Paul
ST 751650	8	Bath, S Michael with S Paul
ST 756651	10	Bath, S Mary Virgin, Bathwick
ST 760663	8	Bath, S Saviour, Larkhall
ST 724647	8	Bath, S Michael, Twerton
ST 749655	8	Bath, Christ Church, Walcot
ST 731664	8	Bath, All Saints, Weston
ST 756642	6	Bath, S Matthew, Widcombe
ST 777665	6	Bathampton, S Nicholas
ST 777679	8	Batheaston, S John Baptist
ST 788666	6	Bathford, S Swithun
ST 682693	8	Bitton, S Mary
ST 503590	8	Blagdon, S Andrew
ST 341569	6	Bleadon, SS Peter & Paul
ST 588730	8	Bristol, All Saints
ST 584726	8	Bristol, Cathedral Church of Holy & Undivided Trinity
ST 589731	10	Bristol, Christ Church
ST 587732	6	Bristol, S John on the Wall
ST 584728	6	Bristol, S Mark (Lord Mayor's Chapel)
ST 595737	4	Bristol, S Paul
ST 595730	8	Bristol, SS Philip & Jacob
ST 587730	12	Bristol, S Stephen Martyr
ST 591728	8	Bristol, S Thomas Martyr
ST 601749	6	Bristol, S Werburgh
ST 621708	6	Bristol, S Luke, Brislington
ST 563788	8	Bristol, S Mary Virgin, Henbury
ST 592767	5	Bristol, Holy Trinity, Horfield
ST 588735	10	Bristol, S James, Horsefair
ST 587741	8	Bristol, S Matthew, Kingsdown
ST 603715	8	Bristol, Holy Nativity, Knowle
ST 665762	8	Bristol, S James, Mangotsfield
ST 592723	12(2)	Bristol, S Mary Virgin, Redcliffe
ST 585733	6	Bristol, S Michael on the Mount, Without, St Michael's Hill
ST 585720	6	Bristol, S Paul, Southville
ST 616760	6	Bristol, Holy Trinity, Stapleton
ST 560755	6	Bristol, S Mary Magdalene, Stoke Bishop
ST 573774	6	Bristol, Holy & Undivided Trinity, Westbury on Trym
ST 618740	10	Bristol, S Ambrose, Whitehall
ST 478593	6	Burrington, Holy Trinity
ST 515619	6	Butcombe, S Michael
ST 687574	6	Camerton, S Peter
ST 577632	8	Chew Magna, S Andrew
ST 557619	6	Chew Stoke, S Andrew
ST 727823	6	Chipping Sodbury, S John Baptist
ST 437602	6	Churchill, S John Baptist
ST 468735	6	Clapton in Gordano, S Michael
ST 788642	6	Claverton, S Mary Virgin
ST 417718	5	Clevedon, All Saints, East Clevedon
ST 393708	8	Clevedon, S Andrew
ST 409726	6	Clevedon, S John Evangelist, South Clevedon
ST 622589	6	Clutton, S Augustine
ST 674807	8	Coalpit Heath, S Saviour

ST 735598	4	Combe Hay, dedication unknown
ST 646647	6	Compton Dando, S Mary Virgin
ST 545570	6	Compton Martin, S Michael & All Angels
ST 435637	8	Congresbury, S Andrew
ST 695652	8	Corston, All Saints
ST 692905	6	Cromhall, S Andrew
ST 720741	5	Doynton, Blessed Trinity
ST 558669	6	Dundry, S Michael
ST 711593	6	Dunkerton, All Saints
ST 742758	6	Dyrham, S Peter
ST 565560	6	East Harptree, S Lawrence
ST 514757	6	Easton in Gordano, S George
ST 716629	5	Englishcombe, S Peter
ST 661606	6	Farmborough, All Saints
ST 603792	6	Filton, S Peter
ST 668820	6	Frampton Cotterell, SS Peter & Paul
ST 789601	5	Freshford, S Peter
ST 645579	6	High Littleton, Holy Trinity
ST 594570	5	Hinton Blewett, S Margaret
ST 766851	5	Horton, S James Elder
ST 352585	5	Hutton, S Mary Virgin
ST 681835	6	Iron Acton, S James Less
ST 699669	6	Kelston, S Nicholas
ST 334634	6	Kewstoke, S Paul
ST 654688	8	Keynsham, S John Baptist
ST 401668	6	Kingston Seymour, All Saints
ST 363596	6	Locking, S Augustine
ST 553710	8	Long Ashton, All Saints
ST 376558	6	Loxton, S Andrew
ST 667623	6	Marksbury, S Peter
ST 782737	8	Marshfield, S Mary Virgin
ST 662542	12	Midsomer Norton, S John Baptist
ST 466699	6	Nailsea, Holy Trinity
ST 533604	6	Nempnett Thrubwell, S Mary Virgin
ST 701649	6	Newton St Loe, Holy Trinity
ST 601873	8	Olveston, S Mary BV
ST 650565	6	Paulton, Holy Trinity
ST 503754	6	Portbury, S Mary Virgin
ST 466760	8	Portishead, S Peter
ST 693604	6	Priston, S Luke
ST 623641	6	Publow, All Saints
ST 699766	6	Pucklechurch, S Thomas
ST 634670	5	Queen Charlton, S Margaret
ST 688546	6	Radstock, S Nicholas
ST 688752	6	Siston, S Anne Mother of BVM
ST 598631	5	Stanton Drew, S Mary Virgin
ST 599594	5	Stowey, S Mary Virgin
ST 756684	6	Swainswick, S Mary Virgin
ST 634906	8	Thornbury, S Mary Virgin
ST 458714	6	Tickenham, SS Quiricus & Julietta
ST 667586	6	Timsbury, S Mary Virgin
ST 704933	6	Tortworth, S Leonard
ST 668884	6	Tytherington, S James Greater
ST 529582	6	Ubley, S Bartholomew
ST 316583	6	Uphill, S Nicholas (Old Church)
ST 425731	4	Walton in Gordano, SS Peter & Paul
ST 714796	5	Wapley, S Peter
ST 674733	8	Warmley, S Barnabas
ST 741584	6	Wellow, S Julian
ST 699797	6	Westerleigh, S James Great
ST 561569	4	West Harptree, S Mary
ST 444741	6	Weston in Gordano, SS Peter & Paul
ST 318619	8	Weston super Mare, S John Baptist
ST 353629	6	Weston super Mare, S Martin, Worle
ST 366655	5	Wick St Lawrence, S Lawrence
ST 723889	6	Wickwar, Holy Trinity
ST 543650	6	Winford, S Mary Virgin

ST 412567	8	Winscombe, S James Great
ST 642810	6	Winterbourne, S Michael
ST 490719	8	Wraxall, All Saints
ST 467627	10	Wrington, All Saints
ST 713828	6	Yate, S Mary
ST 431654	8	Yatton, S Mary Virgin

Bedfordshire

TL 037383	8	Ampthill, S Andrew
TL 192375	6	Arlesey, S Peter
SP 943363	6	Aspley Guise, S Botolph
TL 085304	8	Barton le Cley, S Nicholas
TL 057508	8	Bedford, S Andrew
TL 049496	12	Bedford, S Paul
TL 050501	8	Bedford, S Peter de Merton
TL 014499	8	Biddenham, S James
TL 188446	8	Biggleswade, S Andrew
TL 023583	6	Bletsoe, S Mary
TL 153511	6	Blunham, S Edmund
TL 081588	4	Bolnhurst, S Dunstan
TL 013512	8	Bromham, S Owen
TL 064198	6	Caddington, All Saints
TL 130381	5	Campton, All Saints
TL 086479	8	Cardington, S Mary
SP 952549	4	Carlton, S Mary
TL 034525	6	Clapham, S Thomas of Canterbury
TL 166393	8	Clifton, All Saints
TL 109586	6	Colmworth, S Denys
TL 103485	6	Cople, All Saints
SP 956420	5	Cranfield, SS Peter & Paul
TL 046676	5	Dean, All Hallows
TL 021219	8	Dunstable, Priory Church of S Peter
SP 970207	6	Eaton Bray, S Mary Virgin
TL 049474	6	Elstow, S Mary & S Helena
SP 983325	6	Eversholt, S John Baptist
SP 991578	8	Felmersham, S Mary
TL 059359	6	Flitton, S John Baptist
TL 029342	6	Flitwick, SS Peter & Paul
TL 076510	6	Goldington, S Mary Virgin
TL 134517	5	Great Barford, All Saints
SP 954567	6	Harrold, S Peter
TL 081412	6	Haynes, S Mary
TL 178387	8	Henlow, S Mary
SP 966269	4	Hockliffe, S Nicholas
TL 043414	6	Houghton Conquest, All Saints
TL 018239	6	Houghton Regis, All Saints
SP 944389	4	Hulcote, S Nicholas
SP 955362	8	Husborne Crawley, S James
TL 015480	10	Kempston, All Saints
TL 031190	6	Kensworth, S Mary
TL 073624	5	Keysoe, S Mary
SP 923255	12(1)	Leighton Buzzard, All Saints
SP 912249	8	Linslade, S Barnabas
TL 178570	4	Little Barford, S Denys
TL 107630	5	Little Staughton, All Saints
TL 095212	12	Luton, S Mary
SP 996412	5	Marston Morteyne, S Mary Virgin
TL 058381	8	Maulden, S Mary
TL 028654	4	Melchbourne, S Mary Magdalene
TL 134359	6	Meppershall, S Mary Virgin
TL 020561	6	Milton Ernest, All Saints
TL 149466	6	Northill, S Mary Virgin
TL 011530	6	Oakley, S Mary
SP 966580	6	Odell, All Saints
TL 136443	6	Old Warden, S Leonard
SP 991560	5	Pavenham, S Peter
SP 942628	4	Podington, S Mary
TL 229495	6	Potton, S Mary
TL 089528	6	Renhold, S Mary
TL 039631	6	Riseley, All Saints
TL 153545	5	Roxton, S Mary Magdalene
TL 174491	6	Sandy, S Swithin
SP 993596	6	Sharnbrook, S Peter
TL 123339	5	Shillington, All Saints
TL 082356	6	Silsoe, S James Great
TL 146422	6	Southill, All Saints
SP 982490	6	Stagsden, S Leonard
SP 966242	5	Stanbridge, S John Baptist
TL 012355	4	Steppingley, S Bartholomew
SP 990536	5	Stevington, S Mary Virgin
TL 220367	8	Stotfold, S Mary Virgin
TL 016159	4	Studham, S Mary
TL 219475	4	Sutton, All Saints
TL 058659	5	Swineshead, S Nicholas
TL 162530	6	Tempsford, S Peter
TL 051584	6	Thurleigh, S Peter
SP 975243	6	Tilsworth, All Saints
TL 010289	8	Toddington, S George of England
SP 988208	8	Totternhoe, S Giles
SP 940525	8	Turvey, All Saints
TL 113360	5	Upper Gravenhurst, S Giles
TL 027327	6	Westoning, S Mary Magdalene
SP 012179	6	Whipsnade, S Mary Magdalene
TL 093552	5	Wilden, S Nicholas
TL 106498	6	Willington, S Lawrence
SP 948333	8	Woburn, S Mary
TL 003451	6	Wootton, S Mary Virgin
SP 955644	5	Wymington, S Lawrence
TL 011671	4	Yelden, S Mary

Berkshire

SU 596649	8	Aldermaston, S Mary
SU 757678	6	Arborfield, S Bartholomew
SU 784664	4	Barkham, S James
SU 483782	6	Beedon, S Nicholas
SU 591684	6	Beenham Valence, S Mary
SU 845721	6	Binfield, All Saints
SU 428716	5	Boxford, S Andrew
SU 603726	6	Bradfield, S Andrew
SU 902797	8	Bray, S Michael
SU 427793	6	Brightwalton, All Saints
SU 557648	4	Brimpton, S Peter
SU 553708	8	Bucklebury, S Mary
SU 672684	6	Burghfield, S Mary Virgin
SU 411779	4	Chaddleworth, S Andrew
SU 474741	8	Chieveley, S Mary Virgin
SU 526797	6	Compton Parva, SS Mary & Nicholas
SU 897854	8	Cookham, Holy Trinity
SU 987772	5	Datchet, S Mary Virgin
SU 362771	6	East Garston, All Saints
SU 863676	8	Easthampstead, SS Michael & Mary Magdalene
SU 493809	8	East Ilsley, S Mary
SU 624720	6	Englefield, S Mark
SU 434819	5	Farnborough, All Saints
SU 792637	6	Finchampstead, S James
SU 380754	6	Great Shefford, S Mary
SU 529763	6	Hampstead Norreys, S Mary
TQ 014758	6	Horton, S Michael
SU 334687	8	Hungerford, S Lawrence
SU 794729	8	Hurst, S Nicholas
SU 383669	6	Kintbury, S Mary Virgin
SU 326789	8	Lambourn, S Michael & All Angels
TQ 005795	6	Langley Marish, S Mary Virgin
SU 612793	4	Lower Basildon, S Bartholomew

SU 877808	8	Maidenhead, All Saints, Boyne Hill
SU 556672	6	Midgham, S Matthew
SU 471671	10	Newbury, S Nicolas
SU 993747	8	Old Windsor, SS Peter & Andrew
SU 613661	6	Padworth, S John Baptist
SU 634764	6	Pangbourne, S James Less
SU 457771	6	Peasemore, S Barnabas
SU 667761	6	Purley, S Mary
SU 716729	8	Reading, S Giles
SU 717735	12	Reading, S Laurence
SU 714733	8	Reading, S Mary Virgin
SU 708748	8	Reading, S Peter, Caversham
SU 825618	6	Sandhurst, S Michael & All Angels
SU 475683	6	Shaw, S Mary
SU 730682	6	Shinfield, S Mary
SU 841771	6	Shottesbrooke, S John Baptist
SU 976795	10	Slough, S Mary, Upton with Chalvey
SU 755755	8	Sonning, S Andrew
SU 455678	6	Speen, S Mary
SU 576717	4	Stanford Dingley, S Denys
SU 654645	6	Stratfield Mortimer, S John Evangelist, Mortimer West End
SU 668641	8	Stratfield Mortimer, S Mary Virgin
SU 594808	6	Streatley, S Mary
SU 731647	6	Swallowfield, All Saints
SU 516673	10	Thatcham, S Mary
SU 640713	6	Theale, Holy Trinity
SU 673729	8	Tilehurst, S Michael
SU 788758	8	Twyford, S Mary
SU 635675	4	Ufton Nervet, S Peter
SU 829769	6	Waltham St Lawrence, S Lawrence
SU 880721	10	Warfield, S Michael
SU 782784	8	Wargrave, S Mary
SU 408732	5	Welford, S Gregory Great
SU 854775	6	White Waltham, Blessed Virgin Mary
SU 968770	8	Windsor, HM Free Chapel of S George, Castle
SU 955773	6	Windsor, S Andrew, Clewer
SU 968768	10	Windsor, S John Baptist
SU 904724	6	Winkfield, S Mary
SU 815688	8	Wokingham, All Saints
SU 805690	8	Wokingham, S Paul
TQ 002739	8	Wraysbury, S Andrew
SU 554745	6	Yattendon, SS Peter & Paul

Buckinghamshire

SU 957973	8	Amersham, S Mary
SP 847203	6	Aston Abbots, S James Great
SP 879119	8	Aston Clinton, S Michael & All Angels
SP 817139	8	Aylesbury, S Mary
SP 771371	5	Beachampton, Assumption BVM
SU 945900	8	Beaconsfield, S Mary & All Saints
SP 835153	6	Bierton, S James
SP 778022	8	Bledlow, Holy Trinity
SP 863337	8	Bletchley, S Mary
SP 912344	4	Bow Brickhill, All Saints
SP 832394	6	Bradwell, S Laurence
SP 656138	6	Brill, All Saints
SP 894401	4	Broughton, S Laurence
SP 695337	8	Buckingham, SS Peter & Paul
SU 930823	8	Burnham, S Peter
SP 791390	6	Calverton, All Saints
SU 991937	8	Chalfont St Giles, S Giles
TQ 000909	6	Chalfont St Peter, S Peter
SP 922180	6	Cheddington, S Giles
TQ 016986	6	Chenies, S Michael
SP 956015	6	Chesham, S Mary

SP 904458	6	Chicheley, S Laurence
SP 899514	6	Clifton Reynes, S Mary Virgin
SP 737112	6	Cuddington, S Nicholas
TQ 043870	8	Denham, S Mary
SP 766110	6	Dinton, SS Peter & Paul
SU 924790	6	Dorney, S James
SP 837284	6	Drayton Parslow, Holy Trinity
SP 740254	5	East Claydon, S Mary
SP 970191	6	Edlesborough, S Mary Virgin
SP 836067	6	Ellesborough, SS Peter & Paul
SP 885495	6	Emberton, All Saints
SU 962827	8	Farnham Royal, S Mary
SP 884340	6	Fenny Stratford, S Martin
SU 999856	6	Fulmer, S James
SP 767252	5	Granborough, S John Baptist
SP 901308	6	Great Brickhill, S Mary Virgin
SP 771312	6	Great Horwood, S James
SP 825060	6	Great Kimble, S Nicholas
SP 851424	6	Great Linford, S Andrew
SP 900010	6	Great Missenden, SS Peter & Paul
SP 742080	8	Haddenham, S Mary Virgin
SP 874101	4	Halton, S Michael & All Angels
SU 784866	6	Hambleden, S Mary Virgin
SP 804467	8	Hanslope, S James Great
SP 806190	6	Hardwicke, S Mary
SU 865931	12(1)	High Wycombe, All Saints
SP 686287	6	Hillesden, All Saints
SU 920836	6	Hitcham, S Mary
SU 864955	8	Hughenden, S Michael & All Angels
TQ 040811	8	Iver, S Peter
SP 945163	6	Ivinghoe, S Mary Virgin
SU 806916	6	Lane End, Holy Trinity
SP 875450	5	Lathbury, All Saints
SP 916537	6	Lavendon, S Michael
SP 726379	5	Leckhamstead, Assumption BVM
SP 712405	5	Lillingstone Lovell, Assumption BVM
SP 791309	5	Little Horwood, S Nicholas
SU 921990	6	Little Missenden, S John Baptist
SP 698091	8	Long Crendon, S Mary
SP 837378	6	Loughton, All Saints
SP 660173	5	Ludgershall, S Mary Virgin
SP 706352	6	Maids Moreton, S Edmund
SU 851861	8	Marlow, All Saints
SP 647233	5	Marsh Gibbon, S Mary Virgin
SP 919146	5	Marsworth, All Saints
SP 904197	5	Mentmore, S Mary Virgin
SP 864405	6	Milton Keynes, Cross & Stable, Downs Barn
SP 887392	6	Milton Keynes, All Saints, Milton Keynes Village
SP 812044	6	Monks Risborough, S Dunstan
SP 906418	4	Moulsoe, S Mary
SP 816285	6	Mursley, S Mary Virgin
SP 733123	5	Nether Winchendon, S Nicholas
SP 878439	8	Newport Pagnell, SS Peter & Paul
SP 847314	8	Newton Longville, S Faith
SP 927447	6	North Crawley, S Firmin
SP 777226	6	North Marston, S Mary
SP 889510	8	Olney, SS Peter & Paul
SP 722309	6	Padbury, S Mary Virgin
SU 916933	6	Penn, Holy Trinity
SP 750202	8	Quainton, S Mary & Holy Cross
SU 786979	4	Radnage, S Mary
SP 667067	6	Shabbington, S Mary Magdalene
SP 642365	5	Shalstone, S Edward C&K
SP 832367	6	Shenley, S Mary
SP 890467	5	Sherington, S Laud
SP 884362	6	Simpson, S Thomas Apostle
SP 936206	5	Slapton, Holy Cross

SP 883270	6	Soulbury, All Saints
SP 706266	6	Steeple Claydon, S Michael & All Angels
SP 853261	8	Stewkley, S Michael & All Angels
SP 832492	6	Stoke Goldington, S Peter
SP 834104	8	Stoke Mandeville, S Mary Virgin
SU 975827	8	Stoke Poges, S Giles
SP 784123	6	Stone, S John Baptist
SP 787405	8	Stony Stratford, S Giles
SP 676374	5	Stowe, Assumption of Holy Vigin Mary
SP 802273	6	Swanbourne, S Swithin
SP 743336	5	Thornborough, S Mary Virgin
SP 658331	5	Tingewick, S Mary Magdalene
SP 665266	6	Twyford, Assumption BVM
SP 859467	5	Tyringham, S Peter
SP 740169	6	Waddesdon, S Michael & All Angels
SP 912373	6	Wavendon, Assumption BVM
SP 871073	6	Wendover, S Mary Virgin
SP 859103	5	Weston Turville, S Mary Virgin
SP 863504	6	Weston Underwood, S Laurence
SU 827949	8	West Wycombe, S Lawrence
SP 805341	6	Whaddon, S Mary
SP 803208	6	Whitchurch, S John Evangelist
SP 880225	6	Wing, All Saints
SP 869190	6	Wingrave, SS Peter & Paul
SP 769276	8	Winslow, S Laurence D&M
SP 804413	6	Wolverton, Holy Trinity
SU 909878	8	Wooburn, S Paul
SP 688159	6	Wotton Underwood, All Saints
SP 877376	6	Woughton on the Green, Assumption BVM

Cambridgeshire

TL 228565	5	Abbotsley, S Margaret of Antioch V&M
TL 184762	6	Alconbury, SS Peter & Paul
TL 133959	5	Alwalton, S Andrew
TF 094060	4	Bainton, S Mary
TL 588508	5	Balsham, Holy Trinity
TF 078051	5	Barnack, S John Baptist
TL 396499	6	Barrington, All Saints
TL 407558	5	Barton, S Peter
TL 331441	6	Bassingbourn, SS Peter & Paul
TL 545605	6	Bottisham, Holy Trinity
TL 324563	8	Bourn, SS Helen & Mary
TL 215707	6	Brampton, S Mary Magdalene
TL 082759	4	Brington, All Saints
TL 629548	6	Brinkley, Blessed Virgin Mary
TL 281779	4	Broughton, All Saints
TL 193677	5	Buckden, S Mary
TL 148767	5	Buckworth, All Saints
TL 635555	5	Burrough Green, S Augustine
TL 590660	8	Burwell, S Mary Blessed Virgin
TL 057758	4	Bythorn, S Laurence
TL 455578	8	Cambridge, Our Lady & English Martyrs (RC)
TL 451584	8	Cambridge, S Andrew Great
TL 449583	6	Cambridge, S Benedict
TL 448582	4	Cambridge, S Botolph
TL 449584	6	Cambridge, S Edward King
TL 448585	12	Cambridge, University Church of Great S Mary
TL 489571	6	Cambridge, S Andrew, Cherry Hinton
TL 463596	6	Cambridge, S Andrew, Chesterton
TL 443549	8	Cambridge, SS Mary & Michael, Trumpington
TL 625425	5	Castle Camps, All Saints
TL 124985	6	Castor, S Kyneburgha
TL 089733	4	Catworth, S Leonard
TL 300579	6	Caxton, S Andrew
TL 394861	6	Chatteris, SS Peter & Paul
TL 663699	6	Chippenham, S Margaret

TL 383555	4	Comberton, S Mary
TL 320660	4	Conington (near Cambridge), S Mary
TL 181859	6	Conington (near Peterborough), All Saints
TL 455687	6	Cottenham, S Mary & All Saints
TL 252592	6	Croxton, S James
TL 400905	6	Doddington, S Mary
TL 380619	5	Dry Drayton, SS Peter & Paul
TL 631578	5	Dullingham, S Mary Virgin
TL 480460	6	Duxford, S Peter
TL 139716	4	Easton, S Peter
TL 170588	8	Eaton Socon, S Mary
TL 161718	4	Ellington, All Saints
TF 470069	6	Elm, All Saints
TL 319636	4	Elsworth, Holy Trinity
TL 269598	4	Eltisley, S Pandionia
TL 088935	5	Elton, All Saints
TL 538803	8	Ely, S Mary
TL 184598	6	Eynesbury, S Mary Virgin
TL 482604	8	Fen Ditton, S Mary Virgin
TL 320688	6	Fenstanton, SS Peter & Paul
TL 633708	8	Fordham, S Peter & S Mary Magdalene
TL 422459	5	Fowlmere, S Mary Virgin
TL 412483	5	Foxton, S Lawrence
TL 521562	8	Fulbourn, S Vigor
TL 242523	6	Gamlingay, S Mary Virgin
TL 424623	4	Girton, S Andrew
TL 154861	4	Glatton, S Nicholas
TF 154059	6	Glinton, S Benedict
TL 245707	8	Godmanchester, S Mary Virgin
TL 249641	4	Graveley, S Botolph
TL 422388	5	Great Chishill, S Swithin
TL 117832	5	Great Gidding, S Michael
TL 271556	6	Great Gransden, S Bartholomew
TL 210641	5	Great Paxton, Holy Trinity
TL 459519	5	Great Shelford, S Mary Virgin
TL 124647	6	Great Staughton, S Andrew
TL 217746	4	Great Stukeley, S Bartholomew
TL 548578	5	Great Wilbraham, S Nicholas
TL 280442	6	Guilden Morden, S Mary
TL 464757	6	Haddenham, Holy & Undivided Trinity
TL 137797	6	Hamerton, All Saints
TL 418509	6	Harston, All Saints
TL 255726	6	Hartford, All Saints
TL 403522	6	Haslingfield, All Saints
TL 283712	6	Hemingford Abbots, S Margaret
TL 293709	8	Hemingford Grey, S James
TL 432399	5	Heydon, Holy Trinity
TL 291661	6	Hilton, S Mary Magdalene
TL 436640	8	Histon, S Andrew
TL 336708	6	Holywell, S John Baptist
TL 493627	5	Horningsea, S Peter
TL 613473	4	Horseheath, All Saints
TL 281721	6	Houghton, S Mary
TL 238718	6	Huntingdon, All Saints
TL 241716	8	Huntingdon, S Mary
TL 495439	8	Ickleton, S Mary Magdalene
TL 644744	6	Isleham, S Andrew
TL 044756	5	Keyston, S John Baptist
TL 099679	5	Kimbolton, S Andrew
TL 478653	4	Landbeach, All Saints
TL 116753	5	Leighton Bromswold, S Mary Virgin
TF 445114	6	Leverington, S Leonard
TL 562467	5	Linton, S Mary Virgin
TL 310428	6	Litlington, S Katharine
TL 527842	4	Little Downham, S Leonard
TL 375533	4	Little Eversden, S Helen
TL 189628	4	Little Paxton, S James

TL 566870	8	Littleport, S George
TL 453517	6	Little Shelford, All Saints
TL 209757	4	Little Stukeley, S Martin
TL 399665	8	Longstanton, All Saints
TL 415952	6	March, S Wendreda
TF 119079	6	Maxey, S Peter
TL 382448	8	Melbourn, All Saints
TL 378468	8	Meldreth, Holy Trinity
TF 441149	6	Newton in the Isle, S James
TL 415648	6	Oakington, S Andrew
TL 219671	4	Offord Cluny, All Saints
TL 093772	4	Old Weston, S Swithin
TL 362504	6	Orwell, S Andrew
TL 372708	8	Over, S Mary Virgin
TL 498482	6	Pampisford, S John Baptist
TF 390091	5	Parson Drove, S John Baptist
TL 194986	12(1)	Peterborough, Cathedral Church of SS Peter, Paul & Andrew
TL 191987	8	Peterborough, S John Baptist
TL 196991	6	Peterborough, S Mary
TL 198971	5	Peterborough, S Margaret, Old Fletton
TL 157961	4	Peterborough, S Mary Virgin, Orton Waterville
TL 199975	6	Peterborough, S John Baptist, Stanground
TL 186977	6	Peterborough, S Augustine of Canterbury, Woodston
TL 428681	6	Rampton, All Saints
TL 291851	6	Ramsey, S Thomas a' Becket
TL 310716	8	St Ives, All Saints
TL 185601	10	St Neots, S Mary
TL 488492	8	Sawston, S Mary Virgin
TL 620444	5	Shudy Camps, S Mary
TL 593732	10	Soham, S Andrew
TL 360778	6	Somersham, S John Baptist
TL 183644	4	Southoe, S Leonard
TL 128729	6	Spaldwick, S James
TL 471521	6	Stapleford, S Andrew
TL 642590	5	Stetchworth, S Peter
TL 511746	6	Stretham, S James Great
TL 448790	6	Sutton in the Isle, S Andrew
TL 555622	6	Swaffham Bulbeck, S Mary
TL 568639	6	Swaffham Prior, SS Cyriac & Julietta
TL 363694	6	Swavesey, S Andrew
TF 069006	5	Thornhaugh, S Andrew
TL 441469	5	Thriplow, S George
TF 428165	6	Tydd St Giles, S Giles
TF 093040	4	Ufford, S Andrew
TL 073993	6	Wansford, S Mary Virgin
TL 303798	6	Warboys, S Mary Magdalene
TL 498651	5	Waterbeach, S John Evangelist
TL 616531	5	Weston Colville, S Mary
TL 612492	5	West Wickham, S Mary
TL 606523	5	West Wratting, S Andrew
TL 267969	8	Whittlesey, S Andrew
TL 271970	8	Whittlesey, S Mary
TL 474485	6	Whittlesford, SS Mary & Andrew
TL 577706	5	Wicken, S Lawrence
TL 480750	6	Wilburton, S Peter
TL 405706	6	Willingham, S Mary & All Saints
TL 104806	5	Winwick, All Saints
TF 462097	10	Wisbech, SS Peter & Paul
TF 419082	6	Wisbech St Mary, S Mary
TL 279810	4	Wistow, S John Baptist
TF 056020	6	Wittering, All Saints
TL 660591	5	Woodditton, S Mary Virgin
TL 209821	4	Woodwalton, S Andrew
TL 177918	6	Yaxley, S Peter
TL 262624	4	Yelling, Holy Cross

Cheshire

SJ 632531	6	Acton, S Mary
SJ 419595	6	Aldford, S John Baptist
SJ 788557	8	Alsager, Christ Church
SJ 846616	6	Astbury, S Mary
SJ 660437	6	Audlem, S James Great
SJ 398717	6	Backford, S Oswald K&M
SJ 767524	8	Barthomley, S Bertoline
SJ 939778	8	Bollington, S John Baptist
SJ 918656	6	Bosley, S Mary Virgin
SJ 781648	5	Brereton, S Oswald
SJ 569581	8	Bunbury, S Boniface
SJ 317743	6	Burton, S Nicholas
SJ 368738	6	Capenhurst, Holy Trinity
SJ 819740	6	Chelford, S John Evangelist
SJ 406664	12(1)	Chester, Cathedral Church of Christ & BVM
SJ 404658	8	Chester, S Mary's Centre
SJ 404663	6	Chester, S Peter
SJ 407655	8	Chester, S Mary without the Walls, Handbridge
SJ 418675	6	Chester, All Saints, Hoole
SJ 441658	8	Christleton, S James
SJ 822558	8	Church Lawton, All Saints
SJ 666607	6	Church Minshull, S Bartholomew
SJ 859628	8	Congleton, S Peter
SJ 706556	10	Crewe, Christ Church
SJ 661949	8	Culcheth, Holy Trinity
SJ 581828	8	Daresbury, All Saints
SJ 663713	6	Davenham, S Wilfrid
SJ 975845	6	Disley, S Mary Virgin
SJ 495853	6	Ditton, S Michael (RC)
SJ 362609	6	Dodleston, S Mary
SJ 413627	8	Eccleston, S Mary BV
SJ 413545	8	Farndon, S Chad
SJ 517877	6	Farnworth, S Luke
SJ 521773	8	Frodsham, S Lawrence
SJ 890697	8	Gawsworth, S James
SJ 779700	6	Goostrey, S Luke
SJ 639863	8	Grappenhall, S Wilfrid
SJ 665775	8	Great Budworth, S Mary & All Saints
SJ 472820	8	Hale, S Mary
SJ 466579	6	Handley, All Saints
SJ 638728	6	Hartford, S John Baptist
SJ 762673	6	Holmes Chapel, S Luke
SJ 752785	6	Knutsford, S John Baptist
SJ 598654	5	Little Budworth, S Peter
SJ 743742	6	Lower Peover, S Oswald
SJ 682868	8	Lymm, S Mary Virgin
SJ 914736	10	Macclesfield, Christ Church
SJ 918737	12	Macclesfield, S Michael
SJ 922730	8	Macclesfield, S Peter
SJ 486472	8	Malpas, S Oswald King
SJ 561457	6	Marbury, S Michael
SJ 704663	8	Middlewich, S Michael & All Angels
SJ 790802	6	Mobberley, S Wilfrid & S Mary Virgin
SJ 653523	8	Nantwich, S Mary
SJ 291774	8	Neston, SS Mary & Helen
SJ 842761	6	Nether Alderley, S Mary
SJ 665739	8	Northwich (Witton), S Helen
SJ 650651	8	Over, S Chad
SJ 944792	6	Pott Shrigley, S Christopher
SJ 919836	6	Poynton, S George
SJ 901769	8	Prestbury, S Peter
SJ 375588	8	Pulford, S Mary Virgin
SJ 742837	6	Rostherne, S Mary
SJ 510832	8	Runcorn, All Saints
SJ 759608	8	Sandbach, S Mary
SJ 336718	6	Shotwick, S Michael

SJ	620828	6	Stretton, S Matthew
SJ	930712	6	Sutton, S James
SJ	553625	8	Tarporley, S Helen
SJ	492670	6	Tarvin, S Andrew
SJ	487586	6	Tattenhall, S Alban
SJ	441746	4	Thornton le Moors, S Mary
SJ	457507	6	Tilston, S Mary
SJ	522465	6	Tushingham, S Chad
SJ	709610	6	Warmingham, S Leonard
SJ	462633	6	Waverton, S Peter
SJ	617742	6	Weaverham, S Mary Virgin
SJ	848815	6	Wilmslow, S Bartholomew
SJ	603928	6	Winwick, S Oswald
SJ	681536	8	Wistaston, S Mary Virgin
SJ	594477	6	Wrenbury, S Margaret
SJ	700499	6	Wybunbury, S Chad

Cleveland

NZ	617161	6	Guisborough, S Nicholas
NZ	509320	8	Hartlepool, All Saints, Stranton
NZ	507314	8	Hartlepool, S Aidan
NZ	507335	10	Hartlepool, S Oswald
NZ	634224	8	Marske by the Sea, S Mark
NZ	531167	8	Ormesby, S Cuthbert
NZ	662212	8	Saltburn by the Sea, Emmanuel
NZ	661190	8	Skelton in Cleveland, All Saints
NZ	446193	12	Stockton-on-Tees, S Thomas à Becket
NZ	451176	8	Thornaby on Tees, S Paul

Cornwall

SX	104816	5	Advent, S Adwena
SX	222813	8	Altarnun, S Non
SX	398545	6	Antony, S James
SX	100731	6	Blisland, SS Protus & Hyacinth
SX	073670	8	Bodmin, S Petroc
SX	404613	6	Botus Fleming, S Mary
SX	321920	5	Boyton, Holy Name
SX	162621	5	Braddock, Blessed Virgin Mary
SX	358696	8	Callington, S Mary Virgin
SX	436692	6	Calstock, S Andrew
SW	645400	8	Camborne, SS Martin & Meriadoc
SW	530384	10	Carbis Bay, S Anta & All Saints
SX	123687	8	Cardinham, S Mewbred
SX	036521	6	Charlestown, S Paul
SW	731291	6	Constantine, S Constantine, King of Cornwall
SW	790606	6	Crantock, S Carantoc
SW	646345	8	Crowan, S Crewenna
SW	677213	6	Cury, S Corentyn
SX	151873	6	Davidstow, S David
SX	234581	6	Duloe, S Cuby
SX	000719	8	Egloshayle, S Petrock
SX	125517	8	Fowey, S Fimbarrus
SW	873352	4	Gerrans, S Gerrans
SX	120552	5	Golant, S Sampson
SW	484317	8	Gulval, S Gulval
SW	738401	6	Gwennap, S Weneppa
SW	658277	8	Helston, S Michael
SW	671440	6	Illogan, S Illogan
SX	198958	6	Jacobstow, S James
SS	252113	8	Kilkhampton, S James Greater
SW	894510	8	Ladock, S Ladoca
SW	711127	6	Landewednack, S Winwalloe
SX	431615	6	Landulph, S Leonard
SX	228840	6	Laneast, SS Sidwell & Gulval
SX	085636	8	Lanhydrock, S Hyderock
SX	039642	8	Lanivet, S La

SX	080591	8	Lanlivery, S Brevita
SX	181569	6	Lanreath, S Marnarck
SX	172516	8	Lansallos, S Ildierna
SX	088823	6	Lanteglos by Camelford, S Julitta
SX	145515	6	Lanteglos by Fowey, S Wyllow
SS	244057	6	Launcells, S Swithin
SX	332847	8	Launceston, S Mary Magdalene
SX	328851	6	Launceston, S Thomas Apostle
SX	355823	6	Lawhitton, S Michael
SW	548377	6	Lelant, S Uny
SX	131903	6	Lesnewth, S Michael & All Angels
SX	276807	6	Lewannick, S Martin
SX	338791	6	Lezant, S Briochus
SX	319736	6	Linkinhorne, S Melori
SX	254644	8	Liskeard, S Martin
SW	918721	6	Little Petherick, S Petrock
SX	104597	6	Lostwithiel, S Bartholomew
SW	505330	6	Ludgvan, S Ludgvan
SX	052581	6	Luxulyan, SS Cyric & Julitta
SW	757325	6	Mabe, S Laudus
SW	453317	8	Madron, S Maddern
SX	446520	6	Maker, SS Julian, Mary & Macra
SW	764250	6	Manaccan, S Dunstan
SS	223036	6	Marhamchurch, Sancta Marvenne
SW	709251	6	Mawgan in Meneage, S Mawgan
SX	288628	6	Menheniot, S Lalluwy
SX	260567	6	Morval, S Wenna
SS	204153	6	Morwenstow, S Morwenna
SW	678192	6	Mullion, S Melina
SX	272766	6	North Hill, S Torney
SX	282896	6	North Petherwyn, S Paternos
SX	312973	6	North Tamerton, S Denis
SW	915754	6	Padstow, S Petrock
SW	464271	6	Paul, S Pol de Leon
SX	203550	6	Pelynt, S Nun
SW	475300	8	Penzance, S Mary
SW	779389	6	Perranarworthal, S Piran
SW	770520	6	Perranzabuloe, S Piran
SW	565384	8	Phillack, S Felicitas Matron & Martyr
SX	367643	6	Pillaton, S Odulph
SS	222077	6	Poughill, S Olaf K&M
SX	202994	6	Poundstock, S Neot
SW	899477	8	Probus, SS Probus & Grace
SW	692412	8	Redruth, S Uny
SW	987597	8	Roche, S Gonand of the Rock
SW	720507	6	St Agnes, S Agnes
SW	782257	8	St Anthony in Meneage, S Anthony
SX	014524	8	St Austell, Holy Trinity
SW	977717	6	St Breocke, S Breock
SX	097774	6	St Breward, S Brueredus
SW	786324	8	St Budock, S Budocus
SW	409258	4	St Buryan, S Buryan
SX	247682	6	St Cleer, S Cleer
SW	850439	6	St Clement, S Clement
SX	205844	5	St Clether, S Clederus
SW	912637	8	St Columb Major, S Columba
SW	839624	8	St Columb Minor Rural, S Columba
SW	951583	8	St Dennis, S Denys
SX	399678	6	St Dominick, S Dominica
SW	997787	6	St Endellion, S Endellienta
SW	892570	8	St Enoder, S Enoder
SW	847498	6	St Erme, S Hermes
SW	550350	4	St Erth, S Ercus
SW	871692	6	St Eval, S Eval
SW	978460	6	St Ewe, All Saints
SX	149972	4	St Gennys, S Genesius
SX	359577	8	St Germans, S Germanus

SW 787346	8	St Gluvias, S Gluvias
SW 999423	6	St Goran, S Goranus
SW 595374	6	St Gwinear, S Gwinear
SW 550313	6	St Hilary, S Hilary of Poitiers
SW 928718	6	St Issey, S Issey
SX 309672	6	St Ive, S Ivo
SX 129912	6	St Juliot, S Juliot
SW 810426	8	St Kea, All Hallows
SW 791213	8	St Keverne, S Keverne
SX 021769	6	St Kew, S James Great
SX 242608	6	St Keyne, S Kayna
SX 042732	8	St Mabyn, S Mabena or Holy Mother
SX 260550	6	St Martin by Looe, S Martin of Tours
SW 872659	8	St Mawgan in Pydar, SS Mawgan & Nicholas
SX 388656	6	St Mellion, S Melanus
SW 886741	6	St Merryn, S Merryn
SW 998518	6	St Mewan, S Mewan
SW 964422	6	St Michael Caerhays, S Michael & All Angels
SW 858422	4	St Michael Penkevil, S Michael
SW 965771	6	St Minver, S Menefrida
SX 186678	6	St Neot, S Neot
SW 828563	6	St Newlyn East, S Newlina
SX 201632	4	St Pinnock, S Pinnock
SW 945533	8	St Stephen in Brannell, S Stephen
SX 325857	8	St Stephen's by Launceston, S Stephen
SX 417583	6	St Stephen's by Saltash, S Stephen
SX 064806	6	St Teath, S Tetha
SX 066763	6	St Tudy, S Tudy
SX 140550	6	St Veep, SS Cyriac & Julitta
SW 968649	6	St Wenn, S Wenna
SX 115569	6	St Winnow, S Winnow
SX 431588	6	Saltash, SS Nicholas & Faith
SW 357254	6	Sennen, S Sennen
SX 329726	5	South Hill, S Sampson
SX 309819	6	South Petherwyn, S Paternus
SW 731371	6	Stithians, S Stedyana
SX 360743	8	Stoke Climsland, All Saints
SS 231065	8	Stratton, S Andrew
SX 228516	6	Talland, S Tallan
SX 050884	6	Tintagel, S Materiana
SW 486381	8	Towednack, S Tewinnock Confessor
SX 209881	4	Treneglos, S Werburgh
SW 826448	10	Truro, Cathedral & Parish Church of S Mary
SW 819458	8	Truro, S Keyne, Kenwyn
SW 657407	8	Tuckingmill, All Saints
SX 085542	6	Tywardreath, S Andrew
SW 916396	6	Veryan, S Symphorian
SX 237978	6	Week St Mary, Nativity SMV
SW 679311	6	Wendron, S Michael
SX 328876	8	Werrington, S Martin of Tours
SX 263986	6	Whitstone, S Anne
SW 994654	6	Withiel, S Clement
SW 455385	6	Zennor, S Senara Virgin

Cumbria

NY 374044	8	Ambleside, SS Mary Virgin & Anne
NY 683204	6	Appleby, S Lawrence
NY 052198	8	Arlecdon, S Michael
NY 147419	8	Aspatria, S Kentigern
NY 521180	5	Bampton, S Patrick
SD 631825	4	Barbon, S Bartholomew
SD 195700	8	Barrow in Furness, S James Great
SD 496796	6	Beetham, S Michael & All Angels
SD 403969	8	Bowness on Windermere, S Martin
NY 528610	6	Brampton, S Martin
NY 363034	6	Brathay, Holy Trinity

NY 117337	6	Bridekirk, S Bridget
NY 793139	4	Brough, S Michael
SD 209874	10	Broughton in Furness, S Mary Magdalene
SD 530769	6	Burton in Kendal, S James
NY 398559	8	Carlisle, Cathedral Church of Holy & Undivided Trinity
NY 422545	8	Carlisle, S Elisabeth, Harraby
SD 380788	6	Cartmel, Priory Church of S Mary Virgin
NY 015153	8	Cleator Moor, S John Evangelist
NY 124306	8	Cockermouth, All Saints
SD 446911	6	Crosthwaite, S Mary Virgin
SD 226739	10	Dalton in Furness, S Mary
SD 705871	6	Dent, S Andrew
NY 012105	8	Egremont, S Mary
SD 365760	6	Flookburgh, S John Baptist
NY 553368	6	Great Salkeld, S Cuthbert
SD 268742	4	Great Urswick, S Mary Virgin
NY 443309	4	Greystoke, S Andrew
SD 352981	8	Hawkshead, S Michael
NX 985166	8	Hensingham, S John Evangelist
SD 497834	6	Heversham, S Peter
NY 092005	8	Irton, S Paul
SD 517921	10	Kendal, Holy Trinity
NY 257243	8	Keswick, S Kentigern, Crosthwaite
SD 233822	6	Kirkby in Furness, S Cuthbert
SD 611788	6	Kirkby Lonsdale, S Mary Virgin
NY 775088	8	Kirkby Stephen, S Stephen
NY 321055	6	Langdale, Holy Trinity
NY 549398	4	Lazonby, S Nicholas
SD 171800	6	Millom, S George Martyr
SD 499816	6	Milnthorpe, S Thomas
NY 622084	8	Orton, All Saints
NY 516302	8	Penrith, S Andrew
NX 969121	8	St Bees, Priory Church of SS Mary & Bega
SD 656921	8	Sedbergh, S Andrew
NY 564153	6	Shap, S Michael & All Angels
NY 110537	8	Silloth, Christ Church
NY 324508	6	Thursby, S Andrew
SD 289787	6	Ulverston, S Mary Virgin
NX 977184	10	Whitehaven, S James
NX 997289	8	Workington, S Michael

Derbyshire

SK 407559	8	Alfreton, S Martin
SK 176464	8	Ashbourne, S Oswald
SK 194697	6	Ashford in the Water, Holy Trinity
SK 348631	8	Ashover, All Saints
SK 415294	6	Aston on Trent, All Saints
SK 467652	8	Ault Hucknall, S John Baptist
SK 215685	8	Bakewell, All Saints
SK 207834	6	Bamford, S John Baptist
SK 477772	6	Barlborough, S James
SK 252723	6	Baslow, S Anne
SK 351476	8	Belper, S Peter
SK 444583	6	Blackwell, S Werburgh
SK 473706	8	Bolsover, SS Mary & Lawrence
SK 280581	6	Bonsall, S James Apostle
SK 208527	6	Bradbourne, All Saints
SK 244412	6	Brailsford, All Saints
SK 230543	6	Brassington, S James
SK 378391	8	Breadsall, All Saints
SK 460335	6	Breaston, S Michael
SK 044729	6	Burbage, Christ Church
SK 067742	8	Buxton, S Peter, Fairfield
SK 150829	8	Castleton, S Edmund
SK 057808	6	Chapel en le Frith, S Thomas a' Becket

SK 381304	6	Chellaston, S Peter
SK 116702	5	Chelmorton, S John Baptist
SK 385712	10	Chesterfield, S Mary & All Saints
SK 205337	6	Church Broughton, S Michael & All Angels
SK 293181	5	Church Gresley, S George & S Mary
SK 391633	6	Clay Cross, S Bartholomew
SK 498753	6	Clowne, S John Baptist
SK 526743	8	Creswell, S Mary Magdalene
SK 348546	8	Crich, S Mary
SK 167378	4	Cubley, S Andrew
SK 266629	8	Darley Dale, S Helen
SK 399464	6	Denby, S Mary Virgin
SK 352364	10	Derby, Cathedral Church of All Saints
SK 343357	8	Derby, S Luke
SK 353360	8	Derby, S Peter
SK 392333	6	Derby, S Michael & All Angels, Alvaston
SK 398359	6	Derby, S Werburgh, Spondon
SK 021943	6	Dinting Vale, Holy Trinity
SK 114341	5	Doveridge, S Cuthbert
SK 353783	8	Dronfield, S John Baptist
SK 349428	10	Duffield, S Alkmund
SK 432798	8	Eckington, SS Peter & Paul
SK 251699	6	Edensor, S Peter
SK 222610	5	Elton, All Saints
SK 417329	4	Elvaston, S Bartholomew
SK 269320	6	Etwall, S Helen
SK 218764	6	Eyam, S Lawrence
SK 330265	4	Foremark, S Savior
SK 041948	8	Glossop, All Saints
SK 032935	8	Glossop, S James Great, Whitfield
SK 200719	6	Great Longstone, S Giles
SK 327218	6	Hartshorne, S Peter
SK 231815	6	Hathersage, S Michael
SK 036870	8	Hayfield, S Matthew
SK 435465	8	Heanor, S Lawrence
SK 448671	5	Heath, All Saints
SK 172834	8	Hope, S Peter
SK 375445	6	Horsley, S Clement
SK 465418	8	Ilkeston, S Mary Virgin
SK 461810	6	Killamarsh, S Giles
SK 492338	8	Long Eaton, S Lawrence
SK 215383	6	Longford, S Chad
SK 250130	6	Lullington, All Saints
SK 233297	4	Marston on Dove, S Mary
SK 301598	8	Matlock, S Giles
SK 388250	8	Melbourne, SS Michael & Mary
SK 406601	6	Morton, Holy Cross
SK 283429	6	Mugginton, All Saints
SK 282129	8	Netherseale, S Peter
SK 292206	6	Newhall, S John
SK 005854	8	New Mills, S George
SK 404645	8	North Wingfield, S Lawrence
SK 424357	6	Ockbrook, All Saints
SK 336719	8	Old Brampton, SS Peter & Paul
SK 384752	8	Old Whittington, S Bartholomew
SK 199440	6	Osmaston, S Martin
SK 295155	8	Overseale, S Matthew
SK 389525	5	Pentrich, S Matthew
SK 453550	8	Pinxton, S Helen
SK 504645	5	Pleasley, S Michael
SK 303272	8	Repton, S Wystan
SK 399506	8	Ripley, All Saints
SK 480372	6	Sandiacre, S Giles
SK 473313	8	Sawley, All Saints
SK 495687	5	Scarcliffe, S Leonard
SK 438303	6	Shardlow, S James
SK 400584	6	Shirland, S Leonard

SK 442570	6	South Normanton, S Michael
SK 383558	6	South Wingfield, All Saints
SK 464381	8	Stanton by Dale, S Michael & All Angels
SK 241642	6	Stanton in the Peak, Holy Trinity
SK 433749	8	Staveley, S John Baptist
SK 157321	6	Sudbury, All Saints
SK 237342	6	Sutton on the Hill, S Michael
SK 442689	4	Sutton Scarsdale, S Michael
SK 404532	6	Swanwick, S Andrew
SK 141711	4	Taddington, S Michael
SK 006799	6	Taxal, S James
SK 440609	6	Tibshelf, S John Baptist
SK 351241	10	Ticknall, S George
SK 152758	8	Tideswell, S John Baptist
SK 432411	8	West Hallam, S Wilfrid of York
SK 383674	5	Wingerworth, All Saints
SK 239606	5	Winster, S John Baptist
SK 287539	8	Wirksworth, S Mary
SK 124742	6	Wormhill, S Margaret
SK 212644	8	Youlgreave, All Saints

Devon

SS 424264	6	Abbotsham, S Helen
SX 856687	6	Abbotskerswell, Blessed Virgin Mary
SS 404231	6	Alwington, S Andrew
SS 463306	8	Appledore, S Mary
SS 612404	6	Arlington, S James
SX 755697	8	Ashburton, S Andrew
SS 628135	6	Ashreigney, S James
SX 856847	6	Ashton, S Michael
SX 386952	6	Ashwater, S Peter
SS 591231	6	Atherington, S Mary
ST 133018	6	Awliscombe, S Michael & All Angels
SY 296984	8	Axminster, S Mary
SY 038919	6	Aylesbeare, Blessed Virgin Mary
SS 956222	6	Bampton, S Michael & All Angels
SS 558332	8	Barnstaple, SS Peter & Mary Magdalene
SS 552150	6	Beaford, All Saints
SY 229893	5	Beer, S Michael
SX 619935	6	Belstone, S Mary
SX 459634	6	Bere Ferrers, S Andrew
SS 560467	6	Berrynarbor, S Peter
SX 828610	8	Berry Pomeroy, S Mary
SX 799727	6	Bickington, S Mary Virgin
SS 453264	8	Bideford, S Mary
SX 667466	6	Bigbury, S Lawrence
SS 757237	6	Bishop's Nympton, S Mary Virgin
SS 565300	6	Bishop's Tawton, S John Baptist
SX 911735	6	Bishopsteignton, S John Baptist
SX 804510	6	Blackawton, S Michael
SS 465057	6	Black Torrington, S Mary
SS 651049	4	Bondleigh, S James
SX 821786	8	Bovey Tracey, SS Peter, Paul & Thomas
SS 421072	6	Bradford, All Saints
SS 999041	8	Bradninch, S Dionysius or Denys
SX 381808	6	Bradstone, S Nonna
SS 324140	6	Bradworthy, S John Baptist
SX 927982	6	Brampford Speke, S Peter
SY 195884	6	Branscombe, S Winifred
SX 463918	6	Bratton Clovelly, S Mary Virgin
SS 643377	6	Bratton Fleming, S Peter
SS 488370	8	Braunton, S Brannock
SS 750477	4	Brendon, S Brendan
SX 470804	5	Brentor, S Michael
SX 513894	6	Bridestowe, S Bridget

SX 816864	6	Bridford, S Thomas a' Becket
SS 281031	8	Bridgerule, S Bridget
SX 923561	10	Brixham, Blessed Virgin Mary
SX 553521	6	Brixton, S Mary
SX 982973	8	Broadclyst, S John Baptist
ST 101047	6	Broadhembury, S Andrew A&M
SX 801662	6	Broadhempston, SS Peter & Paul
SS 617059	6	Broadwood Kelly, All Hallows
SX 411892	6	Broadwoodwidger, S Nicholas
ST 123003	6	Buckerell, SS Mary & Giles
SX 740673	12(2)	Buckfast, Abbey Church of S Mary (RC)
SX 742665	8	Buckfastleigh, Holy Trinity
SS 418209	6	Buckland Brewer, SS Mary & Benedict
SS 465091	5	Buckland Filleigh, S Mary & Holy Trinity
SX 720731	8	Buckland in the Moor, S Peter
SX 490682	8	Buckland Monachorum, S Andrew
ST 075166	6	Burlescombe, S Mary
SS 637166	6	Burrington, Holy Trinity
SS 910049	6	Cadbury, S Michael & All Angels
SS 913079	6	Cadeleigh, S Bartholomew
SS 922142	6	Calverleigh, S Mary Virgin
SX 701874	8	Chagford, S Michael
SS 680407	4	Challacombe, Holy Trinity
ST 309044	6	Chardstock, All Saints
SS 687329	6	Charles, S John Baptist
SX 750426	6	Charleton, S Mary
SS 712126	6	Chawleigh, S James
SS 733133	4	Cheldon, S Mary
SX 773935	6	Cheriton Bishop, S Mary
SS 867062	6	Cheriton Fitzpaine, S Mary
SS 635256	8	Chittlehampton, S Hieritha
SX 783387	6	Chivelstone, S Sylvester
SX 836850	8	Christow, S James
SX 867794	8	Chudleigh, SS Mary & Martin
SS 687141	8	Chulmleigh, S Mary Magdalene
SX 712459	6	Churchstow, S Mary Virgin
SX 903564	6	Churston Ferrers, Christ Church
SX 348992	6	Clawton, S Leonard
ST 161156	6	Clayhidon, S Andrew
SS 309251	6	Clovelly, All Saints
SX 989935	8	Clyst Honiton, S Michael & All Angels
ST 035015	6	Clyst Hydon, S Andrew
SX 984889	6	Clyst St George, S George
SY 026999	5	Clyst St Lawrence, S Lawrence
SX 891684	6	Coffinswell, S Bartholomew
SY 081871	6	Colaton Raleigh, S John Baptist
SS 698076	6	Coldridge, S Matthew
SS 769000	6	Colebrooke, S Andrew
SX 864601	6	Collaton, S Mary Virgin
SY 246941	6	Colyton, S Andrew
SX 901714	6	Combeinteignhead, All Saints
SS 586463	8	Combe Martin, S Peter
SX 604593	6	Cornwood, S Michael & All Angels
SX 829555	6	Cornworthy, S Peter
SX 457835	5	Coryton, S Andrew
ST 206022	6	Cotleigh, S Michael
SS 836002	8	Crediton, Holy Cross
SS 873121	6	Cruwys Morchard, Holy Cross
ST 021071	10	Cullompton, S Andrew
ST 102135	8	Culmstock, All Saints
ST 247005	6	Dalwood, S Peter
SX 785626	6	Dartington, S Mary
SX 886503	6	Dartmouth, S Petrox
SX 878513	8	Dartmouth, S Saviour
SX 869515	6	Dartmouth, S Clement, Townstall
SX 953766	8	Dawlish, S Gregory
SX 730635	6	Dean Prior, S George Martyr
SX 823688	5	Denbury, S Mary Virgin
SX 727567	6	Diptford, S Mary
SX 860551	6	Dittisham, S George
SX 739445	6	Dodbrooke, S Thomas of Canterbury
SS 570120	6	Dolton, S Edmund
SS 568103	5	Dowland, S Peter
SS 742044	6	Down St Mary, S Mary Virgin
SX 736909	6	Drewsteignton, Holy Trinity
ST 141077	6	Dunkeswell, S Nicholas
SX 813892	6	Dunsford, S Mary
SX 769483	6	East Allington, S Andrew
SS 867265	6	East Anstey, S Michael & All Angels
SS 942071	6	East Bickleigh, S Mary
SS 677313	6	East Buckland, S Michael
SY 066849	8	East Budleigh, All Saints
SS 601419	4	East Down, S John Baptist
SX 838700	5	East Ogwell, S Bartholomew
SX 748383	6	East Portlemouth, S Winwalloe Onolaus
SS 774136	6	East Worlington, S Mary
SX 638532	6	Ermington, SS Peter & Paul
SS 602019	6	Exbourne, S Mary BV
SX 921925	12(2)	Exeter, Cathedral Church of S Peter
SX 915931	8	Exeter, S David
SX 936934	8	Exeter, S Mark
SX 918923	4	Exeter, S Mary Steps
SX 920926	6	Exeter, S Petrock
SX 912918	8	Exeter, S Thomas Martyr
SX 918899	8	Exeter, S Michael & All Angels, Alphington
SX 938922	8	Exeter, S Michael, Heavitree
SX 956950	6	Exeter, S Michael & All Angels, Pinhoe
SX 946877	8	Exminster, S Martin
SY 007825	6	Exmouth, 7 Bapton Lane (loft)
SY 007825	10	Exmouth, 7 Bapton Lane (garage)
SY 029813	8	Exmouth, S Margaret, Littleham
SY 008818	8	Exmouth, S John Evangelist, Withycombe Raleigh
SY 109994	6	Feniton, S Andrew
SS 662280	6	Filleigh, S Paul
SS 511325	6	Fremington, S Peter
SS 463195	6	Frithelstock, SS Mary & Gregory
SX 686404	6	Galmpton, Holy Trinity
SS 464399	8	Georgeham, S George
SS 700229	4	George Nympton, S George
SX 439941	5	Germansweek, S Germans
SX 671884	5	Gidleigh, Holy Trinity
SS 598341	6	Goodleigh, S Gregory
SS 495192	8	Great Torrington, S Michael
ST 005128	6	Halberton, S Andrew
SX 777532	6	Halwell, S Leonard
SX 427994	6	Halwill, SS Peter & James
SX 778586	6	Harberton, S Andrew
SY 091904	6	Harpford, S Gregory
SS 235247	6	Hartland, S Nectan
SS 541045	8	Hatherleigh, S John Baptist
ST 343004	6	Hawkchurch, S John Baptist
SS 502356	6	Heanton Punchardon, S Augustine
ST 135132	6	Hemyock, S Mary
SX 830809	4	Hennock, S Mary
SS 599205	8	High Bickington, S Mary
SS 689343	6	High Bray, All Saints
SX 851721	8	Highweek, All Saints
SX 612501	6	Holbeton, All Saints
SX 858916	4	Holcombe Burnell, S John Baptist
ST 056190	6	Holcombe Rogus, All Saints
SX 705694	6	Holne, Virgin Mary
SS 343039	8	Holsworthy, SS Peter & Paul
SY 167999	6	Honiton, S Michael Archangel (Old Church)
ST 163007	8	Honiton, S Paul

ST	001204	8	Huntsham, All Saints
SS	569082	6	Iddesleigh, S James
SX	898904	6	Ide, S Ida
SX	894774	6	Ideford, S Mary Virgin
SS	513473	8	Ilfracombe, Holy Trinity
SS	521478	8	Ilfracombe, SS Philip & James
SX	785761	6	Ilsington, S Michael
SX	560995	6	Inwardleigh, S Petroc
SX	833665	8	Ipplepen, S Andrew
SS	587016	5	Jacobstowe, S James
SX	395814	6	Kelly, S Mary
SX	922857	6	Kenn, S Andrew
ST	068081	6	Kentisbeare, S Mary
SS	622438	6	Kentisbury, S Thomas
SX	958833	6	Kenton, All Saints
SY	273980	6	Kilmington, S Giles
SX	733443	8	Kingsbridge, S Edmund K&M
SX	875678	6	Kingskerswell, S Mary
SS	681194	6	King's Nympton, S James Apostle
SX	872728	8	Kingsteignton, S Michael
SX	635477	6	Kingston, S James
SS	827230	6	Knowstone, S Peter
SX	451771	6	Lamerton, S Peter
SS	590311	6	Landkey, S Paul
SS	451155	6	Langtree, dedication unknown
SS	731083	6	Lapford, S Thomas of Canterbury
SX	457862	6	Lewtrenchard, S Peter
SX	386850	8	Lifton, S Mary
SS	443234	6	Littleham, S Swithin
SX	812626	5	Littlehempston, S John Baptist
SS	490167	6	Little Torrington, S Giles
SX	721486	6	Loddiswell, S Michael & All Angels
SS	616387	6	Loxhore, S Michael & All Angels
SS	138439	8	Lundy Island, S Helen
ST	169067	8	Luppitt, S Mary
SX	785812	6	Lustleigh, S John Baptist
SX	508847	6	Lydford, S Petrock
SX	993843	6	Lympstone, Nativity of BV
SS	720494	6	Lynton, S Mary Virgin
SX	706398	6	Malborough, All Saints
SX	749813	6	Manaton, S Winifrid
SS	744220	6	Mariansleigh, S Mary
SX	866636	6	Marldon, S John Baptist
SS	544376	6	Marwood, S Michael & All Angels
SX	434828	6	Marystowe, S Mary Virgin
SX	508787	5	Marytavy, S Mary Virgin
SX	540672	6	Meavy, S Peter
SS	548082	4	Meeth, S Michael & All Angels
ST	276030	6	Membury, S John Baptist
SS	525120	6	Merton, All Saints
SS	759197	6	Meshaw, S John Baptist
SX	407793	6	Milton Abbot, S Aegidius
SX	655515	6	Modbury, S George
SS	807283	6	Molland, S Mary
SS	457207	6	Monkleigh, S George
SS	581055	4	Monkokehampton, All Saints
ST	187031	6	Monkton, S Mary Magdalene
SS	773074	6	Morchard Bishop, S Mary
SS	954250	6	Morebath, S George
SX	755861	8	Moretonhampstead, S Andrew
SS	456452	6	Mortehoe, S Mary
SY	276945	6	Musbury, S Michael
SX	858712	8	Newton Abbot, S Leonard's Tower
SX	550482	6	Newton Ferrers, Holy Cross
SX	879980	8	Newton St Cyres, SS Cyr & Juletta
SS	448290	8	Northam, S Margaret
SX	739838	6	North Bovey, S John Baptist

SX	711565	5	North Huish, S Mary
SY	196958	4	Northleigh, S Giles
SX	505992	6	Northlew, S Thomas of Canterbury
SS	737299	6	North Molton, All Saints
SS	664017	8	North Tawton, S Peter
SS	727006	6	Nymet Tracey, S Bartholomew
SS	910212	8	Oakford, S Peter
SY	194995	6	Offwell, S Mary
SX	582951	8	Okehampton, All Saints
SY	080852	6	Otterton, S Michael & All Angels
SY	098956	8	Ottery St Mary, S Mary Virgin, K Edward Confessor & All Saints
SX	886608	8	Paignton, S John Baptist
SS	296058	5	Pancrasweek, S Pancras
SS	388215	6	Parkham, S James
ST	088017	6	Payhembury, S Mary
SS	478184	6	Peters Marland, S Peter
SX	512777	6	Peter Tavy, S Peter
SS	513092	6	Petrockstowe, S Petrock
SS	556341	8	Pilton, S Mary Virgin
SX	478544	10	Plymouth, S Andrew
SX	487564	8	Plymouth, Emmanuel, Compton Gifford
SX	497577	6	Plymouth, S Edward, Egg Buckland
SX	517530	8	Plymouth, S Mary & All Saints, Plymstock
SX	537563	8	Plymouth, S Mary BV, Plympton St Mary
SX	545557	8	Plymouth, S Maurice, Plympton St Maurice
SX	454593	6	Plymouth, S Budeaux, St Budeaux
SX	463550	8	Plymouth, S Andrew, Stoke Damerel
SX	471608	6	Plymouth, S Mary, Tamerton Foliot
ST	051029	6	Plymtree, S John Baptist
SX	966968	6	Poltimore, S Mary Virgin
SS	856085	6	Poughill, S Michael & All Angels
SX	972844	6	Powderham, S Clement B&M
SS	313029	6	Pyworthy, S Swithun
SS	850181	6	Rackenford, All Saints
SX	740615	5	Rattery, Blessed Virgin Mary
SX	550477	8	Revelstoke, S Peter, Noss Mayo
SX	946992	6	Rewe, S Mary Virgin
SS	576170	6	Roborough, S Peter
SS	727205	6	Romansleigh, S Rumon
SS	787217	6	Rose Ash, S Peter
SX	353907	5	St Giles on the Heath, S Giles
SS	533189	6	St Giles in the Wood, S Giles
SS	632013	6	Sampford Courtenay, S Andrew
ST	030142	6	Sampford Peverell, S John Baptist
SX	534724	5	Sampford Spiney, S Mary
SS	828026	6	Sandford, S Swithin
SY	247906	8	Seaton, S Gregory
SX	542631	6	Shaugh Prior, S Edward
SS	438092	6	Shebbear, S Michael
SX	560676	6	Sheepstor, S Leonard
SS	487063	6	Sheepwash, S Lawrence
SX	779443	6	Sherford, S Martin
SS	597374	6	Shirwell, S Peter
SS	863011	6	Shobrooke, S Swithin
SY	252974	6	Shute, S Michael
SY	125873	8	Sidbury, SS Peter & Giles
SY	252974	8	Sidmouth, S Nicholas
SS	956028	8	Silverton, S Mary
SX	821450	6	Slapton, S James Greater
SX	536903	5	Sourton, S Thomas of Canterbury
SX	695602	6	South Brent, S Petroc
SY	205934	4	Southleigh, S Laurence
SX	697429	6	South Milton, All Saints
SS	714259	8	South Molton, S Mary Magdalene
SX	776404	6	South Pool, S Cyriac
SX	653944	6	South Tawton, S Andrew

197

SX 976924	8	Sowton, S Michael & All Angels
SX 697967	6	Spreyton, S Michael
SX 793639	6	Staverton, S Paul
ST 244045	6	Stockland, S Michael & All Angels
SS 851063	4	Stockleigh English, S Mary Virgin
SX 940980	6	Stoke Canon, S Mary Magdalene
SX 861483	6	Stoke Fleming, S Peter
SX 848571	6	Stoke Gabriel, S Gabriel
SX 915704	6	Stokeinteignhead, S Andrew
SX 808428	6	Stokenham, S Michael & All Angels
SS 633355	5	Stoke Rivers, S Bartholomew
SS 922188	6	Stoodleigh, S Margaret
SX 432870	6	Stowford, S John
SS 346116	6	Sutcombe, S Andrew
SS 620300	6	Swimbridge, S James Apostle
SX 409760	6	Sydenham Damerel, S Mary
SY 067997	6	Talaton, S James A&M
SX 481744	8	Tavistock, S Eustachius
SS 559299	8	Tawstock, S Peter
SX 806945	6	Tedburn St Mary, S Mary Virgin
SX 939731	8	Teignmouth, S James Less, West Teignmouth
SX 944730	8	Teignmouth, S Michael, East Teignmouth
SS 787121	6	Thelbridge, S David
SS 401084	5	Thornbury, S Peter
SS 924021	8	Thorverton, S Thomas of Canterbury
SX 667907	6	Throwleigh, S Mary Virgin
SX 447876	6	Thrushelton, S George
SX 672428	6	Thurlestone, All Saints
SS 951125	6	Tiverton, S Paul
SS 954128	8	Tiverton, S Peter
SX 965880	6	Topsham, S Margaret
SX 819669	4	Torbryan, Holy Trinity
SX 909643	6	Torquay, S Savior, Tor Mohun, (Greek Orthodox)
SX 924653	8	Torquay, All Saints, Babbacombe
SX 913644	8	Torquay, S Mary Magdalene, Upton
SX 918660	10	Torquay, S Mary, St Marychurch
SX 890638	6	Torquay, SS George & Mary, Cockington
SX 802604	8	Totnes, S Mary
SX 856822	6	Trusham, S Michael
ST 068127	8	Uffculme, S Mary Virgin
SX 677556	8	Ugborough, S Peter
ST 015155	6	Uplowman, S Peter
SY 325935	6	Uplyme, SS Peter & Paul
ST 202076	6	Upottery, S Mary Virgin
SX 910977	6	Upton Pyne, Our Lady
SX 536701	6	Walkhampton, S Mary
SS 642227	6	Warkleigh, S John Evangelist
SS 935153	6	Washfield, S Mary Virgin
SS 812118	6	Washford Pyne, S Peter
SS 466220	6	Weare Giffard, Holy Trinity
SS 228184	6	Welcombe, S Nectan
SX 518484	6	Wembury, S Werburgh
SX 723438	6	West Alvington, All Saints
SX 520623	6	West Bickleigh, S Mary Virgin
SS 657313	6	West Buckland, S Peter
SS 516420	6	West Down, S Calixtus
SS 472286	6	Westleigh, S Peter
SS 359156	6	West Putford, S Stephen
SS 770134	6	West Worlington, S Mary
SY 044972	6	Whimple, S Mary
SX 492726	6	Whitchurch, S Andrew
SX 869943	6	Whitestone, S Katharine
SX 719767	6	Widecombe in the Moor, S Pancras
SY 214992	5	Widworthy, S Cuthbert
SS 633080	8	Winkleigh, All Saints
SS 803145	8	Witheridge, S John Baptist
SX 855704	8	Wolborough, S Mary

SY 009872	8	Woodbury, S Swithin
SX 737488	5	Woodleigh, S Mary
SS 332211	6	Woolfardisworthy, Holy Trinity
ST 246082	6	Yarcombe, S John Baptist
SS 561235	6	Yarnscombe, S Andrew
SX 577517	6	Yealmpton, S Bartholomew
SS 720040	6	Zeal Monachorum, S Peter

Dorset

SY 577852	6	Abbotsbury, S Nicholas
SY 914989	4	Almer, S Mary
SY 529926	6	Askerswell, S Michael
ST 479012	10	Beaminster, S Mary of the Annunciation
SY 847947	6	Bere Regis, S John Baptist
ST 696131	5	Bishop's Caundle, SS Peter & Paul
ST 885063	8	Blandford Forum, SS Peter & Paul
SZ 087913	6	Bournemouth, Sacred Heart (RC)
SZ 089913	8	Bournemouth, S Peter
SZ 067921	8	Bournemouth, S John Evangelist, Surrey Road
ST 768303	6	Bourton, S George
ST 587143	6	Bradford Abbas, S Mary
SY 658930	5	Bradford Peverell, Assumption BVM
SY 480943	8	Bradpole, Holy Trinity
SY 465926	8	Bridport, S Mary
ST 437026	6	Broadwindsor, S John Baptist
SZ 028878	8	Brownsea Island, S Mary
ST 875069	6	Bryanston, S Martin (School Chapel)
ST 757247	6	Buckhorn Weston, S John Baptist
ST 687052	6	Buckland Newton, Holy Rood
SY 488895	6	Burton Bradstock, S Mary
SZ 032988	6	Canford Magna, dedication unknown
SY 591995	8	Cattistock, SS Peter & Paul
ST 666012	6	Cerne Abbas, S Mary
ST 901041	4	Charlton Marshall, S Mary
SY 679927	10	Charminster, S Mary Virgin
SY 421929	5	Chideock, S Giles
ST 835127	6	Child Okeford, S Nicholas
SZ 161926	12(1)	Christchurch, Priory Church of Holy Trinity
ST 869184	5	Compton Abbas, S Mary Virgin
SY 960820	6	Corfe Castle, S Edward Martyr
SY 976983	6	Corfe Mullen, S Hubert
ST 522049	6	Corscombe, S Mary
SU 054133	8	Cranborne, SS Mary & Bartholomew
SY 698905	6	Dorchester, S George, Fordington
SY 692907	8	Dorchester, S Peter
ST 859085	6	Durweston, S Nicholas
ST 572045	6	Evershot, S Osmond
ST 865170	6	Fontmell Magna, S Andrew
SY 626949	6	Frampton, S Mary
ST 806266	8	Gillingham, S Mary Virgin
ST 680082	4	Glanvilles Wootton
SY 666974	4	Godmanstone, Holy Trinity
ST 998108	5	Gussage All Saints, All Saints
ST 985113	6	Gussage St Michael, S Michael & All Angels
ST 536083	5	Halstock, S Mary
SZ 055988	6	Hampreston, All Saints
ST 753083	6	Haselbury Bryan, SS Mary & James
ST 781029	6	Hilton, All Saints
SU 014062	5	Hinton Martell, S John Evangelist
ST 699119	5	Holwell, S Laurence
ST 859124	6	Iwerne Courtney (Shroton), S Mary
ST 868145	6	Iwerne Minster, S Mary
SY 955795	8	Kingston, S James
ST 768231	5	Kington Magna, All Saints
ST 617086	6	Leigh, S Andrew
ST 629127	5	Lillington, S Martin
SY 551907	8	Litton Cheney, S Mary

SY 491943	6	Loders, S Mary Magdalene
SY 570906	5	Long Bredy, S Peter
ST 649128	4	Longburton, S James Great
ST 977103	6	Long Crichel, S Mary Virgin
ST 742134	5	Lydlinch, S Thomas a' Becket
SY 343923	10	Lyme Regis, S Michael Archangel
SY 936962	6	Lytchett Matravers, S Mary Virgin
SY 960931	6	Lytchett Minster, dedication unknown
SY 596978	6	Maiden Newton, S Mary
ST 816150	5	Manston, S Nicholas
ST 735059	5	Mappowder, SS Peter & Paul
ST 823187	4	Margaret Marsh, S Margaret
ST 781187	6	Marnhull, S Gregory
SY 647889	6	Martinstown, S Martin
ST 882201	5	Melbury Abbas, S Thomas
ST 596066	4	Melbury Bubb, S Mary
ST 573078	6	Melbury Osmund, S Osmund
SY 801974	6	Milborne St Andrew, S Andrew
ST 798022	8	Milton Abbey, S Sampson
SY 916956	5	Morden, S Mary
ST 849252	6	Motcombe, S Mary
SY 470995	6	Netherbury, S Mary
ST 598172	5	Nether Compton, S Nicholas
ST 807108	6	Okeford Fitzpaine, S Andrew
ST 594169	4	Over Compton, S Michael
SU 033178	4	Pentridge, S Rumbold
SY 715971	6	Piddlehinton, S Mary Virgin
ST 702007	6	Piddletrenthide, All Saints
ST 903094	5	Pimperne, S Peter
SZ 028931	6	Poole, S George Oakdale
SZ 008904	10	Poole, S James
SY 517962	6	Powerstock, S Mary Virgin
SY 705829	6	Preston, S Andrew
SY 758943	6	Puddletown, S Mary Virgin
ST 561021	5	Rampisham, S Michael & All Angels
ST 622210	5	Sandford Orcas, S Nicholas
ST 868226	4	Shaftesbury, Grammar School Chapel
ST 857224	6	Shaftesbury, S James Great
ST 863229	6	Shaftesbury, S Peter
ST 937017	4	Shapwick, S Bartholomew
ST 638165	8	Sherborne, Abbey Church of S Mary Virgin
ST 824115	6	Shillingstone, Holy Rood
SY 498914	4	Shipton Gorge, S Martin
ST 782293	5	Silton, S Nicholas
ST 472066	6	South Perrott, S Mary
ST 909029	6	Spetisbury, S John Baptist
ST 733182	6	Stalbridge, S Mary
ST 454006	5	Stoke Abbott, S Mary
ST 860094	6	Stourpaine, Holy Trinity
ST 794216	4	Stour Provost, S Michael
ST 715152	4	Stourton Caundle, S Peter
SY 650937	5	Stratton, S Mary Virgin
ST 951004	6	Sturminster Marshall, S Mary
ST 788139	6	Sturminster Newton, S Mary
SZ 027788	8	Swanage, S Mary Virgin
SY 630993	5	Sydling St Nicholas, S Nicholas
SY 444936	6	Symondsbury, S John Baptist
ST 925041	5	Tarrant Keyneston, All Saints
ST 376034	8	Thorncombe, S Mary
ST 603133	6	Thornford, S Mary Magdalene
SY 562980	4	Toller Porcorum, SS Peter & Andrew
ST 516015	5	Toller Whelme, S Mary
ST 589185	6	Trent, S Andrew
SY 660852	6	Upwey, S Lawrence
SY 925872	10	Wareham, Lady S Mary
SY 661778	8	Weymouth, All Saints, Wyke Regis
SY 396954	8	Whitchurch Canonicorum, S Candida & Holy Cross

SZ 009999	10	Wimborne Minster, S Cuthberga
SU 032120	8	Wimborne St Giles, S Giles
SY 862976	4	Winterborne Kingston, S Nicholas
ST 834046	4	Winterborne Stickland, S Mary
ST 836001	5	Winterborne Whitechurch, S Mary
SY 899977	4	Winterborne Zelstone, S Mary
ST 988065	6	Witchampton, SS Mary, Cuthberga & All Saints
SY 847864	6	Wool, Holy Rood
ST 594106	6	Yetminster, S Andrew

Durham

NZ 050163	8	Barnard Castle, S Mary Virgin
NZ 093526	6	Benfieldside, S Cuthbert
NZ 218284	8	Bishop Auckland, S Andrew
NZ 097518	8	Blackhill, Our Lady Immaculate (RC)
NZ 101516	8	Blackhill, S Aidan
NZ 224377	8	Brancepeth, S Brandon
NZ 276513	8	Chester le Street, SS Mary & Cuthbert
NZ 107509	8	Consett, Christ Church
NZ 012193	6	Cotherstone, S Cuthbert
NZ 283148	6	Darlington, Holy Trinity
NZ 291144	8	Darlington, S Cuthbert
NZ 296143	8	Darlington, S John Evangelist
NZ 273421	10	Durham, Cathedral Church of Christ & BMV
NZ 274426	6	Durham, S Nicholas
NZ 276419	8	Durham, S Oswald K&M
NZ 169167	6	Gainford, S Mary
NZ 259224	6	Heighington, S Michael
NZ 309101	6	Hurworth, All Saints
NZ 167474	6	Lanchester, All Saints
NZ 356288	5	Sedgefield, S Edmund
NZ 228264	8	Shildon, S John
NZ 292407	6	Shincliffe, S Mary Virgin
NZ 131206	8	Staindrop, S Mary
NZ 185554	8	Tanfield, S Margaret
NZ 208352	5	Willington, S Stephen

East Sussex

TQ 521030	6	Alfriston, S Andrew
TQ 689145	4	Ashburnham, S James
TQ 418143	6	Barcombe, S Mary Virgin
TQ 750158	8	Battle, S Mary
TQ 843237	6	Beckley, All Saints
TQ 445079	4	Beddingham, S Andrew
TQ 746081	8	Bexhill, S Peter
TQ 782262	6	Bodiam, S Giles
TQ 825183	6	Brede, S George
TQ 683210	8	Brightling, S Thomas of Canterbury
TQ 308045	10	Brighton, S Nicholas of Myra
TQ 314049	10	Brighton, S Peter
TQ 308041	4	Brighton, S Mark
TQ 298063	8	Brighton, Good Shepherd, Preston
TQ 677248	8	Burwash, S Bartholomew
TQ 485230	8	Buxted, S Margaret Queen
TQ 392193	6	Chailey, SS Peter & Mary
TQ 544142	6	Chiddingly, dedication unknown
TQ 450338	8	Coleman's Hatch, Holy Trinity
TQ 658191	6	Dallington, S Giles
TQ 402275	6	Danehill, All Saints
TQ 326153	8	Ditchling, S Margaret
TV 608983	8	Eastbourne, All Saints
TV 620997	8	Eastbourne, Christ Church
TV 598995	8	Eastbourne, S Mary Virgin
TV 610988	10	Eastbourne, S Saviour
TV 557977	5	East Dean, SS Simon & Jude
TQ 520162	6	East Hoathly, dedication unknown

TQ 796246	5	Ewhurst Green, S James
TQ 466268	8	Fairwarp, Christ Church
TQ 429235	8	Fletching, S Andrew & S Mary Virgin
TQ 725309	4	Flimwell, S Augustine
TQ 590357	6	Frant, S Alban
TQ 591095	8	Hailsham, S Mary
TQ 439395	6	Hammerwood, S Stephen
TQ 479357	6	Hartfield, S Mary
TQ 839098	8	Hastings, All Saints
TQ 824096	8	Hastings, S Clement
TQ 815106	8	Hastings, Christ Church, Blacklands
TQ 802091	8	Hastings, Christ Church, St Leonards
TQ 599203	8	Heathfield, All Saints
TQ 581123	6	Hellingly, SS Peter & Paul
TQ 683092	5	Hooe, S Oswald
TQ 266053	6	Hove, S Leonard, Aldrington
TQ 881164	4	Icklesham, S Nicholas
TQ 915238	6	Iden, All Saints
TQ 500126	6	Laughton, All Saints
TQ 422103	4	Lewes, S Thomas à Becket
TQ 413096	10	Lewes, S John Baptist, Southover
TQ 471183	6	Little Horsted, S Michael & All Angels
TQ 465240	8	Maresfield, S Bartholomew
TQ 586270	8	Mayfield, S Dunstan
TQ 422208	6	Newick, S Mary
TQ 830245	6	Northiam, S Mary
TQ 887218	6	Peasmarsh, SS Peter & Paul
TQ 647048	6	Pevensey, S Nicholas
TQ 446125	8	Ringmer, S Mary Virgin
TQ 514099	5	Ripe, S John Baptist
TQ 421063	6	Rodmell, S Peter
TQ 556298	8	Rotherfield, S Denys
TQ 921203	8	Rye, S Mary Virgin
TQ 749242	8	Salehurst, S Mary Virgin
TV 483990	8	Seaford, S Leonard
TQ 777188	6	Sedlescombe, S John Baptist
TQ 689301	6	Ticehurst, S Mary
TQ 472214	8	Uckfield, Holy Cross
TQ 641319	8	Wadhurst, SS Peter & Paul
TQ 549193	8	Waldron, All Saints & S Bartholomew
TQ 609182	6	Warbleton, S Mary Virgin
TV 641046	6	Westham, S Mary
TQ 589025	6	Willingdon, S Mary
TQ 493356	8	Withyham, S Michael & All Angels
TQ 338208	6	Wivelsfield, S John Baptist

Essex

TM 054296	8	Ardleigh, S Mary Virgin
TL 483345	6	Arkesden, S Mary Virgin
TL 581415	8	Ashdon, All Saints
TL 578097	4	Beauchamp Roding, S Botolph
TL 798435	6	Belchamp St Paul, S Andrew
TL 827407	8	Belchamp Walter, S Mary
TQ 566967	6	Bentley Common, S Paul
TL 603016	5	Blackmore, S Lawrence
TL 762207	5	Black Notley, SS Peter & Paul
TL 534055	6	Bobbingworth, S Germain
TL 758258	10	Bocking, S Mary
TL 756096	8	Boreham, S Andrew
TM 004069	6	Bradwell on Sea, S Thomas Apostle
TL 756229	10	Braintree, S Michael Archangel
TQ 596937	8	Brentwood, S Thomas of Canterbury
TL 705105	6	Broomfield, S Mary
TL 578273	4	Broxted, S Mary
TQ 948970	6	Burnham on Crouch, S Mary

TQ 897945	5	Canewdon, S Nicholas
TL 784355	6	Castle Hedingham, S Nicholas
TL 708069	12(1)	Chelmsford, Cathedral Church of S Mary Virgin, SS Peter & Cedd
TQ 441937	6	Chigwell, S Mary
TQ 465933	8	Chigwell Row, All Saints
TL 451386	6	Chrishall, Holy Trinity
TL 471318	6	Clavering, SS Mary & Clement
TL 855230	8	Coggeshall, S Peter ad Vincula
TM 013247	6	Colchester, S Leonard at the Hythe
TL 994252	8	Colchester, S Peter
TL 971232	6	Colchester, All Saints, Shrub End
TL 850303	6	Colne Engaine, S Andrew
TL 779052	8	Danbury, S John Baptist
TM 056332	8	Dedham, S Mary Virgin
TQ 730952	6	Downham, S Margaret
TL 861289	8	Earls Colne, S Andrew
TQ 862888	6	Eastwood, S Laurence & All Saints
TL 462397	6	Elmdon, S Nicholas
TL 459021	8	Epping, S John Baptist
TL 444045	6	Epping Upland, All Saints
TL 768167	4	Fairstead, S Mary
TL 481248	6	Farnham, S Mary Virgin
TL 872204	8	Feering, All Saints
TL 676204	8	Felsted, Holy Cross
TL 686328	6	Finchingfield, S John Baptist
TQ 717839	8	Fobbing, S Michael
TL 677168	6	Ford End, S John Evangelist
TL 837447	8	Foxearth, SS Peter & Paul
TL 638001	6	Fryerning, S Mary
TL 573067	6	Fyfield, S Nicholas
TL 704029	8	Galleywood, S Michael & All Angels
TL 812386	6	Gestingthorpe, S Mary
TL 905088	8	Goldhanger, S Peter
TL 627121	5	Good Easter, S Andrew
TL 772295	6	Gosfield, S Catherine
TQ 614777	8	Grays, SS Peter & Paul
TL 730049	8	Great Baddow, S Mary Virgin
TL 678303	8	Great Bardfield, S Mary Virgin
TM 108216	8	Great Bentley, S Mary Virgin
TM 083263	6	Great Bromley, S George
TQ 681922	5	Great Burstead, S Mary Magdalene
TL 505427	6	Great Chesterford, All Saints
TL 630230	8	Great Dunmow, S Mary
TL 606254	6	Great Easton, SS John & Giles
TL 512196	5	Great Hallingbury, S Giles
TM 219193	8	Great Holland, All Saints
TL 972324	6	Great Horkesley, All Saints
TL 738156	5	Great Leighs, S Mary
TL 432089	6	Great Parndon, S Mary
TL 643354	5	Great Sampford, S Michael
TL 892257	8	Great Tey, S Barnabas
TL 862110	6	Great Totham, S Peter
TQ 949875	6	Great Wakering, S Nicholas
TL 696134	8	Great Waltham, SS Mary & Lawrence
TL 757387	6	Great Yeldham, S Andrew
TL 822285	6	Greenstead Green, S James Apostle
TL 558447	6	Hadstock, S Botolph
TL 815307	8	Halstead, S Andrew
TL 483115	8	Harlow, S Mary Virgin
TL 473085	8	Harlow Common, S Mary Magdalene
TM 262326	8	Harwich, S Nicholas
TL 546165	8	Hatfield Broad Oak, S Mary Virgin
TL 522149	6	Hatfield Heath, Holy Trinity
TL 651416	8	Helions Bumpstead, S Andrew
TL 635380	6	Hempstead, S Andrew
TL 544286	6	Henham, S Mary Virgin

TL 620147	6	High Easter, S Mary Virgin
TL 565037	6	High Ongar, S Mary
TQ 635943	5	Hutton, All Saints
TQ 652996	6	Ingatestone, SS Mary & Edmund
TQ 623920	6	Ingrave, S Nicholas
TL 879178	5	Inworth, All Saints
TL 856185	6	Kelvedon, S Mary Virgin
TM 219220	8	Kirby le Soken, S Michael
TQ 678865	6	Langdon Hills, S Mary Virgin & All Saints
TM 034337	6	Langham, S Mary
TL 442352	4	Langley, S John Evangelist
TL 965191	5	Layer de la Haye, S John Baptist
TQ 842857	6	Leigh on Sea, S Clement
TL 764081	8	Little Baddow, S Mary Virgin
TM 123249	5	Little Bentley, S Mary Virgin
TM 091279	4	Little Bromley, S Mary
TL 516395	6	Littlebury, Holy Trinity
TL 961319	5	Little Horkesley, SS Peter & Paul
TL 712128	6	Little Waltham, S Martin
TQ 429969	8	Loughton, S John Baptist
TL 849071	8	Maldon, All Saints
TL 857067	6	Maldon, S Mary Virgin
TL 491266	6	Manuden, S Mary
TL 666005	4	Margaretting, S Margaret
TL 525120	6	Matching, S Mary Virgin
TM 114317	6	Mistley, S Mary
TL 537071	6	Moreton, S Mary Virgin
TQ 541983	6	Navestock, S Thomas Apostle
TL 413070	6	Nazeing, All Saints
TL 521341	6	Newport, S Mary Virgin
TL 495052	6	North Weald, S Andrew
TQ 644820	6	Orsett, S Giles & All Saints
TL 853335	6	Pebmarsh, S John Baptist
TL 814462	5	Pentlow, S George
TL 663143	5	Pleshey, Holy Trinity
TL 842020	6	Purleigh, All Saints
TL 606372	8	Radwinter, S Mary Virgin
TQ 807908	8	Rayleigh, Holy Trinity
TL 733229	6	Rayne, All Saints
TQ 770959	6	Rettendon, All Saints
TL 498315	5	Rickling, All Saints
TL 740408	5	Ridgewell, S Laurence Martyr
TQ 872903	8	Rochford, S Andrew
TL 407103	6	Roydon, S Peter
TL 537386	12	Saffron Walden, S Mary Virgin
TM 123155	6	St Osyth, SS Peter, Paul & Osyth
TL 743048	6	Sandon, S Andrew
TL 724293	5	Shalford, S Andrew
TL 509137	4	Sheering, S Mary
TQ 605951	6	Shenfield, S Mary Virgin
TL 776344	8	Sible Hedingham, S Peter
TQ 777862	6	South Benfleet, S Mary Virgin
TQ 877868	10	Southend-on-Sea, Annunciation BVM, Prittlewell
TQ 916851	8	Southend-on-Sea, S Augustine, Thorpe Bay
TQ 958997	8	Southminster, S Leonard
TQ 571939	8	South Weald, S Peter
TL 719080	6	Springfield, All Saints
TL 721388	5	Stambourne, SS Peter & Thomas
TQ 684823	8	Stanford le Hope, S Margaret of Antioch
TL 521241	8	Stansted Mountfitchet, S Mary Virgin
TL 664240	6	Stebbing, S Mary Virgin
TL 679410	5	Steeple Bumpstead, S Mary
TL 799246	6	Stisted, All Saints
TL 555217	4	Takeley, Holy Trinity
TM 143242	6	Tendring, S Edmund K&M
TL 774148	8	Terling, All Saints
TL 611310	8	Thaxted, S John Baptist
TQ 472994	5	Theydon Garnon, All Saints
TM 179223	6	Thorpe le Soken, S Michael
TM 098196	6	Thorrington, S Mary Magdalene
TL 993038	6	Tillingham, S Nicholas
TL 957103	8	Tollesbury, S Mary
TL 928117	6	Tolleshunt D'Arcy, S Nicholas
TL 739374	5	Toppesfield, S Margaret of Antioch
TL 381006	12(1)	Waltham Abbey, Holy Cross & S Lawrence
TL 514363	6	Wendens Ambo, S Mary Virgin
TQ 736998	4	West Hanningfield, SS Mary & Edward
TL 712312	8	Wethersfield, S Mary Magdalene
TL 562134	5	White Roding, S Martin
TL 827371	5	Wickham St Paul, All Saints
TL 694051	8	Widford, S Mary
TL 596073	4	Willingale, S Christopher
TL 817154	8	Witham, S Nicholas & All Saints
TM 038215	6	Wivenhoe, S Mary Virgin
TL 933323	6	Wormingford, S Andrew
TL 678062	8	Writtle, All Saints

Gloucestershire

SP 243269	5	Adlestrop, S Mary Magdalene
SP 002332	6	Alderton, S Margaret
SO 603007	5	Alvington, S Andrew
SP 065019	5	Ampney Crucis, Holy Rood or Sanctoe Cruis
SO 706107	6	Arlingham, S Mary Virgin
SO 928333	6	Ashchurch, S Nicholas
SO 819252	6	Ashleworth, SS Andrew & Bartholomew
ST 879980	6	Avening, Holy Cross
SO 708081	6	Awre, S Andrew
SO 902193	6	Badgeworth, Holy Trinity
SP 077051	6	Barnsley, S Mary
ST 684990	10	Berkeley, S Mary Virgin
SP 118065	6	Bibury, S Mary
SO 961277	8	Bishop's Cleeve, S Michael & All Angels
SO 904059	8	Bisley, All Saints
SO 703172	6	Blaisdon, S Michael
SP 245226	6	Bledington, S Leonard
SP 165350	8	Blockley, SS Peter & Paul
SP 175325	6	Bourton on the Hill, S Lawrence
SP 167209	8	Bourton on the Water, S Lawrence
SO 942128	6	Brimpsfield, S Michael & All Angels
SP 201278	6	Broadwell, S Paul
SO 891170	6	Brockworth, S George
SO 743337	6	Bromsberrow, S Mary
SP 082360	6	Buckland, S Michael
ST 757993	6	Cam, S George
SO 855307	6	Chaceley, S John Baptist
SO 892026	6	Chalford, Christ Church
SO 964204	8	Charlton Kings, S Mary
SP 052121	6	Chedworth, S Andrew
SO 928220	5	Cheltenham, S Mark
SO 948225	12	Cheltenham, S Mary Virgin
ST 903986	4	Cherington, S Nicholas
SP 155394	8	Chipping Campden, S James
SO 768183	6	Churcham, S Andrew
SO 885197	6	Churchdown, S Bartholomew
SP 027013	8	Cirencester, Holy Trinity, Watermoor
SP 023021	12(1)	Cirencester, S John Baptist
SO 571080	4	Clearwell, S Peter
SO 772017	6	Coaley, S Bartholomew
SP 128199	5	Cold Aston, S Andrew
SP 004134	5	Colesborne, S James A&M
SP 144052	8	Coln St Aldwyns, Decollation of S John Baptist
SP 087109	5	Coln St Denys, S James Great
SP 059166	6	Compton Abdale, S Oswald
SO 788264	6	Corse, S Margaret

SO 965147	6	Cowley, S Mary BV
SO 892123	6	Cranham, S James Great
SO 994050	4	Daglingworth, Holy Rood
SO 871299	6	Deerhurst, Holy Trinity or S Mary
SP 055314	5	Didbrook, S George
SU 099965	5	Down Ampney, All Saints
SP 018358	6	Dumbleton, S Peter
ST 757981	8	Dursley, S James Great
SO 700313	6	Dymock, S Mary BV
SO 783057	6	Eastington, S Michael & All Angels
SP 183400	6	Ebrington, S Eadburgha
SO 948060	5	Edgeworth, S Mary Virgin
SO 967123	6	Elkstone, S John Evangelist
SO 767149	6	Elmore, S John Baptist
SO 920260	4	Elmstone Hardwicke, S Mary Magdalene
SO 582158	5	English Bicknor, S Mary Virgin
SP 221291	5	Evenlode, S Edward
SP 152012	8	Fairford, S Mary Virgin
SO 858326	6	Forthampton, S Mary Virgin
SO 744069	6	Frampton on Severn, S Mary Virgin
SO 831188	12	Gloucester, Cathedral Church of Holy & Indivisible Trinity
SO 831184	8	Gloucester, S Mary de Crypt
SO 829189	6	Gloucester, S Mary de Lode
SO 828187	6	Gloucester, S Nicholas
SO 858178	8	Gloucester, S Lawrence, Barnwood
SO 813170	8	Gloucester, S Swithun, Hempsted
SP 205135	6	Great Barrington, S Mary Virgin
SP 195172	6	Great Rissington, S John Baptist
SO 911148	6	Great Witcombe, S Mary Virgin
SP 096246	6	Guiting Power, S Michael & All Angels
SO 793124	6	Hardwicke, S Nicholas
SO 810104	6	Haresfield, S Peter
SO 780237	6	Hartpury, S Mary Virgin
SO 827276	6	Hasfield, S Mary
SP 154051	6	Hatherop, S Nicholas
SO 568022	6	Hewelsfield, S Mary Magdalene
ST 837980	6	Horsley, S Martin
SO 713196	6	Huntley, S John Baptist
ST 989970	6	Kemble, All Saints
SU 161964	6	Kempsford, S Mary Virgin
SU 215995	6	Lechlade, S Lawrence
SO 943194	8	Leckhampton, S Peter
SO 866258	6	Leigh, The, S Catherine
SO 802032	6	Leonard Stanley, S Swithun
SO 672136	6	Littledean, S Ethelbert
SP 179298	6	Longborough, S James
SO 684198	8	Longhope, All Saints
ST 909924	6	Long Newnton, Holy Trinity
SO 763124	8	Longney, S Lawrence
SP 166226	6	Lower Slaughter, S Mary
SO 633026	10	Lydney, S Mary
SO 814217	6	Maisemore, S Giles
SP 117001	6	Meysey Hampton, S Mary
SP 162435	8	Mickleton, S Lawrence
SO 873007	6	Minchinhampton, Holy Trinity
SO 773170	6	Minsterworth, S Peter
SO 663186	8	Mitcheldean, S Michael & All Angels
SP 206322	8	Moreton in Marsh, S David
SO 779097	6	Moreton Valence, S Stephen
SO 723259	8	Newent, S Mary
SO 553095	6	Newland, All Saints
SO 690115	8	Newnham on Severn, S Peter
SP 019078	6	North Cerney, All Saints
SP 112146	8	Northleach, SS Peter & Paul
ST 735961	6	North Nibley, S Martin
SO 866244	8	Norton, S Mary Virgin

SP 235256	6	Oddington, S Nicholas
SO 866096	12(1)	Painswick, S Mary Virgin
SO 969239	8	Prestbury, S Mary
SP 044009	5	Preston, All Saints
SO 807142	8	Quedgeley, S James
SO 827067	6	Randwick, S John Baptist
SO 752313	6	Redmarley D'Abitot, S Bartholomew
SP 019098	6	Rendcomb, S Peter
SO 622177	8	Ruardean, S John Baptist
SO 558047	8	St Briavels, S Mary Virgin
SP 117394	6	Saintbury, S Nicholas
SO 828234	8	Sandhurst, S Lawrence
SP 169147	6	Sherborne, S Mary Magdalene
ST 892897	6	Shipton Moyne, S John Baptist
SP 035002	6	Siddington, S Peter
SO 740036	6	Slimbridge, S John Evangelist
SU 050973	6	South Cerney, All Hallows
SO 801084	6	Standish, S Nicholas
SP 069344	6	Stanton, S Michael & All Angels
SP 061323	4	Stanway, S Peter
SO 551126	6	Staunton (near Coleford), All Saints
SO 782293	6	Staunton (near Tewkesbury), S James
ST 729988	6	Stinchcombe, S Cyr
ST 684954	6	Stone, All Saints
SO 800051	6	Stonehouse, S Cyr
SP 191257	8	Stow on the Wold, S Edward
SO 852053	10	Stroud, S Lawrence
SO 934248	6	Swindon Village, S Lawrence
SP 092279	5	Temple Guiting, S Mary
ST 891929	8	Tetbury, S Mary
SO 889323	12	Tewkesbury, Abbey Church of S Mary Virgin
ST 556958	6	Tidenham, S Peter
SO 840286	6	Tirley, S Michael
SP 035331	6	Toddington, S Andrew
SP 243363	6	Todenham, S Thomas of Canterbury
SO 905295	5	Tredington, S John Baptist
SO 894361	6	Twyning, S Mary Magdalene
SP 155232	5	Upper Slaughter, S Peter
SO 862149	8	Upton St Leonards, S Leonard
SO 717138	6	Westbury on Severn, SS Peter & Paul
SO 761091	6	Whitminster, S Andrew
SP 107397	6	Willersey, S Peter
SP 023283	6	Winchcombe, S Peter
SP 194131	6	Windrush, S Peter
SO 966093	6	Winstone, S Bartholomew
SP 032157	6	Withington, S Michael
SO 840026	6	Woodchester, S Mary
ST 587994	5	Woolaston, S Andrew
SO 961303	6	Woolstone, S Martin of Tours
ST 756936	8	Wotton under Edge, S Mary Virgin
SP 192215	4	Wyck Rissington, S Lawrence

Greater London

TQ 200801	8	Acton, S Mary
TQ 371640	6	Addington, S Mary BV
TQ 441838	8	Barking, S Margaret
TQ 431887	8	Barkingside, S George
TQ 222766	8	Barnes, S Mary Virgin
TQ 245965	8	Barnet, S John Baptist
TQ 268768	8	Battersea, S Mary
TQ 375697	10	Beckenham, S George
TQ 295653	10	Beddington, S Mary Virgin
TQ 343794	10	Bermondsey, S James
TQ 342825	8	Bethnal Green, S Matthew
TQ 497734	8	Bexley, S Mary Virgin
TQ 419589	6	Biggin Hill, S Mark

TQ 376830	8	Bow, S Mary
TQ 401693	8	Bromley, SS Peter & Paul
TQ 414679	8	Bromley Common, S Luke
TQ 330766	10	Camberwell, S Giles
TQ 279644	8	Carshalton, All Saints
TQ 243638	6	Cheam, S Dunstan
TQ 271775	8	Chelsea, All Saints (Old Church)
TQ 272783	10	Chelsea, S Luke
TQ 479640	6	Chelsfield, S Martin of Tours
TQ 438709	8	Chislehurst, Annunciation BVM
TQ 444697	8	Chislehurst, S Nicholas
TQ 215777	8	Chiswick, S Nicholas
TQ 319811	12	City of London, Cathedral Church of S Paul
TQ 336813	8	City of London, S Botolph Without, Aldgate
TQ 332815	8	City of London, S Botolph, Bishopsgate
TQ 324811	12	City of London, S Mary-le-Bow, Cheapside
TQ 329811	12	City of London, S Michael, Cornhill
TQ 323817	12	City of London, S Giles, Cripplegate
TQ 322812	6	City of London, S Vedast, Foster Lane
TQ 325813	8	City of London, S Lawrence Jewry, Guildhall
TQ 333808	8	City of London, S Olave, Hart Street
TQ 314815	8	City of London, S Andrew, Holborn
TQ 318814	12	City of London, S Sepulchre, Holborn Viaduct
TQ 334811	6	City of London, S Katherine Cree, Leadenhall Street
TQ 319817	5	City of London, S Bartholomew, Smithfield
TQ 300795	10	City of Westminster, Abbey, (College Church of S Peter)
TQ 301805	12(1)	City of Westminster, Liberties of S Martin-in-the-Field
TQ 309810	10	City of Westminster, S Clement Danes, Strand
TQ 301795	10	City of Westminster, S Margaret, Parliament Square
TQ 295790	8	City of Westminster, S Stephen, Rochester Row
TQ 294752	8	Clapham, Redemptorist Church of Our Immaculate Lady (RC)
TQ 292753	4	Clapham, Holy Trinity, Clapham Common
TQ 316823	8	Clerkenwell, S James
TQ 312581	5	Coulsdon, S John Evangelist
TQ 101781	6	Cranford, S Dunstan
TQ 512752	8	Crayford, S Paulinus
TQ 319655	12(2)	Croydon, S John Baptist
TQ 327644	10	Croydon, S Peter, South Croydon
TQ 445600	10	Cudham, SS Peter & Paul
TQ 500845	8	Dagenham, SS Peter & Paul
TQ 339852	8	Dalston, S Mark
TQ 374762	8	Deptford, S John
TQ 432617	6	Downe, S Mary Virgin
TQ 176807	8	Ealing, Christ the Saviour
TQ 176797	8	Ealing, S Mary
TQ 147807	8	Ealing, S Mary, Hanwell
TQ 085736	6	East Bedfont, S Mary
TQ 192917	6	Edgware, S Margaret
TQ 340936	8	Edmonton, All Saints
TQ 426745	8	Eltham, S John Baptist
TQ 328966	8	Enfield, S Andrew
TQ 317968	8	Enfield, S Mary Magdalene
TQ 513779	8	Erith, Christ Church
TQ 508787	8	Erith, S John Baptist
TQ 249906	8	Finchley, S Mary
TQ 476713	5	Foots Cray, All Saints
TQ 242759	10	Fulham, All Saints
TQ 383776	10	Greenwich, S Alfege
TQ 351851	8	Hackney, S John Baptist
TQ 356842	8	Hackney, S John of Jerusalem, South Hackney
TQ 232784	8	Hammersmith, S Paul
TQ 141695	8	Hampton, S Mary
TQ 053895	6	Harefield, S Mary Virgin
TQ 087782	8	Harlington, SS Peter & Paul
TQ 059777	6	Harmondsworth, S Mary
TQ 153874	10	Harrow on the Hill, S Mary
TQ 153917	8	Harrow Weald, All Saints
TQ 512931	6	Havering-atte-Bower, S John Evangelist
TQ 405663	6	Hayes (near Bromley), S Mary Virgin
TQ 097811	8	Hayes (near Southall), S Mary Virgin
TQ 228895	8	Hendon, S Mary
TQ 132775	8	Heston, S Leonard
TQ 282864	8	Highgate, S Anne
TQ 069829	10	Hillingdon, S John Baptist
TQ 299812	8	Holborn, S Giles in the Fields
TQ 313849	8	Holloway, S Mary Magdalene
TQ 544869	8	Hornchurch, S Andrew
TQ 124760	8	Hounslow, S Paul
TQ 448868	8	Ilford, S Mary Virgin
TQ 167761	10	Isleworth, All Saints
TQ 321837	6	Islington, S James Apostle, Prebend Street
TQ 317838	8	Islington, S Mary Virgin, Upper Street
TQ 256797	10	Kensington, S Mary Abbots
TQ 281852	6	Kentish Town, S Martin, Gospel Oak
TQ 254831	8	Kilburn, S Augustine
TQ 205869	8	Kingsbury, S Andrew
TQ 178692	12	Kingston upon Thames, All Saints
TQ 311801	8	Lambeth, S John Evangelist, Waterloo Road
TQ 315799	8	Lambeth, SS Andrew & Thomas, Short Street
TQ 379749	8	Lewisham, S Mary Virgin
TQ 377868	8	Leyton, S Mary Virgin
TQ 394874	8	Leytonstone, S John Baptist
TQ 368810	8	Limehouse, S Anne
TQ 251694	6	Merton, S Mary Virgin
TQ 268701	6	Mitcham, Christ Church
TQ 271687	8	Mitcham, SS Peter & Paul
TQ 250974	8	Monken Hadley, S Mary Virgin
TQ 208759	8	Mortlake, S Mary Virgin
TQ 586848	6	North Ockendon, S Mary Magdalene
TQ 134786	6	Norwood Green, S Mary Virgin
TQ 354704	6	Penge, S John Evangelist
TQ 284784	10	Pimlico, S Barnabas, St Barnabas Street
TQ 290784	8	Pimlico, S Gabriel, Warwick Square
TQ 124896	8	Pinner, S John Baptist
TQ 381809	10	Poplar, All Saints, East India Dock Road
TQ 385785	8	Poplar, Christ Church, Cubitt Town
TQ 242756	8	Putney, S Mary Virgin
TQ 179748	8	Richmond, S Mary Magdalene
TQ 512889	8	Romford, S Edward Confessor
TQ 351798	8	Rotherhithe, SS Mary & Paul
TQ 091875	8	Ruislip, S Martin
TQ 472684	6	St Mary Cray, S Mary
TQ 352807	8	Shadwell, S Paul
TQ 335826	12(1)	Shoreditch, S Leonard
TQ 465715	6	Sidcup, S John Evangelist
TQ 297934	10	Southgate, Christ Church
TQ 266792	10	South Kensington, Imperial College, Queen Anne's Tower
TQ 327803	12	Southwark, Cathedral Church of S Saviour
TQ 325797	8	Southwark, S George Martyr
TQ 337818	8	Spitalfields, Christ Church
TQ 328887	8	Stamford Hill, S Anne
TQ 167922	8	Stanmore, S John Evangelist
TQ 360816	10	Stepney, S Dunstan
TQ 347808	8	Stepney, S George in the East
TQ 329863	6	Stoke Newington, S Mary
TQ 300717	8	Streatham, S Leonard
TQ 258652	8	Sutton, All Saints, Benhilton
TQ 281717	8	Tooting Graveney, All Saints
TQ 333909	8	Tottenham, All Hallows

TQ 158741	10	Twickenham, All Hallows
TQ 164733	8	Twickenham, S Mary Virgin
TQ 059837	8	Uxbridge, S Andrew
TQ 055840	8	Uxbridge, S Margaret
TQ 377892	10	Walthamstow, S Mary
TQ 367879	8	Walthamstow, S Saviour
TQ 325781	8	Walworth, S Peter
TQ 254747	8	Wandsworth, All Saints
TQ 241740	8	Wandsworth, Holy Trinity, West Hill
TQ 403884	8	Wanstead, Christ Church
TQ 062795	6	West Drayton, S Martin
TQ 394838	10	West Ham, All Saints
TQ 389649	6	West Wickham, S John Baptist
TQ 215848	8	Willesden, S Mary
TQ 244714	8	Wimbledon, S Mary
TQ 400907	8	Woodford, S Mary Virgin
TQ 309907	6	Wood Green, S Michael
TQ 430791	8	Woolwich, S Mary Magdalene

Greater Manchester

SJ 760879	10	Altrincham, S Margaret, Dunham Massey
SJ 942989	12(1)	Ashton under Lyne, S Michael & All Angels
SJ 931985	8	Ashton under Lyne, S Peter
SD 613111	6	Blackrod, S Catherine
SD 714109	8	Bolton, All Souls
SD 718087	8	Bolton, Holy Trinity
SD 721093	12(1)	Bolton, S Peter
SD 693081	8	Bolton, S Mary, Deane
SD 693106	8	Bolton, S Peter, Halliwell (Doffcocker)
SJ 758868	8	Bowdon, Blessed Virgin Mary
SJ 931919	8	Bredbury, S Mark
SD 804109	8	Bury, S Mary Virgin
SJ 857887	8	Cheadle, S Mary
SJ 934956	6	Denton, S Anne
SJ 779987	8	Eccles, S Mary Virgin
SD 744058	8	Farnworth, S John
SJ 747940	8	Flixton, S Michael
SD 984043	6	Friezland, Christ Church
SJ 924866	8	Hazel Grove, S Thomas, Norbury
SD 856107	8	Heywood, S Luke
SD 616043	8	Hindley, S Peter
SD 644115	8	Horwich, Holy Trinity
SJ 949944	8	Hyde, S George
SD 655004	8	Leigh, S Mary Virgin
SJ 838987	10	Manchester, Cathedral of Virgin Mary, SS George & Denys
SJ 838981	12(1)	Manchester, Town Hall
SJ 830919	8	Manchester, Christ Church, Barlow Moor
SJ 847904	6	Manchester, S James, Didsbury
SJ 855940	8	Manchester, Holy Innocents, Fallowfield
SJ 889959	8	Manchester, Emmanuel, Gorton (Unitarian)
SJ 833901	6	Manchester, S Wilfred, Northenden
SJ 962880	8	Marple, All Saints
SD 872062	8	Middleton, S Leonard
SD 928129	8	Milnrow, S James
SD 969023	8	Mossley, S George
SD 976030	6	Mossley, S John Baptist, Roughtown
SJ 995953	8	Mottram in Longdendale, S Michael
SD 937117	8	Newhey, S Thomas
SD 927051	12(1)	Oldham, S Mary Virgin
SD 937043	8	Oldham, S Mark, Glodwick
SD 953045	8	Oldham, S Thomas, Lees
SD 951075	8	Oldham, S Thomas, Moorside
SD 812037	8	Prestwich, S Mary Virgin
SD 797076	8	Radcliffe, S Mary
SD 792169	8	Ramsbottom, S Paul

SD 896132	8	Rochdale, S Chad
SD 904116	8	Rochdale, S Mary, Balderstone
SD 904145	6	Rochdale, All Saints, Hamer
SD 886157	6	Rochdale, Christ Church, Healey
SE 007064	8	Saddleworth, S Chad
SJ 835987	8	Salford, Sacred Trinity
SJ 812995	8	Salford, S Thomas, Pendleton
SD 940094	8	Shaw, S James
SD 931168	8	Shore, S Barnabas
SJ 972987	8	Stalybridge, S Paul
SJ 964985	8	Stalybridge, Holy Trinity, Castlehall
SD 803059	8	Stand, All Saints, Whitefield
SD 563102	8	Standish, S Wilfred
SJ 900889	10	Stockport, S George
SJ 898905	10	Stockport, S Mary
SJ 893935	8	Stockport, S Elisabeth, Reddish
SJ 795942	8	Stretford, S Matthew
SD 774018	8	Swinton, S Peter
SD 688020	8	Tyldesley, S George
SD 739030	8	Walkden, S Paul
SJ 705891	8	Warburton, S Werburgh
SD 652060	8	Westhoughton, S Bartholomew
SD 582057	10	Wigan, All Saints
SD 578045	8	Wigan, S James, Poolstock
SD 746007	10	Worsley, S Mark

Hampshire

SU 331436	6	Abbotts Ann, S Mary
SU 869499	8	Aldershot, S Michael Archangel
SU 717397	8	Alton, S Lawrence
SU 299443	6	Amport, S Mary Virgin
SU 365458	8	Andover, S Mary
SU 434412	6	Barton Stacey, All Saints
SU 637517	9	Basingstoke, All Saints
SU 637522	8	Basingstoke, S Michael
SU 582600	6	Baughurst, S Stephen
SU 784447	6	Bentley, S Mary
SU 666403	5	Bentworth, S Mary
SU 771409	6	Binsted, Holy Cross
SU 606320	5	Bishop's Sutton, S Nicholas
SU 468198	8	Bishopstoke, S Mary
SU 556177	8	Bishop's Waltham, S Peter
SU 781336	6	Blackmoor, S Matthew
SU 645590	8	Bramley, S James or All Saints
SU 843329	6	Bramshott, S Mary
SU 154189	4	Breamore, S Mary
SU 305018	8	Brockenhurst, S Nicholas
SU 309329	6	Broughton, S Mary
SU 582398	5	Brown Candover, S Peter
SU 470610	6	Burghclere, Ascension
SU 740200	6	Buriton, S Mary
SU 696146	6	Catherington, All Saints
SU 708370	6	Chawton, S Nicholas
SU 582285	6	Cheriton, S Michael
SU 568503	6	Church Oakley, S Leonard
SU 424348	5	Crawley, S Mary
SU 795484	6	Crondall, All Saints
SU 528139	8	Curdridge, S Peter
SU 107158	6	Damerham, S George
SU 545503	8	Deane, All Saints
SU 607182	5	Droxford, S Mary & All Saints
SU 589460	5	Dummer, All Saints
SU 681223	8	East Meon, All Saints
SU 509323	6	Easton, S Mary
SU 292290	8	East Tytherley, S Peter
SU 405615	6	East Woodhay, S Martin

SU 367125	8	Eling, S Mary
SU 639458	5	Ellisfield, S Martin
SU 779609	6	Eversley, S Mary Virgin
SU 581065	10	Fareham, SS Peter & Paul
SU 872555	8	Farnborough, S Peter
SU 458036	6	Fawley, All Saints
SU 145139	8	Fordingbridge, S Mary Virgin
SU 712266	6	Froxfield, S Peter
SU 756429	6	Froyle, S Mary of the Assumption
SU 366425	8	Goodworth Clatford, S Peter
SZ 601988	8	Gosport, S Mary, Alverstoke
SU 872353	8	Grayshott, S Luke
SU 646152	6	Hambledon, SS Peter & Paul
SU 717062	8	Havant, S Faith
SU 746292	8	Hawkley, SS Peter & Paul
SU 853594	8	Hawley, Holy Trinity
SU 723605	5	Heckfield, S Michael
SU 440603	8	Highclere, S Michael & All Angels
SZ 212959	5	Hinton Admiral, S Michael & All Angels
SZ 274951	8	Hordle, All Saints
SU 428253	10	Hursley, All Saints
SU 439466	6	Hurstbourne Priors, S Andrew
SU 385530	4	Hurstbourne Tarrant, S Peter
SU 525587	8	Kingsclere, S Mary
SU 360310	6	King's Somborne, SS Peter & Paul
SU 493323	4	Kings Worthy, S Mary
SU 487488	6	Laverstoke, S Mary Virgin
SU 374376	5	Leckford, S Nicholas
SU 775279	8	Liss, S Mary
SU 771287	6	Liss, S Peter
SU 299268	6	Lockerley, S John Evangelist
SU 426438	6	Longparish, S Nicholas
SU 358371	5	Longstock, S Mary
SZ 322955	8	Lymington, S Thomas Apostle
SU 298082	8	Lyndhurst, S Michael & All Angels
SU 071196	6	Martin, All Saints
SU 513391	6	Micheldever, S Mary
SZ 291921	8	Milford on Sea, All Saints
SU 281109	5	Minstead, All Saints
SU 608558	5	Monk Sherborne, All Saints
SU 326266	5	Mottisfont, S Andrew
SU 304364	5	Nether Wallop, S Andrew
SU 454089	8	Netley Abbey, S Edward Confessor
SU 589327	8	New Alresford, S John Baptist
SU 724328	5	Newton Valence, S Mary
SU 476637	4	Newtown, S John Baptist
SU 441173	10	North Stoneham, S Nicholas
SU 740509	6	Odiham, All Saints
SU 588337	6	Old Alresford, S Mary Virgin
SU 514500	8	Overton, S Mary
SU 284383	5	Over Wallop, S Peter
SU 561317	4	Ovington, S Peter
SU 515234	6	Owslebury, S Andrew
SU 609582	4	Pamber, Priory
SU 746232	8	Petersfield, S Peter
SZ 633994	10	Portsmouth, Cathedral Church of S Thomas of Canterbury
SU 652009	8	Portsmouth, S Mary, Portsea
SU 607416	6	Preston Candover, S Mary Virgin
SU 677270	8	Privett, Holy Trinity
SU 145054	8	Ringwood, SS Peter & Paul
SU 351212	8	Romsey, Abbey Church of SS Mary & Ethelflaeda
SU 646320	6	Ropley, S Peter
SU 712563	6	Rotherwick, dedication unknown
SU 423503	6	St Mary Bourne, S Peter
SU 742338	6	Selborne, S Mary
SU 562133	8	Shedfield, S John Baptist
SU 624556	6	Sherborne St John, S Andrew
SU 291224	8	Sherfield English, S Leonard
SU 672568	6	Sherfield on Loddon, S Leonard
SU 643623	5	Silchester, S Mary
SU 609168	8	Soberton, S Peter
SZ 158968	6	Sopley, S Michael & All Angels
SU 441139	8	Southampton, Ascension, Bitterne Park
SU 426117	10	Southampton, S Mary
SU 419113	10	Southampton, S Michael Archangel
SU 626086	6	Southwick, S James without the Priory Gate
SU 435312	5	Sparsholt, S Stephen
SU 746253	6	Steep, All Saints
SU 355352	6	Stockbridge, S Peter
SU 696614	5	Stratfield Saye, S Mary Virgin
SU 576164	6	Swanmore, S Barnabas
SU 334524	5	Tangley, S Thomas
SU 288456	6	Thruxton, SS Peter & Paul
SU 568303	6	Tichborne, S Andrew
SU 541059	6	Titchfield, S Peter
SU 481251	8	Twyford, S Mary
SU 538207	8	Upham, Blessed Mary of Upham
SU 357435	6	Upper Clatford, All Saints
SU 698485	6	Upton Grey, S Mary
SU 622227	6	Warnford, Our Lady of Warnford
SU 640241	8	West Meon, S John Evangelist
SU 391408	5	Wherwell, S Peter & Holy Cross
SU 460478	8	Whitchurch, All Hallows
SU 576115	6	Wickham, S Nicholas
SU 482293	12(1)	Winchester, Cathedral of Holy Trinity, SS Peter Paul & Swithun
SU 482290	6	Winchester, College (Chapel of S Mary)
SU 487295	5	Winchester, S John Baptist
SU 481289	5	Winchester, S Michael in the Soke
SU 552586	6	Wolverton, S Catherine
SU 478395	6	Wonston, Holy Trinity
SU 430617	6	Woolton Hill, S Thomas
SU 592532	6	Wootton St Lawrence, S Lawrence
SU 818610	8	Yateley, S Peter

Hereford & Worcester

SO 387303	6	Abbey Dore, Holy Trinity & S Mary
SP 028549	4	Abbots Morton, S Peter
SO 748529	4	Alfrick, S Mary Magdalene
SO 466358	6	Allensmore, S Andrew
SO 333515	6	Almeley, S Mary
SP 027724	8	Alvechurch, S Laurence
SO 802710	6	Areley Kings, S Bartholomew
SO 643415	4	Ashperton, S Bartholomew
SO 997377	6	Ashton under Hill, S Barbara
SO 787676	6	Astley, S Peter
SO 683235	6	Aston Ingham, S John Baptist
SO 422656	6	Aymestrey, S John Baptist & S Alkmund
SO 371323	4	Bacton, S Faith
SP 071431	8	Badsey, S James
SO 976358	6	Beckford, S John Baptist
SO 919769	6	Belbroughton, Holy Trinity
SP 045436	6	Bengeworth, S Peter
SP 066697	6	Beoley, S Leonard
SO 793343	5	Berrow, S Faith
SO 786753	8	Bewdley, S Anne
SO 932432	6	Birlingham, S James Apostle
SO 801355	4	Birtsmorton, SS Peter & Paul
SO 990518	6	Bishampton, S James
SO 663483	6	Bishop's Frome, S Mary Virgin
SO 529509	6	Bodenham, S Michael & All Angels
SO 694434	6	Bosbury, Holy Trinity

SO 609564	6	Bredenbury, S Andrew
SO 931390	6	Bredon's Norton, Chapel of Ease
SO 919369	5	Bredon, S Giles
SO 334445	6	Bredwardine, S Andrew
SP 093439	8	Bretforton, S Leonard
SO 584248	8	Bridstow, S Bridget
SO 755551	5	Broadwas, S Mary Magdalene
SP 097363	6	Broadway, S Eadburgh
SO 957707	10	Bromsgrove, S John Baptist
SO 656548	8	Bromyard, S Peter
SO 479445	8	Burghill, S Mary
SO 875343	6	Bushley, S Peter
SO 449492	6	Canon Pyon, S Lawrence
SO 794373	6	Castlemorton, S Gregory
SO 891736	8	Chaddesley Corbett, S Cassian
SP 074384	6	Childswickham, S Mary Virgin
SP 120440	5	Church Honeybourne, S Egwin
SP 024513	6	Church Lench, All Saints
SO 851588	10	Claines, S John Baptist
SP 088493	6	Cleeve Prior, S Andrew
SO 466379	4	Clehonger, All Saints
SO 929793	8	Clent, S Leonard
SO 251450	8	Clifford, S Mary
SO 714616	6	Clifton upon Teme, S Kenelm
SO 326275	6	Clodock, S Clydog
SO 718427	6	Coddington, All Saints
SO 739423	8	Colwall, S James Great
SO 842801	6	Cookley, S Peter
SO 736472	6	Cradley, S James A&M
SO 887450	6	Croome D'Abitot, S James
SP 000452	6	Cropthorne, S Michael & All Angels
SO 922559	8	Crowle, S John Baptist
SO 917432	4	Defford, S James
SO 415546	6	Dilwyn, S Mary Virgin
SO 903625	6	Droitwich, S Peter de Witton
SO 902637	8	Droitwich, S Augustine of Canterbury, Dodderhill
SO 421585	8	Eardisland, S Mary Virgin
SO 312491	6	Eardisley, S Mary Magdalene
SO 871420	6	Earl's Croome, S Nicholas
SO 658688	4	Eastham, SS Peter & Paul
SO 731372	6	Eastnor, S John Baptist
SO 443392	6	Eaton Bishop, S Michael & All Angels
SO 923414	8	Eckington, Holy Trinity
SO 799312	6	Eldersfield, S John Baptist
SO 982410	6	Elmley Castle, S Mary
SO 865697	6	Elmley Lovett, S Michael
SP 038436	12(2)	Evesham, All Saints & S Laurence, 'The Bell Tower'
SO 387287	6	Ewyas Harold, S Michael & All Angels
SO 497638	6	Eye, SS Peter & Paul
SP 009616	8	Feckenham, S John Baptist
SO 996463	6	Fladbury, S John Baptist
SO 581343	6	Fownhope, S Mary
SO 597283	6	Foy, S Mary
SO 454224	5	Garway, S Michael & All Angels
SO 572190	6	Goodrich, S Giles Abbot & Confessor
SO 963558	5	Grafton Flyford, S John Baptist
SO 955421	6	Great Comberton, S Michael
SP 029431	8	Great Hampton, S Andrew
SO 776458	8	Great Malvern, Priory Church of S Mary, S Michael
SO 836607	6	Grimley, S Bartholomew
SO 921808	8	Hagley, S John Baptist
SO 828579	8	Hallow, SS Philip & James
SO 558380	6	Hampton Bishop, S Andrew
SO 954644	8	Hanbury, S Mary Virgin
SO 838419	6	Hanley Castle, S Mary Virgin
SO 810428	6	Hanley Swan, S Gabriel
SO 841709	8	Hartlebury, S James Great

SO 944389	4	Hentland, S Dubricius
SO 508400	8	Hereford, All Saints
SO 510397	10	Hereford, Cathedral Church of BVM & S Ethelbert
SO 507397	8	Hereford, S Nicholas
SO 512400	5	Hereford, S Peter
SO 947588	4	Himbleton, S Mary Magdalene
SP 025400	8	Hinton on the Green, S Peter
SO 568347	8	Holme Lacy, S Cuthbert
SO 505424	6	Holmer, S Bartholomew
SP 016572	6	Inkberrow, S Peter
SO 946368	6	Kemerton, S Nicholas
SO 848491	6	Kempsey, S Mary Virgin
SO 419256	6	Kentchurch, Blessed Virgin Mary
SO 830769	12	Kidderminster, S Mary & All Saints
SO 526616	6	Kimbolton, S James Less
SO 558287	6	King's Caple, S John Baptist
SO 438506	5	King's Pyon, S Mary
SO 447613	8	Kingsland, S Michael
SO 424356	8	Kingstone, S Michael & All Angels
SO 291568	6	Kington, S Mary
SO 346497	4	Kinnersley, S James
SO 713377	8	Ledbury, S Michael & All Angels
SO 784534	6	Leigh Sinton, S Edburga
SO 405741	8	Leintwardine, S Mary Magdalene
SO 498593	10	Leominster, SS Peter & Paul
SO 660253	6	Linton, S Mary Virgin
SO 967428	6	Little Comberton, S Peter
SO 529317	5	Little Dewchurch, S David
SO 531213	6	Llangarron, S Deinst
SO 838363	6	Longdon, S Mary
SO 551410	8	Lugwardine, S Peter
SO 331563	6	Lyonshall, S Michael & All Angels
SO 420387	8	Madley, Nativity SMV
SO 805475	6	Madresfield, S Mary Virgin
SO 783478	8	Malvern Link, S Matthias
SO 426456	4	Mansell Lacy, S Michael
SO 512471	6	Marden, S Mary Virgin
SO 756598	6	Martley, S Peter
SO 734450	6	Mathon, S John Baptist
SO 316342	5	Michaelchurch Escley, S Michael & All Angels
SP 081470	6	Middle Littleton, S Nicholas
SO 460577	4	Monkland, All Saints
SO 373433	4	Monnington on Wye, S Mary
SO 571374	5	Mordiford, Holy Rood
SO 504456	6	Moreton on Lugg, S Andrew
SO 618472	6	Much Cowarne, S Mary
SO 482312	6	Much Dewchurch, S David
SO 657327	6	Much Marcle, S Bartholomew
SO 381477	5	Norton Canon, S Nicholas
SP 042477	8	Norton, S Egwin
SP 053462	6	Offenham, SS Mary & Milburgh
SO 844634	6	Ombersley, S Andrew
SO 473263	5	Orcop, S Mary
SO 957374	6	Overbury, S Faith
SP 129469	6	Pebworth, S Peter
SO 391580	5	Pembridge, S Mary
SO 600527	6	Pencombe, S John
SO 947457	8	Pershore, Abbey Church of Holy Cross
SO 948458	8	Pershore, S Andrew's Parish Centre
SO 344385	6	Peterchurch, S Peter
SO 503441	6	Pipe and Lyde, S Peter
SO 834515	6	Powick, S Peter
SO 348424	4	Preston on Wye, S Laurence
SO 565598	4	Pudleston, S Peter
SP 042676	8	Redditch, S Stephen
SP 066666	6	Redditch, S Peter, Ipsley
SO 876377	6	Ripple, S Mary

SO 732711	8	Rock, SS Peter & Paul
SO 598241	8	Ross on Wye, S Mary Virgin
SO 496243	6	St Weonards, S Weonards
SO 874621	6	Salwarpe, S Michael & All Angels
SO 565276	5	Sellack, S Tyssilio
SO 856440	5	Severn Stoke, S Denys
SO 731629	6	Shelsley Beauchamp, All Saints
SO 806648	6	Shrawley, S Mary
SO 896539	4	Spetchley, All Saints
SO 702658	4	Stanford on Teme, S Mary
SO 370600	6	Staunton on Arrow, S Peter
SO 375448	6	Staunton on Wye, S Mary Virgin
SO 604407	6	Stoke Edith, S Mary Virgin
SO 621494	6	Stoke Lacy, SS Peter & Paul
SO 949677	8	Stoke Prior (near Bromsgrove), S Michael
SO 520564	5	Stoke Prior (near Leominster), S Luke
SO 862750	6	Stone, Blessed Virgin Mary
SO 904497	12	Stoulton, Campanile
SO 904497	6	Stoulton, Campanile
SO 906498	6	Stoulton, S Edmund King & Martyr
SO 911406	6	Strensham, S John Baptist
SO 633441	6	Stretton Grandison, S Lawrence
SO 721517	6	Suckley, S John Baptist
SO 534454	6	Sutton St Nicholas, S Nicholas
SO 618407	6	Tarrington, SS Philip & James
SO 594684	6	Tenbury Wells, S Mary
SO 379398	5	Tyberton, S Mary
SO 764805	6	Upper Arley, S Peter
SO 650273	6	Upton Bishop, S John Baptist
SO 943544	6	Upton Snodsbury, S Kenelm
SO 852403	8	Upton upon Severn, SS Peter & Paul
SO 796399	6	Welland, S James
SO 497483	6	Wellington, S Margaret
SO 402518	6	Weobley, SS Peter & Paul
SO 584413	5	Weston Beggard, S John Baptist
SO 631232	6	Weston under Penyard, S Lawrence
SO 726569	6	Whitbourne, S John Baptist
SO 268475	5	Whitney, SS Peter & Paul
SO 413691	6	Wigmore, S James Apostle
SO 566436	6	Withington, S Peter
SO 829794	6	Wolverley, S John Baptist
SO 612358	6	Woolhope, S George
SO 848549	12	Worcester, All Saints
SO 849546	12(3)	Worcester, Cathedral Church of Christ & BMV
SO 840544	8	Worcester, S John Baptist in Bedwardine
SO 852550	6	Worcester, S Martin
SO 850550	6	Worcester, S Nicholas
SO 851549	6	Worcester, S Swithun
SO 929658	6	Wychbold, S Michael de Wyche
SO 609426	4	Yarkhill, S John Baptist

Hertfordshire

TL 095022	6	Abbots Langley, S Lawrence
TL 435247	6	Albury, S Mary
SP 963124	6	Aldbury, S John Baptist
TQ 139985	8	Aldenham, S John Baptist
TL 404328	6	Anstey, S George
TL 060051	6	Apsley End, S Mary
TL 308271	6	Ardeley, S Laurence
TL 267398	6	Ashwell, S Mary Virgin
TL 353284	8	Aspenden, S Mary
TL 272225	6	Aston, Blessed Virgin Mary
TL 244338	8	Baldock, S Mary Virgin
TL 383356	8	Barkway, S Mary Magdalene
TL 402384	6	Barley, S Margaret

TL 325136	8	Bengeo, Holy Trinity
TL 297236	8	Benington, S Peter
SP 993078	8	Berkhamsted, S Peter
TL 486213	10	Bishop's Stortford, S Michael
TL 396252	8	Braughing, S Mary
TL 433308	6	Brent Pelham, S Mary
TL 372069	8	Broxbourne, S Augustine
TQ 130952	8	Bushey, S James Apostle
TQ 145944	8	Bushey Heath, S Peter
TL 349024	8	Cheshunt, S Mary Virgin
TL 218187	6	Codicote, S Giles
TL 317292	5	Cottered, S John Baptist
TL 267192	6	Datchworth, All Saints
TQ 179954	6	Elstree, S Nicholas
TL 273087	6	Essendon, S Mary Virgin
TL 078145	6	Flamstead, S Leonard
TL 432279	6	Furneux Pelham, S Mary Virgin
TL 236282	6	Graveley, S Mary
TL 372125	6	Great Amwell, S John Baptist
TL 028113	6	Great Gaddesden, S John Baptist
TL 399296	6	Great Hormead, S Nicholas
TL 355242	6	Great Munden, S Nicholas
TL 145267	6	Great Offley, S Mary Magdalene
TL 215285	6	Great Wymondley, S Mary
TL 133145	8	Harpenden, S Nicholas
TL 234084	10	Hatfield, S Etheldreda
TL 055078	8	Hemel Hempstead, S Mary
TL 328124	10	Hertford, All Saints
TL 323125	8	Hertford, S Andrew
TL 308119	6	Hertingfordbury, S Mary
TL 238403	6	Hinxworth, S Nicholas
TL 185292	10	Hitchin, S Mary
TL 373089	8	Hoddesdon, SS Catherine & Paul
TL 418127	8	Hunsdon, S Dunstan
TL 183316	5	Ickleford, S Katharine
TL 177185	8	Kimpton, SS Peter & Paul
TL 073024	8	King's Langley, All Saints
TL 161235	6	King's Walden, S Mary
TL 231210	8	Knebworth, S Mary & S Thomas a' Becket
TL 080006	6	Langleybury, S Paul
TL 218120	6	Lemsford, S John Evangelist
TL 118264	5	Lilley, S Peter
SP 998138	6	Little Gaddesden, SS Peter & Paul
TL 446227	6	Little Hadham, S Cecilia
TL 334219	6	Little Munden, All Saints
TL 430197	8	Much Hadham, S Andrew
TL 279023	6	Northaw, S Thomas a' Becket
SP 974088	8	Northchurch, S Mary
TL 221044	8	North Mymms, S Mary
TL 232344	8	Norton, S Nicholas
TQ 117953	8	Oxhey, S Matthew
TL 147317	5	Pirton, S Mary
TQ 165993	6	Radlett, Christ Church
TL 099116	6	Redbourn, S Mary
TQ 061942	10	Rickmansworth, S Mary Virgin
TL 358406	8	Royston, S John Baptist
TL 305318	6	Rushden, S Mary
TL 145071	12	St Albans, Cathedral & Abbey Church of S Alban
TL 136074	8	St Albans, S Michael
TL 150076	10	St Albans, S Peter
TL 141061	6	St Albans, S Stephen
TL 177271	6	St Ippollitts, S Hippolytus
TL 192223	6	St Paul's Walden, All Saints
TL 323345	5	Sandon, All Saints
TL 171106	6	Sandridge, S Leonard
TQ 038984	5	Sarratt, Holy Cross
TL 485148	8	Sawbridgeworth, Great S Mary

TL 222012 6 South Mimms, S Giles
TL 396222 6 Standon, S Mary
TL 241262 8 Stevenage, S Nicholas
TL 267143 6 Tewin, S Peter
TL 476188 6 Thorley, S James Great
TL 358173 4 Thundridge, S Mary
SP 924114 8 Tring, SS Peter & Paul
TL 293265 6 Walkern, S Mary
TL 292335 6 Wallington, S Mary
TL 357144 8 Ware, S Mary Virgin
TQ 111963 10 Watford, S Mary
TL 303188 8 Watton at Stone, SS Andrew & Mary
TL 231163 8 Welwyn, S Mary Virgin
TL 369272 5 Westmill, S Mary Virgin
TL 266299 6 Weston, Holy Trinity
TL 176140 8 Wheathampstead, S Helen
TL 413158 6 Widford, S John Baptist

Humberside

SE 953151 6 Appleby, S Bartholomew
TA 072215 8 Barrow upon Humber, Holy Trinity
TA 033220 8 Barton-upon-Humber, S Mary
TA 034220 8 Barton-upon-Humber, S Peter
SE 783063 6 Belton, All Saints
TA 037392 10 Beverley, Minster Church of S John Evangelist
TA 031398 10 Beverley, S Mary
TA 177680 8 Bridlington, Priory Church of S Mary
TA 001072 6 Brigg, S John Evangelist
SE 960086 6 Broughton, S Mary
SE 712362 4 Bubwith, All Saints
TA 228280 6 Burstwick, All Saints
SE 869178 8 Burton upon Stather, S Andrew
TA 048329 8 Cottingham, S Mary Virgin
SE 797300 6 Eastrington, S Michael
SE 944282 6 Elloughton, S Mary Virgin
TA 036126 6 Elsham, All Saints
SE 782038 8 Epworth, S Andrew
TA 226702 4 Flamborough, S Oswald
SE 746235 8 Goole, S John Evangelist
TA 102213 6 Goxhill, All Saints
TA 233098 4 Great Coates, S Nicholas
TA 022580 6 Great Driffield, All Saints
TA 266092 10 Grimsby, S James
SK 764997 6 Haxey, S Nicholas
TA 214101 4 Healing, SS Peter & Paul
TA 188287 8 Hedon, S Augustine
TA 033264 6 Hessle, All Saints
SE 821390 6 Holme on Spalding Moor, All Saints
SE 748282 8 Howden, S Peter
TA 024534 6 Hutton Cranswick, S Peter
TA 176151 4 Immingham, S Andrew
TA 144173 4 Killingholme, S Denys
TA 099285 12(2) Kingston upon Hull, Most Holy & Undivided Trinity
TA 118330 6 Kingston upon Hull, S James, Sutton
TA 101287 6 Kingston upon Hull, S Mary Virgin, Lowgate
TA 020297 8 Kirk Ella, S Andrew
SK 934985 8 Kirton in Lindsey, S Andrew
TA 214066 5 Laceby, S Margaret
TA 107453 4 Leven, Holy Trinity
SE 877418 8 Market Weighton, All Saints
SE 890047 6 Messingham, Holy Trinity
SE 947496 6 Middleton on the Wolds, S Andrew
SE 897327 6 North Cave, All Saints
SE 989258 6 North Ferriby, All Saints
SE 848478 6 Nunburnholme, S James

SE 804003 6 Owston Ferry, S Martin
TA 315225 8 Patrington, S Patrick
SE 802490 8 Pocklington, All Saints
SK 973999 6 Redbourne, S Andrew
TA 150419 5 Rise, All Saints
TA 291296 5 Roos, All Saints
SE 891109 8 Scunthorpe, S John Evangelist
SE 641222 8 Snaith, S Lawrence
TA 195118 4 Stallingborough, SS Peter & Paul
TA 134359 4 Swine, S Mary
TA 088178 6 Thornton Curtis, S Lawrence
TA 104146 6 Ulceby, S Nicholas
SE 998368 6 Walkington, All Hallows
TA 262039 6 Waltham, All Saints
SE 924225 5 Winteringham, All Saints
SE 927186 6 Winterton, All Saints
TA 342276 6 Withernsea, S Nicholas
TA 088162 4 Wootton, S Andrew

Isle of Wight

SZ 534867 6 Arreton, S George
SZ 607873 8 Brading, S Mary
SZ 429827 6 Brighstone, S Mary Virgin
SZ 485883 8 Carisbrooke, S Mary
SZ 483776 6 Chale, S Andrew
SZ 347873 6 Freshwater, All Saints
SZ 527818 6 Godshill, All Saints
SZ 562855 6 Newchurch, All Saints
SZ 499891 12 Newport, S Thomas Apostle
SZ 505768 6 Niton, S John Baptist
SZ 589923 8 Ryde, All Saints
SZ 584813 8 Shanklin, S Saviour on the Cliff
SZ 457830 5 Shorwell, S Peter
SZ 521778 6 Whitwell, S Mary Virgin & S Radigund

Kent

TQ 653588 4 Addington, S Margaret
TR 227543 4 Adisham, Holy Innocents
TR 075362 6 Aldington, S Martin
TR 255423 4 Alkham, S Anthony
TQ 958293 8 Appledore, SS Peter & Paul
TQ 602646 6 Ash (near Gravesend), SS Peter & Paul
TR 288584 10 Ash (near Sandwich), S Nicholas
TR 010427 10 Ashford, S Mary Virgin
TQ 729590 8 Aylesford, S Peter
TR 210500 5 Barham, S Mary
TQ 720542 6 Barming, S Margaret
TQ 798561 6 Bearsted, Holy Cross
TR 195555 6 Bekesbourne, S Peter
TQ 808326 8 Benenden, S George
TQ 928403 6 Bethersden, S Margaret
TQ 861589 4 Bicknor, S James
TQ 849384 8 Biddenden, All Saints
TR 302690 8 Birchington, All Saints
TR 311681 12 Birchington, Waterloo Tower, Quex Park
TQ 681606 8 Birling, All Saints
TQ 888651 6 Bobbing, S Bartholomew
TQ 882630 8 Borden, SS Peter & Paul
TQ 771499 6 Boughton Monchelsea, S Peter, Boughton Place
TR 048586 8 Boughton under Blean, SS Peter & Paul
TQ 775590 6 Boxley, S Mary Virgin & All Saints
TR 104416 6 Brabourne, S Mary BV
TQ 468555 6 Brasted, S Martin
TQ 880603 6 Bredgar, S John Baptist
TQ 679417 8 Brenchley, All Saints
TR 381684 8 Broadstairs, S Peter Apostle

TQ 989258	6	Brookland, S Augustine
TR 101321	6	Burmarsh, All Saints
TR 151578	12(2)	Canterbury, Cathedral Church of Christ
TR 143583	6	Canterbury, S Dunstan
TR 149580	6	Canterbury, Urban Studies Centre
TR 148592	8	Canterbury, S Stephen, Hackington
TR 132568	6	Canterbury, S Nicholas, Thanington
TQ 954494	6	Charing, SS Peter & Paul
TR 107551	6	Chartham, S Mary
TQ 804494	6	Chart Sutton, S Michael
TQ 757684	8	Chatham, Medway Heritage Centre
TQ 501452	8	Chiddingstone, S Mary Virgin
TR 069537	8	Chilham, S Mary
TR 225644	6	Chislet, S Mary Virgin
TQ 736766	8	Cliffe, S Helen
TQ 670684	6	Cobham, S Mary Magdalene
TQ 466405	6	Cowden, S Mary Magdalene
TQ 777362	8	Cranbrook, S Dunstan
TQ 709665	6	Cuxton, S Michael & All Angels
TQ 544740	8	Dartford, Holy Trinity
TR 363518	6	Deal, S Leonard, Upper Deal
TR 319415	8	Dover, S Mary Virgin
TQ 988715	6	Eastchurch, All Saints
TQ 734533	8	East Farleigh, S Mary
TR 333460	4	East Langdon, S Augustine
TQ 965566	6	Eastling, S Mary
TQ 703570	6	East Malling, S James Great
TQ 662522	6	East Peckham, S Michael
TR 311547	5	Eastry, S Mary BV
TQ 827496	6	East Sutton, SS Peter & Paul
TQ 445461	8	Edenbridge, SS Peter & Paul
TQ 905476	6	Egerton, S James
TR 178438	8	Elham, S Mary Virgin
TR 116449	6	Elmsted, S James Great
TQ 541655	8	Eynsford, S Martin
TR 279497	5	Eythorne, SS Peter & Paul
TQ 547669	6	Farningham, SS Peter & Paul
TR 018615	8	Faversham, S Mary of Charity
TR 229359	8	Folkestone, SS Mary & Eanswythe
TR 189365	8	Folkestone, S Martin, Cheriton
TQ 744698	8	Frindsbury, All Saints
TQ 892574	5	Frinsted, S Dunstan
TQ 813409	8	Frittenden, S Mary
TQ 784689	8	Gillingham, S Mary Magdalene
TR 062504	5	Godmersham, S Laurence
TR 255547	6	Goodnestone, Holy Cross
TQ 724378	8	Goudhurst, S Mary Virgin
TQ 889768	4	Grain, S James
TQ 647745	8	Gravesend, S George
TQ 658737	8	Gravesend, SS Peter & Paul, Milton
TQ 979419	8	Great Chart, S Mary
TR 346515	6	Great Mongeham, S Martin
TQ 634497	8	Hadlow, S Mary
TQ 705639	6	Halling, S John Baptist
TR 131582	4	Harbledown, S Nicholas (hospital chapel)
TQ 875530	8	Harrietsham, S John Baptist
TQ 839642	6	Hartlip, S Michael & All Angels
TQ 756294	8	Hawkhurst, S Lawrence
TQ 832442	8	Headcorn, SS Peter & Paul
TR 183658	6	Herne, S Martin
TR 065607	8	Hernhill, S Michael
TQ 476449	6	Hever, S Peter
TQ 713715	6	Higham, S John Evangelist, Church Street
TQ 902372	6	High Halden, S Mary Virgin
TQ 779753	6	High Halstow, S Margaret
TQ 843551	6	Hollingbourne, All Saints
TQ 783718	6	Hoo St Werburgh, S Werburgh
TQ 704382	8	Horsmonden, S Margaret, Lewes Heath
TQ 970446	6	Hothfield, S Margaret
TQ 724497	6	Hunton, S Mary
TR 162349	8	Hythe, S Leonard
TR 222581	4	Ickham, S John Evangelist
TQ 595569	6	Ightham, S Peter
TR 028277	5	Ivychurch, S George
TR 023452	6	Kennington, S Mary
TQ 700352	6	Kilndown, Christ Church
TR 006393	6	Kingsnorth, S Michael
TQ 682366	6	Lamberhurst, S Mary BV
TQ 825534	10	Leeds, S Nicholas
TQ 549466	6	Leigh, S Mary
TQ 899522	8	Lenham, S Mary
TQ 755502	8	Linton, S Nicholas
TR 211579	6	Littlebourne, S Vincent Spanish D&M
TQ 944458	6	Little Chart, S Mary of Holy Rood
TR 043209	8	Lydd, All Saints
TR 161408	8	Lyminge, SS Mary & Ethelburga
TR 120347	6	Lympne, S Stephen
TQ 942609	5	Lynsted, SS Peter & Paul
TQ 760554	10	Maidstone, All Saints
TQ 749553	8	Maidstone, S Michael & All Angels
TQ 744446	8	Marden, S Michael & All Angels
TR 355704	8	Margate, S John Baptist
TQ 645662	8	Meopham, S John Baptist
TQ 660537	6	Mereworth, S Lawrence
TR 053394	8	Mersham, S John Baptist
TQ 908654	6	Milton Regis, Holy Trinity
TQ 956730	6	Minster (Sheppey), SS Mary & Sexburga
TR 311643	5	Minster (Thanet), S Mary
TQ 685522	5	Nettlestead, S Mary Virgin
TR 054314	6	Newchurch, SS Peter & Paul
TR 183374	6	Newington (near Hythe), S Nicholas
TQ 862654	6	Newington (near Sittingbourne), S Mary Virgin
TQ 954576	4	Newnham, SS Peter & Paul
TR 065247	8	New Romney, S Nicholas
TR 334523	6	Northbourne, S Augustine
TQ 625741	8	Northfleet, S Botolph
TR 000603	8	Ospringe, SS Peter & Paul
TQ 527439	8	Penshurst, S John Baptist
TR 131513	5	Petham, All Saints
TQ 927454	6	Pluckley, S Nicholas
TR 244604	6	Preston, S Mildred
TQ 909723	6	Queenborough, Holy Trinity
TQ 817659	8	Rainham, S Margaret
TR 370653	10	Ramsgate, S Lawrence
TR 360483	6	Ringwould, S Nicholas
TQ 743685	10	Rochester, Cathedral Church of Christ & BVM
TQ 740681	8	Rochester, S Margaret
TQ 926618	6	Rodmersham, S Nicholas
TQ 845312	8	Rolvenden, S Mary Virgin
TQ 593393	8	Royal Tunbridge Wells, S Peter
TR 025335	5	Ruckinge, S Mary Magdalene
TR 265667	6	St Nicholas at Wade, S Nicholas
TR 158360	6	Saltwood, SS Peter & Paul
TQ 791273	6	Sandhurst, S Nicholas
TR 333580	8	Sandwich, S Clement
TR 331581	8	Sandwich, S Peter
TQ 550570	6	Seal, SS Peter & Paul
TQ 573552	6	Seal Chart, S Lawrence
TR 004385	6	Sellindge, S Mary
TR 038568	8	Selling, S Mary Virgin
TQ 531543	8	Sevenoaks, S Nicholas
TR 001569	6	Sheldwich, S James
TQ 591523	6	Shipbourne, S Giles
TQ 523616	8	Shoreham, SS Peter & Paul

TQ 691710	6	Shorne, SS Peter & Paul
TQ 909636	8	Sittingbourne, S Michael
TQ 880423	6	Smarden, S Michael
TQ 704618	6	Snodland, All Saints
TQ 614712	6	Southfleet, S Nicholas
TQ 553414	8	Speldhurst, S Mary Virgin
TR 269567	4	Staple, S James
TQ 786429	8	Staplehurst, All Saints
TQ 847617	5	Stockbury, S Mary Magdalene
TQ 940274	6	Stone in Oxney, S Mary Virgin
TR 125418	6	Stowting, S Mary Virgin
TR 176601	6	Sturry, S Nicholas
TQ 486549	6	Sundridge, S Mary
TQ 605740	8	Swanscombe, SS Peter & Paul
TQ 884334	8	Tenterden, S Mildred
TQ 966636	6	Teynham, S Mary
TQ 991557	8	Throwley, S Michael & All Angels
TQ 591468	8	Tonbridge, SS Peter & Paul
TQ 896619	8	Tunstall, S John Baptist
TQ 846493	6	Ulcombe, All Saints
TQ 844675	6	Upchurch, S Mary Virgin
TR 372502	8	Walmer, S Mary
TR 113484	4	Waltham, S Bartholomew
TQ 989325	6	Warehorne, S Matthew
TQ 685537	6	Wateringbury, S John Baptist
TQ 448541	8	Westerham, S Mary
TR 323701	6	Westgate on Sea, S Saviour
TQ 679575	8	West Malling, S Mary Virgin
TQ 991474	4	Westwell, S Mary
TR 117663	6	Whitstable, All Saints
TR 107664	8	Whitstable, S Alphege, Seasalter
TR 220587	6	Wickhambreaux, S Andrew
TR 029415	6	Willesborough, S Mary Virgin
TR 242575	8	Wingham, S Mary Virgin
TQ 897270	6	Wittersham, S John Baptist
TQ 942349	6	Woodchurch, All Saints
TQ 882574	6	Wormshill, S Giles
TQ 713644	6	Wouldham, All Saints
TQ 612592	8	Wrotham, S George
TR 054469	8	Wye, SS Gregory & Martin
TQ 698501	6	Yalding, SS Peter & Paul

Lancashire

SD 760285	12	Accrington, S James
SD 603135	8	Adlington, S Paul
SD 402072	8	Aughton, Christ Church
SD 392054	6	Aughton, S Michael
SD 873234	8	Bacup, Christ Church
SD 866219	8	Bacup, S Saviour
SD 560262	8	Bamber Bridge, S Mary (RC)
SD 513398	8	Bilsborrow, S Hilda
SD 319406	8	Bispham, All Hallows
SD 684280	10	Blackburn, Cathedral Church of S Mary Virgin
SD 666285	8	Blackburn, S Silas
SD 306365	8	Blackpool, Sacred Heart (RC)
SD 306338	6	Blackpool, Holy Trinity, South Shore
SD 309363	8	Blackpool, S John Evangelist
SD 599243	6	Brindle, S James
SD 529344	6	Broughton, S John Baptist
SD 843329	8	Burnley, S Peter
SD 622433	6	Chipping, S Bartholomew
SD 582175	8	Chorley, S Mary (RC)
SD 583178	8	Chorley, S Laurence
SD 741291	8	Church, S James
SD 744420	8	Clitheroe, S Mary Magdalene
SD 462518	6	Cockerham, S Michael
SD 889401	8	Colne, S Bartholomew

SD 561142	6	Coppull, S John Divine
SD 490184	8	Croston, S Michael
SD 694222	6	Darwen, S Peter (formerly Holy Trinity)
SD 784442	5	Downham, S Leonard
SD 516179	6	Eccleston, S Mary
SD 482458	6	Garstang, S Helen
SD 830489	6	Gisburn, S Mary
SD 560369	6	Goosnargh, S Mary Virgin
SD 716389	6	Great Mytton, All Hallows
SD 371103	6	Halsall, S Cuthbert
SD 785236	8	Haslingden, S James Great
SD 782213	8	Helmshore, S Thomas
SD 523290	8	Higher Penwortham, S Mary
SD 578274	8	Higher Walton, All Saints
SD 614259	8	Hoghton, Holy Trinity
SD 585686	8	Hornby, S Margaret
SD 417320	6	Kirkham, S John (RC)
SD 427324	8	Kirkham, S Michael
SD 482615	10	Lancaster, Cathedral Church of S Peter (RC)
SD 474620	8	Lancaster, Priory Church of S Mary
SD 643766	5	Leck, S Peter
SD 541216	10	Leyland, S Andrew
SD 517217	6	Leyland, S James Apostle, Moss Side
SD 357272	8	Lytham St Anne's, S Cuthbert
SD 371271	6	Lytham St Anne's, S John Divine
SD 370272	6	Lytham St Anne's, S Peter (RC)
SD 348280	8	Lytham St Anne's, S Joseph, Ansdell (RC)
SD 327293	8	Lytham St Anne's, S Anne, St Annes
SD 598711	6	Melling, S Wilfrid
SD 440647	8	Morecambe, Holy Trinity
SD 864381	8	Nelson, S Philip
SD 413084	8	Ormskirk, SS Peter & Paul
SD 733264	8	Oswaldtwistle, Immanuel
SD 793340	8	Padiham, S Leonard
SD 502108	8	Parbold, Christ Church, Douglas
SD 403487	5	Pilling, S John Baptist
SD 348394	8	Poulton le Fylde, S Chad
SD 542293	10	Preston, S John Evangelist
SD 811228	8	Rawtenstall, S Mary
SD 834223	8	Rawtenstall, S Nicholas, Newchurch
SD 832218	6	Rawtenstall, S James, Waterfoot
SD 650350	6	Ribchester, S Wilfred
SD 724303	8	Rishton, SS Peter & Paul
SD 590303	8	Samlesbury, S Leonard Less
SD 502486	8	Scorton, S Peter
SD 463754	6	Silverdale, S John
SD 385384	6	Singleton, S Anne
SD 710522	6	Slaidburn, S Andrew
SD 452203	8	Tarleton, Holy Trinity
SD 465543	5	Thurnham, SS Thomas & Elizabeth (RC)
SD 523051	6	Up Holland, S Thomas Martyr
SD 728438	6	Waddington, S Helen
SD 561281	8	Walton le Dale, S Leonard
SD 733362	8	Whalley, S Mary Virgin & All Saints
SD 600762	6	Whittington, S Michael Archangel
SD 578215	8	Whittle le Woods, S John Evangelist
SD 881177	8	Whitworth, S Bartholomew

Leicestershire

SK 818004	4	Allexton, S Peter
SK 549086	8	Anstey, S Mary
SK 318098	6	Appleby Magna, S Michael
SP 617921	5	Arnesby, S Peter
SK 708190	6	Asfordby, All Saints
SK 361168	8	Ashby-de-la-Zouch, S Helen
SK 707120	8	Ashby Folville, S Mary
SK 866137	6	Ashwell, S Mary

SK 859009	4	Ayston, S Mary Virgin
SK 636098	6	Barkby, S Mary
SK 778349	4	Barkestone-le-Vale, SS Peter & Paul
SP 945999	5	Barrowden, S Peter
SK 577166	8	Barrow upon Soar, Holy Trinity
SP 443965	8	Barwell, S Mary
SK 816014	6	Belton, S Peter
SK 720035	8	Billesdon, S John Baptist
SK 596089	8	Birstall, S James
SP 537859	6	Bitteswell, S Mary
SP 560979	6	Blaby, All Saints
SK 807391	8	Bottesford, S Mary Virgin
SK 832066	6	Braunston, All Saints
SK 405233	6	Breedon on the Hill, SS Mary & Hardulph
SK 850058	4	Brooke, S Peter
SP 526926	8	Broughton Astley, S Mary
SK 879231	6	Buckminster, S John Baptist
SP 442927	8	Burbage, S Catherine
SK 757108	4	Burrough on the Hill, S Mary
SP 868937	6	Caldecott, S John Evangelist
SK 397050	4	Carlton, S Andrew
SK 447273	6	Castle Donington, S Edward
SP 724934	8	Church Langton, S Peter
SP 496879	8	Claybrooke, S Peter
SK 391172	8	Coleorton, S Mary Virgin
SK 367054	5	Congerstone, S Mary Virgin
SK 483129	6	Copt Oak, S Peter
SP 547949	6	Cosby, S Michael & All Angels
SK 604136	5	Cossington, All Saints
SK 902136	6	Cottesmore, S Nicholas
SP 585954	8	Countesthorpe, S Andrew
SP 511960	6	Croft, S Michael & All Angels
SK 835295	6	Croxton Kerrial, S John Baptist
SK 479034	6	Desford, S Martin
SK 454245	6	Diseworth, S Michael & All Angels
SP 471982	8	Earl Shilton, SS Simon & Jude
SK 798291	6	Eaton, S Denys
SK 927053	6	Edith Weston, S Mary
SK 951085	6	Empingham, S Peter
SP 538994	8	Enderby, S John Baptist
SK 920112	6	Exton, SS Peter & Paul
SP 351971	6	Fenny Drayton, S Michael & All Angels
SP 699897	6	Foxton, S Andrew
SK 690130	8	Gaddesby, S Luke
SK 695010	6	Gaulby, S Peter
SP 560879	8	Gilmorton, All Saints
SK 896005	6	Glaston, S Andrew
SK 437179	6	Grace Dieu, Manor House Preparatory School
SP 746888	6	Great Bowden, SS Peter & Paul
TF 001087	5	Great Casterton, SS Peter & Paul
SK 742144	5	Great Dalby, S Swithin
SP 849932	5	Great Easton, S Andrew
SP 652978	8	Great Glen, S Cuthbert
SK 924146	6	Greetham, S Mary Virgin
SK 523074	6	Groby, SS Philip & James
SP 786965	6	Hallaton, S Michael
SK 900076	5	Hambleton, S Andrew
SK 747313	5	Harby, S Mary Virgin
SK 503224	8	Hathern, SS Peter & Paul
SK 390109	6	Heather, S John Baptist
SP 383956	6	Higham on the Hill, S Peter
SP 427938	8	Hinckley, Assumption of SMV
SK 669174	5	Hoby, All Saints
SK 736292	5	Hose, S Michael
SK 676033	6	Houghton on the Hill, S Catherine
SK 427127	8	Hugglescote, S John Baptist
SP 645844	5	Husbands Bosworth, All Saints
SK 405106	6	Ibstock, S Denys
SP 707993	6	Illston on the Hill, S Michael & All Angels
SK 487266	8	Kegworth, S Andrew
SK 972043	6	Ketton, S Mary Virgin
SP 684941	8	Kibworth Beauchamp, S Wilfrid
SP 586865	6	Kimcote, All Saints
SK 689004	8	King's Norton, S John Baptist
SK 718182	5	Kirby Bellars, S Peter
SK 521046	6	Kirby Muxloe, S Bartholomew
SK 454003	6	Kirkby Mallory, All Saints
SK 844112	6	Langham, SS Peter & Paul
SK 585044	12(1)	Leicester, Cathedral Church of S Martin
SK 586051	12(1)	Leicester, S Margaret
SK 583042	8	Leicester, S Mary-de-Castro
SK 572010	8	Leicester, S Andrew, Aylestone
SK 593072	8	Leicester, S Peter, Belgrave
SK 628028	4	Leicester, S Denys, Evington
SK 626060	6	Leicester, S Mary, Humberstone
SK 600012	8	Leicester, S Mary Magdalene, Knighton
SP 526900	6	Leire, S Peter
SK 468279	12	Lockington, S Nicholas
SK 722272	5	Long Clawson, S Remigius
SK 538199	10	Loughborough, All Saints
SK 541198	10	Loughborough, Bell Foundry Campanile
SP 705871	5	Lubenham, All Saints
SP 542844	8	Lutterworth, S Mary
SP 876970	6	Lyddington, S Andrew
SK 908044	4	Lyndon, S Martin
SK 407033	8	Market Bosworth, S Peter
SP 733873	8	Market Harborough, S Dionysius
SK 886164	5	Market Overton, SS Peter & Paul
SK 487100	6	Markfield, S Michael
SK 335122	8	Measham, S Lawrence
SP 800931	6	Medbourne, S Giles
SK 752190	10	Melton Mowbray, S Mary
SP 557840	6	Misterton, S Leonard
SK 925008	4	Morcott, S Mary
SK 581150	8	Mountsorrel, S Peter
SK 829379	4	Muston, S John Baptist
SP 541975	6	Narborough, All Saints
SK 522093	6	Newtown Linford, All Saints
SP 616832	5	North Kilworth, S Andrew
SK 934032	5	North Luffenham, S John Baptist
SK 624004	8	Oadby, S Peter
SK 861089	8	Oakham, All Saints
SK 473163	8	Oaks in Charnwood, S James Apostle
SK 674225	4	Old Dalby, S John Baptist
SK 304039	4	Orton on the Hill, S Edith
SK 359145	6	Packington, Holy Rood
SP 594925	4	Peatling Magna, All Saints
SP 589896	5	Peatling Parva, S Andrew
SK 470008	6	Peckleton, S Mary Magdalene
SK 785114	4	Pickwell, All Saints
SK 870023	6	Preston, SS Peter & Paul
SK 578214	8	Prestwold, S Andrew
SK 651121	6	Queniborough, S Mary
SK 561166	8	Quorndon (Quorn), S Bartholomew
SK 513059	8	Ratby, SS Philip & James
SK 631145	5	Ratcliffe on the Wreake, S Botolph
SK 848028	4	Ridlington, SS Mary Magdalene & Andrew
SK 586126	6	Rothley, S Mary Virgin
TF 036108	5	Ryhall, S John Evangelist
SP 658918	6	Saddington, S Helen
SP 488932	10	Sapcote, All Saints
SP 904982	5	Seaton, All Hallows
SP 483919	6	Sharnford, S Helen
SP 541797	5	Shawell, All Saints

SK 327013	6	Sheepy Magna, All Saints	
SK 481197	8	Shepshed, S Botolph	
SK 354009	4	Sibson, S Botolph	
SK 601152	10	Sileby, S Mary	
SK 741026	5	Skeffington, S Thomas a' Becket	
SK 779104	6	Somerby, All Saints	
SK 692103	4	South Croxton, S John Baptist	
SP 604819	5	South Kilworth, S Nicholas	
SK 942019	4	South Luffenham, S Mary	
SK 857249	8	Sproxton, S Bartholomew	
SK 772309	4	Stathern, S Guthlac	
SK 380209	8	Staunton Harold, Holy Trinity	
SP 398972	6	Stoke Golding, S Margaret Virgin	
SP 489948	8	Stoney Stanton, S Michael	
SK 640021	4	Stoughton, S Mary	
SK 368106	6	Swepstone, S Peter	
SP 569794	4	Swinford, All Saints	
SK 555128	6	Swithland, S Leonard	
SK 626112	8	Syston, SS Peter & Paul	
SP 668857	5	Theddingworth, All Saints	
SK 650152	5	Thrussington, Holy Trinity	
SK 565106	8	Thurcaston, All Saints	
SP 502991	6	Thurlaston, All Saints	
SK 610093	6	Thurmaston, S Michael & All Angels	
SK 647039	8	Thurnby, S Luke	
SK 743057	4	Tilton on the Hill, S Peter	
TF 006063	4	Tinwell, All Saints	
SK 762010	4	Tugby, S Thomas a' Becket	
SK 730101	6	Twyford, S Andrew	
SP 867996	8	Uppingham, SS Peter & Paul	
SK 803250	6	Waltham on the Wolds, S Mary Magdalene	
SK 592197	5	Walton on the Wolds, S Mary	
SK 602110	6	Wanlip, Our Lady & S Nicholas	
SP 557975	8	Whetstone, S Peter	
SK 833143	6	Whissendine, S Andrew	
SK 434162	8	Whitwick, S John Baptist	
SP 609991	8	Wigston, All Saints	
SP 586984	8	Wigston, S Thomas Apostle, South Wigston	
SP 575925	5	Willoughby Waterleys, S Mary Virgin	
SK 894030	5	Wing, SS Peter & Paul	
SP 325973	5	Witherley, S Peter	
SK 538151	6	Woodhouse, S Mary in the Elms	
SK 532141	6	Woodhouse Eaves, S Paul	
SK 604235	6	Wymeswold, S Mary	
SK 851186	6	Wymondham, S Peter	

Lincolnshire

TF 551691	6	Addlethorpe, S Nicholas
SK 946802	5	Aisthorpe, S Peter
TF 455761	6	Alford, S Wilfrid
TF 291353	6	Algarkirk, SS Peter & Paul
SK 982436	5	Ancaster, S Martin
TF 116454	4	Asgarby, S Andrew
TF 055547	5	Ashby de la Launde, S Hybald
TF 119693	6	Bardney, S Lawrence
SK 933415	6	Barkston, S Nicholas
SK 879365	6	Barrowby, All Saints
SK 908597	6	Bassingham, S Michael
SK 966285	4	Bassingthorpe, S Thomas a' Becket
TF 113140	6	Baston, S John Baptist
SK 875538	6	Beckingham, All Saints
SK 930395	5	Belton, SS Peter & Paul
TF 396465	6	Benington, All Saints
TF 224379	8	Bicker, S Swithin
TA 059075	6	Bigby, All Saints

TF 118342	8	Billingborough, S Andrew
TF 068600	6	Blankney, S Oswald
SK 853948	5	Blyton, S Martin
TF 327442	10	Boston, S Botolph
TF 097200	6	Bourne, SS Peter & Paul
TF 082133	5	Braceborough, S Margaret
TF 021673	6	Branston, All Saints
SK 915539	6	Brant Broughton, S Helen
TF 501650	8	Burgh le Marsh, SS Peter & Paul
TF 388449	6	Butterwick, S Andrew
TA 116013	7	Caistor, SS Peter & Paul
TF 456672	5	Candlesby, S Benedict
SK 939486	8	Caythorpe, S Vincent
TF 111946	5	Claxby, S Mary
SK 846490	5	Claypole, S Peter
SK 974606	5	Coleby, All Saints
SK 930241	6	Colsterworth, S John Baptist
TF 221580	6	Coningsby, S Michael & All Angels
TF 001250	4	Corby Glen, S John
SK 871916	6	Corringham, S Lawrence
TF 509618	6	Croft, All Saints
TF 241103	6	Crowland, Abbey Church of SS Bartholomew, Guthlac & Mary
TF 157096	6	Deeping St James, S James
TF 217162	6	Deeping St Nicholas, S Nicholas
SK 865325	6	Denton, S Andrew
TF 208360	8	Donington, S Mary & Holy Rood
TF 024794	6	Dunholme, S Chad
TF 063630	5	Dunston, S Peter
SK 875672	6	Eagle, All Saints
TF 382639	6	East Keal, S Helen
TF 062219	10	Edenham, S Michael & All Angels
TF 122472	10	Ewerby, S Andrew
TF 364425	6	Fishtoft, S Guthlac
TF 389236	6	Fleet, S Mary Magdalene
TF 071337	6	Folkingham, S Andrew
TF 325392	6	Frampton, S Mary Virgin
TF 377438	6	Freiston, S James
TF 461554	6	Friskney, All Saints
SK 947504	6	Fulbeck, S Nicholas
SK 814901	8	Gainsborough, All Saints
TF 403244	6	Gedney, S Mary Magdalene
TF 338113	5	Gedney Hill, Holy Trinity
TF 003904	4	Glentham, S Peter
TF 237318	6	Gosberton, SS Peter & Paul
SK 915358	10	Grantham, S Wulfram
TA 087049	4	Grasby, All Saints
TF 408856	5	Great Carlton, S John Baptist
TF 085119	5	Greatford, S Thomas a' Becket
TF 148439	6	Great Hale, S John Baptist
SK 925304	5	Great Ponton, Holy Cross
TF 107253	4	Hacconby, S Andrew
TF 418651	6	Halton Holegate, S Andrew
SK 883326	6	Harlaxton, SS Mary & Peter
SK 972623	8	Harmston, All Saints
TF 143441	8	Heckington, S Andrew
TF 139407	5	Helpringham, S Andrew
TF 009396	8	Heydour, S Michael & All Angels
TF 534722	6	Hogsthorpe, S Mary
TF 359248	8	Holbeach, All Saints
SK 943434	5	Honington, S Wilfred
TF 119352	6	Horbling, S Andrew
TF 258695	6	Horncastle, S Mary
SK 887443	4	Hougham, All Saints
SK 923464	6	Hough on the Hill, All Saints
TF 560688	8	Ingoldmells, S Peter
TF 023267	5	Irnham, S Andrew

TF 304385	8	Kirton, SS Peter & Paul
TF 123125	5	Langtoft, S Michael & All Angels
TF 389703	6	Langton, S Peter
TF 149769	4	Langton by Wragby, S Giles
SK 831867	6	Lea, S Helen
SK 950517	6	Leadenham, S Swithin
TF 057486	4	Leasingham, S Andrew
TF 367844	5	Legbourne, All Saints
TF 400479	6	Leverton, S Helena
SK 978718	12(1)	Lincoln, Cathedral Church of BVM
SK 972698	6	Lincoln, S Botolph
SK 989728	8	Lincoln, S Giles
SK 973709	4	Lincoln, S Mary le Wigford
SK 973704	6	Lincoln, S Peter at Gowts
SK 843439	4	Long Bennington, All Saints
TF 432229	8	Long Sutton, S Mary
TF 326874	8	Louth, S James
TF 433256	6	Lutton, S Nicholas
TF 512845	6	Mablethorpe, S Mary
TF 137103	6	Market Deeping, S Guthlac
TF 106892	8	Market Rasen, S Thomas
SK 893437	5	Marston, S Mary
TF 121600	6	Martin, Holy Trinity
TF 070613	8	Metheringham, S Wilfrid
TF 098240	6	Morton, S John Baptist
TF 307241	6	Moulton, All Saints
TF 515745	4	Mumby, S Thomas of Canterbury
SK 986578	6	Navenby, S Peter
TF 007753	6	Nettleham, All Saints
TF 048362	5	Newton, S Botolph
TF 061641	6	Nocton, All Saints
TF 021464	5	North Rauceby, S Peter
SK 890590	6	Norton Disney, S Peter
TF 350651	6	Old Bolingbroke, SS Peter & Paul
TF 407502	6	Old Leake, S Mary Virgin
TF 242256	8	Pinchbeck, S Mary
TF 224341	6	Quadring, S Margaret
TF 373671	6	Raithby, Holy Trinity
TF 098278	6	Rippingale, S Andrew
TF 082511	6	Ruskington, All Saints
SK 895761	6	Saxilby, S Botolph
TF 033774	6	Scothern, S Germain
SE 888009	6	Scotter, S Peter
TF 443677	4	Scremby, SS Peter & Paul
TA 072059	5	Searby, S Nicholas
TF 106329	6	Sempringham, Abbey Church of S Andrew
TF 354507	8	Sibsey, S Margaret
TF 058430	6	Silk Willoughby, S Denys
SK 896259	5	Skillington, S James
TF 338431	6	Skirbeck, S Nicholas
TF 069459	8	Sleaford, S Denys
TF 369751	5	South Ormsby, S Leonard
TF 250224	8	Spalding, Our Lady & S Nicholas
TF 262238	8	Spalding, S Paul, Fulney
TF 403660	6	Spilsby, S James
SK 875898	4	Springthorpe, SS George & Laurence
SK 905228	4	Stainby, S Peter
TF 028071	8	Stamford, All Saints
TF 032071	4	Stamford, S George
TF 029071	4	Stamford, S John Baptist
TF 031068	6	Stamford, S Martin
TF 031071	8	Stamford, S Mary
TF 343570	6	Stickney, S Luke
SK 921273	5	Stoke Rochford, SS Mary & Andrew
SK 882820	6	Stow, S Mary
TF 251283	12	Surfleet, S Laurence
TF 285355	8	Sutterton, S Mary BV
SK 868632	5	Swinderby, All Saints
TF 237402	8	Swineshead, S Mary
TF 018225	4	Swinstead, S Mary
TF 211575	6	Tattershall, Holy Trinity
TF 158909	4	Tealby, All Saints
TF 463882	6	Theddlethorpe All Saints, All Saints
TF 105168	6	Thurlby, S Firmin
TF 122582	6	Timberland, S Andrew
TF 446186	6	Tydd St Mary, S Mary
TF 061077	6	Uffington, S Michael & All Angels
SK 868867	6	Upton, All Saints
SK 976642	6	Waddington, S Michael
TF 471586	6	Wainfleet St Mary, S Mary BV
TF 060351	4	Walcot, S Nicholas
TF 138924	8	Walesby, All Saints, Old Church
TF 019706	8	Washingborough, S John
SK 969545	8	Welbourn, S Chad
SK 976382	4	Welby, S Bartholomew
SK 982565	6	Wellingore, All Saints
TF 011798	6	Welton, S Mary
SK 851443	4	Westborough, All Saints
TF 109086	6	West Deeping, S Andrew
TF 367637	6	West Keal, S Helen
TF 323240	6	Whaplode, S Mary
TF 263362	6	Wigtoft, SS Peter & Paul
SK 874845	6	Willingham by Stow, S Helen
TF 473719	6	Willoughby, S Helen
TF 559659	4	Winthorpe, S Mary
TF 053166	6	Witham on the Hill, S Andrew
TF 134780	6	Wragby, All Saints
TF 424508	6	Wrangle, S Mary Virgin & S Nicholas

Merseyside

SJ 333839	8	Bebington, S Andrew
SJ 349823	8	Bebington, S Barnabas, Bromborough
SJ 361800	6	Bebington, S Mary BV, Eastham
SJ 283903	6	Birkenhead, S Oswald, Bidston
SJ 262898	4	Birkenhead, Christ Church, Moreton
SJ 301878	10	Birkenhead, S Saviour, Oxton
SJ 335863	6	Birkenhead, S Peter, Rock Ferry
SJ 272881	5	Birkenhead, S Mary, Upton
SJ 276868	8	Birkenhead, Holy Cross, Woodchurch
SJ 348951	8	Bootle, Christ Church
SJ 321999	6	Crosby, S Luke
SJ 266811	8	Heswall, S Peter
SJ 218864	8	Hoylake, S Bridget, West Kirby
SJ 443912	6	Huyton, S Michael & All Angels
SJ 354894	12(1)	Liverpool, Cathedral Church of Christ
SJ 345906	4	Liverpool, Municipal Buildings
SJ 356912	8	Liverpool, S Francis Xavier (RC)
SJ 415891	6	Liverpool, All Saints, Childwall
SJ 404843	8	Liverpool, S Michael, Garston
SJ 450862	8	Liverpool, S Nicholas, Halewood
SJ 339905	12(1)	Liverpool, Our Lady & S Nicholas, Pier Head
SJ 383924	8	Liverpool, S John Baptist, Tuebrook
SJ 359948	8	Liverpool, S Mary, Walton
SJ 395927	6	Liverpool, S James, West Derby
SJ 422866	8	Liverpool, S Peter, Woolton
SJ 593956	8	Newton-le-Willows, S Peter
SJ 338845	8	Port Sunlight, Christ Church, (Undenominational)
SJ 465927	8	Prescot, S Mary Virgin
SJ 422866	8	Rainford, All Saints
SD 478007	8	Rainford, All Saints
SJ 501904	8	Rainhill, S Bartholomew (RC)
SJ 513953	10	St Helens, S Helen
SJ 506954	8	St Helens, S Thomas, Eccleston

SD 357013 8 Sefton, S Helen

SD 357013	8	Sefton, S Helen
SD 337175	8	Southport, Christ Church
SD 356187	8	Southport, Emmanuel
SD 375201	6	Southport, S John, Crossens
SJ 247841	5	Thurstaston, S Bartholomew
SJ 296922	6	Wallasey, S Hilary of Poitiers
SJ 289931	8	Wallasey, S Nicholas
SJ 311923	8	Wallasey, S Mary, Liscard

Norfolk

TG 401103	6	Acle, S Edmund K&M
TM 270873	8	Alburgh, All Saints
TM 450933	5	Aldeby, S Mary Virgin
TF 883041	6	Ashill, S Nicholas
TM 146976	5	Ashwellthorpe, All Saints
TM 156911	5	Aslacton, S Michael
TM 048953	6	Attleborough, Assumption BVM
TG 192270	10	Aylsham, S Michael
TG 010367	5	Bale, All Saints
TM 063881	6	Banham, Blessed Virgin Mary
TG 082077	5	Barnham Broom, SS Peter & Paul
TG 343218	6	Barton Turf, S Michael & All Angels
TM 284934	5	Bedingham, S Andrew
TF 973185	8	Beetley, S Mary Magdalene
TM 310999	6	Bergh Apton, SS Peter & Paul
TM 065956	5	Besthorpe, All Saints
TG 334091	8	Blofield, S Andrew
TM 011796	6	Blo' Norton, S Andrew
TL 931833	5	Brettenham, S Andrew
TM 203795	6	Brockdish, SS Peter & Paul
TM 293995	6	Brooke, S Peter
TM 346931	5	Broome, S Michael
TM 125927	6	Bunwell, S Michael & All Angels
TG 233227	6	Buxton, S Andrew
TF 949021	6	Carbrooke, SS Peter & Paul
TG 339022	4	Carleton St Peter, S Peter
TF 815150	6	Castle Acre, S James
TL 959975	6	Caston, Holy Cross
TG 381212	6	Catfield, All Saints
TG 133238	8	Cawston, S Agnes
TF 589204	5	Clenchwarton, S Margaret
TG 271197	6	Coltishall, S John Baptist
TG 177124	5	Costessey, S Edmund
TF 655038	5	Crimplesham, S Mary Virgin
TG 219422	6	Cromer, SS Peter & Paul
TF 615017	6	Denver, S Mary
TG 050004	5	Deopham, S Andrew
TF 693303	6	Dersingham, S Nicholas
TM 167824	6	Dickleburgh, All Saints
TM 117800	8	Diss, S Mary Virgin
TM 329922	6	Ditchingham, S Mary Virgin
TF 613033	8	Downham Market, S Edmund K&M
TG 180137	6	Drayton, S Margaret
TF 986133	8	East Dereham, S Nicholas
TL 990867	6	East Harling, SS Peter & Paul
TG 051165	5	Elsing, S Mary Virgin
TF 489074	5	Emneth, S Edmund K&M
TG 198313	6	Erpingham, S Mary
TF 919297	8	Fakenham, SS Peter & Paul
TG 251292	6	Felmingham, S Andrew
TG 468132	5	Filby, All Saints
TF 688065	6	Fincham, S Martin
TM 165928	6	Forncett St Peter, SS Peter & Paul
TG 039217	6	Foxley, S Thomas
TM 152969	5	Fundenhall, S Nicholas

TM 004816	6	Garboldisham, S John Baptist
TG 023073	6	Garveston, S Margaret
TF 636204	6	Gaywood, S Faith
TF 770325	5	Great Bircham, S Mary
TM 020971	5	Great Ellingham, S James
TF 799230	4	Great Massingham, S Mary
TF 962272	6	Great Ryburgh, S Andrew
TG 524080	12(1)	Great Yarmouth, S Nicholas
TG 524044	8	Great Yarmouth, S Andrew, Gorleston
TF 958155	8	Gressenhall, S Mary
TF 721218	6	Grimston, S Botolph
TL 943993	5	Griston, SS Peter & Paul
TM 439969	5	Haddiscoe, S Mary
TG 417067	6	Halvergate, SS Peter & Paul
TG 203349	5	Hanworth, S Andrew
TG 379311	8	Happisburgh, S Mary Virgin
TF 788261	5	Harpley, S Lawrence
TM 312934	6	Hedenham, S Peter
TG 160048	8	Hethersett, S Remigius
TG 201223	5	Hevingham, S Mary Virgin & S Botolph
TG 113274	6	Heydon, SS Peter & Paul
TG 414242	5	Hickling, S Mary
TF 825000	5	Hilborough, All Saints
TL 622981	8	Hilgay, All Saints
TF 984364	5	Hindringham, S Martin
TG 021021	8	Hingham, S Andrew
TL 735880	6	Hockwold cum Wilton, S James
TF 878436	6	Holkham, S Withiburga
TF 887075	6	Holme Hale, S Andrew
TF 707434	5	Holme next the Sea, S Mary Virgin
TG 081387	8	Holt, S Andrew
TG 114112	6	Honingham, S Andrew
TG 216151	6	Horsham St Faith, S Mary Virgin & S Andrew
TG 196042	5	Intwood, All Saints
TM 041860	8	Kenninghall, S Mary
TG 164025	6	Ketteringham, S Peter
TF 617198	10	King's Lynn, S Margaret
TF 618204	8	King's Lynn, S Nicholas
TM 373942	5	Kirby Cane, All Saints
TG 307342	5	Knapton, SS Peter & Paul
TG 245232	5	Lamas, S Andrew
TG 355009	5	Langley, S Michael
TF 887177	6	Litcham, All Saints
TF 935365	6	Little Walsingham, S Mary & All Saints
TM 363987	8	Loddon, Holy Trinity
TM 197923	6	Long Stratton, S Mary Virgin
TG 388183	5	Ludham, S Catherine
TG 069178	5	Lyng, S Margaret
TF 708098	6	Marham, Holy Trinity
TG 196237	8	Marsham, All Saints
TG 454184	6	Martham, S Mary
TG 053111	6	Mattishall, All Saints
TL 732949	6	Methwold, S George
TF 922196	5	Mileham, S John Baptist
TG 194011	6	Mulbarton, S Mary Magdalene
TL 800938	6	Mundford, S Leonard
TF 878098	6	Necton, All Saints
TM 088905	6	New Buckenham, S Martin
TF 854377	6	North Creake, S Mary
TF 987215	8	North Elmham, Blessed Virgin Mary
TM 036825	8	North Lopham, S Nicholas
TG 244390	8	Northrepps, S Mary Virgin
TL 756970	8	Northwold, S Andrew
TM 407987	6	Norton Subcourse, SS Mary & Margaret
TG 231082	5	Norwich, All Saints
TG 231087	10	Norwich, S Andrew
TG 225086	8	Norwich, S Giles

TG 227087   6   Norwich, S Laurence
TG 229084 12(1) Norwich, S Peter Mancroft
TG 229090   6   Norwich, S George, Colegate
TG 228089   8   Norwich, S Michael & All Angels, Coslany
TF 513037   6   Outwell, S Clement
TG 323344   6   Paston, S Margaret
TM 196861   8   Pulham Market, S Mary Magdalene
TM 212853   8   Pulham St Mary, S Mary Virgin
TM 028877   8   Quidenham, S Mary Virgin
TG 356147   6   Ranworth, S Helen
TM 397964   5   Raveningham, S Andrew
TM 263843   8   Redenhall, Assumption VM
TG 427025   6   Reedham, S John Baptist
TG 101228   8   Reepham, S Michael
TG 020060   5   Reymerston, S Peter
TG 133140   5   Ringland, S Peter
TL 994960   5   Rockland All Saints, All Saints
TL 923813   6   Rushford, S John
TF 899020   6   Saham Toney, S George
TG 110249   8   Salle, SS Peter & Paul
TM 231972   8   Saxlingham Nethergate, S Mary Virgin
TG 116304   6   Saxthorpe, S Andrew
TF 954122   6   Scarning, SS Peter & Paul
TM 151790   6   Scole, S Andrew
TG 265237   6   Scottow, All Saints
TF 899319   6   Sculthorpe, S Mary & All Saints
TM 107836   6   Shelfanger, All Saints
TG 144418   6   Sheringham, All Saints, Upper Sheringham
TF 957073   6   Shipdham, All Saints
TM 247990   5   Shotesham, All Saints
TF 682089   6   Shouldham, All Saints
TL 985928   5   Shropham, S Peter
TF 855362   5   South Creake, S Mary Virgin
TM 039817   6   South Lopham, S Andrew
TG 256368   6   Southrepps, S James
TG 365133   5   South Walsham, S Mary
TF 939209   4   Stanfield, S Margaret
TM 234843   6   Starston, S Margaret
TM 387941   5   Stockton, S Michael & All Angels
TF 629058   8   Stow Bardolph, Holy Trinity
TG 221208   6   Stratton Strawless, S Margaret
TG 233312   5   Suffield, S Margaret
TG 305065   4   Surlingham, SS Mary & Saviour
TF 820090   8   Swaffham, SS Peter & Paul
TG 287331   4   Swafield, S Nicholas
TG 219009   4   Swainsthorpe, S Peter
TG 019173   5   Swanton Morley, All Saints
TG 199023   4   Swardeston, S Mary Virgin
TM 149956   6   Tacolneston, All Saints
TM 201959   5   Tasburgh, S Mary Virgin
TF 552206   8   Terrington St Clement, S Clement
TF 539159   6   Terrington St John, S John Baptist
TM 190943   5   Tharston, S Mary
TL 869832   8   Thetford, S Peter
TG 261084   8   Thorpe St Andrew, S Andrew
TM 417983   5   Thurlton, All Saints
TM 135898   6   Tibenham, All Saints
TF 568180   6   Tilney All Saints, All Saints
TF 895211   4   Tittleshall, S Mary
TG 308227   8   Tunstead, S Mary Virgin
TF 505028   6   Upwell, S Peter
TG 360317   5   Walcot, All Saints
TF 502176   6   Walpole St Andrew, S Andrew
TF 502169   6   Walpole St Peter, S Peter
TF 477106   6   Walsoken, All Saints
TF 621112   6   Watlington, SS Peter & Paul
TF 921009   6   Watton, S Mary

TF 918432   8   Wells next the Sea, S Nicholas
TF 667021   5   West Dereham, S Andrew
TG 113158   6   Weston Longville, All Saints
TF 471134   5   West Walton, S Mary Virgin
TF 919234   5   Whissonsett, S Mary
TF 597140   4   Wiggenhall St Germans, SS German & Peter
TF 598114   6   Wiggenhall St Mary Magdalen, S Mary Magdalene
TF 582145   6   Wiggenhall St Mary the Virgin, S Mary Virgin
TF 941400   6   Wighton, All Saints
TM 031899   5   Wilby, All Saints
TM 109857   6   Winfarthing, S Mary
TG 491194   6   Winterton, All Saints
TG 043428   6   Wiveton, S Mary Virgin
TM 285946   6   Woodton, All Saints
TM 163989   4   Wreningham, All Saints
TG 296175   6   Wroxham, S Mary Virgin
TG 106015 10   Wymondham, Abbey Church of S Mary Virgin & S Thomas à Becket
TG 007107   6   Yaxham, S Peter

Northamptonshire

TL 021831   4   Achurch, S John Baptist
SP 740469   5   Alderton, S Margaret
TL 006818   5   Aldwinckle, S Peter
TL 025958   4   Apethorpe, S Leonard
SP 755814   5   Arthingworth, S Andrew
SP 573682   4   Ashby St Ledgers, SS Mary & Leodger
SP 794910   5   Ashley, S Mary
SP 765500   5   Ashton, S Michael & All Angels
SP 514331   8   Aynho, S Michael
SP 559588   6   Badby, S Mary
SP 543703   4   Barby, S Mary
SP 888771   5   Barton Seagrave, S Botolph
SP 627505   5   Blakesley, S Mary
SP 725534   5   Blisworth, S John Baptist
SP 754658   5   Boughton, S John Baptist
SP 906592   5   Bozeat, S Mary
SP 586370   6   Brackley, S Peter
SP 647485   5   Bradden, S Michael & All Angels
SP 822591   6   Brafield-on-the-Green, S Laurence
SP 788875   6   Brampton Ash, S Mary
SP 536663   6   Braunston, All Saints
SP 946852   5   Brigstock, S Andrew
SP 748712   5   Brixworth, All Saints
SP 837758   5   Broughton, S Andrew
SP 673573   5   Bugbrooke, S Michael & All Angels
SP 962943   5   Bulwick, S Nicholas
SP 903749   8   Burton Latimer, S Mary Virgin
SP 519530   6   Byfield, Holy Cross
SP 863592   5   Castle Ashby, S Mary Magdalene
SP 491439   6   Chacombe, SS Peter & Paul
SP 545555   4   Charwelton, Holy Trinity
SP 988691   5   Chelveston, S John Baptist
SP 499487   5   Chipping Warden, SS Peter & Paul
SP 718657   4   Church Brampton, S Botolph
SP 639578   4   Church Stowe, S Michael
SP 714816   5   Clipston, All Saints
SP 830610   6   Cogenhoe, S Peter
SP 657763   4   Cold Ashby, S Denys
SP 662535   6   Cold Higham, S Luke
SP 751557   5   Collingtree, S Columba
SP 898888   6   Corby, S John Baptist
SP 791424   6   Cosgrove, S Margaret
TL 049905   5   Cotterstock, S Andrew
SP 710735   6   Cottesbrooke, All Saints
SP 846899   5   Cottingham, S Mary Magdalene
SP 764529   5   Courteenhall, SS Peter & Paul

SP 925773	4	Cranford St Andrew, S Andrew
SP 925771	6	Cranford St John, S John Baptist
SP 706718	6	Creaton, S Michael & All Angels
SP 588725	4	Crick, S Margaret
SP 546335	5	Croughton, All Saints
SP 545470	5	Culworth, S Mary Virgin
SP 575626	10	Daventry, Holy Cross
SP 952927	6	Deene, S Peter
SP 991766	6	Denford, Holy Trinity
SP 803830	8	Desborough, S Giles
SP 770877	5	Dingley, All Saints
SP 613605	6	Dodford, S Mary Virgin
SP 762768	4	Draughton, S Catherine
SP 852638	8	Earls Barton, All Saints
SP 831893	6	East Carlton, S Peter
SP 716848	5	East Farndon, S John Baptist
SP 667682	6	East Haddon, S Mary Virgin
SP 888588	5	Easton Maudit, SS Peter & Paul
SP 702493	8	Easton Neston, S Mary
TF 011048	4	Easton on the Hill, All Saints
SP 828635	6	Ecton, S Mary Magdalene
SP 505479	4	Edgcote, S James
SP 584352	5	Evenley, S George
SP 595574	5	Everdon, S Mary BV
SP 541500	5	Eydon, S Nicholas
SP 536397	5	Farthinghoe, S Michael
SP 613549	5	Farthingstone, S Mary Virgin
SP 912719	8	Finedon, S Mary Virgin
SP 642598	6	Flore, All Saints
TL 060931	4	Fotheringhay, S Mary & All Saints
SP 706547	6	Gayton, S Mary
SP 895830	5	Geddington, S Mary Magdalene
SP 758469	5	Grafton Regis, S Mary
SP 922802	5	Grafton Underwood, S James Apostle
SP 958751	6	Great Addington, All Saints
SP 667652	6	Great Brington, S Mary
SP 828765	6	Great Cransley, S Andrew
SP 882648	5	Great Doddington, S Nicholas
SP 735839	5	Great Oxendon, S Helena
SP 669499	6	Greens Norton, S Bartholomew
SP 879605	5	Grendon, S Mary
SP 899944	5	Gretton, S James Great
SP 676727	6	Guilsborough, S Etheldreda
SP 763577	5	Hardingstone, S Edmund
TL 037707	4	Hargrave, All Saints
SP 701647	6	Harlestone, S Andrew
SP 690609	5	Harpole, All Saints
SP 778806	6	Harrington, SS Peter & Paul
SP 916974	6	Harringworth, S John Baptist
SP 712773	8	Haselbech, S Michael
SP 516582	4	Hellidon, S John Baptist
SP 590432	6	Helmdon, S Mary Magdalene
TL 096850	4	Hemington, SS Peter & Paul
SP 961685	8	Higham Ferrers, S Mary
SP 926660	8	Irchester, S Katharine
SP 948706	8	Irthlingborough, S Peter
SP 885740	6	Isham, S Peter
SP 986789	6	Islip, S Nicholas
SP 735792	6	Kelmarsh, S Denys
SP 867784	12	Kettering, SS Peter & Paul
SP 563711	4	Kilsby, S Faith
TL 007971	6	King's Cliffe, All Saints
SP 497362	8	Kings Sutton, SS Peter & Paul
SP 697596	5	Kislingbury, S Luke
SP 758747	4	Lamport, All Saints
SP 560774	5	Lilbourne, All Saints
SP 633543	5	Litchborough, S Martin
SP 803596	5	Little Houghton, S Mary BV
SP 627677	5	Long Buckby, S Lawrence
SP 988884	6	Lower Benefield, S Mary
SP 977810	6	Lowick, S Peter
TL 112878	4	Lutton, S Peter
SP 749769	6	Maidwell, S Mary
SP 536421	5	Marston St Lawrence, S Lawrence
SP 693860	5	Marston Trussell, S Nicholas
SP 838666	6	Mears Ashby, All Saints
SP 498420	6	Middleton Cheney, All Saints
SP 736555	5	Milton Malsor, Holy Cross
SP 574491	5	Moreton Pinkney, S Mary Virgin
SP 783664	10	Moulton, SS Peter & Paul
SP 689781	5	Naseby, All Saints
TL 063963	5	Nassington, S Mary Virgin & All Saints
SP 659587	6	Nether Heyford, SS Peter & Paul
SP 582597	6	Newnham, S Michael & All Angels
SP 999659	4	Newton Bromswold, S Peter
SP 755604	8	Northampton, All Saints
SP 754609	8	Northampton, Holy Sepulchre
SP 735586	6	Northampton, S Benedict
SP 759605	10	Northampton, S Giles
SP 750603	8	Northampton, S Peter
SP 737617	6	Northampton, S Mary, Dallington
SP 725611	6	Northampton, S Luke, Duston
SP 746632	6	Northampton, S John Baptist, Kingsthorpe
SP 788618	5	Northampton, S Peter, Weston Favell
SP 603637	5	Norton, All Saints
SP 785731	5	Old, S Andrew
SP 859723	5	Orlingbury, S Mary
TL 042882	8	Oundle, S Peter
SP 780394	5	Passenham, S Guthlac
SP 672543	6	Pattishall, Holy Cross
SP 716455	6	Paulerspury, S James Apostle
SP 801546	6	Piddington, S John Baptist
TL 025846	4	Pilton, All Saints
SP 754682	6	Pitsford, All Saints
TL 068871	5	Polebrook, All Saints
SP 763433	6	Potterspury, S Nicholas
SP 575548	5	Preston Capes, SS Peter & Paul
SP 860748	5	Pytchley, All Saints
TL 000731	8	Raunds, S Peter
SP 670703	5	Ravensthorpe, S Denys
SP 985721	6	Ringstead, Nativity of BVM
SP 757518	6	Roade, S Mary Virgin
SP 714566	5	Rothersthorpe, SS Peter & Paul
SP 816812	8	Rothwell, Holy Trinity
SP 957665	8	Rushden, S Mary
SP 841828	6	Rushton, All Saints
SP 768726	5	Scaldwell, SS Peter & Paul
SP 682828	5	Sibbertoft, S Helen
SP 718701	6	Spratton, S Luke Evangelist
SP 588789	5	Stanford on Avon, S Nicholas
SP 916868	4	Stanion, S Peter
SP 980714	6	Stanwick, S Lawrence
SP 541611	6	Staverton, S Mary Virgin
SP 806883	6	Stoke Albany, S Botolph
SP 741498	5	Stoke Bruerne, S Mary Virgin
TL 026863	5	Stoke Doyle, S Rumbald
SP 968821	5	Sudborough, All Saints
SP 557453	6	Sulgrave, S James
SP 631420	5	Syresham, S James
SP 670756	5	Thornby, S Helen
SP 833790	6	Thorpe Malsor, S Leonard
SP 997787	8	Thrapston, S James
TL 022798	8	Titchmarsh, S Mary Virgin
SP 694487	12	Towcester, S Laurence

SP 952782	6	Twywell, S Nicholas
SP 482532	5	Upper Boddington, S John Baptist
TL 009832	6	Wadenhoe, S Michael & All Angels
SP 802720	6	Walgrave, S Peter
SP 624456	5	Wappenham, S Mary
SP 893798	5	Warkton, S Edmund
TL 077910	6	Warmington, S Mary BV
SP 603690	6	Watford, SS Peter & Paul
SP 633593	8	Weedon Bec, SS Peter & Paul
SP 602470	6	Weedon Lois, S Mary Virgin & S Peter
SP 888810	6	Weekley, S Mary Virgin
SP 928893	8	Weldon, S Mary
SP 641803	8	Welford, S Mary Virgin
SP 892679	8	Wellingborough, All Hallows
SP 582660	5	Welton, S Martin
SP 630719	5	West Haddon, All Saints
SP 778914	5	Weston by Welland, S Mary Virgin
SP 636647	6	Whilton, S Andrew
SP 852605	5	Whiston, S Mary Magdalene
SP 607398	5	Whitfield, S John Evangelist
SP 689443	5	Whittlebury, S Mary
SP 745395	8	Wicken, S John Evangelist
SP 812883	5	Wilbarston, All Saints
SP 867663	6	Wilby, S Mary Virgin
SP 909631	6	Wollaston, S Mary
SP 969777	6	Woodford, S Mary Virgin
SP 543528	6	Woodford Halse, S Mary Virgin
SP 762564	5	Wootton, S George Martyr
SP 866571	6	Yardley Hastings, S Andrew
TL 071978	4	Yarwell, S Mary Magdalene
SP 602753	6	Yelvertoft, All Saints

Northumberland

NY 838560	8	Allendale, S Cuthbert
NU 184137	8	Alnwick, S Paul
NU 179350	8	Bamburgh, S Aidan
NT 999529	8	Berwick-upon-Tweed, Town Hall
NY 988644	6	Corbridge, S Andrew
NZ 267769	6	Cramlington, S Nicholas
NU 231225	6	Embleton, Holy Trinity
NY 935641	8	Hexham, Abbey Church of S Andrew
NZ 198860	8	Morpeth, Watch Tower
NZ 038652	6	Newton, S James
NU 058016	8	Rothbury, All Saints
NZ 114647	6	Wylam, S Oswin

North Yorkshire

SE 335921	6	Ainderby Steeple, S Helen
SE 406664	6	Aldborough, S Andrew
SE 735881	6	Appleton le Moors, Christ Church
SD 948911	6	Askrigg, S Oswald
SE 012885	6	Aysgarth, S Andrew
SE 367770	8	Baldersby, S James
NZ 231090	4	Barton, SS Cuthbert & Mary
SE 268532	6	Beckwithshaw, S Michael & All Angels
SE 266884	8	Bedale, S Gregory
SE 239595	8	Birstwith, S James Apostle
SE 595479	6	Bishopthorpe, S Andrew
SE 252992	6	Bolton on Swale, S Mary
SE 397665	6	Boroughbridge, S James
SE 718608	4	Bossall, S Botolph
SE 436701	6	Brafferton, S Peter or S Augustine
SE 325972	6	Burneston, S Lambert
SE 033615	6	Burnsall, S Wilfrid
SD 651721	6	Burton in Lonsdale, All Saints
SE 647241	6	Carlton, S Mary Virgin

NZ 507045	8	Carlton in Cleveland, S Botolph
SE 240980	8	Catterick, S Anne
SE 464899	6	Cowesby, S Michael & All Angels
NZ 443075	4	Crathorne, All Saints
SE 676263	5	Drax, SS Peter & Paul
SE 526701	8	Easingwold, S John Baptist & All Saints
NZ 164098	4	East Layton, Christ Church
SE 147860	6	East Witton, S John Evangelist
SE 701475	4	Elvington, Holy Trinity
SE 628431	8	Escrick, S Helen
SE 468848	6	Felixkirk, S Felix
SE 195541	4	Fewston, S Michael & S Laurence
TA 117811	6	Filey, S Oswald
SD 932539	8	Gargrave, S Andrew
SD 812641	8	Giggleswick, S Alkelda
SE 046984	6	Grinton, S Andrew
SE 302553	8	Harrogate, S Peter
SE 294556	8	Harrogate, S Wilfrid
SE 613839	8	Helmsley, All Saints
SE 673306	6	Hemingbrough, Blessed Virgin Mary
SE 222938	4	Hornby, S Mary
SE 667757	6	Hovingham, All Saints
SE 429536	6	Hunsingore, S John Baptist
SE 615562	8	Huntington, All Saints
SE 393686	6	Kirby Hill, All Hallows
SE 376848	6	Kirby Wiske, S John Baptist
SE 236745	6	Kirkby Malzeard, S Andrew
SE 697866	6	Kirkbymoorside, All Saints
SE 399505	6	Kirk Deighton, All Saints
SE 347572	8	Knaresborough, S John Baptist
SE 232471	4	Leathley, S Oswald
SD 645693	6	Low Bentham, S John Baptist
SE 785717	8	Malton, S Leonard (RC)
SE 227807	8	Masham, S Mary Virgin
NZ 201085	4	Melsonby, S James Great
SE 126879	8	Middleham, SS Mary & Alkelda
SE 093742	6	Middlesmoor, S Chad
SE 782854	4	Middleton, S Andrew
SE 599454	4	Naburn, S Matthew
SE 367942	8	Northallerton, All Saints
SE 794710	8	Norton, S Peter
SE 159658	8	Pateley Bridge, S Cuthbert
SE 799840	8	Pickering, SS Peter & Paul
NZ 174011	8	Richmond, S Mary
SE 314711	10	Ripon, Cathedral Church of SS Peter & Wilfrid
SE 948053	8	Robin Hood's Bay, S Stephen
NZ 472067	6	Rudby, All Saints
TA 009903	6	Scalby, S Laurence
TA 047891	10	Scarborough, S Mary
SE 615324	10	Selby, Abbey Church of S Mary & S German
SD 819639	8	Settle, Holy Ascension
SE 328721	8	Sharow, S John Divine
SE 488335	8	Sherburn in Elmet, All Saints
SD 991519	8	Skipton, Holy Trinity
SE 431814	6	Sowerby, S Oswald
SE 364511	4	Spofforth, All Saints
SE 657560	6	Stockton on the Forest, Holy Trinity
NZ 526085	8	Stokesley, S Peter
SE 630608	6	Strensall, S Mary Virgin
SE 486435	8	Tadcaster, S Mary
SE 427823	8	Thirsk, S Mary Virgin
SD 902483	4	Thornton in Craven, S Mary
SE 399761	4	Topcliffe, S Columba
SE 325772	6	Wath, S Mary
SE 268788	6	West Tanfield, S Nicholas
NZ 901113	10	Whitby, S Mary
SE 724659	6	Whitwell on the Hill, S John Evangelist

SE 442583   6   Whixley, Ascension
NZ 483024   6   Whorlton (Swainby), Holy Cross
SE 252712   4   Winksley, S Cuthbert
SE 965834   5   Wykeham, S Helen or All Saints
SE 605517   6   York, All Saints
SE 601516   6   York, Arts Centre
SE 603522   12(2)   York, Minster Church of S Peter
SE 601519   8   York, S Martin-le-Grand
SE 599522   6   York, S Olave
SE 572514   6   York, S Stephen, Acomb
SE 593531   6   York, SS Philip & James, Clifton
SE 603517   6   York, S Michael, Spurriergate

Nottinghamshire

SK 587462   8   Arnold, S Mary
SK 580451   8   Arnold, S Paul, Daybrook
SK 519343   8   Attenborough, S Mary
SK 768543   6   Averham, S Michael & All Angels
SK 686808   6   Babworth, All Saints
SK 820516   8   Balderton, S Giles
SK 860521   6   Barnby in the Willows, All Saints
SK 522327   6   Barton in Fabis, S George
SK 527367   8   Beeston, S John Baptist
SK 707399   8   Bingham, S Mary & All Saints
SK 586556   6   Blidworth, S Mary Purif & S Lawrence
SK 624873   6   Blyth, SS Mary & Martin
SK 583296   6   Bunny, S Mary Virgin
SK 618491   4   Calverton, S Wilfrid
SK 721430   4   Car Colston, S Mary
SK 618426   8   Carlton, All Hallows, Gedling
SK 726884   6   Clayworth, S Peter
SK 541348   6   Clifton, S Mary Virgin
SK 835545   6   Coddington, All Saints
SK 700333   8   Colston Bassett, S John Divine
SK 647353   8   Cotgrave, All Saints
SK 685355   6   Cropwell Bishop, S Giles
SK 567714   6   Cuckney, S Mary
SK 815745   5   Dunham on Trent, S Oswald
SK 691431   6   East Bridgford, S Peter
SK 776753   6   East Drayton, S Peter
SK 552262   6   East Leake, S Mary Virgin
SK 743726   8   East Markham, S John Baptist
SK 707813   10   East Retford, S Swithun
SK 748501   4   East Stoke, S Oswald
SK 465468   8   Eastwood, S Mary
SK 625669   6   Edwinstowe, S Mary
SK 759480   6   Elston, All Saints
SK 691913   6   Everton, Holy Trinity
SK 768518   4   Farndon, S Peter
SK 646565   6   Farnsfield, S Michael
SK 710780   6   Gamston, S Peter
SK 682474   4   Gonalston, S Laurence
SK 536301   5   Gotham, S Lawrence
SK 752361   6   Granby, All Saints
SK 489472   8   Greasley, S Mary
SK 738907   4   Gringley on the Hill, SS Peter & Paul
SK 738796   4   Grove, S Helen
SK 878706   5   Harby, All Saints
SK 614917   6   Harworth, All Saints
SK 789511   4   Hawton, All Saints
SK 692293   6   Hickling, S Luke
SK 626392   6   Holme Pierrepont, S Edmund
SK 533494   8   Hucknall, S Mary Magdalene
SK 502278   6   Kingston on Soar, S Winifred
SK 676307   6   Kinoulton, S Luke

SK 490559   6   Kirkby in Ashfield, S Wilfrid
SK 815765   4   Laneham, S Peter
SK 721347   5   Langar, S Andrew
SK 722670   6   Laxton, S Michael
SK 535509   4   Linby, S Michael
SK 663468   6   Lowdham, S Mary
SK 541610   8   Mansfield, SS Peter & Paul
SK 540632   6   Mansfield Woodhouse, S Edmund K&M
SK 691949   6   Misson, S John Baptist
SK 799539   10   Newark on Trent, S Mary Magdalene
SK 518229   4   Normanton on Soar, S James
SK 830620   6   North Collingham, All Saints
SK 798587   6   North Muskham, S Wilfrid
SK 762859   6   North Wheatley, SS Peter & Paul
SK 775618   6   Norwell, S Lawrence
SK 564406   8   Nottingham, All Saints
SK 576397   12   Nottingham, S Mary Virgin
SK 573398   12   Nottingham, S Peter
SK 541417   8   Nottingham, S Margaret, Aspley
SK 553427   8   Nottingham, S Leodegarius, Basford
SK 542450   8   Nottingham, S Mary Virgin, Bulwell
SK 554393   8   Nottingham, Sacred & Undivided Trinity, Lenton
SK 525399   6   Nottingham, S Leonard, Wollaton
SK 514445   6   Nuthall, S Patrick
SK 704797   6   Ordsall, All Hallows
SK 769411   6   Orston, S Mary
SK 759651   6   Ossington, Holy Rood
SK 630514   6   Oxton, SS Peter & Paul
SK 645392   8   Radcliffe on Trent, S Mary
SK 799786   6   Rampton, All Saints
SK 575245   6   Rempstone, All Saints
SK 742525   4   Rolleston, Holy Trinity
SK 572331   8   Ruddington, S Peter
SK 785880   5   Saundby, Dedication unknown
SK 628804   8   Scofton, S John
SK 458533   8   Selston, S Helen
SK 662424   5   Shelford, SS Peter & Paul
SK 554809   6   Shireoaks, S Luke Evangelist
SK 764454   4   Sibthorpe, S Peter
SK 826614   5   South Collingham, S John Baptist
SK 848641   5   South Scarle, S Helen
SK 702538   12(1)   Southwell, Cathedral & Collegiate Church of BVM
SK 543221   8   Stanford on Soar, S John Baptist
SK 488374   6   Stapleford, S Helen
SK 805433   5   Staunton in the Vale, S Mary
SK 788838   6   Sturton le Steeple, SS Peter & Paul
SK 681850   5   Sutton, S Bartholomew
SK 504254   6   Sutton Bonington, S Michael
SK 489589   8   Sutton in Ashfield, S Mary Magdalene
SK 800660   8   Sutton on Trent, All Saints
SK 483619   5   Teversal, S Catherine
SK 510312   6   Thrumpton, All Saints
SK 484397   6   Trowell, S Helen
SK 737711   8   Tuxford, S Nicholas
SK 683263   5   Upper Broughton, S Luke
SK 737543   4   Upton, SS Peter & Paul
SK 568688   8   Warsop, SS Peter & Paul
SK 586376   8   West Bridgford, S Giles
SK 566378   5   West Bridgford, S Wilfrid, Wilford
SK 702813   6   West Retford, S Michael Archangel
SK 745396   8   Whatton, S John of Beverley
SK 634254   6   Willoughby on the Wolds, S Mary & All Saints
SK 812564   6   Winthorpe, All Saints & Blessed Virgin Mary
SK 631477   5   Woodborough, S Swithun
SK 590789   8   Worksop, Priory Church of SS Mary & Cuthbert
SK 579788   10   Worksop, S Anne

Oxfordshire

SU 497967	10	Abingdon, S Helen
SU 498978	6	Abingdon, S Nicholas
SP 471354	8	Adderbury, S Mary Virgin
SU 378429	4	Alkerton, S Michael & All Angels
SP 273046	6	Alvescot, S Peter
SP 603194	8	Ambrosden, S Mary Virgin
SU 531938	6	Appleford, SS Peter & Paul
SP 444015	10	Appleton, S Laurence
SU 432883	6	Ardington, Holy Trinity
SP 301186	6	Ascott under Wychwood, Holy Trinity
SU 265849	6	Ashbury, Blessed Virgin Mary
SP 342031	6	Aston, S James
SU 727990	6	Aston Rowant, SS Peter & Paul
SU 557861	6	Aston Tirrold, S Michael
SP 312034	8	Bampton, S Mary Virgin
SP 454405	10	Banbury, S Mary
SP 562113	5	Beckley, Assumption SMV
SU 614917	8	Benson, S Helen
SU 623943	6	Berrick Salome, S Helen
SP 583223	8	Bicester, S Edburg
SP 286043	5	Black Bourton, S Mary Virgin
SP 449148	6	Bladon, S Martin
SP 506180	5	Bletchingdon, S Giles
SU 532859	8	Blewbury, S Michael & All Angels
SP 430356	8	Bloxham, Our Lady of Bloxham
SP 460376	8	Bodicote, S John Baptist
SU 577908	8	Brightwell, S Agatha
SU 653950	6	Brightwell Baldwin, S Bartholomew
SP 299076	6	Brize Norton, S Britius
SP 252042	5	Broadwell, SS Peter & Paul
SU 343983	8	Buckland, S Mary Virgin
SP 253124	8	Burford, S John Baptist
SP 455106	6	Cassington, S Peter
SP 581253	5	Caversfield, S Lawrence
SP 334219	6	Chadlington, S Nicholas
SU 637965	6	Chalgrove, S Mary Virgin
SP 356194	6	Charlbury, S Mary
SP 562158	5	Charlton on Otmoor, S Mary Virgin
SP 249291	6	Chastleton, S Mary Virgin
SU 663831	8	Checkendon, SS Peter & Paul
SU 360877	6	Childrey, S Mary
SU 489859	6	Chilton, All Saints
SP 757008	6	Chinnor, S Andrew
SP 312273	8	Chipping Norton, S Mary Virgin
SU 583870	8	Cholsey, S Mary
SP 380251	6	Church Enstone, S Kenelm
SP 426128	6	Church Hanborough, SS Peter & Paul
SP 283241	8	Churchill, All Saints
SP 283022	8	Clanfield, S Stephen
SU 235938	6	Coleshill, All Saints
SP 414158	6	Combe, S Laurence Martyr
SP 469466	6	Cropredy, S Mary Virgin
SP 601031	6	Cuddesdon, All Saints
SU 502950	6	Culham, S Paul
SP 462042	8	Cumnor, S Michael
SP 468316	8	Deddington, SS Peter & Paul
SU 382918	4	Denchworth, S James
SU 579943	8	Dorchester, Abbey Church of SS Peter & Paul
SU 480942	8	Drayton, S Peter
SU 595963	6	Drayton St Leonard, S Leonard
SP 358076	6	Ducklington, S Bartholomew
SP 457284	5	Duns Tew, S Mary Magdalene
SU 525882	8	East Hagbourne, S Andrew
SU 459886	6	East Hendred, S Augustine
SU 646914	6	Ewelme, S Mary Virgin
SP 433092	6	Eynsham, S Leonard
SU 288957	8	Faringdon, All Saints
SP 414126	6	Freeland, S Mary Virgin
SP 525294	4	Fritwell, S Olave
SP 581020	6	Garsington, S Mary
SU 597807	8	Goring, S Thomas of Canterbury
SU 270934	5	Great Coxwell, S Giles
SP 644017	6	Great Haseley, S Peter
SP 628024	8	Great Milton, S Mary Virgin
SP 327314	6	Great Rollright, S Andrew
SP 399288	8	Great Tew, S Michael & All Angels
SP 435435	5	Hanwell, S Peter
SU 493890	8	Harwell, S Matthew
SU 762827	8	Henley on Thames, S Mary Virgin
SU 375991	6	Hinton Waldrist, S Margaret
SP 354331	8	Hook Norton, S Peter
SP 417439	4	Horley, S Etheldreda
SP 392450	5	Hornton, S John Baptist
SP 572048	6	Horspath, S Giles
SP 526140	8	Islip, S Nicholas
SP 497148	8	Kidlington, S Mary Virgin
SP 258237	8	Kingham, S Andrew
SP 500195	8	Kirtlington, S Mary Virgin
SP 249025	6	Langford, S Matthew
SP 604228	6	Launton, S Mary Virgin Assumption
SP 319153	6	Leafield, S Michael & All Angels
SU 380865	6	Letcombe Regis, S Andrew
SU 716976	6	Lewknor, S Margaret
SP 617007	6	Little Milton, S James
SU 566935	5	Little Wittenham, S Peter
SU 428872	4	Lockinge, All Saints
SU 264907	6	Longcot, S Mary Virgin
SU 548942	6	Long Wittenham, S Mary Virgin
SU 384994	5	Longworth, S Mary
SP 485248	6	Lower Heyford, S Mary
SU 670766	6	Mapledurham, S Margaret
SU 452968	6	Marcham, All Saints
SU 562991	5	Marsh Baldon, S Peter
SP 531232	6	Middleton Stoney, All Saints
SP 451350	6	Milton, S Blaise
SP 442475	6	Mollington, All Saints
SU 698867	6	Nettlebed, S Bartholomew
SU 609966	4	Newington, S Giles
SP 481288	6	North Aston, S Mary
SP 387136	6	North Leigh, S Mary
SP 421029	6	Northmoor, S Denys
SU 562895	5	North Moreton, All Saints
SP 513062	6	Oxford, Carfax Tower
SP 515059	12	Oxford, Cathedral Church of Christ
SP 515062	8	Oxford, Lincoln College
SP 521061	10	Oxford, Magdalen College
SP 517061	8	Oxford, Merton College
SP 517064	10	Oxford, New College
SP 514060	6	Oxford, S Aldate
SP 520066	6	Oxford, S Cross or Holywell
SP 512060	8	Oxford, S Ebbe
SP 511069	8	Oxford, S Giles
SP 512064	8	Oxford, S Mary Magdalene
SP 516063	6	Oxford, S Mary Virgin (University Church)
SP 506061	6	Oxford, S Thomas Martyr
SP 545043	6	Oxford, S James, Cowley
SP 544076	8	Oxford, S Andrew, Headington
SP 527034	6	Oxford, S Mary Virgin, Iffley
SP 527089	6	Oxford, S Nicholas, Marston
SP 495055	6	Oxford, S Laurence, North Hinksey
SP 497098	6	Oxford, S Peter, Wolvercote
SP 640169	5	Piddington, S Nicholas
SU 522994	6	Radley, S James Great

SP 480241	6	Rousham, SS Leonard & James
SP 286280	5	Salford, S Mary Virgin
SP 420266	6	Sandford St Martin, S Martin
SU 319936	4	Shellingford, S Faith
SP 373428	5	Shenington, Holy Trinity
SU 767782	8	Shiplake, SS Peter & Paul
SP 280180	8	Shipton under Wychwood, S Mary Virgin
SU 241891	8	Shrivenham, S Andrew
SP 497286	6	Somerton, S James
SP 523317	6	Souldern, S Mary Virgin
SP 394090	8	South Leigh, S James Great
SP 407333	5	South Newington, S Peter ad Vincula
SU 599836	6	South Stoke, S Andrew
SU 347876	4	Sparsholt, Holy Rood
SP 349215	6	Spelsbury, All Saints
SU 604988	4	Stadhampton, S John Baptist
SP 397036	6	Standlake, S Giles
SU 342935	8	Stanford in the Vale, S Denys
SP 417056	6	Stanton Harcourt, S Michael
SP 577079	5	Stanton St John, S John Baptist
SP 476260	8	Steeple Aston, SS Peter & Paul
SP 448248	5	Steeple Barton, S Mary
SU 464914	6	Steventon, S Michael & All Angels
SP 393170	6	Stonesfield, S James Great
SP 608260	5	Stratton Audley, SS Mary & Edburga
SP 495005	6	Sunningwell, S Leonard
SU 504942	8	Sutton Courtenay, All Saints
SP 378378	6	Swalcliffe, SS Peter & Paul
SP 372311	5	Swerford, S Mary
SP 476201	6	Tackley, S Nicholas
SP 392378	6	Tadmarton, S Nicholas
SP 234135	6	Taynton, S John Evangelist
SP 686015	6	Tetsworth, S Giles
SP 704063	8	Thame, S Mary Virgin
SP 735052	4	Towersey, S Catherine
SU 303894	5	Uffington, S Mary
SU 607893	8	Wallingford, S Mary le More
SU 397879	8	Wantage, SS Peter & Paul
SU 599936	8	Warborough, S Laurence
SP 491463	6	Wardington, S Mary Magdalene
SU 684947	8	Watlington, S Leonard
SU 407927	6	West Hanney, S James Great
SU 447883	6	West Hendred, Holy Trinity
SP 531186	5	Weston on the Green, Blessed Virgin Mary
SP 597058	6	Wheatley, S Mary
SU 635769	6	Whitchurch, S Mary Virgin
SP 356092	8	Witney, S Mary Virgin
SP 535118	5	Woodeaton, Holy Rood
SP 444166	8	Woodstock, S Mary Magdalene
SP 439199	6	Wootton, S Mary
SP 418418	5	Wroxton, All Saints
SP 477116	6	Yarnton, S Bartholomew

Shropshire

SJ 533019	4	Acton Burnell, S Mary
SJ 358144	5	Alberbury, S Michael & All Angels
SJ 809044	6	Albrighton, S Mary Magdalene
SO 759845	6	Alveley, S Mary Virgin
SJ 541092	6	Atcham, S Eata
SJ 422219	4	Baschurch, All Saints
SJ 530069	8	Berrington, All Saints
SJ 447148	6	Bicton, Holy Trinity
SO 323884	6	Bishop's Castle, S John Baptist
SO 597963	4	Bourton, Holy Trinity
SO 717933	8	Bridgnorth, S Leonard
SO 717928	8	Bridgnorth, S Mary Magdalene

SO 482768	6	Bromfield, S Mary Virgin
SJ 678015	8	Broseley, All Saints
SJ 603372	6	Calverhall, Holy Trinity
SO 506951	4	Cardington, S James
SO 721878	6	Chelmarsh, S Peter
SJ 719299	8	Cheswardine, S Swithun
SO 664903	6	Chetton, S Giles
SJ 736213	6	Chetwynd, S Michael & All Angels
SO 261985	6	Chirbury, S Michael & All Angels
SJ 429029	6	Church Pulverbatch, S Edith
SO 452936	8	Church Stretton, S Lawrence
SO 792934	8	Claverley, All Saints
SO 674757	6	Cleobury Mortimer, S Mary Virgin
SJ 514240	6	Clive, All Saints
SO 300804	8	Clun, S George
SO 371806	6	Clunbury, S Swithin
SJ 670044	10	Coalbrookdale, Holy Trinity
SJ 494057	8	Condover, S Andrew
SJ 558049	6	Cound, S Peter
SO 509853	4	Diddlebury, S Peter
SO 608892	4	Ditton Priors, S John Baptist
SJ 720193	8	Edgmond, S Peter
SJ 403347	8	Ellesmere, Blessed Virgin
SJ 397190	6	Great Ness, S Andrew
SJ 594174	8	High Ercall, S Michael & All Angels
SO 741832	6	Highley, S Mary
SJ 694264	6	Hinstock, S Oswald
SJ 613286	8	Hodnet, S Luke
SO 475924	6	Hope Bowdler, S Andrew
SO 564979	4	Hughley, S John Baptist
SJ 593387	6	Ightfield, S John Baptist
SJ 729045	4	Kemberton, S Andrew
SO 711810	6	Kinlet, S John Baptist
SJ 469183	5	Leaton, Holy Trinity
SJ 729153	6	Lilleshall, S Michael & All Angels
SJ 647068	5	Little Wenlock, S Lawrence
SO 512747	8	Ludlow, S Laurence
SO 353860	6	Lydbury North, S Michael & All Angels
SJ 676341	8	Market Drayton, S Mary
SJ 486105	8	Meole Brace, Holy Trinity
SJ 418147	6	Montford, S Chad
SJ 561232	6	Moreton Corbet, S Bartholomew
SO 669939	6	Morville, S Gregory Great
SJ 623000	8	Much Wenlock, Holy Trinity
SO 521878	4	Munslow, S Michael
SJ 745192	8	Newport, S Nicholas
SJ 703387	8	Norton in Hales, S Chad
SO 455791	4	Onibury, S Michael
SJ 288293	8	Oswestry, S Oswald
SJ 399061	6	Pontesbury, S George
SJ 557335	6	Prees, S Chad
SO 756882	6	Quatt, S Andrew
SO 514918	6	Rushbury, S Peter
SJ 394222	6	Ruyton XI Towns, S John Baptist
SJ 760028	6	Ryton, S Andrew
SJ 327368	6	St Martin's, S Martin
SJ 266340	5	Selattyn, S Mary
SJ 558211	6	Shawbury, S Mary Virgin
SJ 758120	6	Sheriffhales, S Mary
SJ 747075	8	Shifnal, S Andrew
SJ 488124	12(1)	Shrewsbury, S Chad
SJ 492126	10	Shrewsbury, S Mary Virgin
SO 495788	6	Stanton Lacy, S Peter
SJ 568238	6	Stanton upon Hine Heath, S Andrew
SO 729997	6	Stockton, S Chad
SJ 638280	6	Stoke on Tern, S Peter
SO 567822	4	Stoke St Milborough, S Milbruga

SO 436817	6	Stokesay, S John Baptist
SO 673829	4	Stottesdon, S Mary
SJ 719014	5	Sutton Maddock, S Mary
SJ 687065	6	Telford, Holy Trinity, Dawley
SJ 696041	8	Telford, S Michael, Madeley
SJ 689081	6	Telford, S Leonard, Malins Lee
SJ 682204	5	Tibberton, All Saints
SJ 796074	6	Tong, S Bartholomew
SO 557870	5	Tugford, S Catherine
SJ 597093	6	Uppington, Holy Trinity
SJ 553124	5	Upton Magna, S Lucia
SJ 651117	8	Wellington, All Saints
SJ 512288	8	Wem, SS Peter & Paul
SJ 355094	6	Westbury, S Mary
SJ 541418	8	Whitchurch, S Alkmund
SJ 326313	6	Whittington, S John Baptist
SO 672992	5	Willey, S John Divine
SO 432856	8	Wistanstow, Holy Trinity
SO 758958	6	Worfield, S Peter Apostle
SJ 328046	6	Worthen, All Saints
SJ 624121	6	Wrockwardine, S Peter
SJ 563082	6	Wroxeter, S Andrew

Somerset

ST 199187	5	Angersleigh, S Michael & All Angels
ST 638329	4	Ansford, S Andrew
ST 472207	6	Ash, Holy Trinity
ST 052213	6	Ashbrittle, S John Baptist
ST 437371	6	Ashcott, All Saints
ST 321173	5	Ashill, Blessed Virgin Mary
ST 151294	6	Ash Priors, Holy Trinity
ST 637484	6	Ashwick, S James
ST 431546	6	Axbridge, S John Baptist
ST 561287	6	Babcary, Holy Cross
ST 395526	5	Badgworth, S Congar
ST 542348	6	Baltonsborough, S Dunstan
ST 389181	6	Barrington, S Mary Virgin
ST 540317	6	Barton St David, S David
ST 689390	6	Batcombe, S Mary BV
ST 079241	4	Bathealton, S Bartholomew
ST 342396	4	Bawdrip, S Michael
ST 802516	8	Beckington, S George
ST 325204	4	Beer Crocombe, S James
ST 811494	4	Berkley, Blessed Virgin Mary
ST 293524	6	Berrow, S Mary Magdalene
ST 111394	4	Bicknoller, S George
ST 382535	4	Biddisham, S John Baptist
ST 615494	6	Binegar, Holy Trinity
ST 205247	6	Bishop's Hull, SS Peter & Paul
ST 168297	8	Bishop's Lydeard, S Mary Virgin
ST 173230	6	Bradford on Tone, S Giles
ST 335507	6	Brent Knoll, S Michael
ST 297370	8	Bridgwater, S Mary
ST 330159	6	Broadway, SS Aldhelm & Eadburga
ST 085323	4	Brompton Ralph, Blessed Virgin Mary
SS 951314	6	Brompton Regis, S Mary Virgin
ST 224320	5	Broomfield, All Saints
SS 919257	6	Brushford, S Nicholas
ST 685347	6	Bruton, S Mary Virgin
ST 755513	6	Buckland Dinham, S Michael & All Angels
ST 271134	6	Buckland St Mary, S Mary Virgin
ST 304494	8	Burnham on Sea, S Andrew
ST 520339	6	Butleigh, S Leonard
ST 257395	6	Cannington, S Mary Virgin
ST 009426	6	Carhampton, S John Baptist
ST 639320	8	Castle Cary, All Saints

ST 354102	6	Chaffcombe, S Michael & All Angels
ST 323082	8	Chard, S Mary Virgin
ST 535286	5	Charlton Adam, SS Peter & Paul
ST 665230	8	Charlton Horethorne, SS Peter & Paul
ST 528283	6	Charlton Mackrell, S Mary Virgin
ST 459530	8	Cheddar, S Andrew
ST 243276	5	Cheddon Fitzpaine, S Mary Virgin
ST 341377	6	Chedzoy, S Mary Virgin
ST 596531	8	Chewton Mendip, S Mary Magdalene
ST 647524	6	Chilcompton, S John Baptist
ST 570222	5	Chilton Cantelo, S James Great
ST 296392	5	Chilton Trinity, Holy Trinity
ST 042271	6	Chipstable, All Saints
ST 467149	5	Chiselborough, SS Peter & Paul
ST 195146	6	Churchstanton, SS Peter & Paul
ST 052309	4	Clatworthy, S Mary Magdalene
ST 563101	5	Closworth, All Saints
ST 150312	6	Combe Florey, SS Peter & Paul
ST 301112	6	Combe St Nicholas, S Nicholas
ST 396554	6	Compton Bishop, S Andrew
ST 232197	6	Corfe, S Nicholas
ST 636226	5	Corton Denham, S Andrew
ST 356403	6	Cossington, S Mary Virgin
ST 181318	6	Cothelstone, S Thomas of Canterbury
ST 275253	6	Creech St Michael, S Michael
ST 439098	8	Crewkerne, S Bartholomew
ST 361115	5	Cricket Malherbie, S Mary Magdalene
ST 591444	6	Croscombe, S Mary Virgin
ST 141367	6	Crowcombe, Holy Ghost
ST 755278	6	Cucklington, S Lawrence
ST 333209	6	Curry Mallet, All Saints
ST 391254	8	Curry Rivel, S Andrew
SS 931392	6	Cutcombe, S John Evangelist
ST 575446	6	Dinder, S Michael & All Angels
ST 625363	8	Ditcheat, S Mary Magdalene
ST 172405	4	Dodington, All Saints
ST 339141	4	Donyatt, Blessed Virgin Mary
ST 646431	6	Doulting, S Aldhelm
ST 375130	5	Dowlish Wake, S Andrew
ST 405248	8	Drayton, S Catherine
SS 914280	8	Dulverton, All Saints
SS 990436	8	Dunster, S George
ST 275361	6	Durleigh, dedication unknown
ST 291281	6	Durston, S John Baptist
ST 344519	6	East Brent, S Mary BV
ST 499132	5	East Chinnock, S Mary
ST 538122	8	East Coker, S Michael & All Angels
ST 597375	5	East Pennard, All Saints
ST 137437	4	East Quantoxhead, Blessed Virgin Mary
ST 083350	4	Elworthy, S Martin
ST 239352	6	Enmore, S Michael
ST 649387	10	Evercreech, S Peter
SS 857385	6	Exford, S Mary Magdalene
SS 925337	6	Exton, SS Peter & Paul
ST 799575	4	Farleigh Hungerford, S Leonard
ST 215406	6	Fiddington, S Martin
ST 119284	6	Fitzhead, S James
ST 353229	6	Fivehead, S Martin
ST 777479	8	Frome, S John Baptist
ST 498388	6	Glastonbury, S Benedict
ST 499390	8	Glastonbury, S John Baptist
ST 256343	6	Goathurst, S Edward K&M
ST 412364	6	Greinton, S Michael & All Angels
ST 140277	6	Halse, S James
ST 512119	8	Hardington Mandeville, S Mary
ST 471109	6	Haselbury Plucknett, S Michael & All Angels
ST 306211	5	Hatch Beauchamp, S John Baptist

SS	861306	6	Hawkridge, S Giles		
ST	160265	5	Heathfield, S John Baptist		
ST	727530	6	Hemington, Blessed Virgin Mary		
ST	723197	6	Henstridge, S Nicholas		
ST	319474	6	Highbridge, S John Evangelist		
ST	425311	5	High Ham, S Andrew		
ST	167246	6	Hillfarrance, Holy Cross		
ST	418127	6	Hinton St George, S George		
ST	157411	5	Holford, S Mary Virgin		
ST	704237	6	Horsington, S John Baptist		
ST	049292	6	Huish Champflower, S Peter		
ST	427266	8	Huish Episcopi, S Mary Virgin		
ST	304454	6	Huntspill, S Peter		
ST	522226	5	Ilchester, S Mary Virgin		
ST	360146	8	Ilminster, S Mary Virgin		
ST	352174	6	Ilton, S Peter		
ST	353209	5	Isle Abbots, S Mary Virgin		
ST	369211	4	Isle Brewers, All Saints		
ST	696524	6	Kilmersdon, SS Peter & Paul		
ST	166441	4	Kilton, S Nicholas		
ST	436211	6	Kingsbury Episcopi, S Martin		
ST	515262	6	Kingsdon, All Saints		
ST	378137	6	Kingstone, S John & All Saints		
ST	223297	6	Kingston St Mary, S Mary Virgin		
ST	525313	5	Kingweston, All Saints		
ST	078223	4	Kittisford, S Nicholas		
ST	111229	6	Langford Budville, S Peter		
ST	422267	6	Langport, All Saints		
ST	692473	6	Leigh upon Mendip, S Giles		
ST	541223	6	Limington, S Mary Virgin		
ST	594547	6	Litton, S Mary Virgin		
ST	469253	6	Long Sutton, Holy Trinity		
SS	910445	6	Luccombe, S Mary Virgin		
SS	974380	5	Luxborough, S Mary Virgin		
ST	128321	6	Lydeard St Lawrence, S Lawrence		
ST	335542	6	Lympsham, S Christopher		
ST	333289	6	Lyng, S Bartholomew		
ST	672261	6	Maperton, SS Peter & Paul		
ST	381478	8	Mark, Holy Cross		
ST	755450	6	Marston Bigott, S Leonard		
ST	593223	6	Marston Magna, Blessed Virgin Mary		
ST	461192	8	Martock, All Saints		
ST	455417	6	Meare, Blessed Virgin Mary & All Saints		
ST	727492	8	Mells, S Andrew		
ST	442129	6	Merriott, All Saints		
ST	375331	6	Middlezoy, Holy Cross		
ST	676185	8	Milborne Port, S John Evangelist		
ST	664378	5	Milton Clevedon, S James Apostle		
ST	121259	8	Milverton, S Michael & All Angels		
SS	966468	10	Minehead, S Michael & S Andrew		
ST	073374	5	Monksilver, All Saints		
ST	496169	6	Montacute, S Catherine		
ST	398369	6	Moorlinch, S Mary Virgin		
ST	429249	5	Muchelney, SS Peter & Paul		
ST	573199	5	Mudford, S Mary Virgin		
ST	197396	6	Nether Stowey, S Mary Virgin		
ST	608294	5	North Barrow, S Nicholas		
ST	635270	6	North Cadbury, S Michael		
ST	687258	5	North Cheriton, S John Baptist		
ST	319256	8	North Curry, SS Peter & Paul		
ST	524231	4	Northover, S Andrew		
ST	472095	6	North Perrott, S Martin		
ST	290330	6	North Petherton, S Mary Virgin		
ST	197260	6	Norton Fitzwarren, All Saints		
ST	772557	6	Norton St Philip, SS Philip & James		
ST	470160	6	Norton sub Hamdon, S Mary Virgin		
ST	737457	6	Nunney, All Saints		

ST	138227	6	Nynehead, All Saints
ST	152252	5	Oake, S Bartholomew
ST	507155	6	Odcombe, SS Peter & Paul
ST	041419	8	Old Cleeve, S Andrew
ST	243217	4	Orchard Portman, S Michael
ST	382316	5	Othery, S Michael
ST	222142	4	Otterford, S Leonard
ST	247432	4	Otterhampton, All Saints
ST	186385	6	Over Stowey, SS Peter & Paul
ST	301426	6	Pawlett, S John Baptist
ST	756314	6	Penselwood, S Michael
ST	589408	6	Pilton, S John Baptist
ST	220191	8	Pitminster, SS Andrew & Mary
ST	444285	5	Pitney, S John Baptist
SS	886466	6	Porlock, S Dubricius
ST	534162	6	Preston Plucknett, S James
ST	377183	6	Puckington, S Andrew
ST	320417	6	Puriton, S Michael & All Angels
ST	607383	6	Pylle, S Thomas of Canterbury
ST	597249	6	Queen Camel, S Barnabas
ST	126200	6	Rockwell Green, All Saints
ST	808534	6	Rode, S Lawrence
ST	482498	4	Rodney Stoke, S Leonard
ST	449586	6	Rowberrow, S Michael
ST	264251	6	Ruishton, S George
ST	065427	6	St Decuman's, S Decuman
ST	107189	6	Sampford Arundel, Holy Cross
ST	089402	6	Sampford Brett, S George
ST	403149	6	Seavington St Mary, S Mary
SS	920468	6	Selworthy, All Saints
ST	418382	6	Shapwick, S Mary Virgin
ST	403172	8	Shepton Beauchamp, S Michael
ST	620436	8	Shepton Mallet, SS Peter & Paul
ST	443574	6	Shipham, S Leonard
SS	986272	5	Skilgate, S John Baptist
ST	490286	8	Somerton, S Michael & All Angels
ST	631255	6	South Cadbury, S Thomas a' Becket
ST	432168	8	South Petherton, SS Peter & Paul
ST	225370	6	Spaxton, S Margaret
ST	263182	6	Staple Fitzpaine, S Peter
ST	212264	6	Staplegrove, S John
ST	060226	5	Stawley, S Michael
ST	240436	6	Stockland Bristol, S Mary Magdalene
ST	098373	6	Stogumber, S Mary Virgin
ST	205428	6	Stogursey, S Andrew
ST	348271	5	Stoke St Gregory, S Gregory
ST	266223	5	Stoke St Mary, S Mary
ST	484173	6	Stoke sub Hambdon, S Mary Virgin
ST	736288	6	Stoke Trister, S Andrew
ST	624535	6	Ston Easton, S Mary
ST	488372	8	Street, Holy Trinity
ST	235244	6	Taunton, Holy Trinity
ST	228249	8	Taunton, S James
ST	229246	12	Taunton, S Mary Magdalene
ST	228255	10	Taunton, Unit 7, Potters Yard, Railway Street
ST	224239	10	Taunton, S George, Wilton
ST	708227	6	Templecombe, S Mary Virgin
ST	283239	5	Thornfalcon, Holy Cross
ST	266211	4	Thurlbear, S Thomas
ST	274304	5	Thurloxton, S Giles
SS	956420	8	Timberscombe, S Petrock
ST	498197	5	Tintinhull, S Margaret
ST	216222	6	Trull, All Saints
ST	461363	5	Walton, Holy Trinity
ST	294077	5	Wambrook, S Mary Virgin
ST	709417	6	Wanstrow, S Mary Virgin
ST	414527	6	Weare, S Gregory

ST	434479	8	Wedmore, S Mary
ST	140209	8	Wellington, S John Baptist
ST	552459	10	Wells, Cathedral Church of S Andrew
ST	547456	8	Wells, S Cuthbert
ST	289380	6	Wembdon, S George
ST	168337	6	West Bagborough, S Pancras
ST	173205	6	West Buckland, Blessed Virgin Mary & Holy Trinity
ST	499487	6	Westbury sub Mendip, S Lawrence
ST	580246	6	West Camel, All Saints
ST	467134	4	West Chinnock, Blessed Virgin Mary
ST	516136	8	West Coker, S Martin of Tours
ST	668433	5	West Cranmore, S Bartholomew
ST	285210	5	West Hatch, S Andrew
ST	565319	6	West Lydford, S Peter
ST	263285	8	West Monkton, S Augustine
ST	352348	6	Weston Zoyland, S Mary Virgin
ST	552383	6	West Pennard, S Nicholas
ST	113420	6	West Quantoxhead, S Audries
ST	734476	6	Whatley, S George
ST	379153	4	Whitelackington, Blessed Virgin Mary
ST	280105	5	Whitestaunton, S Andrew
ST	711284	8	Wincanton, SS Peter & Paul
SS	904350	6	Winsford, S Mary Magdalene
ST	374063	8	Winsham, S Stephen
ST	015413	4	Withycombe, S Nicholas
SS	846356	6	Withypool, S Andrew
ST	083276	8	Wiveliscombe, S Andrew
ST	518458	6	Wookey, S Matthew
ST	348416	8	Woolavington, S Mary Virgin
SS	938434	6	Wootton Courtenay, All Saints
ST	556161	10	Yeovil, S John Baptist
ST	546229	5	Yeovilton, S Bartholomew

South Yorkshire

SE	541086	6	Adwick le Street, S Lawrence
SE	579069	8	Arksey, All Saints
SE	614097	6	Barnby Dun, SS Peter & Paul
SE	344067	8	Barnsley, S Mary
SK	653930	6	Bawtry, S Nicholas
SK	442833	6	Beighton, S Mary
SE	566056	5	Bentley, S Peter
SK	271968	8	Bolsterstone, S Mary
SK	267925	6	Bradfield, S Nicholas
SE	545141	8	Campsall, S Mary Magdalene
SE	285079	6	Cawthorne, All Saints
SK	512988	8	Conisbrough, S Peter
SE	419043	8	Darfield, All Saints
SE	311099	6	Darton, All Saints
SE	574035	8	Doncaster, S George
SE	655131	6	Fishlake, S Cuthbert
SK	494810	8	Harthill, All Hallows
SE	662096	8	Hatfield, S Laurence
SE	260053	6	Hoyland Swaine, S John Evangelist
SE	364076	6	Monk Bretton, S Paul
SE	247033	8	Penistone, S John Baptist
SK	485954	6	Ravenfield, S James
SK	436959	8	Rawmarsh, S Mary
SK	429929	12	Rotherham, All Saints
SK	433932	8	Rotherham, S Stephen, Eastwood
SE	364113	8	Royston, S John Baptist
SK	354872	8	Sheffield, Cathedral Church of S Marie (RC)
SK	354875	12(1)	Sheffield, Cathedral Church of SS Peter & Paul
SK	307811	8	Sheffield, Christ Church, Dore
SK	353942	8	Sheffield, S Mary Virgin, Ecclesfield
SK	411862	8	Sheffield, S Mary, Handsworth
SK	359822	8	Sheffield, S James Great, Norton
SK	319863	10	Sheffield, S John Evangelist, Ranmoor

SK	334884	6	Sheffield, S Mary, Walkley
SE	291058	6	Silkstone, All Saints
SK	519836	8	South Anston, S James
SE	540020	8	Sprotbrough, S Mary Virgin
SE	690132	8	Thorne, S Nicholas
SK	467955	6	Thrybergh, S Leonard
SK	592931	8	Tickhill, S Mary Virgin
SK	432877	6	Treeton, S Helen
SK	569970	4	Wadworth, S John Baptist
SE	433009	8	Wath upon Dearne, All Saints
SK	384981	6	Wentworth, Holy Trinity
SK	451901	8	Whiston, S Mary Magdalene or S James
SK	307994	8	Wortley, S Leonard

Staffordshire

SK	079245	8	Abbots Bromley, S Nicholas
SJ	762279	4	Adbaston, S Michael
SK	167153	8	Alrewas, All Saints
SK	133553	6	Alstonefield, S Peter
SK	073423	8	Alton, S Peter
SJ	799509	8	Audley, S James
SJ	892383	6	Barlaston, S John Baptist
SK	187185	8	Barton under Needwood, S James
SJ	755484	6	Betley, S Margaret
SJ	890590	6	Biddulph, S Lawrence
SK	044240	6	Blithfield, S Leonard
SO	808905	4	Bobbington, Holy Cross
SJ	880180	5	Bradeley, All Saints
SJ	884087	8	Brewood, S Mary Virgin & S Chad
SJ	766337	8	Broughton, S Peter
SJ	905540	6	Brown Edge, S Anne
SK	242218	6	Burton upon Trent, All Saints
SK	251227	8	Burton upon Trent, S Modwen
SK	239234	10	Burton upon Trent, S Paul
SJ	982102	8	Cannock, S Luke
SK	008432	8	Cheadle, S Giles (RC)
SK	006433	6	Cheadle, S Giles
SJ	859286	4	Chebsey, All Saints
SK	028379	6	Checkley, S Mary & All Saints
SJ	971524	6	Cheddleton, S Edward Confessor
SJ	848176	6	Church Eaton, S Editha
SK	024358	6	Church Leigh, All Saints
SJ	866041	8	Codsall, S Nicholas
SK	047204	4	Colton, S Mary Virgin
SK	011212	6	Colwich, S Michael & All Angels
SK	101409	4	Denstone, All Saints
SJ	971433	6	Dilhorne, All Saints
SJ	981402	8	Draycott in the Moors, S Margaret
SK	192092	4	Drayton Bassett, S Peter
SJ	827291	8	Eccleshall, Holy Trinity
SK	185106	6	Elford, S Peter
SK	116434	6	Ellastone, S Peter
SO	823868	8	Enville, S Mary BV
SJ	755212	6	Forton, All Saints
SJ	820208	6	Gnosall, S Lawrence
SK	171279	8	Hanbury, S Werburgh
SJ	866205	5	Haughton, S Giles
SJ	783262	5	High Offley, S Mary Virgin
SK	124231	6	Hoar Cross, Holy Angels
SK	242252	6	Horninglow, S John Divine
SJ	942574	6	Horton, S Michael
SK	132507	5	Ilam, Holy Cross
SJ	976247	6	Ingestre, S Mary
SJ	810452	6	Keele, S John Baptist
SJ	838540	8	Kidsgrove, S Thomas
SK	122171	6	King's Bromley, All Saints
SK	013469	6	Kingsley, S Werburgh

SO 846831	8	Kinver, S Peter
SJ 873129	6	Lapley, All Saints
SJ 983566	10	Leek, S Edward Confessor
SK 115097	10	Lichfield, Cathedral Church of BVM & S Chad
SK 122102	4	Lichfield, S Chad
SK 118097	8	Lichfield, S Mary
SK 124095	6	Lichfield, S Michael, Greenhill
SK 092004	6	Little Aston, S Peter
SK 082142	5	Longdon, S James Great
SJ 773443	6	Madeley, All Saints
SK 138308	6	Marchington, S Peter
SK 082169	6	Mavesyn Ridware, S Nicholas
SK 154448	6	Mayfield, S John Baptist
SJ 725374	5	Mucklestone, S Mary
SK 149235	5	Needwood, Christ Church
SK 135254	5	Newborough, All Saints
SJ 847461	12	Newcastle under Lyme, S Giles
SJ 818467	8	Newcastle under Lyme, S Luke, Silverdale
SJ 856481	8	Newcastle under Lyme, S Margaret, Wolstanton
SJ 787236	4	Norbury, S Peter
SK 010078	6	Norton Canes, S James
SJ 801006	6	Patshull, S Mary
SO 822992	8	Pattingham, S Chad
SJ 921142	8	Penkridge, S Michael & All Angels
SK 181229	5	Rangemore, All Saints
SK 112394	8	Rocester, S Michael
SK 235277	8	Rolleston, S Mary
SK 045186	6	Rugeley, S Augustine of Canterbury
SJ 954294	5	Sandon, All Saints
SJ 882250	6	Seighford, S Chad
SJ 944066	6	Shareshill, S Mary
SK 113614	6	Sheen, S Luke
SK 110044	8	Shenstone, S John Baptist
SJ 921232	10	Stafford, S Mary
SJ 820350	5	Standon, All Saints
SJ 879452	10	Stoke on Trent, S Peter ad Vincula
SJ 905474	6	Stoke on Trent, S Mary Virgin, Bucknall
SJ 869495	6	Stoke on Trent, S John Baptist, Burslem
SJ 891444	8	Stoke on Trent, Christ Church, Fenton
SJ 883479	10	Stoke on Trent, S John Evangelist, Hanley
SJ 894514	8	Stoke on Trent, S Bartholomew, Norton-in-the-Moors
SJ 859517	8	Stoke on Trent, Christ Church, Tunstall
SJ 904338	8	Stone, S Michael
SK 003274	6	Stowe-by-Chartley, S John Baptist
SK 253264	6	Stretton, S Mary
SJ 852355	6	Swynnerton, S Mary
SK 208041	10	Tamworth, S Editha
SO 852943	6	Trysull, All Saints
SK 211291	8	Tutbury, S Mary
SK 094334	8	Uttoxeter, S Mary
SK 159084	6	Whittington, S Giles
SK 267235	6	Winshill, S Mark
SO 877932	8	Wombourn, S Benedict Biscop
SK 142190	6	Yoxall, S Peter

Suffolk

TL 892453	5	Acton, All Saints
TM 463569	8	Aldeburgh, SS Peter & Paul
TL 866712	4	Ampton, SS Peter & Paul
TM 169545	6	Ashbocking, All Saints
TL 936388	6	Assington, S Edmund K&M
TM 053672	6	Bacton, S Mary Virgin
TM 305683	5	Badingham, S John Baptist
TL 989690	5	Badwell Ash, S Mary
TL 941737	6	Bardwell, SS Peter & Paul

TM 137509	4	Barham, S Mary
TM 076536	6	Barking, S Mary
TL 712487	5	Barnardiston, All Saints
TL 871791	4	Barnham, S Mary
TL 760647	5	Barrow, All Saints
TM 397897	5	Barsham, Holy Trinity
TM 103515	6	Baylham, S Peter
TM 421905	10	Beccles, Bell Tower
TM 227663	6	Bedfield, S Nicholas
TM 372618	6	Benhall, S Mary
TL 985492	6	Bildeston, S Mary Magdalene
TM 356568	6	Blaxhall, S Peter
TM 451753	6	Blythburgh, Holy Trinity
TL 962405	8	Boxford, S Mary Virgin
TL 907600	5	Bradfield St George, S George
TM 399737	5	Bramfield, S Andrew
TM 127464	6	Bramford, S Mary
TM 435815	5	Brampton, S Peter
TM 247603	6	Brandeston, All Saints
TL 777861	6	Brandon, S Peter
TM 268530	6	Bredfield, S Andrew
TM 145764	5	Brome, S Mary
TM 338898	8	Bungay, S Mary
TL 907340	8	Bures, S Mary
TM 082756	5	Burgate, S Mary Virgin
TM 223522	6	Burgh, S Botolph
TL 857641	10	Bury St Edmunds, Cathedral Church of S James
TM 003576	6	Buxhall, S Mary
TM 329558	4	Campsea Ashe, S John Baptist
TM 382640	4	Carlton, S Peter
TM 510901	6	Carlton Colville, S Peter
TL 805465	6	Cavendish, S Mary Virgin
TM 358777	6	Chediston, S Mary
TL 789601	5	Chevington, All Saints
TL 770454	8	Clare, SS Peter & Paul
TM 221526	6	Clopton, S Mary
TM 133542	8	Coddenham, S Mary Virgin
TM 051569	4	Combs, S Mary
TM 120416	6	Copdock, S Peter
TM 070669	8	Cotton, S Andrew
TM 523818	5	Covehithe, S Andrew
TL 718550	5	Cowlinge, S Margaret
TM 313747	6	Cratfield, S Mary
TM 226606	5	Cretingham, S Peter
TL 725625	5	Dalham, S Mary
TM 421690	4	Darsham, All Saints
TM 174632	8	Debenham, S Mary Magdalene
TM 282669	6	Dennington, S Mary
TL 960616	6	Drinkstone, All Saints
TM 236663	6	Earl Soham, S Andrew
TM 108589	5	Earl Stonham, S Mary Virgin
TM 070345	5	East Bergholt, S Mary Virgin
TM 283587	6	Easton, All Saints
TL 940421	6	Edwardstone, S Mary Virgin
TL 982636	5	Elmswell, S John
TL 823799	8	Elveden, Memorial Tower of SS Patrick & Andrew
TL 723780	5	Eriswell, S Peter
TL 901785	6	Euston, S Genevieve
TL 621655	6	Exning, S Martin
TM 148737	8	Eye, SS Peter & Paul
TM 293391	4	Falkenham, S Ethelbert
TL 947570	6	Felsham, S Peter
TL 837677	5	Fornham All Saints, All Saints
TL 852669	6	Fornham St Martin, S Martin
TM 285635	8	Framlingham, S Michael
TM 200597	8	Framsden, S Mary
TL 665718	5	Freckenham, S Andrew

TM 261775	8	Fressingfield, SS Peter & Paul
TL 719642	6	Gazeley, All Saints
TM 077718	6	Gislingham, S Mary
TL 835484	6	Glemsford, S Mary Virgin
TL 996678	5	Great Ashfield, All Saints
TL 890660	6	Great Barton, Holy Innocents
TM 014580	6	Great Finborough, S Andrew
TM 339616	5	Great Glemham, All Saints
TL 885714	5	Great Livermere, S Peter
TL 681504	6	Great Thurlow, All Saints
TL 912440	6	Great Waldingfield, S Lawrence
TM 223511	12	Grundisburgh, S Mary Virgin
TM 025425	8	Hadleigh, S Mary Virgin
TM 386774	8	Halesworth, S Mary
TM 194353	6	Harkstead, S Mary
TL 834524	6	Hartest, All Saints
TM 250503	6	Hasketon, S Andrew
TM 026624	5	Haughley, S Mary
TL 672455	6	Haverhill, S Mary Virgin
TL 798530	5	Hawkedon, S Mary
TM 191576	8	Helmingham, S Mary
TM 158513	8	Henley, S Peter
TL 987749	5	Hepworth, S Peter
TL 937619	5	Hessett, S Ethelbert K&M of Kent
TM 333725	5	Heveningham, S Margaret
TM 036352	6	Higham, S Mary
TM 027769	6	Hinderclay, S Mary
TM 088435	6	Hintlesham, S Nicholas
TL 985515	6	Hitcham, All Saints
TM 171361	6	Holbrook, All Saints
TM 353443	8	Hollesley, All Saints
TL 994790	6	Hopton, All Saints
TM 210724	8	Horham, S Mary
TL 825620	8	Horringer, S Leonard
TM 181775	5	Hoxne, SS Peter & Paul
TL 976680	5	Hunston, S Michael
TM 336743	6	Huntingfield, S Mary
TM 412567	4	Iken, S Botolph
TL 855706	5	Ingham, S Bartholomew
TM 168442	6	Ipswich, S Clement
TM 163446	5	Ipswich, S Lawrence
TM 166448	8	Ipswich, S Margaret
TM 160445	5	Ipswich, S Mary at the Elms
TM 165440	6	Ipswich, S Mary at the Quay
TM 164446	12(1)	Ipswich, S Mary le Tower
TM 158447	6	Ipswich, S Matthew
TM 161442	5	Ipswich, S Nicholas
TL 931704	6	Ixworth, S Mary Virgin
TL 705470	6	Kedington, SS Peter & Paul
TM 386652	8	Kelsale, S Mary
TM 002420	8	Kersey, S Mary
TM 527862	6	Kessingland, S Edmund
TL 714828	6	Lakenheath, S Mary
TL 913490	8	Lavenham, SS Peter & Paul
TL 864542	5	Lawshall, All Saints
TM 296724	6	Laxfield, All Saints
TM 438625	8	Leiston, S Margaret
TL 902391	5	Little Cornard, All Saints
TM 346586	5	Little Glemham, S Andrew
TM 112601	5	Little Stonham, S Mary Virgin
TL 924451	5	Little Waldingfield, S Lawrence
TL 865468	8	Long Melford, Holy Trinity
TM 541942	8	Lowestoft, S Margaret
TM 538905	8	Lowestoft, All Saints & S Margaret, Pakefield
TL 990781	5	Market Weston, S Mary
TM 323583	6	Marlesford, S Andrew
TM 269829	6	Mendham, All Saints
TM 106658	6	Mendlesham, S Mary
TM 362900	4	Mettingham, All Saints
TM 430677	5	Middleton, Holy Trinity
TL 710746	10	Mildenhall, S Mary
TM 238585	6	Monewden, S Mary
TL 966478	6	Monks Eleigh, S Peter
TM 213651	5	Monk Soham, S Peter
TL 700641	5	Moulton, S Peter
TL 975342	6	Nayland, S James
TL 645633	8	Newmarket, All Saints
TL 641635	6	Newmarket, S Mary
TL 863604	6	Nowton, S Peter
TM 157773	6	Oakley, S Nicholas
TM 155708	5	Occold, S Michael
TM 066496	8	Offton, S Mary
TM 059625	5	Old Newton, S Mary
TM 422500	5	Orford, S Bartholomew
TM 204549	6	Otley, S Mary
TM 510936	5	Oulton, S Michael
TL 736596	5	Ousden, S Peter
TL 930670	5	Pakenham, Blessed Virgin Mary
TM 116785	8	Palgrave, S Peter
TM 355692	6	Peasenhall, S Michael
TM 298549	6	Pettistree, S Peter
TL 989381	6	Polstead, S Mary
TL 770482	5	Poslingford, S Mary Virgin
TL 946503	6	Preston, S Mary
TL 978590	6	Rattlesden, S Nicholas
TM 057782	6	Redgrave, S Botolph
TM 350645	6	Rendham, S Michael
TM 041746	6	Rickinghall Superior, S Mary
TM 403884	4	Ringsfield, All Saints
TL 912626	6	Rougham Green, S Mary
TM 346818	5	Rumburgh, S Michael & All Angels & S Felix
TM 196461	6	Rushmere St Andrew, S Andrew
TM 299843	5	St Cross South Elmham, S Cross
TM 322812	4	St James South Elmham, S James
TM 314839	5	St Margaret South Elmham, S Margaret
TM 388629	6	Saxmundham, S John Baptist
TM 031385	5	Shelley, All Saints
TL 860514	5	Shimpling, S George
TM 367695	5	Sibton, S Peter
TM 493972	6	Somerleyton, S Mary Virgin
TL 811530	4	Somerton, All Saints
TM 507763	8	Southwold, S Edmund K&M
TM 125451	6	Sproughton, All Saints
TL 783525	5	Stansfield, All Saints
TL 843493	6	Stanstead, S James
TM 115704	5	Stoke Ash, All Saints
TL 741434	6	Stoke by Clare, S John Baptist
TL 986363	8	Stoke by Nayland, S Mary Virgin
TM 133595	10	Stonham Aspal, SS Mary & Lambert
TL 958682	4	Stowlangtoft, S George
TM 049587	8	Stowmarket, SS Peter & Mary
TM 232740	10	Stradbroke, All Saints
TL 748526	5	Stradishall, S Margaret
TM 034338	6	Stratford St Mary, S Mary
TM 134778	4	Stuston, All Saints
TM 162344	6	Stutton, S Peter
TL 871413	8	Sudbury, All Saints
TL 871416	8	Sudbury, S Gregory
TL 874414	10	Sudbury, S Peter
TM 347638	6	Sweffling, S Mary Virgin
TM 242674	6	Tannington, S Ethelbert
TM 135371	6	Tattingstone, S Mary Virgin
TM 437659	6	Theberton, S Peter
TM 018783	5	Thelnetham, S Nicholas

TM 142696	6	Thorndon, All Saints
TM 104714	6	Thornham Magna, S Mary
TM 116765	6	Thrandeston, S Margaret
TL 929652	5	Thurston, S Peter
TL 861698	4	Timworth, S Andrew
TL 960637	4	Tostock, S Andrew
TL 900723	6	Troston, S Mary
TM 193485	6	Tuddenham (near Ipswich), S Martin
TL 738714	5	Tuddenham (near Mildenhall), S Mary
TM 363552	6	Tunstall, S Michael
TM 298522	8	Ufford, Assumption
TM 000711	6	Walsham le Willows, S Mary
TM 466792	5	Wangford, SS Peter & Paul
TM 010742	5	Wattisfield, S Margaret
TM 425755	6	Wenhaston, S Peter
TM 423804	5	Westhall, S Andrew
TM 044692	5	Westhorpe, S Margaret
TL 819706	6	West Stow, S Mary
TM 008628	6	Wetherden, S Mary
TM 127669	5	Wetheringsett, All Saints
TM 241802	6	Weybread, S Andrew
TL 833582	5	Whepstead, S Petronella
TL 753545	5	Wickhambrook, All Saints
TM 303557	6	Wickham Market, All Saints
TM 099693	6	Wickham Skeith, S Andrew
TM 242721	8	Wilby, S Mary
TM 230768	6	Wingfield, S Andrew
TM 180616	5	Winston, S Andrew
TM 366793	6	Wissett, S Andrew
TL 651478	5	Withersfield, S Mary Virgin
TM 179508	6	Witnesham, S Mary
TM 271491	8	Woodbridge, S Mary Virgin
TL 974625	6	Woolpit, S Mary
TM 455899	5	Worlingham, All Saints
TL 691739	5	Worlington, All Saints
TM 233686	8	Worlingworth, S Mary
TM 489830	6	Wrentham, S Nicholas
TM 121739	6	Yaxley, S Mary Virgin
TM 394689	6	Yoxford, S Peter

Surrey

TQ 051476	6	Albury, SS Peter & Paul
SU 897508	6	Ash, S Peter
TQ 073715	5	Ashford, S Matthew
TQ 193580	8	Ashtead, S Giles
SU 906632	8	Bagshot, S Anne
TQ 254596	8	Banstead, All Saints
TQ 211497	8	Betchworth, S Michael
TQ 327508	8	Bletchingley, S Mary Virgin
TQ 008449	6	Bramley, Holy Trinity
TQ 222508	6	Buckland, S Mary Virgin
TQ 313413	6	Burstow, S Bartholomew
SU 865605	8	Camberley, S Michael, Yorktown
TQ 175408	6	Capel, S John Baptist
TQ 343553	8	Caterham Valley, S John Evangelist
TQ 240411	6	Charlwood, S Nicholas
TQ 042670	8	Chertsey, S Peter
SU 960353	8	Chiddingfold, S Mary
TQ 283564	5	Chipstead, S Margaret
SU 974618	8	Chobham, S Lawrence
TQ 108598	8	Cobham, S Andrew
TQ 060391	8	Cranleigh, S Nicholas
TQ 165495	8	Dorking, S Martin
SU 997363	6	Dunsfold, S Mary & All Saints
TQ 096528	4	East Horsley, S Martin
TQ 146679	8	East Molesey, S Mary Virgin

TQ 013714	10	Egham, S John Baptist
TQ 195609	8	Epsom, Christ Church, Epsom Common
TQ 214605	10	Epsom, S Martin
TQ 137647	8	Esher, Christ Church
TQ 220629	8	Ewell, S Mary Virgin
TQ 091405	8	Ewhurst, SS Peter & Paul
SU 839467	8	Farnham, S Andrew
SU 842414	8	Frensham, S Mary
SU 968440	8	Godalming, SS Peter & Paul
TQ 357515	8	Godstone, S Nicholas
SU 986501	12	Guildford, Cathedral Church of Holy Spirit
SU 999495	8	Guildford, Holy Trinity
SU 996493	6	Guildford, S Mary
SU 994493	10	Guildford, S Nicolas
TQ 029507	6	Guildford, S John Divine, Merrow
SU 997507	6	Guildford, S John Evangelist, Stoke Park
TQ 002395	5	Hascombe, S Peter
SU 903334	10	Haslemere, S Bartholomew
TQ 113640	8	Hersham, S Peter
TQ 276427	8	Horley, S Bartholomew
TQ 243556	6	Kingswood, S Andrew
TQ 167561	10	Leatherhead, SS Mary & Nicholas
TQ 224469	6	Leigh, S Bartholomew
TQ 405532	6	Limpsfield, S Peter
TQ 427518	6	Limpsfield Chart, S Andrew
TQ 389437	8	Lingfield, SS Peter & Paul
TQ 290538	8	Merstham, S Catherine
TQ 198421	6	Newdigate, S Peter
TQ 309508	6	Nutfield, S Paul
TQ 095648	8	Oatlands Park, S Mary
TQ 066565	6	Ockham, S Mary & All Saints
TQ 157406	6	Ockley, S Margaret
TQ 021634	6	Ottershaw, Christ Church
TQ 319460	4	Outwood, S John Baptist
TQ 391530	6	Oxted, S Mary Virgin
SU 942559	6	Pirbright, S Michael & All Angels
SU 933478	6	Puttenham, S John Baptist
TQ 145505	8	Ranmore, S Barnabas
TQ 274494	8	Redhill, S John Evangelist
TQ 259502	10	Reigate, S Mary Magdalene
SU 897479	6	Seale, S Laurence
TQ 019543	6	Send, S Mary
SU 999478	8	Shalford, S Mary Virgin
TQ 076667	6	Shepperton, S Nicholas & S John Baptist
TQ 074478	8	Shere, S James
TQ 031718	8	Staines, S Mary BV
TQ 038710	8	Staines, S Peter
TQ 057742	6	Stanwell, S Mary BV
TQ 129584	6	Stoke D'Abernon, S Mary
TQ 106685	8	Sunbury on Thames, S Mary
TQ 374501	5	Tandridge, S Peter
TQ 161673	6	Thames Ditton, S Nicholas
TQ 102665	8	Walton on Thames, S Mary
TQ 044512	8	West Clandon, SS Peter & Paul
TQ 072647	8	Weybridge, S James
SU 946397	8	Witley, All Saints
SU 997592	6	Woking, S Mary Virgin, Horsell
TQ 021568	8	Woking, S Peter, Old Woking
TQ 015451	8	Wonersh, S John Baptist
SU 973536	8	Worplesdon, S Mary

Tyne & Wear

NZ 184634	6	Blaydon on Tyne, S Cuthbert
NZ 287619	8	Felling, S Mary, Heworth
NZ 241678	10	Gosforth, All Saints
NZ 306651	6	Hebburn, S Andrews Centre

NZ 342498	8	Houghton-le-Spring, S Michael & All Angels
NZ 326653	8	Jarrow, Christ Church, Jarrow Grange
NZ 167654	6	Newburn, S Michael & All Angels
NZ 250640	12(1)	Newcastle upon Tyne, Cathedral Church of S Nicholas
NZ 247640	8	Newcastle upon Tyne, S John Baptist
NZ 238642	8	Newcastle upon Tyne, S Matthew AE&M
NZ 218641	6	Newcastle upon Tyne, S James, Benwell
NZ 232633	8	Newcastle upon Tyne, S Stephen, Elswick
NZ 225656	8	Newcastle upon Tyne, SS Basil & James, Fenham
NZ 255668	8	Newcastle upon Tyne, S George, Jesmond
NZ 361671	8	South Shields, S Hilda
NZ 406572	8	Sunderland, Holy Trinity
NZ 393569	8	Sunderland, S Michael & All Angels
NZ 404563	8	Sunderland, S Ignatius Martyr, Hendon
NZ 404594	10	Sunderland, S Andrew, Roker
NZ 354687	10	Tynemouth, Christ Church, North Shields
NZ 210613	8	Whickham, S Mary
NZ 354721	8	Whitley Bay, S Paul
NZ 175619	6	Winlaton, S Paul

Warwickshire

SP 091575	8	Alcester, S Nicholas
SP 230486	6	Alderminster, S Mary & Holy Cross
SP 233564	6	Alveston, S James
SP 290926	6	Ansley, S Lawrence
SP 400837	4	Ansty, S James
SP 283906	6	Arley, S Wilfrid
SP 312702	4	Ashow, Assumption BVM
SP 311893	5	Astley, S Mary Virgin
SP 138599	6	Aston Cantlow, S John Baptist
SP 308979	8	Atherstone, S Mary
SK 296063	5	Austrey, S Nicholas
SP 402502	5	Avon Dassett, S John Baptist
SP 359869	8	Bedworth, All Saints
SP 101518	8	Bidford on Avon, S Lawrence
SP 388577	5	Bishop's Itchington, S Michael
SP 315393	6	Brailes, S George
SP 437796	6	Brinklow, S John Baptist
SP 391868	8	Bulkington, S James
SP 399515	6	Burton Dassett, All Saints
SP 400899	5	Burton Hastings, S Botolph
SP 320500	6	Butlers Marston, S Peter & Paul
SP 349531	6	Chadshunt, All Saints
SP 292366	5	Cherington, S Nicholas
SP 453764	6	Church Lawford, S Peter
SP 510808	4	Churchover, Holy Trinity
SP 198646	6	Claverdon, S Michael & All Angels
SP 198522	6	Clifford Chambers, S Helen
SP 531764	6	Clifton upon Dunsmore, S Mary Virgin
SP 201890	10	Coleshill, SS Peter & Paul
SP 301851	5	Corley, dedication unknown
SP 083606	6	Coughton, S Peter
SP 344684	6	Cubbington, Nativity of Our Lady
SP 486712	6	Dunchurch, S Peter
SP 267490	4	Ettington, Holy Trinity & S Thomas Canterbury
SP 340850	6	Exhall, S Giles
SP 434496	6	Farnborough, S Botolph
SP 283874	6	Fillongley, S Mary & All Saints
SP 423701	4	Frankton, S Nicholas
SP 493670	5	Grandborough, S Peter
SP 250346	6	Great Wolford, S Michael & All Angels
SK 287009	6	Grendon, All Saints
SP 374600	8	Harbury, All Saints
SP 236674	6	Hatton, Holy Trinity
SP 152661	6	Henley in Arden, S John Baptist

SP 536744	6	Hillmorton, S John Baptist
SP 245722	6	Honiley, S John Baptist
SP 261427	6	Honington, All Saints
SP 210435	6	Ilmington, S Mary
SP 286724	6	Kenilworth, S Nicholas
SP 335511	6	Kineton, S Peter
SP 214963	8	Kingsbury, SS Peter & Paul
SP 414589	5	Ladbroke, All Saints
SP 163711	6	Lapworth, S Mary Virgin
SP 445676	5	Leamington Hastings, All Saints
SP 289688	5	Leek Wootton, All Saints
SP 335560	4	Lighthorne, S Laurence
SP 261303	5	Little Compton, S Denys
SP 287331	6	Long Compton, SS Peter & Paul
SP 412651	4	Long Itchington, Holy Trinity
SP 184470	6	Lower Quinton, S Swithun
SP 320967	5	Mancetter, S Peter
SP 341444	6	Middle Tysoe, Assumption BVM
SP 463832	8	Monks Kirby, S Edith
SP 463612	6	Napton on the Hill, S Lawrence
SP 231929	6	Nether Whitacre, S Giles
SP 299571	4	Newbold Pacey, S George Martyr
SP 363908	10	Nuneaton, All Saints, Chilvers Coton
SP 366916	8	Nuneaton, S Nicholas
SP 359658	4	Offchurch, S Gregory
SP 317455	5	Oxhill, S Laurence
SP 170728	8	Packwood, S Giles
SK 263024	6	Polesworth, S Editha
SP 485576	6	Priors Marston, S Leonard
SP 343648	4	Radford Semele, S Nicholas
SP 368481	5	Radway, S Peter
SP 204693	6	Rowington, S Lawrence
SP 326654	8	Royal Leamington Spa, All Saints
SP 317657	8	Royal Leamington Spa, S Peter (RC)
SP 324673	8	Royal Leamington Spa, S Mary Magdalene, Lillington
SP 328638	8	Royal Leamington Spa, S Margaret, Whitnash
SP 504752	8	Rugby, S Andrew, NE Tower
SP 503752	5	Rugby, S Andrew, W Tower
SP 487739	6	Rugby, S Mark, Bilton
SP 487771	8	Rugby, S Botolph, Newbold on Avon
SP 386745	6	Ryton-on-Dunsmore, S Leonard
SP 077510	8	Salford Priors, S Matthew
SK 260074	4	Seckington, All Saints
SP 263612	6	Sherbourne, All Saints
SP 403844	6	Shilton, S Andrew
SP 259406	6	Shipston on Stour, S Edmund
SP 426455	5	Shotteswell, S Laurence
SP 243910	6	Shustoke, S Cuthbert
SP 219601	6	Snitterfield, S James Great
SP 418617	8	Southam, S James
SP 330726	6	Stoneleigh, S Mary
SP 201543	10	Stratford upon Avon, Holy Trinity
SP 081638	6	Studley, Nativity of BVM
SP 299375	5	Sutton under Brailes, S Thomas of Canterbury
SP 114705	8	Tanworth in Arden, S Mary Magdalene
SP 259435	6	Tredington, S Gregory
SP 121672	8	Ullenhall, S Mary Virgin
SP 498618	4	Upper Shuckburgh, S John Baptist
SP 282650	10	Warwick, S Mary
SP 287649	8	Warwick, S Nicholas
SP 143522	8	Welford on Avon, S Peter
SP 277556	8	Wellesbourne, S Peter
SP 360692	4	Weston under Wetherley, S Michael
SP 312347	6	Whichford, S Michael
SP 516675	6	Willoughby, S Nicholas
SP 437841	4	Withybrook, All Saints

SP 409758	8	Wolston, S Margaret
SP 430880	6	Wolvey, S John Baptist
SP 153633	6	Wootton Wawen, S Peter

West Midlands

SK 061007	8	Aldridge, S Mary Virgin
SP 302807	8	Allesley, All Saints
SP 207780	6	Barston, S Swithin
SP 244791	6	Berkswell, S John Baptist
SP 188824	6	Bickenhill, S Peter
SO 950966	8	Bilston, S Leonard
SP 070875	8	Birmingham, Basilica of S Chad, RC Cathedral
SP 070870	12	Birmingham, Cathedral Church of S Philip
SP 073866	16	Birmingham, S Martin
SP 082899	12	Birmingham, SS Peter & Paul, Aston
SP 142898	6	Birmingham, SS Mary & Margaret, Castle Bromwich
SP 057847	8	Birmingham, S Bartholomew, Edgbaston
SP 112923	8	Birmingham, Abbey Church of SS Thomas & Edmund (RC), Erdington
SP 110917	8	Birmingham, S Barnabas, Erdington
SP 056903	8	Birmingham, S Mary, Handsworth
SP 029839	8	Birmingham, S Peter, Harborne
SP 049789	10	Birmingham, S Nicholas, King's Norton
SP 075837	4	Birmingham, S Anne, Moseley
SP 078832	8	Birmingham, S Mary, Moseley
SP 025793	8	Birmingham, S Laurence, Northfield
SP 068920	8	Birmingham, S John Evangelist, Perry Barr
SP 038822	8	Birmingham, S Mary, Selly Oak
SP 148843	4	Birmingham, S Giles, Sheldon
SP 119788	8	Birmingham, S James, Shirley
SP 135863	8	Birmingham, S Edburgha, Yardley
SO 955862	8	Blackheath, Holy Trinity, Old Hill
SO 970874	8	Blackheath, S Giles, Rowley Regis
SJ 997019	8	Bloxwich, All Saints
SK 007018	5	Bloxwich, Christ Church, Blakenall Heath
SK 021031	6	Bloxwich, S Michael & All Angels, Pelsall
SO 916868	8	Brierley Hill, S Michael
SP 317825	6	Brownshill Green, S Thomas
SO 947943	8	Coseley, Christ Church
SP 336790	12(1)	Coventry, Cathedral of S Michael
SP 358795	8	Coventry, S Michael, Stoke
SP 379809	6	Coventry, S Mary, Walsgrave on Sowe
SO 977968	8	Darlaston, S Lawrence
SO 942901	10	Dudley, S Thomas
SO 938881	8	Dudley, S Andrew, Netherton
SP 048958	6	Great Barr, S Margaret
SO 966836	8	Halesowen, S John Baptist
SO 942851	8	Halesowen, S Peter, Cradley
SP 203808	8	Hampton in Arden, SS Mary & Bartholomew
SO 893894	8	Kingswinford, S Mary
SO 892868	6	Kingswinford, Holy Trinity, Wordesley
SP 182767	8	Knowle, SS John Baptist, Lawrence & Anne
SP 252817	5	Meriden, S Lawrence
SO 991895	8	Oldbury, Christ Church
SO 915894	8	Pensnett, S Mark
SP 123748	5	Salter Street, S Patrick
SO 917937	8	Sedgley, All Saints
SP 020876	8	Smethwick, Old Church
SP 153792	12	Solihull, S Alphege
SO 901842	12	Stourbridge, S Thomas
SO 900850	8	Stourbridge, Holy Trinity, Amblecote
SO 924844	8	Stourbridge, Christ Church, Lye
SO 908831	8	Stourbridge, S Mary, Old Swinford
SO 892847	6	Stourbridge, S James, Wollaston
SP 122962	8	Sutton Coldfield, Holy Trinity
SP 110938	8	Sutton Coldfield, S Michael, Boldmere

SP 016984	12(1)	Walsall, S Matthew
SP 024999	6	Walsall, S Michael, Rushall
SO 988954	10	Wednesbury, S Bartholomew
SO 998962	8	Wednesbury, S Paul, Wood Green
SP 011929	8	West Bromwich, All Saints
SO 967985	10	Willenhall, S Giles
SO 914988	12	Wolverhampton, Collegiate Church of S Peter
SO 914973	8	Wolverhampton, S Luke, Blakenhall
SJ 924025	6	Wolverhampton, S Mary, Bushbury
SO 894954	8	Wolverhampton, S Bartholomew, Penn
SJ 891003	8	Wolverhampton, S Michael & All Angels, Tettenhall

West Sussex

SZ 909991	6	Aldwick, S Richard
TQ 037132	5	Amberley, S Michael
TQ 067044	6	Angmering, S Margaret
TQ 339298	6	Ardingly, S Peter
TQ 016073	8	Arundel, S Nicholas
TQ 307309	8	Balcombe, S Mary
TQ 087259	8	Billingshurst, S Mary
TQ 262227	8	Bolney, S Mary Magdalene
SU 803038	6	Bosham, Holy Trinity
TQ 313193	8	Burgess Hill, S John Evangelist
TQ 016131	4	Bury, S John Evangelist
SU 859047	8	Chichester, Cathedral Church of Holy Trinity
TQ 212226	6	Cowfold, S Peter
TQ 268366	8	Crawley, S John Baptist
TQ 303245	8	Cuckfield, Holy Trinity
SU 895225	8	Easebourne, S Mary
TQ 396380	12(1)	East Grinstead, S Swithin
SZ 949999	6	Felpham, S Mary
TQ 116085	6	Findon, S John Baptist
TQ 009193	6	Fittleworth, S Mary
TQ 111026	6	Goring by Sea, S Mary
SU 929167	6	Graffham, S Giles
TQ 213162	8	Henfield, S Peter
TQ 170302	10	Horsham, S Mary
TQ 279164	8	Hurstpierpoint, Holy Trinity
TQ 131288	5	Itchingfield, S Nicholas
TQ 315153	6	Keymer, SS Cosmas & Damian
TQ 018265	6	Kirdford, S John Baptist
TQ 349258	8	Lindfield, All Saints
SU 931227	6	Lodsworth, S Peter
TQ 220275	8	Lower Beeding, Holy Trinity
TQ 023047	6	Lyminster, S Mary Magdalene
SU 887215	6	Midhurst, S Mary Magdalene & S Denis
SU 824283	6	Milland, S Luke
SU 901050	4	Oving, S Andrew
SZ 884975	6	Pagham, S Thomas a' Becket
SU 977218	8	Petworth, S Mary
TQ 047187	8	Pulborough, S Mary
SU 807237	6	Rogate, S Bartholomew
TQ 091343	8	Rudgwick, Holy Trinity
TQ 205373	8	Rusper, S Mary Magdalene
TQ 145227	6	Shipley, S Mary Virgin
TQ 216051	8	Shoreham-by-Sea, S Mary of the Harbour
TQ 257281	8	Slaugham, S Mary
SU 961083	4	Slindon, S Mary
TQ 117316	6	Slinfold, S Peter
SU 783194	6	South Harting, S Mary
SU 863225	6	Stedham, S James
TQ 178114	8	Steyning, S Andrew
TQ 086141	6	Storrington, S Mary
TQ 110173	6	Thakeham, S Mary
SU 837225	4	Trotton, S George
TQ 337353	8	Turners Hill, S Leonard

TQ 253199	5	Twineham, S Peter
TQ 193112	8	Upper Beeding, S Peter
SU 972057	6	Walberton, S Mary
TQ 158336	8	Warnham, S Margaret
TQ 118128	6	Washington, S Mary
SU 756073	8	Westbourne, S John Baptist
TQ 171206	6	West Grinstead, S George
TQ 363328	6	West Hoathly, S Margaret
TQ 131040	6	West Tarring, S Andrew
TQ 052258	6	Wisborough Green, S Peter ad Vincula
TQ 302362	6	Worth, S Nicholas
TQ 137028	8	Worthing, S Botolph, Heene
SU 982035	6	Yapton, S Mary

West Yorkshire

SE 433371	4	Aberford, S Ricarius
SE 085497	6	Addingham, S Peter
SE 302253	8	Ardsley East, S Michael & All Angels
SE 463150	4	Badsworth, S Mary Virgin
SE 401374	6	Barwick in Elmet, All Saints
SE 241245	8	Batley, All Saints
SE 105395	8	Bingley, All Saints
SE 218262	8	Birstall, S Peter
SE 167333	12	Bradford, Cathedral Church of S Peter
SE 177380	8	Bradford, Holy Trinity, Idle
SE 160290	8	Bradford, Holy Trinity, Low Moor
SE 076298	5	Bradshaw, S John
SE 428431	6	Bramham, All Saints
SE 144231	8	Brighouse, S Martin
SE 136254	8	Brighouse, S Matthew, Lightcliffe
SE 208372	8	Calverley, S Wilfrid
SE 192254	8	Cleckheaton, S John
SE 390461	8	Collingham, S Oswald
SE 378182	6	Crofton, All Saints
SE 485202	6	Darrington, S Luke & All Saints
SE 072334	8	Denholme, S Paul
SE 246215	8	Dewsbury, All Saints
SE 225292	8	Drighlington, S Paul
SE 108212	8	Elland, S Mary
SE 387126	6	Felkirk, S Peter
SE 194422	8	Guiseley, S Oswald
SE 092260	8	Halifax, All Souls
SE 098252	12(1)	Halifax, S John Baptist
SE 030372	6	Haworth, S Michael & All Angels
SE 429133	8	Hemsworth, S Helen
SD 986280	8	Heptonstall, S Thomas Apostle
SE 440181	6	High Ackworth, S Cuthbert
SE 143082	8	Holmfirth, Holy Trinity
SE 295184	8	Horbury, SS Peter & Leonard
SE 142168	10	Huddersfield, S Peter
SE 168151	8	Huddersfield, All Hallows, Almondbury
SE 134137	6	Huddersfield, S Paul, Armitage Bridge
SE 118181	8	Huddersfield, S Stephen, Lindley
SE 111166	8	Huddersfield, S Mark, Longwood
SE 116478	8	Ilkley, All Saints
SE 061410	8	Keighley, S Andrew
SE 011459	8	Kildwick, S Andrew
SE 417303	6	Kippax, S Mary
SE 198125	8	Kirkburton, All Hallows
SE 179172	8	Kirkheaton, S John Baptist
SE 362210	6	Kirkthorpe, S Peter
SE 302339	8	Leeds, Cathedral Church of S Anne (RC)
SE 306333	12(1)	Leeds, S Peter
SE 245351	8	Leeds, S Peter, Bramley
SE 278346	8	Leeds, S Matthias, Burley
SE 303374	6	Leeds, S Matthew, Chapel Allerton
SE 273369	8	Leeds, S Chad, Far Headingley

SE 280359	8	Leeds, S Michael & All Angels, Headingley
SE 312314	8	Leeds, S Mary Virgin, Hunslet
SE 286373	5	Leeds, Holy Trinity, Meanwood
SE 350365	5	Leeds, S James, Seacroft
SE 265337	8	Leeds, Christ Church, Upper Armley
SE 202240	8	Liversedge, Christ Church
SE 047116	10	Marsden, S Bartholomew
SE 099107	6	Meltham, S Bartholomew
SE 211204	10	Mirfield, S Mary Virgin
SE 202197	6	Mirfield, S Paul
SE 013260	8	Mytholmroyd, S Michael
SE 166087	6	New Mill, Christ Church
SE 113270	8	Northowram, S Matthew
SE 276211	12(1)	Ossett, Holy & Undivided Trinity
SE 201454	8	Otley, All Saints
SE 030347	8	Oxenhope, S Mary Virgin
SE 462224	8	Pontefract, All Saints
SE 455219	10	Pontefract, S Giles
SE 220331	8	Pudsey, S Lawrence
SE 101301	8	Queensbury, Holy Trinity
SE 041198	8	Ripponden, S Bartholomew
SE 343283	8	Rothwell, Holy Trinity
SE 212113	6	Shelley, Emmanuel
SE 144374	8	Shipley, S Paul
SE 041465	6	Silsden, S James Great
SE 453111	6	South Kirkby, All Saints
SE 043232	8	Sowerby Bridge, S Peter, Sowerby
SE 384305	8	Swillington, S Mary
SE 380405	8	Thorner, S Peter
SE 253188	8	Thornhill, S Michael & All Angels
SD 936241	8	Todmorden, S Mary
SD 935238	8	Todmorden, Unitarian
SE 219306	6	Tong, S James
SE 333208	12(2)	Wakefield, Cathedral Church of All Saints
SE 344182	6	Wakefield, S Helen, Sandal Magna
SD 935220	8	Walsden, S Peter
SE 404484	8	Wetherby, S James
SE 365292	6	Woodlesford, All Saints
SE 319131	5	Woolley, S Peter
SE 408173	6	Wragby, S Michael & Our Lady, Nostell Priory

Wiltshire

SU 263758	8	Aldbourne, S Michael
ST 841830	5	Alderton, S Giles
SU 069615	5	All Cannings, All Saints
SU 152414	8	Amesbury, SS Mary & Melorus
SU 042944	5	Ashton Keynes, Holy Cross
SU 099700	6	Avebury, S James
SU 056313	6	Barford St Martin, S Martin
SU 072392	4	Berwick St James, S James
ST 946223	6	Berwick St John, S John Baptist
SU 038642	8	Bishop's Cannings, S Mary Virgin
SU 244837	8	Bishopstone, S Mary Virgin
ST 950396	5	Boyton, Blessed Mary of Boyton
ST 828613	8	Bradford on Avon, Christ Church
ST 824609	8	Bradford on Avon, Holy Trinity
ST 914519	6	Bratton, S James Great
ST 979730	6	Bremhill, S Martin
SU 013845	6	Brinkworth, S Michael
SU 163284	6	Britford, S Peter
SU 153907	6	Broad Blunsdon, S Leonard
SU 041253	6	Broad Chalke, All Saints
SU 106763	6	Broad Hinton, S Peter ad Vincula
ST 963652	6	Bromham, S Nicholas
SU 233614	5	Burbage, All Saints
ST 999709	8	Calne, S Mary Virgin
SU 146959	6	Castle Eaton, S Mary Virgin

ST	959889	5	Charlton, S John Baptist	ST	837840	4	Luckington, S Mary
ST	970328	6	Chilmark, S Margaret of Antioch	SU	263509	6	Ludgershall, S James
SU	319705	5	Chilton Foliat, S Mary	SU	093860	6	Lydiard Millicent, All Saints
ST	923732	8	Chippenham, S Andrew	SU	104848	6	Lydiard Tregoze, S Mary
ST	919739	8	Chippenham, S Paul	SU	024787	6	Lyneham, S Michael
SU	073577	6	Chirton, S John Baptist	ST	803386	6	Maiden Bradley, All Saints
SU	187799	6	Chiseldon, Holy Cross	ST	933873	8	Malmesbury, S Paul
ST	992440	5	Chitterne, All Saints	SU	086579	6	Marden, All Saints
ST	960784	6	Christian Malford, All Saints	SU	014541	6	Market Lavington, S Mary of the Assumption
SU	075770	6	Clyffe Pypard, S Peter	SU	189693	8	Marlborough, S Mary Virgin
ST	966399	6	Codford St Peter, S Peter	SU	180686	6	Marlborough, S George, Preshute
ST	821711	8	Colerne, S John Baptist	ST	903637	8	Melksham, S Michael & All Angels
SU	242536	6	Collingbourne Ducis, S Andrew A&M	ST	812323	8	Mere, S Michael Archangel
SU	239558	6	Collingbourne Kingston, S Mary	SU	119361	6	Middle Woodford, All Saints
SU	031716	6	Compton Bassett, S Swithin	SU	210695	6	Mildenhall, S John Baptist
SU	029300	6	Compton Chamberlayne, S Michael	SU	190604	6	Milton Lilbourne, S Peter
SU	108263	6	Coombe Bissett, S Michael & All Angels	SU	148484	6	Netheravon, All Saints
ST	874706	6	Corsham, S Bartholomew	ST	816794	6	Nettleton, S Mary
ST	828467	6	Corsley, S Margaret of Antioch	SU	218402	4	Newton Tony, S Andrew
SU	099935	6	Cricklade, S Sampson	ST	854548	8	North Bradley, S Nicholas
ST	980824	5	Dauntsey, S James Great	SU	131578	4	North Newnton, S James
SU	006616	6	Devizes, Blessed Virgin Mary	SU	234490	5	North Tidworth, Holy Trinity
SU	004612	8	Devizes, S John	ST	907433	5	Norton Bavant, All Saints
SU	011614	6	Devizes, S James Great	ST	991936	6	Oaksey, All Saints
SU	009316	6	Dinton, S Mary	SU	188723	5	Ogbourne St Andrew, S Andrew
ST	914248	4	Donhead St Andrew, S Andrew	SU	195747	5	Ogbourne St George, S George
ST	906244	6	Donhead St Mary, S Mary Virgin	SU	059457	4	Orcheston, SS George & Mary
SU	181216	8	Downton, S Lawrence	SU	163598	6	Pewsey, S John Baptist
SU	157448	6	Durrington, All Saints	ST	995585	6	Potterne, S Mary Virgin
SU	117674	5	East Kennett, Christ Church	SU	097872	8	Purton, S Mary
ST	880305	6	East Knoyle, S Mary	SU	273716	6	Ramsbury, Holy Cross
ST	991242	5	Ebbesbourne Wake, S John Baptist	ST	978626	6	Rowde, S Matthew
ST	926533	10	Edington, S Mary, S Katharine & All Saints	SU	146305	8	Salisbury, S Edmund's Art Centre
SU	141516	6	Enford, All Saints	SU	150296	8	Salisbury, S Martin
ST	965539	6	Erlestoke, Holy Saviour	SU	138303	8	Salisbury, S Paul
SU	198541	6	Everleigh, S Peter	SU	143300	8	Salisbury, S Thomas of Canterbury
SU	001386	4	Fisherton de la Mere, S Nicholas	SU	252649	5	Savernake Forest, S Katharine V&M
SU	146495	6	Fittleton, All Saints	ST	867283	5	Sedgehill, S Catherine
ST	996296	6	Fovant, S George	ST	944609	6	Seend, Holy Cross
SU	277643	6	Great Bedwyn, S Mary	ST	892268	6	Semley, S Leonard
ST	980543	6	Great Cheverell, S Peter	SU	209904	6	Sevenhampton, S James
SU	136383	5	Great Durnford, S Andrew	SU	315635	6	Shalbourne, S Michael & All Angels
ST	964832	6	Great Somerford, SS Peter & Paul	ST	854860	6	Sherston, Holy Cross
SU	080355	6	Great Wishford, S Giles	SU	070443	6	Shrewton, S Mary
ST	860800	6	Grittleton, S Mary Virgin	SU	195880	6	South Marston, S Mary Magdalene
SU	329629	4	Ham, All Saints	SU	088343	6	South Newton, S Andrew
ST	973908	4	Hankerton, Holy Cross	ST	833648	6	South Wraxall, S James
SU	181928	6	Hannington, S John Baptist	SU	070374	5	Stapleford, S Mary
ST	999662	6	Heddington, S Andrew	ST	906571	6	Steeple Ashton, S Mary Virgin
ST	925425	6	Heytesbury, SS Peter & Paul	SU	036374	5	Steeple Langford, All Saints
SU	201925	8	Highworth, S Michael	ST	982382	4	Stockton, S John Baptist
SU	020754	6	Hilmarton, S Laurence	ST	776339	6	Stourton, S Peter
ST	871592	6	Hilperton, S Michael & All Angels	SU	179871	8	Stratton St Margaret, S Margaret of Antioch
ST	910329	6	Hindon, S John Baptist	ST	947787	5	Sutton Benger, All Saints
ST	861616	6	Holt, S Katharine	ST	902417	6	Sutton Veny, S John Evangelist
ST	821414	6	Horningsham, S John Baptist	SU	157839	10	Swindon, Christ Church
SU	197374	4	Idmiston, All Saints	SU	143847	8	Swindon, S Mark
ST	917580	6	Keevil, S Leonard	SU	140867	6	Swindon, S Mary, Rodbourne Cheney
ST	846371	6	Kingston Deverill, S Mary	ST	944291	6	Tisbury, S John Baptist
ST	904772	6	Kington St Michael, S Michael	ST	944177	5	Tollard Royal, S Peter ad Vincula
ST	917685	6	Lacock, S Cyriac	ST	856580	12	Trowbridge, S James
ST	928758	4	Langley Burrell, S Peter	SU	135550	6	Upavon, S Mary Virgin
SU	093958	5	Latton, S John Baptist	SU	300540	6	Upper Chute, S Nicholas
ST	958862	4	Lea, S Giles	SU	009912	6	Upper Minety, S Leonard
SU	206812	5	Liddington, All Saints	SU	041573	8	Urchfont, S Michael & All Angels
SU	291662	4	Little Bedwyn, S Michael	SU	207825	6	Wanborough, S Andrew
ST	866413	8	Longbridge Deverill, SS Peter & Paul	ST	869455	8	Warminster, S Denys

ST 874514	8	Westbury, All Saints
ST 813776	4	West Kington, S Mary Virgin
ST 859327	5	West Knoyle, Holy Innocents
SU 006530	6	West Lavington, S Mary Magdalene
SU 133681	6	West Overton, S Michael & All Angels
SU 229325	6	West Winterslow, All Saints
ST 812590	6	Westwood, S Mary Virgin
SU 095312	6	Wilton, SS Mary & Nicholas
SU 175345	5	Winterbourne Earls, S Michael & All Angels
SU 098720	4	Winterbourne Monkton, S Mary Magdalene
SU 077407	4	Winterbourne Stoke, S Peter
SU 066825	8	Wootton Bassett, S Bartholomew & All Saints
SU 197629	5	Wootton Rivers, S Andrew
SU 137802	6	Wroughton, SS John Baptist & Helen
SU 008377	6	Wylye, S Mary Virgin
SU 063715	5	Yatesbury, All Saints
ST 865762	4	Yatton Keynell, S Margaret
ST 781317	6	Zeals, S Martin

Wales
Clwyd

SH 943776	6	Abergele, S Michael
SJ 388453	6	Bangor is y coed, S Dinott
SJ 004764	8	Bodelwyddan, S Margaret
SJ 284647	8	Buckley, S Matthew
SJ 291377	6	Chirk, S Mary
SJ 050661	8	Denbigh, S Mary
SJ 243730	8	Flint, S Mary
SJ 347550	8	Gresford, All Saints
SJ 209713	6	Halkyn, S Mary Virgin
SJ 455398	6	Hanmer, S Chad
SJ 316659	6	Hawarden, S Deiniol
SJ 412541	6	Holt, S Chad
SJ 309584	6	Hope, S Cynfarch
SJ 034371	4	Llandrillo, S Trillo
SJ 217419	8	Llangollen, S Collen
SJ 209281	4	Llansilin, S Silin
SJ 237642	6	Mold, S Mary
SJ 246685	8	Northop, SS Eurgain & Peter
SJ 373418	6	Overton, S Mary Virgin
SJ 021781	6	Rhuddlan, S Mary
SJ 010815	8	Rhyl, S Thomas
SJ 302438	6	Ruabon, S Mabon & S Mary Virgin
SJ 123584	8	Ruthin, S Peter
SJ 418462	4	Worthenbury, S Deiniol
SJ 336502	10	Wrexham, S Giles

Dyfed

SN 453011	5	Burry Port, S Mary
SN 181460	6	Cardigan, S Mary
SN 415203	8	Carmarthen, S Peter
SM 952157	8	Haverfordwest, S Mary Virgin
SN 302114	6	Laugharne, S Martin
SN 534203	4	Llanarthney, S David
SN 599810	8	Llanbadarn Fawr, S Padarn
SN 629223	6	Llandeilo, S Teilo
SN 763341	6	Llandovery, S Dingat, Llandingat
SN 419406	6	Llandysul, S Tyssul
SN 507005	8	Llanelli, S Elli
SN 349107	8	Llanstephan, S Ystyffan
SN 083400	6	Nevern, S Brynach
SM 984015	8	Pembroke, S Mary Virgin
SM 752254	8	St David's, Cathedral Church of S David
SN 082012	6	St Florence, S Florencius
SN 134004	8	Tenby, S Mary

Gwent

SO 301141	10	Abergavenny, S Mary
ST 277871	6	Bassaleg, S Basil
SO 166003	8	Bedwellty, S Sannan
SO 251087	8	Blaenavon, S Peter
ST 339906	8	Caerleon, S Cadoc
ST 483886	8	Caldicot, SS Mary & Bartholomew
ST 536939	10	Chepstow, S Mary
SO 477074	6	Cwmcarvan, S Clement
SO 298233	6	Cwmyoy, S Martin
SO 457103	5	Dingestow, SS Dingat & Mary
SO 519135	4	Dixton, S Peter
SO 168088	8	Ebbw Vale, Christ Church
SO 404243	6	Grosmont, S Nicholas
SO 375108	8	Llanarth, S Teilo
SO 415039	6	Llandenny, S John
SO 233148	6	Llanelly, S Ellyw
ST 321936	8	Llanfrechfa, All Saints
SO 456157	6	Llangattock Vibon Avel, S Cadoc
ST 374967	8	Llangybi, S Cybi
SO 317094	5	Llanover, S Bartholomew
ST 307932	6	Llantarnam, S Michael
SO 398149	8	Llantilio Crossenny, S Teilo
SO 311153	4	Llantilio Pertholey, S Teilo
ST 371878	5	Llanwern, S Mary
ST 424869	6	Magor, S Mary Virgin
ST 262826	8	Marshfield, S Mary Virgin
ST 523908	6	Mathern, S Tewdric
ST 241845	6	Michaelston y Fedw, S Michael
SO 508129	8	Monmouth, S Mary Virgin
ST 343837	6	Nash, S Mary
ST 308897	8	Newport, All Saints
ST 308876	12(1)	Newport, Cathedral Church of S Woolos
SO 523107	4	Penallt, S Mary
ST 424908	6	Penhow, S John Baptist
SO 417118	4	Penrhos, S Cadoc
ST 267800	8	Peterstone Wentloog, S Peter
ST 412842	5	Redwick, S Thomas Apostle
ST 293824	6	St Brides Wentlooge, S Bridget
ST 478936	6	Shirenewton, S Thomas a' Becket
SO 456203	6	Skenfrith, S Bridget
ST 379948	6	Tredunnock, S Andrew
SO 418103	5	Tregare, S Mary
SO 284020	8	Trevethin, S Cadoc
SO 379008	8	Usk, S Mary

Gwynedd

SH 573713	8	Bangor, S David, Glanadda
SH 613159	8	Barmouth, SS John & David
SH 604761	8	Beaumaris, S Mary
SH 727178	8	Dolgellau, S Mary Virgin
SH 601710	6	Llandegai, S Tegai
SH 784822	8	Llandudno, Holy Trinity
SH 565387	8	Porthmadog, S John Divine

Mid Glamorgan

SO 003026	8	Aberdare, S Elvan
ST 171892	6	Bedwas, S Barrog or Baruck
SS 903800	8	Bridgend, S Illtyd, Newcastle
ST 155864	8	Caerphilly, S Martin
SO 032079	6	Cefn coed y cymmer, S John Baptist
SS 924815	6	Coity, S Mary
SS 876799	4	Laleston, S David
SS 858888	6	Llangynwyd, S Cynwyd
ST 047834	8	Llantrisant, SS Illtyd, Tyfodwg & Gwynno

ST 227881 8 Machen, S Michael
SO 049058 8 Merthyr Tydfil, former Church of S Tydfil
SS 969962 8 Pentre, S Peter
SS 893818 5 Pen y fai, All Saints
ST 071902 8 Pontypridd, S Catherine
SS 837774 8 Porthcawl, S John Baptist, Newton
SO 113080 6 Rhymney, S David

Powys

SJ 188008 8 Berriew, S Beuno
SO 044290 5 Brecon, Cathedral Church of S John Evangelist
SO 037284 6 Brecon, S David, Llanfaes
SO 045285 8 Brecon, S Mary
SO 144349 6 Bronllys, S Mary
SO 040510 6 Builth Wells, S Mary
SO 143251 4 Cathedine, S Michael
SO 271940 5 Church Stoke, S Nicholas
SO 213438 5 Clyro, S Michael
SO 089422 4 Crickadarn, S Mary
SO 087643 5 Crossgates, S Paternus
SO 181238 6 Cwmdu, S Michael
SN 929275 6 Defynnog, S Cynog
SJ 227011 6 Forden, S Michael & All Angels
SO 046336 4 Garthbrengy, S David
SO 231551 5 Gladestry, S Mary
SO 177386 8 Glasbury, SS Cynidr & Peter
SJ 219117 4 Guilsfield, S Aelhaiarn
SO 287725 8 Knighton, S Edward
SJ 242060 6 Leighton, Holy Trinity
SO 239204 5 Llanbedr, S Peter
SO 034323 6 Llandefaelog, S Maelog
SO 108357 4 Llandefalle, S Matthew
SO 026885 6 Llandinam, S Llonio
SO 195954 5 Llandyssil, S Tyssil
SO 151667 6 Llanfihangel Rhydithon, S Michael & All Angels
SO 114293 4 Llanfihangel Tal-y-llyn, S Michael
SJ 142195 6 Llanfyllin, S Myllin
SO 133261 4 Llangasty Talyllyn, S Gastyn
SO 211179 8 Llangattock, S Cattwg
SO 135276 6 Llangorse, S Paulin
SN 954847 8 Llanidloes, S Idloes
SH 745009 8 Machynlleth, S Peter
SN 984374 4 Merthyr Cynog, S Cynog
SO 223965 6 Montgomery, S Nicholas
SO 034669 6 Nantmel, S Cynllo
SO 211609 6 New Radnor, S Mary
SO 109913 6 Newtown, S David
SO 250591 6 Old Radnor, S Stephen Martyr
SO 087246 8 Pencelli, S Meugan
SO 316646 8 Presteigne, S Andrew
SO 157338 6 Talgarth, S Gwendoline
SJ 225077 8 Welshpool, S Mary

South Glamorgan

ST 064741 6 Bonvilston, S Mary Virgin
ST 183765 10 Cardiff, S John Baptist
SS 994746 8 Cowbridge, Holy Cross
SS 985740 6 Llanblethian, S Bleddian
ST 052703 4 Llancarfan, S Cadoc
ST 156781 10 Llandaff, Cathedral & Parish Church of SS Peter & Paul
ST 221819 5 Llanedeyrn, S Edeyrn
ST 177818 6 Llanishen, S Isan
ST 044728 5 Llantrithyd, S Illtyd
SS 966687 6 Llantwit Major, S Illtyd
ST 188721 8 Penarth, S Augustine

ST 060767 6 Pendoylan, S Cadoc
ST 058688 6 Penmark, S Mary
ST 084764 6 Peterston super Ely, S Peter A&M
ST 083665 6 Porthkerry, S Curig
ST 133802 8 Radyr, Christ Church
ST 214792 6 Rumney, S Augustine
ST 138715 5 St Andrews Major, S Andrew
ST 017680 6 St Athan, S Tathan
SS 894750 6 St Brides Major, S Bridget
ST 016733 5 St Hilary, S Hilary
ST 002716 4 St Mary Church, S Mary
SS 957793 4 St Mary Hill, S Mary Virgin
ST 228814 6 St Mellons, S Mellons
ST 090743 5 St Nicholas, S Nicholas
ST 152683 6 Sully, S John Baptist
ST 153801 8 Whitchurch, S Mary

West Glamorgan

SS 753923 6 Baglan, S Catherine
SS 738998 6 Bryn Coch, S Matthew
SS 756986 6 Cadoxton juxta Neath, S Catwg
SS 587988 8 Gorseinon, S Catherine
SS 646989 4 Llangyfelach, SS David & Cyfelach
SS 428914 4 Llangennith, S Cennydd
SS 753977 6 Neath, S Thomas
SS 763902 8 Port Talbot, S Mary, Aberavon
SS 656929 8 Swansea, S Mary
SS 627928 8 Swansea, S Paul, Sketty

Scotland

Central

NS 886926 8 Alloa, (Episcopal) S John Evangelist
NN 781014 8(1) Dunblane, Cathedral
NS 791938 6 Stirling, Holy Rude

Grampian

NJ 939088 8 Aberdeen, Cathedral Church of S Machar
NJ 945155 6 Potterton, Butterwells Farm

Highland

NN 1074 4 Fort William, S Andrew
NH 664449 10 Inverness, (Episcopal) Cathedral Church of S Andrew

Lothian

NT 242735 10 Edinburgh, (Episcopal) Cathedral Church of S Mary
NT 254741 8 Edinburgh, S Andrew
NT 248736 10 Edinburgh, S Cuthbert
NT 236752 5 Edinburgh, Fettes College Chapel

Strathclyde

NS 577668 10 Glasgow, (Episcopal) Cathedral Church of S Mary Virgin
NN 095085 10 Inveraray, (Episcopal) All Saints
NS 477642 8 Paisley, S James

Tayside

NO 404303 8 Dundee, (Episcopal) Cathedral Church of S Paul
NO 401301 8 Dundee, S Mary (Old Steeple)
NO 024426 6 Dunkeld, Ruined Cathedral Church of S Columba

Channel Isles

WA 574074	6	Alderney, S Anne
WV 296756	6	Guernsey, S Marguerite de la Foret
WV 335825	6	Guernsey, S Michel du Valle, Vale
WV 337783	8	Guernsey, S Peter A&M, S Peter Port
WV 271762	10	Guernsey, S Pierre du Bois
WV 628554	8	Jersey, S John in the Oaks, St John
WV 655492	6	Jersey, S Mark Evangelist, St Helier

Isle of Man

SC 246840	8	Peel, S German (Kirk German)

Ireland

Antrim

D 106035	12	Ballymena, S Patrick
J 366737	6	Belfast, S Donard, Bloomfield
J 374748	10	Belfast, S Mark, Dundela
J 328723	8	Belfast, S Thomas
J 413874	8	Carrickfergus, S Nicholas

Armagh

J 079585	8	Lurgan, Christ Church

Cork

W 490547	6	Bandon, S Peter
W 668714	8	Cork, Cathedral of S Fin Barre
W 672725	8	Cork, RC Cathedral of Mary Magdalene
R 6007	6	Doneraile, S Mary
W 3034	5	Roscarbery, S Fachtna's Cathedral

Derry

C 850325	8	Coleraine, S Patrick
C 442165	10(2)	Londonderry, S Columb's Cathedral

Down

J 329673	8	Ballylesson, Holy Trinity, Drumbo
J 507817	8	Bangor, S Comgall
J 245587	10	Hillsborough, S Malachi
J 402790	8	Holywood, SS Philip & James
J 378314	6	Newcastle, S John
J 178184	6	Rostrevor, S Bronach

Dublin

O 150340	6	Dublin, S Audoen
O 147338	10	Dublin, SS Augustine & John (RC)
O 152335	12(2)	Dublin, Cathedral of S Patrick
O 152339	10(2)	Dublin, Christ Church Cathedral
O 157354	8	Dublin, S George

Fermanagh

H 234443	10	Enniskillen, Cathedral of S Macartan

Kilkenny

S 5056	8	Kilkenny, Cathedral of S Canice

Limerick

R 5857	8	Limerick, Cathedral of S Mary
R 5857	10	Limerick, Mount S Alphonsus (RC)

Louth

O 0975	8	Drogheda, S Peter

Tipperary

S 1258	8	Thurles, Cathedral of the Assumption (RC)

Waterford

S 6012	8	Waterford, Cathedral of the Blessed Trinity

Wexford

T 0421	10	Wexford, The Immaculate Conception (RC)

Wicklow

T 2473	8	Arklow, S Saviour
N 982143	6	Blessington, S Mary
O 262178	8	Bray, Christ Church

Australia

34.56S 138.36E	10	Adelaide, SA, S Francis Xavier Cathedral
34.56S 138.36E	8	Adelaide, SA, S Peter's Cathedral
34.56S 138.36E	8	Adelaide, SA, Town Hall
34.53S 138.37E	8	Adelaide, SA, S Cuthbert, Prospect
34.58S 138.36E	8	Adelaide, SA, S Augustine, Unley
34.54S 138.36E	6	Adelaide, SA, S Andrew, Walkerville
37.36S 143.58E	8	Ballarat, Vic., Town Hall
37.36S 143.58E	8	Ballarat, Vic., S Peter
33.27S 149.35E	8	Bathurst, NSW, All Saints Cathedral
36.48S 144.21E	8	Bendigo, Vic., S Paul's Cathedral
27.28S 153.02E	10	Brisbane, Qld., S John's Cathedral
27.30S 153.00E	6	Brisbane, Qld., S Andrew, South Brisbane
35.18S 149.08E	8	Canberra, ACT, S Andrew
38.10S 144.26E	8	Geelong, Vic., S Paul
34.47S 149.43E	8	Goulburn, NSW, S Savior's Cathedral
42.54S 147.18E	8	Hobart, Tas., Holy Trinity
42.54S 147.18E	8	Hobart, Tas., S David's Cathedral
32.33S 151.33E	6	Maitland, NSW, S Paul
25.32S 152.36E	8(1)	Maryborough, Qld., S Paul
37.49S 144.58E	8	Melbourne, Vic., S James Old Cathedral
37.49S 144.58E	8	Melbourne, Vic., S Patrick's Cathedral (RC)
37.49S 144.58E	12(1)	Melbourne, Vic., S Paul's Cathedral
37.50S 145.01E	6	Melbourne, Vic., S Bartholomew, Burnley (RC)
37.53S 145.00E	6	Melbourne, Vic., S James, Gardenvale (RC)
37.45S 145.03E	6	Melbourne, Vic., S Pius X, West Heidelberg (RC)
32.55S 151.46E	8	Newcastle, NSW, Christ Church Cathedral

31.58S 115.52W	8	Perth, WA, S George's Cathedral
31.58S 115.49E	15(2)	Perth, WA, University of Western Australia
31.59S 115.48E	6	Perth, WA, Christ Church, Claremont
33.55S 151.10E	10	Sydney, NSW, Christ Church S Laurence
33.53S 151.12E	12(1)	Sydney, NSW, S Andrew's Cathedral
33.53S 151.12E	12(2)	Sydney, NSW, S Mary's Cathedral (RC)
33.55S 151.10E	6	Sydney, NSW, S Benedict, Broadway (RC)
33.54S 151.05E	8	Sydney, NSW, S Paul, Burwood
33.53S 151.12E	8	Sydney, NSW, S Philip, Church Hill
33.52S 151.12E	8	Sydney, NSW, S Mark, Darling Point
33.50S 150.57E	8	Sydney, NSW, All Saints, Parramatta
33.55S 151.13E	8	Sydney, NSW, S Jude, Randwick
33.44S 151.09E	8	Sydney, NSW, S James, Turramurra
33.39S 151.50E	8	Sydney, NSW, S Matthew, Windsor
36.22S 146.20E	8	Wangaratta, Vic., Cathedral
34.51S 148.55E	6	Yass, NSW, S Clement
31.55S 116.45E	8	York, WA, Holy Trinity

Canada

51.05N114.05W	8	Calgary, AB, Christ Church, Elbow Park
49.17N122.21W	10	Mission City, BC, Benedictine Priory (RC)
46.24N90.19W	10	Montreal, PQ, Notre Dame Cathedral (RC)
46.24N90.19W	10	Montreal, PQ, S Patrick (RC)
46.50N71.15W	8	Quebec City, PQ, Branch Library
46.50N71.15W	8	Quebec City, PQ, Holy Trinity Cathedral
49.13N123.06W	8	Vancouver, BC, Cathedral of the Holy Rosary (RC)
48.25N123.22W	10	Victoria, BC, Cathedral Church of Christ

India

18.34N73.58E	8	Poona, The Holy Name, Panch Howd (RC)

Kenya

3.37S 39.50E	6	Kilifi, S Thomas

New Zealand

36.55S 174.47E	8	Auckland, NI, S Matthew in the City
37.53S 175.29E	6	Cambridge, NI, S Andrew
43.33S 172.40E	12(1)	Christchurch, SI, Cathedral Church of Christ
43.33S 172.40E	8	Christchurch, SI, S Paul, Papanui
45.52S 170.30E	8	Dunedin, SI, First Church of Otago
37.46S 175.18E	8	Hamilton, NI, S Peter's Cathedral
41.17S 174.47E	5	Wellington, NI, Old S Paul's Cathedral
41.17S 174.47E	12(2)	Wellington, NI, Cathedral of S Paul
41.17S 174.47E	8	Wellington, NI, S Peter

Pakistan

31.34N74.22E	6	Lahore, Cathedral of the Resurrection

South Africa

33.56S 18.23E	10	Cape Town, Cathedral Church of S George
33.56S 18.28E	8	Cape Town, S Mary, Woodstock
29.53S 31.00E	8	Durban, S Paul
29.53S 31.00E	10	Durban, S Mary, Greyville
33.18S 26.32E	8	Grahamstown, Cathedral of S Michael & S George
26.10S 28.02E	8	Johannesburg, S George, Parktown

USA

32.27N99.45W	6	Abilene, TX, Church of the Heavenly Rest
42.20N71.05W	8	Boston, MA, Christ Church
42.20N71.05W	8	Boston, MA, Church of the Advent
42.20N71.05W	8	Boston, MA, Perkins Institute for the Blind, Watertown
41.24N73.37W	8	Brewster, NY, Melrose School Chapel
40.05N74.51W	8	Burlington, NJ, S Mary
32.48N79.58W	8	Charleston, SC, S Michael
41.50N87.45W	10	Chicago, IL, Mitchell Tower, University of Chicago
42.36N72.05W	10	Groton, MA, Groton School Chapel
35.19N82.28W	8	Hendersonville, NC, S James
42.15N70.53W	10	Hingham, MA, Memorial Hall
29.45N95.20W	8	Houston, TX, S Thomas
29.45N95.20W	8	Houston, TX, Trinity
42.17N85.36W	8	Kalamazoo, MI, Stetson Chapel, Kalamazoo College
41.43N73.28W	10	Kent, CT, Kent School
34.24N92.17W	8	Little Rock, AR, Cathedral of the Holy Trinity
25.45N80.15W	8	Miami, FL, Cathedral of the Holy Trinity
39.30N76.30W	6	New Castle, DE, Immanuel on the Green
40.45N73.59W	8	New York, NY, Holy Trinity, Wall Street
42.19N72.38W	8	Northampton, MA, Smith College
40.00N75.10W	8	Philadelphia, PA, Christ Church
40.00N75.10W	8	Philadelphia, PA, S Mark
40.00N75.10W	8	Philadelphia, PA, S Martin in the Fields
40.00N75.10W	8	Philadelphia, PA, S Mary
40.00N75.10W	8	Philadelphia, PA, S Peter
35.42N78.40W	5	Raleigh, NC, Christ Church
33.28N94.02W	8	Texarkana, TX/AR, First Presbyterian Church
38.55N77.00W	10	Washington, DC, National Episcopal Cathedral
38.55N77.00W	10	Washington, DC, Old Post Office Tower

Zimbabwe

17.43S 31.05E	10	Harare, Cathedral of S Mary & All Saints
18.55S 29.51E	6	Kwe Kwe, S Luke

Dove	Atlas
Aberavon, Port Talbot	Port Talbot, Aberavon
Ackworth	High Ackworth
Aldrington	Hove, Aldrington
Almondbury	Huddersfield, Almondbury
Alverstoke	Gosport, Alverstoke
Amport St Mary	Amport
Anston, South	South Anston
Armitage Bridge	Huddersfield, Armitage Bridge
Ash by Wrotham	Ash (near Gravesend)
Ash in Martock	Ash
Ash next Sandwich	Ash (near Sandwich)
Ashwelthorpe	Ashwellthorpe
Aston White Ladies	White Ladies Aston
Bamber Bridge (Brownedge)	Bamber Bridge
Bamford in the Peak	Bamford
Bangor Is Y Coed	Bangor is y coed
Barkeston	Barkestone le Vale
Basildon	Lower Basildon
Beercrocombe	Beer Crocombe
Belgrave	Leicester, Belgrave
Belton in Isle of Axholme	Belton
Benefield	Lower Benefield
Berkhamsted, Great	Berkhamstead
Berwick on Tweed	Berwick upon Tweed
Bexhill on Sea	Bexhill
Bidston	Birkenhead, Bidston
Bilton	Rugby, Bilton
Birchington on Sea	Birchington
Blackbourton	Black Bourton
Blo Norton	Blo' Norton
Boldmere	Sutton Coldfield, Boldmere
Bolton, Smithills (Halliwell)	Bolton, Halliwell (Doffcocker)
Bow (Nymet Tracey)	Nymet Tracey
Bradford, Tong	Tong
Bradoc	Braddock
Bradwell juxta Mare	Bradwell on Sea
Brandon Ferry	Brandon
Bredons Norton	Bredon's Norton
Broadchalke	Broad Chalke
Broadwood Widger	Broadwoodwidger
Bromborough	Bebington, Bromborough
Burton on Stather	Burton upon Stather
Burton upon Trent, Horninglow	Horninglow
Burton upon Trent, Winshill	Winshill
Caldecote	Caldecott
Cardynham	Cardinham
Carlton Magna	Carlton
Carlton by Bosworth	Carlton
Castle Bromwich	Birmingham, Castle Bromwich
Cefn Coed	Cefn coed y cymmer
Charlton by Malmesbury	Charlton
Cheverell Magna	Great Cheverell
Churchstoke	Church Stoke
Clapham Common	Clapham, Clapham Common
Cliffe Pypard	Clyffe Pypard
Clifton on Dunsmore	Clifton upon Dunsmore
Clifton on Teme	Clifton upon Teme
Coln St Aldwyn	Coln St Aldwyns
Combe in Teignhead	Combeinteignhead
Corbridge on Tyne	Corbridge
Cradley	Halesowen, Cradley
Cranford	Cranford St John
Cransley	Great Cransley
Crossens	Southport, Crossens
Dalby on the Wolds	Old Dalby
Daybrook	Arnold, Daybrook
Downham in the Isle	Little Downham
Driffield	Great Driffield
Dunham Massey	Altrincham, Dunham Massey
Durnford	Great Durnford
Duston	Northampton, Duston
Dyffryn	Bryn Coch
East Ardsley	Ardsley East
East Crompton	Shaw
Eastham	Bebington, Eastham
Ecclesfield	Sheffield, Ecclesfield
Englishcombe or Inglescombe	Englishcombe
Evington	Leicester, Evington
Exeter, Topsham	Topsham
Finborough Magna	Great Finchborough
Fisherton Delamere	Fisherton de la Mere
Fylingdales	Robin Hood's Bay
Gedling	Carlton, Gedling
Giggleswick in Craven	Giggleswick
Glasbury on Wye	Glasbury
Goring on Thames	Goring
Great Catworth	Catworth
Great Creaton	Creaton
Great Crosby	Crosby
Great Marlow	Marlow
Guernsey, Vale	Guernsey, La Greve
Halewood	Liverpool, Halewood
Halifax, Northowram	Northowram
Halton Holgate	Halton Holegate
Handsworth	Sheffield, Handsworth
Haughton, Denton	Denton
Hazelbeech	Haselbech
Helidon	Hellidon
Heworth	Felling, Heworth
Hill Farrance	Hillfarrance
Hopton by Thetford	Hopton
Horsell	Woking, Horsell
Hoylandswaine	Hoyland Swaine
Hucknall Torkard	Hucknall
Humberstone	Leicester, Humberstone
Ile Brewers	Isle Brewers
Isle of Grain	Grain
Kensington, South	South Kensington
Keresley	Brownshill Green
King's Norton or Norton by Galby	King's Norton
King's Sutton	Kings Sutton
Kingsworthy	Kings Worthy
Man, Isle of, Kirk German	Peel
Kingsthorpe	Northampton, Kingsthorpe
Kirkby Ireleth or Kirkby in Furness	Kirkby in Furness
Kirkby Moorside	Kirkbymoorside
Kirkby on the Moor or Kirby Hill	Kirby Hill
Kirton in Holland	Kirton
Knighton	Leicester, Knighton
Laneham	Church Laneham
Langton by Partney	Langton
Leamington Spa	Royal Leamington Spa
Leigh	Church Leigh
Leigh on Mendip	Leigh upon Mendip
Lightcliffe	Brighouse, Lightcliffe
Lillington	Royal Leamington Spa, Lillington
Little Hempston	Liitlehempston
Little Petherick or St Petrock Minor	Little Petherick

Dove	Atlas	Dove	Atlas
Liverpool, Much Woolton	Liverpool, Woolton	St Gerrans	Gerrans
Liverpool, Tue Brook	Liverpool, Tuebrook	St Giles in the Heath	St Giles on the Heath
Liverpool, Walton on the Hill	Liverpool, Walton	St Ippolyts	St Ippollitts
Llanbadarn Fawr	Crossgates	St Laurence in Isle of Thanet	Ramsgate
Llanbedr Ystradyw	Llanbedr	St Leonards on Sea	Hastings, St Leonards
Llandefaelog Fach	Llandefaelog	St Martin	St Martin's
Llandrillo yn Edeyrnion	Llandrillo	St Peter's in Isle of Thanet	Broadstairs
Llandyssul	Llandysul	St Sampson or Golant	Golant
Llanfeugan	Pencelli	Seavington	Seavington St Mary
Llanfihangel Cwm Du	Cwmdu	Sheffield, Beighton	Beighton
Llanfihangel Rhydeithon	Llanfihangel Rhydithon	Sherston Magna	Sherston
Llanfihangel Talyllyn	Llanfihangel Tal-y-llyn	Shirley	Birmingham, Shirley
Llangybi (Llangibby)	Llangybi	Shotesham All Saints	Shotesham
Lois Weedon	Weedon Lois	Skipton in Craven	Skipton
Long Burton	Longburton	South Elmham, S Cross	St Cross South Elmham
Lye, The	Stourbridge, Lye	South Elmham, S James	St James South Elmham
Lytham	Lytham St Anne's	South Elmham, S Margaret	St Margaret South Elmham
Martin by Timberland	Martin	Southleigh	South Leigh
Martinstown or Winterbourne St Martin	Martinstown	South Mymms	South Mimms
		South Wigston	Wigston, South Wigston
Merrow	Guildford, Merrow	Southwold on Sea	Southwold
Michaelston y Vedw	Michaelston y Fedw	Sowerby	Sowerby Bridge
Minety	Upper Minety	Sowerby juxta Thirsk	Sowerby
Monk Okehampton	Monkokehampton	Stalybridge, Stayley	Stalybridge, Copley
Monksherborne	Monk Sherborne	Stamford Baron	Stamford
Moreton	Birkenhead, Moreton	Stanground	Peterborough, Stanground
Morthoe or Mortehoe	Mortehoe	Stanton on Hine Heath	Stanton upon Hine Heath
Newark upon Trent	Newark on Trent	Stoke in Teignhead	Stokeinteignhead
Newbold on Avon	Rugby, Newbold on Avon	Stoke next Guildford	Guildford, Stoke Park
Newburn on Tyne	Newburn	Stowe Nine Churches	Church Stowe
Newcastle upon Tyne, Low Elswick	Newcastle upon Tyne, Elswick	Stratfieldsaye	Stratfield Saye
		Stratford on Avon	Stratford upon Avon
Newchurch Kenyon	Culcheth	Stretton cum Wetmoor	Stretton
Newchurch in Rossendale	Rawtenstall, Newchurch	Sutton cum Lound	Sutton
Newington juxta Sittingbourne	Newington (near Sittingbourne)	Sydenham Damarel	Sydenham Damerel
Newington next Hythe	Newington (near Hythe)	Telford, Coalbrookdale	Coalbrookdale
Newton Hall	Newton	Telford, Dawley Magna	Telford, Dawley
Newton Nottage	Porthcawl, Newton	Telford, Wellington	Wellington
Newton Toney	Newton Tony	Thorn Falcon	Thornfalcon
Norbury (Hazel Grove)	Hazel Grove, Norbury	Thorndon All Saints	Thorndon
Norton in the Moors	Stoke on Trent, Norton-in-the-Moors	Thorpe next Norwich	Thorpe St Andrew
		Tichmarsh	Titchmarsh
Norton juxta Malton	Norton	Todmorden, Walsden	Walsden
Nymet St George	George Nympton	Tregaer	Tregare
Offley	Great Offley	Tuddenham St Martin	Tuddenham (near Ipswich)
Old or Wold	Old	Tuddenham St Mary	Tuddenham (near Mildenhall)
Old Fletton	Peterborough, Old Fletton	Tunbridge Wells	Royal Tunbridge Wells
Oldham, Leesfield	Oldham, Lees	Tysoe	Middle Tysoe
Old Hill	Blackheath, Old Hill	Upholland	Up Holland
Orton Waterville	Peterborough, Orton Waterville	Up Ottery	Upottery
Overton on Dee	Overton	Upton by Birkenhead	Birkenhead, Upton
Pakefield	Lowestoft, Pakefield	Urswick	Great Urswick
Pelsall	Bloxwich, Pelsall	Wadesmill	Thundridge
Pen Selwood	Penselwood	Walsall, Blakenall Heath	Bloxwich, Blakenall Heath
Penwortham	Higher Penwortham	Walsall, Bloxwich	Bloxwich
Petersmarland	Peters Marland	Walsgrave on Sowe	Coventry, Walsgrave on Sowe
Preston next Wingham	Preston	Walton le Wolds	Walton on the Wolds
Pulverbatch	Church Pulverbatch	Waterfoot	Rawtenstall, Waterfoot
Reddish	Stockport, Reddish	Wath juxta Ripon	Wath
Rock Ferry	Birkenhead, Rock Ferry	Wath on Dearne	Wath upon Dearne
Rolleston on Dove	Rolleston	Wellesbourne Hastings	Wellesbourne
Rougham	Rougham Green	Wellington, Rockwell Green	Rockwell Green
Rowley Regis	Blackheath, Rowley Regis	West Kirby	Hoylake, West Kirby
Rudby in Cleveland	Rudby	Weston Favell	Northampton, Weston Favell
Rushall	Walsall, Rushall	Weymouth, Preston	Preston
St Anne's on the Sea	Lytham St Anne's, St Annes	Weymouth, Upwey	Upwey
St Bride's Wentloog	St Brides Wentlooge	Whatton in the Vale	Whatton

Dove	Atlas
White Lackington	Whitelackington
Whitnash	Royal Leamington Spa, Whitnash
Whorlton in Cleveland	Whorlton
Wiggenhall St German	Wiggenhall St Germans
Wigston Magna	Wigston
Wilford	West Bridgford, Wilford
Willoughby Warterleys	Willoughby Waterleys
Winterslow	West Winterslow
Wishford Magna	Great Wishford
Wolford	Great Wolford
Wollaton	Nottingham, Wollaton
Woodchurch	Birkenhead, Woodchurch
Wood Eaton	Woodeaton
Woodston	Peterborough, Woodston
Woolastone	Woolaston
Wootton Glanville	Glanvilles Wootton
Wylam on Tyne	Wylam
York, Bishopthorpe	Bishopthorpe
York, Huntington	Huntington

Atlas	Dove
Altrincham, Dunham Massey	Dunham Massey
Amport	Amport St Mary
Ardsley East	East Ardsley
Arnold, Daybrook	Daybrook
Ash	Ash in Martock
Ash (near Gravesend)	Ash by Wrotham
Ash (near Sandwich)	Ash next Sandwich
Ashwellthorpe	Ashwelthorpe
Bamber Bridge	Bamber Bridge (Brownedge)
Bamford	Bamford in the Peak
Bangor is y coed	Bangor Is Y Coed
Barkestone le Vale	Barkeston
Bebington, Bromborough	Bromborough
Bebington, Eastham	Eastham
Beer Crocombe	Beercrocombe
Beighton	Sheffield, Beighton
Belton	Belton in Isle of Axholme
Berkhamstead	Berkhamsted, Great
Berwick upon Tweed	Berwick on Tweed
Bexhill	Bexhill on Sea
Birchington	Birchington on Sea
Birkenhead, Bidston	Bidston
Birkenhead, Moreton	Moreton
Birkenhead, Rock Ferry	Rock Ferry
Birkenhead, Upton	Upton by Birkenhead
Birkenhead, Woodchurch	Woodchurch
Birmingham, Castle Bromwich	Castle Bromwich
Birmingham, Shirley	Shirley
Bishopthorpe	York, Bishopthorpe
Black Bourton	Blackbourton
Blackheath, Old Hill	Old Hill
Blackheath, Rowley Regis	Rowley Regis
Blo' Norton	Blo Norton
Bloxwich	Walsall, Bloxwich
Bloxwich, Blakenall Heath	Walsall, Blakenall Heath
Bloxwich, Pelsall	Pelsall
Bolton, Halliwell (Doffcocker)	Bolton, Smithills (Halliwell)
Braddock	Bradoc
Bradwell on Sea	Bradwell juxta Mare
Brandon	Brandon Ferry
Bredon's Norton	Bredons Norton
Brighouse, Lightcliffe	Lightcliffe
Broad Chalke	Broadchalke
Broadstairs	St Peter's in Isle of Thanet
Broadwoodwidger	Broadwood Widger
Brownshill Green	Keresley
Bryn Coch	Dyffryn
Burton upon Stather	Burton on Stather
Caldecott	Caldecote
Cardinham	Cardynham
Carlton	Carlton by Bosworth
Carlton	Carlton Magna
Carlton, Gedling	Gedling
Catworth	Great Catworth
Cefn coed y cymmer	Cefn Coed
Charlton	Charlton by Malmesbury
Church Laneham	Laneham
Church Leigh	Leigh
Church Pulverbatch	Pulverbatch
Church Stoke	Churchstoke
Church Stowe	Stowe Nine Churches
Clampham, Clampham Common	Clapham Common
Clifton upon Dunsmore	Clifton on Dunsmore
Clifton upon Teme	Clifton on Teme
Clyffe Pypard	Cliffe Pypard
Coalbrookdale	Telford, Coalbrookdale

Atlas	Dove	Atlas	Dove
Coln St Aldwyns	Coln St Aldwyn	Leicester, Humberstone	Humberstone
Combeinteignhead	Combe in Teignhead	Leicester, Knighton	Knighton
Corbridge	Corbridge on Tyne	Leigh upon Mendip	Leigh on Mendip
Coventry, Walsgrave on Sowe	Walsgrave on Sowe	Littlehempston	Little Hempston
Cranford St John	Cranford	Little Downham	Downham in the Isle
Creaton	Great Creaton	Little Petherick	Little Petherick or St Petrock
Crosby	Great Crosby		Minor
Crossgates	Llanbadarn Fawr	Liverpool, Halewood	Halewood
Culcheth	Newchurch Kenyon	Liverpool, Tuebrook	Liverpool, Tue Brook
Cwmdu	Llanfihangel Cwm Du	Liverpool, Walton	Liverpool, Walton on the Hill
Denton	Haughton, Denton	Liverpool, Woolton	Liverpool, Much Woolton
Englishcombe	Englishcombe or Inglescombe	Llanbedr	Llanbedr Ystradyw
Felling, Heworth	Heworth	Llandefaelog	Llandefaelog Fach
Fisherton de la Mere	Fisherton Delamere	Llandrillo	Llandrillo yn Edeyrnion
George Nympton	Nymet St George	Llandysul	Llandyssul
Gerrans	St Gerrans	Llanfihangel Rhydithon	Llanfihangel Rhydeithon
Giggleswick	Giggleswick in Craven	Llanfihangel Tal-y-llyn	Llanfihangel Talyllyn
Glanvilles Woottton	Wootton Glanville	Llangybi	Llangybi (Llangibby)
Glasbury	Glasbury on Wye	Longburton	Long Burton
Golant	St Sampson or Golant	Lower Basildon	Basildon
Gosport, Alverstoke	Alverstoke	Lower Benefield	Benefield
Goring	Goring on Thames	Lowestoft, Pakefield	Pakefield
Grain	Isle of Grain	Lytham St Anne's	Lytham
Great Cheverell	Cheverell Magna	Lytham St Anne's, St Annes	St Anne's on the Sea
Great Cransley	Cransley	Marlow	Great Marlow
Great Driffield	Driffield	Martin	Martin by Timberland
Great Durnford	Durnford	Martinstown	Martinstown or Winterbourne
Great Finchborough	Finborough Magna		St Martin
Great Offley	Offley	Michaelston y Fedw	Michaelston y Vedw
Great Urswick	Urswick	Middle Tysoe	Tysoe
Great Wishford	Wishford Magna	Monkokehampton	Monk Okehampton
Great Wolford	Wolford	Monk Sherborne	Monksherborne
Guernsey, La Greve	Guernsey, Vale	Mortehoe	Morthoe or Mortehoe
Guildford, Merrow	Merrow	Newark on Trent	Newark upon Trent
Guildford, Stoke Park	Stoke next Guildford	Newburn	Newburn on Tyne
Halesowen, Cradley	Cradley	Newcastle upon Tyne, Elswick	Newcastle upon Tyne, Low
Halton Holegate	Halton Holgate		Elswick
Haselbech	Hazelbeech	Newington (near Hythe)	Newington next Hythe
Hastings, St Leonards	St Leonards on Sea	Newington (near Sittingbourne)	Newington juxta Sittingbourne
Hazel Grove, Norbury	Norbury (Hazel Grove)	Newton	Newton Hall
Hellidon	Helidon	Newton Tony	Newton Toney
High Ackworth	Ackworth	Northampton, Duston	Duston
Higher Penwortham	Penwortham	Northampton, Kingsthorpe	Kingsthorpe
Hillfarrance	Hill Farrance	Northampton, Weston Favell	Weston Favell
Hopton	Hopton by Thetford	Northowram	Halifax, Northowram
Horninglow	Burton upon Trent, Horninglow	Norton	Norton juxta Malton
Hove, Aldrington	Aldrington	Nottingham, Wollaton	Wollaton
Hoylake, West Kirby	West Kirby	Nymet Tracey	Bow (Nymet Tracey)
Hoyland Swaine	Hoylandswaine	Old	Old or Wold
Hucknall	Hucknall Torkard	Old Dalby	Dalby on the Wolds
Huddersfield, Almondbury	Almondbury	Oldham, Lees	Oldham, Leesfield
Huddersfield, Armitage Bridge	Armitage Bridge	Overton	Overton on Dee
Huntington	York, Huntington	Peel	Man, Isle of, Kirk German
Isle Brewers	Ile Brewers	Pencelli	Llanfeugan
King's Norton	King's Norton or Norton by	Penselwood	Pen Selwood
	Galby	Peterborough, Old Fletton	Old Fletton
Kings Sutton	King's Sutton	Peterborough, Orton Waterville	Orton Waterville
Kings Worthy	Kingsworthy	Peterborough, Stanground	Stanground
Kirby Hill	Kirkby on the Moor or Kirby Hill	Peterborough, Woodston	Woodston
Kirkby in Furness	Kirkby Ireleth or Kirkby in	Peters Marland	Petersmarland
	Furness	Porthcawl, Newton	Newton Nottage
Kirkbymoorside	Kirkby Moorside	Port Talbot, Aberavon	Aberavon, Port Talbot
Kirton	Kirton in Holland	Preston	Preston next Wingham
Langton	Langton by Partney	Preston	Weymouth, Preston
Leicester, Belgrave	Belgrave	Ramsgate	St Laurence in Isle of Thanet
Leicester, Evington	Evington	Rawtenstall, Newchurch	Newchurch in Rossendale

Atlas	Dove
Rawtenstall, Waterfoot	Waterfoot
Robin Hood's Bay	Fylingdales
Rockwell Green	Wellington, Rockwell Green
Rolleston	Rolleston on Dove
Rougham Green	Rougham
Royal Leamington Spa	Leamington Spa
Royal Leamington Spa, Lillington	Lillington
Royal Leamington Spa, Whitnash	Whitnash
Royal Tunbridge Wells	Tunbridge Wells
Rudby	Rudby in Cleveland
Rugby, Bilton	Bilton
Rugby, Newbold on Avon	Newbold on Avon
St Anne's	St Anne's on the Sea
St Brides Wentlooge	St Bride's Wentloog
St Cross South Elmham	South Elmham, S Cross
St Giles on the Heath	St Giles in the Heath
St Ippollitts	St Ippolyts
St James South Elmham	South Elmham, S James
St Margaret South Elmham	South Elmham, S Margaret
St Martin's	St Martin
Seavington St Mary	Seavington
Shaw	East Crompton
Sheffield, Ecclesfield	Ecclesfield
Sheffield, Handsworth	Handsworth
Sherston	Sherston Magna
Shotesham	Shotesham All Saints
Skipton	Skipton in Craven
South Anston	Anston, South
South Kensington	Kensington, South
South Leigh	Southleigh
South Mimms	South Mymms
Southport, Crossens	Crossens
Southwold	Southwold on Sea
Sowerby	Sowerby juxta Thirsk
Sowerby Bridge	Sowerby
Stalybridge, Copley	Stalybridge, Stayley
Stamford, S Martin	Stamford Baron
Stanton upon Hine Heath	Stanton on Hine Heath
Stockport, Reddish	Reddish
Stokeinteignhead	Stoke in Teignhead
Stoke on Trent, Norton-in-the-Moors	Norton in the Moors
Stourbridge, Lye	The Lye
Stratfield Saye	Stratfieldsaye
Stratford upon Avon	Stratford on Avon
Stretton	Stretton cum Wetmoor
Sutton	Sutton cum Lound
Sutton Coldfield, Boldmere	Boldmere
Sydenham Damerel	Sydenham Damarel
Telford, Dawley	Telford, Dawley Magna
Thorndon	Thorndon All Saints
Thornfalcon	Thorn Falcon
Thorpe St Andrew	Thorpe next Norwich
Thundridge	Wadesmill
Titchmarsh	Tichmarsh
Tong	Bradford, Tong
Topsham	Exeter, Topsham
Tregare	Tregaer
Tuddenham (near Ipswich)	Tuddenham St Martin
Tuddenham (near Mildenhall)	Tuddenham St Mary
Up Holland	Upholland
Upottery	Up Ottery
Upper Minety	Minety
Upton	Upton by Birkenhead
Upwey	Weymouth, Upwey
Walsall, Rushall	Rushall
Walsden	Todmorden, Walsden
Walton on the Wolds	Walton le Wolds
Wath	Wath juxta Ripon
Wath upon Dearne	Wath on Dearne
Weedon Lois	Lois Weedon
Wellesbourne	Wellesbourne Hastings
Wellington	Telford, Wellington
West Bridgford, Wilford	Wilford
West Winterslow	Winterslow
Whatton	Whatton in the Vale
White Ladies Aston	Aston White Ladies
Whitelackington	White Lackington
Whorlton	Whorlton in Cleveland
Wiggenhall St Germans	Wiggenhall St German
Wigston	Wigston Magna
Wigston, South Wigston	South Wigston
Willoughby Waterleys	Willoughby Warterleys
Winshill	Burton upon Trent, Winshill
Woking, Horsell	Horsell
Woodeaton	Wood Eaton
Woolaston	Woolastone
Wylam	Wylam on Tyne